XULON PRESS

God Sees Me and Loves Me!

Written By Terri Lyn

Illustrated by
Jason Velazquez

Xulon Press
2301 Lucien Way #415
Maitland, FL 32751
407.339.4217
www.xulonpress.com

Printed in the United States of America

Paperback ISBN-13: 978-1-6628-3479-0
Ebook ISBN-13: 978-1-6628-3480-6

Thank you to the Holy Spirit for inspiring me.

Thank you to my family for encouraging me.

GOD sees me and loves me,
no matter where I go.

When I am at home,
GOD sees me and loves me.

When I am at church,
GOD sees me and loves me.

When I go to the zoo,
GOD sees me and loves me.

When I am at school,
GOD sees me and loves me.

When I play at the park,
GOD sees me and loves me.

When I ride in the car,
GOD sees me and loves me.

When I go to the store,
GOD sees me and loves me.

When I am at the doctor,
GOD sees me and loves me.

When I go to the top of a mountain, GOD sees me and loves me.

When I go to the bottom
of the ocean, GOD sees me
and loves me.

When I am with my friends,
GOD sees me and loves me.

When I am asleep in my bed, GOD sees me and loves me.

Can you think of other places that GOD sees you and loves you?

GOD is always with me.
GOD sees me and loves me,
no matter where I go.

CPSIA information can be obtained
at www.ICGtesting.com
Printed in the USA
BVHW012001190223
658820BV00008B/21

9 781662 834790

MANAGING EVENTS

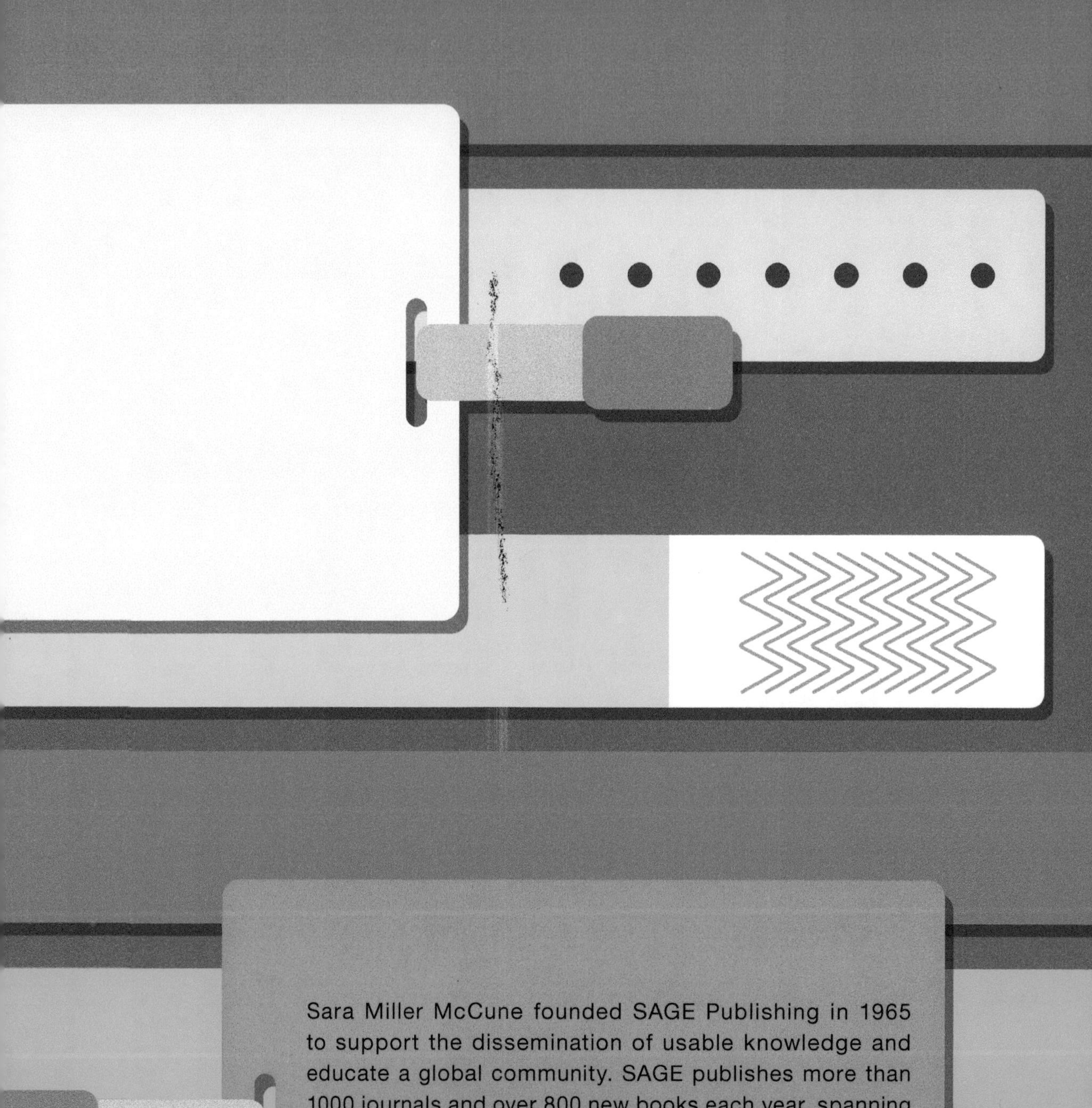

MANAGING EVENTS

REAL CHALLENGES

REAL OUTCOMES

LIZ QUICK

SAGE
Los Angeles | London | New Delhi
Singapore | Washington DC | Melbourne

Los Angeles | London | New Delhi
Singapore | Washington DC | Melbourne

SAGE Publications Ltd
1 Oliver's Yard
55 City Road
London EC1Y 1SP

SAGE Publications Inc.
2455 Teller Road
Thousand Oaks, California 91320

SAGE Publications India Pvt Ltd
B 1/I 1 Mohan Cooperative Industrial Area
Mathura Road
New Delhi 110 044

SAGE Publications Asia-Pacific Pte Ltd
3 Church Street
#10-04 Samsung Hub
Singapore 049483

First published 2020

Editor: Matthew Waters
Assistant editor: Jasleen Kaur
Assistant editor, digital: Sunita Patel
Production editor: Sarah Cooke
Copyeditor: Christine Bitten
Proofreader: Sharon Cawood
Indexer: Silvia Benvenuto
Marketing manager: Abigail Sparks
Coverdesign: Francis Kenney
Typeset by: C&M Digitals (P) Ltd, Chennai, India

Library of Congress Control Number: 2020933406

British Library Cataloguing in Publication data

A catalogue record for this book is available from the British Library

ISBN 978-1-4739-4808-2
ISBN 978-1-4739-4809-9 (pbk)

THE EVENT CYCLE 1

BEFORE THE EVENT 135

THROUGHOUT THE EVENT 219

BEYOND EVENTS 363

LIZ QUICK

Liz graduated from the Goldsmiths, University of London with a BA Honours degree in German and Drama. She began her career working for Lufthansa German Airlines, working as a Ticketing and Passenger Services agent at London Heathrow Airport and undergoing regular training courses at Seeheim in Frankfurt, Germany. She then made the move into the events industry, initially joining GL Travel Incentives, a UK-based Incentive Travel agency. Here she operated a number of overseas incentive trips on behalf of their clients, to amongst other destinations: Kenya, Hawaii, San Francisco, Rio de Janeiro and Monaco. Following this she moved to Talking Point Ltd, where she operated a number of international conferences and incentives for various blue chip corporations. During this time Liz helped set up the first UK event implant office, at the then SmithKline Beecham in Brentford, London, working in a Business Development role. This was the first time event spend had been consolidated through a sole agency and Liz was instrumental in setting this up and liaising with key clients within the Research & Development and Consumer Healthcare divisions of this major pharmaceutical company and securing the retender for sole supplier with the organisation for a number of years.

She later joined Plus Two Communications Ltd, then TMB Marketing Communications in Dorking, where she worked as Account Director on a number of key accounts, including Bristol Myers Squibb, Olswang, Johnson & Johnson and Wella UK. Liz also worked as a freelancer for some years and set up her own event management business. She worked with a key sponsor and partner on the London 2012 Olympics and regularly volunteers at festivals such as Glastonbury, Cornbury and many others.

In 2006, through a chance meeting with a previous colleague at a conference, she got the opportunity to start lecturing on a freelance basis. In 2010 she graduated from the University of West London with an MA in Learning and Teaching in Higher Education. She now brings her industry experience as a Senior Lecturer at the University of West London and over the last decade has gained extensive experience in course development and leadership, teaching on both undergraduate and postgraduate event management programmes. Liz is passionate about blending both the academic and more practical elements of the event management course she teaches, so that students can 'hit the ground running' when they graduate and enter the industry, which is the key motivation for writing this book.

Foreword

A great introduction for students coming into events as Liz offers real-world practical insight with attention on the need-to-know. The book asks a simple question of students and would-be professionals: What do you really need to know to effectively plan and manage an event? Blending a mix of commentaries from industry professionals and event academics, each chapter charts a logical path towards the goal of successfully delivering an event. It's a sound approach as the reader gets to understand some of the conceptual ideas that explain events, harnessed with the practicalities of making the event happen. Practitioner war stories are always fun and interesting to read, but it also helps a student develop their professional outlook if they can see that there are alternative ways of thinking about things, or, perhaps more importantly, that there are ideas and thoughts that explain why something is done, or should be done, in a certain way. The book is packed with case studies that articulate this perfectly and for readers this is one of the biggest benefits as they each pointedly illustrate what key ideas each chapter is trying to get across in the event planning cycle. What is also helpful is the excellent range of thoughtful activities for students to develop their thoughts and ideas. It all adds up to a lovingly nourished treatise on how we can make successful events happen.

Dr Graham Berridge, Head of Department for Events, University of Surrey, UK

Acknowledgements

To all the contributors who have generously spared their time and stories to help bridge the gap from academia to the real events world.

To Graham Louer who first got me started on the events journey over 30 years ago, and Graham Berridge who helped make the journey into academia seamless; to the Talking Point and TMB crews for inspiring me along the way and in memory of Denise Harris, the best events freelancer, who left us much too soon. Lastly, to the students who have made teaching events so rewarding. This book has been written for you to help prepare you to work in this amazing, inspiring and evolving industry.

Preface

Events of all sizes are shaped and influenced by current and contemporary issues, such as the evolution of technology; the increase of new emerging destinations, global terrorism and the need for more robust risk assessment, as well as a change in mindset brought about by renewed emphasis on environmental stewardship and globalisation. All of these issues have been discussed within this book, with the exception of the global pandemic we now know as Covid-19, as final drafts were completed before the emergence of this crisis. The concept of this book is to present real event challenges and outcomes, from various stakeholder perspectives. This crisis may well be one of the biggest challenges the industry has faced, so the way in which venues and events adapt and transform themselves will ultimately dictate the outcome of the recovery phase, both in the short and longer term.

At this stage we can only surmise the economic fallout of this pandemic and how it will continue to affect the events industry and other sectors. It is difficult to see how the industry will be able to recover without a huge injection of financial support and it is already apparent that many companies will not survive. The event calendar for 2020 has literally been wiped out, with cancellations of mass gatherings across all sectors in all countries and some large blue-chip corporations predicting that large scale events will not resume until Spring 2021 at the earliest, as longer lead times and social distancing will inevitably make events more logistically and financially challenging to deliver. This will especially be the case for event types with large attendee numbers, such as festivals, sporting events and exhibitions.

Whilst this has been a time of deep concern and uncertainty, some favourable outcomes have been recorded during the time of lockdown, such as ecological improvements to natural habitats, adoption of paperless solutions and a decrease in air and noise pollution levels, as a direct result of less air and traffic congestion. This reminds us all how quickly environmental sustainability can take place, once we start to implement positive changes.

Over the past decade events have adapted to find ways to downsize and scale back in times of austerity. We have seen how quickly cuts within this high yielding sector can impact economic growth within destinations that depend on events taking place in them, and how adaptable, resilient and versatile this industry is, as seen following the last global recession, when the industry bounced back with renewed efficiency and creativity.

We have also already seen how almost overnight, as the world locked down, the industry managed to adapt and seamlessly morph itself, using digital platforms and social media to communicate to their internal and external clients, generate new leads, share knowledge and best practice and spread positivity. Hardly surprising then that amongst event professionals there is now a feeling of cautious optimism, that

post-lockdown there is an opportunity for the industry to re-evaluate and relaunch itself; to offer stakeholders something more dynamic and more in keeping with the *current zeitgeist*. This transformation would probably have taken place over the next five years or so anyway, but the pandemic has fast forwarded the process and irreversibly altered the events landscape as never before.

So, what changes are we likely to see in the industry post Covid-19? In the short term conferences and events will undoubtedly take place closer to home, eliminating the need for international travel. Smaller and local events are predicted to be the first to re-emerge. These events will be flipped from the norm, starting out as remote or hybrid, then gradually reverting to physical or face-to-face events, once people start to feel more confident and risk assessment allows for group travel and meetings. Some of the more imminent changes might be:

- New capacity charts will be needed to allow for social distancing and venues will draw up new rules for set up, replacing theatre style seating and auditoriums with smaller more intimate spaces
- Venues will reassess their risk assessment to revise minimum numbers; ensure delegates and audiences are not placed in close proximity to each other; install sufficient hand sanitisers and face masks; take delegate temperatures on arrival etc.
- Venue contracts, payment terms and Ts & Cs will need to build in more flexible clauses to allow for a possible resurgence of the pandemic
- Event insurance companies will need to build in cover for global pandemics as part of their offering
- Delegate registration will be conducted pre-event, by means of an online link
- Plenary Q & A sessions, taking audience questions with a roving microphone will be a thing of the past, with all questions now being posed through social media
- Destination Management Companies (DMCs) will offer agencies virtual familiarisation trips, using virtual 360 renderings and interactive content to promote and sell destinations
- Conference keynote speakers will repeat sessions to delegates, who will pre-book slots in advance of sessions
- Conference packs and any joining instructions will be paperless to reduce contamination.

Post Covid-19 we will start to quickly to realise the benefits these new practises afford, so the old way of working will soon become obsolete. Technology will be used to enhance the industry and in the longer term the ‘new normal’ might include a more progressive, sustainable and socially responsible way of working, that considers legacy, integrates virtual and hybrid content, boosts homeworking, self-employment and freelancing and reduces the need for overseas conference travel.

I do not believe that virtual events will be a long-term replacement for face-to-face programmes or live events. Creativity, artistry and innovation will always be valued in this industry and technical solutions alone, even with increased use of artificial intelligence, virtual and extended reality, are not able to deliver creativity and interaction in the same way. There will always be the need to get together with peers, to listen to live music in real time within the setting of a festival, or watch a football match live at a stadium, that no amount of animation or remote transmission could replicate.

Audiences will always want an immersive event experience, but live streaming will be used on an increasing basis to engage more people, whilst not totally replacing the physical event experience. Incentive travel will also never be replaced by cash incentives, as only a memorable travel experience can motivate and boost top talent within an organisation enough to retain them and generate increased performance levels.

During and after this crisis, communication will be more important than ever, both with clients, supply chains and internal and external stakeholders. A variety of digital platforms, applications, social media and portals, such as Zoom, WebEx, Skype, Facetime, Google Meet & Hangouts will continue to deliver virtual and virtual plus hybrid content to virtual audiences, but this will become far more sophisticated, with more interactive and engaging content, including hackathons, gamification, digital avatars, online cooking demonstrations, polling, chillout zones etc.

Other popular communication tools will be WhatsApp broadcasts, Facebook groups and Instagram Television. Project mapping and webcasts will increasingly be used to communicate key messages, educate audiences and drive sales. The use of 2D and 3D animation, infographics, animated pictures, art installations, game engines, Graphic Processing Unit (GPU) renders, motion caption and photo real visual effects will all be used to communicate with key stakeholders. Brand influencers will promote and sponsor event brands and products to target demographics using social media platforms, and sponsors will be happy to have their products endorsed on virtual platforms, without the need to shake hands in real time. All of these mechanisms will be used in the longer term to deliver hybrid event experiences and enhance audience engagement throughout all stages of the event cycle.

How this will roll out in real terms is still to be seen, but it is becoming increasingly evident; in future years event professionals will measure, evaluate and discuss the functionality and delivery of events in terms of pre and post 2020 and the global sea change brought about by this unprecedented occurrence. I hope you will reading enjoy this book and find it a useful and informative retrospective on how this innovative and comparatively new sector, we know as the events industry, has undergone radical transformation over the last twenty years and will continue to evolve and adapt at an even greater speed in future.

GO ONLINE

MANAGING EVENTS **is accompanied by online resources for students and instructors to help support learning and teaching. These resources are available at:**

https://study.sagepub.com/quick

FOR INSTRUCTORS

- **PowerPoint slides** created by the author will help you **easily integrate the chapters** into your weekly teaching.

FOR STUDENTS

- **Extra information** in the **online appendix** will allow you to **expand your knowledge and improve understanding** of the text.

- **Useful templates** for key stages of the event planning process will help you begin **planning and managing your own event!**

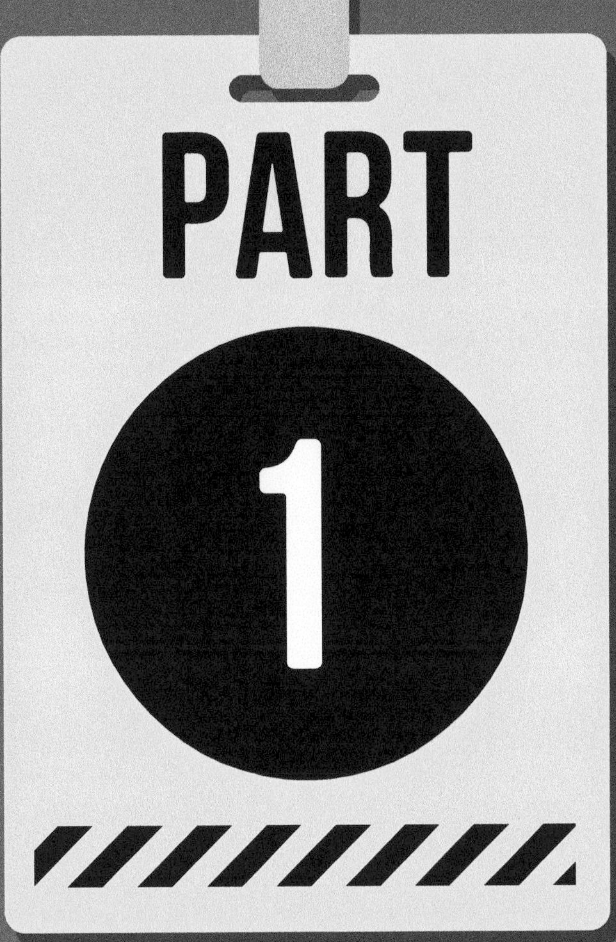

THE EVENT CYCLE

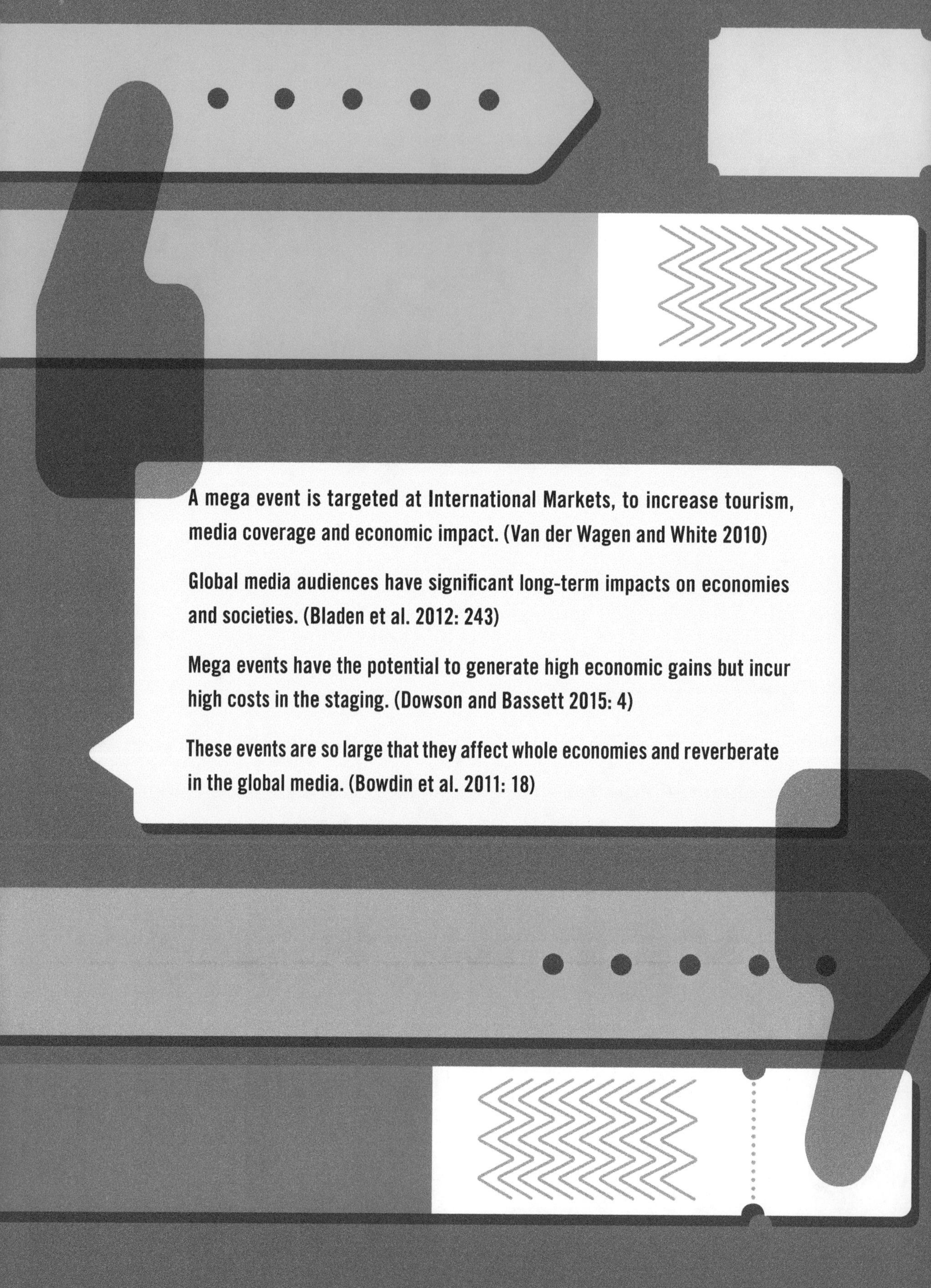

A mega event is targeted at International Markets, to increase tourism, media coverage and economic impact. (Van der Wagen and White 2010)
Global media audiences have significant long-term impacts on economies and societies. (Bladen et al. 2012: 243)
Mega events have the potential to generate high economic gains but incur high costs in the staging. (Dowson and Bassett 2015: 4)
These events are so large that they affect whole economies and reverberate in the global media. (Bowdin et al. 2011: 18)

1

THE PLANNING PHASE

CHAPTER OVERVIEW

This chapter is designed to introduce the concepts of real events from a practical perspective, and to analyse the three distinct phases of the event process, with specific focus on the planning phase. It will also discuss the various sectors of the industry, i.e. corporate, charitable and fundraising events, private parties, weddings, exhibitions, festivals and conferences, and explore the features associated with each of these categories. The chapter will explore the structure of the industry, in terms of the role and relationship between the client or buyer, the supplier and the agency or intermediary, and will examine the progress from early events to the multinational industry it has become today. It will also examine stakeholder liaison. These issues will also be explored further throughout the book.

CHAPTER OBJECTIVES

After reading this chapter, you will be able to identify and understand:

OBJECTIVE 1
The three phases of the event cycle

OBJECTIVE 2
A breakdown of the planning process

OBJECTIVE 3
The need to manage various stakeholders

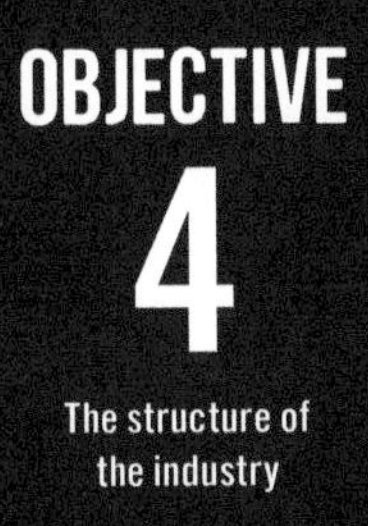

OBJECTIVE
5
How different sectors have evolved and are continuing to grow

Meet JEAN JOSEPH

Hotel Sales and Marketing Consultant

Jean has spent over 30 years working in hotel sales and marketing at property, regional and corporate level for major international hotel chains, including InterContinental Hotels, Kempinski and Kerzner International.

She now works for her own consultancy, which provides sales and marketing support to both larger hotel chains and smaller independent hotels to help them improve their performance. As a consultant, she is conscious of the importance of forward planning and being accountable for the input she provides, and of measuring the effectiveness of the projects worked on.

REAL EVENT CHALLENGE

In my last role at Kerzner International, I was responsible for organising a four-to-five-day road show to a number of UK cities on an annual basis every May. The event was set up for sales and marketing directors from the Kerzner International group of hotels, which consisted of 10 luxury properties. It was important to get sign-off for the budget nearly a year in advance of the event delivery.

As the sales & marketing directors would travel to the UK from international destinations, such as Asia, Dubai and South Africa, part of my remit for organising the road show would be to generate as many quality leads and arrange as many sales meetings as possible for them, whilst they were in the UK. This would be to higher end tour operators, and conference buyers in some of the UK cities, such as London, Preston,

Q&A

FAVOURITE HOTEL CHAIN?

I would have to go for Kerzner, for their high-end brand. It was the only chain I wanted to work for.

CAREER PATH NOT TAKEN?

I thought I wanted to work in Operations, but didn't stay in that area very long before realising it wasn't for me and then transferring into a Sales role.

MOST IMPRESSIVE WORK ACHIEVEMENT?

Working on the launch of the Atlantis Dubai – it will always remain an iconic landmark.

PERSON YOU WOULD MOST LIKE TO DINE WITH?

That's an easy one. John F. Kennedy, for the simple reason he was assassinated on the day I was born.

HOW DO YOU LIKE TO RELAX?

Going to the gym sets me up for the day and helps me relax and get some balance in my life. I now try to do a class four or five times a week.

Chester and Manchester. Because of the volume of sales meetings, it could be very time-consuming and quite a challenge to set up and plan.

My initial challenge, when setting up the roadshow for the first time, was to ensure that the event justified the time and costs involved for each of the directors, in terms of new business generation, and ensuring sufficient appointments were set up for them during the day, in order to ensure continued buy-in from all 10 Kerzner resorts to attend.

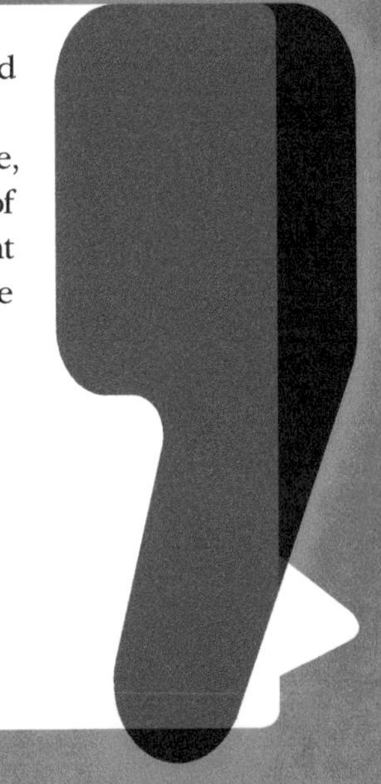

PRACTITIONER VIEWPOINT

Roger Plumpton, Founder and Director of hosmarkhotels

I set up hosmarkhotels 20 years ago, to represent the smaller national hotel brands and independent hotels in the first-class and luxury sectors within the global groups and events market.

Some of the major international hotel chains concentrate their sales resources on the larger event agencies and global corporations. Hosmarkhotels work with a similar strategy, but in addition we focus on the increasing number of smaller agents and companies that still deliver significant volumes of business but are sometimes overlooked by the global giants. We are a team of 12, who all have long-term expertise in the hotel, groups and event industry. Our business model is to charge a retainer fee to the hotels we represent and, just like any sales executive working for a global brand, we have targets to achieve, which can generate a performance-based bonus.

So effectively we are viewed as the regional sales office in the UK for the wide range of hotels that we represent globally. Our portfolio is made up of properties that want to see more business and a stronger profile in the UK groups and event markets. We primarily work with agencies, but we do work with some corporate buyers direct. In addition to our initial core conference and incentive business, the company has also evolved to work with leisure groups and tour operators.

For these buyers working with us helps eliminate risk; they know we understand the market and their business. Moreover, being able to channel enquiries through a centralised UK sales office eliminates any language, cultural or time difference challenges. They can genuinely see the cost savings we can provide for them in both time and money. Our personal and dedicated approach from a team they trust has allowed us to benefit from significant loyalty from these buyers.

Events buyers are always looking for new destinations or a new slant on the more traditional destinations, such as Barcelona and Dubai, and of course, how to better the previous event and destination they used. With more hotels opening annually, this increases the pressure on hotel rates and competition for the business. Direct-flight access can open up new destinations for the UK market. A recent example would be the Mexican Caribbean. This was a tough sell in the UK, but with the arrival of direct flights to Cancun, a whole new range of opportunities for the UK events industry has opened up. Our industry is always looking for new and exciting destinations, or new venues within existing popular destinations, as most events will not return to the same destination year after year.

We operate by maintaining strong relationships with all our clients via solid sales and marketing techniques, including regular sales calls; agency presentations; hosted dinners and networking events. These are also opportunities we extend to our hotel partner sales executives who are visiting the UK. In addition, we use social media to support our sales strategies and have a strong up-to-date database, which we use to provide product updates to our clients. However, we still believe the key to success is through talking and meeting with clients and establishing long-term relationships built on trust and professionalism.

ACADEMIC VIEWPOINT

Julian Robinson, Associate Professor, Coventry University

Marketing is a key stage of planning any event, whether it's a product launch, a private party, a conference or a business networking event. As well as the concept of the event, it is important to establish the aim and objectives and to keep these at the forefront when designing an effective event marketing strategy. Being able to identify who your attendees are is a key aspect of this process as well as thinking about how best to reach them and which medium might be the most effective to attract your target audience. As part of our BA (Hons) Event Management course, our second-year students get to plan and deliver their own live event, which requires them to consider exactly who their target audience are and how they will market their event. Alongside this they will need to liaise with stakeholders such as venue providers, musicians, printers, caterers and possibly the local authority to ensure all the correct licences and regulations are adhered to.

REAL EVENT OUTCOME

Our team made a plan to split up the various resort sales directors between the different cities and arranged back-to-back morning and afternoon sessions on their behalf. These sessions had a speed dating-like format, so that each tour operator or agency representatives would get a chance to meet briefly with the 10 Kerzner sales & marketing directors, who would each have about 10 minutes to present their property to them. When the bell sounded, the tour operators would move on to the hotel representative at the next table. The organisation required constant communication in the planning stage, but this format made the event a lot more manageable.

A clear strategy plan, an overall vision and constant communication with all the resorts, my own team and the UK clients were essential in the lead-up period. This included organising travel arrangements, transportation, accommodation and advising each resort on the costs involved. It took meticulous planning and often a lot of juggling to put this event together.

We also decided to put together a social programme with quite a few activities whilst they were here. This included daily breakfast meetings and training sessions in each of the UK cities where the road shows took place. We also organised a fun quiz evening in Chester, to allow the hotel sales teams to start building business relationships with the tour operators there, plus a hosted dinner at the Cafe Royal, when they stayed in London, so they were able to network with sales reservation agencies, concierge services and conference planners in a more social setting.

Although this meant for a busy itinerary, and a lot of advance planning and coordination, the resort sales directors were very happy to maximise their networking opportunities whilst they were in the UK. This made the time and expense of the visit worthwhile for them, and this event was repeated the following year and actually continued to run successfully for a number of years afterwards.

THE THREE EVENT PHASES

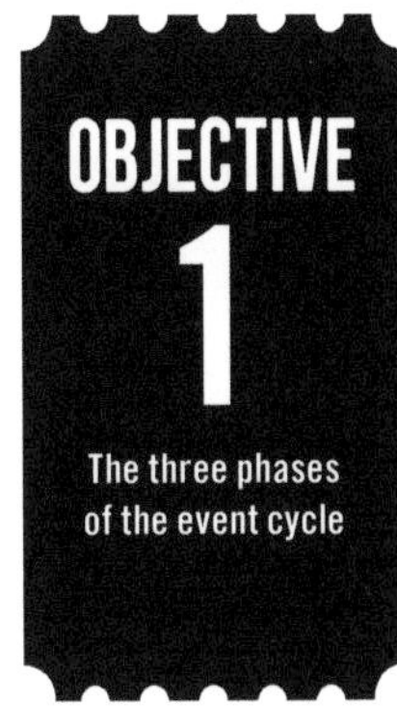

OBJECTIVE
1
The three phases of the event cycle

Events have three distinct phases: the planning phase, the delivery phase and the evaluation phase. Detailed planning is the basic prerequisite of the process and the first task is to establish a formal strategic plan to identify the vision and detail the actions that will fulfil and achieve this vision.

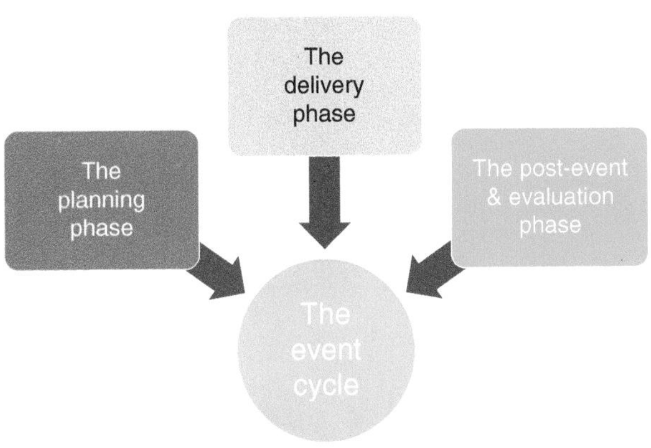

FIGURE 1.1 The event cycle

THE PLANNING PHASE

The planning phase is arguably the most important phase of the event cycle, as invariably it will determine its success. Singh (2009) describes the planning stage as the longest phase of the event, due to the historical tendency for disorganisation. However, by using prescriptive planning techniques and breaking down the event into more 'manageable chunks', the process can indeed become far more organised. A strategic plan involves a number of sequential steps, which, according to Grant (2005), include:

- Establishing the vision
- Developing the event objectives
- Implementing operational plans
- Devising control systems
- Shutdown and evaluation.

If these steps are not undertaken during the planning process, the delivery phase will not align with the overall vision and purpose. A clear strategic plan is needed to identify potential problems and generate alternative strategies where necessary, so that potential errors can be eradicated in the lead-up time, rather than during it.

In the planning phase, it is advisable to involve representation from each organisation in any of the initial meetings that take place. The tasks that need to be executed during this stage will vary considerably, depending on the complexity of the programme, but basically in the planning phase there are certain generic factors that need to be considered in order to scope out the project, as follows:

- Analyse the brief, the timings and what is required
- Work out the tasks

- Map these out
- Decide what resources are needed
- Decide what roles and staff will be required
- Work out a schedule.

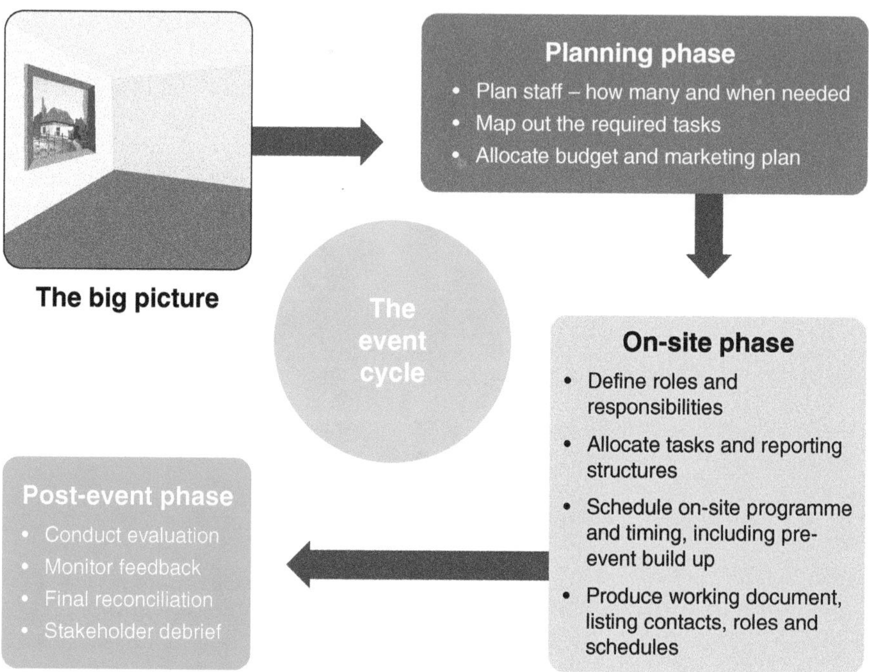
Planning phase
Plan staff – how many and when needed
Map out the required tasks
Allocate budget and marketing plan
The big picture
The event cycle
On-site phase
Define roles and responsibilities
Allocate tasks and reporting structures
Schedule on-site programme and timing, including pre-event build up
Produce working document, listing contacts, roles and schedules
Post-event phase
Conduct evaluation
Monitor feedback
Final reconciliation
Stakeholder debrief

FIGURE 1.2 The event planning phase

Working document a paper-based document generally used as a planning tool, to ensure that everything stays on track on-site

The need for a sufficient lead time to plan is of paramount importance. Although not always avoidable, short lead times can put a lot of pressure on the team responsible for the organisation, as Table 1.1 demonstrates.

As demonstrated in Figure 1.2, once tasks have been defined, a **working document** needs to be compiled. The content of this document, which will become the organiser's on-site guide, will be further discussed in Chapter 2.

- *What happens during the lead-in period:*
  - Planning
  - Venue sourcing
  - Client liaison
  - Research schedule
  - Fact-finding
  - Booking entertainment
  - Sourcing suppliers
  - Liaison with suppliers, such as caterers
  - Producing documents, e.g. production schedule

- *The impact of a short lead-in period:*

– Limits creativity – no time	– Unavailability of suppliers and venues
– Limits choice	– Compromises decisions
– Costs more	– Reactive, rather than proactive management

TABLE 1.1 The lead-in period

THE DELIVERY PHASE

With careful planning in the pre-event planning stage, the execution of the 'delivery phase', often called on-site management, will be easier for all concerned. However, it is true to say that no matter how carefully an event has been planned, some aspects of the programme will always change on-site. For that reason, it is always wise to prepare for the unexpected and think carefully about **contingency planning** in advance. This will be discussed further in Chapter 6 and the whole area of on-site management will be discussed in more detail in Chapter 2.

Contingency planning planning for an unexpected outcome

THE POST-EVENT AND EVALUATION PHASE

The final and extremely important phase of the event cycle is the post-event phase, where evaluation becomes a major factor. In recent times, this area has gained far greater significance, as larger events have started to be evaluated by the impact they have on the wider economy and overall impact on stakeholders, in terms of long-term legacy and regional development. These areas will be further discussed in Chapter 4 and the execution and delivery of post-event evaluation will be further discussed in Chapter 3.

A BREAKDOWN OF THE PLANNING PROCESS

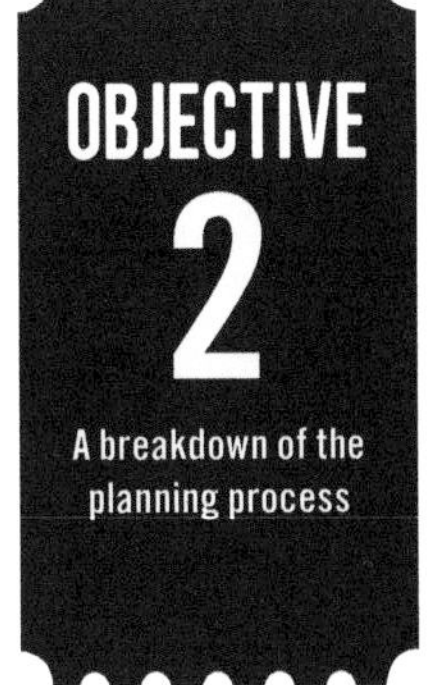
OBJECTIVE
2
A breakdown of the planning process

FACTORS TO CONSIDER IN THE PLANNING PROCESS

Generally, there are nine key elements to consider in the planning process, which are as shown in Figure 1.3.

SETTING AND DEFINING THE EVENT OBJECTIVES

At the outset, one of the key factors to determine is the agreed objectives and overall aim, or, in other words, why is the event actually taking place? Defining and prioritising specific objectives is crucial to the event's success, as objectives should be of value, both to the company or client commissioning it and those taking part in it. For that reason, it is good practice to brainstorm and discuss similar events that have been held before and to decide what the client is trying to achieve. For a number of reasons, it may not be an opportune time to hold the event. This could be due to the fact that there are others of a similar nature taking place around the same time, or in a nearby location, or that motivation within the company is low. Part of the role of a good manager is

Online forum
an online discussion site where delegates can hold conversations on a given subject by posting messages

Virtual event
sharing a common virtual environment on the web, rather than meeting in a physical location

to challenge the objectives and explore other ways of delivering the same message, such as an **online forum**, or a **virtual event**. At times, a newsletter might be just as informative, as well as a more cost-effective way of delivering the message. However, sometimes it is essential to have a face-to-face meeting, in order to achieve the aims and purpose set, that could include the following objectives:

- To increase company retention
- To foster renewed loyalty
- To impart information
- To educate or deliver an educative lecture to the audience
- To introduce a new culture or management structure
- To allow delegates to network and interact
- To launch a new product
- To enhance sales potential and company motivation
- To entertain and have fun.

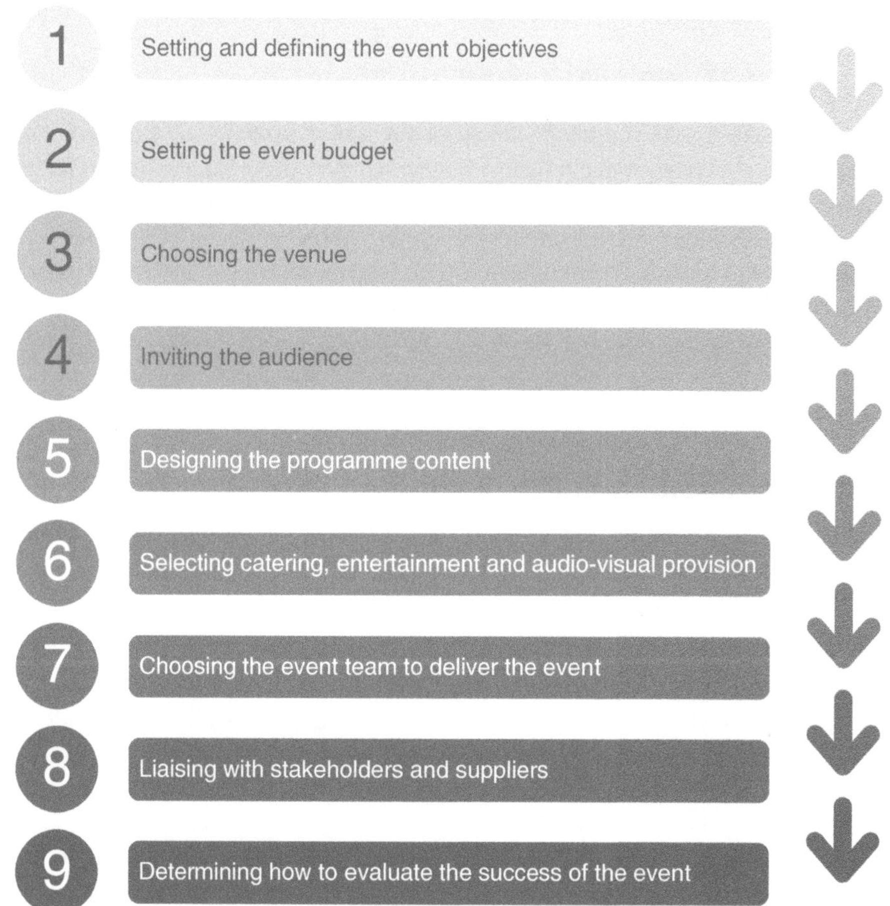
1
Setting and defining the event objectives
2
Setting the event budget
3
Choosing the venue
4
Inviting the audience
5
Designing the programme content
6
Selecting catering, entertainment and audio-visual provision
7
Choosing the event team to deliver the event
8
Liaising with stakeholders and suppliers
9
Determining how to evaluate the success of the event

FIGURE 1.3 The planning process

There may be a number of reasons why the event is being held. However, many fail to learn lessons from previous mistakes, due to insufficient evaluation and monitoring of client feedback. Without this stakeholder feedback, it is impossible to evaluate the **Return on Objectives (ROO)** in the post-event evaluation stage. Defining objectives also allows the organiser to discuss with the budget holder whether this is the most appropriate use of the client's money. This involves taking various criteria into consideration and assessing defined performance benchmarks, and trying to predict whether the event will result in a **Return on Investment (ROI)**.

Return on Objectives (ROO) the measurement of the objectives set at the outset

Return on Investment (ROI) adhering to the financial or other defined performance benchmarks set

SETTING THE BUDGET

Once the aims and objectives have been set, the next vital stage of the planning process is to set the budget and determine who will be responsible for paying it. For the organiser, the most important factor of the planning phase is to ensure that there is enough income to cover any items of expenditure and to constantly review the budget and apprise the budget owner of any areas of concern or overspend. The use of a bespoke financial conference management system and Excel spreadsheets can help monitor spend. More specific areas of budgeting will be discussed in more detail in Chapter 7, where event finance is discussed.

CHOOSING THE VENUE

Choosing a venue that is fit for purpose and indeed choosing the right venue come very high on the list of planning priorities. The selected venue does not have to be the same as that featured in the original bid documentation, but it should at least be of the same standard. Otherwise there may be concerns on the part of key stakeholders, and choosing an appropriate venue is imperative to the overall success. The two main criteria are functionality and the suitability of the venue. As well as being unique, the venue should contain certain features and facilities that will satisfy the customer and audience, not just accommodating the event, but enhancing it. Today, venue sourcing is often conducted online, with available features such as: visual inclusion, bespoke venue search engines and **virtual renderings**. However, one threat to this way of venue sourcing is that the pictures that are featured on the venue website can be misleading and may not accurately resemble the real image of the room or the capacities. For that reason, it is extremely important to conduct a site inspection, before confirming or paying.

Virtual renderings online animation, and exteriors and interior floor plans, which make the process far easier for the organiser than in previous times

INVITING THE AUDIENCE

No matter how successful is the planning and delivery process, the event will only be deemed successful if it attracts an audience. During the planning phase, it is essential to publicise the event, even if it is a corporate conference, where delegates are required to attend. This becomes far more significant when the delegates have to pay their own costs to attend. For this reason, thorough research needs to be conducted during the planning phase, in order to avoid conflict with other similar ones that may be taking place around that time, or in the same area (see Chapter 4). Once the venue has been confirmed and the date has been finalised, it is advisable to send out a Save the Date notification, to alert the target audience to when the event is taking place. This needs to be announced as soon as possible and often before the main marketing and promotion activities commence. The area of promotion and marketing will be further discussed in Chapter 6.

DESIGNING THE PROGRAMME CONTENT

The next stage of the planning process is to prepare a programme with the content and to develop this programme, considering all activities and precise timings throughout the event duration. The programme content will vary depending on the event type; for example, the programme for a corporate event would typically include both a conference programme and a social programme. Once there is relative certainty as to the number of participants attending, the programme can be finalised. At this stage, adjustments can be made to the schedule, for example to the start times or the order of presentations. Ideally, the programme should be printed or posted out to participating organisations and dignitaries one or two weeks ahead of delivery. Other participants may receive their programmes on the day.

Organisers need to balance content with the costs involved of delivering the programme. The conference programme would generally itemise any **keynote speakers** and include the more formal conference and seminar material and topics to be discussed. The social programme would generally detail the scheduled activities, including items such as excursions and off-site dining. The area of programme and content design will also be explored in more detail in Chapters 2 and 6.

Keynote speakers
those speakers who establish the framework for the event agenda

SELECTING CATERING, ENTERTAINMENT AND AUDIO-VISUAL PROVISION

Once the main features have been determined, the fine tuning can begin. At this stage, decisions can be taken about the catering and food and beverage requirements and how this element of the programme will be set up and managed. Again, this will vary considerably, depending on the event type. The topic of catering will be further discussed in Chapter 6.

Complex events use a variety of special effects and will require a specialist production coordinator to manage the audio-visual aspects. Furnishing the function space can range from shifting a few chairs and tables on to the main stage, to constructing flat packs. One of the elements to consider in the pre-event planning phase will be the use of delivery schedules and detailed inventories. The audio-visual (AV) and production elements also range from a basic, but functional AV package of projector, screen and laptop or tablet, to a far more sophisticated arrangement of production equipment. This topic will be further explored in Chapter 8, but it is worth emphasising that production is an important aspect that will have a significant impact on the overall budget and the venue choice and specifications, so it needs to be considered in the early planning stages.

CHOOSING THE TEAM TO DELIVER

An essential part of the planning processes is determining the amount of staff needed to deliver the event, then assigning roles and responsibilities. All events need staff.

The question is how many and of what type? There are any number of factors that will influence the type and number of staff required. Human resource management is the core factor of creating, planning and selecting an appropriate team, with the right skills.

Not all staff receive paid wages. Mega events, such as the Olympic Games, use thousands of volunteers, so the two routes to consider in terms of staffing are: the use of paid staff, and the use of unpaid volunteer staff. When using professional staff, it is most likely that they will be hired for their specific skills, and that they will have already undergone some sort of specific training. One way of ensuring this is to recruit staff using an agency that already has qualified staff on its books. As already mentioned, when recruiting volunteers, the organiser will need to consider how skilled they are to work on that specific event, and whether or not any additional training will be required in advance. Most events with a high public profile will train their volunteers, such as the Virgin London Marathon or the Tour of Britain cycle race. This area will be further discussed later in this chapter.

LIAISING WITH STAKEHOLDERS AND SUPPLIERS

Successful events need to meet the expectations of the many stakeholders involved. A 'stakeholder' is anyone who has an interest in the *value* that the organisation creates. Various stakeholder perspectives should be considered in the planning stage, as events imply and mean different things for different parties and one stakeholder's gain may be another's loss. These varying stakeholder perspectives will influence everything from marketing to funding. All stakeholders are important, because their expectations for and attitudes towards the event will have a considerable impact on the overall experience and success of it. As the price of failure can be enormous, rigorous planning, in-depth research and constant evaluation are needed, together with some key decision-making from approval committees, where appropriate.

In today's market, transparency, accountability and effective public relations (PR) are essential components in stakeholder engagement. The general aim is to set up as many 'win–win' opportunities as possible and to keep in communication with all stakeholders throughout the process. When developing strategic plans, organisations should set objectives that reflect the needs of all their principal stakeholders, some of which are detailed in Table 1.2.

Owners	All event types and sectors have owners. They tend to be company shareholders in for-profit events, corporate and not-for-profit events.
Customers or Consumers	Customers/consumers often pay to attend, e.g. a private exhibition or a festival. They experience a wedding as a guest, or a conference as a delegate. The customer may pay for the consumer to attend, rather than attending themselves. Consumers are generally hosted and do not have to pay out of their own pocket.

(Continued)

TABLE 1.2 (Continued)

Sponsors	Commercial organisations are often *sponsors*, providing the funds. They often seek a return on their investment in the form of promotion and publicity benefits for their company name and products. Government agencies also provide sponsorship to recreation organisations and seek a return on their investment in the form of benefits for the community.
Employees/ volunteers	The industry has a particularly high dependency on volunteers. In large sporting, festival, community and fundraising events, the ratio of volunteers to paid staff is often higher than with other sectors.
The event community	The event community in the host destination is also a stakeholder in the strategic planning process. Organisers should ensure that the services provided are relevant to the community's needs. Communities tend to invest in mega sporting or cultural events through government funding.

TABLE 1.2 Event stakeholders

DETERMINING HOW TO EVALUATE THE SUCCESS OF THE EVENT

Evaluation is the process of measuring the success of an event from a set of key criteria to determine positive and negative outcomes. The evaluation stage tends to take place during the last phase of the event cycle, but it is worth considering that once the event is finished, it will be too late to discuss how it should be evaluated. The evaluation tools and methods need to be determined in the pre-event planning phase, so that it will be possible to monitor the event and pinpoint each stage of its progression, and if necessary, to identify when and how the process started to fail. Deciding and devising a detailed evaluation tool and setting criteria for success are vital components of the post-event planning phase and will be discussed further in Chapter 3.

OBJECTIVE
3
The need to manage various stakeholders

THE NEED TO MANAGE VARIOUS STAKEHOLDERS

MANAGING STAKEHOLDERS

Managing stakeholders involves preparing a detailed stakeholder management plan. In the planning phase, it is imperative for the owner or organisation to determine the role and level of commitment of every stakeholder involved. The stakeholder management plan usually starts by identifying all stakeholders involved in the project and assigning them to groups of primary and secondary categories. The primary stakeholders are usually those that have direct impact, interest or influence and could determine the success or failure of the event. The secondary stakeholders are those that have an indirect impact or influence, but their exclusion would not necessarily determine its overall success or failure.

Once the stakeholders have been identified and categorised, the next step for the project manager is to create a profile for each stakeholder group, in order to fully identify and understand their needs and requirements. It is important to communicate with all stakeholders through regular meetings, special interest groups, consultation, and by keeping them constantly apprised of progress or updates throughout the planning process.

Possible external stakeholders could be the budget holder, local authorities, sponsors, suppliers, corporate partners, government bodies, media or financial affiliates, volunteers, or the delegates or audience. Internal stakeholders could be employees, association members or advisory boards, who may or may not ultimately attend. In the planning stage, it is crucial to discuss how to communicate with all these stakeholders and to set an agenda for regular meetings and reports, to discuss the progress of these meetings and to monitor updates and discuss any new developments with each of the stakeholders. Factors to bear in mind when it comes to dealing with stakeholders are shown in Table 1.3.

- This varies depending on the perspective of the stakeholder, as there are a range of stakeholders.
- All have potentially different aims and objectives.
- It is important to meet these aims with various organisational models.

TABLE 1.3 Stakeholder requirements

MANAGING SPONSORS

Sponsors should be given high priority throughout all stages of the event. Communication with sponsors throughout the planning process is crucial and this communication should be transparent, open and consistent; informing them of any changes, in terms of numbers expected and content of the programme. The agency or client should find out how much involvement the sponsor wants and expects and try to clearly understand each of the sponsor's specific objectives. In the days leading up to the event, full joining instructions should be sent out to the sponsors and any special arrangements should be communicated on-site. In the post-event evaluation phase, feedback should be given to the sponsor, who in turn should attempt to evaluate the success of the sponsorship plan in line with their expectations and the deliverables. This area will be discussed in more depth in Chapter 7.

MANAGING VOLUNTEERS

Volunteers represent a resource for organisers to draw on quickly and cost-effectively. They offer their labour, knowledge, skills and experience, often at no financial cost, so are economically beneficial to all types of organisations. Recruiting voluntary workers has its own challenges and complexities and requires different strategies depending on the size of the event. Mega events, such as the Olympic Games, would not be possible to operate without the use of volunteers, as can be demonstrated by the Games Makers for London 2012 and for Rio 2016. For this reason, organisers of mega events tend to recruit more applicants than they actually require. This is done deliberately as a contingency strategy, in case of no-shows, or last-minute cancellations, but can in turn drive up the overheads involved in volunteer training and expenses.

Organisations where there is a potentially suitable demographic of potential volunteers, such as universities or colleges, need to be identified. In some cases, well-known figures are recruited as ambassadors to boost numbers and the publicity involved with recruitment. Volunteers will often be the first point of contact for the customer, greeting them and directing them around the venue, so it is essential to brief them on any key information and prepare them for any questions attendees might ask. Even for smaller events, the role of the volunteer is paramount. Some local community events are often solely managed by volunteers.

In order to determine what rewards might be appropriate to offer volunteers, it is often advisable to examine motivations for volunteering in the first place. Volunteer motivations are often divided into intrinsic behaviour, driven by internal rewards, and extrinsic behaviour, driven by external rewards or personal gain. Volunteers seem to enjoy the belonging and sense of community that take place when working as part of a team on an event, which often leads them to go on to volunteer at other events. However, as volunteers are generally unpaid for their services, keeping them happy is integral to the recruitment process.

As an unpaid member of staff, it is easy to just walk away if feeling disgruntled or dissatisfied. Recent suggestions to ensure volunteer retention have therefore included sustaining and rewarding volunteers for their contribution. This might include paying volunteers' expenses; offering them tax incentives; free tickets and merchandise; flexible working hours and shorter commitments; and other concessions.

DID YOU KNOW?

Volunteers in the UK currently contribute an estimated £23.9bn to the UK economy per year.

The word 'to volunteer' was first recorded in 1755, originating from the Middle French word 'voluntaire' and derived from the noun 'volunteer', meaning 'one who offers himself for military service'.

EVENT ETHICS

Volunteers are increasingly employed, particularly in the fundraising sector, which is often known as 'the Third Sector'. These volunteers give substantial time and commitment. Many events would not be able to operate without them, as they are integral to charitable and mega events, such as the Olympic Games.

Do you agree or disagree with the view that volunteering is just a source of cheap labour, which takes away paid jobs?

THE STRUCTURE OF THE INDUSTRY: BUYERS, AGENCIES, INTERMEDIARIES AND SUPPLIERS

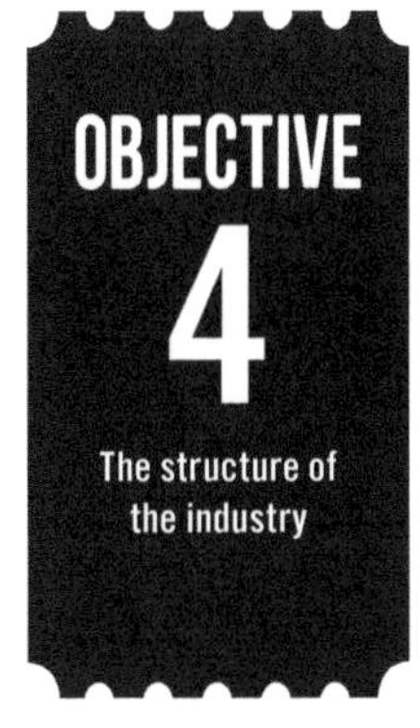

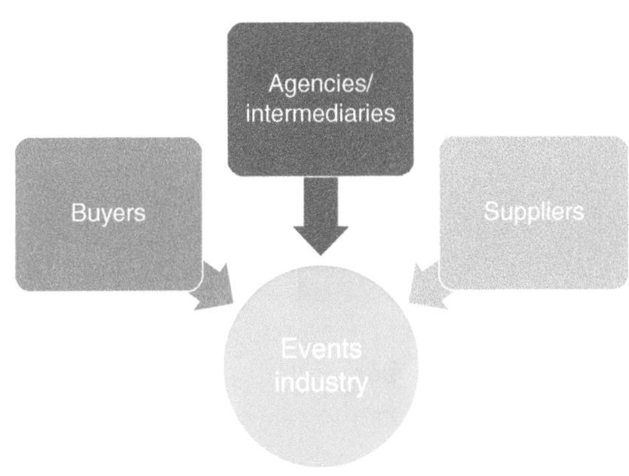

FIGURE 1.4 The structure of the events industry

WHAT IS AN 'EVENT STRUCTURE'?

The industry is fragmented and made up of many different sectors, organisations and suppliers. These sectors are often referred to as the event structure. Essentially, the structure or infrastructure of the industry can be applied, irrespective of size, scale and type. There are a number of functions and roles that exist in the sector, including venue suppliers, destination and accommodation providers and air and ground transportation companies. There are also a whole plethora of specialist suppliers, who provide the industry with products and services, such as: displays, catering, staffing, entertainment services, technical equipment, telecommunications and IT companies, interpreters and translators, speciality caterers, exhibition contractors, production companies and event insurance specialists.

Event management services are also offered through agencies, consultants and specialist planning companies, who offer a seamless 'one-stop shop' approach to the buyer. Some of the sectors are very distinct and specialised, for example: **Destination Marketing Organisations (DMOs)** and **Destination Management Companies (DMCs)**, but still form an important part of the event structure, which comprises buyers, suppliers and intermediaries or agencies, as detailed further in the following section.

Destination Marketing Organisations (DMOs) organisations that promote a town, city, region, or country in order to increase the number of visitors and promote the development and marketing of a destination

Destination Management Companies (DMCs) professional services companies with local knowledge, expertise and resources, working in the design and implementation of events, activities, tours, transportation and programme logistics

THE EVENT BUYER

Entrepreneurial buyer
someone who makes money by starting their own business, especially when this involves seeing a new opportunity and taking risks

End-users
people who ultimately use or are intended to ultimately use a product

An event buyer, as the name implies, is generally the individual, company or organisation that holds the budget and purchases event services. Buyers can come from corporate companies, agencies, associations, the public sector or they could also be an **entrepreneurial buyer**. The common factor is that they 'hold the purse strings' and have control of the budget, whether or not they are paying for the event themselves, or accruing funds from a corporation, other association or body. Generally, buyers are **end-users**, who buy or hire conference venues and related services required to deliver their event.

In the case of private events, a buyer, client or owner could also be the bride or groom, or their family, who are paying for the wedding, or an individual who has decided to outsource elements of a private party. In the sporting arena, a buyer might be a sports' funding organisation, board, committee or an association.

THE CORPORATE BUYER

Consumer
a person who experiences goods and services for personal use but does not necessarily purchase them

A corporate event can be defined as a gathering that is sponsored by a business for its employees, business partners, clients and/or prospective clients. A corporate buyer may also be a conference organiser, working on behalf of a corporate company. In the United States and Australia, conference organisers are also known as meeting planners or professional conference organisers (PCOs). Corporate buyers tend to be known as 'the client'. They are usually the customer, although not necessarily always the **consumer**. Corporate events vary in size and type and could include any of the following:

- Annual general meetings, board meetings
- Exhibitions
- Congresses
- Product launches
- Team-building events
- Sales conferences
- Reward and recognition events
- Training courses and seminars.

Today, large corporate companies tend to be governed by Procurement departments (see Chapters 5 and 10). Their role is to procure event products and services on behalf of their company and employees, without necessarily experiencing these services or products first-hand. Table 1.4 details some of the main corporate sectors that buy conference services.

CORPORATE BUYING PATTERNS

Highest yielding
producing the largest amount; giving the highest return

Outsource
contracting out of a business process to another party

In terms of corporate buying patterns, budgets tend to be more generous than with other sectors, so corporate events tend to be the **highest yielding** sector in the industry. High spending sectors are generally the pharmaceutical, information technology (IT) and automotive industries, with the USA and Europe tending to spend more on corporate events than other countries. Some larger corporate companies have their own teams, but still prefer to **outsource** elements to an agency or event management company, with proven expertise. This allows the corporate team to concentrate on their other responsibilities, such as managing the content and delegate communication.

Corporate Sector	Examples
Petrochemical Industry, including oil and gas suppliers	BP, Exxon or AGL Energy, Australia
Pharmaceutical and Healthcare	Glaxo SmithKline, United Healthcare, Johnson and Johnson
IT and Telecommunications	Microsoft, Samsung, Google
Automotive and Manufacturing	Toyota, Fiat, Tata steel, ChemChina
Financial and Professional services	Ernst and Young, UBS, PricewaterhouseCoopers
Retail including food and drink	Marks & Spencer, Walmart, Subway, Costa Coffee
Travel and Transport	British Airways, Eurostar, Australian Tourist Commission

TABLE 1.4 Major corporate sectors that buy events

In some cases, the event owner or buyer might purchase services directly from the supplier, when organising their company event, often trying to reduce expenditure, as outsourcing to an **intermediary** can be an expensive part of the overall budget and cutting out the middle man or agency can be perceived as a way to make savings in times of recession or austerity.

Intermediary
the person or company who acts as a mediator or agent between parties

Centralised
under a single authority

Within different corporate organisations, buying is not always **centralised**. There are various internal departments that might be responsible for organising the company's conferences or events; ranging from company private assistants (PAs), secretaries, marketing and communications employees to human resources teams, so this can make it challenging to find who is responsible. Some corporate staff charged with organising events may have had very little formal conference training.

The payment of corporate events tends to come from a central marketing budget. For this reason, corporate buyers tend to make quick decisions once they have decided to commission an event, so the process is relatively quick compared to other sectors. Company delegates do not pay to attend internal events, but are expected to attend them, as part of their job function.

Previously, a reasonable average lead time for a corporate event may have been circa three months, but in recent years the trend has been for shorter lead times, sometimes even less than a couple of weeks before delivery. This could be because corporate clients sometimes prefer to hold off commissioning, until they are completely sure they have enough annual budget available to run the event. At other times, they need to act quickly at the end of a year quarter or year end, to use up any residual budget. This can result in putting added pressure on agencies and suppliers to organise and deliver a corporate conference or meeting within a very short time frame. Sometimes corporate organisations need to evaluate whether it is the right time to hold an event, and how this will be perceived in terms of staff morale, for instance that there are no imminent redundancies or staff freezes to detract from the event purpose. The corporate buyer tends to commission events throughout the year, though generally the summer months tend to be quiet, because of the holiday period, and autumn and spring are the busiest months.

In order to ensure a professional execution, corporate events generally tend to be held in hotels or other purpose-built conference centres. In recent years, however, there has been a shift in demand towards a more flexible conference offering, which will appeal to internal and external clients and delegates. Following on from the recent global recession, the trend has been to shorten corporate events, so that they tend to take place during daylight hours, and do not require overnight accommodation. This trend has opened up the possibility of using non-residential or unusual venues, such as a museum, an art gallery or an airline hangar to stage corporate events. In an environment where increased focus is given to budget management and greater innovation, using an unusual venue can create groundbreaking design and better food and beverage selection. It can also increase interest in the venue and the delegates' desire to attend, as well as substantially reducing the overall budget for the corporate buyer. However, this can be a challenging remit for the incumbent agency or the event management company, who are charged with the organisation, as well as for the venue itself.

REAL INSIGHT 1.1

THE INCREASED USE OF UNUSUAL VENUES FOR CORPORATE EVENTS

Demand for unusual venues has risen by almost one-third in the past 12 months, according to venue collective Lime Venue Portfolio, who are based in the UK. The group says that organisers are being 'spurred on creatively' by unique venues. Richard Kadri-Langford, Head of Marketing at Lime Venues, said: 'The unusual venue market is now an established sector of the industry and one that continues to add incremental value to it. In short organisers now have the right venues to have them in and are being spurred on creatively to create more expansive experiences. Organising events involves the buyer placing a lot of trust in the suppliers and venues they choose. We have worked hard to improve the level of trust buyers have in our portfolio of venues by placing a high degree of value in our people and ensuring they are experienced, well trained and supportive. Thus, the perceived risk of using an unusual venue, which was historically quite high, has been eroded over time. We like to think we have been at the forefront of this development.'

The rich historical heritage of the UK lends itself to some amazing and unusual venues, ranging from museums and zoos to prisons. BMW used the Darwin Centre at the Natural History Museum in London to host an event for 100 clients in 2014, where guests were taken on an immersive journey through the David Attenborough studio, before enjoying cocktails, canapés and music in the glass-fronted atrium. The Magic Circle Headquarters in London is also not a traditional corporate venue but has hosted an array of corporate events in recent years for clients such as HSBC, Direct Marketing Association and the Royal Bank of Scotland. This highlights the growing trend to use novelty venues to captivate and engage delegates and make the conference experience more memorable.

SOURCE: meetpie.com

THE ASSOCIATION BUYER

Associations usually commission events to provide a service rather than for financial return. As delegates are often required to pay their own expenses to attend, it is in the interest of the associations to keep the meetings functional and designed to be practical and useful, and to keep costs as low as possible. Unlike corporate events, there is no central budget, so invariably costs need to be as streamlined as possible, with less emphasis on luxury accommodation than with other sectors. For that reason, these events are often held in less expensive conference or convention centres or academic venues out of term time, rather than in hotels. See Table 1.5 for examples of association buyers.

Delegate numbers for association events tend to be higher than for corporate ones. For this reason, the lead time sometimes needs to be a few years in advance, in order to guarantee that a venue sizeable enough to accommodate these large numbers can be secured. Another reason why lead times are often prolonged, is that the decision-making process is often made by a committee, many of whom may be volunteers and only working for the board or association in their spare time.

Association Sector	Examples
Professional or trade associations/ institutions	The American Institute of Certified Public Accountants; Editorial Freelancers Association; National Network of Embroidery Professionals
Voluntary associations and societies	WaterAid; Greenpeace; Child Line India Foundation
Charities	Save the Children; Médecins Sans Frontières; Helen Keller International
Religious organisations	American Jewish Committee; the Inter-Religious Organisation of Singapore; Orthodox Peace Fellowship
Political parties/Trade unions	The Conservative Party; AKEL: Progressive Party of the Working People, Cyprus; African National Congress (ANC)

TABLE 1.5 The association buyer

In order to decide on future host venues and cities, prospective venues and/or destinations are often shortlisted and the host destinations themselves are required to demonstrate the benefits they could offer in a detailed bid proposal (see Chapter 5). Normally different venues and destinations are considered each time at the bid stage, though it is not unusual for a charity or an association to block-book space at the same venue in advance to guarantee securing a space large enough to accommodate large delegate numbers. Cancer Research UK, for example, has a policy of confirming the NEC in Birmingham up to five years in advance for its annual conference.

Several destinations and venues might be involved in the proposal stage and a site inspection or visit is usually made before reaching a final decision. Sometimes these events require that a partner programme runs simultaneously to the conference; delegates' spouses are invited to join, but rather than attending the conference, are hosted in other leisure activities, such as a golf day or shopping excursion.

PUBLIC SECTOR BUYERS

Also known as 'government' buyers, public sector buyers adopt similar buying patterns to those of associations. As these organisations are non-profit organisations, they tend to use surplus of the revenues to further achieve their ultimate objective; rather than distributing income to the organisation's shareholders, leaders or members, the budget tends to come from political party membership fees, or taxpayers' money. They are therefore often required to run on tight budgets, so in a similar way to association buyers, they often opt for less prestigious venues. Sometimes the perception of saving money is more important than the actual cost of the event. For example, it would be highly inappropriate for one of these meetings to take place in a venue or destination that was deemed to be too luxurious or resort-like. This might give out the wrong message or imply that the attendees are having some sort of 'jolly', rather than an essential governmental conference. A local town hall in a business city would therefore be more appropriate than a resort for this type of meeting. Public sector delegates would not expect to pay to attend this type of political or governmental conference. In fact, some public sector delegates receive a 'per diem' allowance, when attending these events.

'Per diem' allowance a daily allowance or specific amount of money an organisation gives an individual, often an employee, per day to cover living expenses when working

REAL INSIGHT 1.2

THE UK GOVERNMENT'S PREFERRED ANNUAL CONFERENCE VENUES

Most years in the UK, the Labour and Conservative Party conferences take place over a period of three weeks during September and October of each year, whilst the House of Commons is in recess. In the UK, political party conferences have traditionally taken place in seaside resorts such as Blackpool, Brighton and Bournemouth. This is primarily for historical reasons and largely due to there being plenty of cheap accommodation available in such towns at the end of the summer holiday season. Notoriously, back in 1984, during the Conservative Party conference, there was a terrorist attack on the British government. This may have been the most ambitious plot since the Gunpowder plot of 1605. The Provisional IRA detonated a bomb at the Grand Hotel, Brighton on 12 October 1984, where the Conservative annual conference was taking place. Most of the government was staying at the hotel at the time. Five people were killed in the explosion, and more than 30 were injured. It came very close to wiping out most of the government, including the Prime Minister, Margaret Thatcher.

Nowadays, in the UK these conferences are increasingly taking place in major cities such as Manchester, Liverpool, Birmingham and Glasgow, with all of the major UK political parties' conferences taking place in towns and cities in 2016. There is an unofficial agreement between the parties that they will stagger the timing of their conferences, to allow undivided media attention, though smaller political parties do not always firmly abide by this rule. In 2012, for example, there was an overlap between the Liberal Democrat and UK Independence Party annual conferences, with the latter concluding on the opening day of the former, and in 2013 the Liberal Democrat and Green Party of England and Wales conferences overlapped by three days.

Similar types of venues are used overseas for government conferences, with Australia hosting the 2016 LNP Annual Convention at the Brisbane Convention & Exhibition Centre and New Zealand's Labour Party conference taking place at the Wigram Air Force Museum Events Centre in Christchurch.

THE INDIVIDUAL BUYER/ENTREPRENEUR

Despite the increasing requirement to have the right licences and training in place to set up events, at this stage there is still no legal requirement to be accredited, or hold a professional qualification, as will be further discussed in Chapter 10. Many individual planners and small concerns still decide to 'go it alone', organising profit-generating events, often termed a 'user conference', where space is offered to anyone prepared to pay to attend. The individual or 'entrepreneur' identifies a 'hot topic' or debate theme and sources subject key speakers, celebrity guests or entertainment that will attract a target audience. This might be because the individual has researched the topic and sourced specific business or industry-related themes to encourage discussion or has access to the latest knowledge or key acts that will entice an audience to purchase tickets.

For these buyers, it is very important to have access to a good quality database: industry contacts or an updated list of potential attendees, who may have previously shown interest in attending. It is possible for the individual buyer to purchase these lists from suppliers, although the latest laws governing data protection and consumer rights in relation to unsolicited emails, are now making this type of data marketing more challenging for the entrepreneurial buyer.

REAL INSIGHT 1.3

'USER CONFERENCE', DURHAM, UK

The 17th Durham Blackboard Users' Conference took place over two days in January 2017. This conference is organised on an annual basis for and by the user community. Whilst attended by various local commercial companies who use Blackboard and sponsor the conference, they have no influence on the conference theme, programme or conference content itself. Therefore, the attendees are free to offer constructive feedback on the various products. This long-standing e-learning event, now in its 17th year, regularly attracts over 120 delegates. The audience is made up of a mix of repeat attendees and first-time visitors, including learning technologists, librarians, academics, administrators and company management. It is a great networking opportunity offered at a low price.

The conference commenced with an 'optional' free half day of pre-conference workshops and user group sessions, followed by the conference itself. The pre-conference afternoon and the two-day conference were held, as in previous years, at the Durham Business School, Durham. The gala dinner on the final evening took place at Durham Castle. During the conference, there were a number of pre-conference workshops and user group meetings scheduled, including the sessions:

- Blackboard Mobile User Group
- Enterprise Survey Workshop.

Durham University signed up to eduroam to facilitate the use of Twitter at the event and each delegate was given a temporary conference ID at registration.

SOURCE: https://community.dur.ac.uk/lt.team/conference

THE ROLE OF THE AGENCY OR INTERMEDIARY

The agency or intermediary is the 'middleman' bridging the gap from the buyer, or budget holder to the supplier. As previously discussed, sometimes the buyer might prefer to purchase products and services direct from the supplier, thus 'cutting out' the middleman, and in doing so, potentially save money. However, it is questionable whether going direct to a supplier does actually cut costs overall.

The advantage of channelling events through an agency or intermediary is that they have both expertise and buying power. It is their everyday business to source products and services from suppliers, on behalf of their clients. In an ever more competitive environment, agencies have the supplier contacts, negotiation skills and expertise to demonstrate savings to their client, using **economies of scale purchasing**, not to mention a certain amount of goodwill.

Economies of scale purchasing
large businesses often receive a discount because they are buying in bulk

Agencies or intermediaries should also have a good understanding as to what qualifies as a fair price within the industry and will be able to benchmark costs with a good degree of accuracy. Another advantage of using an agency is that they generally have up-to-date venue and destination knowledge, as they are liaising with suppliers on a continuous basis. Additionally, event agencies get to experience the facilities and services of many venues and upcoming destinations, through running other programmes, or conducting site inspections and sometimes **familiarisation trips or educationals**, hosted by the destination or venue. There are a number of agencies and intermediaries that exist in the industry, including those listed in Table 1.6.

Familiarisation trips or educationals a free or low-cost trip that travel agents or event staff are provided by suppliers to gain an understanding of the benefits of different trips that they can sell to their clients

Company type	Role
Event management agency/company	The event management company's tasks may include the following activities: • Researching and recommending a suitable destination and/or venue • Planning the conference and social programme • Marketing the conference and handling delegate registrations • Booking delegate accommodation and ensuring meeting-room facilities are sufficient • Planning an exhibition to run concurrently with the conference • Producing a budget and handling all of the conference finances. They are normally paid a management fee by the client organisation. Some also get commission from the venues. They tend to work with corporate buyers, for a minimum three-year contract, issued by the corporate procurement division.
Venue search agency	Generally, offer a more limited service, restricted to researching and recommending a suitable event venue. They put forward a shortlist of three possible venue choices, they receive between 8–10% agency commission from the venue itself once the meeting has confirmed, rather than charging a fee. All other supplier liaison and operational work is handled by the end-client after that point. A volume business, i.e. the more bookings they place, the more commission they will earn. Can prove 'a foot in the door' to procuring other services from the client, e.g. registration or on-site support.
Production company	Involved in the actual design, programme delivery and staging of the conference, rather than the planning and operational delivery. Can be 'all-singing-and dancing', or just the provision of sound and lighting – audio-visual. It is not unusual for a client to issue two separate tenders for the operational and production elements of the same event. The challenge is then for two different agencies to work together on the same project.

(Continued)

TABLE 1.6 (Continued)

Company type	Role
Destination management company (DMC)	A local service organisation that provides consulting services, creative events and logistics management, based on an in-depth knowledge of the destination and local venues. Usually charges commission and/or a management fee. A 'ground-handler' is just involved with providing transportation within a destination.
Corporate events company	Involved with sporting or recreational events and provides corporate hospitality and specialised team-building events. Some clients will go direct to them or can be sub-contracted by a destination management company or an event management company.
Representation company	An agency that represents hotels and venues but is not large enough to have its own sales division in a particular region or country. The representation company may have a portfolio of properties that it promotes and markets to corporate or other agency buyers. It conducts sales visits to present the hotels and venues to potential conference buyers.
Business travel agency	A form of travel agency that deals with business customers only. Business travel usually consists of making arrangements for air, rail, coach, ferry and individual hotel accommodation for the traveller. Some larger corporate organisations have business travel implants based in their offices, to provide a seamless service for their company employees.

TABLE 1.6 Event agencies and intermediaries

WHAT IS AN EVENT SUPPLIER?

The list of event suppliers is extensive, but a few of the principle suppliers to the industry are as follows:

- Venues
- Destinations
- Airline and transportation companies
- Other suppliers to the events industry.

VENUES

The venue product is the standardisation of meeting space, bedrooms and in-house technology. In the current market, event venues can be eclectic and diverse. Kotler and Armstrong (2004) describe venues as 'hybrid places' that have become places of combined recreation and learning, in order to be successful.

The most successful venues are those that consider the needs of the client, strive to match their expectations, and tailor their product and services accordingly. Appropriate venue staff should be proficient at conducting 'show-rounds' and **recreational visits (recces)**. All venue staff should be made aware if any site visits are scheduled and be able to show the client relevant space based on their specific

Recreational visits (recces) visits to a place in order to become familiar with it meeting requirements. Branded hotels offer a guaranteed quality of service, and effective branding and categorisation can reassure clients on expected service-level standards, giving these venues a competitive edge.

DESTINATIONS

The conference location can be essential to the overall success of an event. The destination could be a termed as a country, city or region. Larger events are designed to be of great importance to the destinations they take place in, therefore a competitive bidding process to become the host destination is often the remit of government departments, sporting and other associations. With smaller events, the incumbent agency might use its expertise to influence the buyer, but generally it is the buyer or event owner who makes the final choice on destination. Events are used today to boost the awareness, appeal and profitability of a tourism destination and to harness cultural attractions in the short and/or long term, so that the destination becomes the entrepreneurial city, the creative city, the eventful city or the intercultural city. Destination image and branding will be further discussed in Chapter 5.

Most conference destinations contain a number of suitable venues, facilities, attractions and other support services to attract conference business. It is often the host cities' **convention and visitor's bureau** that promotes the strengths of the destination they represent. Indeed, the features and attractions of a destination may also be a key deciding factor for a bid to host a festival, sporting or mega event. A destination's success often relies on its uniqueness, status or timely significance to create interest and attract attention.

Convention and visitor's bureau
a non-profit organisation that represents a specific city, town or state

REAL INSIGHT 1.4

SINGAPORE'S REPOSITIONING TO BECOME AN IDEAL MICE DESTINATION

Although already a well-established and respected destination, with an excellent infrastructure, Singapore previously only tended to attract overseas tourists for a stopover en-route to Australia or New Zealand. Moreover, Singapore faced stiff competition from other stopover hubs such as Bangkok or Hong Kong, due to the varied activities and sightseeing opportunities that these other destinations offered. Tourists stopping over at these destinations were actually being persuaded to break their journeys and spend a few days, rather than just an overnight stop. This is exactly the type of business sector that the Singapore Tourist Board (STB) wanted to see for Singapore. Over the past few years, they have been working hard to attract longer stay business to the city

(Continued)

by repositioning Singapore as a tourism stop, worthy of spending a few nights. This has included creating more attractions in Singapore to equal those offered in Bangkok and Hong Kong. The Marina Bay area and Sentosa Island have been redeveloped, introducing excursions such as scenic boat rides; the Singapore flyer, a 28-capsule version of the London Eye; and breath-taking venue and transfers, with trishaw rides.

STB have also been working hard to promote and publicise Singapore's Straits Chinese and Peranakans cultural history throughout the Civic District, Chinatown and Little India, with entertainment ideas such as visits to Thiw Kang Pottery jungle; a local vegetable farm; a spice merchant's mansion; and a culinary school set in the grounds of Fort Canning, a nearby tea plantation. The goal has been to push visitor numbers over 17 million and to generate over $4.3 billion in increased tourism, as well as generating new jobs within the city.

A new Convention and Exhibition centre has been completed, including an entirely glass-fronted main entrance and space that can accommodate up to 12,000 delegates theatre-style, with a further 31 meeting rooms to hold between 10 and 400 people. To bolster the new positioning of MICE events in Singapore, a third airline terminal has also been built at Changi airport.

AIRLINE AND TRANSPORTATION COMPANIES

Both airline and transportation companies offer bespoke services for group travel that function quite differently from that of individual bookings. For example, corporate buyers may have business travel implants within their offices, or outsource to a business travel company, who can provide a reliable 24-hours delivery and an out-of-office service for air and ground travel requirements. Conference buyers and intermediaries of group travel have more flexibility with suppliers in terms of fare rates, ticket restrictions and timelines for submitting passenger names, than would normally be permitted. Ground transportation could include the hire of coaches, minivans, limousines, taxis or trains to transport delegates. Again, these ground transportation services offer a more flexible provision for group delegates. Ground handling services include:

- Group representation and obtaining local permits
- Catering and fuel supply
- Transportation and hotel arrangements
- International trip handling
- Private and executive aviation handling
- Special 'Meet and Assist' services
- Crew assistance
- Visa arrangements
- Government and military flights handling
- Medical flights handling.

Other event suppliers are shown in Table 1.7.

Suppliers	Examples
Audio-visual and production companies	Fisher Productions, ON Event Services, USA
Telecommunication companies, including video-conferencing providers	Polycom, Vidyo, Telstra
Catering companies	Emirates Abela Catering Company, Leith's, Compass, Sodexho
Transportation providers, including airlines, coach and rail companies, car hire and taxi companies	Jetstar Airways, SNCF, Golden Tours
Interpreters and translators for international events	ABCO International Translators and Interpreters, Toronto
Speaker bureaus	The London Speaker Bureau, The Harry Walker Agency, USA
Lighting and floral companies	Shenzhen EzPro Sound and Lighting Technology Co. Ltd, A Love Affair Floral & Event Design, Sydney
Event insurance companies	Hiscox Event Assured, Insure my Event, USA

TABLE 1.7 Other event suppliers

HOW DIFFERENT EVENT SECTORS HAVE EVOLVED AND ARE CONTINUING TO GROW

OBJECTIVE
5
How different sectors have evolved and are continuing to grow

WHEN DID EVENTS BEGIN? THE EVOLUTION OF AN EMERGING INDUSTRY

Events in the form of organised acts and performances have their origins in ancient history and have always had an important function within society, providing participants with the opportunity to assert their identities and share rituals and celebrations. In the days before the Internet and social media, communities displayed an anthropological need to get together and socialise and to celebrate certain rituals and traditions. Traditionally, the origins of these special events and festivals were based around special religious holy days, celebrated across various religions and countries around the world. In today's evolving globalised society, with its diverse cultural mix, certain key dates on the calendar are still recognised as an occasion to celebrate individual milestone anniversaries and achievements, such as birthday parties, wedding celebrations, funerals, house warming parties, and so on, but have grown today to include events that may have originated in other parts of the world. For example, hen and stag nights and baby showers were concepts that were first introduced to other cultures and countries from the USA. Carnival, for example, originated in South America and the Caribbean, but is now celebrated globally.

Rites of passage
a ceremony that marks the transition from one phase of life to another

Events, however, are not solely about marking **rites of passage**. In modern times, they make a key contribution to cultural and economic development and can have a major impact on the development of cultural tourism in the destinations where they take place. Some events that have been taking place for many years have become very popular and familiar. These include fairs, festivals, sporting events, exhibitions and other forms of public celebration.

REAL INSIGHT 1.5

THE LORD MAYOR'S SHOW, LONDON

SOURCE: Image courtesy of Yamen via Wikicommons.

One ancient UK event that has continuously evolved, for example, is The Lord Mayor's Show. The City of London was squeezed by the King's taxes and frequently held hostage in baronial disputes, but in 1215 King John gave his support and issued a Royal Charter allowing the citizens to elect their Mayor every year. There was one important condition: every year the newly elected Mayor must leave the safety of the City, travel upriver to the small town of Westminster and swear loyalty to the Crown. The Lord Mayor has now made that journey for over 800 years, despite wars and plagues, and over time has collectively pledged their loyalty to 34 kings and queens of England.

Today, the Lord Mayor's Show is one of the most famous annual events in London and is held to celebrate the newly elected Lord Mayor of London. The show starts with a river pageant, where the new Lord Mayor travels along the Thames on the QRB Gloriana, a traditional barge, along with 24 other boats. This is followed by a parade through the streets of the City of London and ends with an amazing firework finale displayed across the Thames. This provides stunning views for spectators standing along the Southbank and the bridges over the Embankment. The Lord Mayor's Show is the largest parade of its kind in the world, with more than 7,000 participants; 200 horses; 2,000 military personnel; 220 motor vehicles; 56 floats; 26 marching bands; and the renowned state coach. The City's float is one of 144 that travel the two-mile route. The procession includes livery companies, schools, charities and organisations that the Lord Mayor chooses to champion during their tenure.

A list of key dates provides some indication of how quickly the events industry started to evolve, particularly in the 20th century, and clearly illustrates the connection between events and politics.

GO ONLINE

You can access this in the Appendix (as Table 1.1) provided online at **study.sagepub.com/quick.**

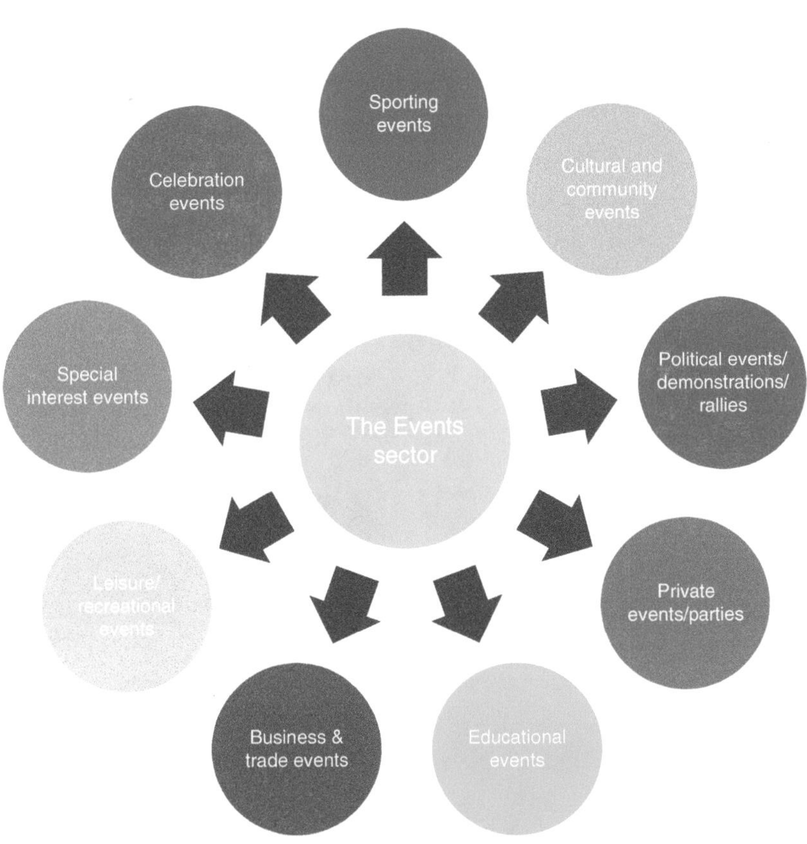

FIGURE 1.5 The events sector

As indicated in Figure 1.5, events can originate from many distinct sectors, often known as typologies. Each one is unique, and it could be argued that they are defined by factors such as: management, length, location, audience, and so on. It can also be the purpose of the actual event or the specific aims and objectives that dictate which category they fall into. However, there are some fundamental features they all have in common. They are all planned and do not happen by chance. All need to be managed and have clear and SMART objectives, i.e. that are Specific, Measurable, Achievable, Realistic and Time-related. From the outset, they all need to have detailed plans of various complexity, under key areas such as marketing, finance, design, and so on. The operational process for all events tends to be fairly similar, and they all need to be measured and evaluated at the end.

There are other ways to categorise events. A common method of doing this is to think about them in terms of their complexity, size, scale, impact and attendance. These categories may appear quite subjective and may not lead to a completely accurate categorisation of typologies; however, knowledge of a category can be beneficial when trying to:

- Promote tourism
- Bring economic benefits to an area or a destination
- Attract media coverage from the event that will be viewed globally
- Organise an event, in order to understand where similar skills can be applied
- Gain recognition for a specific region or area
- Determine spend for the event.

Much has already been written about how events are grouped together. Sometimes we define them according to these various sizes and scale. At other times, the defining characteristic is the event type, or the purpose for holding it in the first place. Further typologies might include the profile of the audience attending, the number of participants, or whether or not they are public or private. If the event is a public one, it is usually open to anyone who pays for a ticket. A private event, however, can only be attended by invitation, e.g. a VIP or a private event, such as a wedding where there is a defined guest list. Table 1.8 shows the various event sectors that exist.

Event sector	Features	Sample event types
Corporate events	Business-related events. Generally paid for by a company or an organisation.	Product launches Sales conferences Incentive travel Exhibitions
Charity and voluntary sector	Not-for-profit events usually held to raise funds and the charity profile. Some paid roles, but are often run by a board of trustees and non-paid voluntary staff. Similar to association and corporate events, but not-for-profit. Most of the funds raised are donated to the charity. Suppliers are therefore often prepared to offer discounts on their services, e.g. waiving their fees for guest speaking, offering a discounted rate on venue hire.	Fun runs Comedy shows, e.g. *Comic Relief* Fashion shows Cake stalls Charity balls Sporting events, e.g. the Virgin London Marathon
Central and local government	Run by local government to discuss local or political issues. Delegates are often required to pay their own fees to attend.	Local government meetings Civic meetings Political forums

Event sector	Features	Sample event types
	The budget needs to be kept as low as possible, with less emphasis on luxury accommodation, more on functionality.	Councillor meetings Election campaigns Political lobbies/rallies
Profit-making events	Run by an organisation or individual entrepreneur to generate revenue. Generally, a 'hot topic' is selected and announced and keynote speakers and topic specialists are sourced. Could be a business or non-business event, designed to attract people to pay to attend for educative or for entertainment purposes. Sometimes known as user-conferences, within the corporate or association sector.	User conferences, e.g. NextGen Government 2016 Conference, Canberra Esri User Conference, 2016, San Diego, California Exhibitions, e.g. The Ideal Home Exhibition, Earls Court
Associations and institutes – education	Includes professional or trade associations; institutions and societies; religious organisations and trade unions. Usually held to provide a service to members or employees, rather than for financial gain. Delegate numbers are usually higher than for corporate events. The lead time is generally longer.	17th International Congress of Dietetics, September 2016, Granada Spain 19th Federation of Asian Veterinary Associations (FAVA) Congress, Ho Chi Minh City, Sept 2016
Sporting events	Come under the umbrella of leisure or recreational events, can include small local events to mega-size events, such as the Olympic Games. Attract international sportsmen and women and in some cases huge crowds of spectators.	Tennis: Wimbledon, Flushing Meadow Golf Championships: The Australian Open Cricket: The Ashes Football: The Euro Championships Motorsports: The Formula 1 Grand Prix
Life cycle/ celebration events	Often private events organised to celebrate or commemorate milestone happenings in the course of the life cycle.	Weddings Funerals
	Generally invitation only – guests are normally hosted by the invitee and do not pay to attend.	Milestone birthdays Hen/stag nights Baby showers Christenings Graduation ball School prom

TABLE 1.8 Features of various event types

EVENT TYPOLOGIES

The following *typologies* are often used when discussing events:

- Mega events
- Special events
- Sporting events
- Hallmark events
- Major events
- Cultural events and festivals
- Minor and small-scale events.

HOW MIGHT WE DEFINE A MEGA EVENT?

In terms of numbers, a mega event is an event that exceeds 1 million visits, with a capital cost of at least $500million and the reputation of a 'must see' show (see Table 1.9).

Olympic Games	Paralympic Games	Commonwealth Games
FIFA World Cup (Fédération Internationale de Football Association)	World Fairs and Expositions	IAAF World Championships (International Association of Athletics Federations)

TABLE 1.9 Mega event examples

REAL INSIGHT 1.6

THE ECONOMIC BENEFITS OF THE FIFA 2014 BRAZILIAN WORLD CUP

In 2014 The Institute of Tourism estimated an $11 billion income spend from visiting tourists during the Brazilian World Cup, with $13.6 billion added to the Brazilian economy and 3.63 million additional jobs created, mostly in the food and beverage, construction, hospitality and tourism sectors. International arrivals increased by 10.1% to 65 million in 2014 (Ernst and Young 2014).

The Brazilian World Cup utilised the potential for bringing 'new' money into the country from outside visitors and significantly contributed to the Brazilian economy from a one-month showcase. However, the cost of staging the World Cup in Brazil equates to £5.4 billion, in a country where 21.4% of the population still live below the poverty line (Index Mundi 2019). In the period leading up to the World Cup, concerns were high, with over 1 million Brazilian residents taking to the streets to protest about the vast amounts being spent to construct new sporting facilities, infrastructure and stadiums, rather than spending on education and healthcare. The sum spent on this event equates to 61% of the country's annual spend on education.

It is difficult to accurately measure the long-term economic benefits of hosting this event. One report predicted that following the Brazilian World Cup consumer spending would fall significantly, due to weaker levels of confidence in the country's global position. However, post event, Euromonitor found more global companies than ever tapping into Brazil's consumer market and predicted that by 2023 Brazil would have the 5th largest consumer market in the world (consumer expenditure is set to rise to £2.7 trillion annually). By promoting health and fitness through sport to the younger generation, it could be argued that the longer term impact on the Brazilian health-funding system will be financially beneficial. Such claims may eventually ease the tensions over the country's controversial spend in the lead-up to the 2014 FIFA World Cup.

HOW CAN WE DEFINE SPECIAL EVENTS?

Getz (2012) suggests that special events are best defined by their context, but generally can be defined as: 'one-time or infrequently occurring, outside normal programmes or activities of the sponsoring or organising body.' To the customer or guest, these special events are an opportunity for a leisure, social or cultural experience outside the normal range of choices, or beyond everyday experience. Attributes that create and define the sense of 'specialness' and make the event particularly memorable include:

- Festive spirit
- Uniqueness
- Quality
- Authenticity
- Tradition
- Hospitality
- Theming
- Symbolism.

These so-called special events can take the form of specific rituals, presentations, performances or celebrations, but all are consciously planned and created to mark special occasions, or to achieve particular social, cultural or corporate goals and objectives. Some examples of a special event are:

- National days and celebrations
- Important civic occasions

- Unique cultural performances
- Major sporting fixtures
- Corporate functions
- Trade promotions
- Product launches.

SPORTING EVENTS

Sporting events generally evolved on a global basis throughout the 18th, 19th and early 20th centuries, with the emergence of recognisable mega and major global events taking place on a regular basis over the sporting calendar. They are often seen as one of the more 'glamorous' event types, in terms of providing stakeholders with an opportunity to travel overseas within a competitive environment, but they can be complex and require a long lead time to organise. In the past two decades, these, probably more than any other event type, have been influenced by PESTEL impacts, some of which will be further discussed in Chapter 4.

Sport provides many of the UK's most significant and enduring events and these events tend to:

- Attract large crowds and media attention
- Help create a national identity
- Have tourism appeal for the host destination
- Generate considerable economic benefit
- Enjoy royal patronage.

REAL INSIGHT 1.7

ALLEGED DISCRIMINATION IN SPORTING EVENTS

Following the Women's World Cup in June 2015, lawyers representing 40 women's soccer teams' players challenged FIFA and the Canadian Soccer Association (CSA), giving them a deadline to open discussion or face them in court over artificial turf planned for Canada's 2015 Cup.

The lawyers told these bodies that they would file a lawsuit against them over staging next year's women's World Cup in Canada on artificial turf. Players from Germany, Brazil, Spain and the USA are among those claiming that the use of artificial turf, instead of grass, for a major tournament is discriminatory, given that the men's World Cup is always played on grass. The 2014 FIFA World Cup for men in Brazil was played on grass and there are no plans to shift future men's tournaments to artificial turf.

SOURCE: Image courtesy of Hmlarson via Wikicommons, provided under the Creative Commons Attribution 3.0 Unported license.

Lawyers said that 'A lawsuit is a last resort, but one that unfortunately appears necessary and will be initiated in coming days'. Hampton Dellinger, the Washington-based law firm representing the players, said in a statement: 'As the already drafted legal papers demonstrate, the players and their attorneys are prepared to put before a judge what we believe is a clear and very unfortunate case of gender discrimination.' Abby Wambach of the USA and Germany's Nadine Angerer, awarded FIFA players of the year for 2012 and 2013, were among those who signed the original letter.

'The discriminatory proposal of FIFA and the Canadian Soccer Association to stage the 2015 Women's World Cup on artificial turf, coupled with their refusal to discuss ways to fix the mistake, have left the players with no choice,' said Dellinger, 'It is now time to ask the courts to stop FIFA and CSA from forcing elite athletes to compete under game-changing, dangerous and demeaning conditions ... world-class games cannot take place on second-class surfaces.'

The Women's Soccer World Cup was staged in six cities: Vancouver, Edmonton, Winnipeg, Ottawa, Montreal and Moncton, where stadia with artificial turf predominate.

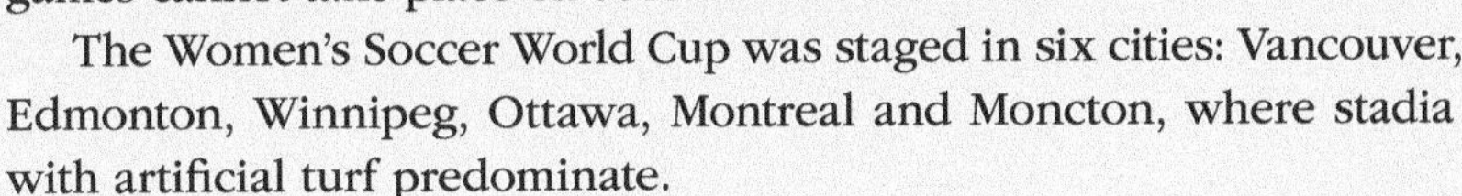

Despite the furore over the turf issue, the event was an overriding success, with the USA qualifying as the eventual winners of the trophy, beating Japan 4–0 in the final match.

HALLMARK EVENTS

Defined by various authors as a one-time or a set of recurring events of a limited duration, these were primarily developed to enhance the awareness, appeal and profitability of a tourist destination in the short and/or long term. They rely on their success or uniqueness, status or timely significance to create interest and attract attention. These hallmark events increase the appeal of a specific tourism destination or region. The hallmark stamp on them is that they have become so closely identified with the ethos of a town, city, or region that they become synonymous with the name of the place and this has resulted in widespread recognition and awareness.

Some examples of hallmark events include:

- Tour de France
- Carnival in Rio
- Oktoberfest, Munich
- Edinburgh International Festival
- Mardi Gras, New Orleans
- Mardi Gras, Sydney.

REAL INSIGHT 1.8

HALLMARK EVENTS

The Edinburgh International Festival is a celebration of the performing arts and is an annual meeting point for a global audience. The Edinburgh International Festival was originally the idea of Rudolf Bing, the then General Manager of Glyndebourne Opera; Henry Harvey Wood, the Head of the British Council in Scotland; and leaders from the City of Edinburgh. It was established in 1947, as a world-class cultural event, to bring together audiences and artists from around the world. The International Festival presents some of the finest performers and ensembles from the worlds of dance, opera, music and theatre for three weeks in August.

The International Festival inspired artists who were not part of the international programme to put on shows of their own, and these events grew into the Edinburgh Festival Fringe. More festivals have grown up around it in August and early September, as well as throughout the year. There are now 12 major annual festivals in Edinburgh, the Festival City.

Over the course of the year, the International Festival team travels the world in search of the most exciting and creative artists working today. Together, it brings unique collaborations, world premieres, exciting new takes on classic works, critically acclaimed productions and more to captivate, thrill and entertain audiences from around the world. It always takes place in Scotland and has done so for the past 70 years, and has become synonymous with the destination of Edinburgh. The objectives are to:

- Present a wide range of performances from the world's leading artists to the widest possible audience
- Offer affordable international culture to audiences from Scotland, the rest of the UK and the world
- Offer an international showcase for Scotland's rich culture
- Present innovative performances and programming and a commitment to new work
- Actively welcome and make it possible for all sections of the Scottish and wider public to experience and enjoy the International Festival
- Encourage everyone to participate in the arts throughout the year.

(**SOURCE:** www.eif.co.uk)

MAJOR EVENTS

Many major events are of a sporting nature, but not exclusively. These are capable of attracting significant visitor numbers from outside the region and of generating large audiences, significant local interest, a large number of participants and substantial tourism revenue to the city or destination. Due to their scale and interest, they can attract:

- Significant visitor numbers
- Considerable media coverage
- Substantial economic benefits.

MINOR AND SMALL-SCALE EVENTS

These tend to be small private or public events, that are held within the community or financed by a private donor, but that do not have a major impact on a community or region, due to their small size and audience numbers. An example of this is an awards ceremony or local sporting event or community fair.

CULTURAL EVENTS AND FESTIVALS

Festivals are a growing and financially significant sector of the industry and play a major part in the economy of a host city and the community spirit of that city. These can foster **civic pride** and identity from within the local community and transform a city into an available tourist and commercial destination. In the USA, it is estimated that around 10,000 festivals take place every year, attracting more than 31 million visitors. In Europe and Australia, the growth of this sector has also been significant. Cultural events and festivals are inextricably linked, and we can define the word 'culture' to mean 'the personal expression of community heritage' (Raj et al. 2017). Cultural events can sometimes take the form of arts or musical festivals, varying in scale from local to national – e.g. Aldeburgh, Chichester – to international – e.g. Edinburgh – and global – e.g. Coachella Valley Music and Arts Festival, California. They can be integrated programmes aimed at achieving urban regeneration and cultural renewal, e.g. Glasgow, Sheffield, Birmingham, Torino, Seville, and can be used to promote destination tourism, the result of which may result in significant improvement in the arts infrastructure, such as concert halls and galleries.

Civic pride
satisfaction with local or community achievements

REAL INSIGHT 1.9

MUSIC OF BLACK ORIGIN (MOBO) AWARDS

Originally the brainchild of renowned international entrepreneur Kanya King back in 1996 and launched by former UK Labour Prime Minister Tony Blair to

(Continued)

stamp out the stereotypical controversy surrounding certain genres of music and to close the 'Culture Gap'. The Music of Black Origin Awards (MOBO) has since become a respected and highly acclaimed event, not only among the West Indian community, but enjoyed by all cultures on a global scale. The prime objective of this event was to promote black and black-inspired music, as well as the West Indian and African culture, music and image. Over time, cultural events have a tendency to detach themselves from their original roots and objectives, but this is not necessarily the case with the MOBO awards. Components of a cultural event can include language, religion, values, social organisation, political disclosure, adoption of technology, education and aesthetics, and can be strongly linked to behaviours and interaction.

The legacy of The MOBO awards is the constantly changing creative backdrop of this event, which in turn stimulates fashion designers, photographers, artists, event managers and marketeers. Since 2002 the event has enhanced the programme by launching exclusively sponsored merchandise. This event continues to be popular, both with the original communities it sought to represent and a wider global audience. Today, the event still continues to consistently promote urban music, using media coverage to publicise the event and to ensure a memorable red carpet, which is broadcast on major TV networks. Stakeholders from the music industry welcome this event to enhance positive impacts and it currently contributes a staggering £3.5 billion to the UK economy and has fans across the world mimicking their idols.

CHAPTER SUMMARY

CHAPTER SUMMARY QUESTIONS

1 What are the three main stages of the event cycle?

2 What is a typology?

3 What is the difference between a mega and a hallmark event?

4 What different types of buyers exist in the events industry?

5 Why do planning lead times tend to be longer with associations?

6 How have corporate buying patterns changed in recent years?

DISCUSSION POINTS

- What do you consider the most important event in the world and why?
- Should mega and hallmark events provide a platform for free speech?
- What is the difference between a destination management company (DMC), a 'ground handler' and a representation company?

ACTIVITIES

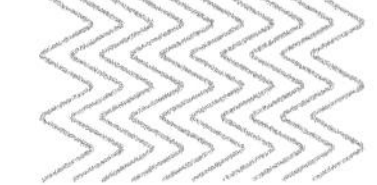

- Draw up a list of reasons why someone would want to hold an event. Try to consider the following when answering:
    - What is the purpose of the event?
    - When do we want to hold it?
    - Where do we want to hold it?
- For each sector detailed in Figure 1.5, provide an example of an event which you think falls within each of the categories listed.
- Draw up a calendar of events (Jan–Dec) that occur in the UK or internationally AND identify the target market that might attend the events you have listed.

REFERENCES

Bladen, C., Kennell, J., Abson, E. and Wilde, N. (2012) *Events Management: An Introduction.* Abingdon: Routledge.

Bowdin, G., McDonnell, G., Allen, J. and O'Toole, W (2011) *Events Management*, 3rd edn. Oxford: Butterworth-Heinemann.

Dowson, R. and Bassett, D. (2015) *Event Planning & Management: A Practical Handbook for PR & Events Professionals.* London: Kogan Page.

Ernst and Young Terco (2014) Sustainable Brazil; Social and Economic Impacts of the 2014 World Cup, publication for Ernst and Young Terco.

FIFA (2015) Benefits of bidding and hosting the FIFA World Cup [online]. Available at: www.fifa.com/governance/competition-organisation/benefits-of-bidding.html (accessed 20 May 2019).

Getz, D. (2012) *Event Studies: Theory, Research and Policy for Planned Events.* Oxford: Butterworth-Heinemann.

Grant, R. (2005) *Contemporary Strategy Analysis.* Melbourne: Blackwell.

Index Mundi (2019) Brazil population below poverty line [online]. Available at: www.indexmundi.com/brazil/population_below_poverty_line.html (accessed 17 October 2019).

Kotler, P. and Armstrong, G. (2004) *Principles of Marketing*, 10th edn. Pearson-Prentice Hall: New Jersey.

Raj, R., Walters, P. and Rashid, T. (2017) *Events Management: Principles and Practice*, 3rd edn. London: SAGE.

Singh, S.R. (2009) *Event Management.* Delhi: APH Publishing Corporation.

Van der Wagen, L. and White, L. (2010) *Events Management: For Tourism, Cultural, Business and Sporting Events*, 4th edn. New South Wales: Pearson.

2

THE EVENT DELIVERY PHASE

CHAPTER OVERVIEW

This chapter will address some of the key issues involved with the delivery of the event on-site and the processes needed to ensure its smooth running. Areas such as: staffing, on-site liaison with suppliers and other stakeholders will be included. It will explore management of the schedule and programme and food and beverage delivery, as well as the use of on-site documentation and online tools. It will also examine best- and worst-case scenarios from events, including health and safety and the execution of emergency and cancellation procedures.

CHAPTER OBJECTIVES

After reading this chapter, you will be able to identify and understand:

OBJECTIVE 1
Managing and monitoring on-site

OBJECTIVE 2
On-site documentation

OBJECTIVE 3
Liaising with stakeholders at the event

OBJECTIVE 4
Event pre-checks, crew set-up and rehearsals

OBJECTIVE 5
Health and safety checks and emergency procedures

Meet JENNY EAVES

Head of Corporate Events at Worldspan

Jenny joined Worldspan in 1997 and is one of the event industry's most senior practitioners. She is used to dealing with complex global logistics, as well as being responsible for account managing some of the agency's key clients. Jenny's role involves overseeing and managing Worldspan's event-delivery teams. She has been awarded numerous accolades, including *Event Magazine*'s 'Best Brand Activity' in 2008 and a major public event she masterminded across Europe for BT Global Services. Away from work, Jenny spends time walking her excitable Boxer or travelling across Europe with her husband.

REAL EVENT CHALLENGE

At Worldspan we often get requests for off-site excursions and managing the risk assessment for this type of potentially dangerous event can be extremely challenging, in an increasingly litigious environment.

This is of particular concern to me, as in my previous company, we ran an event for about 100 people in Cyprus. On the second day of the event, we had planned a jeep safari into the Troodos mountains on four-wheel open-top self-drive jeeps, with a lead and rear vehicle to escort the group.

In the front of each vehicle there was a guest driving, with a passenger seated next to them and two guests at the back. As we took the first corner, two of the passengers in one of the jeeps stood up and overbalanced the jeep, which flipped over and flung all four passengers down the mountain. We immediately stopped all the jeeps and checked for any oncoming traffic. We saw two of the guests walking back up the side of the mountain but could not immediately find the other two delegates. I will always remember the events team having to lift up the flipped jeep, to check nobody was under it!

Fortunately, no one was seriously injured, but all four were badly shaken, with cuts and bruises. As the air ambulance was unable to land on the mountain, we had to lead the four passengers to the side of the mountain and transport them to the restaurant, where the group had planned to have lunch. The air ambulance landed there and took them straight to hospital with one of my colleagues. The next day the local police came to the hotel to interview all parties concerned, to try to establish

THE BEST EVENT YOU HAVE DELIVERED

An incentive for 60 people to Nepal. We stayed in Kathmandu for a couple of nights, then chartered private aircraft and flew over Mount Everest to Pokhara. On this trip we climbed onto local open-top buses, headed to an island for a relaxing lunch, chartered helicopters, went on elephant safaris, and ended with a gala dinner back in Kathmandu in a traditional Nepalese home with everyone dressed in traditional Nepalese costumes. It was the most amazing and memorable event I have ever delivered.

WHAT IS YOUR MANAGEMENT STYLE?

Calm and collected. I like to be prepared, so try to do everything before I go on-site, to be able to deal with the multitude of requests and changes that inevitably occur. No one likes to see the event management team running around like headless chickens, so I try to maintain an aura of calm at all times.

WHAT WAS YOUR FIRST GRADUATE JOB?

I worked in a travel agency in south-west London. It gave me great experience in dealing with individuals and helped me overcome my natural shyness.

WHAT DO YOU KNOW NOW THAT YOU WISH YOU HAD KNOWN AT THE START?

This job isn't brain surgery and no one will die if everything isn't perfect!

WHERE IS YOUR FAVOURITE HOLIDAY DESTINATION?

Hard question ... I love Spain and have toured several times with my husband on his motorbike, but also love the US, Mexico and have just booked for South Africa next year. The world is a big place and there are still so many places I'd like to visit.

whether the guests, the DMC, or the jeep itself were to blame for the accident. Basically, the guests had not realised that the jeep could overbalance so easily. The DMC assisted us in sorting out the insurance claim and paperwork, as the jeep needed to be recovered from the mountain and was subsequently written off. The guests were released very quickly from hospital much to all our relief, but this is an event that I won't easily forget!

PRACTITIONER VIEWPOINT

Debbie Wiggins, Head of Marketing, Ducati UK Ltd

We run high-risk events involving VIPs, customers and staff, such as track days, or corporate ride-outs, so safety is our utmost priority. We conduct a thorough risk assessment prior to each activity, as do all our suppliers. We use the best suppliers possible and assess the needs of our clients, whether they are celebrities or customers, to ensure they have a great time. Their safety is always one of our top concerns.

ACADEMIC VIEWPOINT

Elaine Vyner-Mayes, Senior Lecturer at the University of Northampton

I teach on a module called Risk Management in Events, because as an industry we have started to recognise how important it is to be aware of potential risks in events. There was a time when no one carried out a risk assessment, but today we have such a blame culture, we have to evaluate how events are executed and what could potentially happen. It is about trying to reduce, if not totally eradicate, risk from events. One of the common misconceptions is that risk assessment prevents organisers from putting together interesting events. In fact, it allows event organisers to stage events that are more unusual, competitive and challenging, providing plans and precautions are put in place to mitigate for the outcome. In this way, events today are still as inventive, but nowadays far safer than before.

REAL EVENT OUTCOME

Moving forward to my current role at Worldspan, we still operate jeep drives occasionally; however, an incident like this is far less likely to occur today. A thorough risk assessment is conducted during the site inspection by the event team, for every activity that takes place on-site. Then an event safety plan is put in place. We would now have a professional local driver, or event safe driver, rather than a self-drive vehicle. Moreover for larger events, a security director from the client company would escort us on-site and it would be their responsibility to ensure that any scheduled activities are run safely, to check the risk for any area of concern and deal with any insurance issues.

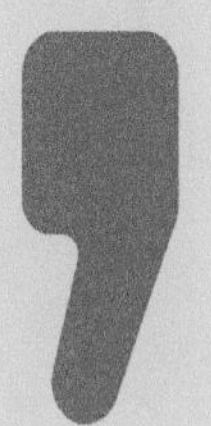

OBJECTIVE 1

Managing and monitoring on-site

MANAGING AND MONITORING AN EVENT ON-SITE

> Investigation, research and decision making will ultimately lead to the development of detailed plans for the successful delivery of an event. (Conway 2009: 46)

With good planning in the pre-event planning stages, the on-site delivery should run smoothly, but invariably there are always elements that do not go according to plan, so the more prepared the event team are in the pre-event planning stages, the better equipped they will be to deal with any eventualities that occur on-site. As will be further discussed in Chapter 6, on-site logistics is basically the process of getting things organised in advance; ensuring people are in the right place at the right time; then pulling everything down when the event is over.

ON-SITE DELIVERY

In advance of arriving on-site, it is advisable to formulate a detailed plan for emergency procedures for all staff and delegates. It is good practice to formulate a precise 'to do list' and concentrate on any elements that are likely to change on-site. As problems can occur at any time, a flexible approach is needed to deal with last-minute changes. Tasks then need to be delegated to team members and measures put in place to ensure that all instructions have been carried out. For example, even though the event management company may have stipulated clear direction on signage, catering requirements, room set up, etc. to the venue, this still needs to be rechecked in person on-site. If the organiser knows the set-up of the venue in greater detail than they do, it will also inspire confidence in the budget holder and delegates attending.

It is therefore recommended that for small meetings, the planning team arrive at the venue in advance of other stakeholders. In cases where the conference or event is overseas, the team should plan to arrive well in advance of the main group, perhaps even a couple of days before the client and delegates arrive, in order to run through last-minute arrangements and final rooming lists, etc. with the venue staff.

MONITORING THE EVENT ON-SITE

The process of monitoring the progress of the event on-site is one that all parties will undertake, including the client, delegates and the team charged with running the event. There are a few important aspects to consider here, which include the following:

- Consult with all parties directly involved in the programme
- Calculate the time of each and every activity
- Ensure that the programme has time for 'ceremonial' activities, e.g. opening and/or closing ceremonies, speeches, entertainment or the presentation of awards
- Confirm that the venue is available for the whole duration of the event
- Choose a date that does not clash with others in the same location or topic area
- Allow for a little 'slack' time between activities
- Plan the structure of the event and order of activities
- Decide how the printed programme will be published.

REPORTING AND RECTIFYING PROBLEMS DURING EVENT TIME

Reporting problems is best administered by keeping a written record of elements, specific to the event, using documentation that is easy to follow and process. Verbal reporting is acceptable as a first stage of communication, but it should be followed up immediately by a written version. This is especially important on-site, as it is not always possible to witness everything that takes place on-site, so some additional tracking procedures are needed. The following are areas of consideration for the crew, which will be further discussed in this section:

- Registration
- Staff scheduling
- Managing staff safety
- Catering
- Serving of alcohol on-site
- Developing an on-site programme schedule
- Making changes to the programme
- Cancellation of the event
- Managing budgetary changes.

REGISTRATION

It is advisable to have a dedicated help desk in the hotel reception area to deal with any accreditation or requirements for room changes. Having a permanent desk in situ, ensures that the team maintain control of the operational procedures and has the additional advantage that staff will get to hear any delegate complaints first-hand. The process of on-site registration can be one of the busiest of the whole event. As this is often the first important activity where delegates, guests and client will come into contact with staff and start to evaluate the experience, it is worth taking extra care and diligence to ensure that the registration process runs smoothly.

The event team should check that there are necessary security points, sufficient staff available and separate desks at the venue to manage delegate registration. For optimum ease and speed, overhead monitors can be used to divide delegates alphabetically. Badges and lanyards and so on should be set out well in advance of guest arrivals and ideally laid out alphabetically with any delegate programme itineraries or conference packs. This may be an opportune time to check flight arrangements; name lists for coaches; dining options or excursions; or to take any additional delegate payments. At the registration point, staff can also re-check room allocations, or register delegates to attend sessions and issue tickets or QR codes, where necessary.

Nowadays, technical advancements make the process of online registration easier and more seamless. The use of swipe cards, RF technology and barcodes has greatly reduced time and resources in this area. However, sometimes it is still worth recruiting additional agency staff on-site, even if it is only for a couple of hours, to ensure that the initial registration process runs efficiently and that any guest queries are answered in the opening stages of the event. There are delegate management companies that specialise in the management and processing of large numbers and can be contracted to oversee registration procedures.

STAFF SCHEDULING

When organising any function, it is crucial to anticipate the amount of support staff needed to deliver a high-quality, well-managed event. The amount of staff required will vary considerably depending on the production and logistical requirements, but, as a 'rule of thumb', there should be at least one organiser on site per 50 delegates. In some cases, more will be needed if the programme is logistically challenging or takes places in an overseas location. In this case, sufficient production crew will also be required to set up, operate and de-rig the set at the end of the conference or event.

From the outset, the organiser will need to:

- Establish a plan for the number of personnel (and any required skills) needed to successfully execute the event
- Develop a recruitment and selection process that is non-discriminatory
- Clarify job expectations and develop the requisite skills needed to complete job responsibilities
- Supervise appropriately
- Compensate equitably and reward outstanding work
- Issue work contracts to all staff.

Generally, more staff are needed to manage on-site than during the pre-planning stages. For this reason, temporary or freelance contractors can be hired to support the core on-site team and will be paid a freelance rate for their services. These temporary or freelance staff will be issued with a contract that stipulates the terms and conditions of their employment; the tasks they will be expected to perform; and any clarification on working hours. Working on-site demands long hours and it is not uncommon for the working day to commence early in the morning and finish very late at night. This should be made clear to staff in advance and agreed measures put in place to compensate them accordingly.

MANAGING STAFF SAFETY

Staff training and on-site briefings will be discussed later in this chapter. However, it is worth mentioning here that the on-site staff briefing procedures should clearly set out and explain any potential hazards that may arise. These could occur at any stage, and might include hazardous areas such as cars in parking areas; the transport of food stuff before or during service; the use of food warmers, chafing dishes, live cooking stations; or any hazards that might occur from handling on-site production equipment, manual handling, and so on.

The *Manual Handling Operations Regulations 1992* (MHOR) define manual handling as: 'any transporting or supporting of a load (including the lifting, putting down, pushing, pulling, carrying or moving thereof, by hand or bodily force; during the preparation of food, with the use of knives and heating appliances.' Other potential hazards to staff could arise from exposure to chemicals and chemical products (COSHH), dry ice, heat sources, cleaning supplies; COSHH stands for 'Control of Substances Hazardous to Health', and under the Control of Substances Hazardous to Health Regulations (2002) employers have a duty of care, either to prevent or reduce their workers' exposure to substances hazardous to their health, and to prevent occupational hazards, such as slips, trips and falls and accidents that may occur. These are all areas that should be covered in the staff training before the event takes place, and at the actual on-site briefing, where these points should be reiterated and any questions answered in full.

CATERING

During the on-site delivery, the catering requirements should be confirmed with the in-house catering division, or external catering company, responsible for food and beverage provision. Timings, menus and food breaks should be thoroughly discussed at this meeting, together with any contingencies for overrunning and how this could impact the catering delivery. The set-up of the catering space, food stations, a buffet area or dining tables should be talked through and visualised.

A system should be devised when serving food buffet style, where guest tables take turns to fill their plates at the buffet. This will help eliminate queues and crowding. In addition, any special dietary requirements should be clarified and relayed to the catering staff. All buffet food should be clearly labelled in advance. During service, food and beverages should be served from different exits to ensure synchronised delivery. Staff should be briefed on-site on the following catering requirements and details, as summarised below:

- Special dietary requirements and who has requested these
- The menu and meal content and any guest allergies, or other special needs
- The use of coloured dots on delegate badges to indicate special dietary requirements
- Serving food and canapés out of different exits to disperse evenly
- Exact buffet layouts and positioning to minimise queuing
- The timings for serving any hot and cold food.

WORKING WITH IN-HOUSE AND EXTERNAL CATERING COMPANIES ON SITE

In most cases, the venue itself can provide in-house catering as part of the event offering. However, sometimes it may be necessary to work with external catering companies, or catering incumbents that are not tied to a specific venue. Additionally, it may be necessary to recruit stewards and hostesses externally, to serve food and drinks at the venue. Staff should receive on-site documentation for all meals that take place on-site, as part of the operations manual, which may look as in Table 2.1.

First Name	Last Name	Requirements specify	Dinner Thurs	Buffet Weds	Day 2 Thurs
Michael	Barber	Vegetarian	yes	yes	yes
David	Barden	Vegetarian	yes	yes	yes
David	Bateson	Requires something to eat that does not contain wheat, onion, garlic, cream, lettuce or chilli.	yes	yes	no
Paul	Bennett	No shellfish	yes	yes	yes
Carol	Cawkwell	Vegetarian	yes	no	yes
Deirdre	Cawthorne	Allergies to mayonnaise and pickle	yes	no	yes
Joanne	Charles	Gluten free	yes	yes	yes
Hasan	Chawdhry	No pork / alcohol content; Halal preferably	yes	yes	yes

TABLE 2.1 Sample on-site catering documentation

RESTAURANTS FOR ON-SITE LUNCHES

Depending on the event type, some lunches can be more formal than others, but generally as part of a conference programme, a lunch break would normally only take around one hour, or even less. For this reason, buffet lunches work well, as they tend to be quicker. Sometimes lunch could be part of an excursion or team-building activity. In contrast to evening dining, conference lunches tend to be more informal, with no set seating plan. As a general rule only, non-alcoholic drinks are served at lunchtime, although this might be dependent on the event type and location.

At a day conference or meeting, lunch is often served in a separate space, or private dining area, away from the main conference. Within a 24-hour delegate package, breakfast, lunch and evening dinner will usually be included in the rate and the same in an eight-hour conference day-delegate package, minus breakfast and evening dinner. There is a growing tendency today, either to save time, costs or sometimes both, for the venue to provide a working lunch, where the delegates break to select dishes from a hot and cold running buffet and move back into the plenary or breakout session to eat, whilst still working.

EVENING DINING, PRIVATE DINING AND 'DINE-AROUNDS' ON-SITE

At a corporate event, a variety of catering options may be adopted for evening dining. On the first night when guests arrive, possibly at different times, at the hotel or venue, it is a good idea to arrange for a hot and cold running buffet to be served in a private room and replenished throughout the evening. This is ideal for staggered guest arrivals and latecomers and will also give guests the chance to meet and mingle before commencement of the event. Although not technically part of the conference programme, details on this 'welcome dinner' should be included in the delegate's joining instructions and this is often included in the overall budget costing.

During the conference programme, there may be a variety of private hosted dinners. For large events, it is sometimes necessary to organise a 'dine around' evening, where organisers pre-book a number of restaurants in the city, offering a selection of cuisines, and invite delegates to sign up to the one they prefer. This allows organisers to accommodate all guests, and also gives separate groups or country groups the chance to discuss matters in private, or in their own language. Transportation to the restaurants is normally organised by the event team, who also inspect all the restaurants in advance and advise delegates on menu choices. Staff are often on hand to escort guests on the night, and to check that all arrangements are satisfactory.

At other times during a conference programme, delegates are at leisure to dine where they choose, either in the hotel or at an alternative restaurant. Guests should be informed in advance of which meals they will be expected to cover from their own costs, or claim on company expenses, and which meal costs will be added to the overall conference master bill.

PLANNING A GALA DINNER

Gala dinners tend to take place on the last night, as a final farewell evening. They often take place in a special historical, unusual or upmarket venue that the general public would not normally have access to for dining purposes. Transportation from and to the venue is normally added to the overall budget cost. The evening usually commences with a cocktail or champagne reception, often held in a separate holding area to the main event, so the 'reveal' of the room set-up for dinner can retain the 'wow factor'. A gala dinner can sometimes also incorporate an award ceremony. This is usually the most formal dinner in the social programme and guests are usually seated according to a fixed table plan and served from a set menu, rather than a buffet. The gala dinner normally has extra embellishments, such as a red carpet, entertainment, floral arrangements, background music, table decorations and parting gifts, formal seating plans, firework displays, and so on.

Table plans are often posted on boards in the foyer or entrance to the dining space, to allow guests to see where they are sitting in advance. The tables are often decorated with candles and flowers, with name cards and branded menus, and the evening can be themed with company speeches, live entertainment, a disc jockey (DJ) and after-dinner dancing. There may also be a raffle or keynote speaker as part of the evening activities. Formal evening attire or even fancy dress tends to be worn at this type of dinner. Recommendations for a successful evening are shown in Table 2.2.

- Arrange food tastings beforehand whenever possible
- Select wines that complement the food
- Arrange to have menus and name cards printed
- Select menu choices to cater for all requirements
- Book separate space for a drinks reception and an after-dinner bar
- Ensure the room has sufficient space for a dance floor and DJ

(Continued)

TABLE 2.2 (Continued)

- Determine a theme for the dinner and how to dress the room in line with the theme
- Assess whether it will be necessary to use a local production company to supply props and equipment
- Have taxis on stand-by or book a coach transportation company
- Check there is sufficient space for coaches to pick up and drop off
- Conduct a thorough risk assessment to include fire & safety regulations
- Source additional security for the night
- Ensure the room is fully air-conditioned and the right temperature for the guests
- Check the latest time that guests and crew can leave the venue
- Check the facilities meticulously, including toilets, disabled facilities and cloakroom space.

TABLE 2.2 Recommendations for a successful gala dinner

SERVING OF ALCOHOL ON-SITE

The organiser will be required to apply for a temporary licence for any event that will sell alcohol. This can be obtained from the local council and will permit up to 500 persons in the bar area at any one time. Strict sales hours will need to be enforced, with clear notification for the last time to purchase alcohol before the close of the event. Other measures that can help limit risk include: ensuring that alcohol outlets are positioned close by food outlets; making sure there are sufficient security personnel and stewards available on-site; checking all bar staff are adequately trained for Challenge 21 & 25 – part of a UK scheme, introduced by the British Beer and Pub Association (BBPA), to try to prevent young people gaining access to age-restricted products, including cigarettes and alcoholic beverages – and are prepared to refuse the sale of alcohol to intoxicated attendees.

It is advisable to have alcohol-free areas on-site, such as children and family zones and to provide safe areas for intoxicated attendees. Drinks should also be served in plastic cups, where possible, to prevent glass breakages and subsequent accidents. In cases where there are motorised sports or other high-risk activities, these should be placed as far away as possible from tents serving alcoholic beverages. Staff should ensure that all participants sign a disclaimer to say they have not been drinking alcohol before taking part in these activities.

EVENT ETHICS

Following an undercover operation carried out in July 2019, the New York State Liquor Authority charged and imposed heavy fines on three businesses for selling alcohol to minors.

Do you think clients or bar staff should be held responsible and charged if they are found guilty of serving minors?

OTHER THINGS TO CONSIDER WHEN SELLING ALCOHOL

- The design of the area for optimum flow of people and to prevent congestion/crushing
- Suitable and sufficient lighting for audience movement around site
- Provision of storage for the delivery and positioning of alcohol tanks, carbon dioxide cylinders and security
- Safe disposal of glass bottles
- Installation of an alcohol plan
- Use of token or application system versus cash.

DEVELOPING AN ON-SITE PROGRAMME/PRODUCTION SCHEDULE

Regardless of the size and complexity of the event, a programme schedule and itinerary that sets out the schedule needs to be devised. Sometimes the venue itself will produce an on-the-day production schedule and itinerary, for all those working on-site. At other times, it will be the responsibility of the client themselves to produce one. The schedule should indicate who is doing what, where and when, from start-up, such as from 08.00 to shut-down, for example at midnight. Everybody working on the event should receive this information and be aware of what is scheduled to happen and when.

In terms of operations, audience requirements need to be taken into consideration. If there are several different activities taking place at the same time, or within a tight time frame, it is essential that guests or visitors know in advance what is going on. Therefore, the audience, delegates or guests need to be issued with a 'programme of activities', which can be posted online in advance, or handed out at registration. This will help them plan their visit before arrival. It is not only guests and visitors who need to be aware of the on-site schedule, all staff including volunteers also need to know when briefing meetings and activities are taking place. Staff will also need to know the details of any site checks, about the arrival of any equipment, emergency procedures, who is handling security, and so on.

A major music festival such as Glastonbury or Coachella, for example, which has many different stages and acts, needs to publish what is going on, where and when in good time, to ensure the audience can plan their movements and ensure they are in the right place at the right time to see their preferred acts or bands.

MAKING CHANGES TO THE PROGRAMME

There are a number of reasons why changes may need to be made to the conference programme, not least travel disruptions; technical problems; external announcements; or other situations, that might impact the attendance of delegates or guest speakers.

The important thing is to make sure that if changes do need to be made to the programme during event time, they are communicated to all key parties. It may be necessary to email delegates, room-drop programme changes, or put a revised schedule on display at the hospitality desk. Organisers will often be busy behind the scenes making calls to change timings or liaising with the venue about changes to the schedule or catering arrangements. All event types experience last-minute changes to the programme, but nowadays social media can provide a useful tool to quickly communicate any schedule changes to the audience.

CANCELLATION OF THE EVENT

In the worst-case scenario, it may be necessary to cancel the event, either just before commencement, or even at the event itself. There are a number of reasons this might happen, for instance a sudden lockdown due to a global pandemic, terrorism threats, sickness or other reasons beyond the control of the budget holder. The key priority is to communicate the decision to cancel to all stakeholders as soon as possible. Depending on the terms of the contract and the time of cancellation, it may be possible to only lose the deposit payment. However, in the late stages of proceedings, it might be that a claim needs to be made against the event insurance cover, to pay for any loss of income resulting from the cancellation.

MANAGING BUDGETARY CHANGES

Changes to the set budget will inevitably occur on-site. Even with the best-planned budget costing, the planner should allow for contingencies and unexpected changes to the budget. Invariably the budget costs will increase on-site, so it is essential to continuously monitor on-site spend and to keep an account of any adjustments or changes that occur. In the rare instance that there has been an overestimation of the overall costs, the client may be able to allocate extra funds where required. Sometimes delegate or audience numbers increase at the event, but generally there are many other unforeseen expenses that occur on-site and should be allowed for in the contingency planning.

The customary industry practice is to issue a standard Price Change Notification (PCN) form, for any on-site price amendments. The event manager should ensure that the client or owner signs this documentation as soon as new costs are known. The client or budget owner should be continuously informed of any substantial changes to the budget, as soon as possible and ideally in event time. Meetings between the management team and the principle suppliers, such as the venue or hotel, should also take place on a regular basis on-site, in order to update on final room or guest numbers and make the necessary adjustments. This will make the whole process of final budgetary reconciliation far easier and will prevent any unwanted financial surprises.

In addition, staff should keep a record of any personal expenditure incurred during the course of the event, especially if they need to claim back any additional expenditure afterwards. The organiser overseeing the event may have set up budget allocations for on-site meetings, publicity, staff expenses, and so on, and there needs to be some way of recording this information and calculating the overall costs while on-site. Producing a cost sheet will help to check that the budget allowance is being adhered to, as well as providing a mechanism for an instant check, to see whether this matches the amount estimated in the initial budgeting process. The area of budgeting will be discussed in more depth in Chapter 7.

ON-SITE DOCUMENTATION AND SOFTWARE TOOLS

OBJECTIVE
2
On-site
documentation

ON-SITE DOCUMENTATION

On-site documentation should be planned and collated in the planning phase and electronic or hard copies of the most essential documents brought on-site by the event team. As previously mentioned, the on-site programme will inevitably change, so it is recommended to have a detailed operations manual or conference working document, as a reference starting point. This documentation should be updated throughout the planning process and finalised with all the latest updates before event commencement and should be made available to all the organising team to access. The types of on-site documentation that will be discussed in this section are:

- The conference working document
- The production schedule
- The venue report
- The on-site report form
- Event contracts and terms and conditions
- Risk management documentation
- Copies of any relevant licences
- Air and transportation reports/flight manifest details.

THE CONFERENCE WORKING DOCUMENT

Producing a conference working document is essential and often termed the event 'Bible'. It is a written account of all on-site activities. The data included under each section is usually collected from previous meetings, critical path documentation and contact reports. If clearly set out and prepared well in advance, this document should be a valuable operational tool, so that even if the project manager falls sick at the last minute, or is not personally able to deliver on-site, the event should still be tenable. The conference working document might contain the following information:

- Contact information for all stakeholders. This key contacts list should include mobile numbers for all clients, staff, suppliers and sponsors
- Destination information and general information on the host city/destination
- Venue capacities; site plans; room specifications and allocations; layout and floor plans
- Accommodation breakdown; locations; and lists of special room requirements
- Air and ground transportation details and **flight manifests**
- Staff duty rosters, with names allocated to each task, timings and briefing notes for staff

Flight manifests detailed documents listing all inbound and outbound flight timings and connections

- Food and beverage details, menus and special dietary requirements, etc.
- Programme content, description of conference and social activities and seminar/breakout details, with precision timings, outlining a step-by-step schedule and corresponding locations
- Conference technical specifications and data, outlining audio-visual, production specifications and technical requirements including set-up and set-down details
- **Risk assessment documentation** and health and safety information
- Contingency planning and emergency procedures
- Budgetary details
- Licensing and contract details
- Additional information such as radio or mobile phone allocations and communication channels.

Risk assessment documentation a document or online folder that identifies potential risks and hazards

THE PRODUCTION SCHEDULE

The production schedule is the main document used for managing on-site activity. This document can be defined as: 'a minute by minute plan to monitor the tasks that lead to the ultimate conclusion of the event itself' (Goldblatt 2014). The production schedule will make up part of the final event manual, to be distributed to all suppliers, contractors and key clients. The schedule includes timings, activities, location, stakeholder involvement and individual and team responsibility of tasks, from the moment the organising team turn up at the venue, until the moment they leave. This is often known in the industry as load-in to load-out, or bump-in to bump-out.

A detailed breakdown of timings, including the start and finish times for specific activities, and a brief description of the planned activity should be included in the production schedule. Additionally, detailed information on equipment and services; the resources required for each activity; corresponding notes on it; responsibility and sign-off, together with an indication of when each activity has been completed, should also feature. Other aspects of this schedule might include:

- The rehearsal schedule
- Team production meetings
- Details on staging and set-up
- The running order for an event, known as the 'run sheet'
- Load-in and load-out times.

Suppliers will use this schedule as the basis to plan their own logistics and budgetary documentation. It is therefore important to forward the most current draft to the distribution list before commencement of the event, to allow any changes or budgeting adjustments to take place before delivery. It is also worth trying to stay ahead of the schedule, and also a good idea to build in some extra 'fat-time', to accommodate any delays or snags that could occur and, where necessary, help bring the schedule back on track. The production schedule will serve as a good gauge of how the event is progressing and allow the organiser to track if it starts to fall behind schedule. This is particularly useful in the build phase, a part of the event delivery process that can often be underestimated and miscalculated in terms of time.

THE VENUE REPORT

The formulation of a venue report, following on from the venue site inspection, should be brought on-site, either in a paper-based or electronic form. Sections of that report may be itemised under various categories, such as:

- Transfers: flights, trains
- Accommodation
- Dinner: table allocations
- Allocation of activities, team games
- VIPs and special guests
- Ticket allocation and name lists
- Seat allocation – especially for a formal dinner, concert or performance.

The venue report will be discussed in more detail in Chapter 6.

THE ON-SITE REPORT FORM

The event planner will often write up a comprehensive report after the event has taken place. A document that can be used for reporting any on-site problems should be designed. The report should be signed off when completed and detail elements.

GO ONLINE

Read through this sample on-site report at **study.sagepub.co.uk/quick**

FILES FOR CONTRACTS AND TERMS AND CONDITIONS (Ts & Cs)

Managing stakeholder contracts is a key component of successful logistics. The content of these contracts and how significant they are to the planning stage will be further discussed in detail in Chapter 7. It is recommended to bring a copy of all supplier contracts on-site, either in paper or electronic form, in case there are any supplier questions or even disputes with suppliers.

RISK MANAGEMENT DOCUMENTATION

Copies of all risk management documentation should also be brought on-site, to help with checks in case of emergencies. The content of this documentation will be discussed further in this chapter.

COPIES OF ANY RELEVANT LICENCES

It may be necessary to bring copies of any relevant licences on-site. These licences will need to be applied for in the planning stage. Licensing objectives are normally put in place to ensure:

- Prevention of crime and disorder
- Prevention of public nuisance
- Public safety
- Protection of children from harm.

In general, all public entertainment at events has to be licensed, to ensure that the performers and the public are safe. Licences are generally obtained from a local authority through the licensing officer, who should advise the licensing committee on whether to grant a public entertainment licence. It is important to take professional advice from this body early in the planning stages, to ensure that there are not going to be any licensing compliance issues. The types of licences most commonly associated with smaller events are the music and dancing licence and the occasional entertainment licence, a temporary event notice, a food hygiene certificate, and a phonographic performance limited licence. For larger events, it may be necessary to apply for licences, such as a notification of a demonstration or a march.

Most venues will have their own public indemnity licence, but the organiser always needs to check this and obtain proof of documentation as a matter of course. If the event is being held in a public place or is free and does not involve the transmission of live amplified music, there is a good chance it will not be necessary to apply for a licence. However, if it is going to be loud and noisy, or if an admission fee is going to be charged, then the organiser should apply for an occasional entertainment licence. Some organisers will be charged a fee to apply for the licence. However, all local authorities, particularly from country to country, will differ, and apply their own rules, as each interprets the regulations differently. Table 2.3 lists some events for which licences are required.

Chugging
the action or practice of approaching passers-by in the street to ask for subscriptions or donations to a particular charity

The sale of alcohol	• Licence or other authorisation needed from a licensing authority to sell or supply alcohol in England and Wales • The law and policy governing this area is overseen by the Home Office • Individuals can also apply for a personal licence to sell alcohol, usually granted by a local council.
The sale and serving of food	• Premises where food operations are carried out, including a home, mobile or temporary premises, such as stalls and vans, must be registered • Licence rules vary from country to country; for example, in the USA the production and sale of processed foods are governed by state and federal regulations • Most US states have cottage food laws now that do not require a licensed kitchen • Goods can be sold at a farmers' market or roadside stand, e.g. jams and jellies as well as baked goods that do not require refrigeration.
The use of door supervisors/security	• Individuals need an on-door supervision qualification that is recognised by the Security Industry Authority (SIA), which includes taking four training modules and passing three exams • The security guard licence enables staff to work in the private security industry as a security guard • The licence is issued by the Security Industry Authority (SIA) and is valid for three years.

Street trading	• Street trading is the selling, offering or exposing for sale of any item or service in the street • This includes stalls, shop-front displays, cafe tables and chairs with service • A licence is required to trade on the public highway, including the pavement or any other area (not within a permanently enclosed premise), within 7 metres of any road or footway.
Public charity collection	• A street collection licence may be required in order to collect money or sell items on the street for charity • This often depends on the presiding local council • Licences are also needed to collect money in public areas, e.g. a shop doorway or car park • Collectors need to apply for a licence if they are ***chugging*** on behalf of a registered charity.
Use of animals in events	• In most European countries, the local council approves an application and provides a certificate confirming the owner's right to keep the animals and use them in performance or at an event • A police officer or other authorised officer may enter any premises where performing animals are kept, at any time, without a warrant, to inspect the premises and to check conditions and can ask to see the owner's certificate of registration • The conditions must meet health, welfare and safety standards.
Holding a lottery	• Small society lotteries do not require a licence, but must be registered with the local authority in the area where the principal office of the society is located • Society lotteries are promoted for the benefit of a non-commercial society • A society is non-commercial if it is established and conducted for charitable purposes; to enable participation in sport or a cultural activity (for example a local theatre); or any non-commercial purpose other than that of private gain.

TABLE 2.3 Event licences

Regulations brought into effect in 2003 changed the amount of permits and licences required for event activities to take place. The Licensing Act of 2003 brought together six existing licences into one. These were for alcohol, public entertainment, cinemas, theatres, late night refreshments and night cafes. To cover these areas, three additional licences were created: **a premises licence, a temporary event notice** and **a club premises certificate**. Many licensing requirements and regulations were introduced to prevent crime and disorder, promote public safety and protect youth and minors at external events.

Premises licence
a permanent licence granted to a specific location that authorises the holder to sell alcohol

Temporary event notice
a temporary licence granted to carry out a 'licensable activity' on unlicenced premises

Club premises certificate
a permanent licence granted to a specific location that authorises the holder to carry on any or all of the following licensable activities: the sale of alcohol; the supply of alcohol by a club to its members and guests

AIR AND TRANSPORTATION REPORTS/FLIGHT MANIFEST DETAILS

Full details of delegate travel arrangements, flight manifests and corresponding transfers also need to be available to access on-site. Many changes to delegate flight arrangements, and flight re-routings take place in event time. Depending on the size, this can be a complex and time-consuming part of the programme, especially in the case of conferences, where it can be the responsibility of the planning team to make the changes to flight reservations and amend transportation arrangements accordingly.

Trained staff should be available to deal with these issues on-site. Group flight bookings have their own rules and regulations and, in some cases, it may be worth recruiting extra staff, or staff with specialist knowledge on reservations and flight ticketing, to deal with this area of expertise.

THE USE OF TECHNOLOGY AND SOFTWARE TOOLS AT THE EVENT

Advanced technology has improved the way that planners are able to track and manage delegate movement around a conference or exhibition. As will be discussed in more depth in Chapter 7, the use of swipe cards, NFC technology and QR codes are an easy and discreet means of storing delegate contact details and other relevant information. This technology can also be used to give feedback and monitor it during the post-event evaluation phase. Using conference-enhanced software means that it is now possible to get instant feedback from clients and delegates.

ON-SITE USE OF TECHNOLOGY

Applications such as Evolero and Pathable have been designed to allow organisers to understand in 'real time' what conference attendees are thinking. Pathable can track which sessions, speakers and exhibitors, delegates are interested in and where managers need to focus their attention in future. This application also contains features that can facilitate use of personalised agendas, note taking, discussion forums, surveys, **live polls**, all conducted in multinational languages. This is a particularly useful tool in an ever increasingly globalised arena.

Live polls
casting audience votes in real time to gauge response

Applications like these are now being used by many **blue chip corporations**, such as Coca Cola, Yahoo and Microsoft, to run their events. Apple's iBeacon, a small, inexpensive **digital transmitter**, which interacts with the mobile application when it comes into range (from 1–50 metres), and can link to a range of Smartphone applications to alert the owner to new products and offers for their mobile device, is now successfully being used at events.

Blue chip corporations
large international corporations that have been in business for many years and are considered to be very stable

Digital transmitter
transmitters are necessary component parts of many electronic devices that communicate by radio, such as cell phones, wireless computer networks, Bluetooth-enabled devices

These are capable of producing automated badges, connecting to the internet from a mobile phone, then sending a signal to the badging point. They can also be used to conduct live polls with the audience for instantaneous feedback. The system even has sensors which are able to control the temperature on seats, so should delegates start to feel cold during the event, the temperature of the seat would automatically increase, thus improving the audience's overall experience.

NEAR FIELD TECHNOLOGY AND QR CODES

Near field technology (NFC) is also continuing to develop, providing low-battery, low-cost options for streamlining the sharing of data and content, allowing event managers to connect to attendees' smartphones and provide and collect information. NFC can allow attendee name badges to be used for transit. City transportation payment cards, such as Oyster cards to travel on the London transport network, use this technology. NFC can also enable attendee tracking; access control; and exhibitor lead retrieval, to allow for the exchange of online social networking data between two key providers at an event. This is an ideal tool for voting and rating products, suppliers and services, and can facilitate a seamless post-event evaluation process. Implementing NFC technology has helped festival organisers communicate to their audiences, thus reducing accreditation, long queues and security costs. By issuing digital tickets, consumers are able to access a festival guide and all the information they need to know about the festival programme, music acts, catering outlets, on-site maps and directions before arriving.

Event organisers are also using quick response (QR) codes on products, to encourage attendees to scan objects for exclusive content and features and follow through on post-event promotions and feedback. QR codes are similar to NFC technology, aiming to streamline the user experience and keep communication and marketing fluid and manageable. QR apps are generally free for mobiles and are easy and fun to use. They can be placed on almost any kind of print publicity or even large video displays. The amount of information that can be stored in a QR code makes tracking easy, and individual codes can be sent to guests to assist follow-up analysis, as well as better lead management.

LIAISING WITH STAKEHOLDERS AT THE EVENT

OBJECTIVE
3
Liaising with stakeholders at the event

MANAGING STAKEHOLDERS ON-SITE

Constant liaison and communication with key stakeholders should be maintained by the planning team during the delivery of the event, as it could impact the complete success of the delivery. There are also various suppliers who need to be managed and monitored on-site, ranging from paid staff and contractors to unpaid volunteers, and all other suppliers and vendors. Additionally, the client or owner, sponsors, VIPs and dignitaries and press will also need to be managed, so that each is aware of their role and responsibilities on-site. The following practices that will be elaborated on in this section, should make the on-site communication process run more smoothly and efficiently:

- Conducting staff briefings
- Issuing duty rosters
- Monitoring of staff performance
- Managing other vendors, suppliers and support services
- On-site client liaison
- Handling press and public relations (PR) requirements at the event
- Managing press and VIP guests
- Managing sponsors on-site
- On-site venue liaison.

CONDUCTING STAFF BRIEFINGS

Experienced and well-trained staff are the crucial link to competency and compliance. Staff and volunteer training should take place before commencement of the event and regular staff briefings should be scheduled to take place during it. All staff should receive a recap on the earlier induction training, on key areas such as: budgeting processes; risk management; licensing and regulations; emergency procedures; and health and safety awareness. More generic training items, such as multicultural awareness, respect, the organisational culture, management practices, best practice, teamwork and a sense of community engagement may also need to be included in the on-site briefing.

It is also advisable to hold a team briefing every morning with all staff to run through the tasks outlined in the duty roster. This will be the optimum time to advise of any changes to the programme and discuss any potential risks and eventualities that might occur on the day. At the briefing, staff will have the opportunity to ask questions about areas that may be unclear. This on-site training should furnish organisers with knowledge on how to deal with all eventualities. Event staff should then follow the detailed duty rosters throughout the event, to allow for breaks, emergencies and contingencies.

At these briefings, a recap of staff duties, who is in charge and who they report to in the chain of command should be communicated. The client should impart this vital information to all those working on-site. It is also good practice to hold a staff debrief at the end of each working day, to discuss how things have gone and to highlight any challenges or unforeseen occurrences that may have arisen during that day.

Any changes to the original programme should be documented throughout the event, as it can be difficult to track amends or incidents on completion. It is therefore recommended to keep a logbook on-site, where staff can record the date, time and description of any incidents. This could prove invaluable when monitoring and evaluating the success of the event, and any possible claims of dissatisfaction or complaints that might arise once it has finished. The briefing process will update or remind staff on emergency procedures and will also provide the opportunity to run through the following:

- Event background, client details and reporting structures
- Who does what and when on-site
- The site access and build
- Facilities and layout
- Arrivals on-site, especially flight arrivals and transportation
- Recap of conference and/or social programme
- Communication of vital information, e.g. delegate profile, budgetary signatories, timings to all those working on-site
- Briefing documents and health and safety and emergency procedures.

ISSUING DUTY ROSTERS

Detailed duty rosters should be compiled in advance for each day of the event, to include full details of all timings, activities, responsibilities and any additional notes.

GO ONLINE

Find a sample duty roster online at **study.sagepub.co.uk/quick**

MONITORING OF STAFF PERFORMANCE

As previously mentioned, situations can build and escalate very quickly on-site and it is not always possible to ascertain who was involved, or how the situation was dealt with during the on-site process. It is therefore advisable to have someone at the helm who retains overall control of the organising team and is able to stand back and monitor events as they unfold and assess how the on-site team are coping.

In some cases, new or externally contracted workers may have been assigned too much responsibility, which they either do not have the aptitude for or sufficient expertise to carry out competently. In other cases, it is clear that staff are able to step up and take more responsibility or work longer hours on-site than originally scheduled. Sometimes it may be that the team dynamics are not working, due to personality clashes or a difference of opinion, or there may be skill shortages in particular areas. In these cases, it may be necessary for the project manager or team leader to make changes to the staffing schedule during event 'real time'. This should balance skills or plug any gaps due to sickness or absenteeism. Detailed feedback to staff and post-event briefings should be conducted after the event has finished, and this area will be further discussed in Chapter 3.

MANAGING OTHER VENDORS, SUPPLIERS AND SUPPORT SERVICES

The logistics of hiring and delivering on-site services requires detailed planning and coordination. All events require people with specialist skills to provide various services, depending on the nature of it. There are numerous event businesses and agencies that will be utilised on-site that specialise in the services listed in Table 2.4.

Catering	Transport	Security	Toilet hire
First aid	Sound & Lighting/AV	Entertainment	Costume design
Staging/props	Signage	Equipment	Insurance
Florists	Cleaning	Transportation/Taxis	Marquee providers

TABLE 2.4 On-site suppliers

This is by no means an exhaustive list but gives some indication of what supplier services may need to be managed on-site. Trade publications, such as *Access All Areas*, provide further information on suppliers, as do the *Purple Guide* and the

White Book Directory, which contains a huge compendium of suppliers and services, mainly employed for outdoor events. Some suppliers provide the equipment itself only, while others also provide the staff needed to operate it, dependent on how big the event is, and the overall budget spend.

It is a good idea to meet with key vendors and suppliers during the set-up phase, to run through relevant documentation and to talk through the event programme, timings, safety procedures and all other relevant items listed in the contract or working document that may apply to them, such as: exhibition set-up; floor plans; set-up and clear-up instructions; on-site radio communication; and access procedures. Set-up of any stands or stalls should be signed off on-site by the venue and client.

Daily briefings with vendors and any other suppliers who have a presence on-site should also be arranged, to run through any changes to the programme or advise on final numbers, and to answer any questions they may have. Regular liaison beforehand, on-site between the event team, supplier and vendors, should also facilitate better overall communication and a smoother billing process at the end of the event.

DEALING WITH FOOD AND CATERING SUPPLIERS ON-SITE

When dealing with catering suppliers on-site, the organiser should ensure that the delivery, storage, preparation and sales of food, together with the provision of all caterers, traders and suppliers, comply with the appropriate legislation (see Table 2.5 for ways to improve supplier compliance). This is not usually a problem when working with licensed venue suppliers, as they will be regularly inspected by the local authorities, but it can present more of a problem when using temporary kitchens or external catering vendors to prepare and serve food.

Anyone handling or preparing food is required to have a 'food and hygiene certificate', which should be clearly displayed at all times and available for inspection by the event team or local authority. The food and hygiene certificate ensures that any staff serving or preparing food to the general public, should be appropriately dressed, with hair tied back and no jewellery. Different-coloured chopping boards should be used, especially when preparing raw and cooked meat in the same space. Staff working within the kitchen should also be appraised on the rules for chilling and storing frozen food on-site.

1. Assess supplier capability	• *Gather information.* This should be pertinent to the service they are providing, or goods supplied before the critical starting point. • *Verify the supplier information.* This evidence should always be up-to-date and instantly retrievable. • *Authorise the information.* Once a supplier has been thoroughly checked and approved to deliver any given product or service, ensure suppliers from this list are used by all company divisions. • *Keep to the approved supplier list.* All too often the reality is that different divisions stray from the approved suppliers list and start to appoint non-approved suppliers, based on cheaper price, which can prove very costly and can increase the overall event risk.

2. Manage supply contracts	• *Set clear policies and rules.* This will enable suppliers to be very clear about exactly what is expected. • *Contracts and specification.* Formalise all requirements so nothing is left to chance. Bring copies of these agreements on-site in the operation manual/working document. • *Controls and restraints.* Ensure suppliers understand any control processes that need to be followed; for example, site-access control on construction sites, trading hours and regulations, security issues, health and safety, etc.
3. Monitor suppliers	• *Behaviour.* Do not allow suppliers to become complacent and lose their sense of responsibility for their own compliance and performance. It is important to be clear about where accountability lies. • *Audit.* Either hard copies or online audits can be used to provide an audit trail. Online auditing is cheaper and can replace sprawling spreadsheets, thus minimising timescales and maximising efficiency. • *Key performance indicators (KPIs).* It is important to gather, measure and analyse statistics that illustrate whether desired outcomes and objectives were achieved; for example, percentages of products and services that were delivered on time.

TABLE 2.5 Three steps to improving supplier compliance

SOURCE: Adapted from: www.cips.org/en-GB/supply-management/opinion/2016/january/three-steps-to-improve-supplier-compliance

ON-SITE CLIENT LIAISON

Event professionals will work with many different types of client during their career. Often this can be a rewarding part of the remit, as clients can sometimes end up being a friend or business advocate; however, managing difficult clients can be challenging and also have its own unique set of problems. A difficult client might monopolise the event team's time or demand outrageous services. In some cases, they are slow to pay or unable to make decisions. This is particularly the case when there is more than one client, or a committee to answer to. Difficult clients in the event industry tend to create emergencies out of minor situations. In the worst-case scenario, the difficult client is all of the types featured in Table 2.6.

The client who thinks everything is an emergency	• Panic about small details • Time-consuming and stressful to deal with
The confused client	• Don't really know what they want • Lack of clear vision for the event
	• Constant changes • Struggle to make decisions
The client who 'knows-it-all'	• Constantly telling you how to do your job • Think they can do your job better than you
The client who constantly moves deadlines	• Provides false deadlines • Gives unclear timelines and can create last-minute urgencies

(Continued)

TABLE 2.6 (Continued)

The client who clearly no longer cares	• Has unspoken expectations but doesn't seem to outwardly care • Difficult to manage
The client who loves to complain	• Constantly finds fault with everything • Unclear on what they want but will let you know exactly what they don't want! • Continuously shoots down your ideas
The client who questions every budget item	• Budget is all that matters • Keen to keep costs down and nothing else matters

TABLE 2.6 Types of difficult clients that may be encountered in the events industry

SOURCE: Adapted from: https://helloendless.com/difficult-clients-in-the-event-industry

It can be tough for organisers to manage any of these client traits on-site, but it is worth remembering that often your client, or the event owner, is also under considerable pressure to deliver a first-class event, and that may influence their behaviour. It is always advisable for the organisers to try to remain calm and in control throughout the delivery process. Building up trust and an understanding with the client takes time; however, there are a few proactive steps that can be taken to ease the client/supplier relationship, as shown in Table 2.7.

1	Establish event goals, objectives and ground rules from the outset
2	Communicate to the client in the right words and unambiguous language
3	Regularly update the client on any changes, especially financial ones
4	Hold regular briefing meetings on-site
5	Record any meetings where necessary
6	Use tangible measurables to quantify
7	Document everything
8	Check the client is happy with their room/facilities etc.
9	Try to build trust and confidence with the client
10	Own your knowledge/expertise
11	Do not be afraid to challenge or disagree with a client, where necessary
12	Under-promise, over-deliver
13	Know when to back off, apologise or simply walk away.

TABLE 2.7 Thirteen steps for improving the client/supplier relationship

HANDLING PRESS AND PUBLIC RELATIONS (PR) REQUIREMENTS AT THE EVENT

Public relations is a communication platform that can convey messages to the public and connect the organisation with its stakeholders. Once on-site, a well-organised PR presence can enhance publicity and boost the reputation of the event. Within the industry, there are varied types of public relations functions, which include some of the following:

- Media relations
- Community relations
- Public affairs and government relations:
    - Lobbying (organisations promoting their causes/interests to lawmakers/governmental regulators – for favours in vote or support)
    - Public diplomacy (between nations – secret or transparent)
    - Public affairs/public information (news, conferences, videos)
- Events as promotional tools for companies
- Employee relations (parties, picnics, incentive travel, charity fundraisers, rewards, etc.)
- Investor/donor relations (annual reports/meetings, CSR, pension programmes, etc.).

Communication within PR is a process that can be divided into the following components of communication: the source; the message; and the channel through which the message is delivered. In terms of on-site practice, this could be a one-way model, which focuses exclusively on the flow of information from the organisation or company to its stakeholders; or a two-way model, focusing on a two-way dialogue and response between the organisation or company and its stakeholders.

It is extremely important to handle press and PR on-site with due care and diligence. As the press will be reporting on the proceedings, this is one aspect that it is extremely important to get right. Often the press will arrive before the main guests and may attend a VIP PR reception before having access to the main event. During the course of an event, it may be necessary to use the PR facility for the purposes listed in Table 2.8.

Internal communication	Employees, board members, executive committee, etc.
Corporate PR	Communicating on behalf of the organisation
Media relations	Journalists, editors, radio, television, etc.
Business to business	Other organisations: suppliers, retailers, etc.
Public affairs	Communicating with opinion formers, e.g. local/national politicians

(Continued)

TABLE 2.8 (Continued)

Community relations/corporate social responsibility	The local community or elected representatives
Investor relations	Financial organisations, investors
Strategic communication	Situation analysis, problem and solution to further an organisational goal
Issues management	Monitoring of the PESTEL environment
Crisis management	Communicating clear messages in a fast-changing situation or emergency
Copywriting	Writing press releases etc. to different audiences to high standards of literacy
Publication management	Overseeing print/media processes, often using new technology
Exhibitions	Organising complex events or exhibitions

TABLE 2.8 The function of public relations at events

HOLDING A PRESS CONFERENCE ON-SITE

Sometimes it is necessary to hold a press conference during the on-site delivery stage. This may be in cases where the event has a prominent speaker or attendee, or when there are significant announcements to make, or an immediate response is required. A press conference can also be set up when there is an emergency or crisis that needs to be communicated during the event. Press conferences are required during the event delivery for the following other reasons:

- To enable the release of more detailed information than a press release could convey
- To provide a platform to be interactive with the audience and to answer any questions
- To announce something unforeseen or unprecedented
- To set the record straight on any matter or issue following negative publicity and/or to boost company morale.

MANAGING PRESS AND VIP GUESTS

A meet-and-greet party would generally be assigned to welcome the press and sign them in on arrival. Often this function will be undertaken by the company's CEO or general manager, or the highest official attending the event, rather than the event manager. This may depend on the event type. For example, at a celebration to mark a factory launch, if one of the guests attending is a local member of parliament, they should be welcomed and greeted by the general manager of the factory. Press and VIPs normally arrive well in advance of the other guests or the audience and are usually dropped off at a separate entrance from the other delegates. They are often then escorted to a private room with drinks and snacks available, together with private cloakroom and washroom facilities before commencement of the event. Each of the press representatives should be given a badge and a press kit. If required to ask questions, they should have access to handheld or roving microphones.

After the registration process, it should be possible to check which of the major media outlets are represented and have registered.

MANAGING VIPS ON-SITE

The event team should be briefed in advance, to avoid any protocol errors. The more information on the VIPs attending available, the better. The organiser should ensure that there is sufficient space and facilities provided for the VIP guests. Transportation for any VIP guests or dignitaries is generally arranged by the organising team on their behalf. In cases where the dignitaries or press are arriving from overseas, the team should make enquiries in the pre-event planning stage about where the VIP comes from and subsequently brief staff at the event on any special customs, religious beliefs or special dietary requirements. All staff should also be informed on how long the VIP will stay and what their first or native language is. It may be necessary secure an interpreter, or simultaneous translation services, or headphones and so on to assist them.

SEATING OF VIPS AND DIGNITARIES ON-SITE

In cases where the VIP is also one of the speakers, it is important to know where they should be seated at the conference. If the VIP guest is part of the audience, a seat should be made available and clearly marked for them in the first row, usually with their full name printed on a piece of paper. When seated at a board table, the VIP's place of honour is the first seat to the right of the person presiding the event, or the host. The VIP guest should subsequently be seated in line according to their ranking, to the left side of the host, and so on. Wherever possible, the event manager should avoid seating two men or two women next to each other at a table.

If the event is a meeting or a conference, the seating will be determined by the programme content and the table layout. In most cases, the seating will be British seating, where the host sits at the head of the table; or French seating, where the host sits at the central part of the longest side of the table. The common practice is for the conference to be launched by the host, who then introduces the VIP guest or guests. All the other speakers who are attending should then speak in order of their importance. Dignitaries, high-ranking officials and VIPs tend to have very full schedules and sometimes thank everyone for attending, excuse themselves and depart immediately after delivering their speech.

MANAGING PRESS ON-SITE

On those occasions when a press conference needs to be held, it is important that the organiser ensures that the environment is fit for purpose and that the press room is correctly prepared and set up. The press representatives should have assigned seats and, where necessary, a dedicated press area. In order to facilitate this, the organiser should carry out the following tasks:

- Check the location of electrical outlets
- Set up a table to seat any spokespeople

- Provide seating for reporters and their equipment
- Display any visuals as a backdrop to the table
- Have a sign-in pad for attendance
- Provide a podium for the moderator/speakers
- Set up a refreshment desk or area.

The spokesperson or team should be seated at a top table facing the reporters. In order to keep to timescales and ensure a professional outcome, the press conference should aim to start no later than five minutes after the scheduled commencement time, and all proceedings should be recorded. Any press questions should be sent through and vetted in advance. At the start of a press conference, the moderator or chairperson should welcome the press and introduce the participants and the issues to be discussed.

Each participant should be allowed to present for a few minutes. After the presentations, the moderator should invite questions and make sure they are directed to the appropriate stakeholders. After questions, the press conference should be brought to an end; the audience or participants should be thanked and, if appropriate, the media should be encouraged to stay for a more informal briefing, refreshments, or in some cases a site inspection. After the press conference, it will be possible to ascertain from the attendance register which major media representatives were not present and, for those who were unable to attend, it may be possible to deliver a press release; press package; video link; or schedule a subsequent meeting.

EVENT PROTOCOL ON-SITE

These are the standards, customs and rules that are commonly acknowledged, or even set down in writing, to ensure that all event personnel know how to treat and manage internal and external stakeholders at the event, from start to finish. This should be made part of the briefing. It is important for the event organiser to be aware of any arrival protocol concerning the meet and greet of speakers; guests at the airport; where to place state flags at government meetings; how to seat guests during meetings at dinners; and whether to present keynote speakers or dignitaries to guests. For the management of senior government officials and state representatives, it is possible to outsource to specific event-protocol departments.

BUSINESS ETIQUETTE AT THE EVENT

REAL INSIGHT 2.1

BUSINESS ETIQUETTE IN CHINA

When conducting business in China, clients will expect the team to be well prepared. This includes collating presentation material in advance of meetings and having at least 20 copies of the bid proposal ready to hand out. Presentation materials should be printed in black and white, not colour. Bright colours should also be avoided in business attire, as they are considered inappropriate, so it is best to opt for dark colours and more conservative suit styles.

Lateness is considered a serious offence in Chinese business etiquette, so suppliers should arrive promptly at meetings and try to make introductory 'small talk', as social niceties are considered particularly important, especially at the beginning of a meeting. Political and controversial conversation topics and strong negative statements should be avoided, as in China these are considered impolite. It is better to say: 'Let's think about it' or 'Shall we see?' rather than a blunt 'no'.

It is important for the bidding team to retain their composure during meetings. Body posture should always be formal and attentive, as it demonstrates self-control and respectfulness. Chinese clients do not like to be caused any embarrassment and showing too much emotion in a professional setting could have an adverse effect on the business negotiation.

Shaking hands is common practice, but the Chinese client should initiate the gesture. Exchanging business cards is also common practice. It is best to have one side printed in English and the other in either simplified or traditional Chinese, preferably in a gold font, as this is the colour of prestige and prosperity in China. Cards should be handed out with both hands, with the Chinese side facing the recipient. In return, when offered a business card it should be received attentively and examined carefully for a few moments. When the meeting has finished, the event team should exit the meeting room in advance of their Chinese counterparts.

In terms of reaching a business decision, in China it is perfectly acceptable to extend the negotiation period far beyond the original deadline date, if

(Continued)

it means any advantage can be gained. The event team should prepare themselves for this and be willing to accept the delays without mentioning deadlines. This patience will be much appreciated and could make the difference between winning and losing the business. Chinese clients prefer to establish a strong relationship with their agency and suppliers before closing a deal, so it might be necessary to arrange to meet up with the client or event owner several times, before reaching a final decision.

In China people usually enter a room in hierarchical order, so anyone walking into the conference room first, will be taken as the head of the delegation. No gifts should be brought to any meeting or formal dinner, as Chinese business etiquette considers this bribery, which is illegal in this country. Understanding this and other cultural etiquette is evidently essential when operating events in China or any other foreign markets.

Within the events industry there is also professional etiquette to consider, such as dressing professionally and respecting boundaries when operating in different cultures, to avoid causing offence. The way that personnel dress on-site is extremely important, especially when operating overseas, or dealing with different cultures and behaviours, so as not to cause offence. All staff should be briefed on cultural norms, such as the exchanging of business cards in Japan, or the appropriate use of jokes, as well as understanding how to generally steer the conversation and what subject areas to avoid.

Other areas of etiquette need to be adhered to when on-site, such as not drinking or smoking in front of clients. Staff should seek client guidance about where to take their meals and seek clarification on whether they will be permitted to mingle with guests while working. Another important aspect of business etiquette is maintaining punctuality at all times.

GO ONLINE

Read through Table 2.1 in the online Appendix (available at **study.sagepub.com/quick**) for an illustration of the summary of rules for dealing with VIPs and dignitaries at events, to ensure the correct protocol and etiquette are adhered to.

The questions listed in Table 2.9 may need to be asked on-site in accordance with business etiquette.

- How should the client staff, guests and planners interact? Should they be permitted to socialise with each other on-site when not working?
- Are staff, suppliers and event planners permitted to use the public and recreational areas during the event, e.g. swimming pool, gym, bars?

- Should planners or suppliers be permitted to fly in the same class as the client to events and to overseas site inspections?
- What is the dress code for planning staff and suppliers on-site?
- What is the company's policy on drinking and smoking?
- Will the planning staff and suppliers eat separately or with the client and guests?
- Will staff members be permitted to bring spouses or partners on-site?
- What hours and duties will staff be required to perform, and will there be a duty roster?
- Will staff working overtime, evenings, weekends and holidays be granted time off in lieu?
- Who will be the key client signatories on-site and who will be permitted to authorise any changes or amend the existing programme or approve additional changes?
- How much cash should be brought on-site and should the venue or other suppliers be offered gratuities?
- Is the company fully insured and covered for any potential legal liabilities?
- Should staff, event planners and suppliers be allowed to post any details or visuals onto social media?
- What will be the implications of staff, planners or suppliers compromising or breaching these codes of conduct?

TABLE 2.9 Business etiquette on-site
SOURCE: Adapted from Allen (2010)

MANAGING SPONSORS ON-SITE

At the event itself, the sponsor should be treated as a VIP. It is a good idea to arrange for a meet-and-greet service for your sponsors. Just as with the client or the event owner, all sponsors should be offered priority accommodation, parking spaces, a separate hospitality area with food and drinks and preferential seating. Often, sponsors are invited to a pre-event reception. The event team should ensure that any signage or merchandise that the sponsor wants to display is erected in a timely fashion that meets their requirements, before commencement. After the event, sponsors should be thanked, both verbally and in writing. Feedback should be given to the sponsor in the post-event phase, to allow them to evaluate the success of the sponsorship plan in line with their expectations and the event deliverables, as will be further discussed in Chapter 3.

ON-SITE VENUE LIAISON

Although much of the venue liaison process will take place in the planning phase, there are always last-minute changes and amends to make with the venue on-site. As will be further discussed in Chapter 6, the planning team should make at least one more site inspection before the start date.

If the organising team plan to arrive to set up at the venue the day before, the space will need to be booked for two days beforehand. This may provide a valuable opportunity to re-inspect all facilities and rooms, to set up any special arrangements with the venue and sort through rooming lists, technical requirements and billing systems. As well as familiarising staff with the main conference venue, visits to all restaurants and other external venues can be conducted during this time. This can also be an opportunity to arrange menu tastings and to make sure the quality of the catering will be of the highest standard.

Once on-site, additional time needs to be allowed for setting up and clearing up. Depending on what type of event is being held, clean-up time can vary enormously, especially if there is food, drink, décor and any kind of sound system involved; it is therefore essential to make sure sufficient time has been booked to clean up afterwards.

Venue preparation often comes under the area of health and safety since it concerns key safety checks. Failure to carry out these checks could put the health and well-being of everyone involved at risk. Moreover, should anything go wrong, it will be the event management company, or owner, that will be held responsible, which in some cases might lead to legal action. These areas will be further discussed under the health and safety section in this chapter. Possible venue checks might include:

- Acquiring any licence or permits necessary
- Providing insurance
- Conducting a risk assessment
- Setting up emergency procedures.

As a conference organiser, it is extremely beneficial to have one point of contact at the venue who thoroughly understands the requirements and audience and who will be on-site for the whole duration. It is a good idea to meet with this person in the set-up phase, to talk through the programme, prepare lists and all items listed in the working document. It is not always possible to set up so early on-site. For example, if it is an evening event, there may be another event being held in the same space during the day. In this case, the organising team may have a finite time to get into the venue and set up and transform the space for an evening function, so they have to be well prepared and have conducted their venue checks earlier. For large events, it may be advisable to hire an event office, fully equipped with computer systems, printers and other office amenities, as a base for any on-site operations.

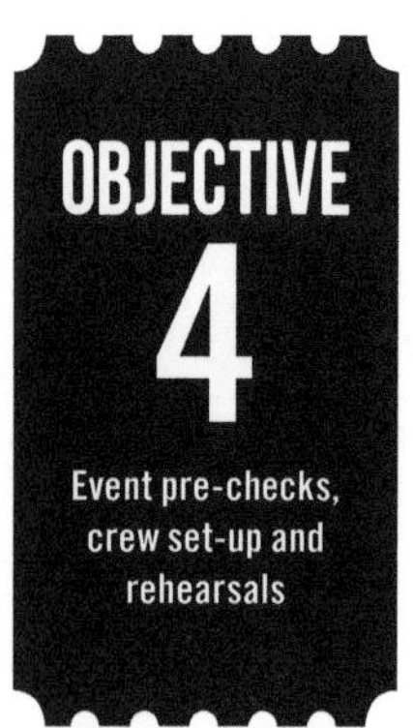

OBJECTIVE
4
Event pre-checks, crew set-up and rehearsals

PRE-EVENT CHECKS, CREW SET-UP AND REHEARSALS

DATA MANAGEMENT

The processing of relevant data management will have been conducted by the event team in the planning phase. Once on-site, it is essential to have access to this data, usually by means of an online portal, laptop or tablet, so that staff can check relevant data pertinent to the event. A data-management system will essentially include information such as:

- Personal details, visa, passport
- Company details: location, country, title
- Travel: airline, train, car, coach

- Accommodation: number of nights, room type, special requirements
- Gala dinner, workshops, special dietary requirements, allergies
- Seating allocation
- Ticket allocation
- Payments, fees, tickets.

PRE-EVENT CHECKS

The on-site set-up phase can be the most hectic time for the operations and productions crew, as this is when many changes need to be executed to the programme. Regardless of the event type and size, there are generally some basic tasks that will need to be completed before delegates arrive; a few simple procedures and checks that can help ensure all runs smoothly on-site are listed in Table 2.10.

• Meet with the venue staff or conference and events manager beforehand to run through the event proceedings, room allocations, layouts and catering provision
• Brief all parties about on-site extra expenditure and master account sign-off procedures
• Liaise with the venue to ensure there is sufficient signage, a registration area, a cloakroom and a welcome desk
• Set up the registration desk with any badges, conference packs, stalls, attractions, etc.
• Check meeting rooms are correctly set up with a screen, microphones, a top table, lectern, the correct audio-visual equipment and enough seats for all attendees
• Make sure the meeting rooms are supplied with paper, pens, water, etc.
• Check the availability of replacement or back-up equipment
• Check all technical equipment and organise technical rehearsals with speakers before commencement of the event
• Check any additional off-site restaurants or venues that will be used
• Ensure the cleanliness of facilities, private and public areas, inside and outside areas and restrooms throughout
• Place products such as waste bins, potpourri, fine-quality hand towels and handwash in the rest rooms to upgrade them
• Arrange any room-drops of delegate gifts or conference packs
• Make any necessary guest announcements or post on in-room monitors
• Brief event and venue staff on communication processes
• Implement contingency plans for routine as well as emergency situations.

TABLE 2.10 On-site pre-event checks

During the set-up phase, the following event checklist for various on-site functions and responsibilities could be used to cover all eventualities.

GO ONLINE

An event checklist for on-site functions and responsibilities can be found at **study.sagepub.co.uk/quick**

CREW SET-UP AND REHEARSALS

At large events with significant production requirements, the advance party and crew will need to monitor and supervise the production set-up and organise technical rehearsals with the crew and guest speakers and make any last-minute adjustments to presentation material and so on. The production crew should ensure that speakers have the opportunity to run through the presentation slides in the set-up phase; arrange a brief technical rehearsal; and ensure that all speakers adhere to timings, so the event does not overrun.

DID YOU KNOW?

Compliance with the Equality Act 2010 includes making it unlawful to discriminate against disabled individuals without justifiable reason.

Employers must make reasonable adjustments to workplace or working arrangements and the event venue.

SOURCE: www.acas.org.uk

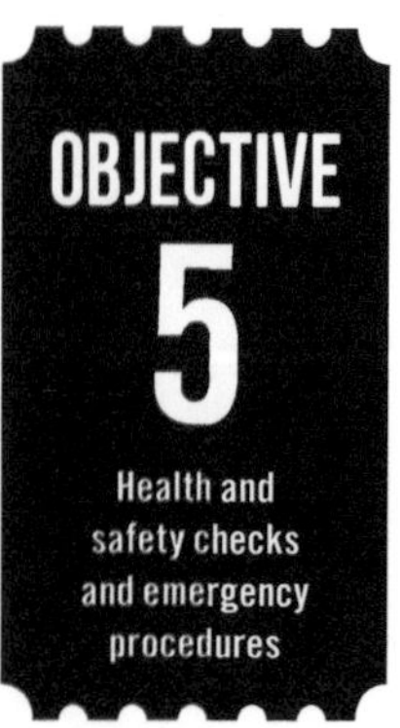
OBJECTIVE
5
Health and safety checks and emergency procedures

HEALTH AND SAFETY CHECKS AND EMERGENCY PROCEDURES

DELIVERING SAFE EVENTS

Providing safety for all stakeholders will help ensure the success of the event and the reputation of all parties involved. An awareness of risk management and health and safety issues needs to commence in the planning stages, and will vary considerably, depending on the type of event and the emergency procedures put in place.

Event managers have a 'duty of care' to adhere to safety regulations. This might be for moral or ethical reasons, but also because if they fail to do so, there may be legal recourse, which could have devastating financial implications for the client. Due to increasing legislation and regulation demands on the industry, ignorance is no longer a defence and all events have had to become more professional and be able to demonstrate that all possible steps have been taken to ensure safety. Businesses must endeavour to control the risks in the workplace, by assessing in advance what might cause harm to people and deciding whether they are taking reasonable precautions to prevent that harm (HSE's *The Event Safety Guide* 2014).

In cases of negligence, those who show a 'gross breach of duty of care' may be prosecuted. Therefore, event organisations need to be proactive in providing relevant health and safety training to all staff, so that they will be able to pinpoint problems as they develop, rather than waiting for them to happen. It is the responsibility of the event management company or owner to ensure that all staff are properly trained, or risk being penalised. For example, anyone serving alcohol at an event must hold a Responsible Service of Alcohol (RSA) certificate and failure to do so may result in loss of their alcohol or liquor licence or, even worse, potential closure.

The main incidents that need to be considered include: threats from fire and smoke; terrorism and bomb threats; threats to VIPs; cyber security threats; natural disasters caused by flood or earthquakes; gas leaks or other biological hazards; incidents caused by crowd congestion and overcrowding; riots and protests; traffic and vehicle accidents; and infrastructure problems caused by collapsing tents, marquees, and so on.

Since key legislation was first established through the Health and Safety at Work Act (1974), the industry has learnt many important lessons from past mistakes and specific tragic incidents. Increased press coverage and the advent of social media have made this area more visible and overall there are better expectations of safety today, possibly due to increased government involvement. However, the most likely reason for the renewed focus on health and safety is the recent emergence of a global compensation culture. The threat of litigation is enough to make any trader think very carefully about the issue of health and safety, in order to survive as a business.

WHAT IS RISK MANAGEMENT?

Basically, this is the process of identifying risks and evaluating their potential consequences, then determining and implementing the most effective way of controlling and monitoring them. Sometimes it may be worth outsourcing this to a specialised risk-management contractor, who will be able to conduct a full risk audit and recommend appropriate measures. Although this may come at a cost to the agency or owner, it may be worth the investment in the long run, in order to maintain the reputation of the company of the provider.

RISK ASSESSMENT

The Health and Safety Executive (HSE 2015) has identified that most fatal accidents and major injuries at events are caused by transportation issues. Other areas to include in a risk assessment are queues, slips and trips, poor lighting, fire hazards and on-site vehicles and transportation to the event or venue.

Part of effective health and safety management involves conducting a risk assessment and then creating a health and safety policy and implementing, monitoring and revising that policy where necessary. It is often a requirement of the venue to carry out regular risk assessments on the property, as well as reviewing the specific requirements of each event, to ensure the overall safety of delegates. This risk assessment is usually carried out in the planning phase. The following steps can be taken as part of a risk assessment:

1 Identify the hazards
2 Assess these as high, medium or low
3 Act to reduce these with methods and measures to reduce the risk
4 Re-assess the risks after action has been taken
5 Monitor the risks and re-assess
6 Consult the experts if necessary
7 Record and report any actions.

Once typical risks have been identified, the likelihood of these occurring will need to be analysed and evaluated by the organising team; they then need to be prioritised and plans put in place to avoid them occurring. Strategies should be devised to eliminate these risks occurring and preventative measures put in place to reduce each risk, as illustrated in Table 2.11.

Risk area	Risk factors	Preventative measures
Event planning	Inexperienced, inadequate or incompetent management Crowd behaviours Staff oblivious to external conditions Lack of policies and procedures	Train staff and managers, take on-site for a recce and briefing in advance of the event Conduct full review of areas, such as: crowd behaviour and likely responses to specific acts or bands Put appropriate policies and procedures in place
Event type and purpose	First time or one-time experience Controversial events Lack of aims or objectives	Research similar events Try to eliminate controversy by adopting a good PR strategy Set clear measurable aims and objectives with the event owner or budget holder
Finances	Lack of funding, inadequate insurance Improper procurement practices Cash handling procedures/areas Insufficient income raised through ticket sales and additional funds, to break even or make a profit	Conduct prior thorough research on income versus expenditure. Source possible sponsors for funding Get sufficient event cover/insurance for event Try to work with ethical companies/procurement organisations Check staff disclosure credentials Establish a safe environment for cash handling and procedures on-site Increase ticket price and other revenue options
Human resources	Insufficient staffing Untrained/inexperienced personnel Incorrect deployment of personnel	Source adequate qualified staff and/or volunteers Ensure on-site briefings are carried out Appoint staff in correct areas with relevant expertise

Risk area	Risk factors	Preventative measures
Infrastructure	Inadequate power/technology/utilities Improper sanitation and waste management Insufficient parking and traffic management	Consult registered electricians and ensure equipment is PAT tested Work with certified waste management companies/source additional staff on-site Recruit enough stewards or marshals for on-site car parks/traffic flow etc. Use pedestrian crossings/access Improve road access, signage and vehicle entrances on- and off-site
Operations	Occupational health and safety Installation, operation and close-down logistics Equipment, décor, special effects	Ensure health and safety training and, where possible, SIA/IOSH accreditation for staff Include full details in conference working documentation Carry out regular equipment checks
Suppliers	Specialist, skilled, union requirements Lack of supplier contract and control Quality control, compliance and insurance issues	Where possible, work with tried-and-tested supplier incumbents Check supplier regulations and certification Consult an external professional, where necessary
Time	Inadequate planning and decision time Event start and end times, duration Arrival and departure modes	Try to work within realistic deadlines and ask for extensions when necessary Consult residents/police if there are potential late-noise issues Make contingency plans for overrunning

TABLE 2.11 Typical event risk factors

SITE SAFETY MANAGEMENT

All phases of site safety, including the planning, build and the breakdown phase, should be considered. The process of site safety management includes the identification of decision makers, who may ultimately decide to stop the event. Other health and safety issues on-site will be the identification of emergency routes; the identification of holding areas; crowd and transportation management; food and beverage safety on-site; and the provision of an emergency plan and first-aid facilities. Accident reporting is also very important on-site, as this may prevent future accidents, as well as providing a written record in cases where compensation may be due.

SITE PLANNING SAFETY CHECKS

Following on from the initial site inspections, robust health and safety checks should be put in place. It will be up to the event crew to forecast key areas such as: capacity and audience numbers, crowd dynamics, plot and site size, access, exits and entrances, and security and CCTV coverage. They will plot the safest layout for various facilities, including ticketing points, security and assembly points for possible evacuation. Any on-site plans will take into account the following:

- Temporary structures, such as marquees
- Fencing and barriers
- Access and search points
- Ticket checks
- Signage and directions
- Emergency route plans.

CAPACITY PLANNING

Most venues will be licensed by the local authority and have strict guidelines on the maximum capacity allowed on the premises at any one time. This is known in the industry as the occupant capacity and exists to ensure that there is sufficient means of escape for the event audience and recognised crowd control. A number of factors will be considered when determining this capacity, such as the number of fire exits, sanitary facilities, venue layout, and so on. The licensing authority may also restrict the number of people that are allowed in a particular part of the venue. When using a temporary or unusual venue to stage an event, it is necessary to apply for a licence, and to state the capacity of the expected audience. For any large event, having clear emergency procedures is essential. This should take the form of written instructions and venue briefings for all staff, so that they are aware of the venue regulations and all exit points within the venue, which should be clearly marked.

FOOD AND BEVERAGE SAFETY ON-SITE

In terms of food safety, a principal factor is to ensure that both hot and cold food is kept at the correct temperature. In addition, there should be appropriate kitchen equipment on-site and sufficient chefs with the expertise to handle the numbers. Food hygiene is extremely important and there should be provision of running hot water and enough sinks and correct layout facilities of kitchens in relation to the other amenities on-site.

Q & A ON SERVICE

Q: How many service points do you need for a fork buffet to serve 500 efficiently?

A: 10 service points – 50 people on each buffet station

That is 30 seconds for each person, which equals 25 minutes of service

CROWD MANAGEMENT

Crowd management techniques have developed from the early theories of Canetti who, as early as 1962, made an attempt to understand 'crowd dynamics' throughout the

20th century. He was one of the first theorists to attempt to classify each crowd by its personality and motivation, and tried to find techniques to predict and manage crowd behaviour and address the fundamentals of the crowd, such as:

- Growth – peak times when the crowd numbers will rise
- Direction – which direction the audience will be coming from/moving to
- Density – the density distribution of crowd members located in a particular area.

Crowd psychology is still an important part of risk assessment today, particularly the effects of drugs and alcohol on crowd behaviour. Today, when developing an 'audience profile', event managers try to understand the 'type' of crowd they are dealing with; their age, sex and profile, in a way that echoes Canetti's theory. Defining crowd behaviour is particularly important with outdoor events, live events, festivals, concerts and sporting events. The distinction between crowd management and crowd control is that the former is the process by which crowd activities are facilitated in the planning stages, whereas the latter concerns the tactical measures that might be implemented to control the event crowd when those activities become undesirable. Mick Upton, former director of Showsec, advises event managers to gather intelligence in advance in order to determine how a crowd may behave. He suggests a number of questions to ask, such as:

- Who is coming?
- How many are coming?
- What are their demographics?
- Why are they coming?
- When will they arrive?
- What will they do at the event?
- When will they leave?
- Where will they go when they have left?

Unruly behaviour is unfortunately something that event organisers have to anticipate. This is usually brought about as a result of overcrowding, congestion and crowd crush. It is therefore important to review the crowd behaviour in advance of the event, to adopt a preventative approach, especially at festivals and music events, to evaluate these risks and try to eliminate them. At major music festivals, a number of measures have been introduced to limit the physical pressures of a large crowd, particularly near the stage area.

Access to the 'moshpit', the area immediately in front of the stage, is limited and provides a separate enclosure from other sections of the crowd. A recent approach has introduced designated areas, primarily aimed at VIPs and celebrity guests, but which also act as a relief area, by breaking up the density of the crowd. Contingency measures need to be developed that can deal with problems as they occur. Most members of the public, although irritated by it, will accept that some problems cannot always be prevented. However, they will expect that the event organisers will have anticipated problems and thought about a response to them in advance.

Q & A ON CROWD INCIDENT

Q: What event has seen the most fatalities and serious injuries in the last 100 years?

A: Sept. 2015: The Hajj, Mecca, 769 dead (officially reported) but unofficial reports put the figure up to over 5000.

SOURCE: Image courtesy of Al Jazeera English via flickr.com. Shared under the Creative Commons BY-SA 2.0 license.

CROWD MOVEMENT

One aspect that can cause problems at any event is queuing and congestion at entrances/ exits or turnstiles. Models for queuing have long been developed by major theme park operators, such as Disney, where attempts have been made to eliminate queues and congestion and illuminate some of the problems associated with them. The key is to prevent impatience, which can lead to confrontation amongst the crowd. One approach is to have plenty of staff on hand to assist people and also to constantly monitor through CCTV what is going on.

When queues are anticipated, the event organiser should arrange facilities, entertainment, or even television monitors at queue points, to inform the crowd and keep people as relaxed as possible. It is also a good idea to keep queuing areas covered from the elements wherever possible. In terms of crowd movement, the following risks should be considered:

- Steep slopes
- Grassy/slippery slopes
- Dead ends, locked gates
- Junctions where routes meet and merge
- Uneven ground, floors or steps
- Damaged surfaces, cracked concrete, loose gravel, etc.
- Narrow doorways/choke points
- Transition points such as the top and the bottom of an escalator
- Reverse or cross flows in a dense crowd
- Crowd flows that are obstructed by queues, or gathering crowds or any large pedestrian flows mixing with traffic
- Moving attractions within a crowd
- Convergence of several routes into one.

Large functions and events need seamless crowd flow and people management. They require the right rooms to be in the right place, especially when moving from break-out rooms or syndicates to plenary and catering areas and back. In addition, local emergency services need to be notified of the numbers and location in advance and to be on standby during the entire event.

STEWARDING AND MARSHALLING ON-SITE

Stewards and marshals are needed for a number of roles, including giving directions; helping with registration; manning lost children's tents; litter collection; and managing car park areas. At festivals and outdoor events, recruits are often made up of volunteers. At larger events, a roving car park supervisor in a vehicle is needed to check at regular intervals at various points on the site, particularly when staff are handling cash. These roving supervisors should carry a supply of water, snacks, basic signage, and be able to transport staff, if necessary, especially during the summer months.

Stewards and marshals usually direct traffic on-site, though they may be required to undertake special traffic regulation training for directing traffic to and from public roads and motorways. It is more likely, however, that organisers would accredit some trained and approved stewards to work under their direction under the Police Accredited Traffic Officers (PATO) scheme. All stewards should have undergone appropriate training and should be issued with fluorescent high-viz weather protection jackets and torches or flashlights in bad or dark weather conditions.

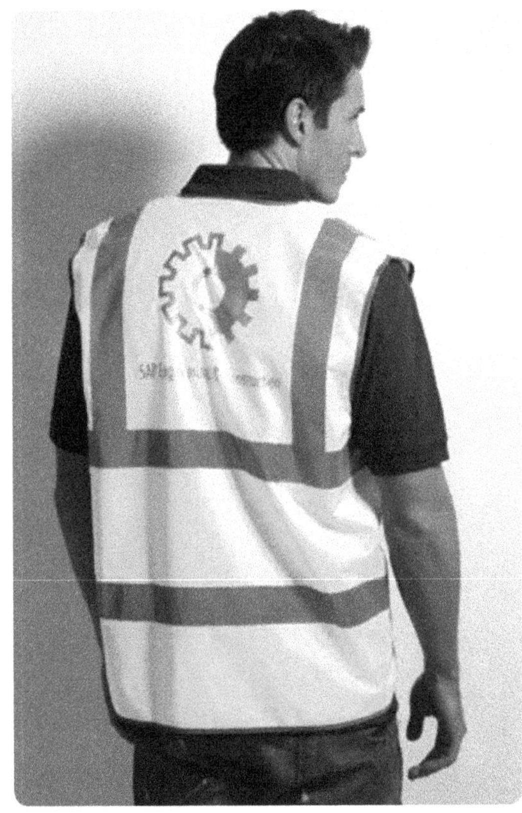

SOURCE: Image courtesy of Jordon B via flickr.com. Shared under the Creative Commons BY 2.0 license.

TRAFFIC MANAGEMENT

This area generally involves devising a plan that covers all eventualities and contingencies to allow traffic to flow, particularly at peak arrival and departure times. Traffic management involves policing all modes of transportation to the event, as well as ensuring the safety of pedestrians, cyclists, crew and emergency vehicles. Traffic management could involve arranging VIP transportation, including limousines and helicopters, should a helipad be available on-site or nearby. Crew at outside events are responsible for ensuring the safety of all access roads for pedestrians and putting the necessary roadblocks and security in place. The traffic manager should have a contingency plan in case larger numbers than expected show. Overflow car parks with appropriate signage should be made available. It is also important to plan ahead for what to do if heavy rain causes flooding or waterlogged, muddy areas.

Part of the traffic management plan for larger events will be to develop traffic networks using computers and simulation models. They can be used to calculate traffic flows and determine whether any temporary road restrictions need to be enforced, such as road or lane closures, temporary crossing facilities, banned turns, speed limits or temporary bumps, one-way streets and access control. This can also show the emergency services who can go through which gates. In some cases, link and junction properties and pedestrian crossings will be required. Signage is an important aspect of traffic management, to notify vehicles in advance of instructions such as:

- 'Coaches Next Right'
- 'Disabled Parking (Badge Holders Only) Turn Left'
- 'All Cars Turn Right'.

CAR PARKING CONSIDERATIONS

Most venue sites will have a choice between adopting self-regulated or controlled parking. Event parking and how the car parks link to the road network need to be planned in advance. For larger events, it may be necessary to have separate car parks that link to the different major roads, to avoid congestion. All car parks should be well signposted and well lit and generally safe for pedestrians who are accessing the site from the car parks. Sufficient stewards are needed to guide cars into parking spaces. Security and CCTV cameras should also be available at these car parks. Where possible, areas designated for children's activities should be kept as vehicle-free zones.

ARRIVING AND LEAVING

The arrival and departure of the event audience is an important health and safety concern and will also contribute to the first and last audience experience and may ultimately influence their overall experience. It is important for planners to plot peak arrival and exit times and to estimate how concentrated the audience arrival will be, as this will have both safety and noise implications. Guest arrivals and departures may have an impact on the venue and local community and in some cases may be a stipulation of the overall venue premises licence.

At larger events, extra staff may need to be recruited, to ensure that guests leave as quickly and quietly as possible. At times, staff may work in conjunction with key transportation providers and emergency services to facilitate this. All pedestrian routes should be marked on access maps and people attending the event should be notified in advance about the safest pedestrian routes. Sufficient staff should be available on-site, to inform waiting pedestrians of the nearest exits and entrances and to answer questions regarding public transportation systems and timetables.

ON-SITE SECURITY

For smaller events, generally the only security required is the vigilance of all staff, well-placed CCTV cameras and sufficient on-site stewards. For larger events, it may be necessary to have a paid police presence and even a temporary control room. Police presence on-site often acts as a deterrent, but this is not a complimentary service and will need to be added to the overall budget. Hiring private security is a less expensive option, but the organiser should still first seek initial consultation with the local police service, to offer initial security advice and recommendations based on size, nature, capacity, and so on.

In the UK, members of the Special Constabulary might also be employed on a voluntary basis. The police control room should ideally be located at a road gate, to allow quick and easy access for police vehicles. Organisers should arrange complimentary meals and drinks and ensure there is sufficient cover to allow them to take regular breaks.

EVENT CASH OFFICE

Any cash office that is required on-site should be centrally positioned for all relevant parties to access for cash distribution, delivery and collection. The cash office should be secured and protected, as this is where any cash floats and incoming cash will be collected, bagged and dispatched for banking. Cash from the gate and car parks should be brought there for storage, so it may be necessary to have a safe or lockable cabinet, or to have regular cash collections made from a security patrol.

REPORTING ACCIDENTS

It is useful to have an accident-report form and a logbook on-site (a sample is shown in Table 2.12). The accident-reporting form can be created and used on-site. Whenever an accident or incident occurs, the organising team should:

- Provide medical assistance to any casualty
- Prevent any other person suffering an injury due to the same cause
- Obtain details of the casualty
- Record details of the accident and the circumstances leading up to it

- Record details of witnesses and obtain a short statement from them
- Report the incident/accident to the venue manager or landowner, as well as the event insurer
- Risk assess the area and equipment, or anything involved with the incident
- Take remedial action to prevent further incidents or accidents
- Record details of the new risk assessment and revised remedial action.

Sunday 24 August 2019
10.23 Car Park 1 – Steward reports a medical emergency
10.24 Car Park 1 – Max Bright calls in casualty details. Male, approx. 65, name Bob Smith collapsed, with suspected heart attack. Wife says he had a previous heart attack in 2017
10.25 First aid called to attend
10.26 County ambulance called
10.30 All staff warned via radios that county ambulance to attend Car Park 1 main gate
10.34 Max Bright, steward at Car Park 1, reports casualty and wife have been taken in county ambulance to All Saints Hospital, Petworth
10.35 Car park supervisor reports the car of casualty to be Red VW Golf, registration TX12 TTA to be secured on-site, until collected by casualty's son at approx. 19.00 tonight

TABLE 2.12 Sample transmissions log

EVACUATION PROCEDURES

Although it is highly unlikely to occur, the event organiser should know how to deal with a possible on-site evacuation and have devised a plan to cover the following:

- Who will inform the emergency services?
- Who will act as emergency services liaison?
- How will staff and the public be notified about the evacuation?
- Who will identify the area under threat?
- Where will the public and stallholders be dispatched to?
- Where will the off-site control be situated?
- Which staff should be placed at which point?
- What will happen to any livestock and animals on-site?
- How should valuables be secured and protected during the evacuation?
- Who will declare the site safe again?
- How will stallholders and the public be allowed to re-enter the site?

ON-SITE EMERGENCY AND FIRST-AID PLAN

The plan should specify who has the ultimate decision to stop or cancel the event. In an emergency situation, the organiser should make a decision, devise a plan after consultation and keep to it. Additionally, the plan should identify emergency routes and evacuation areas and details of local hospitals and emergency services.

Early consultation with the local fire and rescue and medical services is recommended and will reduce workload and eliminate a host of potential problems. At larger events, there should also be extra emergency runners to troubleshoot if necessary.

For a small event, it may be sufficient to bring basic medical supplies on-site, or to outsource to the St John's ambulance or local equivalent representatives. Medical provision at events mostly involves assessing and treating minor injuries and medical conditions. However, nowadays events cannot always risk working with staff who have only a basic medical knowledge. For a larger event, it may be necessary to outsource to paramedics or medical support services and to liaise with local hospitals. At concerts and festivals, exacerbation of attendees' pre-existing medical conditions, such as asthma, epilepsy and diabetes, are common, as well as those resulting from excessive alcohol intake and heat exhaustion; childbirth and serious incidents such as heart attacks or strokes can also occur.

The site first-aid tent should be conveniently located in a central location, accessible to all and, if possible, near a visually identifiable landmark. There is a possibility that serious casualties may need to be removed from the site by ambulance. The first-aid station should therefore be located near a vehicle access point, with sufficient space for ambulances to enter, turn and leave safely, with easy and fast access to main roads. If the event involves risky pursuits, such as motorised sports, it may be necessary to set aside a secure area for an emergency helipad and to have trained medics and paramedics on-site.

CHAPTER SUMMARY

CHAPTER SUMMARY QUESTIONS

1. What checks should the event team carry out at the venue before commencement of the event?
2. What measures should be put in place on-site to ensure the sponsors/partners have a good overall experience?
3. Who should speak first at the conference or event?
4. What is a 'dine around' and when might this be used at an event?
5. What measures can be taken to reduce the risk of intoxication at events?
6. How should any accidents be reported and recorded on-site?

DISCUSSION POINTS

- Why do you think health and safety has become such a major concern for event planners in recent years?
- Do you think all venues have a duty of care to facilitate disabled guests to attend an event?
- Do you think festivals have the right to ban attendees from bringing drinking water into an event?

ACTIVITIES

- Produce a list of information that you could put in a conference working document.
- Design a menu for a hot and cold running buffet dinner for guests arriving at the venue on the first evening.
- Plan a risk assessment document for the most common security issues that might occur at an outdoor event.

REFERENCES

Allen, J. (2010) *Event Planning Ethics and Etiquette: A Principled Approach to the Business of Special Event Management*. New York: Wiley.

Canetti, E. (1962) *Crowds and Power*. New York: Viking Press.

Conway, D.G. (2009) *The Event Managers Bible*, 3rd edn. Oxon: HowtoBooks.

Goldblatt, J. (2014) *Special Events*, 7th edn. New York: Wiley.

The Health and Safety Executive (HSE) (2014) The event safety guide [online]. Available at: www.hse.gov.uk/event-safety/crowd-management.htm (accessed 16 April 2020).

The Health and Safety Executive (HSE) (2015) Annual report and accounts 2015/16 [online]. Available at: www.hse.gov.uk/aboutus/reports/ara-2015-16.pdf (accessed 16 April 2020).

3

THE POST-EVENT AND EVALUATION PHASE

CHAPTER OVERVIEW

This chapter will examine the post-event phase and the evaluation process for different event types and will discuss how to evaluate the data, identify key issues and use the data to underpin future business, staffing issues and any other potential problems that may need resolving. The measurement of Return on Objectives (ROO) and Return on Investment (ROI) will be explored. The chapter will examine the evaluation tools used to collect customer satisfaction feedback after the event and discuss how to deal with negative feedback and the negotiation of discounts and rebates for unsatisfactory service or delivery. Finally, the chapter will explore motivation theory for attending events and monitoring of ethical issues.

CHAPTER OBJECTIVES

After reading this chapter, you will be able to identify and understand:

OBJECTIVE 1
The post-event phase and the importance of evaluation

OBJECTIVE 2
Various evaluation methods used for different event types

OBJECTIVE 3
Supplier debriefs and securing future business with the client

OBJECTIVE 4
The motivation and psychological factors of events

OBJECTIVE 5
The significance of ethical stewardship in events today

Meet SHAUN CASEY

Executive Committee Member

Charity Partner Liaison, Meeting Needs

With more than 30 years' experience in the European MICE industry, Shaun has held a number of management roles in operations as well as sales and marketing for global incentive houses, travel management companies, technology providers and destination management companies. His client focus has centred on automotive, financial/professional services, IT and pharmaceutical.

At BI WORLDWIDE, Shaun's responsibility was to devise and implement a strategy to ensure that the events department achieved the overall objectives of the business, targeting rapid growth to 2020 through organic and strategic acquisition. Core to this strategy is the integration of behavioural economics producing effective and engaging content for clients' audiences, maximising return on objectives, while delivering a best-in-class brand experience for all stakeholders.

Recently, Shaun took a sabbatical from the industry to pursue his interest in CSR. He worked as a Spanish interpreter and lead project manager with the youth development charity Raleigh International. Supporting their community-led WASH initiative in northwest Nicaragua, he led the implementation of a gravity-fed drinking water system to supply more than 400 inhabitants of a remote mountain village with drinking water, in conjunction with the fair-trade cooperative, Juan Francisco Paz Silva.

Having retired from BI WORLDWIDE in June 2019, Shaun's main focus is on Meetings Needs and how he can promote the charity with the meetings industry through social media. He has already visited a beneficiary in Africa to see for himself how funds raised are being used to change people's lives for the better, forever.

REAL EVENT CHALLENGE

I took a 15-year break from BI, the marketing organisation that I had been working with for a number of years and, when I returned, I found the industry and my perception of it had changed radically. The focus had moved away from direct marketing, such as mailshots, vouchers, incentives and merchandising, to digital marketing. The emphasis had shifted to employee and audience engagement, and evaluation on the Return on Objectives; Return on Investment; and even a Return on the Event. These were new areas to me, and my challenge was to embrace the changes and adapt to a new way of working, with new terminology and more focus on the study of audience behaviour than ever before. This meant evaluating the DNA of millennials and younger audiences; their motivation for going on trips; what makes them tick; their need to be recognised and to take selfies and post them on social media. It also meant trying to understand the value of staying connected to the audience 365 days a year through social media and finding ways to incorporate high-quality technical innovation such as Gamification; online registration systems; and virtual and augmented reality into event programmes in order to keep the audience energised.

Q&A

WHAT DID YOU WANT TO BE WHEN YOU WERE YOUNGER?

Cabin crew but I was too short! Seriously, I always wanted to work in tourism or an international job and studied languages at university which led me into that. My first job was for Cosmos.

WHAT'S THE BEST PART OF YOUR JOB ... AND THE WORST?

The best part of the job is seeing how many event-management agencies support our charity and give their time and money. I would say the worst part is seeing falling standards in the industry and it being acceptable to be mediocre.

WHAT QUALITIES DO YOU ADMIRE IN OTHERS?

Integrity, both personally and professionally. Also honesty and generosity of the heart.

FAVOURITE MOVIE OF ALL TIME?

The 1970s spoof Airplane comes to mind. It still makes me chuckle today!

BIGGEST CHANGE IN THE EVENTS INDUSTRY IN THE LAST 10 YEARS?

The increase in administration, health and safety, duty of care, regulations and risk documentation, which has strangled the spontaneity of events to some extent.

PRACTITIONER VIEWPOINT

Richard Bridge, Founder and CEO of Top Banana

The biggest shift in the industry over the last decade has been that events are no longer done for the sake of it, but instead are carefully planned and aligned around measurable business outcomes. Every element is now rooted in the business strategy and links back to an overall purpose. Gone are the days of stand and tell, transmitting information via a slide deck to a seated audience. We are having to work harder than ever before to come up with creative and clever ways to bring messages to life and create an emotional connection between the message and the audience, by involving and immersing them in memorable experiences.

As consumers, we are constantly exposed to the latest trends and technologies, and as such we're finding that the new multi-generational audience are bringing with them a heightened expectation of communication. This is where technology has really impacted our industry as it presents us with new ways of communicating messages, making it more personalised and involving the audience at every stage, whether that be by a bespoke app, gamification, virtual reality or one of the main other technologies that lends itself to our world. However, while we are getting used to the fact that change is the new constant in our industry, my view is that technology will never be able to replace the importance of face-to-face communication, but instead becomes a key tool in how we create new and exciting experiences for our audiences.

Sustainability is becoming more and more prevalent and audiences are demanding and challenging organisers to become more sustainably aware and do more to make a difference. I think in time this will become the norm but for now, it's important to talk about and demonstrate tactics and initiatives that are being done.

ACADEMIC VIEWPOINT

Philip Berners, Events Lecturer and Course Leader for the BA Event Management programmes, Edge Hotel School, University of Essex; author and series editor of *The Practical Guide to Events and Hotel Management* series (Routledge)

The events management modules I teach look at the skills and knowledge required for the planning, delivery and evaluation of events. In the first year, the students learn operational theories in class alongside operational practice in our 4* hotel on campus. In the second year, they learn supervisory and team leadership in class alongside supervising and leading events in the hotel. In the third year, they learn managerial and strategic theories in class alongside management roles of live events in the hotel. This way students graduate with an academic degree while also knowing how to do the job and how to be a successful manager of events – what we call 'industry ready'. This is essential for meeting the increasing expectations of clients and attendees who demand creative experiences – experiential events. This is vital to attract audience engagement and participation at events, especially from 'influencers' on social media sites.

REAL EVENT OUTCOME

Having recognised the changes that had taken place in the industry, as previously outlined, the agency was keen to link up with an academic approach to analyse the science of behavioural economics, and also to view events as the principal part on an overall strategy for the companies we worked with.

We consulted with a professor from the University of Cambridge for a scientific approach to help us understand the more analytical side of the business and to start to evaluate our customers' goals and values. By embracing the paradigm shift in the industry, such as consumer engagement; the analysis of audience behaviour; and the growth of new technology, through use of social media and gamification programmes, we were able to move forward as a business and put the right people in place to facilitate this. This allowed us to embrace a new vision of the industry, rather than lagging behind and not moving with the times, which was the case with some of the other, more traditional, 'old school' event agencies who subsequently floundered.

THE POST-EVENT PHASE AND THE IMPORTANCE OF EVALUATION

OBJECTIVE
1
The post-event phase and the importance of evaluation

THE POST-EVENT PHASE

The last stage of the event cycle is the post-event phase. After the event has taken place, it is time to monitor and evaluate stakeholder feedback and determine the overall success. This is also the time to complete the financial reconciliation, renegotiate with any suppliers where necessary, and to communicate feedback to all stakeholders. The optimum time for an overall analysis is in the period of consultation after the internal and external feedback-debrief meetings have taken place. During this time, the organising team should disseminate the data collected and conduct an assessment of the process and project management through all the event stages.

On completion of the event, an evaluation report should be compiled after the organisers have met with the budget holder or client, for a detailed debrief on the event to ascertain how to improve future delivery and aim to secure future events. In this report, the goals and objectives set at the outset should be measured, to determine whether the event delivered on its objectives or Return on Objectives (ROO) and on its financial projections, or Return on Investment (ROI).

POST-EVENT EVALUATION

In recent years, there has been a shift to evaluate the overall event, particularly in terms of the programme. In previous times, corporate conferences would take place regularly at considerable expense to the company, with no advance analysis of the company's business needs or performance issues. A conference or meeting may have run for an average of two to three days, yet budget holders did not set any specific measurable objectives or conduct any evaluation afterwards. There was little justification required for why the event was being run in the first place and also very little communication with key stakeholders in the post-event phase.

WHY EVALUATE EVENTS?

The general focus tends to be on the organisational aspects and evaluation is often the neglected part of the event cycle. Even multinational event sponsors sometimes forget to include this vital part of the process. Yeoman et al. (2012: 252) describe event evaluation as: 'the process of critically observing, measuring and monitoring the implementation of an event in order to assess the outcomes accurately'.

Regardless of their size and scale, a key reason to evaluate is so that the organisers can learn valuable lessons from the various stakeholders' feedback, and this data can then be used to improve future events. Evaluation is also a useful tool for enabling a better understanding of the audience psychology and motivation for attending events, which will be discussed later in this chapter.

The evaluation process allows the organiser to put together an accurate and detailed evidence-based report, to present to the major stakeholders. It allows mechanisms for monitoring whether the event has been deemed successful overall, but also to pinpoint errors and its possible failings to achieve its objectives. Commitment to investing the time to systematically evaluate will enhance the professional image and reputation of the management company or agency concerned. This has now also become a client expectation. Back in 1998 the author Watt employed a useful **mnemonic device**, designed to help remember the salient features of evaluation, as detailed in Table 3.1.

Mnemonic device techniques used to improve the ability to remember something

Compulsory	Circulated
Concise	Customer focused
Concurrent	Colleague based
Constant	Collected
Customised	Catalogued
Consulted	Complete
Canvassed	Communicated
Copied	

TABLE 3.1 Watt's 15 Cs of evaluation

In most cases, event evaluation is tangible and can be easily measured and interpreted. The amount of interest that has been generated can be easily measured by the amount of tickets sold or accommodation booked. However, there are elements that are harder to measure, such as the '**feel good factor**' of the audience, community or host destination. Therefore, when putting together the initial evaluation plan, planners should specify which aspects of the event will be evaluated and what methods will be used.

Feel good factor a widespread feeling of well-being and financial security, especially viewed as a factor in increased consumer spending

WHEN IS THE RIGHT TIME TO EVALUATE EVENTS?

The event should be constantly monitored, commencing with the pre-event and delivery stages and ending with the final post-event evaluation. Circumstances invariably alter in the lead-up time and this can have a knock-on effect. For this reason, it is important to recognise and log these changes as soon as they occur. As large events normally involve a number of stakeholders, agreement should be sought from them on the evaluation methods from various stakeholder perceptions. The event manager should explain the benefits of adopting an ongoing monitoring system throughout the planning stages, in order to be able to amend any operational oversights and rectify them before they become serious issues. It is also important to determine, in advance, who will be responsible for various aspects of the evaluation process and how the results will be collated and presented in the post-event evaluation phase.

In the planning stages, areas such as staff and supplier performance and the resource available can also be assessed. Any adjustments can be made before the level of resource becomes detrimental to the event and its overall profitability. For any public event, it should also be possible to monitor whether it is attracting appropriate and sufficient interest. If tickets are not selling as quickly as anticipated, this will provide an opportunity to introduce more marketing initiatives, or, in the worst-case scenario, to start discounting.

The following scenario provides an indication of the sort of issues that a project manager may be faced with, in the lead-up time:

REAL INSIGHT 3.1

A SAMPLE PRE-EVENT SCENARIO

The client from a leading household cleaning brand is organising a sales conference to re-launch a new product. In the lead-up to the conference, the company design team decide they want to change the branding slightly. Set panels and some literature have already gone into production. The agency tasked with organising this event then discover that the client has also swapped some of the t-shirt colours for the delegate groups without consultation. The agency has planned the logistics for the breakout session groupings and hotel allocations, based on the previously set colour coding.

Following a site recce four weeks before the event is due to take place, it comes to light that the venue roof has been incorrectly surmised and will not support the weight of the light rigging for the staging of the gala dinner. The client wants the dinner to stay in the same room. The producer wants to move rooms so they can keep to the same layout and design.

There has been an unforeseen error in the delegate booking system and there are now potentially an additional 15 tables (165 pax) to accommodate. The agency team member who designed the system is extremely defensive and upset.

Consider the effects on the following:

- Project plan and timings
- The delegate experience
- The budget
- Client relationship and expectations
- Team morale.

HOW TO EVALUATE EVENTS?

There may only be a short time to conduct questions by customer satisfaction or online evaluation at some events, so it may be necessary to surmise the overall satisfaction, posing key questions to attendees, such as:

- What did you like about the event?
- What did you dislike?
- Any suggestions for improvement?

- What else could have been offered?
- Overall level of satisfaction?

As any experienced organiser will know, in the delivery stage, personal taste, mood and preferences have a large part to play in the individual's evaluation. For this reason, it is generally advisable to provide respondents with an evaluation checklist based on objective performance and tangible deliverables, such as Were there sufficient litter bins on-site? Did speakers deliver key messages? Or: How easy was it to find the venue? rather than intangible and subjective opinions, such as: Was the food good or bad?

HOW TO MEASURE SUCCESS AND ROI AND ROO

A thorough analysis of Return on Investment (ROI) and Return on Objectives (ROO) should be carried out in the post-event phase. Generally, the most important factors to evaluate are whether the event made enough money, achieved its aims and objectives and whether the attendees were satisfied and reacted in a positive way. Corporate organisations have become far more accountable in terms of budgeting since the last major global recession, and conferences have become far more results-driven and linked to specific business needs. It may be possible to analyse what worked and what did not work so well from the audience comments captured through feedback, then try to analyse any significant patterns that emerge from the evaluation.

Specific objectives and performance impacts are now often set well in advance and measured during all three key stages of the event. The first stage is when the meeting is initially conceived. The second is the 'Before meeting' stage, where the various business and performance needs should be assessed. In the third 'After meeting' stage, key objectives should be set. It is necessary to measure whether the programme met the business needs and the objectives set to deliver these outcomes successfully.

LINKING NEEDS WITH EVALUATION

This current shift to results-based programmes means that in today's business events, there is now a comprehensive measurement and evaluation system in place for each programme and impact, and that ROI evaluations are regularly being carried out by event organisations. The ROI process generally generates six types of data, listed in Table 3.2.

1	Reaction to a project or programme
2	Learning skills/knowledge
3	Application/Implementation progress
4	Business impact related to the project or programme
5	Return on Investment
6	Intangible benefits.

TABLE 3.2 Six types of event programme data for evaluation

EVALUATION OF OBJECTIVES

In the post-event phase, the data gathered during the pre-event and on-site phases should be revisited. There are various ways to measure the objectives set, as will be further explored in this chapter. The following key aspects should be considered when conducting a post-event evaluation:

- Audience/participant perception
- Partner or sponsorship deals
- Key messages to impart
- Income
- Media exposure
- Performance or deliverables
- Potential for repeat events
- Other tangible benefits.

Each of these elements should be separately reviewed, so that customer behaviour can be further analysed, under specific deliverable areas, such as: timing, customer response, appreciation, and so on. These factors can then be categorised and documented in the final evaluation report. Even the more intangible areas, such as the atmosphere, ambience and 'the buzz' that the event generated, can be evaluated in the same way. The audiences' general reaction and perception of the event are a significant element to monitor for in an ongoing effort to improve products, services or processes. There are other reasons to conduct an event evaluation and, depending on the nature of the event and purpose, Table 3.3 lists a few questions that might be asked.

Were any key messages aimed at the audience received well?
Was there an increase in company sales or profit as a result of the event?
How many new names and what contact information were acquired?
How much visibility did the event get?
Did the event attract positive or negative media coverage?
Has the event increased awareness of the brand or product, venue or the event location?
Is the event likely to attract more future sponsorship opportunities?
How did the team, suppliers, volunteers, entertainers, speakers perform at the event?
Could their overall performance be improved in any way?
How many participants/sponsors/volunteers said they would get involved next time?
How many stakeholders have asked for more information on the organisation?

(Continued)

TABLE 3.3 (Continued)

How much money was raised?
What was the largest and average gift size?
How well communicated were instructions and event timings, etc. pre-event?
How were the speakers and entertainers received?
How suitable was the venue for the event?
Were the accommodation and conference space comfortable and fit for purpose?
Was the venue easy to find and accessible for parking and transportation?
Was the audience able to hear and see all items of the programme?
How good was the in-house service? Was it too slow or too loud?
How good was the food and beverage delivery?
Did the event programme content inform, motivate or inspire?
Did the event provide overall value for money?

TABLE 3.3 Typical event evaluation questions

WHO BENEFITS FROM EVENT EVALUATION?

Continuous improvement an ongoing effort to improve products, services or processes

In the events world, the adage 'you are only as good as your last event' can be very apt. With this in mind, the organising team is set the challenge of delivering an event that will hopefully exceed expectations. At the very least, the evaluation process will help to monitor the service received and to improve the future offering, working toward **continuous improvement**. A well-rated event experience could mean future business from a repeat or returning customer; a new sponsorship opportunity; a potential future client; and even a possible free marketing opportunity.

Different groups benefit in different ways from the evaluation process. This is why it is so important to gauge the opinion of all key-event stakeholders and ensure that the feedback acquired is unbiased and beneficial to all concerned. Following the evaluation, questions should be raised from all parties involved, in order to assess the viability of holding future repeat events. The attendees are likely to rate elements such as the speakers, venue facilities, entertainers, food and beverage outlets, transportation, accessibility, parking facilities, staff and services provided, and the overall organisation.

DID YOU KNOW?

It takes 12 positive experiences to make up for one unresolved negative experience.

VARIOUS EVALUATION METHODS USED FOR DIFFERENT EVENT TYPES

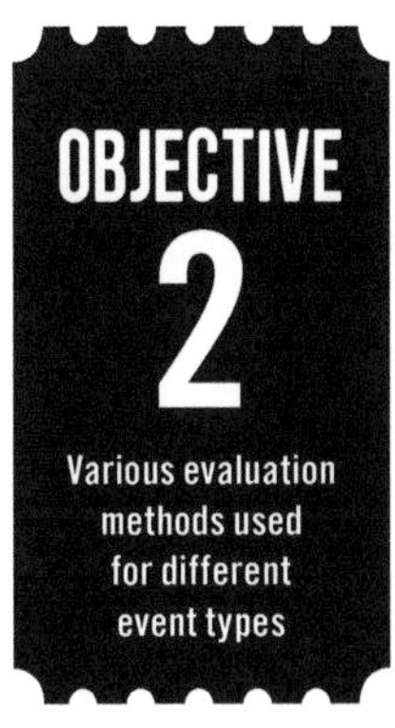
OBJECTIVE
2
Various evaluation methods used for different event types

EVALUATION METHODS FOR SMALL OR MINOR EVENTS

Evaluation methods vary significantly, depending on the event type, and can take the basis of a formal or more informal analysis. The level of evaluation needed for a mega event, such as the Olympic Games or a major football tournament, is far more complex than for a smaller one, such as a business conference, private party or community event. With minor events such as charitable or community events, the evaluation is far simpler to administer and has a different set of criteria. Sometimes the amount of profit generated is not always the most important factor. For example, a **not-for-profit** event might be designed to break even, or even incur a cost, because the other factors, such as raising awareness for a cause, or community involvement and goodwill, are more important.

Not-for-profit
non-profitable or the money generated is to be donated to a worthy cause

Similarly, within a corporate environment, the success might be measured by increased motivation of the company's delegates. It could be an opportunity to share the company's long-term vision; to introduce a new chief executive officer (CEO) to the organisation in a more informal setting; to educate or inform; to motivate staff; or to create networking opportunities. Other, more intangible benefits might be to improve staff loyalty and retention. This could also be considered a part of the overall investment, as the cost of losing trained members to competitors, or recruiting new staff to an organisation, can be a large overhead.

Post-event evaluation should enable managers to gain a clear awareness and understanding of attendee and visitor perceptions, concerns and attitudes. Feedback for this type of minor event could be obtained through means of a brief feedback form, using a tick-box format. Attendees can provide detail on elements they used, or had access to at the event, and rate these facilities or services accordingly. They can also comment on aspects that they enjoyed the most, as well as suggest improvements for future events, or acts or speakers for forthcoming ones, which might motivate them to return the next time. There may also be an opportunity for attendees to leave further detailed comments and feedback on areas, such as: content; food and beverage provision; and entertainment.

This type of evaluation is of paramount importance for planners, as the audience is generally the most important group to keep satisfied. Nowadays it is more typical for attendees to receive an invitation to comment online. This is often done through portals, such as Survey Monkey, or similar online sites.

EVALUATION METHODS FOR MEGA OR MAJOR EVENTS

The evaluation for a mega or major event tends to focus more on a PESTEL impact analysis, using categories such as Political, Economic, Social and Cultural to evaluate the overall success and explore the long-term legacy of the event. This area will be further discussed in the section on impacts in Chapter 4. The list below also gives an indication as to what aspects of a mega or major event might be evaluated on completion:

- Economic impact/financial results
- Social/cultural impacts
- Value of media coverage
- Problem-free operations
- Sponsorship satisfaction
- Volunteer satisfaction
- Generation of employment
- Environmental impacts
- Level of resident and visitor satisfaction.

For events of this size and significance, it is often necessary to involve the government of the host nation in the evaluation process. This could take place at both a local and a national level. As the list above indicates, the post-event evaluation of mega events is more than an evaluation of the social and economic factors. It is also necessary to include factors such as the environmental footprint, public perception and areas of social responsibility.

ECONOMIC IMPACT/FINANCIAL RESULTS

The real cost of a mega event to the host nation may not be fully realised for some years following. Even then it can be difficult to accurately monitor the actual final economic outcome. The full analysis may take as much as a decade to come to light, but a reliable evaluation mechanism needs to be adopted to facilitate this. In the post-event phase of a mega event, a realistic **cost-benefit analysis** should evaluate the cost of all resources, including the cost of infrastructure and training for the paid and unpaid workforce. This mechanism needs to accurately forecast the expenditure versus long-term tangible and intangible benefits to the host community and also the Return on Investment and positive economic impacts that have resulted from hosting the event. This area will be further discussed, under the section on PESTEL analysis, in Chapter 4.

Cost-benefit analysis
a systematic approach to estimate if an investment/decision is sound, and whether its benefits outweigh the costs

SOCIAL/CULTURAL IMPACTS

The social impact can be comparatively harder to measure. This is a difficult area to quantify and tends to be subjective, so it is always important to get an accurate representation from different members of the community. The evaluation of social factors following a mega event needs to involve focus groups and multiple surveys, in order to get widespread representation of opinion and viewpoints. However, in general terms, when an event improves the area and infrastructure, or promotes a sense of sharing and understanding between residents and visitors, social impact perception is mostly positive. However, perceptions can become negative, if the quality of life for the local community is disturbed and impinged upon in the lead-up, during or after an event, as can be demonstrated in the displacement of local residents in the lead-up to and in the aftermath of these larger events.

VALUE OF MEDIA COVERAGE

Media coverage for mega events can be a powerful marketing tool. If used well, it can promote the destination for future tourism and events unlike any other means and is guaranteed to put the host country or city on the world stage. Mega events depend on media and broadcast coverage and are viewed on television by a significantly larger global audience than those attending. The owner or organisation must therefore be assured that proceedings will be available for broadcasting in various formats. The estimated figure for television broadcasting allegedly exceeds all other channels of revenue; however, other forms of media, such as social media, also need to be considered in the evaluation phase. Social media sites, such as Facebook, Instagram and Twitter, are increasingly being used to promote and 'create hype' about the event, and currently play a large part in the evaluation process and stakeholder perceptions.

Following the staging of a mega or major event, government and tourist associations generally attempt to reposition the destination, in order to enhance the overall perception and create an increase in tourism and new expenditure. The amount of media coverage received in the lead-up time and during the event itself, is essential to this process. Most of the time, media attention is welcomed. Major and mega events employ a deliberate strategy to gain regional, national and international press coverage at a free or low cost for the organisers and associated governing bodies.

It is also important that the ruling government receives positive attributes from the event held, as for a mega event such as the Olympic Games, the success or failure of it tends to indicate whether they will be voted in again at the next general election, so it is imperative that the media are on their side and working with them, rather than against them. As mega events attract a global audience, it can also be the political message or protest that is transmitted, through the media. The evaluation of the value of media coverage tends to be more about how the country has fared on balance, in the eyes of the global media, which in some cases could be more about **damage limitation**.

Damage limitation action taken to limit the damaging effects of an accident or error

PROBLEM-FREE OPERATIONS

Events of this magnitude are never free from operational and logistical challenges. In the evaluation phase, detailed criteria to assess the success or failure of the event delivery should be implemented, to help identify when and where problems occurred. An evaluation of what contingency plans were put in place also needs to be carried out. Any external factors such as protests, security provision or terrorist threats that may have occurred and how they were dealt with should also be included in the operational evaluation, as well as the functionality of the improved stadia and new infrastructure, transportation links and so on. to meet the needs of the event. Staffing and other resources, such as venue provision use of facilities and accessibility of the location, should also be evaluated. After an event of this magnitude, it may take some time to be able to accurately measure how well the host destination managed from a logistical perspective. To determine this, consultation with all relevant stakeholders would be required in the post-evaluation stage.

SPONSORSHIP SATISFACTION

Sponsorship of major events has become an important communication tool to promote brand awareness and loyalty. In some cases, the sponsorship of mega sports events, such as the FIFA World Cup and the Olympic Games, can be more effective than any other form of advertising, due to the vast global television audience that they are being broadcast to. In the post-event phase, sponsor and partner satisfaction are also areas to evaluate. As economic income or profit is one of the most important factors, it is essential to ascertain whether the sponsors would be prepared to donate funds or benefits in kind, should the event run again. Even with smaller events that do not receive any public funding, sponsorship is a vital tool to raise funds and can determine financial viability.

While many well-established brands may wish to be associated with major global events, the synergy and sharing of core values and objectives is a vital consideration when aligning the owner with sponsors or partners. Recent studies have concluded that companies sponsor events in order to 'increase or develop product or corporate awareness, to drive sales or to develop market position' (Quinn 2013: 149). This is consequently an area that key sponsors and affiliated partners would want to evaluate in some depth during the post-evaluation phase of a mega event. For event sponsors, Return on Objectives (ROO) might be as significant as Return on Investment (ROI). Suggestions and recommendations for the official sponsors and commercial partners need to be outlined in the bid documentation. In addition, a list of expected activities should be drawn up in the sponsorship proposal, in exchange for possible benefits, as further outlined in Chapter 7.

VOLUNTEER SATISFACTION

Mega events, such as the Olympic Games, depend on the volunteers to contribute and become an integral part of their overall success. This should be followed up with a debrief and to see whether volunteers felt they were equipped with the basic operational skills required to work on it and whether areas such as budgeting processes, risk management, emergency procedures and health and safety awareness, or more generic training, including items such as multicultural awareness, respect, organisational culture, management practices, best practice, team work and a sense of community engagement were adequately included in the induction training.

The term 'pulsating events' describes events that expand and contract, i.e. at times are busier than at other times; for example, festivals or major sporting events generally operate with a small core of personnel for much of the year, expand substantially in the lead-up time, often recruiting volunteers, and then afterwards revert back to the original number of personnel. Event volunteering will be further discussed in Chapter 10 of this book.

GENERATION OF EMPLOYMENT

Employment following mega events can be measured in terms of new job creation, rates and wages, and is closely linked to economic impacts. This is particularly true when the host destination has experienced high unemployment and other economic challenges prior to staging the event. Mega and major events have the ability to create multiple jobs and volunteering opportunities. The general assumption is, therefore, that with an increase in employment, the amount of disposable income available improves and this in turn results in a better general standard of living, and new residual spending, as discussed in Chapter 7. In any host destination, the number of jobs created from mega events is immense, and may vary from building the infrastructure to working on the event itself. However, it could also be argued that many of these jobs are only temporary or casual labour, and do not necessarily lead to permanent employment.

ENVIRONMENTAL IMPACTS

Since the mid-1990s, the requirement to incorporate more environmentally sustainable practices in the delivery of mega events has been far more prevalent. There are many reports of consistent and neglectful waste associated with many major events and the apparent indifference on the part of organisers to address the issues. With ecological concerns receiving more attention today and political activist groups, such as Extinction Rebellion, creating renewed exposure of this issue, host cities now have to consider mechanisms for a wider spread of stakeholder benefits. City planners are under renewed pressure to adopt an 'eventful city' approach as a policy where sustainability is at the core.

It is not possible to evaluate environmental impacts without setting measurable objectives in advance. These are normally clearly set out in the Olympic nation's sustainable promise documentation. This is usually a key part of the host nation's legacy plan, as was seen at London 2012, with its reclaim, reuse and recycle policy. Sustainability will be discussed in detail in Chapter 9, but, in terms of the evaluation of mega events, it tends to be the sustainability, economic and social impacts that are measured; and, in addition to evaluating the impact on biodiversity or ecosystems, it also encompasses analysis on the areas of human rights, inclusivity, anti-corruption, stewardship, ethics and transparency.

LEVEL OF RESIDENT AND VISITOR SATISFACTION

This feedback may need to be gathered over a long time period, through online surveys or forums or face-to-face consultation, which is often conducted through community groups, academics, anti-globalisation protesters, environmentalists and the media. These groups are now starting to hold governments and organisers to account, especially regarding public expenditure.

There is invariably unrest and protest from activist and politically affiliated groups, particularly as the eyes of the world tend to focus on the host destination in the run-up to such large-scale events. Part of the overall analysis includes how these groups were communicated with and how their views and opinions were communicated and acted on throughout the event cycle, and how well the traditions and cultural values of the local, and sometimes marginalised, communities were represented overall. At the very least, group consultation might help organisers gain a better understanding of the host community, as well as resident and visitor perceptions, versus the benefits and costs of staging a large-scale mega event in the region.

EVALUATION METHODS AND TOOLS

There are a number of ways to evaluate an event after it has taken place, including issuing the delegates who attended it with different types of evaluation forms. Head online to study.sagepub.com/quick for more information on this.

NEW TECHNOLOGY BEING USED IN POST-EVENT EVALUATION

On-site voting tools
web-based tools designed for live polling

Ballot methods
using a paper system, voters choose by marking the favoured option or response

Online portals allow for engagement with customers and provide a platform to build a network that increases customer loyalty, drives audiences and provides a useful platform for evaluation. The internet and social media can be used to collect feedback in the post-evaluation phase, in order to gauge overall opinion about the event. Additionally, **on-site voting tools** can be used at award ceremonies, providing a far quicker and more reliable mechanism than traditional **ballot methods**.

SOURCE: Image courtesy of Ibrahim.ID via Wikicommons. Shared under the Creative Commons BY-SA 4.0 license.

Delegate feedback is today often invited from past and future attendees, using bespoke sites to encourage them to leave feedback and post comments. It's also being used increasingly to create 'buzz' and post feedback and photos on festivals and community events.

ANALYSIS OF FEEDBACK FROM THE DATA COLLECTED

Only the significant emerging patterns from the data collected should be measured at this point. It is also necessary to identify how this information will be communicated and used to support the coordination of any future processes and procedures. Event organisers may conduct a 'gap analysis', which involves the comparison of actual performance with the potential or desired performance. This analysis is needed in order to identify effective actions for how to best relay the data and information gathered.

The goal of the agency or event organiser will be to continually improve their offering. The data received should assist them in making an ongoing effort to improve products, services or processes for the future. A customer-driven analysis of past performance should be used to constantly evaluate and improve the efficiency and effectiveness of their delivery. Figure 3.1 illustrates some of the shared values that might be evaluated by the stakeholders in the post-evaluation phase.

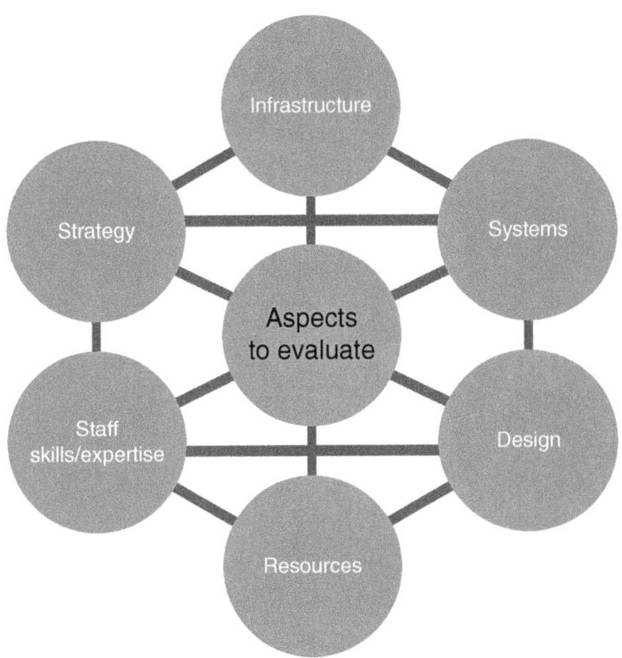

FIGURE 3.1 Aspects to evaluate

THE EVALUATION REPORT

The generation of the evaluation report is usually the final stage in the evaluation process and will present the findings of the data and feedback gathered in the external post-event appraisal. The report format will vary depending on the complexity and detail required.

The report should be written using a clear contents page, headings, bullet points and appendices where appropriate, to help signpost the document and lend structure. As this document provides a major tool for the overall analysis, it should be well presented and professional. If the expertise to provide such a report does not currently exist in-house, it may be necessary to outsource it to a professional service provider. The report should include details on the profile of the event, financial statistics, available resources, attendance numbers and key achievements in line with the event's Return on Investment (ROI) and Return on Objectives (ROO).

The findings and recommendations of the report should be derived from the facts and information presented in the report, rather than based on assumptions and subjective viewpoints. If facts or information are unknown at the time of presenting the evaluation report, or any facts or statistics are missing, it is advisable to state that this outstanding information will be confirmed and relayed in due course.

- Accuracy
- Consistency
- Efficiency
- Effectiveness
- Frequency
- Improvement
- Increases/decreases
- Popularity
- Usage
- ROI
- ROO
- Profitability
- Recall/Retention

TABLE 3.4 Areas to consider in an evaluation report

OBJECTIVE
3
Supplier debriefs and securing future business with the client

SUPPLIER DEBRIEFS AND SECURING FUTURE BUSINESS WITH THE CLIENT

STAFF AND SUPPLIER DEBRIEFING

Once the data collection process is complete and before meeting with the client, it is advisable to set up a debrief meeting with the staff involved in the event. This is often known as an internal or in-house team meeting. A meeting with suppliers and sponsors and the client budget holder, which is known as an external feedback meeting, should also take place after this. Full discussion and a detailed debrief of the proceedings will be required, in order to objectively highlight the success or failure of the event. The subsequent results and overall conclusions gained from this initial meeting, together with the evaluation report, will be used to form the basis of the client debrief.

Facilitator
a person or thing that makes an action or process easy or easier

A representative from each functional area should attend the feedback session to identify any problems that occurred throughout all the event stages. There should be a coordinator or a **facilitator** present, to steer the meeting and summarise the overall proceedings. These meetings should focus on possible areas for improvement and ask questions regarding the event delivery, as suggested in Table 3.5.

- Which things went well and which went badly, and why?
- How could operations be improved?
- Were there any significant risk factors that were not anticipated?
- Was there a pattern to any incidents reported?
- Are there any outstanding legal issues?

- Are there any ongoing implications for staff recruitment and training?
- How was the overall organisation and management?
- What can be learnt for the future?

TABLE 3.5 Questions for the staff and supplier debrief

PROVIDING FEEDBACK TO SUPPLIERS AND VENDORS

Feeding back both the positive and negative feedback to suppliers, partners and performers can be extremely useful; the positive comments can be used as a way of recognising and praising the performance or services provided, and the negative comments can be used to improve these aspects and determine future supplier working relationships. It is therefore somewhat remarkable that this is part of the process that is often overlooked by organisers.

When analysing the data received from the stakeholder group feedback sessions, any patterns that may be evident from recorded comments or customer satisfaction survey forms should be noted. In some cases, event planners may be given permission from the client or budget holder to interview delegates or set up an online feedback forum through social media platforms. It is worth remembering, however, that events are often a subjective experience. Even for delegates attending the same event, it is not always possible to please all of the attendees, all of the time. There may be no real cause for concern if one or two of the attendees criticise the keynote speaker or report feeling unwell after dinner. However, if a significant number of delegates report sickness after eating at the event, or were not impressed with the speaker, then this would require further investigation and action.

Feeding back to suppliers the comments and ratings received from clients and delegates allows them a chance to improve the service they offer, as well as to identify any key areas of concern for immediate attention. Additionally, it might be an opportunity for the event owner to negotiate a discount, rebate or refund in the **financial reconciliation**, either with one of the suppliers held at fault, or with the agency responsible for contracting on their behalf.

As the client or budget holder will trust the agency to work with tried-and-tested suppliers, they may be held responsible by association, should any supplier fail to deliver on any contracted product or service. For example, if an event agency arranges a taxi pick-up for delegates, on behalf of their client, they could be held accountable by that client should the taxi fail to collect delegates from the venue at the appropriate time. For that reason, it is extremely important to regularly review the suppliers worked with and their **terms of service**, before recommending or working with them.

Financial reconciliation an accounting process that matches the money leaving an account with the amount spent

Terms of service rules by which one must agree to abide in order to use a service

GIVING FEEDBACK TO PAID STAFF AND VOLUNTEERS

Paid and unpaid workers or volunteers will be able to provide a first-hand insight into any eventualities or incidents that may have occurred on-site. For that reason, all staff and volunteers should be invited to participate in the review and feedback sessions, and their viewpoints, observations and comments included in the evaluation report. Constructive feedback should also be offered to all staff about their performance at the event and any recommendations for service improvement for future training discussed.

CLIENT DEBRIEFS

The optimum time for a post-event debrief with the owner, client or budget holder is after the evaluation phase has been completed and when the final reconciliation documents and the evaluation report have been prepared. This is also an opportune time to start discussing the next event. If there has been any negative feedback, this is also the opportunity to have an open and honest discussion with the budget holder, as to the possible causes. Negative feedback from attendees does not always signify the end of the working relationship with the client, as long as the agency and client are open to discuss areas of weakness and improve the overall offering, working towards continuous improvement of the service offered.

If the client raises any concerns about the event, or patterns of poor service in one particular area, there might still be time to negotiate discounts with suppliers before submitting the final reconciliation document. It may be that the event organiser or agency needs to offer to reduce the original management fee quoted, as a gesture of goodwill. However, if the feedback is overwhelmingly negative, it could permanently damage the organisation's reputation with the client.

In an increasingly competitive environment, failure to deliver may not just affect the relationship with this particular client. As previously discussed in this chapter, the increase of feedback sites and public forums on social media mean that today any negative feedback is extremely visible in the public domain, so one failure can have disastrous long-term implications for the reputation of any event company. The case study on the cancelled London Oktoberfest featured below, demonstrates how damaging negative publicity can be.

REAL INSIGHT 3.2

LONDON OKTOBERFEST, LONDON TOBACCO DOCK, SEPTEMBER 2015

In September 2015 an event named Oktoberfest London, which was due to be held at London's Tobacco Dock, Wapping was cancelled at short notice after organisers were unable to cope with the unexpectedly large crowds that turned up for the event's opening night.

The event, which was due to run from 28 September until 1 October, was supposed to be London's version of Munich's traditional beer festival. The organisers had received nearly £900,000 in advance ticket sales before it was cancelled. Visitors were promised six different beer tents to rove around in, authentic Oompah bands and food to be provided by the London-based food chain Herman Ze German.

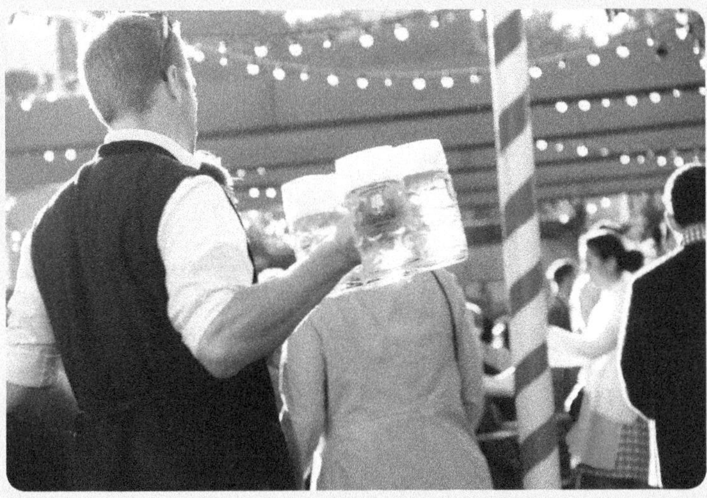

SOURCE: https://www.pikrepo.com/fwhtg/man-holding-beer-mugs-filled-with-beers

There was fury as the four-day Oktoberfest festival was cancelled after just one night, when thousands of customers who had paid up to £1,000 for a table turned up to the event. Organisers of the all-day German-themed drinking festival were completely taken by surprise at the large number of guests that had arrived on the opening night and said they were 'unable to cope', but unfortunately were only able to make the announcement regarding the cancellation about 20 minutes before the first session was due to begin at noon that day.

The venue said there had been 'operational issues' and issued a statement on their Twitter feed, confirming all three remaining days were to be called off.

Later, the venue said the event shut because of low staffing numbers, inexperienced bar staff and health and safety guidelines not being met.

This announcement was made following chaos at the festival's opening night as long queues formed to get in. Revellers blasted the festival, saying it was 'horrific' and badly organised, but the main criticism from the potential audience was the poor and tardy communication of the organisers in alerting the audience to the cancellation of the event. This meant that many guests had already travelled to London from around the country. The announcement sparked anger online, with Twitter users posting many derogatory comments about the event organisation.

(Continued)

Hundreds of people were forced to queue for hours despite having bought tickets for the event, which had cost £10, or £60 for a premium pass, with a VIP table costing £1,000.

The cancelled event was backed by two of the traditional Munich beer suppliers, but the company behind it, OktoberFest UK Ltd, went into administration shortly after, taking with it any hope of a refund for ticketholders, some of whom had spent as much as £1,000 on VIP packages. The company concerned has not attempted to organise any similar events subsequently.

There was some good news, however, as rival organiser London OktoberFest paid out unexpected compensation to these beer fans as a goodwill gesture. This long-standing company, which has no affiliation whatsoever with the ill-fated company of a similar name, has run successful OktoberFest events annually in London since 2011, as well as in other cities, and pledged to grant free general admission to anyone who bought tickets to the previous year's cancelled event, citing 'the spirit of all things Oktoberfest'.

DEALING WITH GRIEVANCES/COMPLAINTS

In unforeseen circumstances such as those as detailed in the above case study, sometimes it is not possible to resolve the issue and settle the dispute merely by refunding or renegotiating costs. It may be necessary to offer the customer or client compensation or future discounts, or to reimburse the budget holder in full. In some cases, when the reputation of the brand has caused irreparable damage to the client, or if there is an ongoing dispute with attendees, it may become necessary for the event organisers to enter into a more formal grievances and complaints process.

Breach of contract a legal cause of action after a binding agreement or bargained-for exchange is not honoured by one or more of the parties

Terms and Conditions the rules and conditions of the contract entered into with the third party

In the worst-case scenario, where there is a serious **breach of contract**, overall dissatisfaction with the delivery of the event may result in expensive court proceedings.

Details of the grievance and complaints procedures should be clearly stated in the **Terms and Conditions** and should be studied intently before entering into any binding financial agreements or signing supplier contracts. In the worst-case scenario, it may be possible to take the issues to a court of law in order to resolve them, which can be a costly, lengthy and time-consuming process.

PLANNING THE NEXT EVENT

On a more positive note, if the event has gone well and matched or exceeded the ROO and ROI, this would be an excellent time to talk about future meetings and to make sure there is an opportunity to tender for the next event. It would be even more preferable to become the existing incumbent, sole or preferred partner of the client, without the ongoing need to tender for each new piece of business with that client.

Presenting the evaluation report and final reconciliation documents will provide the perfect opportunity to ask the client what their plans are for future events, or if the event just delivered will be repeated in future. This debrief meeting is also an excellent opportunity to solicit an **endorsement**. This endorsement or positive testimonial could be added to a company website or any marketing collateral, and will help the agency secure future business with other clients and potential budget holders.

Endorsement giving someone or something written approval

THE MOTIVATION AND PSYCHOLOGICAL FACTORS OF EVENTS

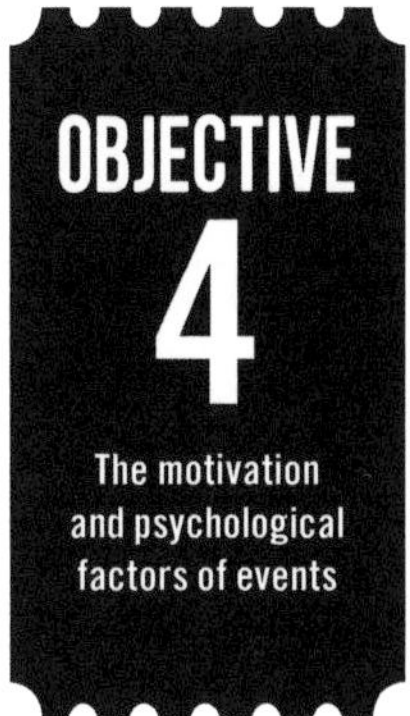
OBJECTIVE
4
The motivation and psychological factors of events

WHY DO PEOPLE ATTEND EVENTS?

An important consideration in evaluation is the link to motivation and the psychological factors of attending events. Psychological perspectives impact the spectators and attendees, the performers and participants who take part. Each group has a different perspective and view that drives them to become involved in the first place. From a psychological perspective, event experiences are often influenced by the level of involvement and the opportunity to participate in the programme. 'While it might be assumed that people are attending an event for the same reason, research shows that attendees often have different motivations and come from a range of backgrounds' (Funk et al. 2004, cited in Bladen et al. 2012: 169).

George Miller, an American psychologist who was one of the founders of the cognitive psychology field, defines motivation as: 'all those pushes and prods – biological, social and psychological – that defeat our laziness and move us, either eagerly or reluctantly to action' (Miller, 1967 in Gross, 1987). This definition of motivation describes the psychological force that drives the audience to action and impacts decision-making, attitude, opinion and influence.

The term 'push and pull factors' is often used in connection with event motivation. Push factors are the internal psychological factors, such as the attendee's personal need for satisfaction and happiness obtained through attending events. Pull factors are the external factors, such as the excitement and anticipation that pull the person towards it. Crompton and Mackay (1997) identify six push factors as: escapism, exploration, relaxation, prestige, regression and socialisation, and two pull factors as: novelty and education. The balance between these push and pull factors may depend on the specific personal circumstances of each person attending.

CONTENT MOTIVATION THEORY

There are several motivation theories that dominate most studies on leisure, sports and tourism, and which can be applied to event motivation. The theories listed in Table 3.6 can all be applied, either from an organiser's perspective, in the pursuit of excellence or to gauge customer satisfaction.

Theorist	Motivation theory	Theory characteristics
Murray (1938)	Needs theory of personality	*Assumes that behaviour is driven by a desire to satisfy the most current needs, which could be:* ***Primary** – instinctive or physiological needs, or* ***Secondary** – learned psychological needs.*
Maslow (1943)	Hierarchy of needs	*Initially developed to link basic human needs and desires.* *According to this theory, the higher needs of **esteem** and **self-actualisation** are only activated when the lower needs, such as **physiological, security** and **social**, have been met.* *Once each level of needs is satisfied, it triggers the motivation for the next level.*
Berlyne (1960)	Concept of optimal level of stimulation	*Uses information from the environment and memory to make choices.* *Comparing and contrasting various stimuli, in order to note differences and similarities.* *Known as **collation** and is central to intrinsic motivation and needed for an optimal level of stimulation.*
Herzberg (1968)	Motivator hygiene theory	*Claims there are two sets of needs that affect individual motivation:* ***Motivators** – are long-term needs, towards a sense of achievement* ***Hygiene** – the content does not necessarily provide satisfaction or motivation.*
Alderfer (1969)	Three-factor theory or Existence, Relatedness and Growth (ERG)	*Compresses Maslow's five need categories into three:* ***Existence** – physiological and material safety needs* ***Relatedness** – social, esteem and interpersonal safety needs* ***Growth** – internal self-esteem and self-actualisation needs.*
Iso-Ahola (1980)	Tourism motivation theory	*Asserts that the internal factors that arouse, direct and integrate a person's need for recreation and tourism are the needs for personal escape and to seek new experiences.*
McClelland (1961)	Achievement motivation theory	*Assumes the three basic principles of motivation are:* *A need for achievement* *A need for affiliation* *A need for power, control or responsibility.*
Aho (2001)	Seven-stage process model	*A seven-stage process model, which an event needs to deliver on, in order to be well perceived as a positive experience by the attendees:* *Orientation* *Attachment* *Visiting* *Evaluation* *Storing* *Reflection* *Enrichment.*

TABLE 3.6 Content motivation theory

AUDIENCE MOTIVATION TO ATTEND VARIOUS EVENT TYPES

Audience motivation to attend varies considerably depending on the event type. Celebration and escape for attendees, resulting in 'family togetherness and socialisation', are often cited as the main motivations for attending mega events. The promise of excitement, novelty, new opportunities and a 'once in a lifetime' experience entices millions of visitors to attend each time a mega sporting event is staged. Special and hallmark events also have the ability to entice and motivate audiences to attend, with their uniqueness and chance to experience an event in a specific and unique setting.

Many people attend a sporting event to escape their daily routine or to experience a uniform identity. Spectators may decide to attend a sporting event because they have a need to belong to a group, or support a team, to give them a sense of belonging and common unity. As humans we have a social need to mix and integrate with others, so other reasons to attend might be to develop relationships, social interaction, for entertainment purposes or a sense of achievement.

For participants, such as athletes, involvement may be more about stress and stimulation-seeking. In a study in 1995, Wann found that male and female sporting fans were motivated by different aspects: male fans tended to engage in sporting events to release stress. Males also valued the entertainment, competitive elements and fan loyalty to a specific team or nation highest, whereas females tended to be motivated by the potential of socialisation and family togetherness that attending sporting events affords. The various motives of sports spectators are demonstrated in Table 3.7.

Authors	Framework	Motives
Wann (1995) Milne and McDonald (1999)	Sports Fan Motivation Scale (SFMS) Motivation of Sport Consumers (MSC)	Eustress, self-esteem, escape, entertainment, economic (gambling), aesthetic, group affiliation, family risk-taking, stress reduction, aggression, affiliation, social facilitation, self-esteem, competition, achievement, skill mastery, aesthetics, value development and self-actualisation.
Trail and James (2001)	Motivation Scale for Sport Consumption (MSCC)	Achievement, acquisition of knowledge, aesthetics, drama, escape, family, physical attraction, physical skills of players, social interaction.
Funk et al. (2004)	Sport Interest Inventory (SII)	Family bonding, friends bonding, drama, entertainment value, escape, excitement, player interest, role model, socialisation, team interest, vicarious achievement.
James and Ross (2004) Mehus (2005)	Entertainment Sport Motivation Scale	Entertainment, skill, drama, team effort, achievement, social interaction, family, team affiliation, empathy, social, excitement.
Koo and Hardin (2008)	Spectators' Motives and Behavioural Intentions	Vicarious achievement, team performance, escape, family, eustress, aesthetics, entertainment value, social opportunities.

TABLE 3.7 Motives of sports spectators

Motivational factors differ again for music festivals. Page and Connell (2011) state that attending festivals contributes to building an identity and a sense of belonging and community for the festival attendee that may be difficult to replicate anywhere else. Malouf (2012) suggests that the main reasons for attending music festivals are socialisation and a chance to meet new people. As audiences can now download and stream most music festivals online, at a fraction of the cost of purchasing a ticket, this need for socialisation and interaction at a music event cannot be discounted.

The motivation to attend corporate or business-related events may not be quite so strong for the audience. In some cases, attendees only attend because they have to as part of their work remit. However, even when this applies, the quality, content, deliverables, and the excitement that is built up in the planning and marketing stage of this type of event, can greatly impact the audience's motivation to attend.

The motives to attend corporate events vary from those of leisure events, in that networking and learning may be the major motives for attending. Beard et al. (1983) discuss intellectual motivation and other cognitive activities, such as learning, exploring, discovering, creating or imagining. They also examine the individual's need for competency and learning to achieve and master a skill through educative or work-related meetings.

PHYSICAL FACTORS OF EVENT MOTIVATION

The psychological motives of attendees need to be analysed as part of the whole event-evaluation process, to ensure that there are enough factors to drive audiences to attend and that satisfaction is delivered through the design and execution of the programme.

When analysing the psychology of a specific event, the feelings and emotions of attendees need to be recalled. For this reason, it is important in the design phase to consider how the environmental setting and design will impact on attendees' behaviour and contribute to the overall event experience. The organiser should therefore identify a reliable mechanism to instantaneously assess the audience's reactions to the setting, environment and design features in the post-event evaluation phase.

Specific physical considerations that are relevant to the psychological perspective include:

- Social interaction
- Capacity and crowding
- Personal space
- Signage
- Physical features
- Sound and lighting
- Colour, temperature and air flow. (Getz 2012)

The design of event settings and how this links to the overall audience experience will be discussed in more depth in Chapter 8. Table 3.8 depicts a model by Brown and Hutton (2013) which attempts to evaluate the audience behaviour during different phases of the event. The purpose of the model is to investigate the audience psyche in the pre-event, on-site and post-event stages, which can be used to gauge and evaluate their reactions at key points and the triggers to their overall satisfaction.

Pre-event	At the event	On event exit	Post-event
Audience motivation Bring with them	Three domains Experience at event	Audience satisfaction Immediate response	Audience satisfaction Remembered/embedded response
Demographic Age Gender Income Lives	Audience behaviour Will either be: Reinforced, or Modified		
Cultural Ethnicity Religion 'Baggage'			
Expectations Been before Marketing			
Survey Face to face Postcard with barcode Online • Blog • Webpage • Facebook	**Survey** Face to face On-site • Weather • Site layout • Still camera Peak experience GPS tracking Experience Hotspots Arousal	**Survey** Face to face Postcard Online	**Survey** Face to face Postcard with barcode Online • Blog • Webpage • Facebook

TABLE 3.8 Early audience behaviour research

SOURCE: Brown and Hutton 2013: 46

THE LINK FROM MARKETING TO MOTIVATION

Motivation has become an area of keen interest to analyse and explore in a market that is growing and becoming increasingly competitive. Understanding the needs of each of these groups can be beneficial to the event organiser and will help to evaluate the psychological needs of all stakeholders involved. Audience satisfaction is an integral part of the marketing process; it is paramount in analysing how to drive audiences to events and what marketing methods to adopt.

The link to customer satisfaction and motivation can be demonstrated by how high-quality service and product deliverables entice the customer back to the same event year on year. It costs far less to attract repeat rather than first-time attendees, which is a further reason to analyse the factors that motivate audiences to attend. Positive word-of-mouth testimonials, good promotion and customer and brand loyalty need to be evaluated, in order to understand the target audience's motivational triggers and therefore satisfy their needs. Figure 3.2 illustrates the elements that can be evaluated from the customer's perspective.

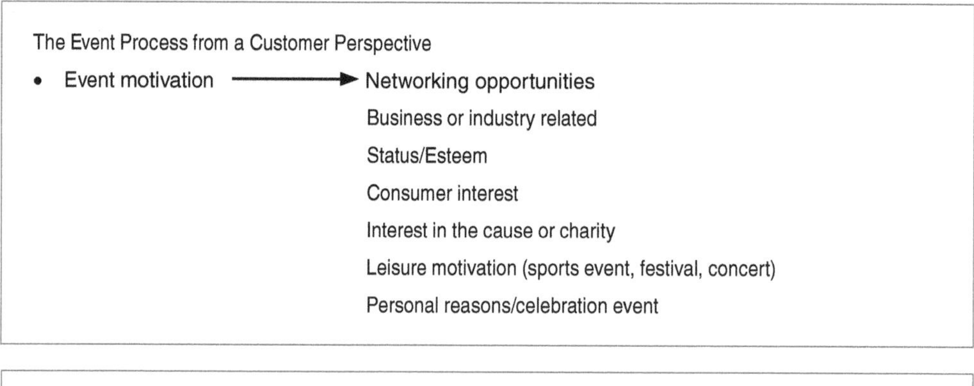

FIGURE 3.2 Customer perspectives for attending events

THE SIGNIFICANCE OF ETHICAL STEWARDSHIP IN EVENTS TODAY

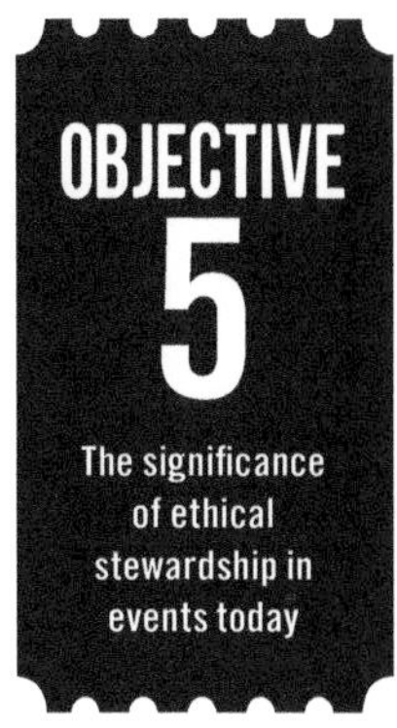
OBJECTIVE
5
The significance of ethical stewardship in events today

WHAT ARE EVENT ETHICS?

As the industry has become more professionalised and procurement driven, ethical considerations have taken on renewed significance and are now a prerequisite for all agencies and organisations operating in this field. In the early years of the events industry, examples of bad practice (overmarking bought-in costs, paying suppliers late, unethical business practices) were common occurrences.

However, in today's litigious environment, reputation and accountability are crucial. It has therefore become more important than ever to form associations and conduct business within an open and transparent environment. Indeed, event-management companies and affiliated suppliers that have been thoroughly vetted and are able to demonstrate clear ethical standards are likely to command respect, boost their reputation and gain a competitive advantage that will ultimately increase their client base.

Organisations now have a duty of care to form alliances and partnerships with preferred or sole suppliers that share their values and ethos, and this involves the following areas where guidelines may be required:

- Personal ethics
- Codes of conduct
- Ethical stewardship in the event environment
- Evaluation of ethical practices.

PERSONAL ETHICS

Good business practice requires high ethical standards on both a personal and professional level. Personal ethics determine individual beliefs on morality and what is right and wrong, that can affect all areas of life, including family, finances and relationships. Some of this can be influenced by cultural customs and religious convictions but it is also about the personal choices that individuals make. While personal ethics are distinguishable from business ethics, it is clear that the two areas overlap.

When recruiting for event personnel, recruiters or employers would look for evidence of personal ethical standards in an applicant's personal or mission statement, their CV and/or their character references and testimonials. Within the industry, personal connections and networking are extremely influential and event stakeholders are likely to engage in business with the same industry contacts and suppliers on a continual basis; so, reputation and positive perception are paramount. Moreover, clients tend to buy services from people they like and trust and who share the same values. For this reason, the area of personal ethics and how individuals present and position themselves can determine to some extent whether the individual has a successful career in the industry.

The characteristics of an ethical person in business include:

- Trustworthiness
- Respect
- Responsibility
- Fairness
- Caring
- Citizenship.

CODES OF CONDUCT

In 1986 The Institute of Business Ethics was established to deal with the increased ethical implications of technological advancement within a globalised economy. Its purpose was to establish a hub for discussion, research and practical advice, in order to promote high standards of professional conduct for all industry sectors. This was set up to help potential investors, customers, suppliers and employees recognise high ethical standards. As with other sectors, the events industry needs to have the assurance that all stakeholders can trust the event organisation they are working with and have some guarantee that they will act with integrity throughout the event process.

- To promote and encourage the highest level of ethics within the profession of the special events industry, whilst maintaining the highest standards of professional conduct.
- To strive for excellence in all aspects of our profession by performing consistently at or above acceptable industry standards.
- To use only legal and ethical means in all industry negotiations and activities.

TABLE 3.9 Codes of ethics in events
SOURCE: The International Special Events Society (ISES)

Self-regulatory codes monitoring its own adherence to legal, ethical or safety codes, rather than have an outside, independent agency such as a governmental entity monitor and enforce those standards

There are many areas of ethical concerns within the events industry that are governed by a basic code of conduct. Some of these are **self-regulatory codes** that may be adopted for one or more of the following reasons:

- As an alternative to direct state regulation
- To avoid having to comply with more stringent government regulation
- To build public trust and consumer confidence
- To avoid legal liability
- To protect children and other consumers
- To exert moral pressure on those who otherwise behave in an 'unprofessional' or 'socially irresponsible' way
- As a mark of professional status and intent
- To raise the public image of their industry
- To develop a set of common standards for services and products within the industry
- To provide a less expensive and faster mode of resolving disputes out of court.

In addition, there may be other, hidden motivations for adopting a code of conduct, such as a conscious or unconscious attempt to exclude competitors from the market by raising barriers to entry. At the same time, a code of conduct is needed to ensure 'a level playing field', particularly during the event bidding process. A code of conduct is needed to ensure a fair bidding process, so that the client is prevented from issuing fake Request for Proposals (RFPs) just to test the water, to benchmark alternative agencies or copy the ideas presented in the tender, while resolutely continuing to place business with friends or former incumbents first, regardless of the proposal content.

ETHICAL STEWARDSHIP IN THE EVENT ENVIRONMENT

Corporate responsibility and business ethics within the workplace are areas of good practice that need to be defined by the company's internal policies and procedures. This is often an area that is dealt with by the human resources division of a company, which is discussed in depth in Chapter 10. Event companies have a duty of care to their staff and employees to provide ethical working practices. Some of these areas are covered by the Health and Safety at Work regulations (HASAW) (HSE 1974) or by other policies that will be further discussed in Chapter 2.

In any case, some basic ground rules and **a chain of command** need to be established between clients, suppliers and planners to establish **due diligence**. It is usually the budget holder who has the ultimate say on how the event is conducted. Within an event management or supplier team, there will also be key decision makers who will make overall decisions on what is permitted by team members at all stages of the process. For the organiser, there are several ethical issues that need to be considered when planning an event, which include some of the following examples:

Chain of command
a system in a military or civil organisation by which instructions are passed from one person to another

Due diligence
reasonable steps taken to avoid corruption or offence

- Confidentiality of information; handling of databases; personal data aspects
- Not overbooking and overpricing
- Disposing of discarded goods, such as boxes
- Handling personal information such as contact addresses
- Looking after celebrity guests; disclosure of celebrity/VIP details
- Environmental issues such as recycling, reusing goods
- Care of guests and staff from health and safety, induction and training, well-being, cultural considerations
- Ensuring finances are kept tight, up-to-date and within budget
- Legal compliances in terms of regulations, with suppliers and authorities
- Control of all areas and equipment in terms of risk assessment, contracts and insurance, to include contracts with all external suppliers.

EVALUATION OF ETHICAL PRACTICES

Even with renewed guidelines and policies, unethical factors may determine the success of the event in the final evaluation. This might affect the decision to use that planner again. Unethical practices that might be included are shown in Table 3.10.

Taking backhanders (gifts, money) for placing business a certain way	Ignoring health and safety and general regulations	Cancelling provisional space held with suppliers, such as conference venues and related services, that is no longer required
Marking up prices or overpricing. Charging for extras on-site without checking or monitoring consumption	Discrimination of guests	Not respecting people's copyright and intellectual property throughout the tender process and not stealing their ideas
Failing to prevent unnecessary waste of resources on-site and following sustainable practice	Unfair working conditions, e.g. hours, food and beverage, transportation, accommodation, sanitation	Not respecting people's time and not turning up for appointments speculatively
Not adhering to confidentiality of information (non-disclosure/data protection)	Overbooking, such as the venue flights or hotel rooms	Accepting supplier invitations for reasons other than genuine business or educational purposes
Not protecting sensitive information, such as governmental, celebrity information or their whereabouts	Approaching the client direct, rather than going through the agency or intermediary where the quote originated	Failure to monitor on-site consumption, and not alerting the client to any additional on-site costs

TABLE 3.10 Examples of unethical practices

Confidentiality of information may include withholding sensitive business information and rigorously checking that there are no conflicts of interest with other customers who may be using the venue or hotel at the same time. The venue should alert the companies concerned about any potential conflict of interest and ensure they never cut the agency or intermediary out of the equation by approaching the client directly. As most of the venue's volume of business comes from event agencies, this would be a very dangerous and short-sighted action but certainly not unheard of in the events industry. This area of ethical conduct of businesses and organisations is closely linked to corporate social responsibility, which will be discussed further in Chapter 9. It also links to the area of corruption and bribery in events, which has already been explored in this book.

LEGISLATIVE ACTS THAT GOVERN EVENT ETHICS

Some of the regulations and policies that have most impact on ethics in the event environment are governed by such legislative acts that affect liability and determine the activities, contracts and supply of goods, some of which are outlined below.

GO ONLINE

Sample legislative acts

You can access a full table of legislative acts that govern ethical events online in the Appendix as Table 2.2.

HOW HAVE THESE ACTS CHANGED THE WAY EVENTS BUSINESS IS CONDUCTED?

For many years, intermediaries have secured commission from hotels and bookings, which has been a major source of remuneration between venue agents and booking agents. The Bribery Act 2010 does not prohibit this practice and still allows the practice of granting rebates and kickbacks to agencies for volume booking. In the area of corporate hospitality, it is also still possible for destinations and venue suppliers to offer familiarisation trips to agencies, providing they are deemed educational in purpose and not just taken as a 'a jolly' or holiday. Familiarisation trips are commonplace in the events industry and the Ministry of Justice general guidance states that where these are designed to showcase the venue operator and to 'establish cordial relations', they are likely to be recognised as an established and important part of doing business.

It can still be acceptable to book rooms and venues for client entertainment and accept gifts from suppliers but only if not offered as an inducement to place business with them as a result of this action. The intention of the gift is more important than its timing; for example, if any gifts or hospitality are given in the time immediately before a contract is awarded, it may appear more likely that the intention was to influence a decision. If the intention is more than a business courtesy, to cement a working relationship and is given as a reward for placing business or to induce the agent to continue placing the booking with the agency, then it could be construed as a bribe. However, activities that might previously have been considered open to misinterpretation or outside the boundaries of proper commercial behaviour, must be considered very carefully in light of the new Act. Agents and venues who comply with the published guidelines will make a strong start in complying with The Bribery Act, which has become an area of growing ethical concern throughout the industry.

As can be seen in Table 2.2 in the online Appendix, The Disability Discrimination Act 2010 has impacted the industry by stipulating the way new staff are selected and recruited. This includes the physical features of the working environment and the way that the work is arranged and performed to make reasonable adjustments for disabled employees when necessary. Examples of these adjustments include:

- Allocating some work tasks to other colleagues where necessary
- Transferring the disabled employee to another post or place of work
- Adjusting work premises
- Allowing more flexible working hours, to allow additional free time for assessment, treatment or rehabilitation
- Providing training or retraining if the disabled employee is no longer able to carry out their role
- Providing modified equipment
- Making instructions and manuals more accessible and easier to read
- Providing a reader or an interpreter.

In practice today, event organisers need to ensure that physically impaired workers or delegates have dignified easy access to all buildings and that event venues adjust or remove any settings or features that make it impossible or unreasonably difficult for a person with a disability to access an event. This includes the access and approach to the venue; the circulation, signs and lighting within the venue; disabled toilets, adequate ramps for wheelchairs, hearing loops and large font for presentations; as well as arrangements for audiences with special needs for pre-seating and exiting of the venue where possible. This should also extend to adequate provision of staff training and evacuation procedures for any physically impaired attendees.

Disabled people are often still portrayed in the media in ways that tend to reinforce negative stereotypes. They are almost exclusively referred to in terms of their disability and frequently as objects of pity. This law also attempts to make disability-related harassment or bullying of disabled workers illegal, including behaviour such as making fun of a person's disability or disabilities in general and is an important ethical consideration for all industries aside from the events industry.

The Data Protection Act 2018 states that personal data can be any information that could be used to directly or indirectly identify a person; for example, contact details, photos or work addresses. For this reason, an ethical approach would be to only collect data for specific purposes; for example, registration. All details should be deleted as soon as they are no longer required, preferably as soon as the event has ended and has been reconciled. In order to process any customer information, it is now necessary to gain consent first and this information must be explicit and current. UK law now empowers individuals to withhold consent for certain uses of their data, so that customers now have the right to request access to information or delete it from companies' records if they so choose.

Any organisation who has access to a customer's personal data should have informed them of this fact before the change in the law was implemented. If they failed to do so, they may be liable for fines up to €20 million or 4% of the organisation's total worldwide annual turnover, whichever is higher. However, according to a recent Mailjet survey, 48% of UK start-ups verified they were GDPR compliant, compared to 38% in Spain, 33% in France and 31% in Germany (EU GDPR Information Portal). Every organisation or sole trader who processes personal information must also pay a data protection fee to the Information Commissioner's Office (ICO) unless they are exempt. The fee varies dependent on the size and turnover of the business. Within the events industry, this has the greatest impact on direct marketing, where viral marketing campaigns are often used in promotions. It is now essential to respect an individual's right to privacy and be diligent with their data, in order to avoid litigation and also to promote ethical values.

The Working Time Directive has also brought about changes to the industry in practice. Historically, a career in events was known to involve long working hours and was not considered a traditional nine-to-five career choice. The nature of the job, with its long hours, early starts and late finishes meant that, in some cases, staff were required to work 'around the clock'. This could mean working an 18-hour day, without breaks and very little 'down time'. Event staff were not automatically entitled to overtime, free weekends or **time off in lieu**. This working pattern was deemed to be part of the job function, which went with the territory of being part of the coveted and so-called 'glamorous' events industry. This is an area that has become clearly linked to ethical awareness and corporate responsibility within the workplace. Today, although the hospitality industry still requires staff to work long shifts, it has also seen a significant improvement since the Working Time Regulations (WTR) first came into effect 20 years ago.

Time off in lieu
time that an employee who has worked extra hours may take off from work

This new act reflects a change in event ethics, where previously event and hospitality staff worked until they reached 'burnout' or collapsed with exhaustion. Nowadays, concern is raised about employees' welfare from a health and safety perspective, which also reflects recent governance policies regarding employee well-being. However, this is unfortunately not the case in all countries, where poor working wages and practices of human slavery and trafficking still exist, and new reports of the maltreatment of employees emerge on a frequent basis. Ethical stewardship of this kind has given rise to an increase in the ethical purchasing of products and services within events, hospitality and related disciplines. Purchasing products that are fair trade certified and adhere to fair trade standards is thought to contribute towards reducing global poverty, by encouraging environmentally friendly production methods and safeguarding humane working conditions. Therefore, ethical purchasing has to be a consideration of best practice within the industry and in deciding which suppliers and nations to work in partnership with.

Burnout
a state of emotional, physical and mental exhaustion

Fair trade certified
a registered certification label for products sourced from producers in developing countries

Copyright infringement
granting rights to the copyright holder, such as the right to reproduce, distribute, display or perform the protected work

The Communications Decency Act has resulted in incidents where content owners, including media giant Viacom, have sued YouTube, the renowned video-sharing site, for copyright infringement. It is also worth considering that any potential employers or educational institutions may have access to the applicant's social media profiles and can therefore make quick decisions on the applicant's suitability based on what they see.

EVENT ETHICS

An ethical professional code can enhance the reputation of those involved with events. Acts, such as The Bribery Act (2010), have changed the way suppliers and clients can exchange gifts.

Do you agree or disagree that it is unethical to accept lavish corporate hospitality, such as tickets for the final of the Rugby World Cup, from a potential or existing supplier?

WHY ARE ETHICS IMPORTANT IN RESEARCH?

Ethics in research developed after the unethical experimentation on humans during the Second World War, which resulted in the Declaration of Helsinki with its aim to protect research participants. Research ethics provide a framework for conducting research, whether it be a short questionnaire devised by an undergraduate student or a multi-million-pound industry project carried out by a group of professional researchers. Secondary research that is focused on journal articles and books would be unlikely to pose serious ethical concerns, except perhaps in relation to the way the researcher might select the articles and report on their findings. However, although conducting primary research does require the researcher to uncover true facts and opinions from a sample audience, it is important to remember that all respondents have a right to their privacy and to remain completely anonymous. This should not prevent the research taking place but rather facilitate good practice; respecting the interests of all parties, mitigating risks and delivering research outcomes that are rigorous, robust and reliable.

Research ethics work to preserve the safety and rights of research participants and to ensure that they are not at risk of any harm by participating in the research project. The researcher has a duty of care to safeguard the information and data collected in any study, and to protect the well-being and integrity of the research and respondents. For this reason, no research should be undertaken without research-ethics approval. Ethical considerations must also be carefully considered in cases where there is a potential risk to the researchers themselves, either through accessing security-sensitive material or reporting on other sensitive material, or travelling to areas where they might put themselves in danger.

EVENT ETHICS

Ethics questions to ask when conducting research:

- How will you contact participants to take part, e.g. by text, email, phone or social media?
- What will you tell them about the research being conducted?
- How will you protect yourself?
- How will you ensure that your participants will be at no risk of harm?
- How will you manage the data collected?
- What will happen to your research afterwards?

For any research involving human subjects, vulnerable individuals or groups, and using personal data, ethical approval should be sought. Meticulous research might be needed to mitigate these factors, especially if the research is being carried out in a sensitive or potentially dangerous location.

Typically, research that involves human subjects, vulnerable individuals or groups, personal data, any type of clinical or physical intervention or research which is conducted in a sensitive or potentially dangerous location, or might raise ethical issues, requires appropriate planning and meticulous research design, in order to mitigate those factors. Researchers, across all disciplines, should be mindful of ethical questions when planning, conducting and reporting on their work. The inclusion of human subjects in any capacity is subject to moral integrity and mutual respect and trust between participants and investigators. These should be in line with professional standards and therefore prescriptive guidelines and processes should be adhered to. Table 3.11 lists some of the areas of good practice that need to be considered.

Confidentiality of information/agreement	• Information regarding confidentiality of identity, names and data. • Encoding of transcripts, so that no written record of the participant's name appears alongside the data. • Data protection for computer material, recordings and photographic material may apply. • Ensuring the information gained is protected and anonymous where appropriate and treated with respect and integrity.
Non-disclosure/data protection	• Explaining to the participants verbally and in writing the purpose of the research, how the data will be used and what will happen to it afterwards. • Protection of information and how it will be used and stored (e.g. on a data storage information sheet) and for how long.
Honesty, integrity and transparency	• Explaining what happens if respondents decide not to take part, or, if they do take part, what may happen in terms of loss of respect, side-effects, dignity, etc. • Ensuring there is no risk to participants or the researcher through loss of reputation, health, security, emotional upset, or danger. • Ensuring that the rights of diverse, religious, ethnic and cultural groups are maintained. • Adhering to gender, race, age and sexual preference equality throughout.
Briefing/debriefing on purpose and findings of study	• Informing potential participants of the nature of the research and any issues that might influence their willingness to take part. • Detailed information about the research (often called a plain English statement), the purpose, procedures and process. • Informing on any available funding/expenses to claim. • Providing enough information to make a valid judgement. • Debriefing the participants on completion of the study, as to the findings, procedures, potential audience and how the findings will be used, and the data will be stored.
Informed consent	• Participant agreement or signed consent form (or assent form). • Those that cannot give consent include anyone who does not speak fluent English, the mentally impaired, acutely terminally ill people, or people who are dying or frail and infirm. • Children under the age of 18 cannot consent, however parents and teachers may sign on their behalf.
Right to withdraw without prejudice	• The sample audience needs to be told that participation is voluntary and they can withdraw from the study at any time. • No attempt should be made by the researcher to persuade or coerce the participants to partake in the study. • The researcher needs to be able to easily identify the participants who decide to withdraw from the study, in order to take their information out of the overall findings.

TABLE 3.11 Good ethical practice in research

CHAPTER SUMMARY

CHAPTER SUMMARY QUESTIONS

1 What is meant by the term evaluation?
2 At what stage is it important to evaluate an event?
3 What factors should be considered when evaluating an event?
4 Why is it so important to feedback to suppliers and vendors after the evaluation?
5 Why is it important to conduct a debrief with the client or event owner after the event has taken place?
6 Why are codes of conduct and ethics important in the events industry?

DISCUSSION POINTS

- What is the difference between formal and informal feedback?
- How successful are electronic feedback methods in assessing events and what are the drawbacks with this type of evaluation method?
- What are the main advantages and disadvantages of evaluating an event using the following methods?
  - Direct observation
  - Visitor surveys
  - Tracking media coverage.

ACTIVITIES

- Explain how each of the following can be a valuable source of information for evaluation purposes:
  - **a)** staff debrief
  - **b)** customer satisfaction surveys/complaints

- c) event revenue
- d) data records, e.g. spectator numbers
- e) SWOT analysis
- f) questionnaires
- g) interviews.

- Produce an event-evaluation plan for a selected event to include the following:
    - a) objective setting
    - b) potential sources of information
    - c) appropriate tools/methods to obtain information.
- Design a customer survey for your event, considering:
    - a) pre-event expectations
    - b) logistics on the day of the event
    - c) customer service
    - d) general expectations.

REFERENCES

Aho, S.K. (2001) 'Towards a general theory of touristic experiences: Modelling experience process in tourism', *Tourism Review*, 56(3/4): 33–7.

Alderfer, C.P. (1969) *Three Factor Theory (ERG) – Organizational Behavior and Human Performance*. London: Elsevier.

Beard, J., Ragheb, J.G. and Mounir, G. (1983) 'Measuring leisure motivation', *Journal of Leisure Research*, 15(3): 219–28.

Berlyne, D.E. (1960) 'Concept of optimal level of stimulation', *Journal of Leisure Research*, 13: 139–58.

Bladen, C., Kennell, J., Abson, E. and Wilde, N. (2012) *Events Management: An Introduction*. Abingdon: Routledge.

Brown, S. and Hutton, A. (2013) 'Developments in the real-time evaluation of audience behaviour at planned events', *International Journal of Event and Festival Management*, 4(1): 43–55.

Crompton, J.L. and Mackay, S.L. (1997) 'Motives of visitors attending festival events', *Annals of Tourism Research*, 24(2): 425–39.

EU GDPR Information Portal (2018) Complete guide to GDPR compliance [online]. Available at: https://gdpr.eu/ (accessed 16 April 2020).

Funk, D.C., Ridinger, L.L. and Moorman, A.M. (2004) 'Exploring origins of involvement: Understanding the relationship between the consumer motives and involvement with professional sports teams', *Leisure Sciences*, 26(1): 35–61.

Getz, D. (2012) *Event Studies: Theory, Research and Policy for Planned Events*. Amsterdam: Elsevier.

Gross, R. D., (1987) *Psychology: The Science of Mind and Behaviour*. London: Edward Arnold

Health and Safety Executive (HSE) (1974) Health & Safety at Work (HASAW). Available at: www.legislation.gov.uk/ukpga/1974/37/contents (accessed 19 October 2019).

Herzberg, F. (1968) 'Motivator Hygiene Theory', in J. Milner (2007) *Organisational Behaviour 4*. New York: Routledge.

Institute of Business Ethics (n.d.) Homepage. Available at: www.ibe.org.uk (accessed 1 November 2019).

The International Live Events Association (2020) Available at: https://www.ileahub.com/Meet-ILEA/Professional-Conduct-Ethics (accessed 2 February 2020).

Iso-Ahola, S.E. (1980) *The Social Psychology of Leisure and Recreation*. Dubuque, IA: William C. Brown.

James, J.D. and Ross, S. (2004) 'Comparing sport consumer motivations across multiple sports', *Sport Marketing Quarterly*, 13(1): 17–25.

Koo, G. and Hardin, R. (2008) 'Difference in interrelationship between spectators' motives and behavioural intentions based on emotional attachments', *Sports Marketing Quarterly*, 17(1): 30–43.

Malouf, L. (2012) *Events Exposed*. London: Wiley.

Maslow, A.H. (1943) 'A theory of human motivation', *Psychological Review*, 50(4): 370–96. Available at: https://doi.org/10.1037/h0054346 (accessed 16 April 2020).

McClelland, D. (1961) *Human Motivation Theory*, 2nd edn. Cambridge: Cambridge University Press.

Mehus, I. (2005) 'Sociability and excitement motives of spectators attending entertainment sport events: Spectators of soccer and ski-jumping', *Journal of Sport Behavior*, 28.

Milne, G.R. and McDonald, M.A. (1999) *Sports Marketing: Managing the Exchange Process*. Sudbury, MA: Jones & Bartlett.

Murray, H. (1938) 'Needs theory of personality', in D.J. Cooper (ed.), *Leadership for Follower Commitment*. Oxford: Butterworth-Heinemann.

Page, S. and Connell, J. (2011) *The Routledge Handbook of Events*. London: Routledge.

Quinn, B. (2013) *Key Concepts in Event Management*. London: Sage.

Trail, G.T. and James, J.D. (2001) 'The motivation scale for sport consumption: assessment of the scale's psychometric properties', *Journal of Sport Behaviour*, 24(1): 108–27.

Wann, D.L. (1995) 'Preliminary validation of sport fan motivation scale', *Journal of Sport & Social Issues*, 19(4): 377–96.

Watt, D.C. (1998) *Event Management in Leisure and Tourism*. Longman: Harlow.

Yeoman, I., Robertson, M. and Ali-Knight, J. (2012) *Festival and Events Management*. London: Routledge.

BEFORE THE EVENT

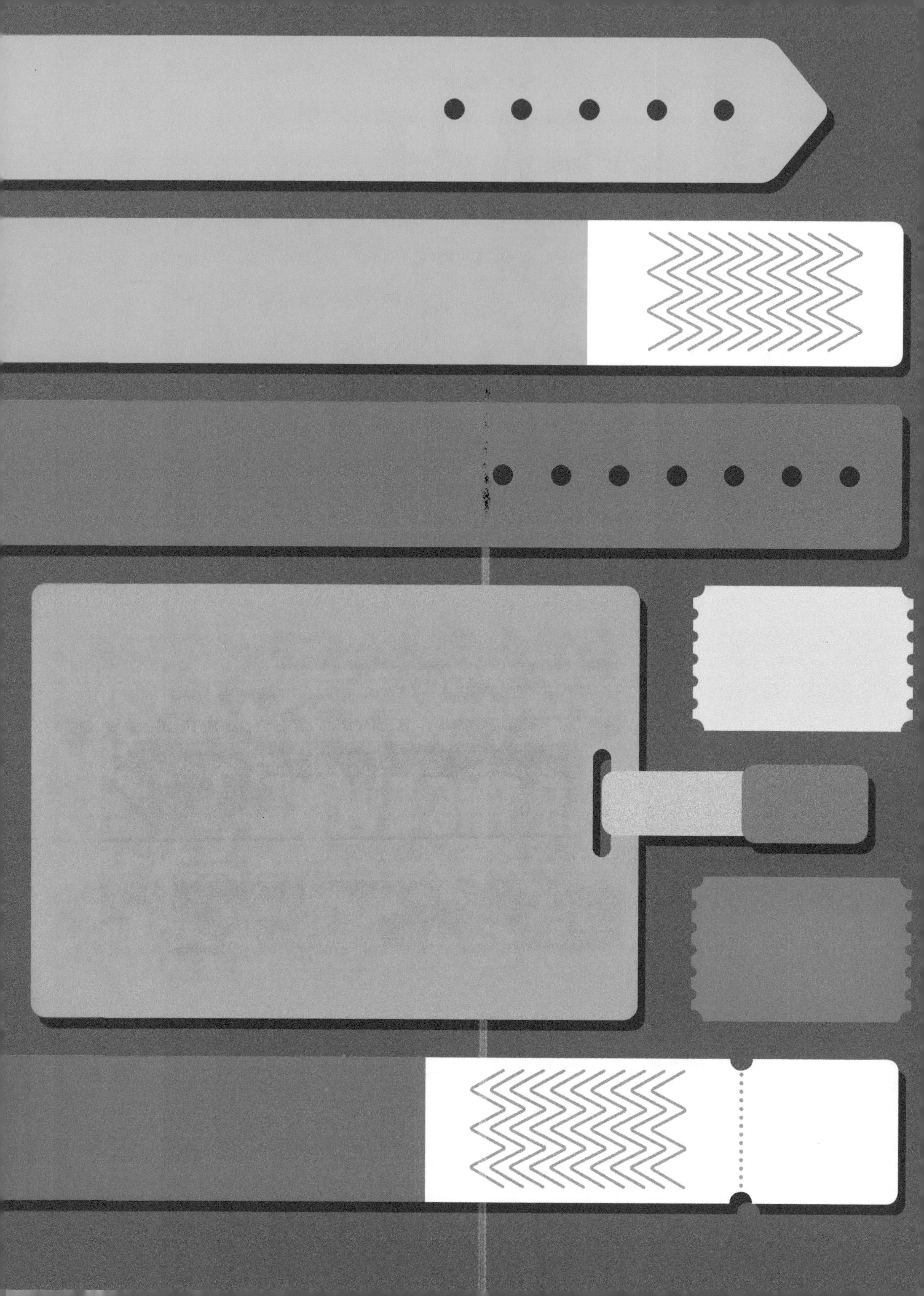

4

EVENT RESEARCH, FEASIBILITY AND IMPACT ANALYSIS

CHAPTER OVERVIEW

This chapter examines the importance of conducting appropriate market and feasibility research, in order to test the market, in advance of launching a new product or service. The chapter will also examine various market research techniques and discuss the importance of understanding the competition within the marketplace. It will also discuss research methods and the tools used in academic research and look at the use of a feasibility study or business plan to assess the marketplace and the competition. The chapter will also analyse the impact of economic, social and cultural factors and examine the progress from the early formation of the events industry to the multinational industry it has become today.

CHAPTER OBJECTIVES

After reading this chapter, you will be able to identify and understand:

OBJECTIVE 1
The need for market research and market awareness in events

OBJECTIVE 2
The different methods to design and conduct research

OBJECTIVE 3
The various research tools used to gather research information

OBJECTIVE 4
Event impact research and analysis

OBJECTIVE 5
Conducting and implementing a feasibility study

Meet ELISABETH BARTON

Onset Solutions Ltd

Elisabeth has been a consultant since 1999 with specialist knowledge of conference, events, sales and marketing and now heads the commercial team promoting conferences and event services to external organisations. Previously, she worked as Sales Director for Marriott hotels for more than eight years, with a corporate career with Bass, Whitbread plc and Allied Breweries. She is experienced in new business income generation, compiling feasibility studies, and implementing strategic reviews of existing operations, including hands-on tactical support. Elisabeth has been a director of Key Locations venue-finding agency since 1999, placing £2 million in conference and events each year, and has also been Director of Tarbay Centre Ltd since 2009, and Onset Solutions Ltd since 1999. She joined the catering and conference consultants Turpin Smale as Associate Director, working at the University of Brighton and the University of Leicester and a range of unusual venues specialising in strategic planning and tactical implementation for conference, events, sales and marketing. Elisabeth has also supported the Russell Partnership as their conference and events specialist for over 12 years, working on various projects including over 40 universities, a range of dedicated conference centres, racecourses, cricket grounds, corporate headquarters and unusual venues.

REAL EVENT CHALLENGE

A leading UK university I was working with as a consultant, identified over four years ago that there was an opportunity to expand both their summer commercial income and also establish a year-round conference centre. The team were looking to double the university's revenue by creating a distinctive brand of south-coast conferences, and were looking to develop a year-round conference offer and range of event management services. The university's management team required specialist conference, event and market positioning advice from the Onset team, giving consideration to the feasibility of future management and operational strategic direction. This was particularly interesting given the diverse cross-sector usage of the sites and heritage context. The feasibility documentation needed to present a plan for potential development for a conference and events venue within a city-centre converted building involved initially establishing the current gap in the market then defining the offer by providing financial projections to understand the viability of the project and the future potential for the region.

WHAT WAS YOUR PATHWAY TO CURRENT CAREER?

After graduating, Allied Breweries accepted me on their apprenticeship scheme, principally in operational roles specialising in events. Moving to Whitbread in F&B management when an inspirational GM offered me a sales director position, from there my career grew. As I was rapidly approaching my 30th birthday, this was a key milestone for me and I decided that if I was to form my own company and work for myself, I had to achieve it by then and have not looked back since; luckily I love what I do.

WHAT WAS THE MOST USEFUL SUBJECT STUDIED AT SCHOOL/COLLEGE?

I was a good generalist at most school subjects and naturally did well in those that interested me. My old home economics teacher who said 'hardly university material, darling' conversely gave me the push to get my head down. At university we had the opportunity for work experience and at the time mine was not the Disney experience I had signed up for at the open day; however, hospitals (special need and maternity wards), rough pubs in Wembley, industrial catering and swish hotels in Harrogate highlighted how diverse this sector is and the opportunity it presents.

FAVOURITE ANIMAL?

Dogs and their unreserved, unjudging boundless love, I adore.

YOUR PROUDEST CAREER MOMENT?

To my utter amazement (and to be honest my brother's too) 'Student of the Year' was special. Striving in a competitive business environment and expanding despite recessions also has to be up there. Developing and creating an amazing events team at the University of Brighton is something I also take pride in, as their quality of delivery is exceptional.

WHAT WOULD BE YOUR FUTURE DREAM EVENT?

Wow, I have in my head a dreamy 'white linen' luncheon set in a wild meadow, with chandeliers in the trees, rambling white roses, ethereal theatrical actors appearing at dusk (dogs allowed obviously), crystal glasses serving the finest wine, and local food all sourced from within a five-mile radius; totally 'over the top' yet stylishly simple.

PRACTITIONER VIEWPOINT

Louise Harrison, Conventions & Events Specialist, International Business Development Manager, Brisbane Convention & Exhibition Centre, Brisbane, Australia

Here at the Brisbane Convention & Exhibition Centre (BCEC), we are well-versed in conducting feasibility studies. Our primary business comes from large congresses, trade shows, exhibitions, international association conventions and large corporate events. Our aim is to attract international conventions to Brisbane and the BCEC. These are mostly existing world congresses, though sometimes we do identify gaps in our clients' market sectors and work with them to develop new events, which we term 'inaugurals'.

We have a very well-structured process for researching and qualifying international convention business, which is linked to subject matter and speciality. We start by conducting a feasibility study, or event analysis. If we feel the project isn't viable or for whatever reason is unlikely to come to Australia, we drop it and this is literally termed a 'dropped' event in our system. It may potentially be re-evaluated at a later date.

Part of the international sales team's role is to identify prospective events to bid for. We consult with industry peak bodies, experts and academics throughout the initial research process, which may take many months and even years. This is a highly structured bidding process, which follows a strict and prescriptive checklist format. For the many congresses and conventions we tender for, the bid team might be made up of academics, centres of excellence, key opinion leaders and official advocates, who can advise on content and appropriate subject matter, and our regional and national strength in a particular field, such as for a worldwide medical, scientific or agricultural congress.

Our team works closely with local, state and federal government departments for the necessary support and funding, and develops the bid in partnership with these organisations for Brisbane to become the next host destination. On completion of the research, the bid document is collated and the bid team presents, together with the local organising committee, to the international organisation's steering committee. These boards or committees liaise with the bid team and further information exchange and a certain amount of lobbying take place before a decision is made. The decision is usually made at the forthcoming congress, and sometimes as far out as two to five years before the year for which we are bidding. The success of the bid determines whether the Brisbane Convention & Exhibition Centre will be selected as the next venue to host the future event.

ACADEMIC VIEWPOINT

Dr Diana (Dee) Clayton, Senior Lecturer (HRM/Leadership – Hospitality, Tourism & Events) at Oxford Brookes University

At the Oxford School of Hospitality Management (OSHM), we encourage students to participate in multiple opportunities to practise writing feasibility studies and getting feedback on those. This includes in areas such as planning events in theory, entrepreneurial pitches, and practical event management.

Through these focused activities, we encourage students to understand what is being asked of them by/through the brief, research comprehensively and appropriately, provide evidence and transparent methodological underpinning, deliver convincing evaluations, and finally concisely summarise robust recommendations and conclusions, all supported by value-added documentation. The key to success is to understand the task and answer it in full, including directly addressing key stakeholders' requirements. When addressing an event's impact, we also encourage students to examine not just numbers (finance, accounting and economics), as increasingly it is important to consider the social and environmental concerns. In each year of study, we provide opportunity to conduct research, not just academic but also using market data, such as market reports and databases. This supporting evidence is essential to underpin a feasibility study, and we teach students to be selective across all types of reliable and valid evidence, both quantitative and qualitative.

Finally, the advice we would offer for a successful bid is to consider 'what is your USP?' This is your 'wow' factor that will make you stand out, which does not necessarily have to be on price. In a customer-centric sector, events students need to question what they are going to add to the overall consumer experience.

REAL EVENT OUTCOME

The first aspect to establish when writing the feasibility proposal for the university was to establish how the report findings were to be used. This helped the team determine what information and detail needed to be included in the document. From previous experience I had learnt that it is advisable not to assume anything and to never hesitate to go back to the client for further clarification on any unclear items in the brief.

Thorough research was needed to prepare the feasibility document and fortunately our team were already familiar with the operational structure and the university facilities. We related the context of the project to our agency's current teams, structures and brands, highlighting the shared values, objectives or aspirations in common with the client. Within the document, the timings of this project and the next stages were also set out.

The credentials section of a feasibility proposal we submitted gave some background detail on our organisation, focusing on our specific skill sets, provenance and proven ability to undertake the brief, including recent examples of events we had delivered within the university and wider environs, to provide confidence in our capacity and expertise. At the start of the document, we included an overview of the brief and scope of the report in order to clarify that we had correctly interpreted the client's wishes and requirements. This included confirmation of the number of consultancy days and the rationale and methodology to be applied. We also detailed any overriding circumstances, risks or opportunities, as well as any motivations for the work to be undertaken, and included a SWOT analysis.

As a site assessment was part of the feasibility proposal, it is essential that we viewed it at different times of day and night, including weekends, and discussed the context of the site in terms of the area, demographics, profile, transport links, building constraints, licence restrictions, the physical description, available space and layout, capacities and sizes. Also, the accessibility of the location to all public regional and national transport was considered, as well as the on-site car parking facilities and charges. Additionally, the proposal summarised and commented on the plans or architect drawings and included elements such as our first impressions, visibility, the street scene and visitor perceptions.

In terms of the financial section of the proposal, we conducted in-depth research to gain current turnover figures, in particular: the sales mix; profile of the users; length of stay; average spends; agency versus direct clients; current marketing spends; key measurements; sales and marketing plans; and the radius of where their current business was coming from, including any denied business caused by 'suppressed demand'. Part of this research involved interviewing relevant stakeholders to canvass opinion and to gain 'hearts and minds' engagement and support for this important opportunity for the university.

THE NEED FOR MARKET RESEARCH AND MARKET AWARENESS IN EVENTS

OBJECTIVE
1
The need for market research and market awareness in events

HOW IS MARKET RESEARCH USED IN EVENTS?

Conducting market research is a structured and coherent way to achieve objectives relating to attendance, satisfaction and profit. Successful market analysis requires a complete understanding of the target audience, both geographically and **demographically**. This understanding comes from undertaking primary and secondary research, and through communication with stakeholders and consumers.

Demography
statistics that measure observable aspects of a population, such as size, age, gender, etc.

Market research relates to communication with potential customers and the target market and is designed to provide necessary information about the event marketplace. This information is needed in the planning phase to develop a rationale and feasibility study for delivering the event. The process of market research determines the needs, wants, aspirations and expectations of the potential target market, before launching a new product or service. This helps to position the product or service and to identify whether there is a gap or requirement, or to determine whether the market is already over-saturated.

In order to better understand the external forces affecting the event and its markets (macro), research is usually conducted before developing the marketing strategy. Market research is also undertaken in order to gain insight into the event or venue's existing and potential consumers and any previous strategies (micro), and helps gauge the level of expectation of all stakeholders. It should be used to pinpoint emerging trends and patterns in the industry and hopefully eliminate any potential problems at the outset, before too much time and resources have been spent on the project. During the process of gathering this background information, the feasibility of the proposed event is usually established.

WHAT QUESTIONS MIGHT NEED TO BE ASKED?

- What is the current position?
- What is the background detail and history of the event, etc.?
- What are the key sources?
- What are the main questions and problems?
- What are the major issues and debates?
- Is there a gap in knowledge?
- Has any other market research been carried out in this area?

GATHERING INFORMATION

When gathering relevant material to inform the feasibility of the event, there are various useful ways to collect information:

- Group meetings and discussions
- Meetings with key people and champions within the community

- Previous written material and other documentation
- Observing the dynamics of the setting, venue or location.

Gathering this information will help finalise the feasibility of the event and also the characteristics or lifestyle of the target market. There are many ways of gathering information, but accessing relevant information is largely dependent upon the financial resources at the organisers' disposal. For example, if the organisation has the budget to outsource to research companies to provide official data, then it should be possible to get an accurate estimate of the potential demand for the event in the marketplace. However, if resources are limited, it may be necessary to research alternative published information that will begin to help identify the status of the market. This data may come from a number of sources, as illustrated in Figure 4.1, which will be useful in the strategic planning process.

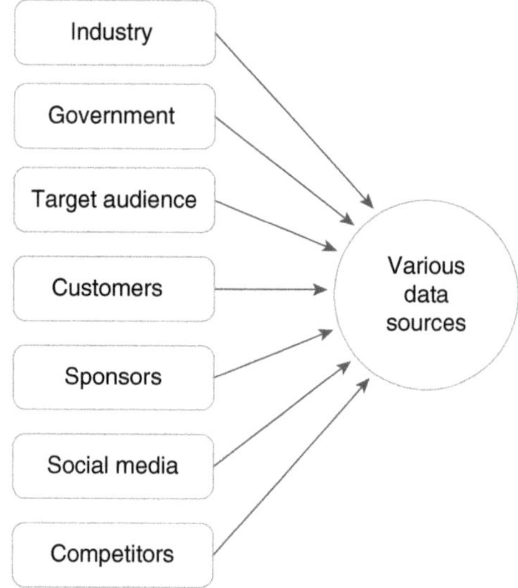

FIGURE 4.1 Data sources for strategic planning

Various sources can be used within the events industry to supply relevant secondary data as follows:

- *Industry* – changes to growth or buying patterns in the industry
- *Government* – any impending changes to funding or policy legislation
- *Target audience* – information on local populations with respect to age, employment, ethnic background and other factors that may be important in determining where to locate a facility or a business
- *Customers* – measuring previous satisfaction levels, preferred activities and suggestions for improvement from past programmes, activities and previous client and supplier details
- *Sponsors* – sponsor information/evaluation, past satisfaction levels and intent to sponsor future events

- *Social media* – information on what is trending, posts on online forums, any shifts in customer buying patterns, preferred events/activities/venue types/destinations, etc.
- *Competitor analysis* – information from other, similar businesses or organisations, with rates and details for benchmarking or adopting best practice.

REAL INSIGHT 4.1

TESTING NEW EVENT PRODUCTS WITH POTENTIAL CUSTOMERS AND TARGET MARKETS

Gamification was the hot topic among many planners at IMEX Frankfurt in May 2018, with a wide range of technical products, services, research and trends showcased during the show. The #IMEXpitch, a firm fixture at IMEX in Frankfurt, was transformed this year from a competition into a showcase with suppliers sharing their innovations. Many planners attended and gained a valuable snapshot of the latest and tech start-ups in the market right now. This is an excellent opportunity for suppliers who have designed new products to showcase them to a potential audience of customers and buyers within the events industry. The TECHknowledge Area, led by an agency called The Meeting Pool, proved to be a popular area for planners wanting to trial new solutions and troubleshoot their technical challenges.

Kim Rhodes from Experient said: 'In response to a surge in demand from my clients, I'm meeting exhibitors to discuss the different new options in gamification.' Tara Thomas from The Meeting Pool said: 'Our one-to-one consulting sessions have shown a real demand for different types of tech designed to drive the event experience.' The EventMobi team shared with planners the different ways in which gamification can drive delegate behaviour. Event Tech Tribe has also seen an increased openness among planners in exploring and trying different forms of technology.

Planners were given the chance to experience new technology and to try it before buying it at the new Tech Café sitting alongside the Technology Pavilion. This was created at the exhibition, specifically in response to buyer requests to explore a greater variety of technical products and features at the show.

Market research from this type of product testing is invaluable and used often in the feasibility stage to test the feedback and response of potential customers who would be a target audience to purchase the product. Based on their reaction and comments, the product might be adapted or tweaked accordingly.

EVENT ETHICS

Adidas ended its multi-million-pound sponsorship of the IAAF in 2017 due to doping and corruption scandals following the Rio 2016 Olympics. The deal had been due to run until 2019 and was reportedly worth £23 million.

Do you agree or disagree that it tarnishes the reputation of a sponsor to align themselves with athletes who may be under suspicion of illegal drug-taking or doping?

HOW IS COMPETITIVE ANALYSIS USED IN EVENTS?

The event environment is a competitive domain, therefore the more knowledge gained about the competition, especially on competitor rate matrix pricing and positioning, the better. By understanding the competitors' offering and their own unique selling point, the incumbent or competing body or agency is better placed to negotiate and bargain with customers and suppliers in the bid process. A good organiser will have researched the competition thoroughly; know exactly who their competition is and what they are currently doing. They should evaluate competitor strengths and weaknesses and marketing strategies. This can be assessed by conducting market research, in order to benchmark the competition's product. This will also help the organisation to work out their next strategy to develop their own product features, pricing schedules or new advertising methods, to gain market share.

This type of competitor analysis or competitive intelligence (CI) can be achieved by making sales calls to the competitors and various target markets, to establish if and where there is a gap in the market, in price, quality and availability. Part of the feasibility process is to analyse the market and the competition, by classifying and evaluating any potential market threats from new and potentially less expensive product offerings, as well as analysing the threat of new entrants to the market. Table 4.1 illustrates the three types of market demand that exist.

Current demand	Events identified as being needed at present
Latent demand	There is a potential untapped market
Suppressed demand	The need is there but may be unfulfilled, for example due to logistical problems or budgetary problems

TABLE 4.1 Various types of market demand

In the planning phase, it is important to recognise any gaps in the market in terms of price, quality and availability, the market potential, pricing and positioning from which recommendations can be drawn. Practical guidelines for defining competitor analysis and setting objectives should be designed; using an acronym borrowed from business and management, these event objectives should always be SMART:

- Specific – to the particular event and particular aspects of that event
- Measurable – able to express the objectives in numbers and quantities
- Agreed – discussed by all team members and stakeholders
- Realistic – set objectives that the team can realistically achieve
- Timed – set a timescale for achievement of the objectives.

Porter (1989) designed a framework known as the five forces model, focusing on where competition comes from and the potential risk of entry by competitors, to highlight the rivalry that exists within any given industry. In an increasingly competitive environment, it is essential for event managers to gain an edge over competitors, by committing investment of capital, revealing plans for future regeneration and renewed employment within the host city or nation, and gauging customer opinion throughout the feasibility stage. It is also essential to continuously keep an eye on the market, to note any changing developments or trends. When evaluating the competition, it is advisable to segment the market into similar clusters and select one or more segments to target, using a specific marketing mix and positioning the product or service so that it is perceived by each target market segment as 'satisfying their needs better than that offered by the opposition'.

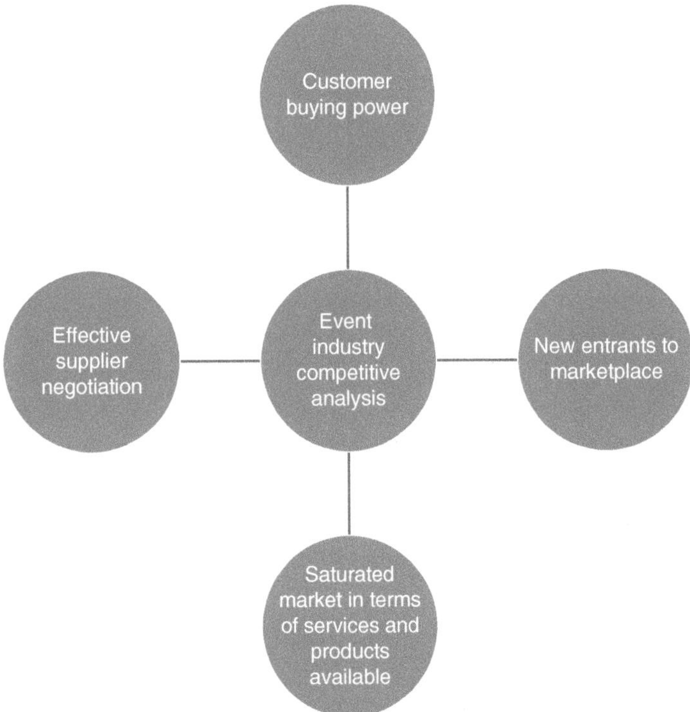

FIGURE 4.2 Event industry competitive analysis

OBJECTIVE 2

The different methods to design and conduct research

THE DIFFERENT METHODS AND APPROACHES USED TO DESIGN AND CONDUCT RESEARCH

WHAT ARE PRIMARY AND SECONDARY RESEARCH METHODS?

When conducting market research and gathering information, the two types of research used are primary and secondary research. As well as conducting primary research in the pre-event planning stages, it is important to conduct secondary research to inform on current trends affecting consumption. The primary findings are conducted and written by the researcher, while secondary research is a re-examination of already published data and findings, as demonstrated in Figure 4.3.

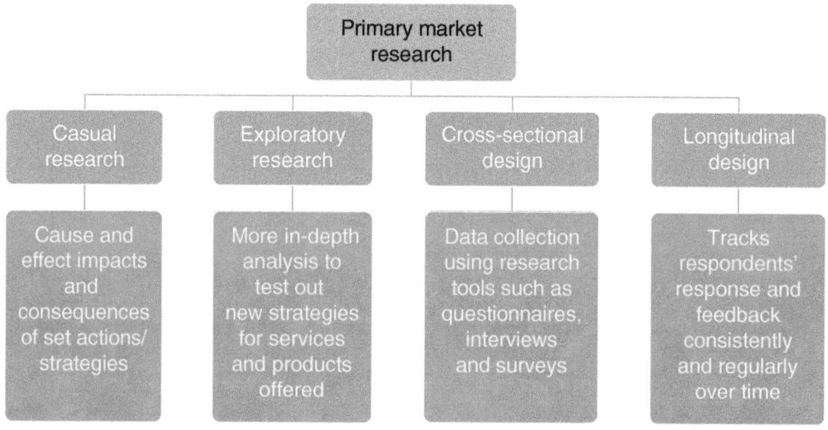

FIGURE 4.3 Primary market research design

PRIMARY RESEARCH

Behavioural information aimed at increasing the effectiveness of marketing and advertising using behaviour information, also known as 'audience targeting'

Target situation analysis provides information about objective and product-oriented needs

Primary data includes demographic and **behavioural information** about prospective customers' attitudes to and opinions on events or event products. It is often needed when an organisation needs to make a specific decision and collate information directly from respondents, in order to answer the questions or issues raised. This type of research investigates a **target situation analysis** and draws conclusions based on canvassing a large sample of participants. This can be expressed in terms of averages, percentages or other statistics. The following research methods may be employed:

- *Casual research* – tends to examine cause-and-effect relationships, for example analysing whether the fact that a venue has extended its opening hours has resulted in the venue becoming more popular with groups.
- *Exploratory research* – is set up as an area for subsequent research, to review at a later stage using more rigorous studies, to test out new strategies and products.
- *Cross-sectional design* – usually involves data collection from many different consumers or respondents, using a tool such as a survey or questionnaire.

- *Longitudinal design* – tends to track the responses of the same sample of respondents over time, using consumer panels, focus groups, online forums or regular questionnaires and surveys.

Primary research may evaluate, for example, whether or not a particular demographic has more leisure time, resources and disposable income, which may be a key factor in putting on events within a specific category. It tends to be conducted to a specific sample audience using face-to-face or telephone interviews, online surveys or focus groups. It can be time-consuming and expensive to conduct this type of research, so it is not always feasible.

SECONDARY RESEARCH

Secondary research is information and data that has already been conducted on the subject and is available as published material to provide background information. This might give the researcher more of an understanding of the facts, historical background and issues before conducting primary research. As with the materials and tools already reviewed in the section above on market research, secondary data may take the form of company reports, previous research studies, stakeholder feedback, blogs, reports published in trade press and journals, and published research. Sometimes it is more appropriate to make an assessment on the feasibility of the event by studying secondary sources, current trends or published data on consumer patterns of behaviour, by outsourcing to research agencies like Mintel, the GfK group, or other national marketing-research agencies. These agencies charge a fee to conduct research on clients' behalf and then publish business reports on current trends in a particular area and are able to supply useful data on local demographics and the overall mood of the global or regional economy. This might include the status of the stock market, the perception of the economy by consumers, and the current availability of jobs and market opportunities.

Generally, when collecting secondary data, it is a good idea to identify the key sectors to target and report specific, not generalised, findings for each of the relevant sectors, such as local corporate, association charities, weddings, exhibitions, and so on. The next stage is to attempt to relate the findings to the future recommendations, drawing from the work undertaken in the **situation analysis**. As previously discussed, secondary data can be obtained from a number of sources, including those listed in Table 4.2.

Situation analysis refers to a collection of methods used to analyse an organisation's internal and external environment

Government statistics and reports on venue consumption, or the Office for National Statistics (ONS)
Media coverage on event types and venues
Industry magazines and trade press, such as *Conference & Incentive Travel* (www.citmagazine.co.uk), *Conference news* (www.conference-news.co.uk), *Event* (www.eventmagazine.co.uk) and *Meetings & Incentive Travel* (www.meetpie.com)
Historical and current data from other events, venues, event management websites

(Continued)

TABLE 4.2 (Continued)

National sector industry reports – EVCOM, MPI, BVEP, Tourism Alliance, Hot stats, PKF, UKEMTS, HBAA, British meetings and events surveys
National publications, newspapers and magazines and online forums
Local reports – usual council profile, tourism strategy, local business and development plans
Destination management marketing consortiums
Internet research into the area, press releases, announcements, developments, competitor new builds or expansions.

TABLE 4.2 Sources of secondary data

During the market analysis stage, all of these factors can be used and may include a mixture of primary and secondary sources. The secondary data tends to help the researcher design the questionnaires or interviews for the primary research. Event-based research might inform and allow the event planner to draw meaningful conclusions on current demand, related facts and figures, occupancies, average customer spend and rates. For more precise detail, further research calls can be made to potential customers within various sectors, such as agents, wedding planners, sponsors or exhibition organisers, in order to get feedback on the gaps and opportunities in the market, current challenges, anecdotal comments, or reaction to rates and proposed pricing strategies.

RESEARCH METHODS

In the event life cycle, the five critical stages necessary to ensure a successful event are shown in Figure 4.4.

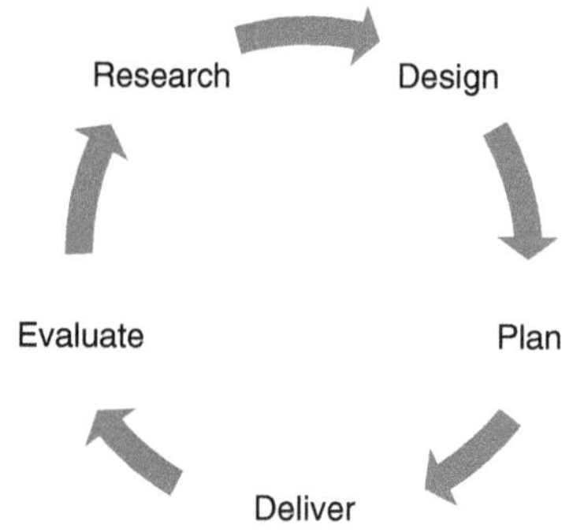

FIGURE 4.4 The five critical stages of the event life cycle

As already discussed, it is necessary to conduct thorough research in the planning stage, in order to reduce the risk and to test the market. The three pre-event research methods, which are also used in any other form of research are:

- *Quantitative*: number of participants, event profit, return on investment (ROI)
- *Qualitative*: delegate satisfaction, feedback, return on objectives (ROO)

- *A mixed-method approach*: a combination of both the above, with some statistical information and some research gained from participant interviews, feedback, etc.

GO ONLINE

The main differences between these types of research approaches are detailed in Table 4.1, included in the Appendix and available online at **study.sagepub.com/quick.**

There are some instances where, in order to get a more rounded picture of what is required, it is necessary to combine both methods of study, which can be termed a mixed-method approach. This involves combining quantitative and qualitative approaches, either sequentially or concurrently, to generate a new body of knowledge or follow a new line of inquiry. It is up to the event owner or organisation to determine the most suitable method of research, dependent on timing, budget, the nature of the study and the depth and complexity of the information required. All three types of research could be considered throughout the event cycle, particularly in the pre-event and post-event stages, and a qualitative methodology can also be very effective on-site. The example below demonstrates how all methods may be effectively used in research:

REAL INSIGHT 4.2

RESEARCH APPROACHES

A QUANTITATIVE APPROACH IN EVENT RESEARCH

An event organiser of the New York Association of Realty [Property] Managers, wanted to find out how participants had rated the annual convention meeting. This year the venue had been changed from Boston to Maine, to save costs, but numbers were down on the previous year and a questionnaire was devised to hand out to delegates after the conference to gauge feedback. The questionnaire was brief and asked them to rate on a scale of one to five, where one was excellent and five was poor, how they rated the new destination, venue and transportation to get there.

Also, closed questions were asked about the quality of the conference programme, appropriateness of the keynote speakers and levels of service at the venue, including accommodation, venue facilities and food and beverage. Afterwards the event team collected all the questionnaires and analysed the numerical data gained from them. They devised a spreadsheet to plot the percentage of high and low scores for each question given by the respondents. They then compared these responses to those they had collected the previous year.

(Continued)

This showed that satisfaction levels were 20% lower overall compared with last year and scores were over 40% lower for ease of travel and venue accommodation. This persuaded the team to revert back to their original venue in Boston. Despite the reductions in cost, the team still felt by moving the event back to Boston, they would be able to increase attendees and levels of satisfaction for the following year.

A QUALITATIVE APPROACH IN EVENT RESEARCH

An event organiser wanted to put on a charity fashion show in Edinburgh, using local models and asking people to bring good-condition clothes to demonstrate on the catwalk and swap with other attendees. She planned to donate a large proportion of the money raised to local charities. She conducted her own research on local women's groups and by asking friends and contacts if they would be interested in this event.

Over a period of three weeks, she conducted telephone research with over 100 people, asking respondents for a series of views through semi-structured interview questions about the proposed event. She collated the comments, analysed them and the key findings were:

a) yes, people were interested but, significantly
b) they did not like the venue she was proposing.

Acting on this information, instead of using the local pub they always used, they booked space in a more upmarket hotel foyer, which agreed to offer a complimentary room and a significant discount on food and wine. The result was that 200 people, mostly female, attended, paying £30 per ticket, and brought their used clothes with them. As a result of this, after deducting expenditure she made an excellent profit of £7,500 to donate to local causes.

A MIXED-METHOD APPROACH IN EVENT RESEARCH

A wedding planning company wanted to conduct research to find out how many couples planning to get married the following year were influenced by celebrity weddings when making their own wedding purchasing decisions. At the National Wedding Show in Excel, London, the company conducted short questionnaires with attendees visiting their stand.

The wedding planners realised that the most cost-effective way to conduct this research was to use a quantitative method, but then probe the future brides and grooms surveyed on their aspirations and needs, using a qualitative approach.

Some of the questions posed in the questionnaire were designed to find out statistical information, such as how many brides and grooms were using social media, by asking them to use a Likert scale to rate a series of statements from one to five.

Other questions in the survey were open-ended and designed to capture opinions and comments from the respondents. The questionnaire was completed by 150 attendees and a report was generated by the wedding planning agency following the wedding show, which presented the findings of the survey. The report used a mixed-method format, representing the quantitative data, using tables, graphs and pie charts. It also used a qualitative approach, using some of the verbatim comments recorded from the attendees. The final findings revealed how celebrity weddings and their depiction through social media had influenced the couples' choice of wedding theme, bridal wear and jewellery, flowers, food and beverage, and in some cases even their venue and destination choice.

This information helped the wedding planners eventually design their own online application, featuring some of the most prestigious celebrity couples to 'get hitched' in the last five years, and showcasing some of the workable celebrity wedding concepts that the agency would be able to replicate on behalf of any potential new customers at a fraction of the original cost.

QUANTITATIVE SURVEYS

These are generally conducted through online questionnaires. A quantitative survey tends to contain structured and precise questions prepared in advance to facilitate quantitative analysis. The literature review or background research conducted on the subject before, allows the researcher to design a framework for the research method and to formulate relevant questions to ask respondents in the survey or interview. The wording of the questions is significant. The questions can be open, which do not usually require a choice of options, or closed, where there are several response options from which to choose. It is advisable to keep the questions clear and concise and avoid asking too many. Researchers should refrain from using event terminology or jargon, or asking respondents questions that they may not understand, or may prove misleading. The researcher should not steer or influence the respondents by using subjective expressions or answer choices but try to include answer responses that are as neutral as possible. In some cases, it may be necessary to include a category answer option of no opinion or not applicable (n/a) in the questionnaire, in case some questions are not relevant or understood by the respondent.

QUALITATIVE SURVEYS

In cases where the research questions are more concerned with the customers' feedback, ideas or feelings, the research tool adopted should be a qualitative survey. Research methods such as interviews or a focus group should be employed with the target population, to gather comments to the questions and areas being researched. This type of survey can be more flexible than a quantitative one, as it tends to use semi-structured questions, rather than concrete or fixed ones, and there is often an opportunity to amend questions during the research. As with quantitative surveys, it is important to link the academic review to the questions being asked in the survey. It helps to identify key themes that emerge from published secondary sources, to discuss in the interviews or focus groups.

MIXED-METHOD SURVEYS

In some cases, it is necessary to use a mixed-method approach for data collection. Although this method might take longer to complete, it can be an excellent way to allow the researcher to triangulate their findings, which means to measure a phenomenon that can be analysed from multiple perspectives. Using a mixed-method approach can help the researcher validate the authenticity and reliability of the responses and allow for a deeper understanding of the issues involved.

The survey provided with the online resources was commissioned by Kilkenny Heritage in Ireland, for some research they were conducting on behalf of Jerpoint Abbey. They were trying to establish whether there is a market for events at the venue. This questionnaire had been sent out to outside caterers who work in the area, to gauge how interested they might be in the prospect of working at this new unusual venue, by supplying catering services at weddings, conferences and other potential events to be held there, once the project to turn the Abbey into an outdoor venue has been completed, as can be seen in the following link to the survey.

GO ONLINE

Head online to **study.sagepub.com/quick** to access this sample survey.

OBJECTIVE
3
The various research tools used to gather research information

THE VARIOUS RESEARCH TOOLS USED TO GATHER RESEARCH INFORMATION

RESEARCH TOOLS

There are various research tools that the researcher might choose to use when conducting research in the events field or writing a dissertation or thesis. The main tools that are employed by researchers to elicit set responses from a sample or target audience are as follows:

- Interviews
- Online surveys
- Case studies
- Observation/participation
- Focus groups.

INTERVIEWS

Interviews can be conducted either by telephone or face to face. Telephone interviews usually consist of a brief telephone conversation, where the interviewer reads out a short list of questions to the respondent. Although conducting telephone interviews generally has a low cost, some respondents are not willing to answer questions over the phone and may be suspicious that there are other motives for the research. Also, poorly written or designed questions can elicit misleading information or disproportional responses from respondents. Furthermore, it is not possible to use visual aids while conducting this type of research or to build up a rapport with the respondent or to detect their body language or other non-verbal signs.

With an increase in voicemail being used by employees to screen unessential calls, it is recommended to set an appointment at a specific date and time to conduct telephone research in advance. Face-to-face interviews allow the interviewer to adapt the questions to the specific situation and gain a deeper insight. However, this option is more time-consuming and expensive and may be more prone to bias, such as when the respondent tells the researcher what they think they would like to hear, rather than being entirely truthful.

ONLINE SURVEYS

Online surveys are often designed to collect quick snapshot responses and to collect demographic information on gender, age and income data. They are generally used to gather instant data and can be a flexible and low-cost option, and particularly useful for conducting research over a wide geographical area. Online surveys are especially popular when trying to reach a large number of people and have the advantage of allowing respondents to answer questions at their own pace and in their own time. They are generally easy to administer and offer a high degree of anonymity to respondents.

However, there are some negatives to this research method: generally, questions are restricted in terms of length. It is also not always possible to gauge whether respondents have really understood the questions or are being genuine in their responses and it is sometimes unclear who is responding. Respondents might not answer the questions honestly, but as they think is required. Also, this type of survey could alienate respondents who do not have access to a computer, Smartphone or the internet. It can take a long time to get a response and there is generally a lower response rate with this method than with others, because it is quite easy for respondents to just ignore them.

CASE STUDIES

This method is often used to identify comparable characteristics and can provide a comprehensive examination of an event organisation or company. A case study usually focuses on an individual or organisation and uses anecdotes and real-life examples. This approach allows the researcher to fully understand the issues involved. There are different types of case studies that can be used, depending on the topic and approach, which are: **exploratory**, **descriptive** and **explanatory**.

Exploratory individual, business or organisation to develop research questions and aims and objectives

Descriptive individual, business or organisation to describe a defined project

Explanatory individual, business or organisation to explain the cause or phenomenon being presented in the case study

OBSERVATION/PARTICIPATION

For observation research, the group or individual are informed in advance that the research is taking place and the researcher is given permission to observe them.

Mystery shopping
a tool used by market research companies, watchdog organisations, or internally by companies themselves to measure quality of service, or compliance with regulation, or to gather specific information about products and services

This is known as overt observation. In special cases, the researcher is permitted to record the consumer's behaviour, often without their knowledge, which is known as 'covert observation', and may take place without informing the participants of their presence. In the events, tourism and hospitality industries, this sometimes branches into the area of **mystery shopping**.

For an event planner, observation or participation could involve visiting a venue, or a specific event, to get an idea of what works well and what ideas could be adapted for their own events. This method is often used when the researcher is trying to examine a specific culture or community. For observation to be reliable and robust, it must reflect the original aims and objectives of the research proposal, and due diligence should be given to ethical considerations.

There are generally two types of observation. Unobtrusive observation is where researchers are placed in a hidden area to watch the behaviours of others, sometimes by placing cameras or one-way mirrors to observe participants. The other type is participant observation, where the researcher becomes part of the group and interacts with them to try to understand their experiences.

Sometimes impromptu conversations with venue staff or delegates can elicit the most useful and revealing information. Also, observing the levels of service being delivered and trying to troubleshoot potential problems can be a useful way to improve the next planned event. As an event organiser, there could be many suitable opportunities to observe several of the processes, including registration, waiting times, service levels, the quality of food and beverage within the venue, as well as the attitude and levels of service provided by the venue staff. In order to get a realistic and honest overall picture of levels of service and quality of the venue, event organisers should consider arriving at the venue without giving notice, or at different times of the day. It is also advisable to take detailed notes or record conversations that they will be able to refer to at a later stage during the feedback process.

FOCUS GROUPS

Focus groups are generally set up to collect information about the attitudes and opinions of respondents. They usually consist of a small group of participants who are interested in or have some knowledge of the subject being discussed. These respondents should be made up of a representative sample from the market. Overall this method can yield large amounts of valuable qualitative data, not just from individual responses, but also from the resulting group dynamic and interaction. Typically, the focus group consists of five to nine people, who are guided by a facilitator. The moderator should have some knowledge of the topic, but not proffer any of their own personal views. They should guide the group objectively and impartially in the discussion, maintaining order and allowing everyone in the group to express their opinions. The facilitator or researcher leading the group should prepare some semi-structured interview questions that will allow the focus group to remain focused, and ensure that similar questions are asked to all stakeholders in all focus groups being conducted for the study.

Sometimes the moderator may observe other behaviour such as body language and attitudes of the focus group, as well as the verbal content of the discussion. The most important factor is to determine who would be best-suited to attend the focus group. The session is often recorded either by audio or visual tools, but these days most often by Smartphone or tablet, and can be transcribed in writing at a later stage if required (see Table 4.3). The duration of the focus group can vary according to the complexity of the topic being discussed, but sufficient time should be allowed to achieve all the objectives and to capture a representative viewpoint from the whole group. A scribe should be appointed to take notes and a timekeeper may be required to make sure the focus group is adhering to the time allotted for the session.

Q1. What additional suppliers would you like to see at the wedding fair?

R01 – Well, for me I think that ...

R02 – I think it would be great to have florists there so that people could discuss floral arrangements.

R03 –

R04 –

Q2. What type of activities should we provide at the event?

R03 – Well, I have noticed that there is less importance on bridal wear at other wedding fairs in the area ...

R02 – That's a hard one to answer because I have never been to a wedding fair.

R04 – Yes, I think a fashion show would be great.

R01 – It would be good to have a look at some sample wedding breakfast menus ...

TABLE 4.3 What does a transcript of a focus group look like?

WHAT IS A SAMPLE POPULATION IN RESEARCH?

Sampling is the process of selecting respondents for a study. The word 'population' can be used when referring to everyone who has responded to a survey, but provided the sample population is representative of the whole population, then the results of the survey on the sample population can be inferred to the whole population. The total number of survey respondents is the 'sample' population. For example, when researchers want to find out the opinion of a whole population, such as all delegates that attended a specific event, they do not need to *survey* everyone, but a sample population that may be only a few hundred or perhaps a thousand people.

GO ONLINE

There are two main types of samples, probability and non-probability samples, as can be viewed in the Appendix available online as Table 4.2.

WHAT IS A PILOT STUDY?

In order to evaluate and test the validity of the questions being posed to respondents, event managers should use a small focus group or interview to test and review the questions. This enables them to identify any flaws before launching them. It also provides an indication of the likely response rate and range of responses to be expected. The pilot stage will help the researcher to ascertain how long the survey or interview will take to complete. It will also establish whether the research questions are understandable and valid for the research being conducted and not likely to cause any misunderstanding.

The questions asked in a survey or questionnaire should have a logical flow and avoid any awkward or repetitious words. They should not be written in a way that leads or encourages the respondents to answer in a certain way, but allow for impartiality and personal opinion. The text should also be written out in full to ensure that all questions are answered in the correct order. For an interview or a focus group, the questions designed by the researcher may be semi-structured and allow for some flexibility, and are often designed to be less prescriptive and more of a guide to ensure the same topic areas are discussed in each interview or focus group.

WHAT DOES RELIABILITY AND VALIDITY MEAN IN RESEARCH?

When conducting research, it is essential that the researcher produces valid and reliable information that can be defended when challenged by any of the event stakeholders. Validity primarily confirms an accurate measurement and concerns data accuracy, credibility and the wider body of knowledge to which the research will ultimately contribute. Accurate representation is central to the area of validity in research. For example, when researching a university fresher's reaction to an induction event, a sample of university freshers must be included in the sample to ensure the findings are valid. Furthermore, the questions posed to this sample of fresher students should be adapted specifically to them. They should also be presented in language and terminology that they are able to understand, in order to ensure their responses are truthful and accurate.

Reliability is a mechanism that allows the researcher to ensure that the research remains truthful and accurate and free from errors over time: for example, if the researcher decided to replicate a survey or interviews; if they conducted the research using the same processes and mechanism to groups of event management graduates from the same university and course, the responses generated should not be significantly different for each cohort. With qualitative research, there is always some degree of subjectivity in the findings. For this reason it can prove a challenge to design a data collection tool that will produce a high reliability and validity. However, by following the same process, and ensuring good practice and transparency within the research procedure, a rigorous and consistent interpretation of the data should be ensured.

Researchers try to maximise reliability by posing questions in a variety of ways, or by asking the same questions on different occasions, or by outsourcing to expert analysts to interpret the responses and look for consistency and stability. As already discussed in the section on focus groups, by keeping to same-question format, and adopting the same, consistent semi-structured interview questions for all focus groups, the researcher should be able to ensure that the data collected is reliable.

Event managers who need to conduct research and gather reliable and valid data, often outsource to universities or colleges to get assistance. Alternatively, they may decide to pay to outsource the research to consultants or experienced researchers, in order to develop a reliable instrument and collect and analyse the data on their behalf. To outsource in this way can sometimes add credibility to the overall findings.

ACQUIRED DATABASES

External databases can provide a large amount of marketing information, to inform event owners when making decisions and allow suppliers to canvass for new business opportunities, by phone, email or other communication. Event companies can acquire database lists and marketing leads from a number of sources, including government sources, specific marketing lead generation companies, associations, and so on. However, Data Protection Legislation and the new General Data Protection Regulations (GDPR) that came into force in May 2018 have significantly changed the way the events industry, among others, is able to communicate with their customers and clients.

The new regulations mean that the use of such lead generation, through database and mailing lists, has become far more strictly governed and monitored, in order to prevent outbound unsolicited emails and phone calls. This now gives the end-user the opportunity to opt out of receiving promotional mailings or receiving further sales, marketing calls or invitations. This legislation protects individuals or companies that decide to opt out and to receive no unsolicited contact, or have their details passed to third-party marketing agencies or companies. Moreover, the fines for contravening these new regulations have increased substantially; therefore, it is in the event owner's interests to be fully conversant with Data Audit and Privacy Statements. They also need to understand the new rules regarding the use of Data Protection legislation.

Any suppliers and organisations who are not fully aware of how these changes will impact their business operationally, should seek further guidance or training on compliance issues and solutions for both data protection and other marketing legislation, and ensure they comply with these revised policy guidelines and regulations.

INTERPRETING RESEARCH FINDINGS

Deciding on the most appropriate research methodology and tools is only the first part of the process. After the design of the questionnaire, survey or focus group, the data needs to be carefully analysed, with a view to presenting the findings, any implications from the research and overall recommendations. The information gathered needs to be sufficiently robust to present to relevant stakeholders. Analysing and communicating research findings is an essential part of the research process and the data needs organising, either in chronological or thematic order.

The findings need to present a clear statement of intent that supports the goals and objectives of the research plan. In qualitative research, the first part of this analysis involves reading through the sample question responses from the focus groups, or interviews, and trying to decipher what themes and issues emerge from the transcripts. The next stage is to analyse the findings in order to ascertain what this reveals about the issues raised and the audience or delegates' perceptions and attitudes. The presentation of qualitative findings primarily identifies the main themes and applies these to the data itself. Often, it helps to adopt a model or framework method here. The framework method, adapted from Brunt et al. (2017), has five key stages, which are:

1 Familiarisation
2 Identifying a thematic framework/model
3 Indexing the data
4 Charting the data
5 Mapping and interpretation.

For a quantitative approach, it is the numerical and statistical data that need analysis. Software applications such as 'NVivo' can also be used to support a qualitative approach and may provide the researcher with a more complete set of data to interpret than when working manually. This enables the researcher to provide a logical sequence in the presentation of the qualitative findings. This and other software packages have been designed to interpret qualitative data, and are generally flexible, versatile and allow the researcher to focus on the original aims and objectives of the study.

Histograms
an accurate representation of the distribution of numerical data

Quantitative data is generally presented using tables, line graphs, bar charts, pie charts or **histograms**, or a mixture of all these. Software applications, such as Microsoft Excel, are often used for data analysis. More bespoke packages, such as ATLAS.ti, SAS, Minitab, Stata, Statistica and SPSS, can also be used in cases where the researcher needs to analyse more complex data. These packages are primarily used to code the data and to ensure that all of the data is assigned the correct value.

Quantitative data can be categorical, where the answers to respondents' questions are classed into groups or categories, for instance festival planners, event suppliers, wedding planning. It can be ordinal, where data is arranged in a specific rank order, such as from highest to lowest, and cardinal, where data can be measured against a scale that has a specific numerical value, such as the amount of events taking place in a specific region per annum.

DATA COLLECTION METHODS

It is important when compiling survey questionnaires to hand to delegates or attendees at the end of an event to consider design considerations, such as:

- Formatting of questions
- Phrasing of questions
- Sequence of questions
- Categories of questions.

Areas to consider are whether the questions posed require a fixed response, or whether they will require the following types of response:

- *An alternative response* (the respondent is given a selection of alternatives to choose from)
- *Multiple choice* (the respondent needs to select ONE answer from a series of specified responses)
- *Multiple response* (the respondent needs to select all the applicable answers from a series of specified responses)
- *Likert scale* (a scale used to represent people's attitudes to a topic, by selecting the statement that best represents their viewpoint)
- *Rating scale* (using numbers to rate the audience, attendee or delegate response to all elements of the programme, e.g. where scoring 1 = highly satisfied and scoring 5 = extremely dissatisfied)
- *Stakeholder feedback forms.*

Different forms will need to be prepared in advance. These should be designed to be relevant to the various stakeholders and will ask for feedback under appropriate sections. These questions may be open or closed, as can be seen in the sample evaluation form online.

GO ONLINE

Find the downloadable sample customer evaluation form online at **study.sagepub.com/quick**

EVENT IMPACT RESEARCH AND ANALYSIS

OBJECTIVE
4
Event impact research and analysis

WHAT ARE EVENT IMPACTS?

As the industry has grown, it has emerged as an academic discipline with an increasing number of undergraduate and postgraduate courses now being offered. The study of event impacts has been driven by a need to examine both the positive and negative impacts of holding events. This is particularly the case with mega or hallmark events. Planners must now consider the impacts of an event throughout each stage of the planning process and beyond. This is also implicated in the decisions of funding organisations and policy makers in order to justify public spending and to evaluate how the communities can best be served by these events. The term 'legacy' is often used to assess how these events offer the best possible benefits for the communities that host them. Nowadays, for these reasons, the majority of bids for large-scale events and mega events, such as the Olympic Games, are often won due to the regeneration opportunities which hosting the event will offer. This may be one reason why so many academic papers and journals are concerned with the area of event impacts.

In an events context, there could be a variety of positive benefits and negative factors, generated as a result of an event taking place. They may be experienced by a variety of stakeholders, including participants, local businesses and the host community itself. An event will affect people in different ways, thus there may be inequity in the distribution of impacts and benefits. Typically, within this discipline, studies focus on one or more of the event impact areas shown in Table 4.4.

Political	• Use of the mega event to reposition the city and/or the country on the world stage • Legacy tends to be an afterthought rather than planned • Part of a process of change in global or regional politics.
Economic	• Injection of 'new money' into a destination • Can be a risk of poor assessment such as misrepresenting visitor numbers and expenditure and the additional costs to the community • Often difficult to predict 'Return on Investment' from event funding (Dwyer et al. 2006) • Difficult to measure without also considering the social and environmental impacts of the event.
Social	• Enhancement of national processes – health through to economic imperatives and national pride • New initiatives on coaching, sports medicine, sports science, skills development • Time for change and improvement – The Games as an exemplar in defined areas • The need for a coordinated approach among all agencies.
Cultural	• Development of social interactions • Traditions, customs, beliefs • Community values and interests of local residents.
Environmental	• Use of brown field (derelict) sites • Waste management and recycling • Sustainable suppliers • Improvements in bio-diversity • Use of the event venues/village as examples • High profile of the event can be used to good effect.
Physical infrastructure	• Transport infrastructure, roads and hospitals • Stadium construction and other new buildings • Landscape improvements • Housing developments.
Tourism/ destination image	• Increased visitation • Destination image enhancement • Reduce seasonality; and increased economic impact.

Urban regeneration	• Upgrading of facilities within a city • Creating better housing/reusing event facilities • Helping to finance local economic development of a region • Regeneration of city image • Community development • Destination repositioning.

TABLE 4.4 Event impacts

Generally, when considering an analysis of these hallmark, major or mega events, it is the economic analysis that is given priority. This may be because it appears easier to predict economic outcomes, rather than conduct painstaking and time-consuming research on the social, physical, environmental and tourism impacts of these one-off events, and their long-term impacts and legacy on a destination or community. Some authors, for example Hiller (1998) and Ritchie (2000), have attempted to put together an evaluation framework for these mega events. Ritchie's work on the Calgary Olympics (1984) is the earliest and most commonly cited example. In this he sets out the key frameworks used to analyse event impacts and guides readers through the range of impact-analysis topics.

Generally, the local and regional economy of the host nation is said to benefit greatly through the per-head spending of visitors and participants. The three main economic impacts that mega events have on the host nation are economic development, destination marketing and new expenditure within the destination. There is generally a reported increase of 20% in foreign trade and investment within the country hosting the Olympic Games. However, even for the Olympic Games, the biggest event of all, there is no guarantee of economic benefit. Due to the investment required to stage mega events on this scale, it could be the difference between economic growth and prosperity or potential bankruptcy for the host nation. It is worth noting that, in the post-event evaluation of mega events, benefits are usually exaggerated and costs are usually underestimated. Although such events can stimulate tourist flow in the short term, this may drop off relatively quickly and the wider implications for the host city or country are far more difficult to measure.

A number of authors argue that it is only the injection of '**new money**' into a destination that counts as economic impact. Furthermore, any revenue coming from tax-paying residents to fund the event are merely a reallocation of funds. These funds could have been used by governments to benefit the country in other ways; for example, investment in education, housing, health, welfare, law enforcement and security. Indeed, as already mentioned, economic impact as a stand-alone factor is very difficult to accurately measure and needs to be considered in conjunction with the social and environmental impacts, or **Triple Bottom Line**, of an event.

New money
money that would otherwise not have been generated

Triple Bottom Line
an accounting framework with three parts: social, environmental and financial

SOCIO-CULTURAL IMPACTS

Over the past few years, there has been a shift from economic focus to social and cultural fields. This has led to an examination of social impacts on host communities where events take place. Therefore, the socio-cultural implications also need to be considered in the post-evaluation phase of mega events. This involves measuring how the national communities and the local communities fared and how they benefitted in terms of social impacts, such as an increase in **community spirit** and **civic and national pride**. The 'community' is often seen as one of the key stakeholders of an events programme.

Community spirit
a feeling of involvement in and concern for one's local community

Civic and national pride
Feeling proud of your city or country

According to Richards and Palmer (2010: 165), 'Community is often a combination of individual local residents and others who inhabit, work in and otherwise have a commitment to the local area.' McLeod (2010) suggests that changes in the quality of life of local communities, participants and stakeholders within the host destination need to be included in the overall analysis of socio-cultural impacts, as is illustrated in Table 4.5.

Social benefits	Social costs
Community benefits	***Quality of life concerns***
Celebration of community	Increased crime/vandalism
Enhanced community identity	Unacceptable increase in vehicular/pedestrian traffic
Enhanced community image	Overcrowding
Increased community cohesion	Litter/ecological damage
Increased community well-being	Reduced privacy
Improved quality of community life	Disruption to noise levels
Individual pride through participation	Overuse of community facilities.
Shared ideas among community.	
Cultural/educational benefits	***Community resource concerns***
Experience of new activities	Increased disagreement within community
Participants learn new things	Event is 'all work and no play'
Event showcases new ideas	Excessive demand on community human resources
Development of cultural skills/talents	Highlights cultural stereotypes
Exposure to new cultural experiences	Unequal sharing of benefits of the event
Strengthening of community friendships	Weakened community identity
Lasting positive cultural impact	Excessive demand on community financial resources
Achievement of common community goals.	Potential sense of failure within community.

TABLE 4.5 Socio-cultural impacts of events
SOURCE: adapted from Delamere et al. 2001

What is a legacy?
Regardless of the actual form that a legacy may take, the idea underlying legacy creation is that it represents something of substance. (Ritchie 2000: 156)
'Legacy' applies to all that remains or is left over from the event as a positive inheritance, or as a challenge for future generations to deal with. (Getz 2012: 285)
Mega events are usually sold to the public on the basis of their many benefits, plus the creation of a permanent legacy, which acts as a catalyst for economic regeneration or some other social, environmental or political imperative of the destination. (Casey 2010: 366)
There is a tendency for hard legacy to become iconic and significant as monumental and tourist attractions. Soft legacy becomes hard as feel-good factors, governance structures and can-do attitude evolve to form productive social networks. (London East Research Institute 2007)

TABLE 4.6 What is a legacy?

The definitions of legacy put forward from various authors and sources in Table 4.6 give some indication of what this word means in real terms in the events industry. However, as Quinn (2013) states, there is a tendency to focus more on the positive benefits rather than the negative impacts that result from these mega events. Positive impacts tend to generate power and opportunities for community development and cohesion. However, in addition to these positive impacts, it is also important to measure the negative impacts that can result from such large-scale events.

Negative impacts might include the displacement of residents, higher property prices, crowding and congestion that alienate local people and populations. The event might cause possible disruption to traditional businesses. Non-sponsored outlets or small vendors operating in the area may experience financial loss as a result of the event. Other negative factors could be the potential displacement of residents or tourists, who may have been deterred from visiting the city or country at this time.

Displacement tends to occur when any household is forced to move from its normal residence by conditions affecting the dwelling or immediate surroundings, and which are not possible for them to control or prevent. The factors to measure here would be how the absence of those tourists, who deliberately choose not to visit at a time of increased rates and hype, affected the destination's overall tourism revenue. More negative social impacts should also be evaluated; for example, whether local residents felt inconvenienced by the increased traffic congestion during the event, particularly if they had no real interest in the event or the new sporting facilities in the first place. It is essential that event managers address the concerns of the local community and try to reduce these negative impacts.

Legacy is often thought of in terms of tangible benefits such as physical infrastructure or the new jobs that will be created; the following criteria list for the London 2012 Olympic Games, compiled by the International Olympic Committee (IOC), indicates what values can be involved in a legacy plan:

- To make the UK a world-class sporting nation, in terms of elite success, mass participation and school sport
- To transform the heart of East London

- To inspire a new generation of young people to take part in local volunteering, cultural and physical activity
- To make the Olympic Park a blueprint for sustainable living
- To demonstrate that the UK is a creative, inclusive and welcoming place to live in, to visit and for business.

The above mission aims comprise five different areas and are essentially concerned with the imprint that the 2012 Olympic Games will leave on the destination, the surrounding area and the host community, before, during and after the event. Although it may be possible to measure the short-term legacy in the years following on from a mega event, most of the longer term impacts may take many more years to accurately monitor.

COMPONENTS OF A LEGACY PROGRAMME

Following a mega or major event, an attempt should be made by all interested parties to predict the overall short-term and long-term impacts, particularly in relation to the overall legacy. It is possible to talk about legacy in terms of hard and soft benefits, with hard benefits being those that are largely direct and relatively easy to isolate and assess; for example, the impact on the labour market, business and infrastructure investment (Kearney, 2005). Soft benefits involve aspects such as destination image gains, improved civic pride, better health provision, and the acceleration of secondary investment. It is clear that whether hard or soft, all these benefits have a direct impact on the stakeholders within the host community or destination.

As already discussed in Chapter 3, there are many ways to measure the potential benefits and lasting legacy of a mega event, including analysis of tourism revenue, new jobs, better infrastructure or the revenue generated. A further factor of the overall legacy programme that needs to be measured in the post-evaluation phase and beyond is what use is made of the infrastructure and stadiums in the years following the mega events. It may be that the facilities provide future athletes with new improved '**state of the art**' facilities to train in, which benefits the local community. The facilities could also be used for other purposes, such as conference and concert venues and visitor attractions. In this instance, the value of this residual future income would also need to be included in the long-term evaluation. However, it may also be that these facilities are not being redeployed and in a few years are lying dormant and unused.

State of the art incorporating the newest ideas and features

For any robust research, inclusion of the impacts from a stakeholder perspective is necessary and the subsequent primary and secondary findings should be included in the case study or feasibility proposal compiled in the planning phase.

OBJECTIVE
5
Conducting and implementing a feasibility study

CONDUCTING AND IMPLEMENTING A FEASIBILITY STUDY

WHAT IS A FEASIBILITY STUDY?

A feasibility study analyses the viability of an idea and focuses on helping answer the essential question of 'should we proceed with the proposed project idea?' All activities of the study are directed towards helping answer this question. Feasibility studies can be used in many ways but focus primarily on proposed business ventures. The feasibility review assesses the required resources and the means to deliver the event and puts forward a business case on the financial viability of running the event, before committing to the bid. Determining early on that a business idea will not work saves time, money and heartache later, therefore companies and individuals with a business idea should always conduct a feasibility study to determine the viability of their idea before proceeding with the development of the business.

The complexity of a feasibility study and the required research will depend on the event size and scale. For example, the feasibility phase for a major or mega event will be far longer and require a more thorough assessment of the event in terms of the short- and long-term impacts on the local community. For these types of event, an existing infrastructure and purpose-built facilities are required before the event can proceed, and a far more detailed, strategic, long-term plan, which attempts to evaluate the longer term benefits or risks to the community, needs to be drawn up.

REASONS TO CONDUCT A FEASIBILITY STUDY

A feasibility study must be undertaken so that the owner or organiser can examine what tasks need to be carried out to achieve the event objectives. Sometimes this will provide opportunities to develop the event beyond what was first envisaged; at other times the study will discover factors that could seriously threaten its existence. The key purpose at this stage is to assess how feasible it is to put on the event. Conducting a feasibility study helps to narrow the scope of the project to identify and define two or three scenarios or alternatives or methods of achieving business success, thus narrowing the scope of the project by identifying the best business model, which is generally good business practice. The consultant conducting the feasibility study may work with the group to identify the 'best' alternative for their situation, and this becomes the basis for the finalised business plan, which tends to only include one alternative or model.

One of the most crucial aspects to research in the initial stages, are actual and possible sources of funding. A local-community committee is likely to go about researching this in a different way to a paid consultant, but, in either case, the process needs to be completed in a relatively short period of time.

Some events are limited by tradition and provenance so may always run at the same time of year, such as the Homebake festival in Sydney or The Dubai World Cup. These types of high-profile events are already well-established. They can either present an opportunity, to act as a trigger for another event, or present a threat, because they soak up all the interest within a region or community. Global event organisers running events during the FIFA World Cup in Russia 2018 should have been mindful of the fixture dates, especially when their country was in the frame to win a match. A direct clash could see attendances fall because so many people would be watching the football. Being aware of what else is happening is vital, and even the smallest event needs to take this factor into account.

REAL INSIGHT 4.3

THE IMPORTANCE OF BACKGROUND-EVENT RESEARCH WHEN PLANNING AN EVENT

A multinational computer-graphics company once planned to organise a series of seminars on advanced computer-generated graphics, kicking off in Paris, and to charge delegates, who would mostly be graphic designers, over €500 to attend. They anticipated that more than 200 delegates would attend and booked a suitable venue in Paris to accommodate them. However, unknown to them, a local governmental organisation was also planning to run a series of free seminars on that topic in the same region that week. As a result, hardly any delegates registered for the seminars on computer-graphic skills, which forced the company to eventually cancel the event, incurring large cancellation charges. The best an event organiser can do is to at least make sure they know what else is taking place and plan their event round it. This means taking into consideration the season, the day of the week, the time of the event and of course how long it will run for.

In summary, there are many reasons why it is important to conduct a feasibility study before embarking on a project, or even evaluating the merits and worth of planning the event. Some of these reasons are listed below:

- It gives focus to the project and outlines alternatives
- It narrows business alternatives
- It identifies reasons not to proceed
- It enhances the probability of success by addressing and mitigating factors that could affect the project early on
- It provides quality information for decision making
- It helps to increase investment in the company or organisation
- It provides documentation that the business venture was thoroughly investigated
- It helps in securing funding from lending institutions, sponsors and other sources
- New opportunities can surface through the investigative process.

The feasibility study is a critical step in the business assessment process. If properly conducted, it may be the best investment a company can ever make.

DID YOU KNOW?

The wise man looks ahead. (Proverb)

Failure to plan, is planning to fail. (Watt and Stayte 2004)

Investigation, research and decision making will ultimately lead to the development of detailed plans for the successful delivery of an event. (Conway 2009)

WHAT TO INCLUDE IN THE FEASIBILITY PROPOSAL

The feasibility proposal should contain the following items in no particular order, although the executive summary should appear at the beginning of the document. It may be necessary to include more specific detail, depending on the complexity of the project and study required.

- Executive summary/mission statement
- Contents page/lists of tables and figures
- Synopsis/understanding of the brief
- Company credentials/background details
- Existing client profile/testimonials
- Operational and logistical details
- Critical path analysis/timescales
- Financial projections/management costs/projected savings
- Risk management plan and SWOT analysis
- Recommendations
- Business licences/registrations, contract terms, and terms and conditions
- Appendices, acknowledgements and report references.

EXECUTIVE SUMMARY OR MISSION STATEMENT

An executive summary or mission statement describes in broadest terms the task that the organisation has set itself. Such statements seek to define an event's purpose and the overall operating philosophy or values of the organisation conducting it. It serves a similar purpose to the abstract in an educational dissertation, should always appear at the beginning of the document and needs to be summarised to be succinct and to the point, as it may well be the only part of the proposal that is actually read.

Once established, the mission statement acts as the basis upon which goals and objectives can be set and future strategies established. For that reason, a coherent mission statement can be an invaluable tool for establishing common direction within a team and promoting unity among its members. This study should be impartial, so if the consultant or agency does not think that the project is viable, they should say so within the rationale. If the research conducted indicates that support from participants, officials, helpers, sponsors and other interested parties is not forthcoming, then the consultant or agency should state that there may be considerable doubt about the feasibility to stage this event at this time. An executive summary or mission statement might include the following:

- A one- to two-page summary. Summaries should appear within a paragraph on each of the report sections

- A summary of recommendations
- Recognition of the benefits, both financial and non-financial
- Suggested next stages.

CONTENTS PAGE/LISTS OF TABLES AND FIGURES

This should show the page numbers of each major section. These can be generated by software, such as Microsoft Word, which will allow the writer to update the report automatically. Where tables or figures have been included in the report, they should be titled and listed consecutively in the contents page.

SYNOPSIS/UNDERSTANDING OF THE BRIEF

It is a good idea to reiterate the brief and present your understanding of what is required in the feasibility study, to ensure both client and agency are in agreement about what will be included in the feasibility proposal. Additionally, the consultant or agency should confirm how many days and what costs will be incurred to research the document.

COMPANY CREDENTIALS/BACKGROUND DETAILS

This section of the document should provide the agency an opportunity to sell itself, highlighting the specific skills that exist within the team and any core competencies to deliver the project. Profiles and biographies of the organisation team and evidence of expertise in this area should be included. Within this section, further background detail could include details on the number of personnel required, from event-director level to volunteers, drawing up a plan to assess if the organisation currently has sufficient numbers of trained staff to deliver all tasks. To a certain extent, inexperienced event staff can be trained, provided there is enough time.

Aside from manpower, this section might discuss whether there is additional support for the project. Complex events often need support from outside the hosting organisation if they are to be successful. Evidence of existing support can be accrued through setting up organisational meetings and one-to-one consultations with relevant bodies and parties. This background research will gauge the amount of support and interest in the event and the amount of potential income that may come from sponsorship and funding.

EXISTING CLIENT PROFILE/TESTIMONIALS

Proven expertise can be an important factor in choosing an organisation or agency to partner with, so it is a good idea to include details of similar projects worked on and any positive testimonials, or contact details from previous satisfied customers or client organisations. This can reassure the event owner or organisation that they are outsourcing to experts in the field and is especially important in the competitive events environment.

OPERATIONAL AND LOGISTICAL DETAILS

Part of an event-feasibility rationale must consider the operational and logistical aspects for the event or events scheduled. Having a suitable venue that is fit for purpose is essential, as the venue should be equal to or better than the standard expected by all participants and stakeholders. The lack of a suitable venue can have a major effect on the overall feasibility.

Additionally, details and availability of other facilities, such as exhibition stands, marquees and portable toilets, need to be included in the feasibility study. It is the responsibility of the organiser to provide details and costs for these and other types of technical equipment, such as projectors, lighting and timing equipment, including whether they can be bought, borrowed or hired. There may be a feasibility problem if insufficient or substandard equipment cannot be locally sourced, as it may be too difficult or expensive to transport equipment from other places. All other information concerning the operational and logistical details of the event or project should be thoroughly investigated and included in this section of the proposal.

CRITICAL PATH ANALYSIS/TIMESCALES

Some events can only take place at certain times of the year and **seasonal adjustments** should be discussed in the rationale. The sheer number of tasks to be performed explains the need to draw up a realistic time frame for completing these tasks in order to plan and host the event. This time frame or schedule is often called a **critical path** and will have a direct bearing on the feasibility of staging the event.

Within the critical-path analysis, various tasks should be prepared according to the requirements and all milestone activities prioritised according to importance. A **Gantt chart**, or other task-scheduling system, such as a computerised project-management package or project-planning software, can be used to complete this schedule and show the timescale over the whole project. By clustering tasks together and plotting them on a horizontal and vertical chart, or spreadsheet, the interdependence of these tasks can be clearly seen at a glance. These tools facilitate a robust analysis of the nature of the task, work responsibilities, the product and resource requirements, and the recommended deadlines for completion. The most important factors to consider in this analysis are:

Seasonal adjustments a statistical technique designed to even out periodic swings in statistics or movements in supply and demand related to changing seasons

Critical path the sequence of activities in a project plan which must be completed on time for the project to complete on its due date

Gantt chart provides a graphical illustration of a schedule that helps to plan, coordinate and track specific tasks in a project

- Booking a suitable venue
- Giving participants an appropriate length of notice
- Daylight hours available
- Weather, especially for an outdoors event
- Conflict of interest with other events
- Community consultation
- Any design, construction, site planning and development
- Contingency plans for unexpected eventualities or the implications of delays.

The analysis should also consider what trade-offs and compromises will have to be made and whether the proposed timelines are realistic for all key suppliers and stakeholders to deliver products and services. Regardless of the venue type, all venues should be booked months in advance. This is particularly true in the case of the largest or most popular venues, which may be booked out more than one year in advance. It is also essential to allow sufficient time to promote the event and ensure that delegates or guests are able to attend. If insufficient notice is given, they may be unable to book air flights or arrange for leave, due to other engagements. For this reason, there needs to be sufficient planning time to enable the event date to be diarised.

Contingency plans plans designed to take account of unforeseen events or circumstances

For mega events, such as the Olympic Games and the FIFA World Cup, the time needed to liaise with all relevant stakeholders and committees and put together the relevant infrastructure is significantly longer, which is why the bidding phase takes place five to seven years before the mega event is scheduled to take place. When preparing a critical analysis of large sporting or mega events, the timeline needs to factor in opportunities to test the proposed events in the facilities beforehand, to monitor running times for a timely delivery of the event. **Contingency plans** for unexpected situations and the cost implications of overrunning should be included, so that local authorities and other groups involved in site planning and development have a clear understanding of their own roles and responsibilities in the process and appreciate that any delay on their part could have implications for the wider schedule plan, as the case study below demonstrates.

REAL INSIGHT 4.4

UNFORESEEN CHALLENGES WITH THE STADIUM BUILDS FOR THE 2018 RUSSIA FIFA WORLD CUP

Completion of the stadiums used for the 2018 Russia FIFA World Cup went mostly according to plan and were completed in good time for the commencement of the tournament. However, as with many projects of this size and scale, there were a few challenges and setbacks for the host destination, which impacted the original plans to complete the necessary infrastructure work. The biggest problem was with the Samara Stadium, which staged one of the semi-final matches. This stadium was riddled with delays, resulting in soaring costs by 2015, when it was reported to be more than £40 million over the original budget.

A new construction company was appointed in 2016, who were forced to tweak the original plans, downscaling the dome, in order to cut costs and stop the project falling further behind schedule. A small fire in August 2017 added to the list of problems. Eventually, the stadium was signed off on 27 April, which was only one day before the first test match between local side Keylia Sovetov and Fakel Voronezh. At the Mordovia Arena, construction was also delayed when there was a suspension of work from 2013 to 2015. The Saint Petersburg Stadium also ran into building problems, which included the discovery of a seriously leaky roof, allegedly caused from damage by cormorants, and a pitch that initially vibrated several times more than the permissible limit.

Concerns were also raised about the levels of formaldehyde and ammonia used in some of the materials within the internal structure. Construction was also delayed at the Ekaterinburg Arena, where it took time to settle plans to retain the old facade, a renowned work of art. Some expensive reconfigurations were needed at this stadium, notably the removal of the roof, in order to comply with FIFA regulations. Contingency plans were also adopted for the Rostov Arena, which was initially designed in the shape of a teardrop, with a unique look and feel. However, spiralling costs meant that this projection had to be downsized, as it was not possible to deliver it in its original form. This meant that final completion was more than seven months after the original proposed date.

Ironically, despite paring down the plans, reports indicate that the final cost of the build was only 15% less than the original and far more lavish design. The Kaliningrad Stadium also ran into financial problems. Plans to include a retractable roof and space for a larger capacity audience had to be shelved when the design company went bankrupt. A revised simplified project was put forward and completed by September 2015.

Concerns about some of the stadiums' location on previous wetlands were increased when, at the Volgograd Stadium, one of the concrete beams that supported the upper roof appeared to have a large crack. Images were instantly circulated via social media and a statement was quickly issued to assure the public of its safety.

Small fires tended to be one of the most persistent challenges, with small fires breaking out in many of the stadiums during the build process. In October 2015 a fire broke out in the Luzhniki Stadium, which eventually staged the final between Germany and Argentina, causing much alarm. At the Nizhny Novgorod Stadium, plumes of black smoke were also seen rising from the site in October 2017, and at the Volgograd Stadium a small fire broke out at the site in June 2017 after a welding accident. Moreover, after an unexploded bomb, dating back to the Battle of Stalingrad, was found and detonated at this site in 2014, the whole site had to be thoroughly combed in case other unexploded bombs were located.

Fortunately, none of these small fires or incidents caused serious delay or injury to those working on the project and, despite having to undertake many revisions and contingencies, Russia managed to deliver an impressive and memorable World Cup.

FINANCIAL PROJECTIONS

During the feasibility process, the cost of hosting the event, opening a new venue, or other objectives need to be considered. It can be difficult to predict the final outcome, but the cost of all resources needs to be meticulously considered, including the cost of infrastructure and training of the potential paid and unpaid workforce needed to work on the event. Being able to identify sources of revenue and capital will enhance profit maximisation, as well as enabling improvements to possible financial and resourcing approaches.

The financial section of the feasibility proposal can be worked out by creating models in a Microsoft Excel spreadsheet. This entails developing a budget where all expected revenues and all known costs are listed. It is most important that would-be organisers exercise a high degree of realism when estimating possible revenues and note any assumptions in commentary boxes or costing notes. It is not generally a good idea to make assumptions about the amount of market demand, as the financial section of the feasibility study needs to be able to predict the financial outcome of staging an event to a reasonable degree of accuracy. The following four typical situations could spell financial disaster:

- A major source of income, e.g. sponsorship, turns out to be significantly less than planned or a funding submission to government fails
- An unexpected cost arises, e.g. venue costs escalate, but it is too late to cancel or change the event
- Errors are made in calculating the original costs, or extra equipment has to be bought at the last moment
- Fewer delegates or guests than expected attend the event.

RISK MANAGEMENT PLAN AND SWOT ANALYSIS

Events such as major sporting or mega events tend to focus on financial loss or loss of reputation, negative public image, loss as a result of physical damage, injuries, death, property damage and litigation and lawsuits. Often, the larger the project or the size of the event, the greater the potential risk. In terms of measuring risk, the main criterion is to evaluate the potential risks that might negatively impact an organisation's ability to successfully deliver the original mission or objectives in the feasibility stage.

As previously discussed, the owners need to feel confident that the event will not result in financial loss and that the event will be organised to the satisfaction of all stakeholders. In order to ensure this, the feasibility study should contain a detailed plan using fault diagrams and work-breakdown structures, to determine the possible causes of potential risk effects. The risk assessment should outline how to minimise the identified risks as much as possible, and outline the contingency arrangements to ensure the safety and well-being of all participants and to ensure the reputation of all parties. The feasibility analysis should also aim to identify risks such as:

- The length of time needed to organise the event
- The date of the event and whether it clashes with others taking place in the same area
- The budget and whether the event can run without incurring a financial loss
- The amount of buy-in and support from relevant stakeholders, e.g. the local community, government and parent bodies

- Additional resources such as venue facilities, suitable infrastructure, equipment and manpower
- Environmental concerns and potential damage to the surrounding area
- Legal considerations such as permits, permissions and appropriate licences.

By association, the risk implicates not only the organising committee for an event, but all internal and external stakeholders. For this reason, during the feasibility stage, event managers need to assess not only the risk to the host organisation or nation, but also the wider implications of the potential PESTEL risks for the environment in which it operates. The environmental risks to the host destination may include traffic congestion and parking problems, noise pollution, water and waste pollution, and possible danger to flora and fauna. All these need to be considered and the long-term impacts of the event evaluated in the feasibility stage.

ASSESSMENT OF RISK EXPOSURE

Major and mega events have the potential to generate great internal and external risks, due to their size and scale. Committing to such a huge investment for such a short-lived event is a risky strategy, as it may turn out to be a great success or a complete disaster. As previously stated, events of this magnitude could mean the difference between making a healthy profit, even after extensive regeneration of infrastructure, and the potential risk of the city going bankrupt.

For this reason, organisers for mega and major events need to identify and predict all the potential risks well in advance of the bidding stage. They also need to assess, as accurately as possible, how these events will impact the nation and what both the potential short- and long-term risks might be. By association, the risk implicates not only the organising committee, but also all internal and external stakeholders. These are all areas that should be evaluated in the post-event phase.

During the feasibility stage, Allen et al. (2011) suggest alleviating possible risk or problems by working backwards, through the use of fault diagrams and work-breakdown structures, in order to determine the possible causes of potential risk effects. The risks should be managed so that the benefits are optimised and the negative impacts are minimalised, to ensure the overall impact is positive. The risks associated with larger events tend to focus on financial loss. Glaessner (2006: 154) defines risk, as 'the product of magnitude of damage and the probability of occurrence'. In terms of assessing risk, there are many factors to consider in the feasibility stage, such as loss of reputation, negative public image, loss as a result of physical damage, injuries, death, property damage, and litigation and lawsuits.

What is a SWOT analysis?

SWOT is an acronym that stands for Strengths, Weaknesses, Opportunities and Threats.

It is essentially a process for evaluating the present condition or situation of an organisation in terms of external factors and the environment, and enables the event organiser to see at a glance how feasible the event is going to be, and to implicate the areas that need more focus and attention. It is important for all organisations to make use of their strengths, improve their weaknesses, recognise opportunities when they arise and eliminate threats. Performed on a regular basis, the SWOT analysis is an excellent basis for good decision making.

A successful SWOT analysis requires considerable energy and commitment. Essentially, it is a brainstorming activity, where questions are posed to provoke team ideas and information that need to be quickly captured and recorded clearly and concisely. Ideally it is not an activity undertaken by just one or two people in the organisation. It is best achieved when there is a wide diversity of opinion from a cross-section of organisation personnel and other stakeholders.

However, if the SWOT analysis team is too large, then the processes can be too slow, and opinion divided. A team of eight to ten persons is an optimal number. It can be beneficial, however, for the event management company or organisation to communicate the findings to a wider audience after it has taken place. For best results, a SWOT meeting should not last more than four hours, and careful time management is therefore essential to ensure that all areas of the SWOT analysis are equally covered.

Table 4.7 provides a hypothetical result of a SWOT analysis carried out by an event organisation that is evaluating the employment of volunteers at a forthcoming event.

Strengths	• The event has a lot of volunteers • The volunteers are happy to work on the event without payment.
Weaknesses	• The volunteers are unskilled, with limited skills in planning events • They are not local and will need to travel to the event venue, thus incurring costs.
Opportunities	• The volunteers may be able to offer new and innovative ideas • They may be able to work in conjunction with a sponsor.
Threats	• There might be competing events on the same day, so poor volunteer attendance • The volunteers might not be prepared to be out of pocket by travelling to the venue • They may need training in health and safety and event procedures.

TABLE 4.7 A SWOT analysis assessing risks and benefits

Event managers may prefer to focus on risks and benefits only in the feasibility study or present a cost-benefit analysis.

RECOMMENDATIONS SECTION

This is an important part of the feasibility study, which allows the consultant or agency to make evidence-based recommendations on the viability of the event or project, having conducted thorough research. This should be presented in a concise way and be summarised whenever possible by the use of bullet points, either at the end of each section of the study, or at the end of the document. The following items should be included in the recommendations:

- Size/capacities
- Branding and sponsorship opportunities
- Identification of primary target markets
- Pricing and funding structures, including consideration given to outsourcing elements
- Sales and marketing
- Risks, benefits or unknown factors
- Any interdependencies or joint ventures for both management or marketing
- Next steps for proceeding with the project and timescales involved.

From the outcomes of the business analysis conducted on the feasibility of using the Certaldo Town Hall, Italy for Civic Town Hall wedding ceremonies and receptions, there are a number of key recommendations that can be brought forward in regard to the capital project development of the Town Hall and its continued development:

- More staff should be hired to market and promote the venue, in conjunction with the local tourist office
- Contacts should be made with local suppliers, e.g. florists, musicians, prop and decoration companies, to form joint business ventures
- Introduce a minibus shuttle partnership to Florence and Siena train station to take guests to the funicular entrance
- Venue should negotiate with funicular company for better rates for transporting wedding guests
- Horse-drawn carriages should be sourced to transport the bride and groom to the Palazzo Pretorio, as no cars allowed in the old town
- Air conditioning should be available in the indoor room, for guests who prefer to have the ceremony indoors.

TABLE 4.8 Sample recommendations section

BUSINESS LICENCES/REGISTRATIONS, CONTRACT TERMS, AND TERMS AND CONDITIONS

Within this section, any additional licences, agreements, accreditation and permissions should be detailed in full. The agency or team responsible for submitting the feasibility study should ensure that the content conforms to the legal requirements of the event owner, in particular:

- Licence requirements
- Use of symbols
- Government permissions
- Contractual agreements with partners, sponsors and suppliers
- Agency accreditation
- VAT, rates of exchange, and tax implications
- Customs and immigration
- Company terms and conditions.

APPENDICES, ACKNOWLEDGEMENTS AND REPORT REFERENCES

Any acknowledgements and appendices generally appear at the end of the feasibility proposal, together with a list of references, sources and useful websites referred to in the body of the report. It is normal practice to get permission from the individuals, companies and organisations to be mentioned in the acknowledgement section. The appendices should be presented at the back of the report and labelled in the order they appear in the report. Within the report, the appendices should be referred to as 'see Appendix 12', and so on.

The report references should include all references cited in the report, and be presented in alphabetical order, either using the Harvard referencing system or footnotes.

PREPARING THE FEASIBILITY PROPOSAL

It is essential that the report document is prepared in time to allow for printing and collation. A complete project plan with timelines will help to ensure the bid is delivered on time. In most cases, the feasibility report is submitted to a panel or board rather than one person in the organisation. The supporting presentation needs to be highly professional, rehearsed and supported with multimedia.

CHAPTER SUMMARY

CHAPTER SUMMARY QUESTIONS

1 What is the difference between primary and secondary research?
2 What does competitive intelligence mean in market research?
3 What does the acronym PESTEL stand for?
4 Who might be the stakeholders in a mega event like the Olympic Games?
5 What event impact is often given priority and why?
6 Why is it important to include an executive summary at the start of any feasibility study?

DISCUSSION POINTS

- How have new GDPR regulations impacted the way you can contact the public to conduct research?

- Do you think it is possible to conduct market research based only on secondary data rather than primary data?
- Is it right that mega events like the Olympic Games sometimes have a political undertone, and is there any way this could be avoided?

ACTIVITIES

- Think of an event you would like to organise and randomly pick a time and date. Now do some research and find out about other local or competing events on the time and date you have chosen. Is the time of your event still feasible?
- Prepare a SWOT analysis for using a specific venue for an event.
- Put together a brief statement defining what you think the word 'legacy' means in the events industry, what types of event it applies to and whether politicians just use the word 'legacy' to make people feel better about the money spent.

REFERENCES

Allen, J., O'Toole, W., Harris, R. and McDonnell, I. (2011) *Festival and Special Event Management*, 5th edn. Brisbane, QLD: Wiley & Sons.

Brunt, P., Horner, S. and Semley, N. (2017) *Research Methods in Tourism, Hospitality and Events Management*. London: Sage.

Casey, D. (2010) 'The impact of mega events', in D. Tassiopoulos (ed.), *Event Management*, 3rd edn. South Africa: JUTA.

Conway, D. (2009) *The Event Manager's Bible*, 3rd edn. Oxon: HowtoBooks.

Delamere, T.A., Wankel, L.M. and Hinch, T.D. (2001) 'Development of a scale to measure resident attitudes towards the social impacts of community festivals', *Event Management*, 7(1): 11–24.

Dwyer, L., Forsyth, P. and Spurr, R. (2006) 'Economic evaluation of special events', in L. Dwyer and P. Forsyth (eds), *International Handbook on the Economics of Tourism*. Cheltenham: Edward Elgar. pp. 316–55.

Getz, D. (2012) *Event Studies: Theory, Research and Policy for Planned Events*. Oxford: Butterworth-Heinemann.

Glaessner, D. (2006) *Crisis Management in the Tourism Industry*. Oxford: Butterworth-Heinemann.

Hiller, H.H. (1998) 'Assessing the impact of mega-events: a linkage model', *Current Issues in Tourism*, 1(1): 47–57.

Kearney, A.T. (2005) *Building a Legacy*. Chicago: AT Kearney.

London East Research Institute (2007) Assessing the legacy of the Olympic Games and Paralympic Games [online]. Available at: www.london.gov.uk/about-us/london-assembly/

london-assembly-publications/lasting-legacy-london-assessing-legacy-olympic (accessed 4 August 2018).

McLeod, S.A. (2010) Concrete operational stage [online]. Available at: www.simplypsychology.org/concrete-operational.html (accessed 2 November 2019).

Porter, M.E. (1989) 'How competitive forces shape strategy', in D. Asch and C. Bowman (eds), *Readings in Strategic Management.* Basingstoke and London: Macmillan.

Quinn, B. (2013) *Key Concepts in Event Management.* London: SAGE.

Richards, G. and Palmer, R. (2010) *Eventful Cities: Cultural Management and Urban Revitalisation.* Oxford: Butterworth-Heinemann.

Ritchie, J.R.B. (1984) 'Assessing the impact of hallmark events: Conceptual and research issues', *Journal of Travel Research*, 22(1): 2–11.

Ritchie, J.R.B. (2000) 'Turning 16 days into 16 years through Olympic legacies', *Event Management*, 6(2): 155–65.

Solomon, M.R., Marshall, G.W., Stuart, E.W., Mitchell, V., Barnes, B. and Mitchell, V-W. (2009) *Marketing: Real People, Real Choices*, 5th edn. London: Prentice Hall.

Watt, D.C. and Stayte, S. (2004) *Events: From Start to Finish.* Reading: ILAM.

5

EVENT CONCEPTION AND BIDDING

CHAPTER OVERVIEW

This chapter will examine the bidding process for a range of global events from mega sporting to smaller private and corporate events and evaluate who commissions tenders and some of the reasons why. The chapter will also discuss the process of coming up with a creative concept and brand image for events. Additionally, it will discuss the various stakeholders involved in the bidding process and the documentation and delivery of a bid. It will also analyse the competitive aspects of bidding, the involvement of the host city in major bids and the role of procurement in corporate events. It will also examine the increased reports of corruption and bribery in global bidding and the need for increased transparency in this area, particularly for large sporting events.

CHAPTER OBJECTIVES

After reading this chapter, you will be able to identify and understand:

OBJECTIVE 1
The bid process within various sectors of the event industry

OBJECTIVE 2
Destination branding and factors that influence destination choice

OBJECTIVE 3
The selection criteria of a Request for Information (RFI) and Request for Proposal (RFP)

OBJECTIVE 4
Proposal writing and delivering effective pitches

OBJECTIVE 5
Transparency and corruption in bidding

Meet SIMON KING-CLINE

Simon King-Cline

Agency Event Creative Director

Simon King-Cline is a serial entrepreneur, having founded Aspect Ltd, Dell London and Theupside.biz. A regular entrepreneurship speaker, he is also an Honorary Visiting Fellow and 'Business Mentor in Residence' in the Faculty of Management at the Cass London Business School. In this role, he advises a number of start-ups and young businesses on a consultancy basis.

'Aspect Ltd' inspires business performance through the delivery of extraordinary live events, experiences and multi-channel communications, and for over 23 years has turned over in excess of £100 million. 'Dell London' is a successful property and lettings business.

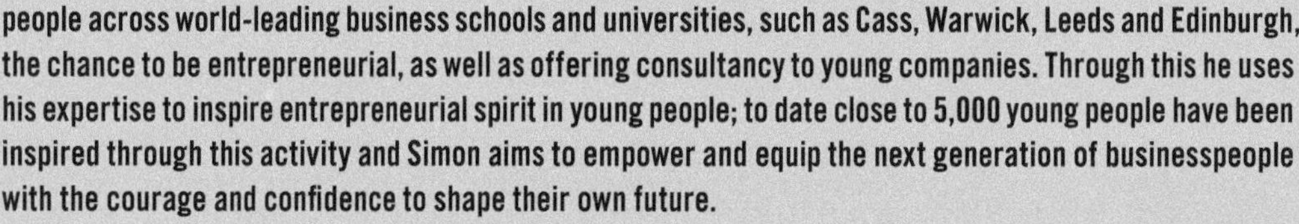

This success has granted Simon the freedom to broaden his passions. His most recent business is Theupside.biz, which works to inspire and give young people across world-leading business schools and universities, such as Cass, Warwick, Leeds and Edinburgh, the chance to be entrepreneurial, as well as offering consultancy to young companies. Through this he uses his expertise to inspire entrepreneurial spirit in young people; to date close to 5,000 young people have been inspired through this activity and Simon aims to empower and equip the next generation of businesspeople with the courage and confidence to shape their own future.

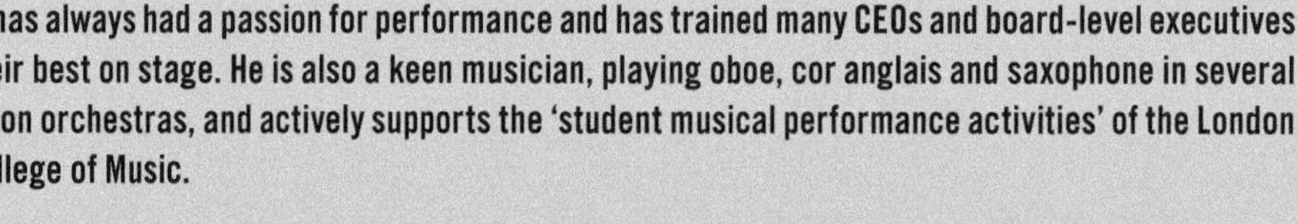

Simon has always had a passion for performance and has trained many CEOs and board-level executives to be at their best on stage. He is also a keen musician, playing oboe, cor anglais and saxophone in several London orchestras, and actively supports the 'student musical performance activities' of the London College of Music.

REAL EVENT CHALLENGE

My agency was once invited to pitch for an event overseas, where the client brief clearly stated they wanted a James Bond theme. This was the first time we'd been asked to pitch by this client. We knew it was a good pitch list, made up of four other leading creative agencies, and that we were probably number five on that list, as we did not have a previous working relationship with them. Our initial dilemma was whether or not to actually respond to the brief, as we did not want to waste time, money and effort on

MOST INTERESTING CLIENT BRIEF?

I get most excited about the launch of large communications projects, such as the repositioning of an organisation's brand or strategy; to reach out to all their stakeholders on a global basis. Those projects open the door to a relationship you can build and expand in the future.

BIGGEST EVENT SETBACK?

Recently for a large event for 500–600 delegates, the venue was flooded literally the day before the event. In a day we managed to find and reorganise the whole event to a new venue.

FAVOURITE MUSICIAN?

Albrecht Mayer – an oboist that not many readers will have heard of, but is my favourite music to listen to.

MOTTO FOR LIFE?

If you're in it, you should be in it to win it.

FAVOURITE VENUE FOR EVENTS?

Big theatre venues like the Albert Hall or Royal Festival Hall

the creative pitch and bid documentation if we were just making up numbers. Having done the qualification on the brief, however, we thought the event was just the sort of size that might be worth going for and that we wanted to establish a longer term working partnership with this particular client. Our challenge was to find a way to stand out from the rest of the competition.

PRACTITIONER VIEWPOINT

Sara Cant, CEO at Talking Point Inc., Greater Chicago Area, USA

It is interesting to see how Aspect challenged the client's brief in this way. In our Chicago-based agency, we sometimes make the decision not to pitch, depending on our time commitments and the other events we are working on. Recently I was filling in some forms issued by the procurement division for a new client. There was a series of three online forms to complete, but they were generic vendor forms, so didn't really make much sense for an events service provider. It would have taken me about a week to complete the forms, and this was just the initial RFI stage, before even reaching the shortlist, so I decided to decline.

There is actually only so much business we can physically do, and as a small company we can't justify having someone just working on developing new business all the time. We made a decision not to diversify, as we don't want to waste time and money pitching for business we might not win. Instead we prefer to work with existing clients in sectors we understand and on repeat business, which mostly comes from the IT and financial sectors, where we have over 22 years' experience.

We would not tender for pharmaceutical events, for example, as we have no previous experience in that sector, so know we would never make the shortlist, let alone the final cut. Mostly we gain work through referrals and from past clients who have moved companies and then contact us. Through the production company we use, we have also recently picked up business in real estate and this also led us to other clients in the same sector.

I was surprised when Visa contacted us, as we had been working with Diners club for some time on their events. I thought there might be a conflict of interest, but Visa were very happy to use us, because we completely understood their business and the sector they operated in. Being able to decide which clients and projects to accept or refuse is a pretty nice stage to be at.

ACADEMIC VIEWPOINT

Kevin Chambers, Course Leader, Festivals & Events at Solent University

Every brief needs to be interrogated. Find the space in the brief and understand the aims and objectives that the client has defined, but also those that they have merely hinted at. Once you understand your prospective audience, you can start the design stage. On our courses we teach experience design and those that excel at designing creative solutions to client briefs emerge as experience architects. More often than not, they can find space within the brief that stimulates a creative response and leads to a design solution that surpasses the expectations of the client. Forging creative solutions to complex problems requires resources, a supportive environment and inspiration. After engaging with a design process, potential solutions emerge. Those processes typically include problem recognition, goal setting, idea generation and evaluation. A successful process enables you to redefine problems, encourages critical analysis and stimulates divergent thinking. You need to explore your imagination and create a tolerance for mistakes while evaluating the suitability of your proposed solutions against risk. Outsiders often deliver the most creative solutions in a pitch situation. They are free from the constraints of what has gone before, happy to question any direction and have little to lose by challenging the client expectations. The ultimate creative process is to conceive a unique experience that stands out from the crowd.

REAL EVENT OUTCOME

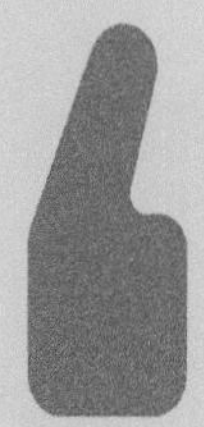

After an initial brainstorm with the creative team, we decided we needed to come up with a creative solution that would differentiate our agency from the other four agencies pitching in the competitive tender. This would involve taking a risk to be bold and brave and ultimately challenging the RFP issued by the client, in order to increase our chance of winning the business. So, we pitched a totally different creative solution and theme, which had nothing to do with James Bond. It was a risky strategy, as we knew the other four agencies would respond to the set brief, but we had nothing to lose. In the end we won the pitch because the client loved it that we had challenged the brief and had scored high on the originality and memorability factors. They felt that as a creative agency we had shown real creativity in coming up with a better concept for the event that would engage the audience in a more innovative, constructive and productive way. We proved our creativity at that event and established a long-term working partnership with that client. So, in this case the risky strategy we adopted paid off.

THE BID PROCESS WITHIN VARIOUS SECTORS OF THE EVENT INDUSTRY

OBJECTIVE
1
The bid process within various sectors of the event industry

THE BID PROCESS

It is normal practice for any representative body responsible for selecting an agency, to ask each competing organisation to supply a formal written offer to undertake work or provide services for a stated price. This information may take the form of an event proposal, containing full details of how the event will be organised and staged. The process of supplying a proposal is often referred to as the 'bid process'. When organisations are required to enter into a formal bid process, the first task they normally need to complete is the bid documentation, to submit to the client or event owner by the required date. Second, a meeting or formal presentation is usually set up to the selecting client or authority, which will draw out the key points or highlights of the proposal and answer any questions that may arise.

The main purpose of the bid process is to:

- Identify in an accurate and reliable fashion, the contractor likely to deliver the best value and achieve the best results
- Demonstrate that the bidding organisation has the capability and resources to stage the event
- Provide additional reasons as to why the bidding organisation should be selected over other bidders.

It is often the case that more than one agency will be contacted to deliver their concept and discuss how they propose to manage an event. This is normally a healthy situation, which eradicates complacency and overpricing on behalf of the incumbent agency. Furthermore, it generally leads to each bidding organisation striving to be as creative and innovative as possible, in order to demonstrate they have the credentials to deliver the best event. The client or organisation usually makes the decision as to which agency will be appointed. In the case of sporting events, the final decision might be made by the local or national sports governing body. For example, in the case of a world championship, the decision as to which nation will host, usually comes from the World Federation, who are comprised of elected officials drawn from the member nations.

TYPES OF TENDER

- *Public Sector*: this refers to central government, regional and local authorities. All these authorities are subject to directives implemented on a national level through regulations and other forms of legislation, e.g. procurement rules.
- *Private Sector*: this refers to corporate companies and small to medium-sized companies (SMEs).

In the tourism, events and hospitality sector, public sector bids have increasingly become a part of strategic and policy initiatives by destinations to attract new business.

These public bids follow standard procurement rules, and are intended to secure open and fair competition, transparent and auditable contracting procedures and equal access to contract opportunities for all suppliers. The bidding process is generally managed through portals that enable potential contractors and suppliers to download pre-qualification material, tender documentation and other relevant files, such as copies of company policies.

Private sector clients tend to be less prescriptive about the format and structure of bids, giving contractors more scope to provide an individual approach, tailored to the requirements of the contract. The process is usually conducted through meetings, presentations, and by submitting hard copies of documents and email correspondence. The process is normally as follows:

- Set up organising committee
- Review available resources/budget
- Determine possible event dates
- Research potential venues
- Contact suppliers
- Set a draft budget
- Develop a bid proposal

FIGURE 5.1 The bid process

There are many factors to consider when deciding to host for a public sector event, whereas the decision process to tender for a private event is far less complex and variable, as detailed further on in this chapter in Figure 5.3, bidding analysis.

FACTORS TO CONSIDER WHEN DECIDING ON WHETHER TO BID FOR A PUBLIC SECTOR EVENT

- Return on Investment (ROI)
- Return on Objectives (ROO)
- The geographical, political and historical background of the event
- Social, economic and environmental impacts
- Urban regeneration
- Environmental development
- Destination image
- The overall cost
- National opinion
- Potential displacement of funds, grants, taxpayers' money.

A major sporting event will typically involve some type of funding or public subsidy. The actual amount spent is invariably higher than the original projected spend, as demonstrated by the 2014 FIFA World Cup in Brazil. The huge cost of US$15 billion to stage it was alleged to be the most expensive in FIFA history and overran the original budget by at least 75%. The cost of the 2016 Rio Summer Olympic Games was estimated at US$4.58 billion, but final costs also overran by about 50% (Varano 2017). That type of large expenditure has become hard to justify in times of austerity and cuts, which may be one of the reasons that recent years have seen withdrawals from the bidding process by Boston, Budapest, Davos, Hamburg, Krakow, Munich, Rome and Stockholm.

REAL INSIGHT 5.1

CWT MEETINGS AND EVENTS' SUCCESSFUL BID TO TENDER FOR THE ISU 2018 WORLD FIGURE CHAMPIONSHIPS

CWT Meetings and Events, Carlson Wagonlit Travel's meetings and events division, were selected by the International Skating Union (ISU) and the Italian Ice Sports Federation (FISG) to run the ISU 2018 World Figure Skating Championships, which took place at Milan's Mediolanum Forum di Assago in March 2018.

CWT's sporting events specialist division M&E Sport won the bid and was awarded responsibility for coordinating the logistics of the five-day event, including all the public relations and marketing activities. The agency was also involved in overseeing the construction of the skating rink at Piazza Gae Aulenti, and the presentation of the gala dinner at the Palazzo del Ghiaccio.

On successfully winning the bid, Raffaele Calia, head of sales and marketing at CWT Meetings and Events and M&E Sport, said, 'Working to successfully deliver an international event at the heart of one of the most dedicated sporting communities is a once-in-a-lifetime opportunity.'

Stefano Abram, general manager of the ISU organising committee, said, 'This is an extraordinary opportunity to combine sporting passion with the values of Made in Italy … I am pleased to work with an experienced, reliable partner like CWT M&E. Hosting a World Cup in Italy is a dream come true for those who live sport and its values.'

The ISU 2018 World Figure Skating Championships is another addition to CWT M&E's portfolio of sporting events. The division already partners with UEFA, Dorna and the Italian National Olympic Committee, where it won a tender to organise the ticketing, logistics and hospitality for the 2018 Pyeongchang Winter Olympics in South Korea.

OBJECTIVE 2

Destination branding and factors that influence destination choice

DESTINATION BRANDING AND THE FACTORS THAT INFLUENCE DESTINATION CHOICE

WHY DO DESTINATIONS WANT TO BID TO HOST MEGA AND MAJOR EVENTS?

There are many reasons why a destination might want to bid to host a major or mega event. In the past, bidding was usually restricted to cities or destinations in developed economies. These cities were considered **fit for purpose** because they had the previous experience, reputation, necessary resources, skills, expertise, facilities and infrastructure required to deliver on this scale. Budget holders and event owners felt reassured that these cities possessed the necessary features, infrastructure and track record to deliver successful events on their behalf. This meant, however, that there was a finite number of host destinations that could be considered viable. This shortage of functional, workable destinations meant that at peak conference times, agencies and buyers sometimes struggled to find available space, at optimum rates, on behalf of their clients. Moreover, the lack of suitable destinations offered little choice for unusual, untried and innovative event programmes that corporate clients, associations and organisers so often sought.

Fit for purpose well-equipped or well-suited for its designated role or purpose

Since the decline of industrial economies, there has been a shift from production – from former traditional industries, such as manufacturing, textiles, mining – to consumption – such as the new markets involved in the buying and consuming of all manner of experiences that have evolved since the decline of industrialisation. In the events industry, this growth has seen a number of widespread events now staged in new emerging destinations, such as Eastern Europe, China, India, Africa and South America. These countries would have never previously been considered, but have now become feasible options to host a multitude of global events. These new emerging destinations have the advantage of being able to provide clients, delegates and attendees with innovative and creative ideas and unique programme recommendations, rather than churning out the same repetitious social excursions, sightseeing tours and dining suggestions, as was previously the case.

As already mentioned in Chapter 4, events play an important role in the economic development of international communities. This economic growth is boosted and supported by regional development agencies, and marketed by governments, tourism marketing organisations, public relations and other related agencies. Their role is to create a positive image of the destination and develop a brand image. This involves marketing, positioning and pitching their region against other destination brands, which become very important in this competitive arena.

THE LINK FROM CITY REGENERATION TO EVENTS

Long-term and strategic development can benefit destinations by identifying gaps in the market and proactively developing event products and offerings to fill them. It is therefore understandable that, in recent years, new emerging destinations have undergone substantial regeneration and revitalisation in order to enter this competitive market arena and reap these direct and indirect benefits. Today, as previously mentioned, this includes the many developing countries who have invested heavily in their region or city's physical infrastructure, in a bid to host in the future.

Events and regeneration are concepts which occur in specific places, but they are also both important mechanisms through which places are made ... In a more abstract sense, the two concepts are synonymous. Regeneration can be viewed as an event – a planned spectacle which takes place at a certain time. (Smith 2012: 10)
Regeneration can be defined as renewal, revival, revitalisation, or transformation of a place or community. (Evans and Shaw 2006: 9)

TABLE 5.1 Definitions of regeneration

The opportunity to become an 'eventful city' and generate economic impact into the region through an increase in **new expenditure**, justifies the time and effort that go into tendering to win a competitive bid. The benefits of **urban regeneration** for a city might include the design and build of new stadiums or a convention centre, or improving hotel standards, venues, shopping facilities and the overall destination infrastructure.

New expenditure
new funds that boost the local economy, as a result of event income or funding

Urban regeneration
a programme of land redevelopment in cities, often where there is urban decay

The subsequent funding and renewed focus on the city or region chosen to host a major or mega event, can transform run-down, derelict and polluted cities and communities, into revitalised host destinations with a new vision, feel and multiple opportunities for future events and future growth. In real terms, this means that private and governmental organisations, tourist agencies, destination management companies and destination marketing organisations are in competition with other similar destinations, as never before, to boost the image of that destination to create new events or competitive pricing strategies, in order to target specific market segments. This is bringing about an exciting new era for the whole industry.

REAL INSIGHT 5.2

PLOVDIV'S BID TO BECOME 2019 EUROPEAN CITY OF CULTURE (ECOC)

Plovdiv, the second largest city in Bulgaria and the oldest city in Europe, became the first Bulgarian city to be awarded European City of Culture (ECoC)

(Continued)

in 2019. The ECoC programme, the European Union's (EU) most acclaimed cultural initiative, was first set up in 1985 to offer aspiring cities the chance of regenerating and rebranding in order to enhance the quality of life for their residents, and boost their international visibility and cultural heritage. The programme has been described as a 'significant catalyst for culture-led regeneration' that has helped countless cities over the last 30 years.

Plovdiv, like many other older cities, has struggled with the process of de-industrialisation, and faced the major challenge of how to regenerate the once-thriving industrial city; to revive a derelict land and a depressed and disadvantaged community. The redevelopment of brownfield sites and historical monuments, such as the famous ancient amphitheatre dating back to the reign of Emperor Tajan at the beginning of the 2nd century, has great cultural and historical significance. Much of the original architecture was demolished by fire or earthquakes at the end of the 4th century. Following Plovdiv's appointment as ECoC in September 2014, a restoration project called 'Beautiful Bulgaria' was launched, where, through careful planning and expert craftsmanship, this ancient monument was preserved and restored back to its former glory.

Most cities who bid to become an ECoC have several objectives. These may include a desire to raise their international profile; to become culturally renowned; to increase their funding for art and cultural events; to attract increased visitation and tourism; to develop relationships with other European cities and regions; to promote creativity and innovation; and lastly to boost employment and the talent of local craftsmen and artists (Palmer Rae Associates 2004). In addition to Plovdiv, the beautiful Italian city of Matera was also chosen as twin ECoC for 2019. Since winning the prestigious tender in September 2014, both cities have launched collaborative activities, joint ventures and project initiatives. Other cities who were not successful in the bid were Sofia, Varna and Veliko Tarnovo.

Plovdiv first decided to apply for the title of ECoC in 2010 when a group of artists called The Art Today Association formed a committee, the initiative being supported by the local government. In September 2011 the Municipal Foundation of Plovdiv was established to implement the ECoC bid process. During the bid process, numerous meetings, conversations and consultations with national and international organisations took place. More than 35 creative teams applied with ideas during the first stage. This helped shape the conceptual framework of the programme, and some of those ideas and concepts were included in the eventual bid document.

Plovdiv was largely successful in being appointed ECoC due to its balanced and well-presented programme, and its realistic budget. Other determining factors included:

- The objective vision of the challenges facing the city
- The number of projects dedicated to schools and young people

- The strong engagement and involvement of the city's socio-cultural and economic environment
- The diverse nature of the Cyrillic and Roma integration projects
- Supporting the development of the creative industries and multi-culturalism.

After winning the bid, the second crucial process commenced during 2015. This involved engagement and interaction with several European partners, in order to develop and shape the programme. The finalised suggestions were presented in front of an international jury. All contributing members of the Plovdiv 2019 bid team played a crucial role in contributing to the development of the project, both from within the core team or as representatives of partner organisations.

Plovdiv's ancient theatre is now renovated and opening for shows, concerts and events, and is now being visited by hundreds of tourists, who come to see the oldest preserved theatre of its kind in the world. Other ancient buildings such as the Boris Hristov House of Culture have also been renovated and restored. The International Fair and Trade show in Plovdiv takes place annually and in April 2017 the city hosted a Technological Entertainment Design (TED) event, where many global delegates gave speeches on interesting topics, entertaining the audiences who attended the event.

Preparation for the bid and the accolade of being awarded European City of Culture has been an important phase in the development of this city. It has been instrumental in contributing to a new cultural self-awareness among its citizens and communities. Moreover, it has strengthened Plovdiv in terms of its artistic and cultural heritage, urban reconstruction, social integration, national and international business and tourism growth.

WHAT IS DESTINATION BRANDING IN EVENTS?

Destination image and branding is becoming an important part of 'selling places' for those agencies and organisations who come together in the bid process to ensure the bid is successful. This collaborative effort to sell destinations is succinctly described by Kearns and Philo (1993: 3) as:

> The various ways in which public and private agencies – local authorities and local entrepreneurs, often working collaboratively – strive to 'sell' the image of a particularly geographically defined 'place', usually a town or city, so as to make it attractive to economic enterprises, to tourists and even inhabitants of that place.

In the events industry today, place or location have increasingly become associated by their visitors, investors and residents with what each city sells, creates and represents. It is these perceptions, attitudes and impressions towards tourist destinations or aspects of destinations that give it a competitive edge. Historical occasions such as sports events, expositions, carnivals and other cultural festivals play a specific role in selling cities. The perceived image of the destination should be holistic, as Waitt (2008: 513) says: 'this holistic view of destinations is evident in the view that city image is cultivated to communicate dynamic, vibrant, affluent, healthy, tolerant, cosmopolitan and sexy places.'

Destination branding has become synonymous with cities such as New York, London, Tokyo and Paris, where the destination brand is about more than just a logo, a series of images or a place. It is about the brand message and it is up to the tourist authorities to communicate that message to the target market, whether they are internal or external visitors, investors or potential residents of that community. Some destinations have created branded events to boost their image. One prime example is Dubai, which has launched the following branded sporting events: The Standard Chartered Dubai Marathon; the Omega Dubai Desert Classic; The Dubai Duty Free Tennis Championship; the Dubai World Cup; Dream racing F1; and the Emirates Airline Dubai Rugby Sevens. Other destinations have linked with a strong corporate sponsor's brand to boost their image brand, e.g. Red Bull Formula 1, The Virgin London Marathon and The Samsung Golfing World Championships.

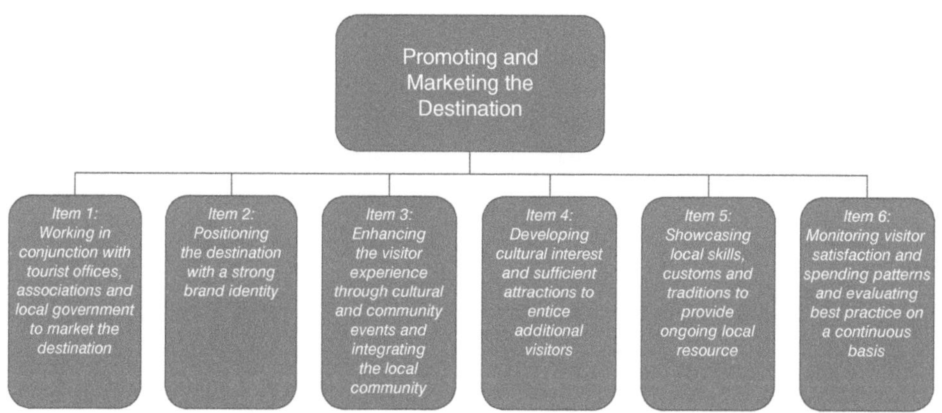

FIGURE 5.2 Promoting and Marketing the Destination

KEY FACTORS THAT INFLUENCE DESTINATION CHOICE

There are several determining factors to consider when deciding which destination is the most appropriate to host an event. The most frequently identified factors are:

- A high level of economic development and strong economy
- Support of governmental free-trade policies
- Seasonality and climate
- Destination image/perceived atmosphere and ambience
- Reputation for quality, efficiency and reliability of services

- Accessibility and distance from market to the destination
- Current market trends
- An innovative, new and emerging destination
- Types of event held in the destination
- Favourable currency exchange rates
- Political stability, safety and security
- Affordability/low cost of living/value for money
- Shared cultural or business interests
- Potential to attract both international and domestic markets
- History of the destination
- Availability of venues and other facilities.

All these criteria mentioned above are important factors for the bid organisation or committee, but each organisation will have its own ideas on which of the factors they value and would prioritise. Generally, event owners consider geographical spread when selecting destinations. This means that diverse cities that have not recently hosted other events may stand a better chance than those cities that have just done so, or will be doing so, during the same period or in the near future. It is therefore important to assess these implications when deciding to bid, as although the actual event might only last for a few days, the preparations will take much longer, even years in the case of a major event.

BIDDING FOR LARGE-SCALE MEGA AND MAJOR SPORTING EVENTS

Most academic studies have looked at bidding in relation to sports events. This is possibly because these often involve public bodies in the process and require a high degree of transparency, and this tends to raise their profile. Mega or major sporting events are also likely to require considerable funding, planning and resources to organise, and hence carry associated risks. Understanding the potential risk factors and demonstrating that the host nation can reduce these factors, will greatly improve a destination's chances of selection. The bid process varies according to the size, budget and nature of the events and the complexity of the stakeholders involved. For larger events, it tends to be a far longer and more complex process than that of other smaller, association or corporate events.

In the case of mega and major events, an existing infrastructure and purpose-built facilities are required before the event can proceed. This requires an initial strategic long-term plan and appropriate legacy planning to ensure that any rise in participation can be sustained in the following years.

As previously discussed in this chapter, this type of bid is highly competitive. There are likely to be several cities and nations bidding to host major international sporting events at one time. The right to host an international event is now one of the most valuable prizes in sport. For example, research undertaken by Sheffield Hallam University in 2017 shows that The World Snooker Championship, which takes place annually at the Crucible Theatre, has boosted Sheffield's economy by £100 million over the last 40 years. The event generates around 40,000 spectator admissions each year and spectators from outside Sheffield spend £1.8 million in the city; on accommodation, food and drink, shopping, local travel and other entertainment. Spectator spending coupled with that of the players, the media, officials and the costs of running the championship, generate an annual economic impact of £2.6 million (SIRC 2017).

KEY STAKEHOLDERS INVOLVED IN THE EVENT BIDDING PROCESS

The stakeholders involved in the selection process of sporting mega events could be made up of sport organisations, government agencies and event owners and organisers. The bid process for mega events generally has a four-year cycle. This commences with the feasibility and rationale stage, when the requirements of the bid, the strategy and policy of the bidding city are evaluated, together with the impact a successful bid would have on the economic, social, political and cultural environment of that destination.

In mega and major events, there are many stakeholders who might be involved in the initial consultation and bid process, and may include:

- Event 'owners' or rights holders
- Organising committees (e.g. FIFA, IOC, UEFA)
- Regional/local government within the host city
- National government agencies for tourism promotion/branding
- National government department for sport and recreation
- Regional tourism destination promotion agency
- National service providers
- Business and investment promotion agencies
- Event sponsors.

Mega events also require different levels of public sector organisations to work, budget and plan together in order to add cohesion and unity for a combined 'energy to inspire outstanding results' (Spracklen 2012: 121-22).

BIDDING FOR SMALLER SCALE AND MINOR EVENTS

With smaller scale corporate and association events, bidding or tendering is different from larger scale events, but is also an important process. A potential shortlist of agencies or organisations, all of whom are considered to have the credibility, resources and expertise to run the event on behalf of the owner, are usually drawn up in the initial selection process.

The feasibility phase for smaller events also requires evaluation in terms of short- and medium-term social, economic and environmental impacts on the local community or business (see Chapter 4). However, the planning time for these may be considerably shorter as public scrutiny and transparency tend not to be such an issue for this type of bid.

THE SELECTION CRITERIA OF A REQUEST FOR INFORMATION (RFI) AND REQUEST FOR PROPOSAL (RFP)

OBJECTIVE
3
The selection criteria of a Request for Information (RFI) and Request for Proposal (RFP)

SUBMITTING AN RFI AND RFP

There is usually a structured process for inviting suppliers or agencies to bid in the events industry: a Request for Information (RFI) is a standard business process, whose purpose is to collect written information about the capabilities of various suppliers. Normally it follows a prescriptive format and is used for comparative purposes. An RFI is generally a fact-finding mission on behalf of the organisation or company's procurement division that may contain sensitive financial and company information. The RFI tends to be issued when the client or event owner needs more information from the vendors. It is often followed by a Request for Proposal (RFP). An RFP is a solicitation or invitation to bid, often made by an agency or a company interested in the procurement of a commodity, service or valuable asset, to potential suppliers to submit business proposals.

Submitting an RFI or RFP always has a cost implication, but may eventually be worth the investment. There are many factors to consider in the tendering process. The first major decision is deciding whether to tender in the first place or not. This may be a case of realistically assessing the chances of being successful as an individual, agency or supplier, or to evaluate whether the invitation to bid is just 'making up numbers' to satisfy a procurement requirement. Some agencies will conduct a bidding analysis to help them reach a decision on whether to tender, as illustrated in Figure 5.3.

An RFI is normally issued every three years, initially to a number of agencies, but usually no more than ten, who have been selected to tender, usually to run multiple events on behalf of the client or event owner. If the solicited agency decides to submit an RFI, they should ensure they are clear about the set criteria for completing it and contact the client if more precise information is needed. Table 5.2 lists further questions that might be asked at this stage; Table 5.3 shows information that may be included in an RFI.

- Does the RFI ask for an internal audit or confidential material?
- Is this a genuine pitch or is the agency just making up numbers?
- Are the deadlines for completion realistic?
- Will they get a chance to present in person?
- What are the agency's strengths and weaknesses?
- How can they best market themselves to ensure preferred or sole supplier status?
- Who is the decision maker on operational factors?
- Has the venue already been selected or is securing suitable space one of the important elements in the agency selection process?
- Will the agency be required to work together with the event organiser or their own in-house team?
- What budget is available for this event? Where is the budget coming from?

TABLE 5.2 Questions to ask on receipt of an RFI/RFP

A cover letter	A courtesy letter should state full contact details and thank the client for giving the agency the opportunity to tender.
Executive summary/statement Company credentials, accreditation and qualifications and organisational structure	The executive summary should summarise the proposal contents. All important aspects including situation analysis and recommendations should be included. This may be the only part of the proposal that is read.
Company financial details/ projected target forecasts	Clients need to know the financial status of the agency they appoint to eliminate any risk. This includes past financial statements and any future business on the books, residual funds and savings. This could by association impact the event owner or organisation, who may be paying deposits to the agency in advance.
Quality assurance	This section will describe company expertise, accreditation and outline processes. This ensures quality standards are met and reduces potential risk to the event owner or client.
Previous event case studies	It is useful for a new client to see examples of the agency's previous work and samples of events. These should represent a range of size, scale and complexity to reassure them that the agency has worked on similar events in the past with successful results.
Client testimonials	Any positive client testimonials will enhance the proposal and may make the difference in the final selection process. It is advisable to provide contact details of previous clients, for use in case the new client or budget holder would like to call them to discuss the agency's performance and delivery in further detail.
Management costs/projected savings/rebates	Within the RFI there will normally be a section detailing the agency costs for managing one or a series of events. This section should outline projected savings made through economies of scale purchasing and projected savings, which will be passed on to the client or company. There may be kick-back, or rebates included for hitting targeted volumes of business.
Business licences/registrations/ terms and conditions	Any business licences, registrations or agency terms and conditions are normally included in the RFI.

TABLE 5.3 Information that may be included in an RFI (Request for Information)

A Request for Proposal (RFP) usually follows on from the RFI. It is generally issued for each separate event, once the initial information about the agency has been collected and analysed through the RFI process and the agency has been appointed as preferred or sole supplier. In an RFP, artistic renderings, hotel brochures, mood boards and visuals can help convey the creative concept, and the documentation for an RFP contains more specific suggestions and recommendations for the event itself.

ANALYSING THE CLIENT BRIEF OR RFP

The client brief or RFP may be sent out by email or delivered in person. It is always preferable to try to set up a meeting to take the brief from the client in person, so that there is a chance to ask relevant questions. For example, it might be that the decision maker has a dislike of certain destinations or venue types but does not specify this in the brief. By asking detailed questions at the briefing stage, the agency stands a better chance of meeting the specified and unspecified expectations of the budget holder, and therefore has a better chance of winning the bid.

Client briefs or RFPs vary considerably. Some are a lot more detailed than others. This can often depend on the expertise of the client or budget holder. Sometimes the brief might detail the performance measurement criteria and production details, as well as logistical requirements. Other clients might provide the incumbent with information about the travel and logistical elements. It is often necessary to go back to the client with a list of questions before starting the proposal, as the more detailed the information gained from the outset, the better equipped the agency generally is to match the requirements of the brief.

It is always good policy to ask for a deadline date for submission. It takes time and resources to receive responses from suppliers and collate the proposal, therefore if the agency pitching is given an unrealistic deadline date for when to submit by the event owner, they might deduce that they are being considered a serious contender. It is always better not to promise to deliver if that deadline is not feasible. Indeed, that may be an opportune time to walk away from the bid process, or it may be possible to renegotiate a date to submit the RFP that is more realistic and allows sufficient time to research and complete the document.

As part of that negotiation process, it is always advisable to try to arrange to deliver the proposal in person, preferably by means of a face-to-face presentation. As much of the bid process is about relationship marketing, it is preferable to present in person whenever possible, rather than just emailing or putting a copy in the post. This allows the agency or supplier to engage with the budget holder and start to form a bond with that client. It also provides an opportunity for the agency to demonstrate their expertise and impress the potential client with their destination or venue knowledge and creative and logistical capabilities.

During the presentation, the agency should convey enthusiasm and passion for the project, which may be the deciding point for selection. It is often surprising that, despite working days and weeks on a proposal, the agency or supplier who is pitching for the job fails to ask fundamental questions about the decision process for the bid. For example, it would be appropriate at this stage to enquire who will ultimately make the final decision, and when and what will be the defining criteria for the selection. It may be pertinent to conduct an event bidding analysis, as detailed in Figure 5. 3 below, before committing too much time and resource.

PREPARATION OF THE BID DOCUMENTATION

Responding to an RFI or RFP takes time, needs careful consideration and a detailed project plan. This will help to ensure the bid documentation is delivered on time. In order to assess how realistic the timelines are, it is advisable for the agency to put together a critical path document. The work breakdown should be prepared according to the event requirements, and key milestone activities should be prioritised in terms of importance leading up to the event delivery. There are a number of methods generally used to prepare work timelines to help achieve deadlines when putting together the bid documentation, including those shown in Table 5.4.

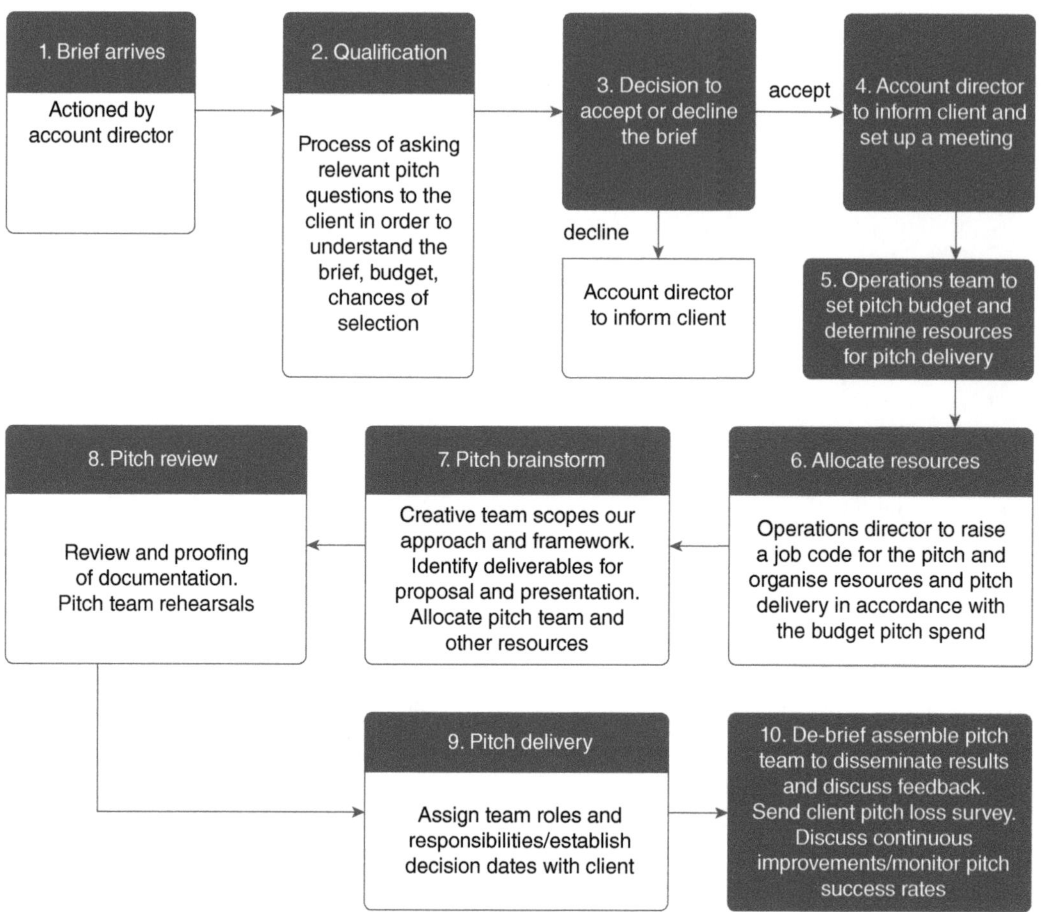

FIGURE 5.3 Event bidding analysis

A Gantt chart	A Gantt chart is a horizontal bar chart, first developed as a production control tool in the USA in 1917 and now frequently used in project management. A Gantt chart provides a graphical illustration of a schedule that helps to plan, coordinate and track specific tasks in a project.
Critical path analysis	Critical path analysis (CPA) is a widely used project management tool that uses network analysis to help project managers to handle complex and time-sensitive operations.
Assigning roles and responsibilities	Make sure that the pitch team are all assigned roles and responsibilities leading up to the submission of the RFI and RFP documents and delivery of the bid presentation.
Bespoke project management systems	A number of bespoke project management systems are available that aim to provide event clients with tailor-made solutions to assist with project management. Often used in the tendering process to assist with time management of the documentation.

TABLE 5.4 Processes used for time management of bid documentation

In most cases, both documents are submitted to a panel or board rather than one person in the organisation, and the presentation needs to be highly professional, rehearsed and supported with a multimedia presentation. Items that may be included in an RFP are listed in Table 5.5.

Synopsis/understanding of the brief	When commencing the proposal document, it is a good idea for the agency or organisation bidding to summarise their understanding of the client's brief and event objectives.
Previous experience/ credentials	As with the RFI, it is good practice to include case studies of previous events and details on the agency's credentials.
Destination and venue rationale	A rationale of preferred destinations and shortlisted venues and facilities within that host destination. State which of these are 'fit for purpose'. This is an area of expertise that clients often expect the agency to provide.
Event concept or theme	A concept/theme is often developed for the event, as well as a specific strapline that reflects the nature of the event.
Event dates and schedule	The event bidding team should state the provisional dates that the agency is holding on the client's behalf. Should preferably include a few different options and a schedule for confirming or releasing the provisional space being held.
Programme overview	To include: A detailed outline of the activities and timings of the programme. Set-up and de-rig times and the actual delegate or attendee programme. Might include ceremonial events with visiting dignitaries, or any keynote speakers required to make speeches or present awards. Could also include any proposed entertainment 'extras' that may start or finish the proceedings or fill any gaps during the event.
Air and ground transportation details/rationale	Details of transportation and a rationale for accessing the various hubs and types of transportation to be utilised.
Critical path (project activities)	Should contain an at-a-glance schedule of key milestone activities leading up to the event. Explain how the activities link to each other in terms of priority and chronological order.
Budgetary details	Any budgetary details will be shown as a draft or a cost estimate. Projected income from any sponsorship or merchandise deals should be itemised, as well as any predicted expenditure.
Event staffing	Details on how the event will be manned and a list of paid and unpaid or volunteer roles should be included in this section.
Technical requirements	A list of technical specifications should be included, together with the number of event crew needed to operate the technical aspects of the event, including the set-up and de-rig phases.
Risk management plan *Event evaluation methods*	To include details of how the event bidding team will conduct a risk assessment before the event, and conduct post-event evaluation after the event has finished. This will demonstrate the expertise and professionalism of the bid team or agency tendering.
Testimonials	As with the RFI, any testimonials from previous or existing clients should be included in the proposal.

TABLE 5.5 Items that may be included in an RFP (Request for Proposal)

THE IMPORTANCE OF DEVELOPING AN EVENT CONCEPT IN THE RFP

Strapline
a definition that denotes a distinctive motto or phrase, used in events to convey a purpose or theme

Within the bidding process, the first stage of creating the concept is the initiation stage, as has been illustrated in Table 5.5. This is the starting point for developing the event identity. Analysing the brief, objectives, brainstorming various ideas, themes and devising a **strapline**, start to form an event concept. This concept can be the underlying principle that establishes the whole vision and experience. The creative concept for weddings, parties and sales conferences are often linked to a strong thematic, celebratory or entertainment element, as opposed to more functional corporate events that have no creative inclusion.

Design is a critical tool for event management, as it relates directly to development of the event concept and overall experience. The design of the creative concept can be the blueprint for the event environment, as well as giving the event a visual identity and recognition, to create enhanced meaningful impact for the audience or participants.

Outlining the creative concept as part of the overall event design is an important part of the live pitch presentation. Bid teams may come to the pitch presentation equipped with props, visuals, video footage, entertainment previews and mood or storyboards, used to convey the design theme and narrate the event programme to the client. In addition, technology and virtual renderings or mood boards are often used to convey a flavour of what the audience will experience at the actual event.

The creative concept can set the event management company apart from the competition and therefore should be subject to confidentiality, trademark and copyright clauses. This is especially important in the pitching process, as it is not unheard of for an event client or owner to invite agencies to pitch in order to gain their creative insight and concept ideas in relation to the brief set, then attempt to deliver the ideas put forward, using their own in-house resources or existing incumbent. Although this is clearly unethical, unfortunately it still often occurs in practice.

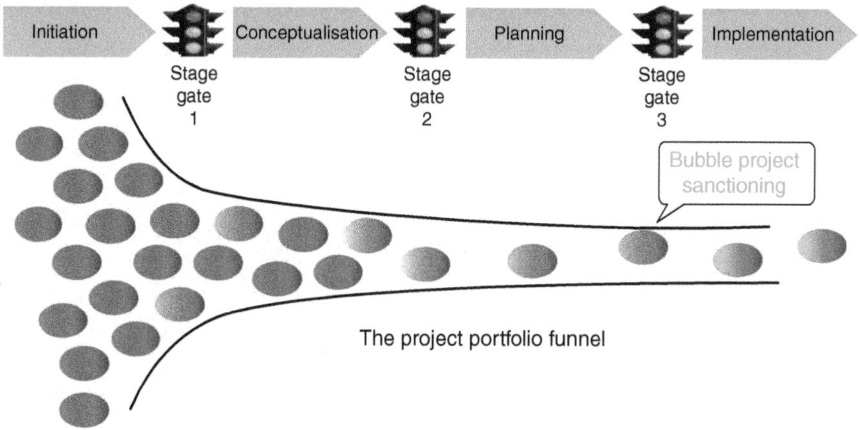

FIGURE 5.4 The project process

REAL INSIGHT 5.3

C2C'S CONCEPT FOR A NEW EDUCATION EVENT

In a bid to design an innovative and 'revolutionary' new concept, Italian event planner Monica Balli, from the agency Concept 2 Creation (C2C), designed an event to be held at Disneyland Paris in February 2019, aimed at the 140 top organisers from all over the world. The purpose of the event was to offer master classes and education. Balli described the creative concept in the following way:

> C2C's teaching will be authentically experiential, one-to-one, with peer-to-peer learners and speakers, one to benefit from the inputs of the others. In this sense, the event will turn out to be a dream: for the first-time participants will face the real gurus of the meeting industry and will be able to fully interact with them.

The event was designed to run over three days, with the aim of breaking down barriers and allowing a cross-cultural experience, leading to a reciprocal understanding of key basic requirements for organising global events. The format is based on the continuing education offered to the Association of Young Presidents, of which Monica Balli is a member, featuring entrepreneurs, CEOs and top managers from companies including Ferragamo, Fendi, Perini, Google, Facebook, Hotels.com, Unilever and Morgan Stanley.

Balli added:

> The aim of C2C is to deepen the areas of interest for organisers, as well as for the business of their companies and for their personal lives, as they are closely linked to work. For this reason, teachers and learners will have a very high profile. There are 10 seminar areas, with 12 to 20 learners expected for each and an opportunity for seamless networking and interaction between the participants and teachers, which is the core of the overall concept.

THE VALUE OF A STRONG CONCEPT IDEA

As already discussed, in an increasingly competitive arena, coming up with innovative ideas and concepts that will deliver memorable experiences and engage attendees is more important than ever in the bidding stage. The concept put forward may indeed seal the overall success of the bid. This is even the case with mega events; the concept put forward by the UK bid team, headed by Lord Coe, was at the heart of the tender for the London 2012 Olympics. The promise to make this Olympics the first 'Green Games' is reputed to have given London the edge over the Paris tender back in 2005.

With smaller, minor and private events, many new concepts are currently being explored in the industry, such as virtual conferences, which are conducted remotely, as detailed in Chapter 9. Another concept that is currently gaining popularity is the so-called 'unconference'. Unlike a traditional conference, which is fairly rigid and prescriptive in its format, an 'unconference' is a loosely structured event, with no formalised agenda, speakers or assigned topic areas. Instead, the delegates write down any topics or issues they may wish to discuss on the day on a whiteboard. Delegates are divided into groups to discuss these issues further during breakout sessions and a facilitator may be engaged to guide the discussion.

Further concepts have been borrowed from the leisure and entertainment field and transferred into the events area, such as: secret events; secret cinema; and escape rooms. 'Secret events' are staged at a secret location that is only announced shortly before the conference commences, sometimes proving a logistical challenge for event organisers. The concept of 'secret cinema' is to make the audience feel like they are in a movie with a specific role to play. They are enhanced using the latest digital technology, such as **projection mapping** and interactive installations. With the escape room concept, delegates normally have to answer key questions or puzzles to solve as part of the overall conference or team-building programme, in order to be able to secure their release from the venue.

Projection mapping a projection technology used to turn objects, often irregularly shaped, using spatial augmented reality

Following on from the gaming trend that the younger generation has become so familiar with in recent years, immersive theatre is now being used in events, as well as the theatre, as a form of escapism and release, in the same way as social media and virtual reality. Often guests have the opportunity to dress up in fancy dress costume with props and move through a series of rooms with interactive actors, so that the audience becomes part of the play or action.

In recent years, the concept of speed networking, which came originally from the dating industry, is being applied in a business sense to the events industry. Attendees can meet up with other, like-minded guests to exchange information and ideas and swap contact details, creating a viable sales opportunity for all parties. Furthermore, the concept of lightning-speed presentations, using TED-style talks or Pecha Kucha presentations, has increased in popularity. In a Pecha Kucha presentation, each presenter is only permitted to show a maximum of 20 images and explain each image in only 20 seconds. This way of delivering short, on-message presentations has created a new phenomenon in the events industry, as has the growth of 'knowledge cafes', which allow for the interactive exchange of ideas and discussion in an informal environment.

All the innovative concepts mentioned above are now being utilised by event professionals, to create dynamic events for an array of event types, to roll out within the pitch process, with the ultimate goal of securing future business.

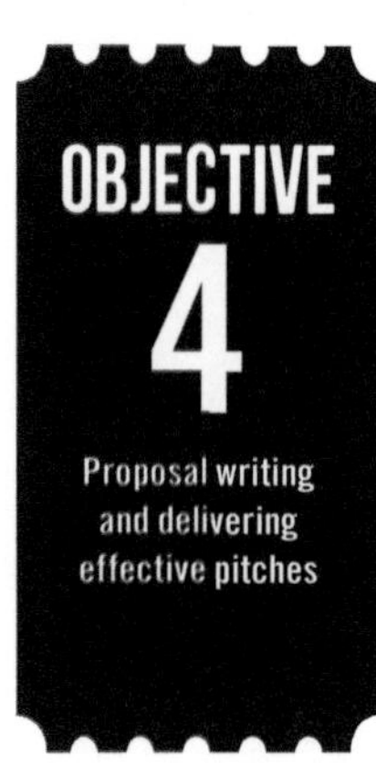
OBJECTIVE
4
Proposal writing and delivering effective pitches

PROPOSAL WRITING AND DELIVERING EFFECTIVE PITCHES

THE PURPOSE OF AN EVENT PROPOSAL

Generally, the purpose of the proposal in response to the RFP, is to provide the client or end-user with an overview of the event. It should also demonstrate a general understanding or interpretation of what the client or event owner's requirements are. Full details, or a description of the target audience and the key event aims and deliverables, should be included in the document. The complexity and amount of detail in the proposal will depend largely on the scale and importance of the event. However, most agencies who bid for multiple events will tend to have an online proposal template for responding to a brief, to save the agency time as well as providing greater assurance of completing the task successfully. As specified above in Table 5.5, several standard items should be included in the proposal. The following items should also be included in the proposal, and will be further detailed in the next section:

- Finance/sponsorship
- Sponsorship deals
- Agency credentials and previous event experience
- Venue and other supplier details
- Programme and content
- Marketing to local stakeholders
- Technical production
- Food and beverage provision and catering arrangements
- Security/risk assessment
- Cancellation/postponement.

FINANCE/SPONSORSHIP

Once the budget is known, and it is evident where the starting capital is coming from, a budget estimate should be included in the pitch proposal. A costing estimate or draft budget can be started once the tasks to be performed have been identified. In order to produce an accurate draft budget, a record of all income and expenses should be monitored. It is also advisable to set up a simple Excel document to show the budgeting structure and predicted costs of the event. Every item must be listed, but at proposal stage it is generally acceptable to allocate an allowance or '**guesstimate**'. Each item then should be categorised, such as income, expenditure, miscellaneous costs or expenses, and it made clear whether these budget items are fixed or variable, so that numbers can be adjusted accordingly, should delegate numbers increase or decrease. Every item must have a likely expenditure or income placed next to it.

Guesstimate
an estimate based on a mixture of guesswork and calculation

When issuing a brief to the agency or suppliers, it is often the case that the client may initially be reluctant to give the agency a budget amount. This is generally because they know that if they specify the estimated amount to deliver the event in the brief, the agency or suppliers will tend to come just under or even exactly on that budget amount. The danger of not setting specific budgetary guidelines is that the agency pitching for the event might arrive at an overall costing that is significantly over or under the amount the client or event owner anticipated.

The agency or suppliers involved in the pitch need a benchmark to work with, as the venue choice, concept and all corresponding items will be governed by the overall budget estimate. This could make the difference between choosing a prestigious 5-star hotel or the local town hall to host the event, and save both the time and embarrassment of the event owner and the agency or suppliers involved.

It is therefore essential that, wherever possible, when responding to a Request for Proposal (RFP), the respondent should try to get an indication of at least a ball-park figure of the overall spend the client is comfortable with. If the agency is an incumbent, they will probably have a reasonable idea of the type of budget rates that the client would find acceptable. However, with a new client or a new piece of business, it might not be so easy to accurately gauge this.

One way to overcome this problem is to suggest an indicative delegate rate to the client. Alternatively, the agency or supplier could conduct some background research by speaking to previous venues used, or delegates who have previously attended similar events in the past. A direct question to the budget holder is normally the best approach and might prompt them to think through this important area in advance. It is worth noting, however, that not all clients determine their selection criteria on cost alone. Quality, innovation and reputation are also very important factors in the decision process. Sometimes an agency is selected because the event owner or organisation likes the company and their ethos, and feels they will be able to work well together.

It is good practice when budgeting during the tendering stage to contact the various outsourced suppliers, in order to obtain quotations for specific elements in the brief. Unfortunately, the tendency for short lead times today, means that it is not always possible to wait for these 'real costs' to arrive. It can sometimes be possible to estimate the likely cost of a specific item. In this instance, however, it is good practice to add a disclaimer to the costing notes, stating that the rates included are assumptions or estimates, to be confirmed in due course. With less-experienced event agencies or suppliers, the standard problems with budgeting can create difficulty in getting the right information at the right time, and an inability to forecast prices correctly.

When the budget is tight, it may be necessary to include the essential items required to deliver the event, but also to include additional recommended enhancements should more budget become available. The final budget for the event is invariably far higher than the initial budget quotation (see Chapter 7). The initial draft budget included in the pitch proposal may change greatly once the tender process has been completed and the agency or supplier appointed. This is often the time to attempt to **upsell** miscellaneous items. It is important for the agency to strike a balance between not pricing themselves out of a competitive pitch, and not cutting on quality and resource. As previously mentioned, it is worth noting that even in these procurement-driven times, event buyers do not always buy on price alone.

Upsell
persuade a customer to buy something additional or more expensive

SPONSORSHIP DEALS

When outlining the financial aspects of any sponsorship deals, the proposal should include a draft budget outlining the potential income and expenditure of the event. During the proposal stage, it may be difficult to attribute actual amounts of revenue through sponsorship deals, in terms of cash or benefits in kind. However, even at this early stage, it is important to make the budget as realistic as possible, and to avoid including income from sponsorship agreements that have yet to be formalised in the overall event income.

Additional margins gained from other income, such as food and beverage items, raffles, auctions, donations, ticket sales and other merchandising, should be included in the budget in the response to brief proposal, even if these amounts are estimated.

AGENCY CREDENTIALS AND PREVIOUS EVENT EXPERIENCE

The organisation bidding to run an event should include credential details in the proposal, outlining its experience and capability. This is necessary to reassure the event owner that they are working with the right agency, who will be able to deliver a first-class event. This section of the proposal should contain relevant information and the skills of the proposed event management team.

If the experience that the agency has secured to date is limited, then the team should outline any transferable skills, managerial and project management and communication and coordination expertise, even if obtained in another field or discipline. It would also be worth outlining any qualifications and accreditation of the bid team. Details of any training programmes for paid staff and volunteers should also be included in this section of the proposal.

VENUE AND OTHER SUPPLIER DETAILS

It may be that the venue is in a competitive bid with other similar venues within a shortlist of chosen venues. It is important to detail the venue location in the proposal document and how to make best use of the venue and space. It could be that the RFP requires the agency to put forward a selection of destinations, to match the requirements of the brief. In some cases, it is the destination itself that is bidding to host the event. As previously discussed in this chapter, this is particularly the case with mega sporting events, such as the Olympic Games, or other major sporting events. The destination puts itself forward in order to secure the hosting rights for a mega event. This is due to the increased finance and funding available and potential improvements to the destination's infrastructure. This will ultimately leave a legacy of improved facilities; urban regeneration; global recognition; and greater awareness of the destination, which will subsequently boost tourism and spend within that destination, as discussed earlier in this chapter.

Once the destination has been selected, a number of shortlisted venues within that destination are detailed in the proposal, though usually no more than three. The reader of the proposal will need assurance that the selected venues are 'fit for purpose'. Therefore, details on the venue facilities, including everything from toilets to car parking, lighting, air-conditioning, signage, seating and built-in conference equipment should be included in the proposal.

In the case of outdoor events, details such as spectator seating, fencing, drainage and power supplies should be included. With both indoor and outdoor events, it is a good idea to include photographic images and detailed layout plans, where possible, and details of previous similar events that the venue has staged. Venue detail included in a proposal should include:

- Accessibility of the venue, its proximity to airports, motorways and public transportation railway links
- Details of the infrastructure and a clear site plan of the venue, ideally with virtual renderings of the space
- Layout plans for public and private areas
- Room configurations, capacities and layout of meeting rooms
- Available car parking space.

The venue section of the proposal should also clearly state how each venue would cater to the needs of the event and the various stakeholders involved, including the audience, performers, staff and officials. It is important for decision makers to know how many hours a day the venue is available, also in the set-up and de-rig phase and the provisional dates being held by the agency and when these options will expire.

Other supplier details

There are many other suppliers that may be involved in a competitive event bid, whose details need to be included in the proposal:

- Audio-visual and production companies
- Catering companies
- Transportation providers, including coach and rail companies, car hire and taxi companies
- Lighting and floral companies
- Other stalls/attractions.

PROGRAMME AND CONTENT

Within this section of the bid documentation, there would be a detailed breakdown of the type of events proposed, how many and over what period they would run. Details on timings for the conference and social programmes would be included, with recommendations for activities, social excursions, team building and a partner programme if required. A detailed conference programme, outlining all content for plenary and breakout sessions and suggested keynote or guest speakers should also be included in this section. Details on staffing resource, target audience and creative concept, together with strapline, theming and props might also be included.

MARKETING TO LOCAL STAKEHOLDERS

An important part of the bidding process is getting 'buy-in' and approval from local stakeholders, who may be involved with the event. Communication is key throughout the planning phase as is devising an effective marketing strategy that is clear and detailed. In the bidding stage, the team will need to decide which modes of marketing to employ in order to attract the required target audience. Researching potential stakeholders in the bidding phase is important, in order to assess whether there is a demand for the event in the first place and to canvass public opinion.

TECHNICAL PRODUCTION

Within the proposal, it can also be useful to include a breakdown of the technical resources that will be needed. This should specify the breakdown of resources and crew and any cost involved with outsourcing and audio-visual and production requirements and how this area will be sourced within the host destination.

FOOD AND BEVERAGE PROVISION AND CATERING ARRANGEMENTS

Details on catering throughout the event need to be included with budgetary details; also details on food stalls or buffet equipment, furnishings and linen should be included in the proposal, as well as any themed menu suggestions, detail on service styles and areas where the catering will be served.

SECURITY/RISK ASSESSMENT

As the owner or organisation needs to be assured that the event will not incur security issues, it is important to detail the following considerations in the bid documentation:

- *Emergency plans*: including identification of emergency routes, holding areas and decision makers; evacuation plans for venues and accommodation; information on how to stop the event if necessary; and details of local hospitals and emergency services and access control.
- *Event health and safety*: including crowd control and well-being; protection of attendees from harm; electrics; food and drink hygiene; and construction issues.
- *Crime prevention*: including prevention of crime and disorder; prevention of public nuisance; public safety and security procedures within the venues and host city; and security plans for high-profile or high-risk groups.
- *Risk assessment*: including identification of potential hazards and methods and measures to reduce these risks.

CANCELLATION/POSTPONEMENT/INSURANCE, TERMS AND CONDITIONS

In this section of the proposal, details of cancellation cover, contractors' insurance and broker details should feature. Additionally, product, public and employers' liability and insurance of staff and performers and entertainers should be detailed, together with any licences and permits required for the agency terms and conditions, including payment terms.

DID YOU KNOW?

The famous author F. Scott Fitzgerald said this in his 1936 work *The Crack-up*: 'No grand idea was ever born in a conference, but a lot of foolish ideas have died there.'

If your pitch sounds and looks like everyone else's, you are not fully demonstrating your creative potential.

PITCHING FOR THE EVENT

This is the physical act of presenting the design concept of the event to the client, often in a competitive bid. As well as the creative aspects, the pitching process allows the event management company to demonstrate its organisation expertise with events of this size and scale, which is an essential part of the bidding process. As has already been mentioned in this chapter, it is always preferential to conduct the pitch to the client or budget holder in person. As part of the preparation for the pitch, the agency or organisation should define in advance their answers to the following:

- The bidding team and who in the team will be responsible for the meet and greet
- Who will set up the audio-visual equipment?
- Who will introduce the team and agenda?
- Who will present each topic or section?
- Who will conclude and summarise?
- Who will answer client questions and ask when the decision will be reached?
- When should a copy of the event proposal be handed out, if the client has not already been sent this in advance?

The bid team should spend some time before the pitch rehearsing, deciding what tools they will use for the presentation, how they will set up, who will greet the client, predicting questions they may be asked and who within the team will answer them. They should agree on objectives in advance, and the overall message and impression they will leave the client with. The pitch should have a distinct beginning, middle and end, starting by sparking interest and ending by recapping and summarising, ending with impact. The pitching team should own the material and convey their positivity on the concept they are presenting. It is often advisable to use PowerPoint or Prezi to signpost a presentation, but not essential.

The team should communicate that they have understood the requirements and objectives of the brief and that they have conducted thorough research. The bidding team should demonstrate a well-structured pitch and, wherever possible, relate the message to the audience. It is generally advised, if unable to answer a client's question in the pitch, rather than trying to guess at an answer, to agree to check on that point and get back to the client in due course, once completely sure of the facts or information.

WHAT IS PROCUREMENT'S ROLE IN THE EVENT TENDERING PROCESS?

Procurement is generally understood as the acquisition of goods from an external source, at the best price. Silvers (2008: 56) describes procurement management as: 'the sourcing, selection and contracting of the suppliers and vendors from whom goods and services will be procured using accurate solicitation materials and quality criterion'. It was initially set up as a process to ensure that goods, services or works were appropriate in terms of quality, quantity, price, time and location. Nowadays, procurement is more about finding an overall solution that includes all aspects of service and customer satisfaction.

The function and role of procurement is to ensure the identification and management of external resources that help an organisation fulfil its strategic objectives.

The term is often used in the bidding process, where there is involvement from corporate, association and public sector purchasing or buying divisions who intervene to help an organisation select the appropriate partners to work with, on one or a series of events as a preferred or sole supplier. The Public Contracts Regulations were revised in 2015 to simplify and streamline current procurement rules.

- 82% of procurement professionals and 86% of event planners currently operate a preferred supplier list.
- 100% of the event agencies MPI spoke to have a place on one or more preferred supplier lists.
- 100% of procurement professionals, 83% of event planners and 73% of event agencies said that preferred supplier lists made their job easier.
- 58% of all respondents said that appointing preferred agencies is a team decision.
- 85% of these respondents said that this team included the event planner and the procurement professional.
- Cost, professionalism and experience are the three most popular factors that event planners and procurement professionals look for when appointing a supplier.
- The same three qualities were identified by event agencies as those they assume clients look for when appointing a supplier.
- The majority of all respondents feel that they are suitably equipped to deal with the changes in the way events are procured.
- 89% of procurement professionals, 67% of event planners and 93% of event agencies knew of instances where event services had been provided by someone not on the preferred supplier list.

TABLE 5.6 Procurement in the events industry

SELECTION CRITERIA IN THE BIDDING PROCESS

There are a number of factors that the client, governing body or organisation or procurement division considers when selecting an agency or event organisation to work with, which may be as follows:

- The bid team could be holding better provisional venues, space or facilities than other rival bidders
- The event has greater financial backing or sponsorship opportunities than other agencies
- The agency has secured favourable rates with suppliers
- The client has been pitching for a number of years and is a popular choice
- The client or organisation is looking for a new incumbent agency to partner with.

The increase of procurement in setting and selecting agency bids has not been without controversy in recent years. The report detailed in Table 5.6 suggests some supplier and agency frustration with procurement involvement; however, as the statistics indicate, this viewpoint is not held by all stakeholders in the industry,

Event management agencies and contractors have raised complaints that the procurement and purchasing divisions of large organisations do not fully appreciate the specific rules and issues surrounding the industry and may need more guidance and understanding when putting business out to tender. However, one clear impact that the role of procurement has brought to the industry is reinforcing awareness of Return on Investment methodologies and meeting the objectives set. This includes being accountable for the success and failure of an event and putting measures in place to evaluate after it has taken place to work towards continuous improvement, as already explored in Chapter 3.

REAL INSIGHT 5.4

PROCUREMENT SELECTION

A leading US Information Technology (IT) company initially issues a Request for Information (RFI) to a number of events management agencies to tender to handle all their internal and external events. The agencies receive an invitation by letter from the IT company inviting them to submit a proposal and providing them with some background information about the company and the four major business sectors that exist.

The IT company states that currently off-site meetings are decentralised with few experienced meeting planners involved and that their objective for the proposal is to qualify a limited number of event management agencies, covering both logistics and production to help manage all meetings and events as generated by UK budget holders within the organisation. They also give statistics on the volume of meetings and the previous year's annual spend on events.

The IT company requests that the agencies provide details on their background, fees and organisational structure, and that they demonstrate their ability and experience to handle meetings, conferences and group air requirements. This information should include a full description of services and a summary list of projects managed over the last two years. They also invite the agencies to explain their vision for the IT company's global meetings.

The IT company states that they have formed a 10-member team to coordinate the implementation and roll-out of the programme and the task force will evaluate and select proposals that best fit the company's overall business needs and adhere to their corporate culture. They stipulate that seven agencies have been selected to participate in this process and they give a deadline date for submission. Following this process, a more specific document, focusing on the actual events, is sent out by the IT company to the seven shortlisted event agencies, to submit their specific concepts, destination and venue detail and full costing. This document is known as a Request for Proposal (RFP).

THE FUTURE OF PROCUREMENT'S ROLE IN THE EVENTS INDUSTRY

All evidence would indicate that the role of procurement in selecting preferred suppliers is here to stay and will only increase in the future and become an industry standard. There needs to be improved communication between procurement professionals and for agencies to understand selection criteria and how smaller agencies need to evolve and work hand-in-hand with procurement in order to survive.

TRANSPARENCY AND CORRUPTION IN EVENT BIDDING

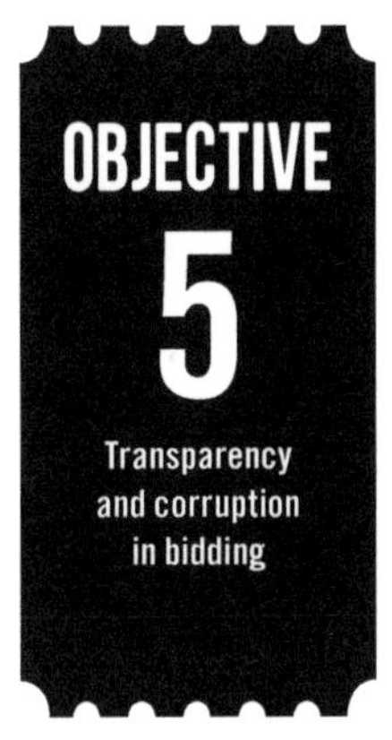
OBJECTIVE
5
Transparency and corruption in bidding

ALLEGED CORRUPTION IN SPORTING EVENTS

Despite the role that procurement plays in monitoring the event tendering process, and the tight ethical protocol involved with the bid tender for major and mega global sporting events, allegations of corruption, bribery and vote-buying within the sporting arena have never been higher. This was demonstrated in the recent corruption allegations concerning the Fédération Internationale de Football Association (FIFA), a private association known to be the international governing body of association football. Following the outcome of the 2018 Russian and 2022 Qatar FIFA World Cup bids, allegations about financial transactions were rife. Subsequently, there was initially speculation about awarding these events to alternative host destinations. Despite ongoing investigations by UEFA, MI6 and the FBI to uncover evidence that these financial transactions took place in the run-up to the event, the 2018 FIFA Sochi World Cup went ahead as planned in Russia. However, these allegations threaten to tarnish international sporting events, and they emphasise the extreme lengths some countries will go to acquire an opportunity to host a mega event of this kind in terms of regeneration, financial reward and creating a lasting legacy.

While the stakes for the host community remain so high, it is very likely that corruption and bribery will continue to cast a cloud over major and mega sporting events in the foreseeable future, until the bid process is subject to more thorough external scrutiny. It will also be interesting to see how, in future, key stakeholders react to events that are tarnished with negative impacts. The case study below illustrates how sponsors of such events do not want to be associated with the bad reputation and are prepared to pull out of their contracts to avoid any negative publicity that might come their way by association with such an organisation.

ALLEGED CORRUPTION IN THE OLYMPIC GAMES

There was further controversy within the International Olympic Committee (IOC) after the head of the Brazilian Olympic Committee, Carlos Nuzman, was detained amid claims he was a key figure in a bribery scandal, which led to Rio de Janeiro being awarded South America's first Olympics in 2014. He was arrested on suspicion of corruption, money laundering and participating in a criminal operation, after

REAL INSIGHT 5.5

ALLEGED CORRUPTION WITHIN FIFA

In 2015 VISA, who was one of FIFA's key sponsors, pulled out of its contract with FIFA (football's world governing body) as Sepp Blatter, President of FIFA from 1998 to 2015, faced increasing pressure not to seek re-election as its president. Nine senior officials at the organisation, as well as five sports media and promotions executives, were charged by US prosecutors over alleged bribes totalling more than US$150 million (£100 million) over 24 years.

This sparked a series of federal corruption investigations of FIFA. Since then more than 40 officials and marketing executives have been charged by US authorities, with 23 already pleading guilty. This followed multiple arrests of officials during a morning raid at a Zurich hotel and the announcement of a separate Swiss investigation into the awarding of the 2018 and 2022 World Cups. Sepp Blatter is currently serving a six-year ban from participating in FIFA activities.

The accusations of 'rampant, systemic and deep-rooted' corruption sent shockwaves through the industry. In a trial in New York in November 2017, three former South American football administrators were accused of taking millions of dollars in bribes and sparked a series of other allegations of racketeering, fraud and money laundering at the heart of the sport's governing body, FIFA. This caused the European football governing body, UEFA, to consider boycotting FIFA, and the sporting world to question whether FIFA was in a position to continue as the football-governing organisation.

Other FIFA sponsors include Adidas, Visa and Coca-Cola, all of whom demanded, following the incident, that the body reform its practices. Visa issued a statement expressing its 'disappointment and concern with FIFA', stating that unless football's world governing body rebuilt a corporate culture with 'strong ethical practices' at its heart they would reassess their sponsorship contract, which at that time was worth at least $25 million a year.

Brazilian prosecutors alleged his estate increased in value by 457% between 2006 and 2016. Further widespread corruption was uncovered during Operação Lava Jato or Operation Car Wash. It was alleged that executives at state-controlled oil company Petrobas accepted bribes in return for awarding construction contracts at inflated prices, and channelled funds into the accounts of Petrobas executives and politicians, which funded the electoral campaigns of senior Brazilian politicians.

In the lead-up to the 2014 Winter Olympics in Sochi, the President of Russia, Vladimir Putin also faced criticism over allegations of corruption and the Russian opposition leader Boris Nemtsov told reporters: 'In preparing for the Olympics $25 to $30 billion was stolen'. Another Putin critic alleged that the most expensive sports facilities built for the Games were commissioned without a competitive bid or public tenders. 'Only oligarchs and companies close to Putin got rich,' he wrote in his blog. 'The absence of fair competition, cronyism … have led to a sharp increase in the costs and to the poor quality of the work to prepare for the Games.'

It is not unusual to see such negative publicity and allegations surrounding these mega events, which is not to say that these allegations are necessarily true. Public opinion is invariably divided on events of this size and scale. Perceptions vary between stakeholders, depending on how much they stand to lose or gain. In terms of the IOC awarding bids to Brazil and Russia, both mega events were deemed poor investments. Brazil faced its worst recession in 25 years, there were cuts in healthcare and education and the police went unpaid for weeks at a time. In Russia, following the 2014 Olympics, the expenditure for the infrastructure and its subsequent under-utilisation were unparalleled. The government will have to subsidise the operation and maintenance of venues and tourist and transportation infrastructure to the tune of $1.2 billion for the foreseeable future, in order to meet the total $55 billion spent to host the event.

Some nations have expressed concerns that these corruption allegations are slowly beginning to taint the Olympic Games and have an impact on potential host nations' decisions on whether to bid for these events. A lack of candidates meant the 2022 Winter Olympics was awarded to Beijing, a city not renowned as a winter sports hub. Away from the Olympics, London made a last-minute decision to pull out of hosting the start of the 2017 Tour de France; and less-fashionable Düsseldorf stepped in. Emerging economies such as Brazil, as well as Russia and Qatar, hosts of the FIFA World Cup in 2018 and 2022 respectively, do not have the same economic rationale to consider. For them, such sporting events are an investment in their global brand and overrunning costs are the price they are willing to pay for that privilege. The International Olympic Committee (IOC) has started to realise the declining appeal of hosting, which is why it delivered its Olympics Agenda 2020, a plan intended to provide cost-saving measures, reduce complexity and red tape, and simplify the bidding process.

EVENT ETHICS

Some agencies announce their company vision and mission statement to their staff, clients and suppliers in order to boost morale, perception and retention, yet still carry out practices that go against these statements.

Do you think this is ethical? Could it be justifiable in some circumstances?

CHAPTER SUMMARY

CHAPTER SUMMARY QUESTIONS

1 What are the typical phases in any bid process?

2 What is the difference between an RFI and a RFP?

3 What issues would you consider before deciding whether to bid for an event?

4 What does the term procurement mean?

5 What is a preferred and sole supplier?

6 What part of the events industry is most susceptible to event corruption and bribery?

DISCUSSION POINTS

- How has corruption in bidding to host mega sporting events impacted the industry over the last decade?
- What does legacy planning mean, as part of a destination bid to host a major or mega event?
- Do you think agencies should charge the event owner or budget holder for the time and resources needed to put together a bid document?

ACTIVITIES

- Identify a list of skills and attributes needed to become a bid writer.
- Make a list of items you would include in a corporate RFI document.
- Put together a critical path document, highlighting the key tasks and timelines needed to prepare a bid proposal and pitch presentation.

REFERENCES

Evans, G. and Shaw, P. (2006) 'Literature review: Culture and regeneration', *Arts Research Digest*, 37.

Kearns, G. and Philo, C. (eds) (1993) *Selling Places: The City as Cultural Capital, Past and Present*. Oxford: Pergamon Press.

MPI report on Procurement (2011) Procuring meetings and events [online]. Available at: www.hbaa.org.uk/sites/default/files/ProcuringMeetingsEvents.pdf (accessed 2 May 2019).

Palmer Rae Associates (2004) *European Cities and Capitals of Culture Study*. Prepared for the European Commission. Available at: https://ec.europa.eu/programmes/creative-europe/sites/creative-europe/files/library/palmer-report-capitals-culture-1995-2004-i_en.pdf (accessed 6 November 2018).

Sheffield Hallam University (2017) Available at: https://www4.shu.ac.uk/mediacentre/news (accessed 14 May 2019).

Silvers, J. (2008) *Risk Management for Meetings and Events*. Oxford: Butterworth-Heinemann.

SIRC (2017) 4th Biennial Society for Implementation Research Collaboration (SIRC 2017): Implementation mechanisms: What makes implementation work and why? [online]. Available at: https://societyforimplementationresearchcollaboration.org/4th-biennial-society-for-implementation-research-collaboration (accessed 20 April 2018).

Smith, A. (2012) *Events and Urban Regeneration: The Strategic Use of Events to Revitalise Cities*. London: Routledge.

Spracklen, K. (2012) 'Special issue on the unintended policy consequences of the Olympics and Paralympics', *Journal of Policy Research in Tourism, Leisure and Events*, 6(1): 15–30.

Varano, J. (2017) 'Major sports events: Are they worth it?', *The Conversation*, 9 August. Available at: https://theconversation.com/major-sports-events-are-they-worth-it-80691 (accessed 5 December 2018).

Waitt, G. (2008) 'Urban festivals: Geographies of hype, helplessness and hope', *Geography Compass*, 2(2): 513–37. Available at: https://doi.org/10.1111/j.1749-8198.2007.00089.x (accessed 17 April 2017).

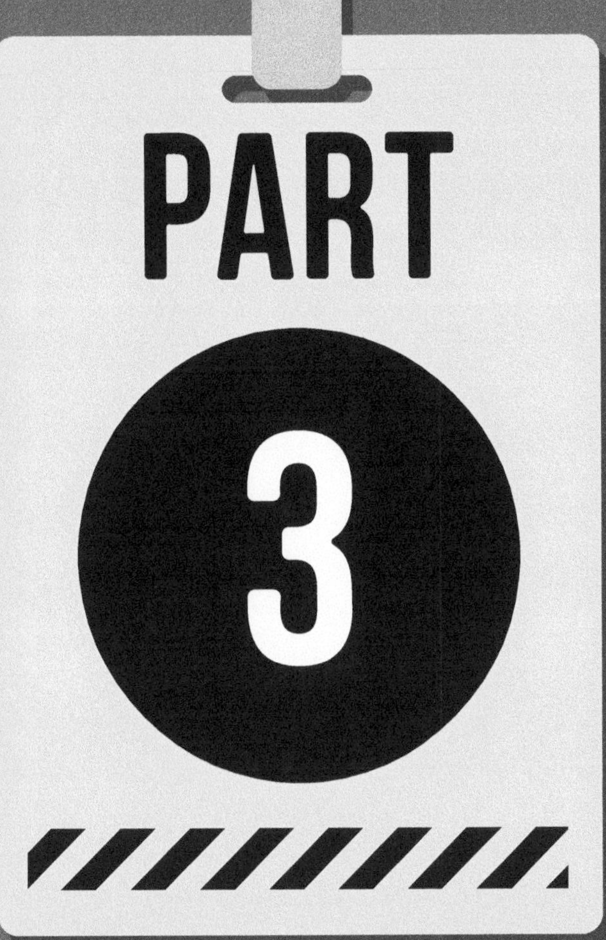

PART 3

THROUGHOUT THE EVENT

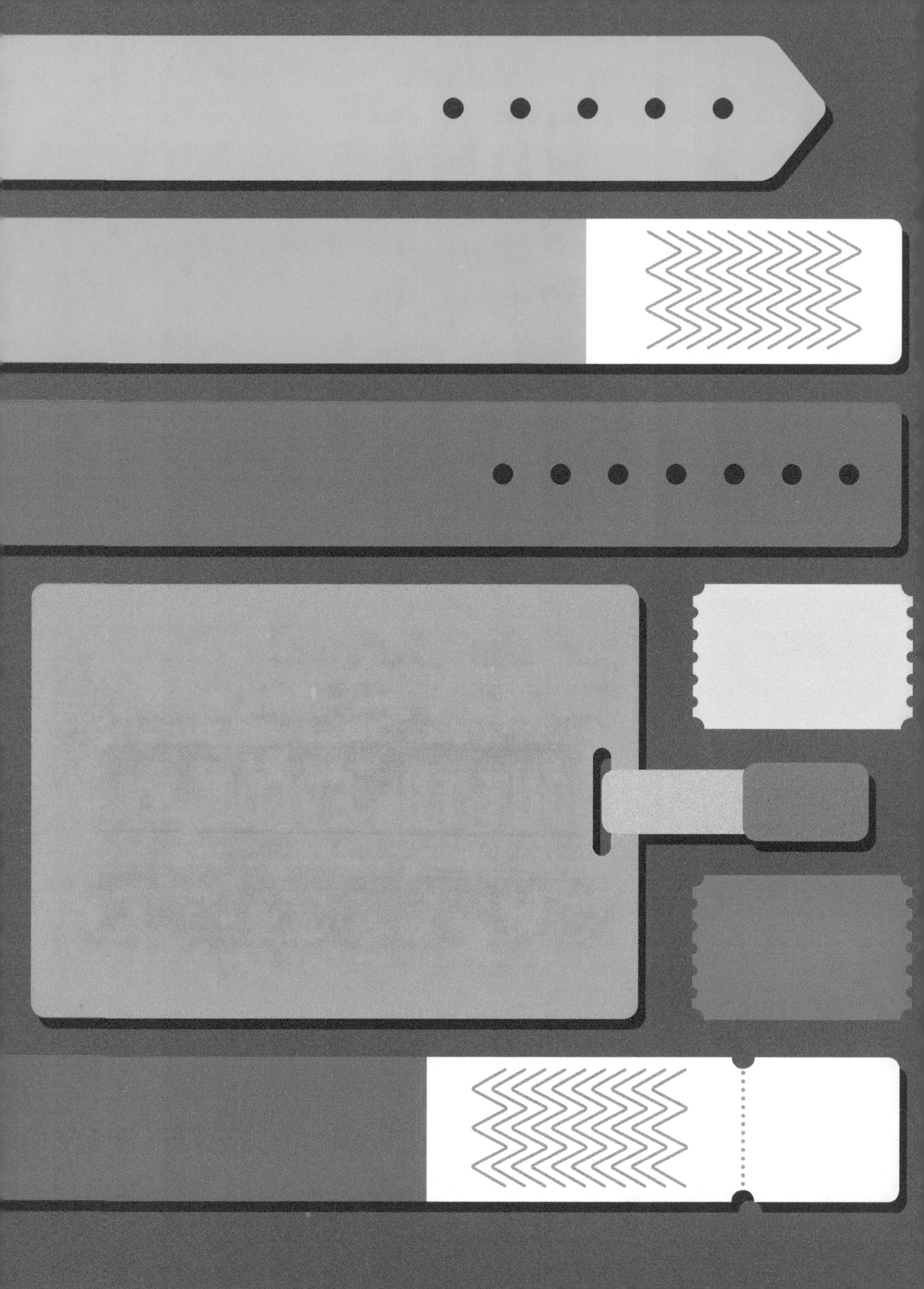

6

EVENT OPERATIONS, LOGISTICS AND MARKETING

CHAPTER OVERVIEW

This chapter will examine the operational factors involved in event planning and delivery, including logistical requirements, for example: project management; destination knowledge; venue sourcing; conducting site inspections; supplier liaison; risk assessment; health and safety; administration; and the invitation and registration process. It also examines the development of the event schedule and programme. The chapter also discusses marketing; sponsorship; public relations and promotion; and aims to develop awareness of professionalism and best practice in the organisation of events, using relevant examples and case studies.

CHAPTER OBJECTIVES

After reading this chapter, you will be able to identify and understand:

OBJECTIVE 1
Operational and logistical aspects

OBJECTIVE 2
Effective project management

OBJECTIVE
4
Plotting resources, tasks and assigning roles and responsibilities

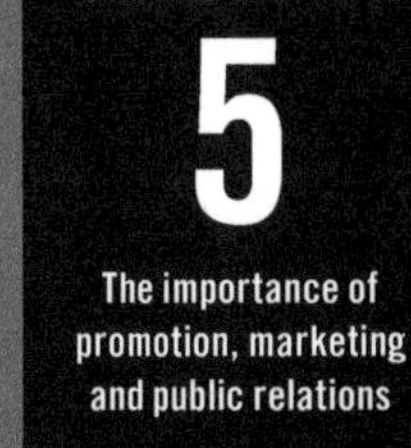

OBJECTIVE
5
The importance of promotion, marketing and public relations

Meet LEE THOMSON

Freelance Event Producer

Lee started her event career on the client side, first running UK roadshows for an IT company based in the USA, then as Head of Events for a major pharmaceutical company, before moving on to work with some of the largest and most prestigious event management agencies in the world. During this time she moved to New York, creating and delivering events for incoming groups to Manhattan. She then moved to Australia for two years and worked with Telstra, a national Olympic sponsor, to develop and deliver its hospitality programme for the 2000 Sydney Olympics.

On arriving back in the UK, Lee joined the production company Indeprod as Director of Live Events, leading a large and diverse team to produce full-service creative event solutions. After five years, she returned to what she loved best: Olympic and football sponsorship activation and managing hospitality programmes, working on sporting mega events in both Beijing and Johannesburg. Her last Olympic programme was for London 2012, where she set up and ran a DMC department for Sportsworld, servicing their eight partner sponsors and guests. This not only included organising and managing a number of elite London-based activities for them during their stay, but also booking and coordinating pre- and post-Olympic travel arrangements and extensions throughout the UK and Europe. Lee now produces creative client proposals for a number of agencies on a freelance basis.

REAL EVENT CHALLENGE

Producing a live festival culminating in a Jamiroquai concert at Le Mans, France, a 24-hour Grand Prix race for an audience of approximately 50,000 people and exclusive VIP hospitality for 200 guests. This was the first time that this type of event had ever been done, so the organisers needed to be convinced that it was a positive and worthwhile undertaking.

The main challenges were the limited access to the site, as it was located in the middle of the race circuit. There was no infrastructure on-site, and the crew basically had four weeks to convert a field into a state-of-the-art concert and festival environment, complete with power, drainage, backstage areas with fully fitted bathrooms, showers and toilets, VIP and crew catering and security. Afterwards, we had a week to de-rig and put everything back as

Q&A

WHAT IS THE MOST PRESTIGIOUS EVENT YOU HAVE EVER WORKED ON?

I have worked on many, but unfortunately due to the sensitivity and signed confidentiality agreements I am not able to divulge any information on these. Always remember, don't ever be afraid to knock on doors; sometimes the most unlikely ones open and you are welcomed in. At the very worst they might say no . . . !

WHO WAS YOUR MOST DEMANDING CLIENT AND WHY?

MTN, South Africa's main mobile provider, was a national sponsor of the 2010 Football World Cup and invited 6,000 guests to attend the Confederations Cup in 2009 and 8,000 VIP guests to the 2010 Football World Cup in South Africa. This incorporated both international and regional VIP hospitality programmes. I delivered these prestigious events by working closely with my client to develop and tightly manage the overall guest programmes and budget.

PREFERRED MODE OF TRANSPORT?

Boat, any type, anywhere.

FAVOURITE COLOUR?

Purple.

DO YOU HAVE ANY UNFULFILLED WORK AMBITIONS?

There are still some countries I would like to explore, but I am ready now to enjoy mentoring the next generation of event professionals.

it was, including the trees. Health and safety were of paramount importance throughout for the crew, the band and the audience.

PRACTITIONER VIEWPOINT

Jamie Ross-Hulme, Senior Producer, Events, Film & Content

Music events can sometimes turn into a logistical nightmare in my experience and I have worked on quite a few of them in the past! A particularly challenging one that springs to mind was a Halloween event in Glasgow, back in 2011, to promote a major alcohol brand. I was working for the experiential marketing team of a large advertising agency and this event was organised on behalf of an existing client. Our team was tasked with curating and theming a ticketed event for an audience of 2,500, which was essentially a late-night rave. It took place in Ashton Lane, a bar area in Glasgow, so the road had to be closed to traffic that night. We knew this was feasible, as it had previously been done for a New Year's event in the same street, but we still had to go through the process of applying for licences from scratch in the pre-production phase. This included securing music and alcohol licences for outside use and a licence for road-traffic closure. Due to the complex logistics involved, e.g. controlling the access and flow of 2,500 drunken revellers and moving from venue to venue to watch various music acts into the early hours, we needed to appoint a health and safety advisory team to work with us on this event. We also had to have a full medical team and ambulances on standby.

In addition, the booking agency for the headline act told us two days beforehand they were double booked and would have to pull out. We then had to source and book an alternative headline act for that night, before finding out that the original band could make it, providing we hire them a private jet to take them from our gig in Glasgow on to Leeds where they would be performing later that night.

The real stress of this type of bespoke event is that, although you can apply for provisional licences in advance, the licensing officer only comes on-site and signs it all off on the night, so we only got the 'green light' about two hours before the event began. Amazingly the delivery went pretty well. We then had to do the whole thing again for the same client the next night in Dublin!

ACADEMIC VIEWPOINT

Owen Grainger-Jones, Principal Teaching Fellow (Events Management), University of Surrey

This was a very complex event to stage in so many ways. There were the venue's requirements and conditions to consider and local and, national licensing and legal requirements. Most venues will have contractors that they prefer or will allow onto their venue site and, for someone who is not fully aware of all such internal, local and regulatory issues, taking on an event such as this would present significant challenges. Perhaps one of the most important considerations within the initial stage of such a complex event project would be to identify experienced professionals who could be depended upon to support the event director and ensure that all the communications, agreements and planning documents are able to be developed in a manageable way.

While health and safety considerations have to 'some extent' become more standardised within the event industry in recent years, the event team would need to ensure that the event complies with all local and national requirements; in addition to local and national requirements, any UK staff working on the event would be theoretically covered by UK health and safety at work legislation and thus ensuring compliance with 'home' requirements while needing to meet local requirements could be challenging. On top of all the aforenoted event planning and logistics challenges, the event will host 50,000 visitors and will therefore have to consider all aspects of crowd management, safety and security and also, and not least, the many issues with working with any artist and their entourage.

The fact that the event went so well is testimony to the event director's experience in working around the world and being able to create and lead high-performing teams able to successfully deliver such an event. At the University of Surrey where I work, we teach students about event planning from an event project perspective with real focus on the contents of key event-planning documents. The event planning is comprehensively linked to key areas of legislation and official guidance documents so that students see the links between practice and regulation and areas of law. In the latter part of their degree course, students are expected to produce high-quality event management plans and risk assessments for the live events that they stage as part of their programme of learning.

REAL EVENT OUTCOME

Working closely with the event producer and production manager, the team managed to deliver a prestigious event, including stage build, lighting, sound, projection and live camera relay rig, car displays, tree removal and replacement and a nearby chateau refurbishment, for the artists and their entourage. This included managing contract negotiations and specific rider requirements for the overall event, undertaking extensive risk assessments, setting up 24-hour on-site security and instructing the whole team on health and safety management throughout the event. The entire production, from crew arrival to departure of the last truck, lasted five weeks.

Our team brought in 'rock and roll' catering for the crew, plus the band's private chef. It was by far the best catering on-site! In addition, the team was responsible for all budgetary management, on-site reporting and putting together a full financial reconciliation on completion of the event.

Despite the initial logistical challenges, the crew worked tirelessly to get it right. Subsequently the event created massive impact for the whole site and stood out from all the other corporate activities taking place around the track, which fulfilled our client's aim. The 24-hour Le Mans organisers repeated the event again in 2018.

OPERATIONAL AND LOGISTICAL ASPECTS

OBJECTIVE
1
Operational and logistical aspects

WHAT IS EVENT LOGISTICS?

Logistics could be described as the network of activities that brings together all the required resources for an event to take place. For that reason, event logistics are an important part of maintaining and delivering customer satisfaction.

Logistics is the science of developing and managing the capabilities and protocol that are responsive to customer-driven service requirements. (Manrodt and Davis 1992: 82)
Event logistics is about getting things organised, getting things and people in the right place at the right time. (Van der Wagen 2011: 229)

TABLE 6.1 Definitions of logistics

IDENTIFYING LOGISTICAL ISSUES

Part of the operational planning process is being able to plan ahead and to consider the logistical aspects of the programme that will be required during the event day, such as:

- Load-in timings for access to the venue and delivery of materials and supplies
- Guest arrival times and patterns and the implications these will have for transport, parking, registration process, queues, staff requirements, etc.
- The flow of people around the venue at key or busy times and the avoidance of on-site congestion
- A plan for on-site communication that identifies how the team is going to communicate
- Space for amenities and a plan for restocking, removal of waste and cleaning during the event
- Determining requirements for VIPs, artists and media representatives and listing whether particular groups have specific requirements that need to be considered
- Emergency planning and risk assessment; identifying any particular concerns related to specific aspects of the event and suggesting contingency plans.

As can be seen from the items listed above, any logistical requirements must be identified early in the planning process. The site or venue has to be completely suitable and fit for purpose. A fine balance is required between the creative and functional aspects. Brainstorming with the whole planning team will help identify any issues that could affect the running of the event.

Additionally, logistics involves managing the processes of manufacture, supply and distribution, including the storage and transport of products and merchandise, which all require an organised and structured alignment of the key logistic functions, such as: procurement, transportation, storage, inventory management, customer service and database management.

LOGISTICAL CONSIDERATIONS

The operations manager should have the skills to look at all activities and tasks that need to be executed in the planning phase and to assign tasks to the various team members. They will have a clear idea of what the event aims and objectives are and make sure relevant questions are asked in the planning stage and that all team members are briefed as to their roles and responsibilities. The event manager should also be able to keep the big picture in sight and retain an overview of all the different areas that need to be carried out at the event, as it is their remit to pull all those strands together and to ensure all the documentation, including budget spreadsheets, have been updated as much as is possible before the delivery stage.

Supply chain analysis analysis of the management of the flow of goods and services

The logistics involved with moving large quantities of food can be highly problematic, particularly if there is a system that limits access to the site. Most large-scale events have to develop a delivery schedule for the early hours of the morning, with limited times available for each operator. **Supply chain analysis** is a useful tool to estimate the time needed for delivery and off-loading of supplies and equipment. This might allow the venue hire period to be extended if necessary, to ensure adequate delivery time. Sufficient storage is another important logistical consideration, as strict food storage rules apply in accordance with health and safety food hygiene regulations.

POTENTIAL LOGISTICAL ISSUES WITH OUTDOOR EVENTS

Outdoor events that take place in an open field, the grounds of a stately home or other open expanses, can often cause the most logistical challenges. This is because all the necessary equipment, power and infrastructure and food and beverage provision has to be brought on to the site in advance and may take some weeks to set up. This may be the case for a number of event types, including corporate events, such as fun days, wedding receptions, festivals or concerts. The logistical elements that need to be considered for outdoor events are access to the site, including the physical limitations and dimensions of the site; refrigerated storage; physical space for food preparation; toilet facilities; cleaning areas; safety restrictions; potential damage to the site; and provision of basic services. These are just a selection of possible factors to consider when choosing a venue or open space that is suitable.

OBJECTIVE
2
Effective project management

EFFECTIVE PROJECT MANAGEMENT

WHAT IS EVENT PROJECT MANAGEMENT?

Project methodology is about managing change, or, in other words, putting some 'order into the chaos'. This could manifest itself in many ways, not least the development of new practices and getting people to change their current working behaviours. Within the events industry, projects come in many shapes and forms, depending on the type, size and complexity of the event, the lead time and the budget and resources available.

A system that describes the work before the event actually starts, the event itself and finally the shutdown of the event. (Allen et al. 2011: 154)
The production of a festival or event is a project. Project management oversees the initiation, planning and implementation of an event. (Bowdin et al. 2011: 257)

TABLE 6.2 Definitions of project management

WHAT MAKES EVENT PROJECTS SUCCEED?

In order for event projects to succeed, project and functional managers must develop good working relationships. A process of negotiation and leadership is needed to accomplish the project, and in the events world a successful operation depends largely on the attitudes, actions and activities of the people involved. The following guidelines will help ensure a successful project outcome:

- A good project charter
- Good use of project tools
- Strong project management
- The right mix of team players
- A good decision-making structure
- Good communication
- Team members working towards common goals
- Project sponsorship set up at executive level.

The process of project management includes constant monitoring, ongoing re-evaluation and communication of the event progress with the organising team (see Figure 6.1). Sometimes it is necessary to go back to the beginning, or revisit part of the schedule during the planning process. If the project shows signs of not being able to achieve its original objectives, or not able to deliver a return on investment, corrective action will need to be taken. This may be due to a number of issues. Certainly there are many aspects and issues that may change the goalposts, such as any amends to the initial brief or requirements; a reduction in numbers; a decrease in the overall budget; changes to staff resources; other resource issues; a change of venue or location; or any other unforeseen circumstances that may impact the course of the event and its progress.

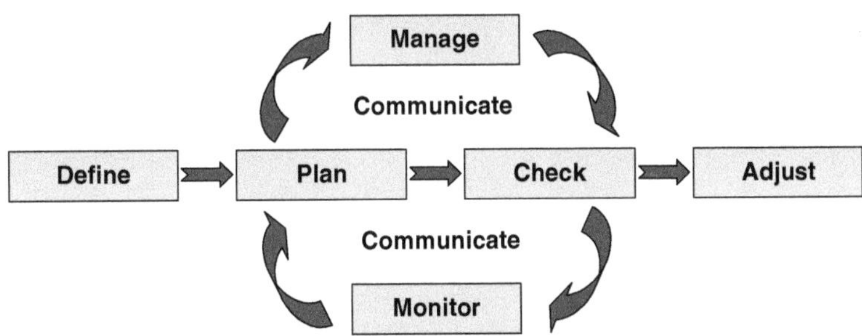

FIGURE 6.1 The project management process

A good project manager is able to identify these needs in advance and to make the necessary changes quickly and spontaneously, before the event becomes at risk.

PROJECT MANAGEMENT SKILLS

Project management requires expertise. It is a skill that is acquired usually only after first making a few mistakes. Excellent communication skills are required in order to be a good project manager and an ability to convey the overall event vision to the team or other colleagues, and to motivate and manage them. Attention to detail is essential for any project manager, as is the ability to be able to bring all the strands of the event together and administer project planning, risk assessment, budget control, as well as resource allocation, in a timely and efficient manner.

- Leader
- Negotiator
- Organiser
- People manager
- Mediator
- Team player
- Problem solver
- Diplomat
- Trouble-shooter
- Decision maker
- Good listener
- Financial controller
- ...and normally a bit of a control freak!

TABLE 6.3 Attributes of a good project manager

STAGES IN PROJECT MANAGEMENT

The first stage of managing the project is to clearly understand the scope and environment and the constraints of the project. It is advisable at this stage to draw up a detailed operational plan, which should include all tasks. These tasks may include choosing the destination, conducting a site inspection, booking the venue, specifying and sourcing technical equipment, room allocation and transportation, contacting sponsors and other suppliers, and so on.

The next stage is to be able to use the items of this operational plan to define the tasks that need to be executed leading up to event delivery, then to confirm the requirements with all stakeholders involved in the project. The operational plan might evolve gradually after a series of client and staff briefings, or a committee meeting with all other interested parties. Throughout the management of any event, it is the responsibility of the event team leader to supervise, support and offer motivation and encouragement to the operations team and to ensure all project tasks are completed within the specified deadline. There may be numerous changes recorded to the overall strategy, so it may be necessary to revisit and amend the operational plan accordingly on an ongoing basis. After this consultation period, the project plan is ready to be rolled out.

Following on from this, a number of key tasks will be assigned and implemented by the team. It is therefore important to check the available resources at this stage and to take appropriate action, should resources or manpower need to be increased or decreased. During this planning stage, the manager, with overall responsibility for the project, will need to monitor, review and control all key tasks on a weekly basis. This will include conducting a regular review of what tasks have been achieved, and those that have fallen behind schedule. Following this, the original operational plan and critical path may need to be adjusted and corrective action implicated where applicable. If more serious challenges or problems occur, they should be immediately reported to superiors, budget holders, committee members, potential sponsors and any organisational board members. The last stage of the operational plan is the technical execution and delivery, which has already been discussed in Chapter 2 of this book.

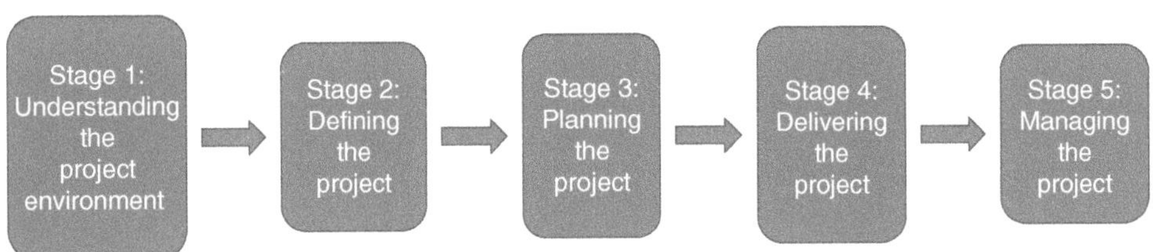

FIGURE 6.2 The five key stages of project management

CRITICAL PATH ANALYSIS

In order to plot the tasks that need completing and to assess how realistic the timelines are, it is advisable for the event manager to put together a critical path document, detailing key milestones leading up to the delivery. The work breakdown should be prepared according to the event requirements, and key milestone activities should be prioritised in terms of importance. The best tool for compiling a critical path analysis is a Gantt chart, which will list the tasks that need completing and assign dates for completion in sequential order, as has already been detailed in Chapters 4 and 5 of this book.

ON-SITE SCHEDULING

The project management phase includes all stages of the planning process, leading up to the final delivery. It is advisable to prepare as much as possible in advance. The more preparation that goes into scheduling, the easier it is to deliver it, allowing for the unexpected eventualities that will invariably occur on-site. The delivery of events has already been detailed in Chapter 2, with further analysis of the key components of an on-site working document. However, as part of the operational process, the event schedule should be drawn up by the organisers and should include the following key functions:

- Venue facilities/lay-out plans
- Staff resources, contact details and duty rotas
- Registration
- Event programme and timings
- Speakers or entertainment
- Food and beverage details
- Signage
- Cloakroom, toilet facilities
- Transportation/parking
- Accommodation and rooming lists
- Movement and distances and audience flow
- Technical and production aspects
- Audience disabilities and any special requirements
- Emergency procedures.

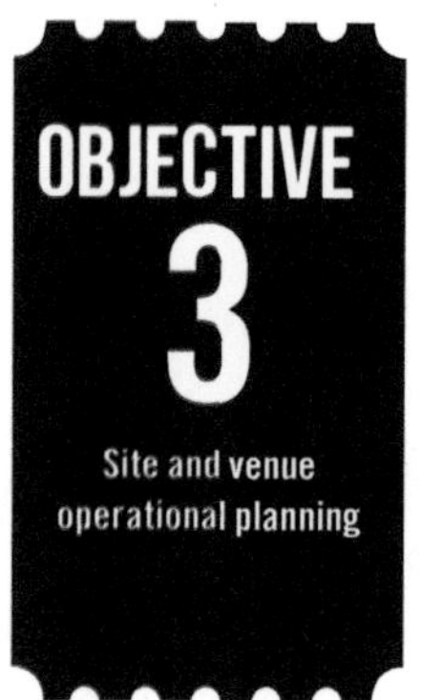
OBJECTIVE
3
Site and venue operational planning

SITE AND VENUE OPERATIONAL PLANNING

As previously discussed, the process of operational site and venue planning will start some time before the actual event takes place. The operations team should try to get an understanding of the general resource requirements and to design initial plans to facilitate an overall blueprint for the infrastructure. This will include making one, two or maybe numerous visits to the site to familiarise the team with the space, dimensions and potential layout. During this time, the team will undergo a period of consultation, feedback and amends before the master site plan is finalised. Once this has been produced, it will be possible to produce specific and more detailed site plans for various groups and interested parties from the master document. In the run-up time and throughout the planning process, the following logistical elements need to be managed by the operational team, which will each be detailed further within this section:

- Destination knowledge
- Venue sourcing and accommodation
- Site inspections

- The venue report
- The infrastructure
- Meeting rooms/layout plans
- Air and ground transportation
- Pre-event catering planning
- Provision of drinking water
- The invitation and registration process
- Financial management.

DESTINATION KNOWLEDGE

Being equipped with a widespread and current destination knowledge, and a realistic geographical idea of where cities and countries lie in relation to each other, is part of the required overall expertise of an event manager. If a client or event budget holder is outsourcing to an event agency, it is reasonable to presume that they would expect them to have a sound idea of the best cities and countries that are suitable to host their meeting or conference. Event managers should also know how accessible these destinations are, and the key facilities and venues that set each destination apart. Further details and precise information can also be obtained from the overseas destination management company, as to special venue and programme suggestions. The agency attending the initial brainstorming sessions with the budget holder or client in the pitch stage should be furnished with enough knowledge to be able to discuss the merits of various suitable destinations, and be able to match the destination features to the demographic of the group and the specific event, with accuracy and confidence. Part of this destination knowledge can be acquired by reading relevant directories, websites, trade press and event publications, or by consulting specialist agencies, tourism organisations, or from word-of-mouth and colleague recommendations.

HOW FAMILIARISATION OR INSPECTION TRIPS CAN INCREASE DESTINATION KNOWLEDGE

Familiarisation trips, hosted by the destination tourist associations, bureaus or other representatives of the destination, can be an excellent way to become familiar with the layout and opportunities of various key destinations, and the venues within them. This allows event planners to keep abreast of trends and changes and developments and to familiarise themselves with newly emerging destinations. These familiarisation trips are a useful tool to conduct a general information search, at little or no cost to the agency. They also provide the professional planner with an opportunity to gain an overview of what a destination can offer, even if, at that point in time, there is no particular event in mind.

These inspection trips are usually hosted by the sales team of a venue, a destination management company (DMC) or a venue or destination representation company or tourist association. It is good practice to write to the host after the familiarisation trip, to thank them for their hospitality and to file a report containing general details on the venues visited and the sightseeing and social activities that exist in the destination.

This information can provide a useful reminder when responding to a client brief and can be logged online for others within the agency or event organisation to access when necessary.

CHOOSING THE DESTINATION

The following factors for destination choice have already been highlighted in Chapter 5. The client may prefer to choose a destination they are already familiar with and where they feel confident that the destination will deliver on the event objectives set. Conversely, many clients may want to try out new and untried destinations that offer innovative programmes, different from the normal leisure or holiday destination that delegates would normally experience. As recently regenerated and revitalised city hubs, these destinations could provide new options for conferences and other events.

Recent research, according to a report published by the Mayor of London's official promotional agency, has revealed that pubs, galleries, theatres, restaurants and a city's wider cultural offerings are key factors when choosing a destination for meetings and events. Around 93% of international event planners report that a destination's cultural highlights are significant when choosing where they host meetings and events. According to Hanneke Dannhorn, President at Brook Green UK DMC: 'A good turnout is what defines success and delegates will be keener to attend an event in a city that has more to offer than just functional hotels and venues.' It is the attractions, culture and arts in a destination that offer 'unforgettable experiences' when visiting cities that humanise an event, ensuring the content is remembered long after the final PowerPoint slide or post-show drink.

VENUE SOURCING AND ACCOMMODATION

In addition to destination knowledge, the agency will be expected to have a good understanding of the various venues that exist in the chosen event destination that adhere to the requirements. Booking adequate accommodation and meeting rooms is part of the operational process. The venue and accommodation should always reflect

www.venuedirectory.com
www.squaremeal.co.uk
www.booking.com/hotels
www.venuesworld.com
https://hirespace.com
www.venuescanner.com
www.headbox.com
https://venuu.com
https://venuereservations.co.uk
www.canvas-events.co.uk

TABLE 6.4 Sample UK venue booking websites and portals

the status of the meeting and the invited guests. For example, the CEO of a company would expect to be accommodated in a 5-star suite as a minimum requirement, but a junior member of staff might be happy with a 3- or 4-star hotel rating and even be prepared to share accommodation.

Tools for choosing an appropriate venue have already been discussed in the event planning process section in Chapter 1. It is worth noting here that part of the overall logistical delivery in the operational planning phase is constant communication between the organiser and the venue itself. Table 6.4 shows a few of the leading websites and portals currently being used to find suitable venues.

SITE INSPECTIONS

The first site inspection to the venue should take place while working on the preparation of a proposal, following receipt of a brief. Ideally the organiser will plan to visit several suitable venue options and, during that time, gather as much specific information on facilities, services and potential costs as possible. When conducting the site inspection in the operational planning phase, the event manager should endeavour to speak to as many divisions of the venue as possible, and compile a comprehensive venue report, with relevant information on each function area containing contact details of email and mobile phones of the following venue personnel:

- Conference/duty manager
- Catering manager
- AV/technical manager
- Security manager
- Health and safety manager.

First impressions should be documented within the report, noting aspects such as décor, cleanliness, the friendliness and efficiency of staff, and commenting on venue facilities such as restaurants, spas, fitness areas and other amenities, such as shops and hairdressers. The overall impression should also make reference to the location for registration desks, including any electronic registration signage, cloakrooms, concierge and porter services. The report should also provide arrival, departure and access details and a breakdown on local transport access by rail, air, public transport or car or coach. Details on parking facilities for coaches, cars and taxis should also be recorded, including disabled access, car park charges and details on courtesy or shuttle buses. Within the report, notes on the provision of external and internal venue signage should be made, itemising what the venue provides, any additional signage that will be needed, as well as any further restrictions that the venue may have stipulated.

Some factors that should be considered at the site inspection are as follows:

- How many rooms does the venue have of the same standard to accommodate delegates?
- How many suites and junior suites does the hotel have?
- Is there Wi-Fi and fast connectivity in each room?
- What other events will be taking place in the venue at the same time?
- Has the venue/hotel had previous experience dealing with similar groups?

- Is there an early check-in, late check-out facility for group bookings?
- What car park facilities are on-site?
- How long is the transfer time to major transport links?
- What discounts is the hotel prepared to offer for delegates and crew?
- How long will the hotel hold provisional space?
- What are the hotel payment terms?

It is advisable for the agency to ask the venue manager conducting the site inspection, if it will be possible to set up a hospitality desk in the hotel foyer and whether they will be permitted to display branded material from their agency, client's organisation, partners or sponsors on pop-up stands or banners in the hotel lobby area or conference plenary area. They should also enquire whether there are any other events scheduled at the same time, or whether the group will have exclusive use of the venue or **run of house**. It would be useful to know whether it will be necessary to share space in any public and refreshment areas, and, most importantly, whether there are any conflicts of interest with other clients and their products or business offering. For example, if a client were launching a new pharmaceutical product within the venue, it would be of paramount importance to ensure there were no competitive industries, such as consumer healthcare, pharmaceutical or medical clients, in the hotel at the same time, or any press presence.

Run of house
use of the hotel rooms available at the time, but not specified in advance

The agency should find out from the venue if any decorating or building works are scheduled in the foreseeable future. They should ask for verbal and written confirmation on the start and finish dates for completion and what areas of the hotel are to be refurbished, to ensure that this will not interfere in any way with their proposed event.

THE VENUE REPORT

On completion of the site inspection, the venue report should detail all the available meeting rooms that the venue has offered. The report should state their location and position to each other, so that it will be possible to anticipate delegate movement and flow at the event.

At this stage, the organiser should consider if any additional stewards or hostesses will be required to guide delegates, particularly at peak times, for example during morning registration, lunch and coffee breaks and at the start of any new sessions. They should detail what items of furniture will be in situ at the venue and what will need to be hired and brought in, together with the potential costs involved. It should be noted whether there is extra space for storage of computers, PCs or merchandise that might be required and whether the venue has offered space for an event office to use as a secure base on-site.

Technical considerations should also be noted, including a list of equipment in each meeting room and a list of audio-visual equipment that might be offered in the venue contract, and equipment that will be hired in. The report should contain detail on sound speakers and microphones, including any restrictions on decibels. Also, the lighting for each meeting room should be detailed, including what rigs are in place, with hanging points and weight loadings recorded. It should be noted whether the room can be blacked out, or whether it might be necessary to hang drapes to darken the room. The organiser should make reference to whether each meeting room has a lectern or staging, and detail the power sources that are in the room, the room ceiling heights and whether each room has manual air conditioning and light switches and dimmers. Also, the condition of the floors should be documented and whether any of the spaces will need to be recarpeted.

GO ONLINE

Items that should be documented in the venue report are detailed in the Appendix, available online as Table 6.1.

The venue report should highlight any areas of the offering that might need revisiting and amending. This is a good opportunity to negotiate savings with the venue. Even if the venue is not prepared to make any further reductions on the overall costs offered, they may well be prepared to offer a few non-monetary incentives to seal the deal, such as a complimentary event office, guest leisure club access, complimentary delegate parking, shuttle buses or even drinks on arrival.

Following documentation of the venue report, the event company, or agency, should make an overall recommendation to the client on the shortlisted venues or preferred venue. They should ensure that provisional space is being held with all venues featured in the proposal for the required dates, until the client is in a position to confirm or cancel the space held.

THE INFRASTRUCTURE

This is particularly relevant when operating in an outside space. Specialist structures can make a more appropriate setting than an established venue. Unlike indoor events where there is a building, outdoor ones have to create their own 'temporary' venue space. This solution provides the freedom of creating the perfect space that is totally unique and bespoke to the client.

Temporary or pop-up structures could also be considered in cases where a venue is not available in a particular area that the client wishes to hold the event. They can also meet a specific client-brief requirement, such as when a very high roof or loading of equipment is needed for an event such as a car launch or factory opening. Usually the cost of building a temporary, pop-up or specialist structure is comparable to the cost of using other venues that have a lengthier construction period and more requirement for production crew both before and during the delivery stage.

Large city parks frequently serve as a venue for music events and festivals. Usually the only way to successfully deliver them is to create a perimeter fence within these parks. A marquee or a perimeter fence can be created to establish the event 'zone'. Fences are usually around three metres in height and enable the organiser to direct the flow of spectators into the venue. Some fences include some kind of entrance system, either gates or turnstiles, or some method of allowing controlled access at the exit and entry points, as well as providing security points. A fence will also cut the event off visually from non-spectators, although they may well be able to hear the music from further out. The construction, erection and operation of a perimeter fence require specialist suppliers and so they become a vital part of the supply chain.

GO ONLINE

The following resource requirements for venue set-up have been adapted from Dowson and Bassett (2015) and include the items listed in Table 6.2, included within the Appendix document available online.

INFRASTRUCTURE PLANNING

Infrastructure planning involves consideration of the structures, space and power supplies needed for the serving and storing of alcohol and food at the event. One of the most important factors when serving food is to ensure that it is maintained and kept at the correct temperature. A constant power supply is mandatory and operational staff should ensure that appliances do not overload the electrical system, or the generators used on the event site. When using temporary kitchens on-site, attention needs to be given in the planning phase to:

- The placement of emergency exits
- Power requirements and safe distribution around the kitchen
- Provision of fire equipment and fire-retardant materials
- Hot-surface signage
- Hand-washing facilities
- Staff access points.

Staff need to ensure that there is sufficient back-up power available for chillers. Cold food should be stored below 5 degrees centigrade and hot food at above 63 degrees centigrade. This should be constantly checked and monitored on-site, especially in an outdoor environment. When using chillers or refrigerator containers on-site, parking for catering services needs to be organised and controls need to be put in place to prevent food contamination or deterioration.

When planning the infrastructure, it is also important to look at the layout of fixed items in relation to each other. This includes planning where to position event attractions; marquees and tents, the toilet cubicles, food and beverage outlets; the public address (PA) system; and stalls and vendors. Sometimes it is more practicable to have all the food outlets placed together in a catering village, and a separate area for children's activities, motorised activities, exhibition tents, toilets, and so on. At other times, however, it works better to split up the facilities, such as placing catering outlets and registration areas around the site, to prevent unnecessary queuing and congestion. Planning the layout and signposting the areas are part of the operational planning and need to take place in the early operational phase, and to be conveyed and communicated well to the audience on-site.

PESTS AND UNSANITARY ENVIRONMENTS

Insects and vermin are common, especially in outside spaces, where there may be supplies of food stored on-site. This includes rats, mice, silverfish, cockroaches, wasps, and so on.

The main issue of concern is the transmission of food-poisoning organisms, so it is important to ensure that the area is treated in advance by a professional pest control service.

SANITARY FACILITIES

These will vary depending on the target audience. There are many commercial companies that supply temporary toilet units, which range from trailers to portacabins and portaloos.

Festival toilets tend to be quite basic and sustainable concerns are often more important than cosmetic ones to that audience. However, for those that prefer festival **glamping**, it may be necessary to source more upmarket and ultimately expensive toilet facilities. These may be furnished and fitted with mirrors, toiletries, baby-changing facilities and disabled toilet access. Hand-washing areas are essential and, in some cases, additional sinks for hand washing and food washing are required. When planning the site layout, the location and positioning of sanitary facilities need to be considered. Wherever possible, blocks of toilets should be stationed around the whole site, but well away from catering areas. Enough room should be allowed on-site for the sewage tanker to get in, drive around, collect the waste matter and leave the site. Toilets for catering team and staff should also be provided, which may or may not be separate from the audience toilet facilities.

Glamping
a fusion of the words 'glamorous' and 'camping' to describe a style of camping with more facilities and amenities than traditional camping

ELECTRICAL TESTING

Electricity can be an unseen hazard to all staff and stakeholders. Electrical failure on-site is also a risk to the event itself and may include any of the following negative outcomes:

- The floodlights do not work
- There is no public address system
- The exhibition stands have no power
- There is no refrigeration or ovens
- The on-site CCTV does not work
- The projector or other AV equipment has no power
- There is no power within the medical facilities.

The risks of mechanical faults and failure within the electricity circuit on-site are manifold and may potentially result in injury, electric shocks, electric burns, explosions, fire, radiation, inhalation of harmful fumes or even fatalities in the worst case. In wet, hot, perspiring conditions, the effects of electricity are worse. The causes of electrical hazards may be:

- Damaged insulation; bare wires; metalwork
- Inadequate circuit protection
- Incorrect earthing; earth leakage currents
- Inadequate systems of work; lack of maintenance and testing; and human error
- Loose, unprotected contacts and connectors
- The overheating of equipment.

It is therefore necessary in the pre-event stages to make operational checks on the site and to secure an Electrical Safety Certificate, which will be part of the premises licensing requirement. All venues should have an annual inspection of electrical equipment and wiring, including fire alarm and emergency lighting, conducted by qualified electricians with relevant experience and qualifications. They should be affiliated to independent bodies such as The National Inspection Council for Electrical Installation Contracting, or a member of an electrical contractors association in the country of operation.

Serious outages or hazards may cause damage to equipment and property, which is why it is essential to carry out regular Portable Appliance Testing (PAT), to ascertain whether the appliance is hazardous to use. A 'portable' appliance could range from a large amplifier or dimmer rack to hairdryers or kettles. It is also important to consider any venue stipulations for these appliances, as well as ensuring the safe transportation of equipment through appropriate containers, flight cases, and so on.

Other on-site fire hazards also need to be considered as part of the logistical planning process. These may include aspects such as malicious ignition or arson; faulty vehicles; campsite fires; the use of cooking equipment; candles or naked flame torches; fuel leakages and the risk of fire starting on non-flame-retardant materials, such as drapes, backdrops, décor or even the event stage or set.

Fires at any event are extremely dangerous as they can spread very rapidly, as seen in countless event disasters, such as the Santa Maria nightclub fire in Brazil in 2013, which resulted in over 200 fatalities. Smoke can cause limited visibility and toxic fumes can lead to asphyxiation. On-site fires can result in high temperatures and burns, and extensive damage can lead to structural collapse and limitation of escape routes. These areas of health and safety on-site have already been outlined earlier in Chapter 2 of this book but need to be monitored as part of the overall checks on a suitable event infrastructure.

MEETING ROOMS AND LAYOUT PLANS

Any operational layout plans need to stipulate the event type and state whether it is taking place inside or out. Getz (2016) highlights three key considerations in determining layout:

- Controlling risk and safeguarding crowd safety (primarily looking at space and movement)
- Creating atmosphere and ambience
- Maximising sales, exposure and publicity.

Successful layout of a site will consider an understanding of capacity, i.e. the number of people that the space can hold, as well as crowd movement, and the way in which the attendees move around. Various layouts and furniture requirements will lead to different capacities for the same space. Estimates of room capacity are usually conservative, as they need to take account of different room features, such as aisles, doorways, furniture, structural pillars. In cases where there are dedicated spaces (e.g. for seats, table spaces, props), **capacity plotting** can be used to accurately determine a specific room capacity.

Capacity plotting determining the number of people who can be seated in a specific space, in terms of both the physical space available and limitations set by law

When deciding on workable capacities, there are three key issues that need to be considered:

- *Safety* – How many people the space can safely hold before issues of crowd movement, crushing and evacuation time make it untenable.
- *Safe capacity* – This is determined by the usable floor area and number of exits needed to evacuate the premises or space.
- *Legal capacity* – Every venue is constrained by its ability to evacuate an audience (in sports grounds and other indoor spaces, the maximum time requirement is four minutes).

The Purple Guide, a published guidebook for health, safety and welfare at music and other events, cites an expected evacuation rate for standard exits and people per minute, which equates to 66 people per metre per minute, where steps or escalators are involved, and on flat ground, 100 people per minute or 82 per metre per minute. However, this may depend on other audience demographics; for example, at the Ideal Home Exhibition, where the target audience is largely comprised of families, the abundance of buggies, prams and wheelchairs may slow the evacuation rate down.

AIR AND GROUND TRANSPORTATION

Air and ground transportation considerations and the compilation of flight manifests are also required in the operations planning process. One of the most time-consuming aspects of on-site management is the coordination of delegate flights. This is an area that often requires constant changes and amends, which can also impact transportation from the airport and hotel and may require a bespoke team to manage in the lead-up time. Areas to manage in the operational phase are as follows:

- Check all airline details in advance with airline carriers
- Put together flight manifests listing arrival and departure times
- Communicate any special requirements, such as delegates' seat preferences, status or dietary requirements to the airline
- Arrange for delegates or guests to have a meet-and-greet service at the airport, if requested
- Coordinate delegate transportation from the airport to the venue, according to arrival times
- Manage any lost baggage or visa issues that may occur on-site
- Notify the airline if any delegates make changes to their bookings on-site
- Coordinate taxis or coaches back to the right airport terminals at appropriate times
- Liaise with ground transportation companies throughout on coach transfers to off-site venues and dinners
- Keep an updated list of local taxi and private limousine companies available.

PRE-EVENT CATERING PLANNING

During the operational stage, planning for adequate provision of food and beverage is essential. Event catering is one area that can make or break the event in terms of the attendee expectations. This seems to be an area that guests pay particular attention to and it can influence the overall customer experience. It might be the cold cup of coffee that stays in the memory of the delegates, no matter how good all other aspects of the event were.

The extent of the catering will depend on the type of event being planned, the delegate profile and the available budget. Generally corporate events require fine dining. The service is prepared by a chef and served by waiting staff with experience of delivering a complex menu to large numbers of guests in a timely fashion. Most conference package rates include food and beverage provision as standard, although food might be charged on a consumption basis at festivals, sporting and other outdoor events. In terms of on-site catering, the event organiser might ask the following questions:

- What is the occasion?
- What time of day is the event taking place?
- How many guests are expected? (children, special dietary requirements)
- How many staff are required? (duty manager, head waiter, bar)
- What is the event duration? (in hours)
- What budget has been allocated for catering provision?

Catering provision can be broken down into the following subsections.

PREFERRED CATERING SUPPLIERS

In many cases, the venue selected will provide the event catering in-house. Some venues have incumbent caterers that have tendered and been appointed as a preferred supplier to that venue. The organiser may be obliged to use that supplier, even though there are other catering companies they are used to working with. It is always worth asking the venue if they are prepared to let you bring in alternative catering companies. They might charge you extra, but it may still be worth it to guarantee a tried-and-tested service. Venues are normally happy for you to arrange a tasting evening to sample the food and wine with the preferred supplier before the event takes place.

OUTSOURCING TO CATERING COMPANIES

With the increase of festivals, concerts and cultural events, the requirement for good outdoor catering companies has grown significantly. These events generally require a high-volume, low-cost menu that can be delivered to a mass audience through multiple food outlets or stalls. Contemporary audiences and delegates expect to be offered a range of cuisines at outside events that cater for all religious and ethical requirements. Guests also expect excellent quality from these catering providers. The provision of festival catering has become far more sophisticated today, with the advent of festival pop-up restaurants, street food and test kitchens.

In the same way, catering provision within the chosen venue has to deliver at all levels and have enough range and variety to suit all dietary and ethnic preferences. With any overseas programme, it is also important to consider the cuisine that guests and delegates will be offered as an essential part of any agenda. Gastronomy now contributes greatly to tourism revenue and is considered an integral part of any programme and the overall guest experience. When organising overseas events, the chosen destination will have its own individual and personal gastronomic identity, shaped by the geographical conditions and climate. Organisers need to be aware of the catering requirements of the delegates or attendees, to ensure that a variety of cuisines are offered to the guests that suit all ages, preferences and budgets.

REAL INSIGHT 6.1

TEST KITCHEN AT HAWKERS BAZAAR – FESTIVAL FOOD OUTLET

A local food festival called Hawkers Bazaar took place in Windsor, Berkshire just a week after the town had celebrated the marriage of Prince Harry to Megan Markle in 2018.

Test Kitchen is Windsor in Berkshire's very first gourmet food truck. The owners Milly and John have brought together their Portuguese and Chinese heritages to create deliciously eclectic seasonal menus. Food options include a range of vegetarian and vegan specialities, to suit the ever-growing demand for meat-free options among festival and event goers. Their recent menu specialities include vegan dirty sweet potato beignets, topped with homemade hot sauce and Coyo paprika dressing, and the Garden Special, a delicious mix of ras el hanout cous, marinated and charred fennel, cuca melon and Peruvian cucumber in a coriander and buttermilk dressing. Whenever possible, ingredients are locally sourced from a large array of farms that are available in the Berkshire area, to adhere to sustainable objectives. Test Kitchen's food is also served in containers made from compostable recycled sugar cane.

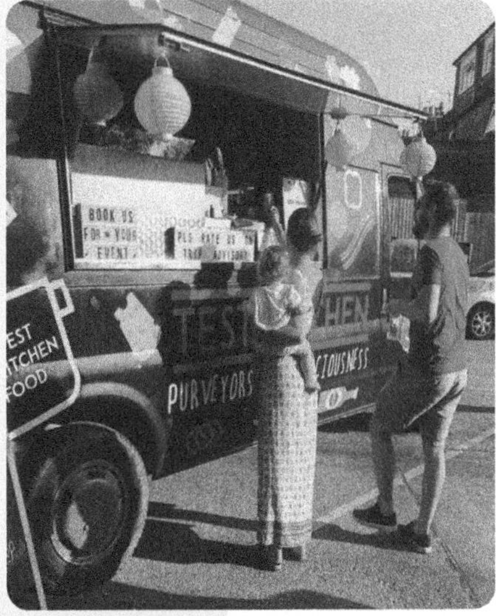

Hawkers Bazaar was an event organised and managed by Test Kitchen in recognition of the owner Milly's yearly family reunion in Malaysia, which she had had to miss that year. It was designed to replicate the feel of her family house there and all of the local hawkers who come along to trade and feed the family. This was an opportunity for vendors to sell local products and for local bands to play in an outside environment and to serve food which, on that occasion, was totally south-east Asian and not their usual offering.

The event was a great success, with local foodies enjoying both the delicious and unique meat and vegetarian food options being served throughout the night at reasonable prices.

SELECTING THE MENU

It is normally standard practice to liaise with the budget holder or event owner about menu choice during the planning phase. This would include all aspects including the style of service, the choice of dishes served and the selection of wine and beverages to complement them. Once the caterer has been established, it is customary to ask the chef to prepare some sample menus, but usually no more than three, and to arrange a tasting. The tasting is very important, as it is usually the last chance the organiser will have to ensure that the right caterer has been selected and that the food and beverage will be delivered to the expected standard. Staff will be appointed to prepare and cook the food with a sufficient number of waiting staff to serve it.

Staff should also find out if the guests or delegates have any special dietary requirements or allergies. Provision should also be made for any additional function requirements, including any crew catering. This may require a different menu and service style and be staggered to provide a hot and cold running buffet throughout the event, in order to ensure that all the crew are fed, as and when they are able to take breaks. In addition, the organiser will need to plan for any necessary furniture hire, crockery and linen hire. In the case of outdoor events, this will include mobile refrigerated trucks, vans or lorries and electric generators for food provision.

WINE AND BEVERAGES

An accompanying choice of wine often needs to be selected to complement the menu. It is advisable to ask the chef at the tasting to recommend a selection of wine or to seek professional advice from a wine specialist or sommelier on this matter, and to consult with the client or budget holder before reaching a final decision.

FOOD AND BEVERAGE THEMING

Designing the catering to match the overall theme or concept can add extra appeal and contribute to the overall feel of the event. The crockery and linen used should be selected to blend in well and to look as appealing as the food itself. Themed catering can be more expensive to source and produce, but it can warrant a higher selling price for tickets and is now often a basic expectation for corporate events.

CONSIDERATIONS FOR CATERING

The following aspects will need to be considered in the planning stages:

- Theming (decoration, flowers, centrepieces, other equipment)
- Table settings, table plans and personalised menus
- Buffet equipment
- Glassware and crockery
- Tables (buffet tables, poseur tables)
- Linen (colours/textures)
- Venue (location, access, capacity).

Styles of service
Canapé – Strawberry dipped with white chocolate
Bowl food – Oriental shredded duck with egg-fried rice
Food stalls – Hand-carved smoked salmon with bagels and cream cheese
Fork buffet – Stir-fried beef strips with mixed peppers 
Full buffet – Roast pork with roast potatoes and vegetables
Silver service – Breast of chicken wrapped with parma ham and chateau potatoes
Full plated – Lamb shank with cheddar mash

TABLE 6.5 Sample service styles

PROVISION OF DRINKING WATER AT THE EVENT

This is a logistical 'must-have' that is crucial from conferences to concerts. Provision of free drinking water is vitally important, particularly at open-air concerts, sporting and dance/music events, due to the volume of people, confined conditions and weather. Recently there has been adverse publicity due to drinking water running out at festivals and dehydration and even fatalities caused by security not permitting guests to bring in water to festivals.

Water should ideally be provided from a mains supply, but bowsers are permissible if they are fit for purpose. The location of these drinking water supplies should be clearly signed and accessible to all. It is also important in the operational planning to ensure that all water-dispensing equipment is clean, well maintained and tested for chemical/biological contamination. In addition to drinking water for audiences, water should be available for animals, such as the provision of a plastic bowl for guide dogs.

Provision of water in the pit areas of concerts and festivals should include an adequate supply of drinking water points and a supply of paper or plastic cups. The number of drinking points available should be determined by the initial risk assessment. Any storage containers used should be of sufficient capacity and meet the needs of people within the first five metres of the pit barrier. As an operations manager, it is also important to think about the additional hazards that water provision can create on-site, for example:

- Problems with on-site drainage
- Hazards caused by queuing for drinking water
- Weather (where high temperatures are present)
- The need for attendees and staff to be clearly differentiated and signposted water provision on-site for sanitary facilities, e.g. drinking water and non-drinking water.

THE INVITATION AND REGISTRATION PROCESS

The registration process can be one of the most challenging aspects of operations, as well as an area that requires the most time and resources. The invitation process varies dependent on the type of event and will be very different, for example, between a public and a private event, but this is an area where careful preparation in the planning stage will ensure a seamless registration process on-site. Event registration has already been discussed in detail in Chapter 2.

FINANCIAL MANAGEMENT

This is an important part of the operational and planning process that needs to start in the very early stages of the process and culminates with the final budgetary reconciliation after the event has finished. This area will be further discussed in detail in Chapter 7.

PLOTTING RESOURCES, TASKS AND ASSIGNING ROLES AND RESPONSIBILITIES

OBJECTIVE 4

Plotting resources, tasks and assigning roles and responsibilities

MANPOWER AND ON-SITE STAFFING

As already discussed in Chapter 1, part of the planning processes involves determining the amount of staff needed on-site, then identifying key tasks and assigning roles and responsibilities. Human resource management is the core factor in creating, planning and selecting an appropriate team with the right skills to deliver the event. All events need staff. The question is: how many and of what type? There are any number of factors that will influence the type and number of staff required, but it is worth remembering that not all staff expect to be paid wages. Mega events, such as the Olympic Games, use thousands of unpaid volunteers.

SOURCE: https://pxhere.com/en/photo/1558103

A core factor of every event's success is selecting the right team with a range of skills. Competencies such as financial and organisational skills, as well as more creative aspects, are required to deliver a successful outcome. Sometimes it is the range of skills and attributes within a team that count, as it does not always help to have everyone with the same skills, or too many strong personalities or leaders within one team.

Before commencement, it is essential to run one or more training sessions for all staff who will be involved in the delivery. It is likely that both paid staff and volunteers will have already undergone some sort of specific training. This training should furnish the team with knowledge of how to deal with all eventualities. Detailed duty rosters should be drawn up to allow for breaks, emergencies and contingencies.

Experienced and well-trained staff are the crucial factor for delivering successful events and complying with any regulations, therefore using tried-and-tested staff, or manpower agencies with qualified staff on their books, is recommended. These agencies are also an excellent place for students to register to get 'hands-on' experience.

Roles need to be carefully assigned, so that there is no duplicity of the tasks executed and that all eventualities are covered on-site. It is usual to require more staff on-site than in the planning phase. At the event, the ratio tends to be one planner per 50 delegates. To get an overview of staffing needs and responsibilities, it helps to produce an organisational chart, clearly setting out team tasks and the skills required to execute these roles. Managing of the event workforce on-site has already been discussed in depth in Chapter 2.

IDENTIFYING AND SETTING EVENT TASKS

An event manager rarely works alone, but as part of a team, who each have separate roles and responsibilities. Usually the director or manager is at the head of the team and needs to keep everyone working well together in the planning stage, which could be for a considerable length of time. It may be necessary to recruit additional staff resources to support the existing core team. When selecting and recruiting the team who will deliver the programme, it is worth considering:

- Who is in charge?
- Who will liaise with the client or budget holder?
- What specialist skills are required to deliver the event?
- How many additional staff or freelancers will need to be recruited?
- What tasks will the various team members carry out?
- Who in the team will do what?
- What will the support staff do?
- What will support staff and any volunteers do?
- What do they need to know?
- Who are the key supplier contacts and who within the team will they liaise with?

Members of the operations team may be involved on a full-time basis in the lead time, or on more of a part-time or contractual basis. Within any team there are usually permanent paid staff and also more casual staff and volunteers. The organisational chart in Figure 6.3 indicates the level of complexity that there might be in an event team.

ASSIGNING ROLES AND RESPONSIBILITIES

Part of the operations process involves drawing up a list of tasks, as already discussed under critical path analysis in Chapters 4 and 5. Within the events team, clear roles and responsibilities should be assigned. At this stage, it is worth determining what additional freelance staff members and suppliers will be required in order to deliver the event. Arrangements need to be put in place to secure the additional personnel required and to check their availability for the event dates held.

GO ONLINE

A duty roster for the event should also be drawn up in the operational stages, which should be part of the on-site working document. You can find a sample blank duty roster in the Templates section online at **study.sagepub.com/quick**.

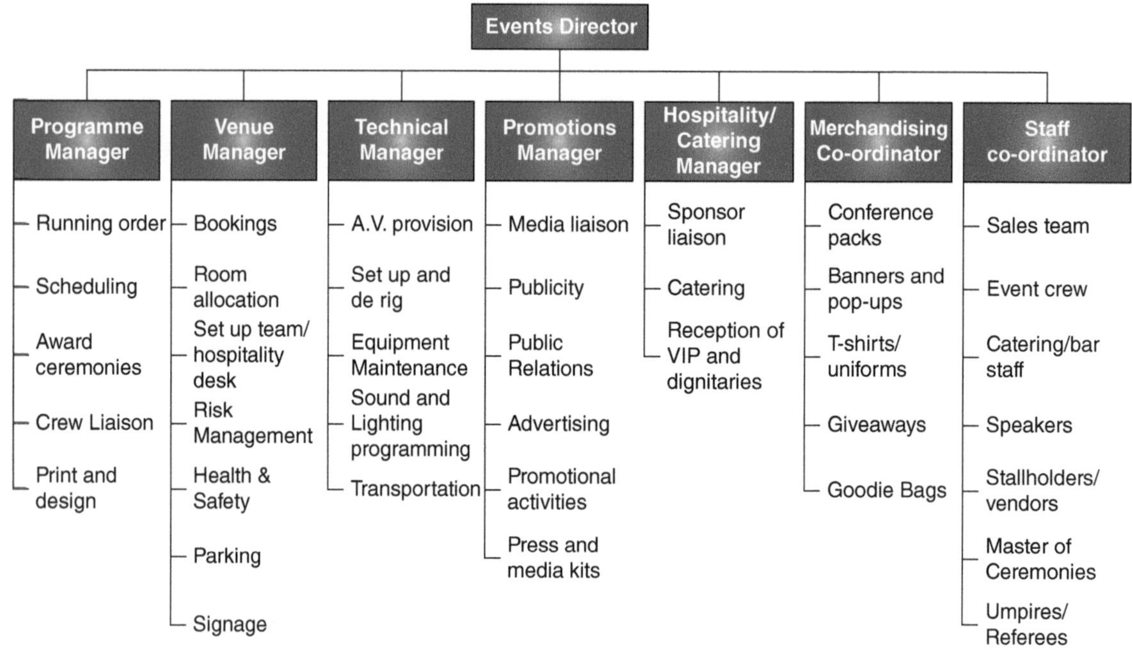

FIGURE 6.3 Sample event organisational chart

ON-SITE STAFF TRAINING

The content of these training sessions may vary depending on the complexity of the event. The training should be designed to cover all aspects of relevant event management as temporary or freelance staff may not have expertise, or any specific knowledge of the client or the event in question. Areas such as the following should be covered:

- Overview of the budget holder or commissioning corporate client or association and the delegate or guest profile
- Event detail and programme overview
- Introduction to core planners and other staff and relevant stakeholders
- Roles and responsibilities of freelancers and the tasks involved
- Health and safety details and risk management
- Duty rosters, team structures, shift patterns and timelines
- Code of conduct and any on-site rules and regulations

- Uniform and dress code
- Any permits and licences required
- Reporting and complaints procedures
- Detailed question and answer (Q & A) sessions.

RULES OF TIME MANAGEMENT

In order to get tasks completed in the run-up to an event, time management is critical. A few points to help with this are:

- Take time to think things through
- Decide on long- and short-term goals
- Set objectives
- Sort out what tasks have to be completed
- Prioritise the tasks
- Allow time for unscheduled interruptions
- Set out to complete all tasks
- Keep a record of the progress made
- Revisit the plan regularly, change it or tick off any completed tasks
- Make sure the team take time out to rest and relax.

HOW TO PRIORITISE

In the planning phase, it is important to know what tasks are essential to complete and which others could be delayed if necessary, without causing a knock-on effect to the overall event planning process. As well as completing a Gantt chart (see Chapter 4), it is possible to prioritise tasks as itemised in Table 6.6.

- Must do items
- Should do items
- Nice to do items
- Urgent and important items
- Important, but not urgent items
- Urgent, but not important items
- Not urgent or important items

TABLE 6.6 How to prioritise tasks

DEVELOPING AN ON-SITE PROGRAMME SCHEDULE

Regardless of the size and complexity of the event, a programme or an itinerary of the schedule needs to be compiled. Sometimes the venue itself will supply production schedules and itineraries for all those working on-site each day. This will indicate who is doing what, where and when from start-up, e.g. 8.00, to shut-down, e.g. 22.00. It is not only guests and visitors who need to be aware of what time certain activities are scheduled; all staff, including volunteers, should know when briefing meetings are taking place. They will also need to know details of any site checks, arrival of any equipment, who is handling security, and so on.

Guest requirements also need to be taken into consideration. They should know in advance what is planned and should be issued with a 'programme of activities' in advance, on arrival or at registration, to ensure they are at the right place at the right time. For example, a major music festival such as Glastonbury, which has many different stages and acts, should publish the various acts and bands and set timings, so that the audience can plan ahead to watch their preferred bands or acts.

GO ONLINE

A sample online schedule can be viewed online in Table 6.4 in the Appendix at **study.sagepub.com/quick.**

CLIENT LIAISON AND PRE-EVENT CLIENT AND TEAM MEETINGS

During the planning stages, ongoing verbal and written communication with all stakeholders, including suppliers, sponsors and the client, are required. It is also advisable to schedule client and team meetings with the client, to run through the detail and discuss any changes to the original programme, or to note any challenges that might be anticipated. This may take the form of regular meetings in the lead-up time through means of virtual tools, such as Skype and FaceTime, social media or by phone. Sometimes a face-to-face meeting is needed to ensure optimum interaction and clarity. A good relationship with the client is invaluable for accruing repeat business and referrals to new clients.

MANAGING MEETINGS

In order to make effective use of the meeting time, the team leader is advised to prepare an agenda in advance, specifying the meeting date and location and where the meeting will take place, plus the expected length of meeting and who from the event team is invited to the meeting. A critical path document can be used to work out what items to discuss. Time should be allocated in the meeting to deal with each agenda item and to decide who will be responsible in the team for overseeing the task. This document will also set a timeline for completing tasks and state how the action will be followed up. After each meeting, it is advisable to agree on the next meeting date and what the next steps are. After the meeting, it is also good practice to complete a meeting contact report, detailing all aspects discussed and any items to be completed before the next meeting.

CONDUCTING RISK ASSESSMENT

In the UK, a person or an organisation that creates risk is required to manage and control that risk, so that it is reduced 'So Far As Is Reasonably Practicable' (SFAIRP). Event planners have a duty to demonstrate that they have taken action to ensure all risk is reduced SFAIRP. They must have documentary evidence, for example a risk assessment report or safety case, to prove that they can manage the risks that the activities create. The UK Health and Safety Executive (HSE) does not tell organisations how to manage the risks but does inspect the quality of risk identification and management. The area of risk assessment has been previously discussed in Chapter 2 of this book.

EVENT ADMINISTRATION

Compiling contracts, lists and joining instructions as part of the operations administration process, can be arduous and time-consuming, even when using electronic systems or online portals. For larger events, it may be worth subcontracting to secure additional secretarial support to assist with this area. The advent of bespoke conference management systems, which are able to generate a multitude of delegate lists and special requirements, have greatly reduced the amount of event administration that needs to be generated before or at the event itself.

FILE MANAGEMENT

Nowadays details will invariably be saved to disk, the cloud, a hard drive or a USB stick. However, there are still occasions when it is useful to resort to traditional methods, such as compiling a meeting file, containing paper copies of all meeting minutes and relevant documentation. To allow for ease of use, the file should be organised so that anyone can find anything by ensuring:

- The file is indexed and the pages numbered
- The most recent correspondence is on top
- The corresponding notes on any section are placed in a logical order and dated.

CONTACT REPORTS

Following a team briefing or meeting, or even a telephone call to discuss key issues in the run-up to an event, it is good practice to record the conversation and any matters that were verbally agreed. The completed contact report should then be emailed out to all relevant stakeholders, to clarify the agreed issues and arrangements and to prevent any misunderstandings. The contact report should specify the date, title, location of the meeting and the people that attended. Items discussed, with details and proposed action and subsequent timelines for completion, should also be recorded.

OBJECTIVE 5

The importance of promotion, marketing and public relations

THE IMPORTANCE OF PROMOTION, MARKETING AND PUBLIC RELATIONS

EVENT MARKETING

The first essential phase of event marketing is to analyse the marketing environment. The marketing plan should be a document that examines the macro and micro marketing environment and outlines the marketing objectives and overall strategy. The development of an effective marketing and communications plan is essential. As has already been discussed in Chapter 4, the concept, theme, programme, and so on, should reflect the needs of the audience who will attend or participate. The next stage is to have an effective plan of action and the necessary resources to implement it.

Marketing is a social and managerial process by which individuals and groups obtain what they need and want through exchanging products and values with others. (Kotler and Armstrong 2010: 6)
The management process responsible for identifying, anticipating and satisfying customer requirements profitably. (CIM 2000: 2)
Marketing is that function of event management that can keep in touch with the event participants and visitors, read their needs and motivation, develop products that meet these needs and build a communication programme which expresses the event's purpose and objectives. (Hall 1997: 136)

TABLE 6.7 Definitions of events marketing

A FRAMEWORK FOR A MARKETING PLAN

The template featured in Figure 6.4 could be used as a guide or framework around which organisers can create their own plan. The elements contained within it are not a mandatory or an exhaustive list, however it is recommended that all marketing/PR plans contain the following items:

- A summary of the event
- An overall vision/mission statement
- Definition of target markets
- Objectives and key performance indicators (KPIs)
- Key strategies and initiatives
- Marketing, public relations and budgetary information.

DEVISING A MARKETING PLAN

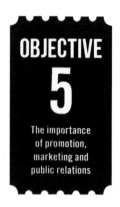

The marketing plan, like the operational plan and the financial budget, should be developed after the event objectives have been established, and the plan should set out and list the actions needed to achieve them. The nature of the event, consumer-buying decisions and other influencing factors can make targeting potential visitors relatively complicated, so perhaps the most essential purpose of a marketing plan is

Strategic planning	Functional planning	Operational planning
1. Define the mission	1. Perform a situational analysis	1. Develop action plans to implement the marketing plan
2. Evaluate the internal and external environment	2. Set marketing objectives	2. Use marketing metrics to monitor how the plan is working
3. Set organisational goals	3. Develop marketing strategies	
4. Establish a business plan, if applicable	4. Implement marketing strategies	
5. Develop growth strategies	5. Monitor and control marketing strategies	

FIGURE 6.4 Levels of marketing planning

to plot how the event can become a reality. The plan should include factors such as which customers to target and how to reach them; how to win their business and retain it afterwards; as well as continually reviewing and improving everything required in order to stay ahead of the competition.

A marketing plan analysis is a tool that illustrates the individual tasks of a project and estimates the time each task will commence and finish and how long the whole project will take to complete. It is a way of displaying graphically the activities that comprise a planning or research project. Like the critical path document, a spreadsheet or Gannt chart approach, a marketing plan reveals how many activities are taking place at once, and indicates all activities in relation to each other, each how long various activities are in progress. In order to prepare a marketing plan, the following steps should be taken:

- List all activities in the plan and, for each, show the earliest start date
- Sequence each activity into a logical order based on when it should, or is most likely to, occur
- Estimate the time required to perform each activity
- Draw up a spreadsheet activity plan or Gantt chart.

Throughout the planning phase, it is also important to keep motivation and momentum high, by sending out regular teasers or communication pieces to the audience. There may not always be large resources available to promote and sell the event, so a marketing campaign is often dependent on volunteer effort and carried out with small budgets.

At this stage, it is advisable to start to create a database and keep building on this in the pre-event marketing stage. Contact details should also be recorded at the event itself, subject to revised GDPR regulations, which will reinforce post-marketing activities and boost numbers for the next time. The infamous 7Ps of promotion can be applied to the marketing process in the ways shown in Table 6.8.

PRODUCT
Encompasses all elements of an event, i.e. venue, food and beverage, entertainment, music, brand, merchandising

PRICE
The price consumers are willing to pay to attend, the perceived value

(Continued)

TABLE 6.8 (Continued)

PLACE Location and channel of distribution, e.g. online tickets, marketing portals
PROMOTION Advertising, agents selling, direct mail, e-shot, logo
PEOPLE Staff, event team, client, attendees, volunteers
PROCESS Within the service industry, planning and operations and consumption
PHYSICAL EVIDENCE Facilities, delegate numbers, feedback

TABLE 6.8 The 7Ps of promotion

SEGMENTATION, TARGETING AND POSITIONING

The key to creating and designing a successful marketing strategy is to create a unique selling point (USP) or distinct brand, to attract people to attend. Other recommended processes to attract an appropriate audience are segmentation, targeting and positioning.

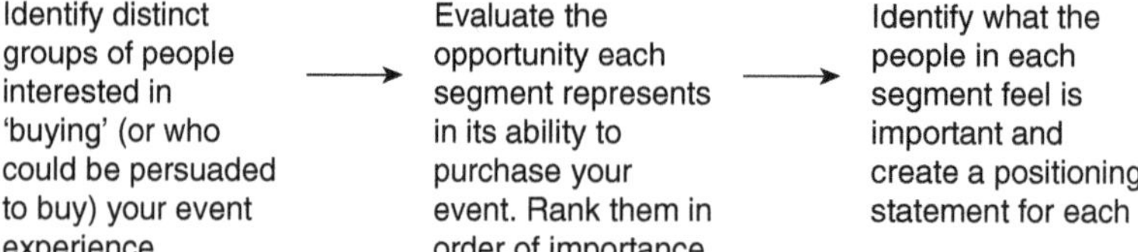

FIGURE 6.5 Segment, target, position

SEGMENTATION

A market segment is a distinct group of customers in a specific market. Very few events accommodate all potential market segments, but few serve only one segment. Methods of segmenting a market are usually:

- By needs, motivations and benefits sought
- By buyer/user characteristics
- By demographics
- Economic or price-related
- By geographic location
- By purpose of purchase.

The process involves identifying different market segments and classifying customers into groups with different needs, characteristics or behaviour. There are various different types of market segmentation, as indicated in Table 6.9.

Behavioural segmentation	The risks, benefits or gains of the products or services to the end-users
Psychographic segmentation	The lifestyle of the audience and their personalities, and what drives them
Profile segmentation	Demographical information, such as age, gender, social class, level of education, number of children, income, geographical location, etc.

TABLE 6.9 Different types of segmentation

According to Boone and Kurtz (2016), even going through this process does not necessarily guarantee success. They recommend that every market segment identified needs to demonstrate measurable economies of scale buying power, and appropriate levels of profit. Products and services that can be effectively marketed should be delivered to this segment at the right price. According to their model there are four parts to the process, listed in Table 6.10.

Identify the basis of segmentation	Select the most appropriate and promising segment and conduct market-driven research on this particular segment based on observation
Develop a segment profile	Find out more specific information on the various segments, so that similarities and differences between each category can be identified and start to define typical customer profiles
Forecast the potential	Identify the market potential for each segment
Forecast market share	Forecast a probable market share based on the competition's market position and marketing strategies designed to reach each segment and cost and resources needed versus potential benefits.

TABLE 6.10 The segmentation process
SOURCE: adapted from Boone and Kurtz (2016)

TARGETING

Following the segmentation process, event marketers are in a stronger position to make more informed decisions about whom they choose to target. In some cases, a mass marketing approach, which targets a widespread and varied selection of potential attendees, is the surest and most cost-effective method of event marketing. This particularly applies to those that appeal to a wide demographic. In the case of more niche events, it may be necessary to target a more specific audience base. The market segments to be targeted can also be selected on the basis of their attractiveness to the organisation. When targeting different segments, the following should be considered:

- The resources available
- Product and service characteristics
- The stage in the event or product life cycle
- Existing market conditions
- Competitor activities
- The external environment.

POSITIONING

In its simplest terms, this means understanding the market and target audience and the factors that are important to them when making a decision to attend. It is also being fully aware of what the competition is offering and being able to select the determinant attributes sought, and to deliver or provide those that will be perceived as better than your competitors. Good positioning involves:

- Creating an image
- Differentiating your product or service
- Guaranteeing to deliver a promise.

This is largely dependent on the specific market. Clarity in the eyes of the target consumer is important, as is credibility, such as creating a brand by stealth that is consistent; for example, Milan Fashion Week, the Cannes Film Festival Coachella or the Primavera Sound Festival in Barcelona might be considered credible event brands. The positioning also needs to be competitive in the eyes of the target market, to ensure that they will respond well to the differential advantage. Events can be positioned:

- By attributes, features or customer benefits
- By price or quality
- According to the end-users or product class
- To offer a competitive edge.

PRE-EVENT MARKETING

When marketing an event, it is important to first forecast how many people will attend, and then estimate what price they will be willing to pay. Next, establish how much is going to be spent on the promotion and start to design collateral with an eye-catching logo and strapline. Once details are known about the event, for example the date and venue, it is advisable to send out an initial marketing communication piece, which could take the form of a *save the date* email, so that potential delegates or attendees can block that date off in their calendars. Throughout the pre-event planning stages, the organisers need to create awareness and generate a positive image and 'buzz'. If it is a ticketed event, it is a good idea to inform target markets of details, including list of attendees, content, any guest or keynote speakers and pricing. Some marketing methods are listed in Table 6.11.

'Buzz' marketing: Using high-profile entertainment or media coverage to stimulate conversation and 'buzz' around the brand
Word-of-mouth marketing: The act of consumers providing information to other consumers and giving people a reason to talk about your products and services, e.g. through social media
Viral marketing: Creating entertaining or informative messages to be sent by email to a potential target audience.

TABLE 6.11 Marketing methods

RELATIONSHIP MARKETING

'"Relationship marketing" is both a philosophy that puts customer retention at the heart of the business process and a marketing strategy, with a set of tools and practices which a company uses to implement relationship marketing objectives successfully' (Bowie and Buttle 2016: 298). In general terms, repeat purchasers have a high lifetime value (LTV), based on their overall long-term spend with the company or agency. It is easy to understand why any event owner or agency would want to build up a long-term and mutually rewarding relationship with the client, to encourage long-term loyalty and a partnership agreement with them. As already discussed in Chapter 5, it is far better to work in partnership with a client as a long-term incumbent, rather than constantly have to tender to work with new clients. In events, as with other industry sectors, people often talk about customer relationship management (CRM). This aims to identify profitable customers or clients and try to develop effective ways to continue building on those working relationships.

REAL INSIGHT 6.2

CREATING 'BUZZ AND HYPE' AROUND A LAUNCH EVENT

SOURCE: https://pixabay.com/photos/ford-fiesta-st-ford-fiesta-st-blue-3160717

In 2017 the agency Touch Associates won the contract to work with the client Ford on the campaign for the media launch of the new Ford Fiesta in Spain.

(Continued)

To create some hype around this new brand, the agency organised a launch event, to take place over four weeks in Valladolid, Spain. The event was designed to host more than 600 media and VIP guests, from over 20 countries, making it Ford's largest media launch in 2017.

David Bottrill, Touch Associates' board director, said:

> We are delighted to be working with Ford and to support them with such a high-profile event. The project is being delivered by a dedicated, knowledgeable and passionate team who have a vast experience of delivering media events, including previous ones for Ford Europe.

The aim was to engage the audience in a different way from other unveilings, attempting to make the experience warmer and more emotional. In a departure from the norm, the first group to attend the launch was made up of a group of influencers, lifestyle media and bloggers, who were given the first chance to experience the new car. The launch was executed with a high degree of creativity to create some excitement and buzz leading up to it.

Stephane Cesareo, of Ford's product communications team, said: 'We are only in the first of four weeks, but so far the feedback has been excellent from both the client and their media guests.'

SOURCE: www.meetpie.com

The main aim of any marketing campaign is to create a desire to attend the event and prompt the delegate to take action, i.e. book and pay for tickets. Use of the AIDA acronym is explained in Table 6.12.

A stands for Attention	• A student sees a poster at university for the summer ball • The instinctive consideration is whether the date is free and the cost affordable
I stands for Interest	• The student talks to friends in class to see if anyone else is interested • If lots of people are interested, do the benefits outweigh the cost factors? • The student also weighs up the practical aspects, e.g. is there anything else going on that night?
D stands for Desire	• The primary motives for going are to have a good time, socialise, meet new friends, have a few drinks, etc.
A stands for Action	• This is the most critical part • As there was a ticket seller stationed in the university refectory, the purchasing process was easy, and the student decided to buy a ticket.

TABLE 6.12 The AIDA acronym

WHAT IS EVENT PROMOTION?

The main purpose of event promotion is to attract an appropriate number of spectators or delegates to attend. No matter how well organised the event is, if there are no attendees, it will not be deemed successful. For some organisers, any shortfall in expected revenues can have a disastrous effect on the organisation's overall profit. This can, in the worst-case scenario, result in major financial loss and even bankruptcy. So clearly promotion is essential to the event's overall success.

Sometimes first-class event promotion can be a victim of its own success. For example, if too many people purchase tickets, it may be deemed to be unmanageable or unsafe and likely to be considered poorly promoted, just as much as a badly attended one. There are many ways to promote the event to the target audience, but the five main promotional methods or tools are advertising, publicity, sales promotion, personal selling and direct marketing. Throughout the planning process, it is important to communicate through mixed methods of promotion in order to:

- Increase awareness
- Create or enhance a positive image
- Position the event relative to its competition
- Inform target markets of core details
- Generate demand
- Remind the target market of the event date and details.

Event promotion represents all of the communication methods that may be used in the marketing and generally has four distinct elements: advertising; public relations; word of mouth; and point of sale. Promotional strategies include using the modes of publicity listed in Table 6.13.

Free publicity through television, radio, print media or word of mouth from sponsors or influencers
Free publicity from online means, including the internet and social media
Paid advertising from television, radio or print media
Paid-for online advertising
Promotional and PR activities and merchandise leading up to the event
Merchandise, signage and banners.

TABLE 6.13 Publicity modes and promotion methods

Publicity is generally free, whereas advertising is paid for and can cover any form of communication. For large events, this may include promotion and advertising through television and cinema commercials, radio and internet adverts through print media and billboards. Table 6.14 shows some of the advantages and disadvantages of promoting an event through these various means.

Modes of advertising	Advantages	Disadvantages
Television/radio	Wide-reaching	Expensive
Magazines/newspapers	Can be targeted	Message can get lost
Posters	Inexpensive	Can be defaced/may be seen by a small minority only
Flyers	Can deliver a lot of detail/relatively inexpensive	Distribution can be expensive/not environmentally friendly
Direct mail	Quick to send out to whole distribution list in one single hit	GDPR regulations make this difficult
Social media/internet	Widespread/targeted/inexpensive	Lots of competition/may exclude some demographic groups.

TABLE 6.14 Event promotion modes of advertising

WHAT ARE PUBLIC RELATIONS?

Public relations, commonly abbreviated to PR, is where the communication is not directly paid for and may include press releases and sponsorship deals at exhibitions, conferences, seminars or trade fairs.

'Word of mouth' marketing entails any informal communication about the product by ordinary individuals, satisfied customers or people, specifically engaged to create word-of-mouth momentum. With the advent of social media, this communication is far more accessible to everyone. Generally, there are four different types of media release that might take place in the planning stages:

- General information
- Press release
- Media invitation
- Public relations in the planning stages.

The type of public relations employed is very dependent on the size and scale of the event. For mega events such as the Olympic Games or FIFA World Cup, for example, the media play a large role in the public relations coverage. Organisers will use professional communication methods to simultaneously deliver messages to large audiences over large geographic areas. Using this type of mass media can be an enormous asset, as it employs delivery systems capable of transcending the time and space for optimum publicity.

Although, according to the old adage 'there is no such thing as bad publicity', this is not always the case. Negative publicity can be damaging for the image and reputation of any business. Events are so visible today that there is literally nowhere to hide, and no way to mandate the content of the circulating media. This can create a huge liability for the organisations involved, as can be seen in the real insight on London Oktoberfest presented in Chapter 3.

WRITING A PRESS RELEASE

Journalists and editors are constantly looking for new stories. Generally, it is not up to you whether the press release will get published, but if the press release is well written and informative, then they might decide to put it in their publication. Writing a press release is a bit like re-visiting the initial planning ideas and trying to capture the most salient details of the event. Press releases need to be informative but simple. All contact details should be included and completed to reach the publication before its print deadline. All sentences should be short and focused, avoiding jargon and obscure language. The press release should be written in paragraphs, in a logical order, with the most important item first, and so on. Headlines should be used to emphasise key points. They should be written in a way to attract the reader's attention, rather than giving them technical advice, or entering into a complex discussion.

GO ONLINE

The press release should contain information that is succinct and summarises the main points of interest and details on the forthcoming event, as can be seen in this sample press release available online in the Appendix as Table 6.5.

EVENT ETHICS

Some event venues employ 'brand ambassadors' to drive results through communication tools, such as social media, or privately including emails, messaging and further one-to-one channels, but do you think it is ethical to use these ambassadors to influence audiences to book a venue or an event?

Is it ethical to use fake consumer reviews as part of an online venue marketing campaign? Could it be justifiable in some circumstances?

MARKETING TOOLS

As already discussed under the section on event promotion, there are many traditional media functions that are employed as marketing tools within the marketing mix, which are often used to promote smaller events. For larger events, traditional mass media functions are also used in the creation, coordination and organisation of information and the dissemination of it to the public, through tools such as those shown in Table 6.15.

These tools also have the means to create both positive and negative publicity. Newspaper publicity can be less costly and more credible than other methods of promotion because the airtime or print space is free and consumers know that the event organisation is not paying for the message. However, this approach relies on

Minor/smaller events	Major/larger events
• Television • Print • Radio • Outdoor posters • Cinema • Direct mail • Internet • Flyers • Brochures	• Newspapers • Magazines • Television/radio • Blogs/websites/social media

TABLE 6.15 Sample marketing tools

pushing sales to a large volume of people and advertising is a costly marketing tool compared to other, newer digital and online marketing tools. Despite this, according to the 2012 Edelman Trust Barometer survey, these traditional media outlets still remain the most trusted sources of distributing information.

THE USE OF TECHNOLOGY IN EVENT MARKETING

Traditional forms of marketing, such as paper-based invites and tickets, were previously used to raise awareness and market events. However, companies that continue to rely on traditional practices, such as paper marketing, with no online presence, are fast becoming obsolete. With the advance of digital technology and internet marketing, together with the development of bespoke event-management applications, the events industry has seen a radical change in marketing practices in recent years.

Internet marketing is able to identify, anticipate and satisfy marketing needs and to achieve the necessary strategic marketing criteria to raise awareness for an event in far less time than ever before. It is clear to see why these modern marketing tools have replaced traditional methods, such as television and radio and press platforms, with the high costs associated with them and the fact that any detail on printed material can quickly become out of date and therefore not relevant. Nowadays it is word-of-mouth marketing, public relations (PR) and 'event buzz' generated via social media that is most commonly used, while the invitation process has been completely digitalised.

ONLINE MARKETING

Online marketing is becoming an increasingly popular and cost-effective marketing tool, particularly for the younger entrants to the industry, who are more disposed to technical and digital media methods. One advantage of using online marketing to promote an event is that computer software technology can be designed to attract potential customers with specific, measurable and targeted communication. Specific digital media marketing tools include **search engine optimisation**; mobile marketing; interactive online advertisements; opt-in email; and online partnerships, such as affiliate marketing and sponsorships. A key component of digital marketing tools is **web analytics**, which provide information on an internet user's online activities or IP address by keyword searches. Companies can outsource to digital media marketing agencies or utilise the appropriate software as a service application.

Search engine optimisation
the process of affecting the online visibility of a website or a web page on a web search engine

Web analytics
the measurement, collection, analysis and reporting of web data for purposes of understanding and optimising web usage

SOCIAL MEDIA AS A MARKETING TOOL

The use of social media sites has also changed the consumer buying and decision-making process, allowing end-users to research products and services online, share anecdotes, give instant feedback, recommend products, provide promotional material and testimonials and answer consumer questions in advance. Social media marketing is a subset of digital media marketing and, in the promotion of events, is often used in the planning and marketing stages to develop online interactive relationships with potential customers and attendees, communicating information and 'creating buzz' about the event. Specific examples of social media marketing tools are blogging, tweeting, posting, sharing, networking, pinning, bookmarking, media sharing and commenting on social media websites.

By connecting the activities of the attendee to their social media accounts, organisers have formed partnerships with various mobile service providers, encouraging attendees to post and share their experiences instantly online. It is easy to see how this free publicity could benefit any organiser's marketing campaign. Moreover, this has brought about many new sponsorship opportunities, offering attendees discounts and exclusive promotions to share links on their social media page, thus boosting the sponsor's brand image.

SOCIAL MEDIA MARKETING AT FESTIVALS

At festivals, sponsors take full advantage of social media to market them. Latest newsfeeds and information on the festival line-up and initiatives are posted out on festival websites. In the lead-up to Glastonbury 2010, the main sponsor, the mobile phone provider Orange, started a new trend by inviting the festival, attendees to publish a photo on their website of the festival, encouraging people to zoom in and tag themselves through websites like Facebook and Instagram. Over 8,000 people tagged themselves in a 70,000-person crowd within days, making it the world's most tagged set of photos. This started a trend that is continuously growing over time.

SOCIAL MEDIA MARKETING AT CORPORATE EVENTS

Videos and applications that facilitate the posting of photos, videos and **streaming media** are also being used in a corporate environment. After Facebook introduced the auto-playing video, video posts jumped by a substantial 5% and are now used regularly at events. Twitter users who tweet with an image are nearly twice as likely to be retweeted and this can be a great publicity tool. Over the past five years, Instagram has doubled

Streaming media
multimedia that is presented to an end-user while being delivered by a provider

in usage, allowing delegates to get more involved and engaged with the event in the planning stages. Twitter walls commonly include Instagram feeds, as well as Twitter images. A version of Snapchat called 'Live Stories' allows attendees and stakeholders to submit photographs and videos from various destinations and events, which ends up contributing to a story or destination from a varied community perspective.

SOCIAL MEDIA MARKETING FOR FUNDRAISING EVENTS AND CAMPAIGNS

In 2014 the renowned ALS ice bucket challenge demonstrated how quickly a social media campaign could reach a target audience. This highly publicised viral fundraising campaign originated in the USA but was quickly replicated throughout the world. Social media sites were inundated with videos of people throwing freezing cold buckets of water over celebrities and the public alike. This succeeded in raising millions and raising awareness of the disease amyotrophic lateral sclerosis (ALS), a progressive neurodegenerative disease, so that the charity introduced its own successful hash tag on Twitter, enabling it to reach global influential and wealthy online communities, which demonstrates how powerful and influential social media has now become.

SOURCE: Image courtesy of Angelin Song via flickr.com. Shared under the Creative Commons BY 2.0 license.

PROMOTIONAL ITEMS

Promotional products, such as brochures, business cards, press kits, websites, informational videos and merchandise, are also a popular tangible marketing tool today. Promotional merchandise is a mobile form of advertising, which helps with brand recognition. In addition to increasing sales, promotional items contribute to building brand awareness, but cost is a factor when selecting these items.

Some of these items include large amounts of detailed information and highlight attributes of the product or service. Business cards and trade show giveaways may display only a company logo and provide contact information. These are useful items that are distributed to targeted audiences with no obligation attached. In 2013 The British Promotional Merchandise Association (BPMA) conducted the first independent national survey into the power of promotional merchandise in the UK and found that promotional merchandise can deliver a higher or equal return on investment than television, radio, outdoor and print advertising. Stephen Barker, BPMA board director, said: 'Promotional merchandise influences purchases and repeat exposure to a brand has a positive effect on how businesspeople react to that brand.'

Preferred items among the survey respondents were USB sticks, writing instruments and mugs. The BPMA's survey calculates 'cost per impression' for a mug is £0.001, a mid-range pen £0.001, a calendar £0.004, a USB stick £0.005 and an umbrella £0.003.

However, two-thirds of respondents said they could remember the brand on the promotional product they received during the last year. More than half (56%) said their opinion of the brand or company was more favourable after receiving the promotional product, with 79% saying they were likely to do business with the company in the future. (Source: www.meetpie.com)

REAL INSIGHT 6.3

COMPLIMENTARY EVENT PROMOTIONAL PRODUCT

Throughout 2016 Branded Promo Gift partnered with UK Cycling Events, the UK's leading provider of cycling events, to produce T-shirts for their events. As cycling continues to increase in popularity, more companies are looking to arrange corporate cycling events, as they provide an excellent platform for team building, networking, client entertaining and the general engagement of staff and clients. In 2016 UK Cycling Events launched the new 'Black Series', where cyclists were pushed to the limit over gruelling routes taking them over the entire length and breadth of the UK. A couple of these rides were held on the continent.

Branded Promo Gift designed and produced a range of bespoke T-shirts for the 2016 event calendar and supplied each rider with a 'Finishers' T-shirt upon successful completion of all the 'Wiggle Super Series', 'UKCE', and 'Black Series' events in and around the UK.

In addition to corporate events, UK Cycling Events has helped host a range of charity rides to test even the most experienced cycling enthusiasts. During one of these events, a rider was involved in an accident that changed his and his family's lives forever. Just after 10am on 15 August 2015, Jordan Glasspool was

(Continued)

involved in a road accident and urgently required the help of the Great Western Air Ambulance Charity. As a way of saying thanks for helping Jordan recover, with the help of UK Cycling Events, his family arranged a fundraising event in 2016, where all proceeds went to the Great Western Air Ambulance Charity, a charity that runs solely on fundraising and donations. Each time they attend an accident, it costs £1500 to £2000.

As a gesture to riders on the day, UK Cycling Events rewarded each rider with #TeamJordan buffs, to show their support for Jordan's family and the members of the Great Western Air Ambulance Charity. The agency Branded Promo Gift was chosen to produce the buffs, which were well received and sported by the riders on the day.

DID YOU KNOW?

The target market is areas where the company wishes to compete, and differential advantage is how the company wishes to compete. (Jobber 2010: 346)

CHAPTER SUMMARY

CHAPTER SUMMARY QUESTIONS

1 What are the main logistical challenges when organising an outdoor event?
2 What are the four key stages in event project management?
3 What is the best way to increase destination knowledge?
4 What are the main factors to note in a site inspection?
5 What social media applications are being used to promote festivals today?
6 What do the 7Ps in event marketing stand for?

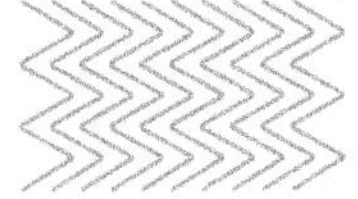

DISCUSSION POINTS

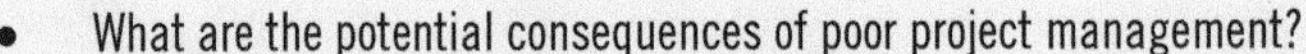

- What are the potential consequences of poor project management?
- Why is relationship marketing as a marketing means so important in the events industry?
- How are online marketing and registration changing the way events are operated today?

ACTIVITIES

- List some key items that should be included in an on-site working document.
- Write a press release for a charity fundraising event you are organising.
- Design a form to help you assess the strengths and weaknesses of a venue, to use while conducting a site inspection of a selection of hotels in a preferred destination.

REFERENCES

Allen, J., O'Toole, W., Harris, R. and McDonnell, I. (2011) *Festival and Special Event Management*, 5th edn. Brisbane, QLD: Wiley & Sons.

Boone, M. and Kurtz, D. (2016) *Contemporary Business*, 16th edn. Hoboken, NJ: Wiley & Sons.

Bowdin, G., McDonnell, G., Allen, J. and O'Toole, W. (2011) *Events Management*, 3rd edn. Oxford: Butterworth-Heinemann.

Bowie, D. and Buttle, F. (2016) *Hospitality Marketing*, 3rd edn. London: Routledge.

British Promotional Merchandise Association (BPMA) Homepage. Available at: www.bpma.co.uk (accessed 2 November 2019).

Chartered Institute of Marketing (CIM) (2000) Homepage. Available at: www.cim.co.uk (accessed 3 July 2019).

Dowson, R. and Bassett, D. (2015) *Event Planning & Management: A Practical Handbook for PR & Events Professionals*. London: Kogan Page.

Edelman (2012) 2012 Edelman Trust Barometer, 23 January. Available at: www.edelman.com/research/2012-edelman-trust-barometer (accessed 30 June 2020).

Getz, D. (2016) *Event Studies: Theory, Research and Policy for Planned Events*. Oxford: Butterworth-Heinemann.

Hall, C.M. (1997) *Hallmark Tourist Events: Impacts, Management and Planning*. London: Belhaven Press.

Health and Safety Executive (HSE) Homepage. Available at: www.hse.gov.uk (accessed 5 October 2018).

Jobber, D. (2010) *Principles and Practice of Marketing*, 3rd edn. London: McGraw-Hill Education.

Kotler, P. and Armstrong, G. (2010) *Principles of Marketing*, 17th edn. London: Pearson.

Manrodt, K.B. and Davis, F.W. (1992) 'The evolution to service response logistics', *International Journal of Physical Distribution and Logistics Management*, 22(9): 3–10.

SFAIRP, So Far As It Is Reasonably Practicable. Available at: www.hse.gov.uk/risk/theory/alarpglance.htm (accessed 10 December 2018).

Van der Wagen, L. (2011) *Event Management*, 4th edn. Melbourne, VIC: Pearson.

7

EVENT FINANCE, ONLINE PAYMENT SOLUTIONS AND BUDGETING

CHAPTER OVERVIEW

This chapter aims to cover the key financial requirements of an event, including an analysis of the value of the industry to the economy. The chapter will explore the key financial skills appropriate for students entering the events world; for example, how to manage budgets, balance income and expenditure, profit margins, mark-ups and payment schedules. It will also discuss effective negotiation skills and examine best practice. The areas of e-ticketing, online financial tools and software will be discussed, as well as pricing strategies, economies of scale purchasing, discounting and rebates and the impact of recession on pricing. The chapter will also discuss how to create sponsorship packages to gain revenue and will explore the costs associated with outsourcing to event management companies and freelancers, as well as agency commissions and fees.

CHAPTER OBJECTIVES

After reading this chapter, you will be able to identify and understand:

OBJECTIVE 1
The value of events to the global economy

OBJECTIVE 2
Budgeting and the financial terminology used in events

OBJECTIVE 3
Expenditure, revenue streams and income sources

OBJECTIVE 4
Negotiation, cost saving, discounting and adding value

OBJECTIVE 5
Administering contracts, payment schedules and agreements

OBJECTIVE 6
Online financial tools and technological advancements in payment solutions

Meet KATHRYN MARKBY

Director at Uniqua Ltd from March 2006 to April 2018

As a highly experienced event professional in the events industry, Kathryn has been working for over 20 years to help organisations achieve their goals through the provision of flawless event management services. During her career, she has been employed at Digital Equipment Corporation, Talking Point, Conference Creations and has freelanced for many other companies. During this time she has worked on a wide variety of events including meetings, conferences and incentive travel.

Kathryn is now working for an IT company as Senior Event Manager where she manages events in the EMEA region, ranging from 10–3,000 attendees. Responsibilities include setting event objectives and metrics, venue sourcing, budgeting, client and stakeholder liaison, delegate management, contract negotiation, vendor management, event execution and on-site management.

She is married with two children.

REAL EVENT CHALLENGE

Back in March 2014 I project managed 'UK Brazil Health Week' for the UK Trade & Investment Department. The event saw the largest ever delegation of Brazilian state health secretaries gathered at a series of events over three days within the UK. The aim of the event was to get health professionals together to meet with British businesses to discuss opportunities for the health sector across Brazil. As there were over 200 health officials invited, it was necessary to ensure that all aspects of the planning went well. In the planning stages, various UK venues were visited and booked and contracts were entered into with Windsor Castle, the House of Commons, Kensington Palace and

CAREER HIGH?

Logistics Manager for Microsoft UK VIP visits, spanning six years – hosting top executives including Bill Gates and Steve Ballmer.

AND THE MOST CHALLENGING?

Microsoft 'Tech Ed' Europe 2010 in Berlin – from April to December 2010 – this was a multi-faceted event attended by 6,500 delegates; the role included management of a $12.5 million budget in three currencies.

BUSINESS BOOK YOU'RE CURRENTLY READING?

Playing Big by Tara Mohr – the founder of the global big leadership programme for women.

YOUR FAVOURITE TIPPLE?

Champagne.

WHERE IS YOUR FAVOURITE CONFERENCE DESTINATION?

Rio de Janeiro, hosting city of the Diageo World Class Bartender of the Year Competition in 2012.

various nearby hotels. However, in the run-up to the event the organising committee informed me that the event was over budget and asked us to cut the existing budget by 20%. This proved extremely challenging as we had already confirmed and contracted venues and other suppliers. We did not want to compromise the quality of the event by moving the dinners and social events to less prestigious venues, and if we did, we would potentially lose deposits stipulated by the venues' terms and conditions. However, I was mindful that we were under scrutiny to save money and deliver the event within the revised budget. As project manager, I had to think long and hard about financial decisions that would secure jobs for my event team and guarantee any future business with the association, but also without cutting on the quality and efficiency of the event being delivered.

PRACTITIONER VIEWPOINT

Michelle Fanus, Event Director, Owner, Dynamyk Events

Financial aspects of the event are always a challenge; however, with clients I create 12-week, 6-week, 1-week and Flash (on the day) budget forecasts. This is the best way to manage costs and forecast revenues. If companies have the resources then I would recommend this approach. It tends to flag up any dips in revenue, takes into account any unanticipated costs and highlights any unforeseen issues that were not apparent during the planning stages but may have appeared without any warning. This approach to budgeting is magical and does absolute wonders for your planning abilities – not only for the current phase but also for repeat events.

In the throes of planning any event, it may emerge that actual revenues were not as rosy as first anticipated so cost savings or reductions are going to have to be made to prevent the event from making a loss. This is where the detailed budget really comes into its own. Having itemised lines for each cost really helps re-think each cost and revenue figure – for example, is £2,000 really necessary for décor?! Are the expensive venues selected absolutely necessary for the success of the event? Nine times out of ten, a change in venue or the selection of a lower budget option, does not affect the overall event experience. At times like these, this is where the 'nice-to-haves' can be removed and cut-backs in specific areas can be made without losing the event integrity and core essence.

Budget management is essential for successful event management. It helps you think and plan ahead, re-think and adjust your plans, but also be prepared for any unforeseen mishaps and any changes in the landscape throughout the planning and execution of the event.

ACADEMIC VIEWPOINT

Peter Petrides, Senior Lecturer and Course Leader, Events Management, University of West London

Given this difficult situation that Uniqua faced, I would advise that the event management company try to renegotiate costs with those suppliers that they have not already contracted with. I would also look at the payment terms detailed in the venue's terms and conditions to see what the stipulated 'get out' clauses are in terms of the payment schedule. I would also be honest and up-front with the venues concerned, about being over budget, and ask if there was any way they could look at making a reduction to the overall charges, although at this late stage, it may be difficult to renegotiate. It may also be possible to look at alternative, less expensive hotels and venues to host the event. I would also revise the budget and see if there were any other potential areas of savings that could be made, in terms of flight costs or ground transportation, which are also always high-spend areas of a conference programme. Within the event management course at our university, we are committed to furnishing students with budgetary skills and opportunities to put real costings together, balancing income and expenditure and negotiation skills on the modules they study.

REAL EVENT OUTCOME

I met regularly with my colleagues during the lead-up time and had several meetings with The UK Trade & Investment Department organising committee to discuss cost-saving measures.

We looked at trying to attract new sponsors, but decided against this as it was too close to the event. We decided to keep the existing venues, as we felt that they were fundamental to the overall success of the event and social programme. We were able to work closely with the venues to reduce per-person spend by negotiating lower day-delegate rates and dinner and drinks packages. We also reduced overall staff numbers and days working on the event. Although this added increased pressure on the remaining team, we were able to meet our client's request of reducing the overall budget by 20%! The event was deemed an overriding success by delegates and stakeholders involved and we were appointed to run it the following year by the organising committee. Therefore, overall a successful outcome was achieved for all parties.

THE VALUE OF EVENTS TO THE GLOBAL ECONOMY

OBJECTIVE
1
The value of events to the global economy

THE VALUE OF THE EVENTS INDUSTRY

Events play an important role in the economic development of international communities. Recent economic growth in event tourism is due to a renewed emphasis on regional development and destination marketing by governments and tourism marketing organisations. Special events increase the opportunities for new expenditure within a host region by attracting visitors to the area. As a result, business activity is stimulated which ultimately creates income and jobs and longer term related investment. Funding for these special events often comes from governments to provide the required facilities and infrastructure at the outset. For this reason, it is important for organisers to be able to predict realistic financial forecasts, or **net economic benefits**.

Net economic benefits the benefit received from paying less for a good than the maximum amount that the person is willing to pay for it

This is particularly the case with mega events and global meetings and conferences, where the resulting spend can be a significant factor in the future growth of the global economy, and are important for the following reasons:

- They play an important role in supporting other businesses
- They have replaced other depleted industry types, such as manufacturing
- They promote investment, trade, communications and technology
- They boost education and professional development in the local community
- They create jobs and retain a community profile
- Meetings are generally a 'clean' industry and promote environmental stewardship
- They represent 'high end' visitor spend
- They can attract global expertise and awareness
- They can be used to create and spread knowledge worldwide
- Meetings can be used to promote global understanding.

POSSIBLE WAYS TO MEASURE AN EVENT'S WORTH

- *Sponsorship potential* – the value of events to sponsors, as properties for investment or branding, or by paying for benefits in-kind
- *Media value* – the value of the media coverage and advertising opportunities this affords
- *Psychological benefits* – the desirability of this event to the host community, which might be equal to the monetary costs
- *Multiple perspectives on value* – analysis of a multi-stakeholder approach.

When considering the economic benefits of any major event, the perspectives of all stakeholders need to be considered, as there are often financial winners and losers in a host country after any event of magnitude has taken place.

HOW IS ECONOMIC IMPACT MEASURED?

Economic impact is measured by the total amount of additional expenditure generated within a defined area, as a direct consequence of staging the event. For example, an impact analysis might consider how changes to a region's existing infrastructure, such as the building of a stadium, the hosting of the Commonwealth Games, the improvement of public transport links, will impact the local region and its economy.

Some authors argue that the economic contributions of events are often exaggerated and that only the injection of 'new money' into a destination counts as economic impact. It is often difficult to predict the real 'return on investment', with a risk of poor assessment, such as misrepresenting visitor numbers and expenditure. It is also often claimed that economic impact is difficult to measure without also considering the social and environmental impacts. In Table 7.1 some potential positive criteria for developing events into a region have been identified.

Impacts of new facilities	Other benefits
• Visitor spend	• Innovation/design
• Increased expenditure	• High-value employment
• Increased tourism	• The 'knowledge' economy
• Business investment/overseas interest	• Civic pride, feel-good factor, reputation
• Media coverage	• Skills, learning opportunities
• Physical infrastructure benefits	• Partnership affiliations/joint ventures
• Better transportation structure	• Sponsorship opportunities
• Associate retail/services, hospitals, etc.	• Branding opportunities

TABLE 7.1 Assessing the benefits of mega/major events

The government or ruling bodies of some host nations maintain that, even when events make a financial loss, they can still bring in additional economic benefits to the host region or country. All types of events, from mega sporting events to festivals, corporate and special events, have the capability to increase opportunities for new expenditure within a host region by attracting visitors to the area. Consequently, destinations today are often marketed for their attributes and aspirations, such as their style, uniqueness and authenticity.

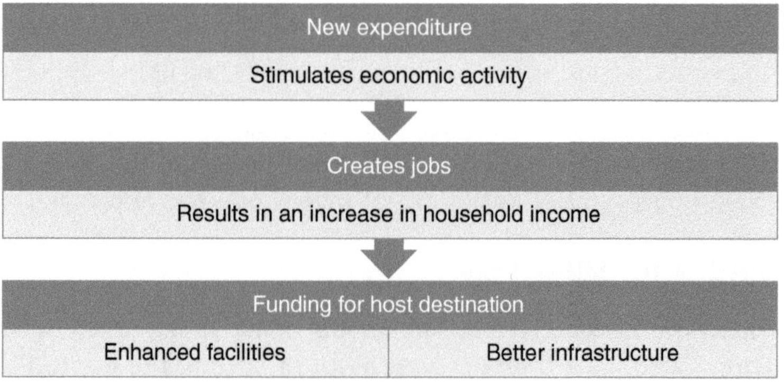

FIGURE 7.1 Multiple stakeholder perspectives on the value of hosting events

Events and festivals are being given more significance due to their contribution to economic development and place promotion. As a result of this increase in visitor spend, business activity is stimulated, which ultimately creates income and jobs and longer term related investment for the region.

REAL INSIGHT 7.1

ASSOCIATION OF DESTINATION MANAGEMENT EXECUTIVES INTERNATIONAL (ADMEI)

A recent study released by the Association of Destination Management Executives International, with headquarters in Dayton, Ohio, shows that member DMCs are optimistic about business in the foreseeable future.

Almost 60% of DMCs that belong to ADMEI reported a stronger third quarter in 2018 compared with the third quarter in 2019. Some 77% of destination management companies reported that their third quarter was as good as or better than the previous year. This continues the trend of increasing business that member DMCs are experiencing all over the globe. Some 89% project that the fourth quarter will be even better. For the past three years, 75% of member DMCs reported that they were experiencing a better year than the year prior and with the increase in business, a demand for more staff.

Survey sources ADMEI member DMCs are located on five continents, with members in Africa, Asia, Europe, North America and South America. Almost a quarter of all member DMCs are located outside of the USA. Survey participants represent 43% of ADMEI's global membership. The mission of ADMEI is to define the DMC industry; uphold the highest level of professionalism; establish standard business and ethical practices; and promote the value of local destination management.

- Creates the ability to bid for BIG events
- Increased infrastructure
- New money brought into the economy
- More jobs created
- Brings about a more professionalised industry.

TABLE 7.2 Impact on the future global events industry

OBJECTIVE
2
Budgeting and the financial terminology used in events

BUDGETING AND THE FINANCIAL TERMINOLOGY USED IN EVENTS

This section will look at some of the financial terminology used in the delivery and management of events, including: budget forecasting; charge-out rates; agency fees; payment schedules; conference packages; commission structures; and financial reconciliation, which will all be reviewed.

INTRODUCTION TO EVENT BUDGETING

The first time an event budget is put together is usually in the preliminary bidding stage. When costs are not known, it is usually fine to provide an estimate, but as soon as new or revised costs come in, the budget spreadsheet should be amended accordingly, with revised costs from the various suppliers. Each amount should be recorded under headings and updated and revised constantly with any costing changes throughout the planning process.

Events are like any other business and usually need to make a profit. Accurate accounting and a financial plan can help to achieve this. The first question that any manager might ask at the outset is whether the aim is to make a profit, or whether there are other factors to take into consideration. It is worth mentioning that an event might not always make a profit, particularly in the initial set-up stages.

In some cases, the return on objectives (ROO) is more important than the return on investment (ROI). With fundraising events, for example, the aim might not be just to make an overall profit, but also to raise funds for a charity, a good cause, another external body or the local community. Fundraising events are also sometimes known as the Third Sector. They are often run by unpaid committees on behalf of registered charities. The general aim is to keep the outgoings as low as possible, in order to generate maximum funds for the cause. Speakers, volunteers and other suppliers will often donate their services for free.

Other sources of revenue may include raffles, an auction, the selling of merchandise, donations and ticket sales. These not-for-profit events are often organised to foster a sense of community integration and engagement, and to raise awareness, rather than just generate income. Here, the objectives or social-cultural factors are usually as important as the economic ones. In some cases, the end goal might be just to break even, where the income matches the expenditure, neither making a profit or a loss. Income can vary in line with attendee numbers, depending on the size and scale. A simple financial model can help to work out what the break-even point is likely to be.

TIPS FOR EFFECTIVE BUDGETING

A control system should also be put in place to monitor expenditure through a recognised authorisation process. The budget information should be regularly updated and available to all parties. The following are useful budgeting tips:

- One person should have overall control of the budget and expenditure
- A budget must be reviewed on a regular basis

- Always allow for a contingency amount
- Ensure all income is invoiced and has come in before paying suppliers, i.e. that income exceeds expenditure at all stages of the financial process
- Hold back final payments to suppliers until after the final reconciliation
- Allow for currency fluctuations and programme changes
- Watch miscellaneous expenses and install a robust monitoring and authorisation system
- Allow for staff expenses in the budget
- Ensure suppliers send their invoices in as quickly as possible
- Agree a deadline date for completion in advance and attempt to reconcile the budget within a few weeks, wherever possible.

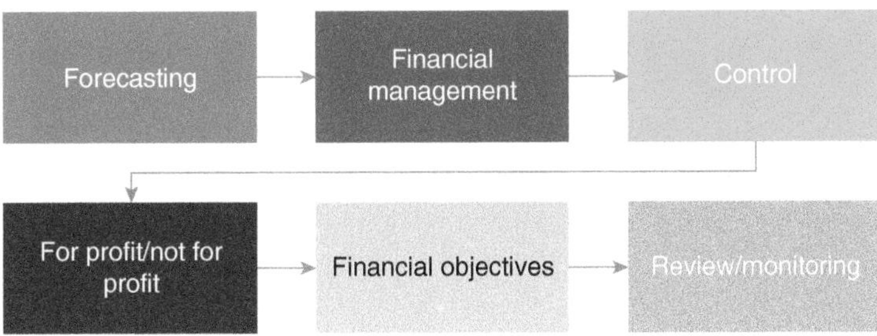

FIGURE 7.2 Budgeting objectives

EVENT BUDGETING

The budget should take into consideration all anticipated costs and then show a **bottom-line figure**. This should match the allocated spend for the event, but in reality it is never quite that simple. The financial process varies greatly, depending on the event type. For example, a corporate event is generally financed from a central budget. This budget usually covers corporate marketing eventualities, including those held on an annual basis. Delegates working for the company will generally be expected to attend, but would not expect to cover the cost of attending themselves. For the organiser, it is usually much easier to work with this kind of arrangement. Once the event has been confirmed, a **pro forma invoice** will be issued by the agency, to ensure that there are sufficient funds in their account to pay any initial deposits to secure items from suppliers, such as venue costs and conference space.

This is not always the case with a **user-conference**. Here delegates often attend an externally organised, non-company event, are required to pay a fee to attend, and recharge costs to their company afterwards. From a budgetary perspective, this is far more difficult to administer, as the process of **cross-charging** can be complicated. Without meticulous planning, there may be insufficient funds in the central budget account to pay suppliers when they are due. The situation has become far more seamless today with the advent of **encrypted online payment solutions**, but this purchasing mechanism still needs to be carefully monitored.

Bottom-line figure
a company's income after all expenses have been deducted from revenues

Pro forma invoice
a document that states a commitment from the seller to sell goods to the buyer at specified prices and terms to the client

User-conference
a conference where delegates or users pay their own fees to attend

Cross-charging
invoicing fees out to each individual delegate or company attending the conference

Encrypted online payment solutions
a secure online payment system

For some events away from the corporate arena, such as sporting and entertainment events, ticket sales will be the main source of revenue. Some of the questions the organiser might need to pose before putting together a budget costing would be:

- What type of event is it?
- Is the aim to make a profit or is it a not-for-profit?
- Where is the starting capital coming from?
- Will the delegates pay to attend?
- How else could additional income be raised, e.g. through ticket sales, merchandising, sponsorship packages, donations, venue commissions or negotiated discounts and savings?

PROBLEMS WITH BUDGETING

The challenge of event budgeting is the same as for any other sector. The principle problem is the difficulty in getting the right information in a timely fashion from suppliers in the planning stage. Sometimes it is necessary to adhere to the client's deadlines, which means occasionally making assumptions on unknown costs, which can turn out to be inaccurate. This is particularly the case when inexperienced managers are responsible for price forecasting and may happen for a number of reasons, such as when a quick quotation is sought over the phone, the supplier costs received are ambiguous, or if there is no paper or email trail to verify the initial costs quoted.

The biggest problem with budgeting is the amount of times the costs change throughout the planning process; sometimes increasing, sometimes decreasing. The final budget rarely resembles the amount depicted in the original budget forecast. In the worst-case scenario, if the client has already signed off on a budget, the management company or agency might have to swallow the loss.

Indeed, one of the biggest financial challenges that organisers face are problems with cash flow. Ironically, the agency or event company might have plenty of business in the pipeline, but because of having to pay their suppliers and staff up-front, and cover the cost of their overheads, they are forced into liquidation or bankruptcy. It is therefore crucial to regularly monitor cash flow throughout the event cycle.

While it is advisable to negotiate a favourable deposit payment schedule with the supplier, which would normally be due as soon as the booking is confirmed, industry standards dictate that supplier invoices should be paid within 30 days of receipt. It is not good practice to default on this. Online solutions mean that paying invoices can be instant today, and habitually paying late can damage the relationship with suppliers in the long run, and potentially tarnish the company's reputation.

EVENT ETHICS

Many smaller event companies have a policy of paying suppliers, freelancers and contractors as late as possible, moving their payment terms from 30 to 60 days.

They will often do this in order to manage cash flow, even if the monies have already been received from the client. This means that suppliers are often constantly chasing invoice payments after the due date.

Do you think this policy is ethical? Could it be justifiable in some circumstances?

WHAT IS PRICING IN EVENTS?

Price setting, negotiation and the ability to produce a clear and transparent budget document are all important management skills, and can be important criteria for selecting agencies and buyers. Sometimes it is the organiser or in-house team of a company who manages the financial aspects of the event; or the agency or intermediary might manage the budget as part of the overall event management services offered. Once the client has confirmed the venue, and decided which suppliers and agency to work with, it will be possible to start to compile a more detailed costing, which will include all items of the confirmed programme. Table 7.3 lists some definitions of pricing.

Price fixes the terms of the voluntary exchange transaction between customers willing to buy and producers wishing to sell. (Middleton and Clarke 2000: 86)
... customers attempt to maximise their perceptions of benefits and value for money as they choose from competitor's products on offer. (Blythe 2006)
Producers are aiming simultaneously to achieve targeted sales volume, sales revenue and market share while optimising their return on investment. (Middleton and Clarke 2000: 90)

TABLE 7.3 Definitions of pricing

It is possible to set up a simple document in the planning phase, using an Excel spreadsheet, to show the estimated budget. This makes the process easier, as the formats set up in advance allow for any cost updates and reformatting. It is essential to keep the spreadsheet up-to-date and avoid duplication. It generally helps if this is managed overall by one person. The client or budget holder also needs to be updated as to any financial amends throughout the process. This may influence their decision to spend on other items, or reduce the overall spend, and could prevent any unwanted surprises in the financial reconciliation stage.

FIXED AND VARIABLE COSTS

When putting together a budget, it is important to know which items are fixed and which are variable costs, as this can impact the budget significantly:

- Fixed costs do not alter, dependent on numbers, and include items such as the venue, costs, event staffing, marketing and insurance.
- Variable costs are subject to change, dependent on numbers, such as conference delegate packs, food and beverage and accommodation.

The cost of hiring meeting space remains the same, whether 30 or 300 delegates attend, however the cost of catering could vary, dependent on how many delegates attend on the day. For that reason, it is extremely important to keep abreast of final numbers and liaise with the venue, or any other relevant suppliers, in order to ensure the variable costs are kept as accurate as possible.

	Fixed	Variable
Definition	Costs that DO NOT CHANGE according to the number of people attending an event	Costs that CHANGE according to the number of people attending an event
Examples	• Venue hire • Staff (event manager) • Entertainment IT/audio-visual (stage, screen, speakers) • Insurance • Overheads	• Food and beverage • Staff (event assistants) • Gifts/merchandise

FIGURE 7.3 Fixed versus variable costs

CONFERENCE PACKAGES

As the conference and events industry has evolved, so has the requirement for conference and meeting packages. In the United States, and other countries, it is still the custom for venues and hotels to present conference costs as separate line-by-line items, based on the detailed and specific needs of each meeting. In Europe, unlike the US and other parts of the world, it is common practice for venues and hotels to package conference and meeting rates.

The idea behind this pricing option is to combine all the various elements of meeting room space, food and beverage, plus any basic audio-visual needs, into a flat day, or a day delegate rate. A packaged day delegate rate might look as illustrated in Table 7.4.

Day delegate rate ***£80 per person inclusive of VAT*** to include:
Hire of main meeting room
Tea and coffee with pastries on arrival
Mid-morning tea and coffee break with biscuits
Hot and cold buffet lunch in separate area
Afternoon tea and coffee break with biscuits
Projector and screen and sound system
Flipchart
Notepads, pens and mints in meeting room
Free Wi-Fi access throughout meeting

TABLE 7.4 Sample day delegate rate

The popularity for price packaging has changed over time. Initially, corporate planners preferred flat pricing for meeting rooms and food and beverage, but in recent years, this bunching of elements has started to include many more items. In many venues, especially throughout Europe, conference package rates are often presented as a 24-hour delegate rate, and include additional items, such as evening dinner in the venue, overnight accommodation and breakfast the following day.

While these packages cover a majority of requirements, planners still need to negotiate for additional requirements, such as exhibition space, breakout rooms, cocktail receptions and other agenda items. It could be argued that the practice of packaging conference rates makes managing conference venue costs both more straightforward and also more appealing to the client. A set price for conference services may offer more perceived value for money than a breakdown of every individual item. Price packaging is also often used within the wider industry, to bunch programme elements together, as in Table 7.5.

Budget based over three-month delivery period/two days on-site
Budget Total estimated fee £12,875.00 Plus VAT
(Excluding Accommodation & Subsistence at actual event)
Production as per specification
Budget Total estimated production package £28,795.00 plus VAT
(Excluding Accommodation & Subsistence)
Catering Package as per specification budget £32.00 per head inclusive (Equipment/food/drink/service) 350 guests @ £11,200.00 plus VAT
Main Budget
£52,870.00 plus VAT
(Excluding Accommodation & Subsistence/Production expenses)

TABLE 7.5 Estimated event package costs

COSTING NOTES

At the end of the budget spreadsheet, or in a separate document, additional notes on the costs are often included, when further clarification is needed. The costing notes should clearly identify exactly what is and what is not included in the budget. Items that need further qualification might include:

- ***Realistic costs*** – this prevents any misunderstanding with the client or budget holder.
- ***Any allowances/estimates*** – when cost assumptions have been made, while waiting for the actual rates to come in from suppliers. The costing notes should make it clear that these will be updated as soon as the real costs are known.

- ***Minimum numbers*** – the costing notes should specify whether the venue or supplier has based their costs on presumption of a guaranteed minimum number of delegates attending. If the minimum numbers are not reached, the suppliers have the right to adjust their rates accordingly.
- ***Enhancements*** – extras that do not appear in the budget, but could be added to enhance the programme, should more funds become available in due course.
- ***Currency rates/fluctuations*** – it is advisable to mention that exchange rates fluctuate and therefore the final costing may need to be adjusted accordingly. This means the overall costs could go up or down, depending on whether the currency rises or falls.
- ***Bank charges*** – charges and interest on financial transactions need to be accounted for. Any bank charges or fees need to be added to the final reconciliation and this should also be stated in the costing notes.
- ***Contingencies*** – needed to protect against the unknown, and any changes or amends that may take place which affect the overall budget costing. It is advisable to factor in a 'buffer' or contingency amount.
- ***E & OE*** – an abbreviation of 'Errors and Omissions Excepted' and is basically a disclaimer to allow for any human error or mistake incurred in the costing process, so is definitely an important one to include in the costing notes.

COMMISSION STRUCTURES

Commission
a form of payment to an agent for services rendered

Payment of commission was initially introduced by venues and hotels to recognise registered agencies and planners for the volume of business they brought to them. A commission structure was set up, to pay out between 8–12% **commission** on all pre-booked accommodation and food and beverages, to reward the agencies for their continued loyalty, and to incentivise them to put further business their way.

This practice primarily tends to apply to hotels and venues within the UK, and not all venues within Europe offer this type of commission scheme. It is therefore advisable for the agency to check each proposed venue in advance, to see what commission rates are offered. This is particularly important in the case of venue search agencies whose sole income comes from venue commissions.

The commission rates are normally calculated excluding VAT and service charges, if applicable. Normally it is acceptable for agencies to keep commission payments, in addition to the management fees they charge out to the client. However, in some cases, the commission needs to be declared to the client or company's procurement division and may become part of a larger negotiated rebate commission structure.

VALUE ADDED TAX (VAT)

VAT rates vary within different companies and are also subject to change. Not all bought-in items are subject to VAT. Some suppliers quote inclusive and some exclusive of VAT, so it is important when presenting costs to the client that the financial planner states which rates apply. In the UK at this present time, VAT represents 20%, so it could make a substantial difference to the overall budget.

As an agency, it is also worth finding out whether it needs to register for VAT, depending on its size and the nature of the event. It is worth noting that voluntary organisations and charities are usually exempt from VAT, as well as certain items, such as transport, taxis, coaches, and so on. As the industry is a global business, the planner should also be aware of VAT charges and any local taxes levied on conference items when operating overseas. For example, participants paying a fee to attend a conference organised in Denmark, will be subject to Danish VAT. It is therefore advisable to include VAT rates, and a disclaimer to explain these additional charges, within the costing notes.

LOCAL TAXES

In some countries, local taxes are levied on bought-in goods, for example the USA adds sales taxes to purchased goods. In many European cities, a city tax is also charged for hotel stays, which guests need to pay on a per person, per night basis. In cities such as Berlin, Amsterdam and Cologne, city tax is charged out at 5% of the total hotel bill. In addition, some destinations now charge tourists a Green tax. This tax is levied for environmental purposes, in an attempt to conserve resources and to offset the possible negative effects of tourism. These hidden costs could add a lot to the overall budget, so it is essential that planners are aware of the financial implications of any local taxes and add these costs into the overall budget to prevent any unexpected increments.

GRATUITIES AND SERVICE CHARGES

It is common practice in the events and hospitality industry to pay service-sector workers a gratuity or tip for the service performed. This often depends on the country or location and is often a matter of social custom and etiquette. Whereas in some countries tipping is discouraged and considered insulting, in other countries tipping is expected from customers, and forms an important part of their overall remuneration package.

The customary percentage amount can also vary between countries; for example, in some European countries it is acceptable to round up the bill, or add on a 10% tip to the overall bill, whereas in the USA a 15 to 20% gratuity would be expected, or even more based on the perceived quality of the service given.

Either way, as a conference planner gratuities for many suppliers will have to be considered and added as an area of expenditure when compiling the budget. In some countries, tipping is still proactively used to obtain preferential treatment, such as upgraded accommodation, reservations or better seats. However, care should be taken for this not to be seen as a bribe. While this practice may be overlooked, or even encouraged in some regions of the world, bribery is a larger and more complicated issue, which may have legal consequences.

CURRENCY RATES

When budgeting for an overseas programme, the event manager should be specific about the exchange rates used. As it is often necessary to put a provisional costing together some time before the actual event takes place, the budget notes need to clearly stipulate the current rates of exchange used, as rates may fluctuate. In fact, it is worth clarifying anything that has a date on it, such as a price based on an option until a certain date.

Sometimes in turbulent economic times, or changing markets, it may be a good idea to buy currency up front, in order to secure a favourable rate of exchange, but of course this comes with an element of risk attached. A contingency amount should be allowed to cover currency changes and the client or budget holder should be aware of what items would be subject to change, should the currency fluctuate.

BANK ACCOUNTS AND TRANSFERS

Most event planners will have business accounts and fixed rates set up with their banks, through which all funds will pass through, and will receive advice on how to set up the account and the costs of borrowing, bank charges and interest, and so on. Normal practice would be to set up signatories for that bank account. When paying for items or currency overseas, the organiser should check whether there are any commissions, transfer fees or bank charges and allow for these. Nowadays online banking has made these sorts of financial transactions much easier and more flexible. Payment cards, such as Revolut, help manage overseas financial transactions with the minimal amount of fuss and a guarantee of optimum exchange rates.

FINANCIAL RECONCILIATION

Sometimes it is necessary to add items to the budget when on-site. In these cases, the organiser needs to obtain client approval for any extra expenditure. The general process is to ask the client to sign off a Price Change Notice (PCN) to authorise any new purchases. For example, if the client has ordered 25 bottles of champagne for dinner but then requests an additional five bottles, the extra bottles will need to be signed off by the client whilst still on-site. The extra expenditure should be itemised in the final costing reconciliation, which will be presented to the client in the post-event stage. It may also be necessary to keep hold of any receipts for this type of miscellaneous expenditure.

EXPENDITURE, REVENUE STREAMS AND INCOME SOURCES

THE VALUE OF A BUSINESS PLAN

OBJECTIVE
3
Expenditure, revenue streams and income sources

The event industry could cite many instances of both small- and large-scale organisations that have run into financial difficulty and even bankruptcy as a result of staging an event. Generally events should not run at a loss, except in special and planned circumstances. Organisers should ensure the initial budgetary information is as accurate as possible. In addition, it may be necessary to produce a feasibility or business plan in the early stages (see Chapter 4). A business plan serves to communicate the strategic direction, providing it is not a one-off proposition, over a period of around three to five years. Advance planning is needed in order to secure funding for the project, from a bank or other lender. Regardless of the scale, age or history of the event, the business plan is an essential tool that should:

- Communicate the vision, purpose and benefits of the event to others
- Enable the event's potential to develop and grow

- Illustrate and help secure the event's viability and sustainability in the longer term
- Show how much money is needed and what it is needed for
- Help plan the resources, delivery, funding and operating structure
- Provide a tool to measure the event's success.

GO ONLINE

A sample business plan template can be viewed in the Appendix available online as Table 7.1.

BUDGET FORECASTING

Net rates
the price without the commission of the travel agent

For any event manager or budget holder, the key factor is to forecast as accurately as possible how much it will cost to stage the event; then to allocate revenue streams and to balance the income and expenditure. If expenditure is greater than income at any stage, a review must take place. Income forecasts should be cautious, while costs should be accurately worked out and negotiated with suppliers to maximise profit. It is vital to monitor the budget forecast throughout the process and to ensure that there is enough residual capital to secure deposits and fulfil payment schedules.

In the financial projection section, target markets and the trading periods should be clearly defined. The number of available days should be established and average **net rates** justified from the competitor and market analysis included. Throughout this stage, rates should be challenged and negotiated. If entering into a long-term contract with a supplier or client, it is advisable to build in interim pricing reviews. Never assume the success factors of this venture, but take time to understand areas such as profile, reputation and demand. When making financial projections, it is advisable, rather than just putting forward one plan, to make alternative recommendations to support the pricing feasibility. The report should not be based on personal preferences or choices, but on research and findings. At the end of the proposal, key findings should be summarised in relation to the occupancy, average rates, margins and mark-ups, fee structure, income and expenditure, cash flow, gross and net profit and any agency commissions.

SOURCE: Image courtesy of © NBC Television, 1963, via wikicommons.

Within this section, it is also recommended to include any management and staffing costs that may be incurred, and whether there are any projected savings to be made in the short to longer term. It may be advisable to include a one to five year financial plan in this section, as the initial set-up costs are likely to be highest at the start of the project, but may result in eventual savings and income in the longer term.

BALANCING INCOME AND EXPENDITURE IN A BUDGET DOCUMENT

When putting together a costing, the essential part is to balance the income (money coming in) with the expenditure (money going out), and to keep an updated record of all income and expenditure throughout the entire process. When compiling a detailed budget, different subheadings can be used. Every item of expenditure must be listed and broken down to the exact activity; for example, accommodation, transport costs, food and beverage printing costs, under each section. Every item must have a likely expenditure or income placed next to it. The main expenditure items included in a budget might be:

- Venue costs
- Food and beverage costs
- Staffing costs
- Design and production costs
- Marketing and promotional costs
- Branding and rebranding costs
- Hidden and miscellaneous costs.

Under each heading of the budget, a more detailed breakdown of costs is required, as detailed below.

VENUE COSTS

These costs could include the main conference venue and any off-site restaurants used for the social programme. Dependent on the size and complexity of the programme, it may be necessary to have more than one conference venue and/or accommodation provider. Venues are like any other business; they need to make a profit and they need a business plan and accurate budgeting. Income forecast should be cautious, while costs should be accurately worked out. Budgets must be reviewed on a regular basis and negotiation with suppliers is key in maximising profit. It is not unusual for the venue to offer potential clients and buyers introductory or discounted rates to win new business.

FOOD AND BEVERAGE COSTS

A substantial part of the overall budget is often the cost of providing food and beverage for delegates and attendees. For corporate events and private parties and weddings, the cost of this is usually covered by the budget holder. At festivals or other public events, this can be a lucrative area to generate extra revenue, making food and beverage a profitable area of extra income. When compiling a budget, it should be made clear exactly what items of food and beverage provision will be covered in the overall budget. The questions shown in Table 7.6 regarding food and beverage provision will need consideration when preparing a budget.

Drinks	• Are these included in the drinks package? • If so, how many drinks per person are included in the package, e.g. has just half a bottle of wine per person been allocated, or is it all drinks on consumption? • What types of beverages are included – soft drinks and all alcoholic beverages or just wine and beer and soft drinks?

Food menus	• Is this a set menu, which is normally required for large numbers, or an à la carte menu? • Will the food be served buffet style or is it a sit-down menu? • How will the serving style impact the overall budget? • Will a bespoke printed menu be required?
Catering staff	• How many catering staff will be needed? • Will the catering staff be required throughout the event, or only at set times? • Will uniform be provided? • Will staff be provided with a meal?
Table decorations, linen, crockery, cutlery, etc.	• What decorations will be required? • Where will these items be sourced? • What will the cost of these items be?
Additional catering costs	• Will there be any extra requirements? • At an off-site event, will a generator, separate water supply and outsourced catering services be required?

TABLE 7.6 Questions for food and beverage budget items

REAL INSIGHT 7.2

CATERING COSTS AT THE WORLD ECONOMIC FORUM

The World Economic Forum (WEF) is an international, not-for-profit foundation, established in 1971, with its headquarters in Geneva, Switzerland. It is independent and impartial, and is committed to improving the state of the world. The WEF works closely with many major international bodies and engages business, political, academic and other society leaders in an effort to shape future global and regional agendas. It works in the 'spirit of global citizenship' with 'moral and intellectual integrity' (World Economic Forum 2014) at the heart of its decision making.

Catering for this unique group of people presents an interesting challenge, with many private parties being hosted around the town, as well as the official receptions. In the main hotel, the Belvedere, over 320 parties took place over five days in 2014, generating 35% of the hotel's annual revenue, with staff serving:

(Continued)

1594 bottles of Champagne and Prosecco

3088 bottles of red and white wine

3807 cups of coffee and tea

80kg of salmon

16,805 canapés

1565 mini pizzas

1350 chocolate-covered strawberries.

Meticulous planning goes on throughout the year with key staff from the WEF, but also with representatives of the following year's delegates, who may wish to hold their own party. The expert kitchen brigade needs to be totally flexible, with Maik Baatsch, Sous Chef, reporting of having 20 minutes to arrange an unexpected party for 50 people at a previous forum. 'We had 40 chefs in the kitchen; each of them made a dish for five and that was that'. He spent the Tuesday night with 20 Korean chefs preparing for the Korean party, which included the country's president, top Samsung executives and the international pop-star, Psy.

Inevitably, when catering for an international, diverse, prestigious and demanding clientele there are challenges – providing food of an exceptional quality whilst meeting complex ethnic and dietary requirements. Kosher, halal, vegetarian, vegan, gluten-free, lactose-free menus are all in a day's work for the catering team and if special ingredients are needed, they will be sourced regardless of cost.

STAFFING COSTS

This may include the costs for full-time paid staff, on-site freelancers, contractors, production crew and possibly unpaid staff, such as volunteers. Charge-out rates for event managers may vary and also the rates that they are paid, dependent on their skill set and expertise. Full-time employees will not be paid extra for working on-site. They are normally expected to cover any extra hours as part of their role, but may be compensated with time off in lieu, on completion of the event. They will also claim for any 'out-of-pocket' expenses incurred. Freelancers and contract staff will charge for each hour worked in the lead-up time, on-site and in the post-event phase, together with any additional expenses incurred. Sometimes it is advantageous for the hiring agency to fix an overall project rate, or a daily flat rate for the freelancer, which will cover all hours worked.

DESIGN AND PRODUCTION COSTS

The cost of the design and production tends to be one of the highest costs of any budget. In times of economic austerity, this is often the first area to be cut from the budget of a corporate event. However, design and production elements are one of the most essential items of a festival, wedding or mega event and therefore generally the highest cost and the one that tends to change the most frequently. It is important for the production company to negotiate with suppliers throughout the process. For example, when operating abroad, they should work out whether it is cheaper to transport equipment by road freight, or to source equipment locally.

MARKETING AND PROMOTIONAL COSTS

The marketing or events team should decide in the planning stages on the type and quantity of promotional activities required, to inform the target market about the event and set the marketing budget accordingly. The calculation can be worked out by considering factors, such as affordability, competitor analysis and the overall objectives. All marketing and promotional costs, including the design of invitations and marketing collateral, should be included in this plan. It is also advisable to set up a bespoke website for promotion and a cost allocation for distribution of tickets to the target market. With a new event, it is logical to spend more funds on the promotion of the event initially, but once it grows in popularity and reputation, it may be possible to scale down the marketing and promotional spend for repeat events, as the following Real Insight demonstrates.

REAL INSIGHT 7.3

VOX CONFERENCE CENTRE AT RESORT WORLD, BIRMINGHAM

The Vox Conference centre at Resort World Birmingham, part of the NEC Group, is managed by the same team behind the ICC Birmingham. It was allocated a large budget to market its facilities in the lead-up time to its opening in September 2015, and hosted more than 50 events and welcomed more than 20,000 delegates through its doors in the first six months of opening. It had over 23 repeat events confirmed for the following quarter, including conferences, exhibitions and private dinners.

Nick Waight, MD of the NEC Group Convention Centres, said,

> The Vox is a very special venue ... It's designed to be contemporary, user friendly and centred on customer needs and requirements. The fact that nearly half of the customers that have used the Vox to date, have already confirmed repeat bookings is something we are very proud of.

As a result of this overwhelming success, it has been possible for the venue to scale down its marketing spend year on year.

BRANDING AND REBRANDING COSTS

The cost of rebranding products or an existing event can be high and may require outsourcing to expert marketers familiar with running these types of campaigns. Sponsors generally take a keen interest in all pre-event promotion carried out. This is to ensure maximum exposure of their name, brand, product or service. They will also carefully monitor the amount of promotional tools, such as signage and product displays, clearly displayed at the venue for all participants to see, which may increase their profile and potentially drive more sales for their products and services.

Whilst branding is generally allowed on-site at corporate events, sponsors are sometimes required to remove logos at festivals, as over-marketing is not appropriate for every type of event. According to Glastonbury Festival Commercial Manager, Hannah Rossmorris: 'the type of people that attend this festival are media savvy and don't like being told what to buy' (Virtual Festivals, 26 June 2018).

HIDDEN AND MISCELLANEOUS COSTS

When putting together a budget costing, careful proofing of each costing item is needed. There are some less obvious costs to include in the budget costing, for miscellaneous items such as:

- Printing
- Stationery
- Mobile phone, two-way radio costs
- Photocopying
- Couriers
- Floral displays.

A nominal amount should be allocated in the draft budget to cover these miscellaneous costs, as it may be too late to advise the budget holder and difficult to absorb these costs into the overall budget at a later stage. There are also sometimes hidden costs, which also need to be included, such as:

- De-rig costs
- The cost implications of going over the allotted time in the contract
- Registration costs
- The cost of any AV equipment not included in the package rate
- The cost of on-site technical support
- Insurance
- Event management fees
- Staff/crew expenses
- Other expenses.

It could make a significant difference to the budget, whether or not the venue is charging an additional daily rate, to cover the cost of setting up the conference the day before the event commences, or for de-rigging after the conference has taken place.

The venue or suppliers contracted may add a disclaimer into the payment terms, stating that if the facilities or services are required for longer than stipulated, they reserve the right to charge accordingly.

In some cases, the venue will include some basic audio-visual provision in the conference package. For more complicated technical requirements, it is important to itemise all items under the relevant headings. Cost items such as conference production and technical support are often the most expensive factors. The cost of delegate management, or registration, can also be high, as this can be a lengthy and time-consuming process.

Any costing spreadsheet should clearly specify what fees the management agency will charge the client and whether this includes any additional commissions or rebates. In today's market, transparency and accountability have become important factors, so it is essential to be open and honest about the fees that are being charged out.

The more complimentary or discounted items the agency is able to secure with the venue or other suppliers the better. It may be possible to secure complimentary items – such as set-up and de-rigging charges, a conference office or drinks on arrival – should the hotel or venue be prepared to offer them when they are no longer able to discount on the conference rates.

- Check prices of similar events and increase ticket sales costs if possible
- Try to bring the venue costs down, by effective negotiation
- Itemise what sponsorship opportunities are available and attempt to increase these
- Negotiate a better deal on menu choices, or cheaper catering options
- Put in a limit on complimentary drinks and add a cash bar
- Accurately work out the ratio of waiters, operations and hostesses needed, before recruiting

TABLE 7.7 Ways to make the event more profitable

INCOME SOURCES

As well as itemising the main costs or income in a budget document, it is important to provide an accurate projection on revenue streams and adjust accordingly as changes to these projected amounts are made. The main sources of income generation at events tend to be:

- Tickets
- Merchandise
- Vendors' fees and commissions
- Sponsorship packages.

TICKETS

For any ticketed event, the main source of revenue will inevitably come from the ticket sales. It is therefore essential to work out how many must be sold in order to break even. One of the biggest challenges for any event organiser is to set a ticket price that will be perceived as desirable and good value for money by the target audience, but will also guarantee profitability.

MERCHANDISE

This can be another opportunity to raise revenue at an event by selling products or items of clothing or merchandise. This can be popular at sporting events, but is increasingly seen with other, smaller ones as well, such as a university graduation, where sweatshirts, baseball caps and other merchandise bearing the university or college logo, are sold to the attendees.

VENDORS' FEES AND COMMISSIONS

Vendor and stallholder fees can be a good source of residual income for the client or owner. Vendors are charged a flat fee or percentage of their takings for having a presence at an event or festival but are permitted to keep any other income raised through product sales. In return, they are normally allocated a pitch to set up with necessary power supplies and amenities at the venue.

SPONSORSHIP PACKAGES

Sponsorship is a promotional technique used by business for purely commercial reasons and is a mutual transaction that offers the sponsoring company a communication link to its target audience, usually in return for financial remuneration or benefits in kind. Sponsorship can best be defined in economic and marketing terms as an exchange relationship, for specific benefits. It can also be defined as a 'partnership' or form of contractual agreement, in which the sponsor publicly endorses an activity and ties its reputation to that of the organisation or the event being sponsored.

Mega and major events in particular need a substantial level of financial funding from the host state, committees, partners and corporate sponsors. It is therefore vital to determine potential financial sources in advance. This is especially relevant within the sporting arena, which has become 'an enormously complicated mechanism', so it is often in the interest of both parties to design sponsorship packages to drive a product or service to consumers on a global scale.

EVENT SPONSORS

Figure 7.4 shows likely event sponsors, dependent on the nature of the event, size and scale.

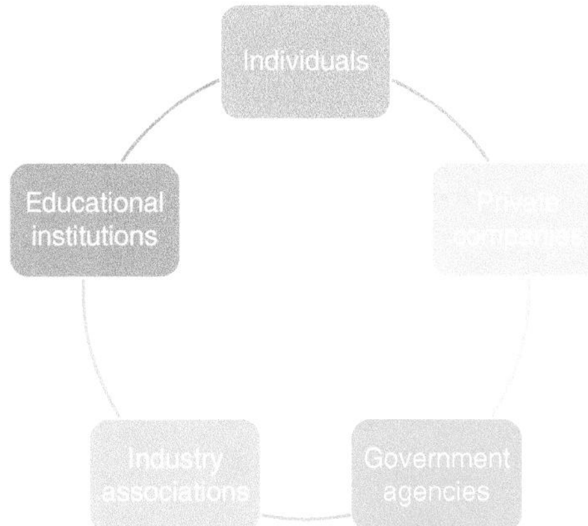

FIGURE 7.4 Who sponsors events?

There are a number of reasons for the bodies featured in Figure 7.4 to sponsor an event, or part of one, which might be:

- Interest in the cause
- To create goodwill or perception
- To enhance or change their existing image
- Interest in the product or brand
- To achieve more positive media and public relations exposure
- To reach a precise target market
- To entertain important clients
- For taxation purposes.

It could be a combination of reasons, but questions the companies will basically want to have answers to when considering sponsorship opportunities, are shown in Table 7.8.

THE CUSTOMER AUDIENCE – Is it the right event? Does it have the right demographic?
THE EXPOSURE POTENTIAL – How much publicity will the company receive? Posters, Press release, Television, Radio, Internet

TABLE 7.8 Sponsorship opportunities

How much sponsors donate will vary depending on the type of event and audience; typical gifts are shown in Figure 7.5. See Table 7.9 for the steps to be taken to attract sponsors.

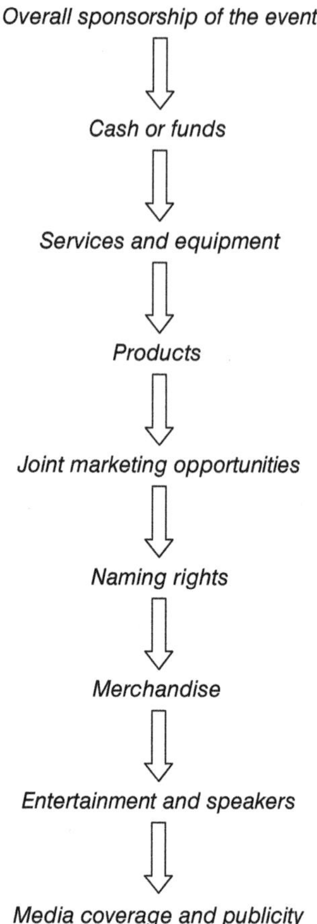

FIGURE 7.5 What do sponsors donate?

Step 1. Create the package	• Define the client/agency's needs • Why is sponsorship necessary? o Money o Publicity o Equipment o Charity
Step 2. Make the pitch	• Plan the sponsorship packages • Identify key players • Choose a setting • Gather supplies • Develop specific measurable objectives • Negotiate and finalise the agreement

Step 3. Write the sponsor agreement	• Overview of the event • Issues of exclusivity • Detailed list of what the sponsor gets • Detailed list of what the agency gets • First right of refusal issues • What other sponsors will be involved?
Step 4. Stay in contact with the sponsor	• Know how much involvement they want • Post-event evaluation to evaluate the success of the sponsorship plan • Sponsorship should be measured in terms of specific objectives • Provide feedback to the sponsor

TABLE 7.9 How to attract sponsors to get involved

The normal process would be to put together a sponsorship proposal, agreed by all interested parties. Before drawing up the proposal, questions that should be explored by the event owner are shown in Table 7.10.

Who will look after the sponsorship?
Is exclusivity being offered?
What signage opportunities are available?
Are celebrities or champions available?
Is there opportunity for client entertainment?
Is there media interest?
How will sales growth be provided for the sponsor's products or services?
How will involvement with the organisation help enhance the sponsor's image?
How much will the sponsor's market share increase and how will this be managed?
Is the organisation trustworthy and credible?

TABLE 7.10 Sample questions to consider before confirming sponsors

Once these questions have been asked and the sponsor and event owner can confirm a mutually beneficial arrangement, the sponsorship proposal can be compiled and is likely to include the following sections:

- A concise description of the opportunity, e.g. if the event is likely to be repeated or take place on a regular basis
- The dates and times that sponsorship will commence and be valid
- Estimated attendance, including evidence from market research if applicable
- An estimate of media exposure based on previous marketing campaigns or forecasts
- The value of television coverage, spot packages, radio, press, signage, all backed up with statistics

- Background details on the event owner or the rights holder, listing their previous experience
- A Mission Statement and long-term goals for the event.

SCALE OF BENEFITS

When working out the scale of benefits for a sponsor, it is advisable to start with a basic package, then increase the benefits with additional incentive items, at each level of donation. The benefits scale should finish with the ultimate package to secure the most income from one or several sponsors. Sample sponsorship packages are shown in Table 7.11.

Premier Sponsor £25,000

Exclusive benefits

- logo on tickets
- titled main entertainment stage with banner
- company booth near main stage
- £500 in tickets
- 15 event T-shirts and framed poster
- Event title

Gourmet Sponsor £10,000

Benefits

- a titled entertainment stage with banner
- company booth in community corridor
- 10 event T-shirts and framed poster
- £250 in tickets

Standard Sponsor £5000

Benefits

- company booth in community corridor
- 5 event T-shirts and framed poster
- £125 in event tickets

A la carte sponsors

- T-shirts £1200
- billboards £750
- printing .... discount

TABLE 7.11 Sample sponsorship packages

REAL INSIGHT 7.4

VISA SPONSORING FIFA

In 2015 Visa, one of FIFA's key sponsors, threatened to pull out of its contract with the football's world governing body, as Sepp Blatter faced increased pressure not to seek re-election as its president. Nine senior officials at the organisation, as well as five sports media and promotions executives, were charged by US prosecutors over alleged bribes totalling more than $150m (£100m) over 24 years. It followed the arrest of senior officials at a Zurich hotel and the announcement of a separate Swiss investigation into the awarding of the 2018 and 2022 World Cup.

Following on from these allegations, FIFA sponsors, including Adidas, Visa and Coca-Cola, called for the body to reform its practices. Visa issued a statement expressing its 'disappointment and concern with FIFA'. It said that unless football's world governing body rebuilds a corporate culture with 'strong ethical practices' at its heart, 'we have informed them that we will reassess our sponsorship'.

The credit card company's contract with FIFA is worth at least $25 million a year.

NEGOTIATION, COST SAVING, DISCOUNTING AND ADDING VALUE

OBJECTIVE
4
Negotiation, cost saving, discounting and adding value

THE IMPACT OF RECESSION ON EVENT FINANCE

In times of financial recession and austerity, events tend to be either postponed or pared back to the basics. It could be argued that this is exactly the time they are needed, in order to stimulate sales effort and economic growth, but sometimes events are viewed as a non-essential part of the organisation's overall marketing spend. Certainly, in times of austerity, budget holders tend to demand more value for money, discounting and optimum rates for all 'bought-in' goods.

It is not uncommon at these times for corporate companies to cut out the intermediary, or 'middleman', and bring the operations back 'in house', or buy direct from the supplier. It can therefore be a very challenging time for the event management agency, who in turn are often forced to put pressure on suppliers to cut their rates. It is not unknown for agencies to drastically reduce their fees at these times, in order to survive.

NEGOTIATING WITH SUPPLIERS

There is often scope for an agency to negotiate a preferential rate with a venue or other service provider, especially when large numbers are involved. The venue will normally publish **rack rates**, to give an indication of optimum rates they can obtain for the room from passing trade. However, a conference buyer would never expect to pay a rack rate, only in exceptional circumstances, where market demand is driving the rate that high.

Rack rates
the published full price of a hotel room

The budget owner will assume the agency or intermediary will have proven negotiation skills, which may be the reason they appointed them in the first place. In most cases, agencies or intermediaries will secure preferential rates for all bought-in items, such as accommodation and conference costs, based on their agency status and the volume of business they generate. However, it is always worth checking whether any preferential supplier rates exist that may have been set up by the procurement division of an organisation, just in case they are favourable to those the agency is able to secure.

ECONOMIES OF SCALE PURCHASING

Basically, this means that businesses often receive a discount because they are buying in bulk. There are many examples of suppliers offering reduced costs for larger volumes of sales, such as group conference items or venue space. In the events industry, an agency will have more buying power than an individual budget owner or corporation, based on the fact that they are usually buying group conference products and services for a multitude of clients on a regular basis. Consequently, the supplier will reward the agency for their loyalty by passing on optimum rates and discounts to them.

TIPS ON HOW TO NEGOTIATE WITH SUPPLIERS TO SECURE OPTIMUM RATES

- Research published rates before beginning to negotiate with suppliers
- Be clear exactly what is included in the rate
- Let the supplier know your budget at the outset (whether real or not)
- Negotiation should always be a win/win situation on both sides
- Planners should only negotiate rates with decision makers
- The more information background detail on your client and proposed event you can provide the supplier with, the better
- Flexibility on dates might help ensure favourable rates
- Seasonal adjustment and delegate numbers can affect rates, so be prepared to consider holding the event at quieter off-peak times
- Negotiate for other benefits beside rates – e.g. free conference office, room upgrades, welcome drinks on arrival – when the supplier refuses to move any further on the rate
- Sometimes it is better to get a packaged day delegate or 24-hour delegate rate, and sometimes better to get separate item costs.

CHARGE-OUT RATES AND AGENCY FEES

Outsourcing to an agency allows the client to concentrate on the many other roles and responsibilities they may have, both at the event and in their other, non-event-related work tasks. The savings and discounts that the agency may be able to negotiate on behalf of the client are generally good. It is in the interest of the agency to pass on those savings to their client to demonstrate value. Even notwithstanding the agency fee charged to organise the conference, the management agency or provider can often still offer excellent value for money to the budget holder or client.

Throughout the 1980s and 1990s, the process for putting together a budget was very different than it is today. Agencies would put together a costing on behalf of the client, often marking up individual items and keeping any commissions payable to them by the venue. They would tend to represent their fee by marking up a straight percentage at the end of the costing; an industry average was between approximately 15 and 20% on the total turnover

GO ONLINE

See the Appendix Table 7.2 online at **study.sagepub.com/quick**.

However, as the industry became more procurement driven, the buyers wanted to see that agencies were adding extra value. It seemed a strange concept that, by utilising a percentage of expenses, a fee approach, and by driving the turnover up, the agency or intermediary would actually earn a higher fee. In previous times, some agencies or intermediaries also became 'greedy' with the fees they charged and tended to mark up item costs and levy high percentage fees on the bottom line of the costing for the services they provided.

As the industry evolved, the emphasis changed to a more transparent fee structure. Clients became better informed and demanded to see the agencies they outsourced to secure better rates through their global purchasing power and the volume of business they secured with suppliers, to provide 'added value' with the services they offered.

GO ONLINE

The ways that planners charge a fee tend to vary considerably but can be roughly split into four different methods of quoting fees to clients, as detailed online in the Appendix as Table 7.2.

A CONSULTANCY APPROACH TO MANAGEMENT FEES

Whilst there are no set parameters or regulations on how to charge a fee for working on an event project, in time it began to make more sense to charge a fee based on the actual time and hours worked on a project, as any external professional consultant would charge for their services, and thus be able to demonstrate to the client the savings they were making to the overall event.

Based on the time worked on the project versus their daily rate, event agencies started to calculate their management fee on the same basis, charging for their time by submitting staff time, based on a daily rate calculation of project time multiplied by the daily rate of the staff concerned. It could be that various different positions in one agency had different charge-out rates, for example an account director might have a daily charge-out rate of £800, whilst an account executive might only have a daily charge-out rate of £300 a day.

Sometimes the cost of managing a project in the pre-event stages incurs different charge-out rates to those for on-site management. In addition, most event agencies will charge a handling fee for any services charged through the company. These can vary and are typically from 12.5% up to 25%.

CONTINGENCY PLANNING

As an event planner, it is worth setting aside a financial amount for any contingencies that might be required. Some organisers allow a 5–10% contingency of the costs overall and add this amount to the overall budget to cover unforeseen eventualities, or any unexpected delays or setbacks that may arise. This is particularly critical if there are unknown costs or a number of estimated cost inclusions in the budget.

PROBLEM IDENTIFICATION

Planned events may incur problems for one of the following reasons:

- A key attendee, celebrity, donor or guest speaker cancels at short notice
- Damage to the venue
- Weather disruption
- Transport problems, e.g. flight or rail strike disputes or delays
- Security threats
- Health and safety concerns.

Most outdoor events take out insurance in case they become unable to stage due to poor weather conditions. In some cases, this is an unavoidable risk. If, during the Notting Hill Carnival it rains, despite being held on August Bank Holiday, there is very little that can be done about it. The event has become so iconic in London that there is likely to be more than 750,000 people celebrating in that area, regardless of the weather. Whilst some community halls and centres could be used to house some activities, the event itself is based around a particular part of London and is very much a street carnival. The organiser can only ensure that as many elements of the programme are protected as possible, for example providing rain cover for electrical equipment and the main stage areas. Other smaller events, such as a school fête, can be salvaged by moving some of the stands and stalls inside the school hall, or to another indoor area, to allow some aspects of the fête to continue.

CANCELLATION POLICIES

The event planning contract should include terms for event cancellation. This is an important part of the contract, designed to protect both the agency and budget holder. Within the cancellation documentation, the planner should clearly specify that the initial deposit and all payments made up until the point of cancellation are non-refundable. This will ensure that the agency will be paid for the work already completed. In event planning this is critical, as most of the work is completed prior to commencement of the delivery. For that reason, it is advisable to put a clause in the contract stating that the client is responsible for paying any services rendered, up until the time that written notification is received regarding cancellation. This is particularly helpful if the payment schedule has been structured to be staggered.

GO ONLINE

It may be necessary to put some specific financial clauses into the terms and conditions, as detailed in the online Appendix as Table 7.3.

EVENT INSURANCE

All events need public liability insurance, but generally it is the responsibility of the venue itself to cover this. The event planner should check exactly what cover the venue, and other vendors or suppliers, hold, especially when hiring equipment such as projectors, sound systems, lighting rigs, and so on.

Issues of client cancellation can be insured against, and event insurance is becoming more and more important since terrorism threats, airline delays and natural disasters have caused events to be curtailed, rescheduled or cancelled at short notice. The most important point to remember here is that the contract will have clauses relating to cancellations. Many companies, such as Insurex, Travel, Hiscox and Insuremyevent, provide specialist event insurance and understand the specific challenges associated with events. The following figures, provided by Mark Blair of Insurex UK, demonstrate some revealing statistics related to event insurance and cancellation in the UK last year:

- 41% of organisers have cancelled an event
- 67% of the cancelled events were not insured
- 48% of organisers are not insured
- 51% of organisers buy insurance to protect reputation.

DID YOU KNOW?

An investment in knowledge pays the best interest. (Benjamin Franklin)

ADMINISTERING CONTRACTS, PAYMENT SCHEDULES AND AGREEMENTS

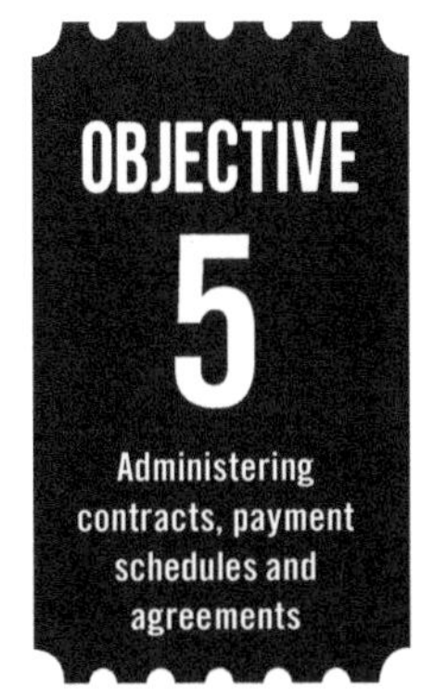

WHAT IS AN EVENT CONTRACT?

Contracts are agreements between two or more parties, with the intention to make a binding and legal working partnership, based on the key aspects and deliverables of the event. A contract is a written document that outlines in precise detail what has been agreed and promised between various stakeholders, and clearly states the terms of the agreed deliverable products and services that have been booked or hired (see Table 7.12 for definitions of contracts).

A contract is an agreement with specific terms between two or more persons or entities in which there is a promise to do something in return for a valuable benefit known as consideration. (Anon)
The Law of contracts is at the heart of most business dealings and therefore is highly significant. (Hill and Hill 2005 cited in Bowdin et al. 2011)
A contract is a legally binding document or an obligation in which each party mutually acquires a right to what is promised by the other. (Hiscox Business Insurance Glossary)

TABLE 7.12 Definitions of contracts

DRAWING UP AN EVENT CONTRACT

The issuing of contracts and terms and conditions is an essential part of the event administrative process. In business, there are usually two types of contracts: a unilateral contract and a bilateral contract. A unilateral contact is, for example, when an insurance company promises to pay out a specific sum of money if the event or occurrence does not take place, whereas a bilateral contract is an agreement between two or more people or groups. In the events industry, a contract could be drawn up between a client and the producer; a producer and any supplier; or direct between the event client and the supplier.

Event contracts can be complicated because of the range of suppliers and contractors involved, and the organiser needs to understand where contracts need to be produced, but will most likely be drawn up with the following suppliers:

- Venue
- Suppliers of equipment
- Entertainment providers
- Catering including drink providers
- Technical support
- Security services
- Activity providers
- Staff and/or crew
- Marketing and promotions agencies
- Ticketing providers
- Stewards.

If the organiser is uncertain about what to include in a contract, it would be advisable to seek professional help, or to outsource to a contract specialist. Although this may be costly, it may save money in the long run should any potential dispute arise.

The contract should be drawn up by mutual consent and both sides should be in agreement (offer and acceptance) and clear as to the details, rights and obligations. Contracts will vary dependent on the nature, size and scale of the event, the number of stakeholders and country of operation; however, it may contain contact details for all concerned parties, event specifics, which may include venue details and services to be provided, insurance details and written confirmation of compliance with relevant regulations and standards; financial details, including fees, compensation, costs, VAT and payment terms; any rider information-specific clauses, such as cancellation schedule, termination of contract, limited liability or **force majeure** and full Terms and Conditions (Ts & Cs).

Force majeure non-acceptance of liability for unavoidable situations, such as weather, acts of God, strikes, natural disasters

The contract should be issued in a standardised format. All details are negotiable until signed by both parties. The contract should clearly state the deadline for sign and return, and all signatures should be dated. A signed contract is effective as soon as it is posted or emailed out. The date of posting or emailing is the effective date of the contract agreement. The email copy of the contract should be safely filed. Any changes to the contract must be authorised and signed as an amendment, or a revised contract should be issued. It is worth noting that an unsigned contract may still be defended in court, as can verbal agreements, but a paper trail is always advised.

In the same way as for licences, there are many occasions when permissions are needed to run an event and a binding contract required. This should cover all areas and state who is contractually responsible if things go wrong, or if any of the following misdemeanours occur:

- Someone sustains an injury on-site
- Food poisoning occurs
- Permission has not been given to use the land for the event
- Police permission and correct licences have not been applied for
- The sound is too loud or music played too late in a residential area
- A fire is caused by faulty electrical equipment.

For this reason, there are key elements which should be stipulated in an event contract which include:

- Buyer or client obligations
- Arrival and departure times of suppliers
- Standards of behaviour
- Clearing up instructions
- Compliance with laws
- Corkage charges
- Use of the venue's name.

An event contract issued by third-party suppliers, such as the venue, should also mention the venue's rights to:

- Move the event to another room of equal size and suitability
- Approve any third-party entertainers or service providers in advance
- Eject unruly guests if necessary.

BREACH OF CONTRACT

Sometimes contractual disputes occur between interested parties, which can lead to a breach of contract. Some of the main areas that can cause problems with contracts are:

- Unfairness of terms
- Unequal obligations
- The supplier's right to increase prices without the consumer being able to cancel the service
- The supplier's right to change what is delivered.

Breach of contract occurs when one party does something against the good intent of the contract or fails to stick to their part of the agreement or promise. It can also occur when one of the parties involved either refuses to carry out their agreed duties or makes it impossible for the other to perform their stated duties. This can be fairly common within the events industry.

Where possible, an amicable resolution to the conflict needs to be found and it may be possible for all parties to consider alternative solutions to the problem. In cases where it is not possible to resolve a dispute between two parties, it may be necessary to seek neutral and unbiased third-party assistance through mediation or arbitration. Wherever possible, an attempt should be made by both parties to conclude the event and then continue to resolve any differences in writing. If conciliation cannot be reached at this stage, it may be necessary for both parties to put their grievances to a small claims court, or seek legal advice for litigation against the other, which can be a very expensive and time-consuming process, but nevertheless is becoming increasingly common as the industry continues to expand.

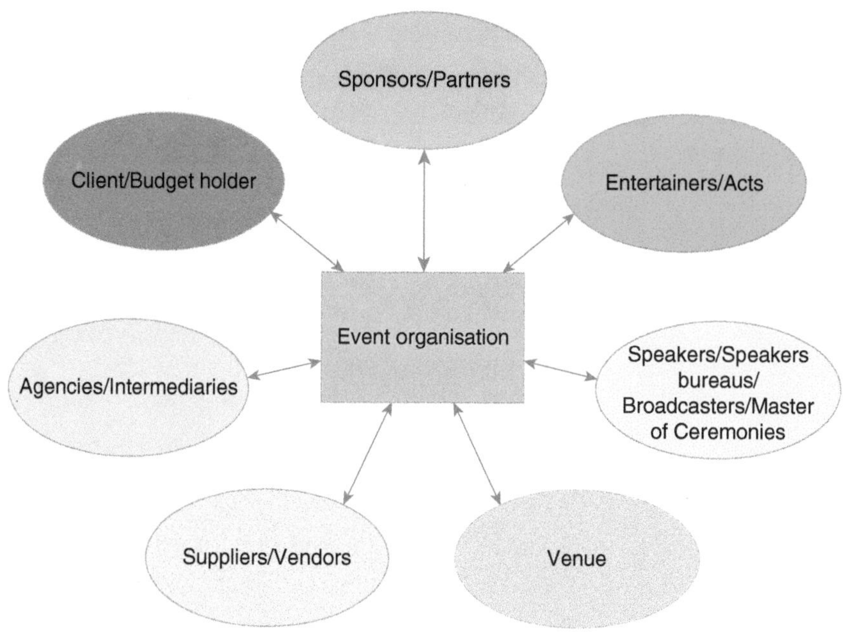

FIGURE 7.6 Sample contracts needed for events

It is worth remembering that even for repeat business the content of verbal contracts can be ambiguous, confusing and hard to enforce in disputes. Both parties will have different recollections of what was promised. It is therefore important to get contracts typed out and signed and stored securely. It is also important to ensure that appropriate signatories are used, particularly as contracts can be declared invalid if evidence proves that signatories are minors, under the influence of alcohol or drugs, or mentally incompetent at the time of signing. A contract generally needs to be in exchange for something: money, property or rights, and mutual assent needs to be both clear and in agreement with all corresponding details.

Within the events industry, a contract could be:

- An offer
- An acceptance of that offer, resulting in a meeting of minds
- A promise to perform
- A value consideration, i.e. a payment
- A time stated for the performance or event, which meets a prescribed time commitment
- Terms and conditions, including fulfilling promises for performance/event delivery.

Contract agreement forms should contain clear writing and uncluttered unambiguous language, clauses that protect mutual interests, a detailed agreement and sufficient information and detail to withstand scrutiny.

TERMS AND CONDITIONS (TS & CS)

Event details are the core of the Terms and Conditions contract and should contain a summary of:

- Contact information and details, stating authorised signatories
- Venue details – times, location
- Details of service or products
- Specifics of any additional services
- Additional insured elements
- Compliance with regulations and standards.

Within the Terms and Conditions, there should be precise detail concerning the venue name, allocated room names, space held, all venue start and finish times, stating set-up and breakdown time for suppliers, artists, technical and rehearsal, and length of performance. The document should list all details in order of occurrence, lights, music, and specify the number of people involved. Corresponding emails and any other documents exchanged between parties should be included in the document. It is also important to include more minor details in the Ts & Cs, such as the need for a changing room or catering for crew. Both contracts between the client, intermediary or supplier, should include the word 'us' as part of their commercial insurance. Supplier contracts should be attached, which state they have to comply with all regulations and standards within the law, for example certified electricians working under BSI, ISO or best practice procedure, or caterers following required food hygiene procedures.

It is also a prerequisite to include event financial details within the Terms and Conditions, and this should be specific and very clear and include items such as compensation values, details of taxes and local service charges, and deposit schedules and deadlines for payment terms. Usually deposits around 30% are due on signing and the balance of 50–70% due before the event date. Ongoing payments can sometimes be an option, depending on the client and contract agreement.

In the case of an international contract, the currency and date and calculation of currency exchange rate and any additional taxes which are part of the contract, should be clearly stated. For international events, it may be possible to refund this tax amount back to the hosting country which could be large sums of money for major and mega events.

Any riders, as part of the entertainment specifications, should be attached to the original contract and retained by the client, supplier and intermediary. When booking high-profile bands or musicians for events, the rider can become a large factor in the cost of the act and may include more outlandish demands. In many instances, the act will demand backline technical equipment to be set up. Additional security may need to be provided for the artist or performer. The level of security and cover required should be discussed in detail with the agent prior to signing the contract. It is not unusual for some event riders to take up to six pages of requirements, with flights, accommodation, catering requirements, and so on. This can all come to a considerable amount in budgetary terms, as can be seen in the case study below.

REAL INSIGHT 7.5

SOME OF THE CRAZIEST RIDERS IN THE USA

SOURCE: Image courtesy of Walt Disney Television via flickr.com. Shared under the Creative Commons BY-ND 2.0 license.

Jennifer Lopez, nicknamed 'J-Lo', the American actress, singer, dancer, fashion designer, producer and businesswoman is often known to promoters as the pale rider, as her rider asks for everything in her dressing room to be in white. This includes a white room, white flowers (lilies and roses), white tables and tablecloths, white drapes, white candles, white sheets and white couches.

The 80s' American rock band Van Halen put M&M's on their rider but requested absolutely no brown ones! They have since explained that they did this to test whether their promoter had read the whole rider, believing this could be an indication of how the rest of performance would be managed, such as the lighting, staging, security and ticketing.

American pop diva Mariah Carey stipulated in her rider that she wanted crystal champagne glasses and 'bendy straws'. The furniture in her living space had to be black, dark grey, cream or dark pink, with no busy patterns and no harsh ceiling lights, only a lamp or clip light.

Barbara Streisand, who completed a tour of New York and London in 2019, emphasised security on her rider – she regularly requests a police K-9 team to sweep the arena before she performs, and wants metal detectors on all doors, 10 torchiere-style floor lamps and 150 folding chairs. She insists that all security personnel are smartly dressed, with strictly no T-shirts worn.

Christina Aguilera demands a police escort to prevent any traffic delays. She also asks for 8-foot tables with tablecloths, plants, flowers, carpet, chewable vitamins, soy cheese and Nesquik as part of her rider.

PAYMENT SCHEDULES

Part of the financial management process of the organiser planner is to ensure that payment schedules are clearly outlined in the contract and that payment due dates are communicated to all parties. As previously mentioned, many event companies have plenty of new business opportunities in the pipeline, but go out of business because they are unable to pay suppliers, and so on. This is often because invoices have not been sent out to the client or settled in a timely fashion. It is normal practice to issue the client or budget owner with a pro-forma invoice to ensure the payment is received, before paying out any supplier deposits, and so on.

Supplier Terms and Conditions should also be thoroughly checked. It is advisable to allocate one person to monitor all supplier contracts for the due deposit dates, then work out a financial schedule, noting when payments are due in and out. Sufficient time should be factored in for monies to clear the bank. One way to manage this is to set up online calendar alerts, to flag up payment reminders and any future payment dates, well in advance of when they are due. Any extras to the budget should be formally agreed in writing. It is also essential to consider how legal and taxation obligations will be met.

Every agency, supplier venue, and so on, will have their own payment schedules, which must be adhered to. Financial managers also need to be aware of the payment schedule set out in the client contract and the payment terms stated in any sponsorship agreements. They should establish a payment schedule that best suits their business and cash flow and make sure that this schedule includes any taxes, service charges and added fees.

EVENT INSURANCE

For events that require insurance, the organiser should contact one of the bespoke insurance companies to take expert advice on the best policy cover. They should also check what insurance provision the budget holder already has in place within their company or organisation and what it covers. The client or budget holder should be advised whether the cost of event insurance has been included in the provisional costing and if so, exactly what this includes and for how much.

All events need public liability insurance to basically cover attendee bodily injury and the venue's loss of revenue through organiser negligence. Generally it is the responsibility of the event owner or agency to check what the venue is covered for. The supplier's own insurance cover should also be checked, especially when hiring production equipment, such as sound and lighting boards. If an event management company needs to arrange insurance, it should always use a specialist broker who knows and understands events. This may include items such as:

- Public liability of £5 million; increased for larger events
- Employers' liability
- Motor-business cover
- Volunteers
- Equipment hire
- Contactors' insurance
- Professional performance artists, groups, etc.
- Products liability
- Cash/money cover
- Cancellation cover.

In some cases, such as with the hire of local authority venues, the authorities' own insurance may cover the event. There are several insurance features to consider, such as:

- Cancellation/abandonment (including terrorism free)
- Material damage
- Liabilities
- Optional travel and money cover
- Travel regulations, including passport and visa applications
- IATA bonding, etc.
- Additional expenses cover
- Failure to vacate premises
- Return of fees (to exhibitors/delegates)
- Non-appearance of speakers or VIPs – many insurers exclude this
- Enforced reduced attendance
- Weather
- Property damage
- Buildings, machinery and plant equipment at the venue.

Each insurance policy will vary, dependent on the event type, its size and significance and the associated risks.

ONLINE FINANCIAL TOOLS AND RECENT TECHNOLOGICAL ADVANCEMENTS IN PAYMENT SOLUTIONS

ONLINE PAYMENT SOLUTIONS

Cashless payment technology is increasingly being demanded by both government offices and the public to meet consumer demands and expectations. Today festival attendees are much more likely to just carry cards, rather than large amounts of cash. Contactless payment, including payment by credit cards and debit cards, key fobs, smart cards or other devices that use radio-frequency identification (RFID) or near field communication (NFC), are now being used to make secure payments. This has many benefits for organisers, as it allows them access to their target audience's details and to track their movements and preferred zones on-site. It is also estimated that customers spend up to 20% more when using cards rather than hard cash.

Event vendors have also facilitated the use of products that allow the visitor to pay directly using PayPal, Apple Pay or QR codes on their smartphones. This transformation of on-site payment methods encourages attendees to leave their wallets at home and to minimise risk, such as on-site theft and security costs. Festival organisers in conjunction with leading banks have introduced cashless wristbands to eliminate having to wait for change, thus reducing queuing times at food and beverage outlets, other vendor stalls and ATM machines.

FINANCIAL MANAGEMENT PACKAGES

Various bespoke financial systems are being used to formulate costing, including market leaders Wrike, Attendify and Oracle's Netsuite and a host of others, which can be specifically tailored for each event organisation to make the financial process far more accurate, and quicker and easier to manage.

E-TICKETING AND FINANCIAL PORTALS

Online portals such as Eventbrite and Billeto are increasingly being used by delegates and attendees to sign up and purchase tickets in a safe and secure way. Eventbrite offers a platform to purchase different packages and search for events in a specific location. The site allows the user to select and save chosen events in a favourites tab which can be retrieved once the user has finished browsing. Unlike sites such as Ticketmaster, Seetickets, Getmein and Stubhub, which sell tickets for mainstream concerts and comedy shows and levy exorbitant transaction fees, these new sites sell tickets for no upfront fee and only take a small percentage of the overall ticket profit. Billeto sells over 2 million tickets each year from events created in over 12 countries and with over 30,000 active organisers.

Despite the positive attributes of online ticket booking, problems can occur with online registration, as illustrated in the case study below. Some secondary sites such as eBay and Amazon are now not allowed to authorise ticket sales on their sites due to the risk of scammers reselling them at inflated prices. This poses a threat both to the industry and the attendee alike. In order to stem this practice, some artists have recently teamed up with a new site launched in 2017 called Twickets. The site was originally set up for purchasers of tickets no longer able to attend musical and other events, to provide a platform to resell their tickets at face value.

REAL INSIGHT 7.6

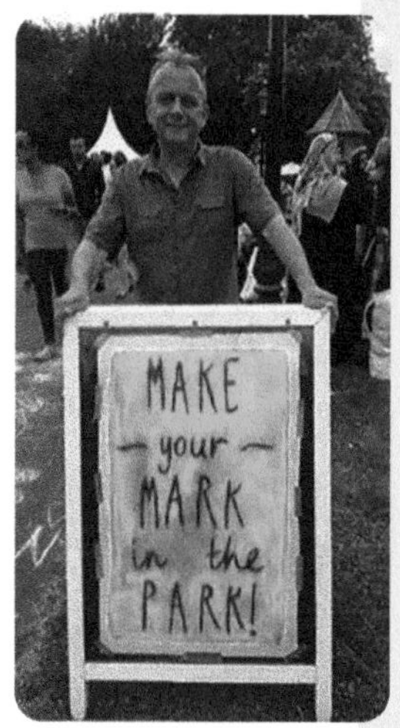

BUYING CONCERT TICKETS ONLINE

Mark was trying to register to attend on the morning the tickets went on sale for a popular festival. He was aware that there would be a short timeframe in which to purchase the tickets. However, despite registering as soon as the tickets were released, it took him over 3 hours to get through to the site. As there were too many people online at one time, the site kept shutting down. In the end he got three confirmations and his credit card was charged twice. This reflects the current instability of online registration, which can lead to frustrated guests. This could in turn lead to poor attendance for the next event, resulting in a negative impact. It is difficult to police how many people go on to the website to register at one time; however over time, errors such as charging customers twice could be eradicated, or an alternative method for purchasing tickets for these types of large events could be made available.

Indeed, recent media reports of data protection leaks of personal and financial details resulting from purchasing, or even just browsing, online have raised renewed concerns about the safety and anonymity of online banking and shopping. However, even with the challenges that exist with contactless payment, it cannot be denied this technology has revolutionised the way we pay for items, travel and attendance at events, and as a result this has ultimately enhanced the overall guest experience.

CHAPTER SUMMARY

CHAPTER SUMMARY QUESTIONS

1 What is the difference between fixed and variable costs in an event budget?

2 Which items should you include in the costing notes?

3 Which items should be shown as miscellaneous costs in a budget spreadsheet?

4 What are commissionable rates?

5 What items are usually included in a 24-hour delegate rate?

6 Which additional items might an event venue be prepared to offer the event management company in order to secure a group conference booking?

DISCUSSION POINTS

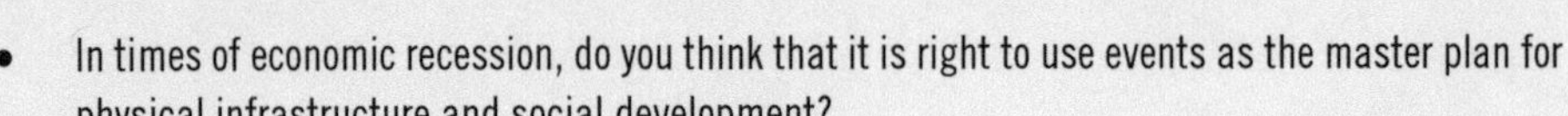

- In times of economic recession, do you think that it is right to use events as the master plan for physical infrastructure and social development?
- As the financial manager of a major event, what questions might you ask at the outset of the event?
- Why is Return on Objectives (ROO) sometimes as important as, if not more so than, Return on Investment (ROI) in events?

ACTIVITIES

- List key items of income and expenditure for an evening awards dinner with 50 guests which will make £2000 overall profit.
- Write to a local pizza delivery company, inviting it to sponsor your student event by supplying the event with complimentary pizzas, in return for some sponsorship benefits of your choice.
- Draw up a list of factors to include in an online application form that might convince a charitable trust to consider a grant application for your cause over others.

REFERENCES

Association of Destination Management Executives (ADMEI). Homepage. Available at: www.admei.org (accessed 4 October 2019).

Bowdin, G., McDonnell, G., Allen, J. & O'Toole, W. (2011) *Events Management*, 3rd edn. Oxford: Butterworth-Heinemann.

Blythe, J. (2006) *Essentials of Marketing Communications*, 3rd edn. London: Pearson.

Eventbrite (2018) Homepage. Available at: www.eventbrite.co.uk/about (accessed 2 June 2019).

Hill, G. and Hill, K. (2005) 'Contract', Legal Dictionary [online]. Available at: http://dictionary.law.com (accessed 19 September 2019).

Hiscox.co.uk. Business insurance terms glossary. Available at: www.hiscox.co.uk/business-insurance/faq/business-insurance-terms-glossary (accessed 20 November 2019).

Middleton, V.T. and Clarke, J.R. (2000) *Marketing in Travel and Tourism*, 2nd edn. London: Butterworth-Heinemann.

Twickets (2017) Twickets.co.uk [online]. Available at: http://edsheeran.twickets.co.uk (accessed 25 June 2017).

World Economic Forum (2014) The Global Competitive Report. Available at: www3.weforum.org/docs/WEF_GlobalCompetitivenessReport_2014-15.pdf (accessed 8 October 2019).

8

EVENT DESIGN AND PRODUCTION

CHAPTER OVERVIEW

This chapter deals with a range of issues relating to event design and concept planning. It will explore experiential design across a range of events from sporting, music events and festivals to corporate events and exhibitions, and will include aspects such as venue design and layout, design of marketing collateral and catering to reflect the event theme, and will explore the use of props, decor, costumes and staging to create the environment. It will also discuss the use of production and audio-visual in events, and content and presentation design, speaker support, and the health and safety issues associated with event production.

CHAPTER OBJECTIVES

After reading this chapter, you will be able to identify and understand:

OBJECTIVE 1
Event design theory and practice

OBJECTIVE 2
Design domains for the event mix

OBJECTIVE 3
The creation of the event experience

OBJECTIVE 4
The various types of audio-visual and production effects

OBJECTIVE 5
The role of audio-visual and other production companies in design

Meet MATTHEW WALL

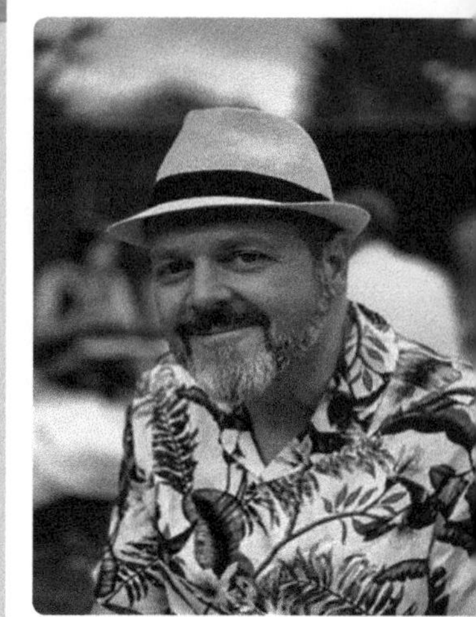

Chief Creative Officer at upstage

Matthew is an industry veteran, with more than 25 years' experience across a range of disciplines, from operations and logistics to audience engagement and creative production. His career began in the voluntary sector, with highlights including the tenth annual Walk for Life (for the HIV/Aids fundraising charity Crusaid) with special guest Archbishop Desmond Tutu. He went on to serve as Head of Events for Bloodwise, running a nationwide series of Bikeathons, including a three-year partnership with the BBC's *Blue Peter* programme. In the private sector, Matthew served as EMEA Vice President for Operations for the global meetings company BCD Meetings & Events, working with a diverse range of clients including Sony, Bank of America and Pfizer. He is the Chief Creative Officer of upstage, a global engagement agency with offices in the UK and US, working with a wide variety of clients to help them create genuine connections between their message and their audience. He edits the blog *Wall's World* (www.wallsworld.co.uk) and is in demand as a speaker and host at industry events, including Confex, HBAA, SITE and many more.

REAL EVENT CHALLENGE

An existing client's annual internal all-hands meeting had got into a bit of a rut. It was always held at a local hotel, and had unfortunately become just another meeting, with too much PowerPoint, lacklustre presentations and an unengaged audience. The real challenge of this event was finding a way to make the programme more immersive and engaging. Because all the employees were in the audience, it was difficult, if not impossible, to find the right content to share. As there was little or no room for employees to actively participate,

HOW DID YOU GET INTO EVENTS?

More by accident than by design! I had a natural affinity with events from having acted, produced and directed in the theatre. My first 'proper' job was with a publishing company looking to breathe some more life into their events, and I really enjoyed applying what I had learned from the Arts to commercial challenges.

WHAT NEW TRENDS ARE YOU SEEING?

Thankfully, smart companies are now beginning to think more about 'experiences' rather than one-off 'events'. Creating meaningful engagement between a brand and its customers takes time, and delivering impactful experiences is a vital building block in that process.

FAVOURITE RESTAURANT?

Probably because I've been going there for so long, it's tough to beat The Ivy.

WHO HAS INSPIRED YOU MOST IN LIFE?

I get inspired by so many people, it's tough to pick just one. I do find this a very inspirational industry to work in, so I'll choose the dozens of peers, colleagues and friends I've made over the years in our crazy business.

ADVICE FOR WOULD-BE EVENTERS?

Events are not what you do, they're how you do it. You inspire people, teach them, motivate them, enthuse them, amaze them, make them think, learn, share and grow. And you do it with events.

the meeting wasn't a conversation or exchange of views, but more just a series of lectures, and our creative team needed to think how we could change the existing format to make the conference more interesting and participative.

PRACTITIONER VIEWPOINT

David Clement, Creative Director/Producer: Live events, Author of *Corporate Event Production – Effective, Face-to-Face, Corporate Communication or Reaching 'The guy at the back' with bad eyesight – who'd rather be in the bar'*. (Entertainment Technology Press; see www.etbooks.co.uk/product/corporate-event-production-9781904031840)

A recent Conference & Incentive Travel (C&IT) magazine industry forum defined 'The Event Experience – an industry in transition'. This however is hardly front page news; the difference is that now all parties, clients, agencies and audiences/attendees are talking about it and sharing thoughts. When corporate events really got off the ground, back in the 1970s, it was sometimes referred to as 'industrial theatre'. Not a bad reference point. Apart from staging, lighting, sound, projection and effects, it also implied a shape and flow to any event (think of a play in three acts, for example, whether in a theatre, a custom-built location or in a field).

It's a creative process. Taking any audience with you depends on how well aligned the agency is to client, audience and take-out message. Not as obvious as it sounds. Success is largely based on the relationship and rapport the production team have with their end client. This will sometimes mean encouraging clients to step outside their comfort zone in order to create the most impact and memorability. If mutual trust, a smoother pre-production and event ensues. And yes, it may even be possible to have fun doing it.

A quote from Carl W. Buecher, US writer and theologian, is a great maxim for any speaker: 'They may forget what you said, but they will never forget how you made them feel.' I'd suggest the principle could equally apply to designing and delivering an effective event experience.

ACADEMIC VIEWPOINT

Matt Bunday, Event Production Manager and University Academic in Event Management

Event design can be tricky to get right. The challenge of using the right combination of colours, props, set, drapes, costume and production elements to improve your event theme can be complicated. Sometimes just a few hanging Chinese lanterns or a blue colour scheme will be enough, with much more probably being overkill, whereas at other times the event requires that your audience be fully immersed in it as they walk into that mystery room. This then means that every part of the event needs to be consistently supporting the theme.

I believe it is so important to teach effective event design and production elements within academia. I think most events have some design aims to them when broken down and learning how these are achievable within time and budget is crucial.

The production elements that we use in the industry are also regularly being updated, with new lighting, sound and AV technology regularly being made available. Our industry trends are regularly changing with new interests, expectations and requirements from our audience.

With all this in mind, we must be teaching students the basics in this area, signposting them where to go to keep their knowledge up to date, and ultimately how to apply it well and to a consistently high standard.

REAL EVENT OUTCOME

Part of our role as events professionals is to challenge our clients in order to understand their objectives more clearly. So the first question should not be: 'What do you want to do?', but rather: 'Why do you want to do it?' By understanding our client's objectives and building relationships between employees in different parts of the business, encouraging storytelling as a way to engage customers and trying to develop new skills, we were able to create a completely different all-hands experience that inspired as it informed.

Instead of transporting people to a local hotel, we held the event on their own premises. We knew that people must be involved in order to be engaged, so rather than a conference we gave them a festival. This was a festival with a difference, because instead of dancing in a field or watching bands, every employee participated in a series of activations designed to connect them with the company they worked for and each other. Some teams made guerrilla-style promotional videos, roaming about their campus filming short adverts; others took part in storytelling workshops to learn how to bring their corporate message to life. There were groups writing radio jingles and groups building pop-up shops – all focused on expressing the company's values and drawing on the experience of the collective team. Everyone learned new skills, networked with people they might otherwise never have met and emerged a better storyteller. That's what I call a very happy ending.

EVENT DESIGN THEORY AND PRACTICE

WHAT IS EVENT DESIGN?

The study of event design rests on three premises:

- All event environments are created
- All experiences within event environments are purposefully designed
- All stakeholders are the direct recipients of the designed experiences.

Design can be viewed as a critical tool for event management, as it relates directly to development of the event concept and experience, enabling the event manager to envision and implement the event message. Event design is embodied through a process of planned deliberation to produce a specific outcome or set of outcomes, or experiences.

Events are designed to satisfy all manner of needs and diverse global audiences. The process of design requires a creative imagination and can be defined as 'design thinking' or 'imagineering'. Bladen et al. (2012) remark that when designing an event, the creative and thinking processes are aligned. They go on to define three types of design thinking – adapted from Edward De Bono's (2016) *Six Thinking Hats* – as Analytical, Logical and Lateral. These are made up of a combination of analysing a suitable creative response to the initial brief, then coming up with a logical or feasible solution for the delivery of the concept, and lastly, lateral thinking, which is coming up with ideas and solutions that may appear more random or 'out of the box'. All three modes of this conceptual thinking are necessary for a successful design plan to evolve.

Design takes many forms and can be used to create values or lifestyle through products, where differentiation is often based more in the image, than the function alone. Getz (2012) refers to it as a combination between science and art. Environmental design is about space, flow and location and will be explored in more depth later in this chapter. The process of transforming a space through design begins with a vision, followed by a strategic plan to implement the desired ambience and images, using fabric, furniture, decoration, colour and props to create the final appearance of the event.

In a fast-changing and ever increasingly competitive area, the design of the event needs to demonstrate uniqueness, originality and authenticity. This could be one of the biggest challenges the industry now faces. Today's clients are commanding ever more, so the producer or designer is now under great pressure to create new and exciting design environments and put forward new and appropriate theme ideas to create unforgettable and memorable experiences. Table 8.1 explores some of the design terminology that will be used in this chapter, to help define the design process.

One of the theoretical concepts of design presented in Table 8.1 is that of Dramaturgy, as explored through the academic writings of Erving Goffman (1956), who believes that when an individual's environment is altered, so would their behaviour be, in order to reflect the new environment. This theory goes on to suggest that the environment of a play or an event can be purposefully manipulated in

Dramaturgy	Stage performance used to create an experience Actors and audience in a co-creation of social reality Storytelling Theming Service personnel: Actors Customers: Audience/attendees Uniforms = costumes of the drama Physical equipment = props Property = physical settings
Atmospherics	Artificial environments – designing of space Deliberate manipulation of environment to produce a reaction Emotional connection to the space via experience
Servicescapes	Built or man-made environments, e.g. exterior and interior design, temperature, noise, smells, tangible objects Physical elements, e.g. dramatic elements used to orchestrate the environment The five senses: vision, smell, touch, taste, sound emitted through colours, fabrics, scents, etc. Relationship of physical to action, e.g. consumer experiences
Symbolic interaction	Human beings respond to meaning and personal associations Meanings shape experience Interaction in an event or shared meanings Events designed to create a memorable experience
Flow	Flow is the sense of effortless action of a core experience, described by many people as the moments that stand out as the best in their lives, moments of powerful concentration and deep enjoyment

TABLE 8.1 Event design terminology

order to control how the attendees will react emotionally to it. Just as in a theatrical context, the use of actors, stage design, lighting, music and other design aspects help produce a specific audience reaction, a conference producer is able to apply these features to an event to elicit a predetermined audience response.

Atmospherics, as referred to Table 8.1, are used in the design of events, to manipulate the audience and engage their senses and perceptions. This could be through content, production and environmental design. The word servicescapes is often used in relation to the design of the environment. Servicescapes are man-made environments, where tangible objects, such as temperature, noise, smells and music, are deliberately placed within the event environment. The producer should design the servicescape of the event, whilst ensuring that the audience will still be sensorially engaged in the whole event experience. This concerns the service received and the delivery of it. The idea focuses on the relationship between the physical complexities and the performance factors needed to deliver a successful event.

Table 8.1 also mentions the term symbolic interaction whose origins trace back to Max Weber, a German sociologist, who stated that individuals act according to their interpretation of the world. Rossmann and Ellis (2008) identify six features of symbolic interaction, as interaction between people, relationships, rules, objects, physical settings and animation. In an event setting, it is how individuals attach meaning and emotion to objects, symbols and settings, which affects their behaviour, perceptions and ultimately their overall experience of the event.

DESIGN OF MARKETING COLLATERAL

Creating products such as applications or merchandised products is also part of the design process. This includes the use of graphic design and the technical and software tools used to design and produce marketing collateral, such as virtual renderings and other printed or electronic materials. The marketing collateral used to promote an event needs to be designed well in advance, once the essential features of the event, such as venue dates and keynote or guest speakers, have been confirmed. This is used to support the sales of a product or service. In the past, the term marketing collateral referred specifically to brochures and flyers, or any printed material used to promote and sell the event. It was often designed by professional artists or designers to reflect the theme, content and programme of the event and enhance the overall brand message, or used as a **teaser** to promote and sell the event. Nowadays marketing collateral is far more likely to be the design of a bespoke website or online portal to promote the event and sell tickets at the same time. This area will often be outsourced to creative agencies, with specific design skills and software to create the 'look and feel' of the marketing material, who will come up with a creative direction, vision and brand identity for the event marketing campaign. However, with the advent of inexpensive and easy-to-use software packages such as Adobe Photoshop, this is increasingly being brought back 'in-house'. Events also use merchandise and printed material to market and promote events, as has been discussed in Chapter 6.

Teaser
an advertising or promotional device intended to arouse interest or curiosity, especially in something to follow

CULTURAL INFLUENCES ON DESIGN

As events are diverse in form and content and have an international reach that brings people, populations and different cultures together, it is important that cultural sensitivity is demonstrated in terms of catering, content, entertainment, environment, production, programme and theme. This is significant because cultural norms vary in different parts of the world, so that what may be appropriate in one country may be considered inappropriate in another. Event planners should be attuned to areas of cultural sensitivity, such as the attitudes and values of a specific society, use of body language and gestures, religious beliefs and legal requirements, relating to the observance of cultural or religious laws.

According to Kim and Jang (2016), people who are open to different cultures are more likely to recollect and remember experiences; however, although event concepts often have a global appeal, the way they are staged may differ, depending on which country is hosting the event.

DESIGN DOMAINS FOR THE EVENT MIX

DESIGN MECHANISMS

Design is essential to the overall experience, as it enhances it and allows the guests to engage in sensory and emotional interaction. The mechanisms presented in Table 8.2 are used within an event, principally to provide content, but also to provoke an audience reaction and heighten the overall experience. Design elements can be exploited to bridge experiences and emotions, for both the host and guests, through drama, atmosphere and service delivery.

The practical tools to deliver the theme or event concept are props, decorations and costumes, which help create ambience and authenticity, and to provide a feeling of escapism, or venture into an imaginary, fantasy world, what is known in the theatre as '**suspending disbelief**'. The entertainment features also allow the designer to tell the story, set the scene, or engage the audience and allow them to interact with the proceedings. For some events, costumes are provided, or the audience is encouraged to dress up. These types of creative events are devised to be multisensory, engaging all senses and providing either an emotive connection with the music, or speaker content, as well as being purposefully designed to elicit an element of surprise, which can also be used to enhance the audience experience.

Suspending disbelief the sacrifice of realism and logic for the sake of enjoyment

Gobo a stencil or template placed inside or in front of a light source to control the shape of the emitted light

Lighting, staging, visual aids, such as a **gobo**, dry ice and floral displays, sound systems, and technical props and equipment are all design mechanisms that are used to create ambience and dramaturgy.

THE EMBOK DESIGN DOMAINS

In her *Event Management Body of Knowledge* (EMBOK), Silvers (2008) explores the various design mechanisms, categorising them under design domains, saying, 'The design domain focuses on the artistic interpretation and expression of the event project and its experimental dimensions.' Various elements of design are categorised, as illustrated below.

Factors of Design	Description
Concept or Theme	Development of a core theme, strapline, message, brand identity or overall concept, which determines all other elements of the event
Content and Activities	Sourcing and selecting appropriate content and activities specific to the event, i.e. keynote topics, discussion forums, live music, multimedia presentations, team-building activities

Factors of Design	Description
Programme /Running order	The agenda, schedule and running order of the event, from the time the audience arrives until they depart to ensure there is a continuous flow of activities throughout
Setting and Environment	Appropriate setting or event environment, which includes infrastructure, facilities, placement of props, furnishings, signage, exhibits and food and beverage outlets
Production and AV elements	Sourcing and supplying necessary staging, multimedia, lighting, sound, special effects and audio-visual requirements, which will vary in complexity depending on the event type
Entertainment/Speakers/Acts	Sourcing and managing appropriate and sufficient entertainment and leisure activities which match the type of event being staged
Food & Beverage/Catering	Planning and implementing appropriate catering provision to suit the nature of the event, including menu selection, accurate scoping of quantities, choice of service styles, beverage selection, etc.

TABLE 8.2 Factors of design

The design domains which are used to create the overall event experience, can be broken down into the following areas, as represented in Table 8.2. They will be further explored in the following section.

DESIGN OF THE THEME OR CONCEPT

'The theme of an event must be supported in every aspect, including the decor, lighting, sound and special effects' (Van der Wagen, 2010). The event theme or concept is what gives it meaning and can be a 'take-home message' for guests. Some events are designed more for pleasure, whilst others are more educative in purpose. An overall theme or concept is initially developed through consultation with the client, or by a brainstorming session with the agency's creative team. It often starts to take physical shape through the manifestation of staging, props, décor, costumes, entertainment, and food and beverage design. Developing an overall theme requires creativity and innovation and is often the most enjoyable part of the planning process, as it provides both the organiser and the owner with the opportunity to open up their minds to various ideas and to try something different. Thematic interpretation can be stimulating and can embody both tangible and intangible elements to ensure that guests have a memorable experience. Brown and James (2004: 60–61) identify five principles which can be applied to theme design management:

- Scale – the size of the event, utilising the venue space
- Shape – the layout of the event
- Focus – directing the attendees' gaze to physical elements such as colour or movement
- Timing – the programme, schedule or agenda
- Build – the peaks and flows within the proceedings.

Silvers (2008) discusses the thought process behind coming up with an appropriate theme and concept. The principles of determining a theme or concept for the event can be manifold, but are essentially to create audience interest and to launch a programme that is both creative and innovative. Once the theme has been decided, the conference producer needs to find ways to thread the theme through a number of design dimensions, with attention paid to cultural traditions, icons, symbolism, imagery, enhanced creativity and overall inclusion of the five senses within a practical and logistical framework.

Table 8.3 shows a basic way of deciding upon a suitable theme or design concept and illustrates some sample theme ideas that could be easily adopted. It is worth considering the audience demographic and how they might respond to it. By participating in the theme, the audience can become part of the entertainment, but this may depend on how prepared the audience is to integrate themselves in the theme, or dress-up in appropriate costume and participate in the themed activities (Bowdin et al. 2011). It is also important not to alienate the audience, or push them too far out of their comfort zone.

Theme	Ideas/Theme
Cultural/National Identity	African Egyptian Moroccan
Dance	Line Dance Barn Dance Salsa
Food and Drink	British Pub Boston Tea Party Cadillac Diner
Film	Film Legends Bollywood James Bond
Literature	Ali Baba Narnia Harry Potter
Music	Jazz and Blues Rock 'n' Roll Boogie Nights

Theme	Ideas/Theme
Nature	Fire and Ice Rainforest Tropical
The Past	Legends of the 20th Century Medieval Titanic
Sport	Cricket Rugby Sporting Heroes
Travel	Orient Express Out of Africa Around the World

TABLE 8.3 Sample theme ideas

Theming within the event environment can often be viewed as a form of escapism and is often aligned to the imagination and human psyche and the subconscious world of the audience or attendee. Table 8.4 indicates some of the factors needed to bring an event theme or concept to life.

1 *Theme names*	Inspiration could come from storybooks, music, movies, television, sports and culture and even board games
2 *Colours*	Flags for international event themes, athletic team colours for sporting event themes, wristbands and corporate logos
3 *Flowers and plants*	Floral arrangements that reflect the theme or host destination and incorporate theme colours
4 *Venue*	The right venue can reduce decoration costs, e.g. venues for tropical events, winter events and garden parties
5 *Seating*	Can foster engagement and inspire a comfortable learning environment, e.g. using bean bags for an informal meeting setting, or divan seating and low tables for an Arabian night theme
6 *Chair covers*	These can be specially designed and ornate, and are often used at weddings and parties, or more formal events, such as conferences and business meetings
7 *Linen and napkins*	Can be used to convey a theme, decorate a table and incorporate colour

(Continued)

TABLE 8.4 (Continued)

8 *Table centrepieces*	These do not have to be expensive and can be created with toys, scrap or objects from nature, etc.
9 *Music, film clips or entertainment*	Can be used to create the right event ambience and reflect the theme, for example a roaring '20s party could have a rolling film clip of *The Great Gatsby* playing in the background. Note appropriate licences are required for any public performance
10 *Catering*	Menu selection can be a powerful vehicle in theming design and how the food will be served, for example using Bento boxes for a Japanese theme
11 *Backdrops and draping*	Creating a photo backdrop or wall. Draping adds a dramatic or formal touch to events and can be used to transform an empty space quickly and inexpensively
12 *Lighting and candles*	Can be used to create instant ambience; for example, flashlights or torches could add a fun factor to entertainment elements at a camping themed event and candles could be used to light gala dinner areas for added ambience.

TABLE 8.4 Twelve key ingredients of event theming

REAL INSIGHT 8.1

A THEMED HARRY POTTER FUNDRAISER

A well-known Australian charity organised a fundraising event to raise money on behalf of a registered charity for people suffering from disabilities. A local hotel with excellent disabled facilities offered the charity the main ballroom at a discounted rate and gave them permission to theme the event as they planned. Due to the fact there was a conference taking place in the ballroom during the day, the charity's organising team only had two hours to transform the space into an environment that would reflect the Harry Potter theme.

At the entrance to the ballroom they recreated Platform 9¾. They designed the space so that on arrival the guests would walk through the gateway to the reception area, where they would be served 'Butterbeer' or cauldron punch as a non-alcoholic option. Toward the back of the reception area, a screen projector was set up, showing highlights of the Harry Potter film franchise on a loop. Guests then proceeded to the maze, which was the key attraction.

Located in the maze area were a variety of stalls, activities and entertainment ideas designed for guests to get fully immersed in the Harry Potter experience.

On completion of the maze, guests were led through to the bar area. Here trestle tables were set up as portrayed in the films and novels. There was also a ramp set up for disabled guests and a stage area for the guest speaker from the charity, who introduced the cause and the fundraising targets set. In order to enhance the theme, the following design features were set up:

- Harry Potter soundtrack playing throughout the evening to create ambience
- Dim lighting to add a dramatic and spooky effect
- Walls painted black
- All staff dressed in Harry Potter costumes
- Guests received a site map, representing the Marauders Map
- Giant spider webs, made from balloons and cloth, pinned to the walls
- Most Wanted posters, featuring Harry Potter, Bellatrix and Sirius
- Education decrees with Umbridge Rules posted on the maze walls
- Antique mirrors from charity shops, with iconic messages from the Chamber of Secrets written in red lipstick
- Old suitcases, books and potion jars used to decorate the bar and trestle tables
- Harry Potter props available to use in the photo booth to capture photos of all invited guests
- Harry Potter face painting
- Replicated Quidditch game as an event activity.

The theme extended to the catering, where the menu included a Harry Potter style banquet on the trestle tables, and confectionery items designed for the event were presented on the table, such as Golden snitches and Olivanders chocolate wands and frogs.

DESIGN OF CONTENT AND ACTIVITIES

Design of the content is an important part of the design domain and involves either psychomotor outcomes, that relate to physical activities, or cognitive outcomes, that relate more to knowledge-based and learning activities. This is supported by Bowdin et al. (2011), who state that an event concept is the foundation on which the design process must be built. They also advocate that the concept needs to serve the event purpose or its objectives. Silvers (2009: 243) describes the area of content design as: "The selection of the appropriate topics, formats and presenters to achieve the communication objectives and educational obligations of the event project, incorporating the principles and dynamics of adult learning."

The content of any event is extremely important, as there needs to be structure and a mix of activities to ensure overall success. The content should be both complex and creative. As an event designer, the challenge is to design content that differs from the norm and is also innovative, which is usually what both the client and the audience want. This can be risky, as by thinking laterally or outside the box, it may end up dividing the audience or eliciting negative feedback. However, on the positive side, it can create the opportunity for surprise, mystery and the 'wow effect.' At a wedding, for example, the bride and groom's preferences on format and structure, including special content such as poetry, musical performance and ceremony, are part of the content design. A good combination for event content is to include a mixture of elements that will educate, entertain as well as provide an element of surprise. In determining content, it is important to understand and articulate the values of the attendees or customers, and evaluate what kind of experience they should have and how to deliver content that will result in a positive response. Table 8.5 demonstrates some of the key content functions of an event and the performance elements that can be adopted within them.

Major Functions	Performance Elements
Objectives and Obligations	Determine purpose of event and review goals Specify communication and learning objectives Identify needs and interests Analyse industry, education, economic, and other trends
Learning Principles	Recognise various learning styles and strategies Incorporate adult learning principles Specify continuing education and accreditation requirements Develop assessment methods for content delivery
Topic and Format Selection	Specify content scope and topic requirements Identify and evaluate programme formats

Major Functions	Performance Elements
	Select appropriate delivery system
	Develop appropriate programme tracks
Speaker Selection	Determine types of content delivery personnel
	Solicit speakers and presentations
	Establish speaker guidelines
	Secure and incorporate support services as needed
Speaker Arrangements	Manage contract fulfilment and contractual relationship
	Arrange logistics and hospitality requirements
	Establish and enforce intellectual property rights
	Manage speaker product marketing activities

TABLE 8.5 Content functions and elements of activity

As the content of a conference is extremely important, it is one of the areas that a conference producer might work together with the client, to ensure appropriate content, which will be delivered through a range of media platforms to deliver the conference message. The content needs to reflect the event's overall objectives, and the purpose might be to:

- Present the company's vision for the future
- Discuss key issues and challenges facing the business
- Encourage debate and discussion within an organisation or a team
- Help with sales kick-off and motivation
- Provide education or training
- Launch or re-launch a product or elevate the perception of the brand
- Entertain or reward staff.

As detailed in Table 8.5, content design is about selecting appropriate activities and topics that will enable the presenters, acts or speakers to achieve their communications, entertainment or educational requirements for the event. The case study below highlights the emergence of content marketing in conferences today.

DESIGN OF THE PROGRAMME

> Programme Design Management concerns the formation and choreography of the agenda of activities, elements, exhibits, and amenities that shape the composition of the event experience to address the ceremonial, hospitality, and communication requirements of the goals and objectives of the event project. (Silvers 2005: 9)

REAL INSIGHT 8.2

NICKY BALESTRIERI, MANAGING CREATIVE DIRECTOR, BMF MEDIA

At the Event Innovation Forum in New York, Nicky Balestrieri, Managing Creative Director of BMF Media, explained why an editorial approach to creating live experiences is essential to brand storytelling and guest engagement. He said that a rise in content marketing has shifted the way industry professionals think about events and meetings, and it's also changing the way live experiences are designed. Producers and designers are thinking more like editors, looking at events like they would a magazine or a website: as a long-term communication strategy with layered messaging and visuals. Nowadays the use of market research and experiential narratives can form concepts that engage guests and create lasting impressions. Balestrieri offered a glimpse into his process, sharing examples from his experience with Paper magazine and work for clients such as Lanvin, Cointreau and Target.

A critical part of the event product is designing an attractive and engaging programme. Generally, there should be some established criteria or structure for the programme content; for example, How many times has this guest or act appeared in the country? Is the event new and original? How will the programme be received by the target audience? Above all, any programme should reflect the overall event mission. The desired level of quality and the design of the programme should match the profit objectives set and resonate with the audience. When designing the programme and content of any event, it is important to align the environment setting to the programme activities. For example, whilst a fine dining event or banquet would work very well in a heritage building or livery hall, it would not be fit for purpose for a festival or concert. Design of the programme and content often depends on the approach of the producer and artistic director, just as it would do in the theatre or ballet.

The design of the programme is the core of the design process and concerns the deliverable items, structure and logical sequence of the event. The programme should always reflect appropriate timings and the flow of scheduled activities, or sessions. It should plot when they will take place sequentially, so that people have enough activities to keep them occupied. However, the programme should also be flexible enough to allow for any unforeseen changes, or more ad hoc or spontaneous programme items. It is also important to ensure that there is sufficient time for a social agenda, which may include free time for breaks, networking and refreshments. The conference producer should always consider the audience reaction and try to find a spread of varied activities that could run simultaneously, to allow for all tastes.

'As well as the tangible activities programmed, there should always be some intangible aspects, or surprise elements for the audience' (O'Toole 2011: 185). In order to entice the audience to attend, it is a good idea to reveal aspects of the main event programme by means of a **teaser**, or social media. However, it is advisable to keep some elements of the programme unannounced to reveal on the day or night of the event. Some of the most important factors of programme design are listed in Table 8.6.

Teaser
a promotional piece designed to reveal only a little about the event, but enough to arouse attention, build excitement and curiosity

1 Consultation with all parties directly involved in the programme
2 Calculating the time of each and every activity
3 Ensuring that the programme has time for 'ceremonial' activities, e.g. opening and/or closing ceremonies, speeches, the presentation of awards or entertainment interludes
4 Ensuring that the venue is available for the FULL duration of the event
5 Choosing the date(s) so that the event does not clash with other local or major ones
6 Allowing for a little 'slack' time between activities
7 Structuring the order of activities
8 Determining whether the programme should be printed, available online or by app, containing programme details, etc.

TABLE 8.6 Important programme design factors

Events often have a prescriptive order or a format. This is sometimes based on written rules or guidelines, or, at other times, on what worked well in the past and has now become a standard format. For example, many academic conferences do not have designed interactions beyond food and wine gatherings. 'Inserting something like a speed dating research session into the programme creates a new experience' (Berridge, 2010: 186).

Table 8.7 shows a programme for a dinner designed to be quite loose to allow for changes and some flexibility.

Times	Activity	Speaker	Venue
Outward			
09:30-10.00	Registration, Coffee, Networking and Pastries	Mark Avebury CEO, PDR Creative	The Auditorium The National Space Centre

(Continued)

TABLE 8.7 (Continued)

Times	Activity	Speaker	Venue
Outward			
10.00-10.15	Participant Welcome and Introduction	John Field Head of Facilities, National Space Centre	The Gallery
10.15-10.30	The Next Millennium in the Space Centre	Charlie Holmes CEO, The National Space Centre	The Gallery
10.30-11.15	Customer Experience in New Advertising	Garry Flower Senior Advisor Merlin and Chairman of Brand Vista	The Auditorium
11.15-11.45	**COFFEE BREAK**		
11.45-12.05	Social Media for 2020 and Beyond	Marketing & Content Training Director	Syndicate rooms TBC
12.05-12.15	Immersive Technology Forum	Paul Bradford Director of PDR Creative	Syndicate rooms TBC
12.15-13.00	Dealing with Data Protection: A GDPR Masterclass	Sally Spencer	The Auditorium
13.00-14.00	**LUNCH WITH EXHIBITORS**		
14.00-15.00	The Delegate Showcase	Series of short talks from our own expert in-house marketing team	The Gallery
15.00-15.30	**TEA/COFFEE BREAK**		
15.30-16.10	Panel Discussion: How we Combine Science and Learning with Marketing to Create Enticing Programmes	Chaired by Rose House Marketing	The Auditorium

Times	Activity	Speaker	Venue
Outward			
16.10-16.55	Engaging Schools and Families with Science	John Sykes Executive Producer, BBC Learning	The Auditorium
16.55-17.00	Closing Remarks and Acknowledgements	Mark Avebury CEO, PDR Creative	The Auditorium

TABLE 8.7 Sample draft event programme

Once at the event, the audience should receive access to the full programme of activities, with a map of rooms and timings, so that they know exactly what is happening and where. This can be designed through a printed programme, room plan, or nowadays through a mobile application. For the guests, the programme is the guide to the event agenda. For the organising team, the programme helps them manage the flow of guests, as well as manage on-site staff, at any specific time. It is also important to remember that as first impressions are vital, the programme should commence from the moment the audience enter the space, until they leave it. Careful consideration should be given to how to create impact for guests or the audience on arrival, sometimes even commencing outside the venue itself, for example having entertainers or a 'meet and greet' team to welcome the audience on arrival at the event.

DESIGN OF THE VENUE AND ENVIRONMENT (FOCUS, SPACE, FLOW)

The design of the event environment should allow for space and flow, so that the audience can move seamlessly through the event. Flow, as detailed in Table 8.3, can determine the ambience and also the audience's attitude and perception of the event. It is therefore an integral part of the design process. The organiser or designer should understand the best use of the environment and how the elements placed within it can impact the audience's overall experience. In the operational planning phase, it is important to consider how the space will be used and whether it will be comfortable as well as functional for the audience.

Designers need to be aware that events often experience extreme peaks of demand, and therefore need to be able to control the flow of customers in, around and outside the site or venue accordingly. Where possible, the site or venue should be designed to cope with peak traffic, by ensuring there is more staff positioned at entrances during this time. It is also important to plot and monitor where the audience will be at certain times, for instance just before kick-off at a sporting event, or at a festival when one main act has ended and another is due to start playing in another area of the site. The resulting surge of guests and increased crowd movement can consequently impact safety implications and therefore needs to be included in the risk assessment.

It is also essential that sightlines are designed so that the audience can see the main activities, as well as being able to navigate and understand the space. As far back at the '60s, Kevin Lynch in his iconic book *The Image of the City*, suggests using landmarks and pathways to indicate activity points, zones and districts. By subdividing the site into functional areas in this way, the site becomes more legible to the audience and ultimately enhances their overall experience.

Zoning concept a method used for dividing event space up by its function

The layout should be designed to enhance atmosphere and flow, to create a **zoning concept**, or to increase sales and footfall, by placing elements in such a way that the audience are forced to stop or pass by an area. Large brands such as Disney stores and IKEA have successfully engineered this technique, creating audience flow and directional movement, to optimise sales opportunities for their brand.

Whilst it is not possible to ensure that the audience or attendees will all have the same experience, placing elements within the environment so that the audience will pass or stop in the same places will at least ensure they have access to the same elements. This may also result in residual income from food and beverages, or merchandise. Revenue also needs to be considered in terms of the cost of the space, as any unused capacity can be an expensive waste of resources. The placement of the following need to be considered when designing the layout of a meeting room or space:

- Workstations
- Security
- Signage or signposts
- Queuing or waiting space
- Provision of disabled facilities
- Reception, foyer or main arena
- Food stations or serving areas
- Staging and lecterns
- Props and décor
- Waiting areas
- VIP or Green rooms
- The event or cash office
- Merchandise points of sale.

Goldblatt (2008) maintains that an event environment is designed to provide a dynamic setting, in which guests can receive a multi-layered experience that engages all the senses. Environmental design also involves the creation or acquisition and arrangement of décor items, props, furnishings, decorative embellishments, wayfinding and signage systems to enhance the attractiveness and functionality of the event environment.

Getz (2012) talks about the the Kaplan model which helps predict delegates or audience's preferences for various types of environment. Here Coherence is understood as when the setting has been organised and everything fits together, so that it may be categorised or clearly perceived as Legible. Kaplan (1987) then describes Complexity as a variety of diverse elements that exist in a setting, and the idea of Mystery is when the audience become drawn in by hidden information, yet to be revealed.

The environment is largely dependent on the nature of the event; however, all these factors influence the end-user and contribute to the overall experience. Legibility is crucial in all 'servicescapes', because customers arrive with pre-determined expectations of how the site will function. For example, guests attending festival sites will expect the site to deliver on a number of levels, often employing 'a zoning concept'. This is the provision of separate areas, including a main stage, a food and beverage outlet area, or in the case of a major festival, such as Glastonbury, various zones such as: the Pyramid Stage, Left Field, The Common, Shangri-La and Silver Hayes, which all represent different vibes, audience preferences, ambience and entertainment offerings.

As early as 1960, Kevin Lynch stressed in his work, that effective site planning should allow people to easily understand the layout, and be able to efficiently navigate within that space. Lynch (1960) recommends that all events should have various recognisable environments.

In this case, say within a festival, such as Glastonbury, the 'nodes' may be the Pyramid stage, or the Other Stage; the paths would be the main thoroughfares or different routes from the various campsites; the landmarks would be recognisable icons, such as the large helter-skelter in the festival site which audiences could use as a reference point when giving directions, or as an easy meeting place; the districts might be the food halls or vintage market stalls areas; and the edges might be listed as the green field, the red field, the yellow field or gate, and so on, in order to colour code parameters and boundaries.

Venue design concerns choices and decisions on the quality and value of the product, which may give one venue a competitive edge over another. In terms of an ideal event environment, today's delegates expect essential facilities, such as event offices, press rooms, car parks, adequate access for the physically disabled, and Wi-Fi in all areas of the conference centre. The major design challenges tend to stem from the fact that many venues are either halls or arenas with no aesthetics. It is a challenge for a purpose-built venue, such as a conference centre, to balance functionality and aesthetic appeal, as they may have ugly structural features, like pillars and room divides. Venues may therefore require substantial modification on technical or creative grounds to be suitable to host the event. This can create an opportunity for unique and unusual venues, for example an art gallery, a museum or livery hall, which may have a more inspiring look and feel, as well as other provocative features.

The more practical or functional aspects of design, for example, within a congress or convention centre, need to meet the demands of the delegate on the move. The space should therefore be designed to function at a number of levels, including the provision of facilities such as business centres, event offices and ample breakout rooms, well situated near the main plenary room. In some cases, if no other space is available within the venue, it is necessary to transform the same room that has been used for the main plenary room during the day, into an area for entertainment or even a gala dinner in the evening. A further factor of environment design is to create separate conference entrances and registration areas within the venue and, wherever possible, to provide separate conference and catering holding areas, ensuring that there is a good use of signage in each.

REAL INSIGHT 8.3

DESIGNING THE ENVIRONMENT IN THE IDEAL HOME SHOW, LONDON, UK

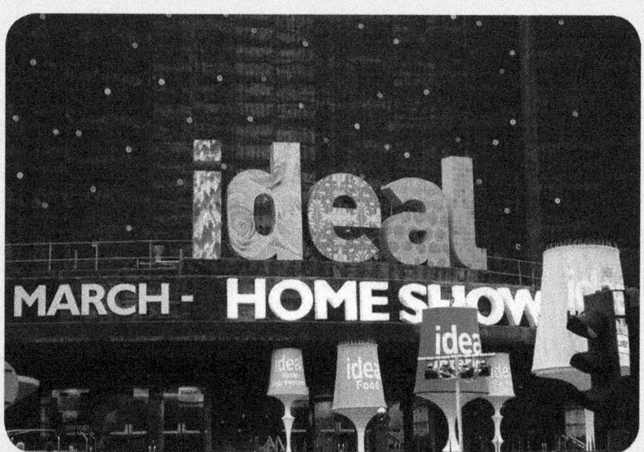

SOURCE: Image courtesy of Mark Hunter via flickr.com. Shared under the Creative Commons BY 2.0 license.

The Ideal Home Show, formerly Exhibition, can be traced back to 1908. It was originally founded by the *Daily Mail* as a publicity tool for the newspaper to increase its advertising revenue. The show is now owned by Media 10 and held at London Olympia, and brings the latest innovations and brightest ideas to the thousands of visitors that attend. From kitchens and bathrooms, to bedrooms and basements, fixtures and fittings, to fine foods, gardens, the latest technological gadgets, to fashion, beauty and gift ideas (Ideal Home Show, 2017).

The key to this award-winning event's success is that it is possible to find and experience all these items under one roof and the show provides multiple opportunities for the attendee to engage in both sensory and emotional interaction whilst there. In order to create a suitable, but ambient space to host this annual event, the designers need to consider the décor, design, artefacts and zoning of different areas, so the space can operate at many levels and appeal to all demographics.

Due to the large venue and audience size, the designers also need to ensure that there is sufficient signage and maps available in all areas, to allow the audience to navigate the venue with ease and to be able to locate various features such as the public toilets and food courts, quickly and easily. Barriers, ropes and coloured pathways are also installed to segregate the different zones and allow the attendees easy access. The site design also needs to allow the attendees to flow seamlessly from one section to another, according to their specific interests and requirements.

In order to create various environments under one roof, the designers have replicated rooms to resemble 'real life' size and scale, such as could be found in everyday homes, and have brought them to life within a specific area of the venue. Features such as garden furniture and real grass are used to create an impression that attendees are in a real garden, which engages all the senses.

In order to encourage participation, celebrity chefs appear within the food and drink theatre. Here attendees can watch celebrity chefs, such as Dean Edwards and Aldo Zilli, prepare delicious dishes from scratch and offer tips on how to prepare restaurant standard food using everyday ingredients. The aromatic smells and sounds that are created within this theatre environment stimulate all of the human senses that enhance the overall attendee experience.

Props and furniture are displayed throughout each created environment. Ambient lighting design is used to create the impression of a sunny day in the back garden, or low lighting in a three-dimensional living room, to give the feeling of a cold winter's day. In addition, the designers integrate an array of new, state-of-the-art technology and contemporary must-have gadgets, showcasing new products within the layout and design of the space. In this way, the audience become part of the event, as they interact with the different props and technology. This encourages them to try out and purchase the products on show. Over the years, the Ideal Home Show designers have considered all aspects of exhibition design and incorporated them into the live show. It is clear to see why this event has been successful for over 100 years and why attendees keep returning year on year.

PRODUCTION DESIGN

> Production Design Management deals with the incorporation, sourcing, and selection of the appropriate sound, lighting, visual projection, multimedia, special effect, and other theatrical elements and services to meet the communication objectives and create the desired impressions and ambience of the event project. (Silvers 2005: 9)

This is an area where the event borrows from theatre and performance. 'The design produces spectacle and show, for example ... production of multiple settings within an environment, or a stage design' (Berridge, 2010: 186).

As previously explored in this chapter, production is an essential part of design and it is possible to detect very clear links between live events and the theatre, as Berridge (2010) discusses through the production of multiple settings within stage or set design. Production design requires expertise, with designers or a creative team who have the necessary skills to plan and plot the technical requirements, content and programme of any event, as demonstrated in the case study below.

REAL INSIGHT 8.4

PRODUCTION DESIGN – HUGO BOSS FASHION SHOW, BERLIN, GERMANY

SOURCE: https://www.pikrepo.com/fejan/female-fashion-models-walking-towards-white-lit-room

The client, Hugo Boss, asked for an 'outstanding and surprising show' to be produced by agency Villa Eugenie. Situated on the 'Buhne' (Stage) of the German

Opera House, 1000 people were treated to a show that combined fashion and opera. The entrance to the event held a surprise in itself as guests were ushered in through the back door and not the main foyer entrance.

This was further enhanced by the seating arrangement which, rather than use the house seating, was in fact set out on the empty opera stage facing the invisible audience. The producers also chose to twist tradition in other ways, by separating the audience from the performance space with a black velour curtain and omitting any sign of a catwalk. Instead, there was just a glistening black floor. In an effort to create the tension, suspense and drama associated with opera, the fashion show was split into several acts.

With scenery changes between each act, guests were plunged into darkness at each set changeover before the next group of models emerged. Structures were used to infuse each act with a special element. Act 1 started with a lowering of a 14m-high steel staircase for the models to enter the stage, whilst Act 2 saw an 82m glistening white walkway emerge that then folded into nine tiers to create a suspended catwalk operated by hydraulic lifts for perfect timing and safety. The finale, Act 3, featured 25,000 gem-like components reflecting a dazzling light that created a tunnel for models to walk through. The aim was to produce a show that was 'illusion', creating surprise, appearance and disappearance.

ENTERTAINMENT DESIGN

> Entertainment Design Management encompasses the sourcing, selection, and control of suitable entertainment, ancillary programs, and recreational activities for the event project and coordinating the support requirements for the entertainers and activities in a manner that delivers the desired entertainment experience and that benefits the audience and organisation. (Silvers, 2005: 9)

Conference entertainment can be varied, often depending on budget, the purpose of the event and the specific target audience. These factors determine the type of performance planned. For example, a cocktail reception may require a simple string quartet but a music festival would require something more technological and innovative. Allen (2009) says that entertainment enhances an event and is a powerful icebreaker, and suggests researching modes that are special or tailored to the region where the event is being hosted. Roche (2000) states that, in the case of mega events, such as the Olympics, there is a huge opportunity to design a ceremony of personal, national, cultural and historical significance. This is certainly what the creative designers of Cultural Olympiads set out to achieve, finding cultural associations and traditions with the host nation and presenting nostalgic areas of civic pride as part of the entertainment of the opening ceremony, as is illustrated in the case study below.

REAL INSIGHT 8.5

DESIGN FEATURES USED IN THE LONDON 2012 OLYMPIC OPENING CEREMONY

SOURCE: Image courtesy of Matt Lancashire, via wikicommons. Shared under the Creative Commons BY 2.0 license.

The theme that was employed for the London 2012 Opening Ceremony was called 'The Isle of Wonder'. Designed by artistic director Danny Boyle, the theme focused on the history of Great Britain, from the beginning of the country's history into the 21st century. Danny Boyle, award-winning film director of many films including *Trainspotting* and *Slum Dog Millionaire*, said he got his inspiration from Shakespeare's *The Tempest*, in which one character sings the praises of a hypothetical magical island. Boyle said that when designing a concept he decided to concentrate on Britain's unique features, rather than attempting to compete with the monumental magnificence of Beijing 2008's opening show. Although the London stadium had the same number of seats as in Beijing, it was only half the size, allowing for a more intimate and personal environment.

The ceremony consisted of a play, telling a story and bringing together the UK's past heritage, traditions, values and historical achievements, and contrasting this with the more modern and less formal traits of British culture.

The story started with a look at rural scenes from the 18th century, with testimonies of Britain's agricultural-based identity of those times, complete with the bright green countryside, a model of Glastonbury Tor, and a water wheel. Actors depicted working villagers playing cricket and drinking ale to represent Merry England of the Middle Ages. Then followed a noisy scenographic play entitled 'Pandemonium', evoking the advent of the

Industrial Revolution in the 19th century. The bright greenery was slowly removed and replaced with the dark colours of industry, in what Danny Boyle described as 'the biggest scene change in theatrical history'. The oak tree situated on top of the model of Glastonbury Tor lifted to reveal volunteers dressed as factory workers, who emerged from there and from the other entrances of the stadium. Industrial machinery then rose from the ground, including seven smoking chimneys, six looms and five engine beams, all designed to celebrate the technological advancements of this era. The cast members then began to drum on buckets and bin lids in order to echo the sense of fear and chaos that was felt in rural communities during the upheaval of the Industrial Revolution. At the end of this scene, a single piece of green is revealed to be covered in red poppies, a symbol of the war dead, from the two world wars. In the following scenes, the audience is transported into the vibrant swinging sixties when London in particular became the centre of a cultural revolution.

Borrowing many items from theatre, the time lapse between each story told, allowed the production crew to change the scenery, staging and design and to switch props, ready for the next act. The sound, music, entertainment, acts, lighting, décor and staging and final fireworks were all designed to reflect the theme. British music and culture were highlighted through musical acts such as The Spice Girls, Jessie J. and Elton John. Extracts from famous British West End musicals and soundbites and clips from the soap series *EastEnders* and popular British songs were used. Design elements were also shown through multiple clips of past Olympic Games, which told the story of how the Games have progressed throughout the years, and presenting nostalgic flashbacks of these Olympic events and past British culture.

The story also presented some of the country's greatest achievements, showcasing the country's prized National Health Service (NHS) and renowned children's hospital Great Ormond Street, the computer scientist and inventor of the world wide web Sir Tim Berners Lee; and featured iconic film and literary classics, such as *Peter Pan*, *Chitty Chitty Bang Bang* and *101 Dalmatians*, as well as the works of J.K. Rowling and characters from the Harry Potter franchise. The ceremony also paid homage to other national treasures, such as the comedian Rowan Atkinson playing the character of Mr Bean, and sports personalities, such as footballer David Beckham and cyclist Bradley Wiggins, past champion of the Tour de France. The closing act saw Paul McCartney inviting the audience in the stadium to join in with a rendition of 'Hey Jude', and the bells of Big Ben peeling out across London, culminating with an airshow by the world-famous Red Arrows, painting the sky with the colours of the Union Jack.

(Continued)

In order to present the surprise element of the show, a short comedic sketch entitled 'Happy and Glorious' featuring the renowned British fictional hero James Bond with the Queen apparently arriving by helicopter, before skydiving together into the arena, was pre-recorded and shown as part of the ceremony. This interlude, showing some of London's iconic landmarks in a more informal context, was purposefully designed to soften the impact of the element of self-celebration. On a practical level, although the film piece was only three minutes long, it allowed the production crew to clear up the main stadium area to allow for the following acts and to prepare the special effects, dancers and actors to enter the arena for the next sequences.

The design concept for the 2012 logo was created by Wolf Olins. He designed a colourful modern depiction of the 2012 numerals, bringing together many iconic features of London, using bright colours and a modern feel. The firework finale, brought about through a partnership between the Mayor of London's Office and the corporate telecommunications giant Vodafone, lit up the renowned venues of the City of London, such as Tower Bridge, the Houses of Parliament and Big Ben. Revellers who were positioned on the banks of the River Thames witnessed a multi-sensory firework display. Exotic fruit flavours were used and synchronised special effects and colour-changing LED wristbands were added to further engage the audience's senses at the midnight firework spectacular. Four flaming rings representing the four nations of the United Kingdom appeared above the stadium, finally connecting with each other to form a single image of unity, that later transformed into the traditional five rings of the Olympic emblem. The display itself was a collaboration between renowned conference production company Jack Morton and Titanium Fireworks. The music soundtrack used to choreograph the display was created by Jack Morton's creative director David Zolkwer and produced by Bounce Ltd. The electric soundtrack was designed to be a fun and quirky rhythmical mix.

Seven and a half thousand people participated in the ceremony, and over 2000 props and 57,000 garments were worn. These acts were selected to be suitable and to represent people of all ages and nationalities. The ceremony saw young children singing and dancing in the stadium and different military forces marching together, under the raised flag of Great Britain, whilst the national anthem was played. Youth bands sang each of the four nations' own anthems – 'Jerusalem' for England; 'Danny Boy' for Ireland; 'Flower of Scotland' for Scotland; and 'Bread of Heaven' for Wales, celebrating Britain's unity, whilst paying homage to its differences and regional peculiarities.

The essential part of creating the entertainment programme is to choose acts or performances that are appropriate for the audience, the tone or theme of the event and the practicalities of the venue itself. The key factor is to involve the audience with the event, using entertainment to create memory points around key messaging. This can be formal or informal, and can be linked to an element of surprise for the guests.

> Such things as look-alikes have become popular as have roving street entertainers or magicians. Reference to popular culture and television shows appeal to many people as does the inclusion of musical acts, comedians or extravagant shows. (Berridge 2010: 186)

The design of the entertainment realm can be divided into ambience and interactive entertainment, as detailed in Table 8.8.

Ambience entertainment
• *Provides atmosphere*
• *Mood-making*
• *Sets the stage for the event*
Interactive entertainment
• *Actively and passively engaged*
• *Memory-making*
• *Emotional take-away*

TABLE 8.8 Ambience and interactive entertainment

It is important to make sure when designing the entertainment programme, that there is a mixture of both ambience and interactive entertainment, as without ambience, interactive entertainment is a lot harder to successfully deliver. It is the ambience which creates the first important impression and then the interactive which impresses the audience. Without the ambience to set the tone, creating memories becomes much harder. The interactive entertainment is vital to get the crowd involved. When they start to participate, the memory becomes far greater. The types of activities that may fall into these two categories are illustrated in Figure 8.1.

CATERING DESIGN

> Catering Design Management includes the determination of suitable catering operations and the selection of the menus, quantities, and service styles to meet the food and beverage needs of the event, including the specific requirements associated with the serving of alcohol. (Silvers 2005: 9)

The design of the catering is an important part of event design. The artistic interpretation and expression make up the experiential dimension, to create the experience. Whilst this can provide an overall culinary experience, a poor dining experience will detract hugely from the positive memories of the occasion.

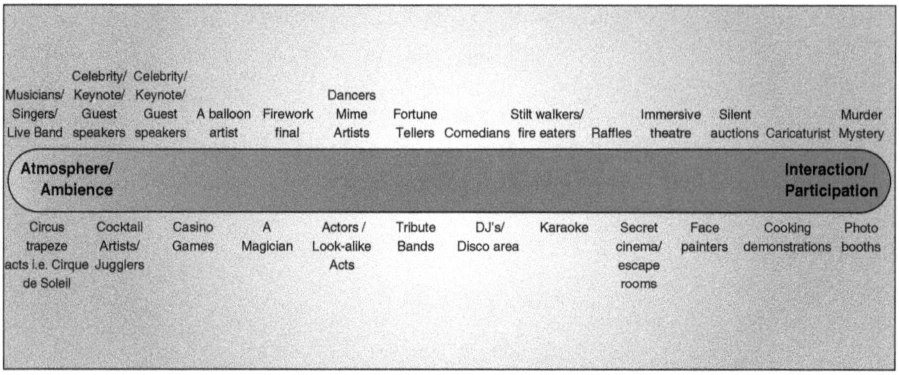

Musicians/ Singers/ Live Band
Celebrity/ Keynote/ Guest speakers
Celebrity/ Keynote/ Guest speakers
A balloon artist
Firework final
Dancers Mime Artists
Fortune Tellers
Comedians
Stilt walkers/ fire eaters
Raffles
Immersive theatre
Silent auctions
Caricaturist
Murder Mystery

Atmosphere/ Ambience
Interaction/ Participation

Circus trapeze acts i.e. Cirque de Soleil
Cocktail Artists/ Jugglers
Casino Games
A Magician
Actors / Look-alike Acts
Tribute Bands
DJ's/ Disco area
Karaoke
Secret cinema/ escape rooms
Face painters
Cooking demonstrations
Photo booths

FIGURE 8.1 Types of popular entertainment

Shock and Stefanelli (2008) comment that planning food and beverage, as part of the design experience, uses more creativity and planning than often initially thought. It takes skill not only to create menus and assemble the food dishes, but to devise a food concept that is going to promote the event well.

Food and beverages are nearly always present at events, as they are often associated with celebration and ceremony. The production and service of food allows for creativity, as food engages all the senses, i.e. scent aroma, taste and sight. As Getz (2012) suggests, the best advertisement for the food and beverage at the event, is often the smell of the cooking. Examples where design can be a prominent feature include food stations, edible centrepieces, menus, dessert shapes, drink mixes and cocktails.

> Part of the logistical design of catering aspects includes determining menus and quantities and service styles to meet the food and beverage requirements of an event, and taking into account special dietary requirements, religious and cultural requirements when designing the catering. (Gasche and Ellis 2010: 226)

Venues need to prepare themselves for event catering provision, ensuring the optimum layout and space utilisation. In some cases, organisation and provision for off-premises catering is required. The food needs to be ordered and purchased in advance and adequate equipment and staff need to be booked. On the day, the food stations or serving areas may need to be creatively themed in keeping with the overall event concept.

When designing catering that will provide a culinary experience at the event, artistic interpretation and expression are an essential part of the experiential dimension. A poor dining experience will detract hugely from the memories of the occasion. It is often the cold cup of coffee that stays in the mind of the delegate when evaluating the event, despite all other successful aspects. Part of the catering design process involves planning suitable menus, quantities and service styles, to meet the food and beverage requirements and deliver within the set budget. Food is often associated with networking, social gatherings and celebration, as a basic physiological level of requirement. It is therefore

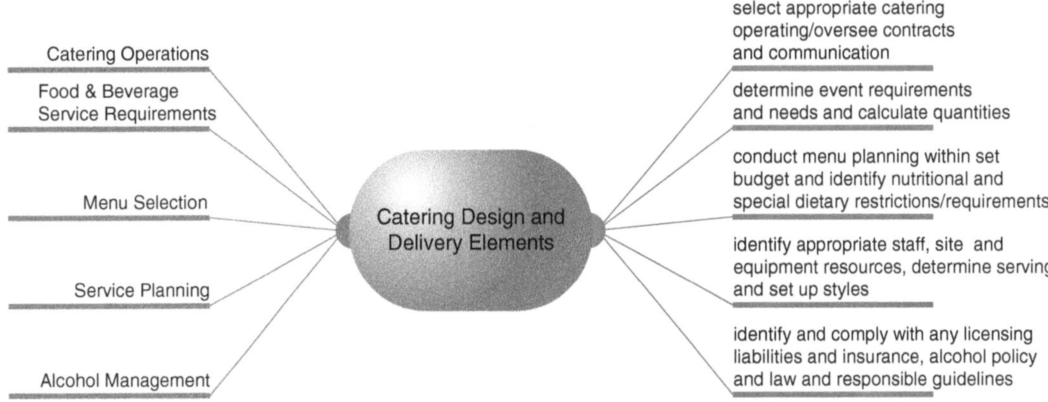

FIGURE 8.2 Catering design and delivery elements

crucial that the food and beverage provision is designed to appeal to all the senses. It is also vital to correctly estimate attendance in relation to staffing levels, in order to save costs and avoid wastage. The event caterers should be able to provide appropriate service styles that take into account special dietary, religious and cultural requirements, and should be able to provide alternative meal options where necessary.

THE CREATION OF THE EVENT EXPERIENCE

WHAT IS EVENT EXPERIENCE?

When designing an event, we aim to create an experience, where the audience will become physically, mentally, emotionally, socially and/or spiritually engaged. Getz (2012) talks about two dimensions of experience, which are conative – influencing behaviour and physical activities – and affective – focusing on feelings, preferences and personal values. Research indicates that delegates and spectators become more engaged in an event when they participate in it, becoming active, rather than passive, spectators. The design of the event, if successfully crafted, is powerful enough to make a change in the audience's skill, memory or emotions, or what is often termed a transformative experience. By creating a 'wow factor' for the audience, events can create memorable or even life-changing experiences. There are three levels of experience that have been identified by Hover and Van Mierlo (2006), and adapted from an Experience model by Van Gool and Van Wingaarden (2005):

- *Basal experiences* – an emotional reaction to a stimulus, but with insufficient impact to stay long in one's memory
- *Memorable experiences* – the emotion created can be recalled at a later time
- *Transforming experiences* – these emotions result in durable changes on an attitudinal or behavioural level.

- Theme
- Story
- Authenticity
- Interactive/Engaging
- Uniqueness
- Surprise
- Multisensory
- Emotive

...can also be added to factors associated with effective and rewarding customer experience

- Easy to access
- Opportunities to be social
- Personal relevance
- Learning opportunities

FIGURE 8.3 Factors associated with creativity, design and experience

DID YOU KNOW?

> The design of an event is both an experience-maker and experience-enhancer, which provides ample opportunity for the attendee to engage in sensory and emotional interaction with the event. (Ali 2010: 52)

Experience is about .... dreams, emotions, imagination.

As an event designer, it is important to create an event where the audience have access to the same experience, even if their individual perceptions of it are different. For this reason, it is important that the design elements created are open to a variety of interpretations.

Csikszentmihalyi (1991) advocates the most crucial component for a successful event experience is to be able to satisfy all the audience on an individual and subjective level.

Nowadays visits to leisure sites become experience outings. The promise of the experience is what helps attract us to venues and events such as:

- The Disney Store
- Tea at the Waldorf
- The Jack the Ripper London Tour
- David Bowie Exhibition
- The Shard.

To design a rich, compelling and engaging experience, you don't want to select and stay in just one realm. Instead you want to use the experiential framework to creatively explore the aspects of each realm that might enhance the particular experience you wish to stage. (Pine and Gilmore 1999: 39)
Every time an event is offered, the experiences of those involved will be different. Expectations, moods and behaviour will be different. (Getz 2012: 414)

TABLE 8.9 Definitions on the 'sweet-spot' of experience

Wood and Masterman (2007) write of the Seven I's of Experience – Involvement, Interaction, Immersion, Intensity, Individuality, Innovation and Integrity – all of which are fundamental when engaging the audience in a memorable event experience.

1	Put the attendees first
2	Pay attention to all five senses
3	Look for spaces that have character, or that can transform easily
4	Introduce conversation starters to proceedings
5	Remember that branding does not have to be expensive
6	Pay attention to the music
7	Fresh flowers are much appreciated
8	Do not be afraid to try something new
9	Pay attention to the guests' arrival and commencement of the event
10	Lighting is key, but should be subtle
11	Try out non-traditional seating arrangements
12	Get people talking in any way possible

TABLE 8.10 Crafting an unforgettable event experience in 12 simple steps

Participation can be passive or active, depending on whether the event attendees directly impact the event experience being created. Pine and Gilmore's (1999) Experience Realm provides an understanding of the combination of immersion and absorption in relation to the participation levels at the various stages of the event experience. This model makes a distinction between Absorption, where the audience of either an entertainment event, like a concert or an educational event, like a training workshop, are passive spectators who take in and become engrossed in the content; and, at the other end of the spectrum, Immersion, which is more prevalent in an aesthetic event, like an art exhibition or an escapist event, like a karaoke night. In this type of event, guests become completely immersed in the event experience, by actively participating in the event. Pine and Gilmore (1999: 39) maintain that: 'the richest experiences encompass aspects of all four realms.'

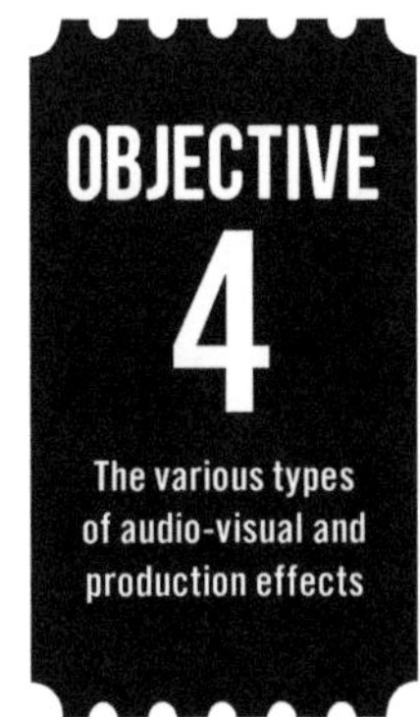

THE VARIOUS TYPES OF AUDIO-VISUAL AND PRODUCTION EFFECTS USED IN EVENTS

WHAT IS EVENT PRODUCTION?

Production varies, depending on budget and often the type of event. Clearly, a simple, functional and low-budget meeting like a small functional conference or an Annual

General Meeting (AGM), where it is important to keep costs to the minimum, might not require a great deal of production, other than basic audio-visual provision. The role of a production team in the planning stage is:

- To draw up a checklist and site supervision
- To appoint roles and responsibilities for all personnel and sub-contractors
- To apply for necessary licences and agreements where appropriate
- To administer training where appropriate and comply with risk assessment.

The production crew will be responsible for producing the multimedia and visual imagery and sound bites needed and installing all pre-recorded footage. This may include designing and formatting speaker slides and supporting conference speakers with their presentation, including content run-throughs and technical rehearsal.

Once on-site, the production team will be responsible for 'calling the show' and managing all technical content and the proceedings of the event. A high-end or larger scale event, such as a corporate sales kick-off to launch the company's strategy for the forthcoming year to the sales team, may have a higher budget allocated and require more technical production elements, as detailed below:

- Audio (sound)
- Lighting
- Visual production
- Front projection
- Back projection
- Special effects technology.

AUDIO (SOUND)

Regardless of the size of the event, it is essential that the audience can see and hear the conference. The required sound provision for a conference tends to be heavily weighted towards amplifying speech, rather than music, so the type of sound system used for this type of event is completely different to that utilised for a concert or festival. The important factors to consider when providing sound are clarity and range. The audience needs to be able to clearly hear what the speaker is saying throughout the whole venue. Enhanced clarity will come from using good equipment, operated through an appropriate sound desk, by a qualified technician. As it is essential for all delegates to be able to clearly hear all the participating conference speakers, this is an area where budget should never be sacrificed for the cheaper option.

In order to ensure that the sound quality is equally audible throughout the whole area, it may be necessary to install delay or full speakers down the side of the main conference plenary area. Multiple smaller speaker stacks are always more preferable than one big system front of house. Experienced speakers generally have a preference as to what type of microphone they prefer to use, which falls into the following four categories:

- Lapel microphone – fixed to the speaker's clothing
- Lectern microphone – mounted on a static lectern on the stage

- Handheld microphone – held by the speaker
- Roving microphone – allows the audience to ask questions or be amplified during the conference.

Less experienced speakers should probably opt for the lapel microphone, as it is easier to control the sound levels should the speaker decide to wander around the stage, or vary the strength of their voice throughout the presentation.

Technical sound rehearsals before the actual show are vital, as this gives a chance for the technicians to make necessary sound checks and adjust microphone heights, and so on. The audio technician needs to set the sound to an appropriate level for each of the speakers involved in the conference, as they will each have a different voice tone and level. Sound engineers can amplify the sound according to the artist or the bands' requirements at a musical event. Technical checks are key as are permitted decibel levels. A professional sound desk can cost in the region of £250,000, therefore adequate insurance liability is vital.

LIGHTING

Lighting can offer much to an event in terms of setting a mood and creating atmosphere. Light has two functions during events – it allows the guests to see what is happening and is also central to the design. Within musical events, effective performance lighting has become a necessity, as producers realised that a wash of colours and lighting had a dramatic effect on the enjoyment of the audiences. Music venues, both in closed venues and outdoors, are the biggest users of light. Professional lighting engineers at large outdoor music events can sometimes be working with up to 30–50 individual lighting units arranged on a lighting rig above the stage. Some lighting rigs can be static or mechanically operated and pre-programmed to work in orchestrated tandem with the music and performance.

Lighting is also used to create an explosion of colour, with elements of design that are created specifically to create a visual mood, to immerse both the performer and the audience. Choosing the right lighting can set the tone for the event and contribute towards evoking ambience, mood and scenic elements. Lighting has the ability to transform a single set space into a room with character and depth, created through selective visibility and creating the perfect atmosphere.

Lighting is one of the fastest growing and changing technical fields in events. Good lighting design should enhance the event experience, rather than drawing too much attention as a separate entity. This means that lighting should be subtle and almost absorbed by the audience on a subconscious level. It should be a natural part of the staging, rather than the focus of attention, which could potentially detract from the content.

Event lighting in practical terms generally refers to the beams or rays used at a range of events which control the selected visibility of a stage area or a venue; in artistic terms, it refers to taking a client's or event planner's dream and creating it by using a large assortment of highly technical lighting fixtures. In terms of event design, there is a psychological aspect to lighting. On a practical level, it is important that the speaker is well lit and that the lighting design considers suitable colour tones that do not wash out the speaker. It is often a case of merging the more practical with the artistic aspects of conference lighting to create the right effect. As Van der Wagen (2007: 219) observes:

> Lighting can be used to create spectacular effect and for this reason, events held at night provide the opportunity for more dramatic results than the ones held in the morning.

For example, whilst bright or fluorescent lighting might be suitable for a professional business meeting, this type of lighting can appear harsh. When attempting to create ambience for a more social function, like a dinner or show, soft and low lights or perhaps moving lights tend to be far more suitable.

Skill and creativity are needed in the design of event lighting, as using different colours to light the venue can transform a dead or empty space into a shining and interesting space, full of possibilities. The audience will have a reaction to colour and light and this will form part of the overall sensorial experience, so it is not an area to skimp costs on from the overall production budget.

The introduction of light-emitting diode (LED) means that a lower voltage is required and the lights also emit less heat. The most important benefit of these lights is that they provide the versatility for a number of colour changes from one light source. In today's events arena, lighting plays a major role in the composition of production, through invisible techniques, position, visual elements and style. Lighting can effectively enhance the desired ambience and transition of a set space. It can act as a tool to bring out other decorative components of the event set, such as colour schemes, and can therefore make or break an event. Additionally, effective use of lighting can enhance the performance or performers by highlighting and defining certain parts of the body and focusing on movement and the core muscles used.

SOURCE: A Martin MAC 550 intelligent light. Image courtesy of Martin Röll Martinroell, via wikicommons.

LED lighting is now being used to replace normal projection function for high quality presentations at outdoor events, fashion shows and sporting events. In past times, black drapes were used to hide areas in standard conference venues. However, nowadays the whole background can be changed in an instant, using lighting to project images on to buildings, so that these large intricate visuals create theatricality as well as ambience. Creative LED is becoming the number one choice for big and impactful global outdoor shows, such as the Dubai and Paris air shows.

Today's lighting is very advanced, often termed intelligent lighting**.** This is the same term that is used for stage lighting, where the lights are pre-programmed through a computer to have automated or mechanical abilities. These lights are far more sophisticated than standard stationary illumination. Although the most advanced intelligent lights can produce extraordinarily complex effects, the intelligence lies with the programmer of the show or lighting operator, rather than the lights themselves. For this reason, intelligent lighting is also known as automated lighting, moving lights or moving heads.

VISUAL PRODUCTION

Visual projection ranks as of equal importance to the sound aspect elements of conference production. Event visuals can take the form of moving or still pictures and videos, either in 2D or 3D dimension. Kenney (2015) defines visuals as a number of varying forms, including pictures, drawings, videos, film, computer-generated graphics, animated and virtual reality displays. As Matthews (2015) says, entertaining crowds with impressive visual displays is a powerful way to encapsulate the audience in the story being told, capturing minds, attention and feelings. If correctly designed, visual displays can transfer the audience away from a mundane room into an entertaining and extraordinary dimension that they would not normally have the chance to experience. Generally conferences require as large a format of projection, or screen vision, as possible. The best and most cost-effective way of achieving this is by using a projector-based system. There are two ways of projecting: front and back.

FRONT PROJECTION

Front projection becomes a necessity when the layout does not provide sufficient space for the crew and the required audio-visual equipment behind the screen to facilitate back projection. Generally the projector is placed as high as possible in the conference space, often on a ceiling mount, and the correct image is projected by adjusting the setting menus on the projector.

BACK PROJECTION

Back projection generally requires a distance of at least 3 metres behind the screen to project the image on to. This dimension may vary depending on how large the screen is and the image that is being projected. Generally this is a far more favourable way of projecting, as it allows the whole stage to be used by the presenter, without the risk of cutting across the projector beam, thus causing shadows on the screen. Rear or back projection also has the advantage of producing a brighter image, because the ambient light can be controlled better by the lighting crew in a backstage environment.

Within a conference setting, it tends to work best to have two identical projectors. This eliminates risk, as, for example, in the case of a projector malfunction, the technician would simply switch over projectors, hopefully without causing too much disruption or being noticed by the audience.

SPECIAL EFFECTS TECHNOLOGY

Today special effects technology has taken on renewed significance and has radically changed the face of the industry. Nowadays special effects and visuals can contribute towards the interpretation or performance at any given event. Examples of this technology might include two- or three-dimensional figures appearing on the screen, prior to or during a performance, and matching the themes and movements of the artists or performers.

It could be argued that visuals and special effects can now deliver a message more effectively than the written or spoken word. Visual design is more successful in capturing a modern audience's attention, particularly a younger generation audience, whose sensory perceptions will tend be more advanced and sophisticated. Due to the increase in gamification, a younger demographic audience have learnt to interpret visual content for a deeper and more impactful event message or impression.

Technology can be used for an assortment of things, from creating shapes and figures on LED screens, to projecting on buildings using holograms and mirrored projections. For example in a live musical set, the visuals used can be as influential as the music itself, transforming the performance into an unforgettable and sensory experience. In this visual event arena, the future seems to be Projection Mapping, which can be used to turn dance music shows into a visually stimulating experience within the mind of the artist and audience alike.

LIVE EVENT PRODUCTION FOR FESTIVALS AND CONCERTS

Live music events currently generate 50.1% of events industry revenue and in the past, events have been the fastest growing sector of the events industry. Sound and visual effects are considered the two major factors in the overall live music experience, as well as the staging and special effects, which enhance the overall guest experience.

Music concerts can be defined as live events that contain multiple artists, and are often aimed at a particular target audience. Gibson and Connell (2005) recognise festivals as events that allow crowd engagement, whilst creating a unique and immersive environment. For live events, it may be necessary to build a stage from scratch, or extend the existing one. It is crucial that any structure is able to support the act being staged, and must therefore be tested or certified to meet the appropriate health and safety requirements. Various systems are specifically designed as solutions to stage building and are considered fit for purpose by the events industry. Advanced technology has become a prerequisite for these events, in order to keep them relevant.

PRODUCTION AND DESIGN BUDGETS AND ASSOCIATED COSTS

An important factor to consider when creating a design concept for any event is that there is sufficient budget to deliver the items put forward, in order to save time and potential embarrassment with the client or event owner. The budget for event design and production can be extremely high and needs to be carefully considered as part of the overall financial planning process. In the same way that operational costs are calculated in the pre-planning phase, all budget items and cash flow forecasts for production need to be prepared and presented to the client, well in advance of booking or committing to any specific technical items, props, staging or equipment.

In times of austerity and recession, it is often the more complex aspects of design and production that are pared from the budget, allowing for a more functional delivery to the set and staging of the event.

THE ROLE OF AUDIO-VISUAL AND OTHER PRODUCTION COMPANIES IN EVENT DESIGN

OBJECTIVE 5

The role of audio-visual and other production companies in design

AUDIO-VISUAL COMPANIES

Many event managers will work with incumbent audio-visual (AV) suppliers, so they can be assured the equipment is safe and is regularly checked and upgraded. Generally audio-visual agencies or intermediaries are only concerned with hiring out equipment for events and do not get involved in a consultancy production role. The type of technical equipment that will be hired tends to be lighting and sound and multimedia presentation. The basic requirements for any event would be provision of a screen projector and a Mac or PC. The more complex the event, the more likely it is that a producer would be required to manage the show.

In some cases when an event is taking place overseas, it can be more cost-effective to use '**dry hire**' audio-visual equipment from the destination, rather than submit to the costly process of transporting the equipment by road. However, there is a risk factor to this, in ensuring that the quality of the equipment is of the highest standard. Some planners prefer to transport their own equipment by van, and bring their own production team to deliver the show, regardless of the costs involved. Even in terms of the dry hire of audio-visual equipment, it is necessary to liaise with a technical co-ordinator who fully understands the technical requirements of the event, as well as experienced sound and lighting engineers, who are familiar with all the equipment. Other, more complex audio-visual requirements might be a high-quality **front of house** speaker system, a professional mixing desk and various microphones.

Dry hire
the hire of equipment or a venue without any accompanying operators or staff

Front of house
usually the parts of the theatre or room in front of the proscenium arch

PRODUCTION ROLES/AGENCIES

For larger events with more complex production requirements, a producer or production company may be required. The role of the producer is varied and includes full conference production through to technical support, as detailed in the description of the agency below. The tasks of an event producer may include the following:

- Technical support and audio-visual
- Concept design and theming of set and staging
- Communicating the brand message
- Designing and building the set with staging tools and communications devices
- Video production, computer graphics generation and multimedia
- Production meetings/debriefs
- Production schedule/producing documents for staging events
- Designing the running order for an event/a run sheet

- Planning load-in times and load-out times
- Rehearsals and speaker support – 'getting it right on the night'
- Managing the on-site crew and calling the show
- De-rigging and get out (of venue)
- Managing on-site event health and safety.

LIGHTING COMPANIES

Lighting should be one of the first items on the venue selection checklist to consider and to decide whether there is a need to outsource to a professional lighting company. This can vary greatly depending on whether indoor and/or outdoor lighting is required, and the overall concept or theme of the event. The priority from a producer's perspective would be to create a detailed lighting plan that will deliver the requirements of the specific event and setting, depending on the complexity of the lighting system required and the budget available. It would not be necessary, for example, to invest in a huge lighting rig, when a simple colour wash effect would suffice.

Any lighting equipment that needs to be erected above a height of 3.3 metres will require a qualified and experienced rigger to install it and make it safe and complicit with the venue's own health and safety policy. Once the design of the lighting has been finalised, the key concern is to ensure that professional and trained operators are in place to operate the lighting.

Existing venues should have secure rigging points, located in key places around the venue, for example above the stage or in the ceiling. The loading on each point should be clearly marked. The venue should be able to advise the conference client on areas like power supply so that the organiser can gauge whether they match the event requirements. They should also be able to provide details on expected weight loading from the lighting projector, to ensure that the rigging will be able to support them.

At the 2017 Australian Eurovision show, an experiential digital and video specialist agency called Monkey Cobbler was used to design flooring, created with LED panels, transforming the venue and enabling the background to be changed for each of the participating countries' performing artists.

Lighting rigs are generally supported using a system called 'Trussing'. A Truss is a universal beam that is designed to be hung from a ceiling or roof rigging point, or to be supported from the ground. Other factors to consider when designing lighting for an event are the power requirements and possible interference, and how many light operators will be required. This will be largely driven by the complexity and effects required. Another important factor to consider is the safety and security aspects. These will require a full risk assessment from external experts or the lighting company used, in order to be covered under the venue's indemnity clauses.

Pre-programmed programmed into a computer or other electronic device before use

Due to the complexity of the majority of event programmes today, most of the lighting special effects will be '**pre-programmed**' and set up before the event takes place. This includes all lighting changes and sound levels, as well as the cueing of video or slides. A computer will be used to generate the show, which means that fewer technicians and production crew are needed than in previous times. However, this can also result in technical glitches if the computer fails. Some venues will only work with certain accredited conference production and audio-visual companies, as the case study featured below illustrates.

REAL INSIGHT 8.6

LIGHTING COMPANIES EMPLOYED AT THE ROYAL COURTS OF JUSTICE

When a historic building is open to the public, it is important that lighting meets all regulations without detracting from the visual splendour of the environment.

Those were the twin challenges that the agency Dernier & Hamlyn faced at the magnificent Royal Courts of Justice, where they were commissioned by consultants Mott MacDonald to create emergency lighting for the building's celebrated Great Hall.

The Great Hall is used as a spectacular venue for a wide range of national and international events and is renowned for its beautiful mosaic marble floors, stunning stained-glass windows and imposing lighting.

SOURCE: Image courtesy of Igerrak, via wikicommons. Shared under the Creative Commons BY-SA 4.0 license.

The agency had previously worked on the original corona ring chandeliers that hang from the ceiling, some 80 feet from the ground. Their team suggested that a circle fitting should be manufactured to sit inside the corona rings to hold the driver and battery packs required to power LED lighting for use in emergencies. This solution provides high light levels, while being virtually invisible from the ground. Mike Palmer, technical director at Mott Macdonald, said:

> We had worked with Dernier & Hamlyn on other schemes including the Palace of Westminster. This experience, combined with their extensive knowledge of the Royal Courts of Justice's lighting, made them the natural choice for this project.

Dernier & Hamlyn has a long association with the Royal Courts of Justice, who will only ever work with accredited preferred suppliers at their events. They manufactured chandeliers for various areas, including the famous Bear Garden. This project saw them meet the Royal Courts' aim to combine practicality, legal requirements and aesthetic beauty.

EVENT ETHICS

It is not uncommon for a big artist's rider to cost over and above £20,000 in addition to their performance fee. Although to some extent this is negotiable, the rider must be delivered to ensure that the artist actually performs at the event.

Do you agree or disagree that it would be unethical for a celebrity speaker or act to charge a large fee at a charitable or fundraising event?

Do you think all acts or speakers should completely waive their performance fee at fundraising festivals?

CONDUCTING TECHNICAL RECCES

Technical site inspections, often know as recces, shortened from the word 'reconnaissance', are as important as any logistical or operational site inspection. The technical site appraisal may follow on from an initial operational site inspection, where information on the logistical suitability of the venue may already have been determined. However, the conference or event producer will view the venue space with a completely different set of criteria than the logistics manager. They will be more concerned with whether the space will work from a technical and production perspective and consider elements such as:

- The proposed occupant capacity versus the available space
- The audience and artiste profile
- The duration of the event and timings
- The venue specifics – power (is 3-phase power available?), water supply, crew access
- Venue health and safety
- The event concept suitability within the venue
- The required technical resources
- Available audio-visual/production facilities and in-house technicians at the venue
- Any restrictions, for example areas for company branding and own signage
- Whether the venue has crew access, parking and lifts for production equipment
- Delegate flow to and from plenary rooms, breakout rooms, and registration and catering areas
- An available production area, office and secure storage area.

The site recce involves physically arranging to view the venue space and the facilities available. For this type of site inspection, specific information needs to be gathered. At any site appraisal, you would be likely to see a conference producer with a tape measure and camera measuring up and evaluating the potential of the space or venue. The operations team needs to work with the production team, so that both teams are in agreement on the suitability of the venue to host the event from both an operational and a technical perspective.

Following on from the technical recce, a full inspection report based on the visit should be compiled, which should contain detail on each area, record first impressions and highlight any areas that may need working on. It should then be possible to start to develop the programme. Areas of special attention should be detailed and include aspects such as the venue access and sufficient entry and exit points for attendees and emergency services. This is also a chance to list the facilities already on site, such as toilets, power, water supplies, fixed seating. In the case of an outdoor space or green-field site, details on the site drainage and site gradient should be recorded, and the producer should evaluate what equipment will need to be brought in, for example electric generators, water, marquees, and so on. In the case of an indoor venue, a conference producer will need to record the dimensions of all available space and ascertain whether the venue has sufficient room for front or back projection and seating requirements.

GO ONLINE

They should also note what disabled facilities are available, in terms of ramps, equipment and other disabled facilities, as can be seen in the technical considerations checklist for the site inspection, which can be found online at **study.sagepub.com/quick**.

MANAGING MULTIMEDIA AND PRE-RECORDED FOOTAGE

The contracted production team will be responsible for mixing live and pre-recorded media to show throughout the event, using a combination of new technologies and video links, and will balance the use of live plenary and recorded media throughout the delivery of the event programme.

MANAGING CELEBRITY AND KEYNOTE SPEAKERS

The sourcing and booking of various acts is normally handled by an agent or agency. Entertainment agencies are quite diverse and represent a variety of acts. Generally the event organiser would decide upon their preferred act first and then make contact with the agency that represents them.

Artists and performers tend to be signed to a number of different agencies. The process of booking an act would normally start by providing a brief on what the performer will be expected to do throughout the event, or with realistic timescales. From the initial brief, the agency will be able to put together a costing and subsequently issue a contract. An experienced agency would be able to recommend the newest and hottest acts available, as originality and uniqueness are always high on any client's agenda.

Included in the contract will be a technical rider, which will be a list of technical equipment that the artist will expect to be provided in order to be able to perform as required, as has already been discussed in the previous chapter. There will also be a personal rider, which is the non-technical support that an artist might request in advance. The extent of the demands depends on the artist and their expectations. Requests might include simple necessities, such as a dressing room with a mirror and access to a shower. International artists, however, might ask for flights, travel and accommodation, to a certain specification, which may include excess baggage claims for instruments or other equipment.

SPEAKER AND PRESENTATION SUPPORT

This might involve attending meetings with the client or event owner in the pre-event stage to brainstorm and offer advice on the concept, programme content or overall brand message. The production team may also support keynote or guest speakers in the design of event content or presentations, often writing and editing material and advising on visual content. It is not uncommon to find that even the most experienced CEOs of a global organisation have little idea how to deliver a presentation or devise an effective speech, and need help to craft their own presentation. Therefore, this is often outsourced to a production team to work on the scripting and editing of keynote speeches, interviews or even video links. In some cases, there is sufficient time for the production team to offer presentation coaching or training, which may require a few sessions and constant tweaking and editing of the material. Once on-site, the production team should guide the speakers through on-stage rehearsals, including blocking and delivery. The production crew will also carry out technical rehearsals and warm-up sessions on the day of the event, including instruction on the use of microphones and a teleprompter or autocue, where necessary.

CHAPTER SUMMARY

CHAPTER SUMMARY QUESTIONS

1. What are the seven key design domains according to Julia Rutherford Silvers' (2008) EMBOK model?
2. Name the three levels of experience, as discussed by Hover and van Mierlo (2006), adapted from a model by Van Gool and Van Wingaarden (2005)?
3. What two types of active interaction do Pine and Gilmore (1999) present in their Experience Realm?
4. What different types of microphones are used in conferences?
5. What is the difference between front and back projection?
6. What is sensorial design?

DISCUSSION POINTS

- Why is the provision of good audio and visual equipment so important to a concert or conference?

- Explain how the experience of one event you have attended was 'enhanced' by a specific creative element.
- What is the difference between an audio-visual company and a production agency?

ACTIVITIES

- Create an event experience, themed in one colour. Justify what type of event it will be, why that colour is suitable and what type of audience such an event is likely to attract.
- Plan a themed Christmas meal for 150 guests, called 'Winter Wonderland', which should include the following:
  - Hot and cold snacks
  - Cocktail list for pre- and post-dinner drinks
  - Alcoholic and non-alcoholic drinks
  - Three-course menu for dinner
  - Beverage menu for dinner
- Develop a production guide for ONE of the following events and decide on the event setting and production 'tools' that you will need for the event:
  - School Nativity (Christmas) play
  - Wedding reception
  - Speed-dating Valentine event
  - '80s disco night
  - Business dinner.

REFERENCES

Ali, N. (2010) 'Event design', in N. Ferdinand and P. Kitchin (eds), *Events Management: An International Approach*. London: Sage, pp. 51–69.

Allen, J. (2009) *Event Planning*. London: John Wiley & Sons.

Berridge, G. (2010) 'Event design', in D. Tassiopoulos (ed.), *Events Management*, 3rd edn. Claremont: Juta, pp. 185–206.

Bladen, C., Kennell, J., Abson, E. and Wilde, N. (2012) *Events Management: An Introduction*. Abingdon: Routledge.

Bowdin, G., McDonnell, G., Allen, J. and O'Toole, W. (2011) *Events Management*, 3rd edn. Oxford: Butterworth-Heinemann.

Brown, S. and James, J. (2004) 'Event design and management: Ritual or sacrifice?', in I. Yeoman, M. Robertson, J. Ali-Knight, S. Drummond and U. McMahon-Beattie (eds), *Festival and Events Management: An International Arts and Culture Perspective*. Oxford: Elsevier Butterworth-Heinemann.

Csikszentmihalyi, M. (1991) *Flow: The Psychology of Optimal Experience: Steps toward Enhancing the Quality of Life.* New York: Harper Collins Publishers.

De Bono, E. (2016) *Six Thinking Hats.* New York: Penguin Life.

Gasche, J. and Ellis, M. (2010) 'Catering management design for events', in D. Tassiopoulos (ed.), *Events Management*, 3rd edn. Claremont: Juta, pp. 225–248.

Getz, D. (2012) *Event Management and Event Tourism*, 2nd edn. New York: Cognizant Communication.

Gibson, C. and Connell, J. (2005) *Music and Tourism: On the Road Again.* Toronto: Channel View Publications.

Goffman, E. (1956) *The Presentation of Self in Everyday Life.* Edinburgh: University of Edinburgh Press.

Goldblatt, J. (2008) *Special Events.* Hoboken, NJ: Wiley & Sons.

Hover, M. and Van Mierlo, J. (2006) Imagine your event: Imagineering for the event industry. Unpublished manuscript, Bread University of Applied Sciences and NHTV Expertise, Event Management Centre, Netherlands.

Ideal Home Show (2017) Homepage. Available at: www.idealhomeshow.co.uk (accessed 12 July 2017).

Kaplan, S. (1987) 'Aesthetics, affect, and cognition: Environmental preference from an evolutionary perspective', *Environment and Behavior*, 19(1). Available at: https://doi.org/10.1177/0013916587191001 (accessed 6 December 2019).

Kenney, K. (2015) *Visual Communication Research Designs*, 2nd edn. London and New York: Routledge.

Kim, J.H. and Jang, S. (2016) 'Memory retrieval of cultural event experiences: Examining internal and external influences', *Journal of Travel Research*, 55(3).

Lynch, K. (1960) *The Image of the City.* New York: MIT Press.

Matthews, D. (2015) *Special Event Production: The Resources*, 2nd edn. New York: Routledge.

O'Toole, W. (2011) *Events Feasibility and Development: From Strategy to Operations.* Oxford: BH.

Pine, B.J. and Gilmore, J.H. (1999) *The Experience Economy: Work is Theatre & Every Business a Stage.* Boston: Harvard Business School Press.

Roche, M. (2000) *Mega-Events and Modernity: Olympics and Expos in the Growth of Global Culture.* London: Routledge, pp. 1–30.

Rossman, J.R. and Ellis, G.D. (2008) Creating value for participants through experience staging: Parks, recreation, and tourism in the experience industry [online]. Available at: http: researchgate.net. (accessed 10 December 2018).

Shock, P. and Stefanelli, J. (2008) *A Meeting Planner's Guide to Catered Events.* Hoboken, NJ: John Wiley & Sons.

Silvers, J.R. (2005) The Potential of the EMBOK as a Risk Management Framework for Events. Las Vegas Conference.

Silvers, J.R. (2008) 'EMBOK: A theoretical and practical model for the event world', in U. Wunsch (ed.), *Facets of Contemporary Event Management – Theory and Practice for Event Success.* Bad Honnef, Germany: Verlag K.H. Bock.

Silvers, J., Bowdin, G., O'Toole, W. and Nelson, K. (2006) 'Towards an international event management body of knowledge (EMBOK)', *Event Management*, 9(4): 185–98.

Van Gool, W. and Van Wingaarden, P. (2005) *Beleving op niveau. Vrij tijd von vermaak tot transformative.* Amsterdam: Pearson, Prentice Hall.

Van der Wagen, L. (2007) *Event Management for Tourism, Cultural, Business and Sporting Events,* 3rd edn. Melbourne, VIC: Pearson Education.

Wood, E.H. and Masterman, G. (2007) 'Event marketing: Experience and exploitation', at *Extraordinary Experiences Conference: Managing the Consumer Experience in Hospitality, Leisure, Sport, Tourism, Retail and Events,* Bournemouth University, 3–4 September.

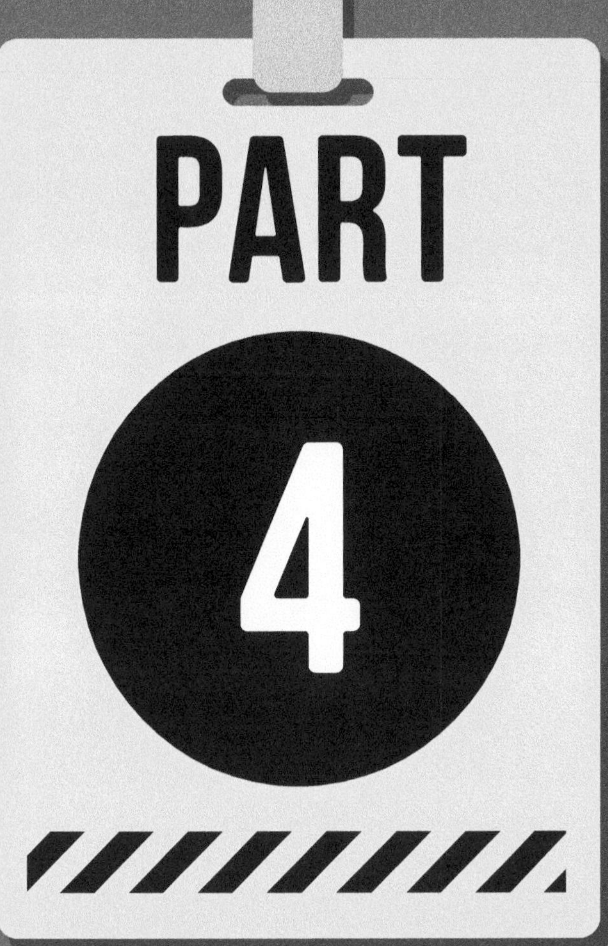

BEYOND EVENTS

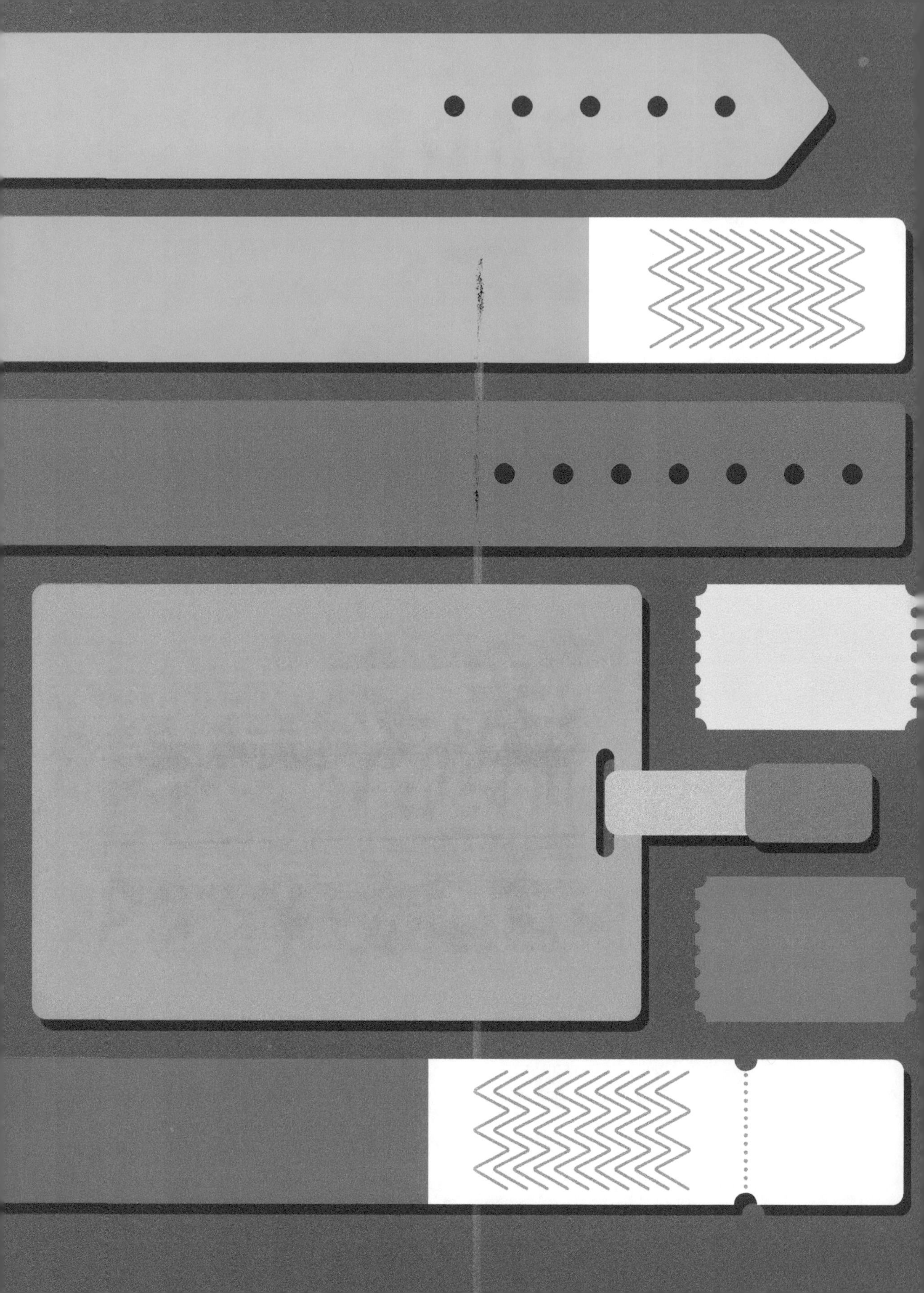

9

EVENT TRENDS AND ISSUES

CHAPTER OVERVIEW

This chapter is concerned with how the events industry is evolving and will examine current global issues that are impacting the industry. It will focus on recent innovations, specifically changes in event technology, sustainability in events and the growth of corporate social responsibility (CSR), globalisation and legislation. It will look at decision making in organisations and how decisions can be made based on different options and alternatives. It will examine the factors that may impact these decisions and will also consider best practice within the industry and the increase in ethical awareness and transparency. The chapter will also discuss how the industry might continue to change in future years.

CHAPTER OBJECTIVES

After reading this chapter, you will be able to identify and understand:

OBJECTIVE 1 Evolving technological innovation

OBJECTIVE 2 Sustainability issues impacting the industry

OBJECTIVE 3 Globalisation within various sectors of the events industry

OBJECTIVE 4 Current international legislation and regulatory requirements

OBJECTIVE 5 The link to social responsibility

Meet SAM WILSON

Director of EcoEvents

Director of EcoEvents, Sam, together with her trusted team of associates, provide expert support for the creative industry, such as the integration of various international standards including ISO 9001 (Quality), ISO 14001 (Environment), ISO 50001 (Energy) and ISO 45001 (Occupational Health and Safety). Her specialities include environmental and sustainability consultancy, lecturing, workshops and event sustainability. Sam has developed a 26-week module in event sustainability that is currently being used by a number of universities to ensure students are able to effectively communicate the issues and apply sustainability best practice through a specifically designed 'toolkit'. Sam presented the 2015 CSR awards in Beijing and is the author of numerous industry articles relating to sustainability and environmental management. Sam specialises in meeting client requirements through strategic business development, integrated operational controls and creative engagement.

REAL EVENT CHALLENGE

The biggest challenge is working out the best way to embed sustainability into the event journey, to help our clients self-regulate in a way that is more than a tick-box exercise, which just stifles creativity! Our clients are often integrated media or event agencies; every one of them is different, but they are all time-poor and lack experience in this area. Rather than becoming too prescriptive, agencies need to retain their creativity whilst still operating within a strategic organisational framework. This ensures that all the intended outcomes are met and everyone in the organisation is involved. It is therefore important to have a management system that draws all the strands together. In terms of the sustainability impact of an event, there are two important elements to consider:

WHAT PART OF YOUR JOB DO YOU MOST ENJOY?

Helping people to navigate the often confusing journey to sustainability, take measurable action to make a difference and witness the legacy of these actions as they turn into tangible outcomes.

WORST JOB-RELATED MISTAKE?

There is not one job I do where I do not learn something new! We are riding the crest of evolution and things are constantly changing. Added to which, every client is different, and the work needs to reflect that. I would have to say the worst mistake I have made is choosing the wrong associate for a client project – they were a cultural misfit and it went horribly wrong. Luckily, I have worked with the client successfully for years and as with all mistakes, it is the way you handle it that matters!

PREFERRED SUPERPOWER?

A carbon sucker.

FAVOURITE MEAL?

Lemon meringue pie.

PINNACLE OF CAREER SO FAR?

Presenting the China CSR awards in Beijing.

1) Ensuring our event operations are as sustainable as possible by managing key activities such as transport, materials and waste, and ensuring an inclusive and socially progressive event which can be measured and audited. Any activity analysis MUST include potential pollution at events, which can have catastrophic effects on people and wildlife.
2) Embedding sustainability into the event activation and engagement process, so that these values are experienced by all attendees, who are becoming increasingly more concerned about issues such as climate change.

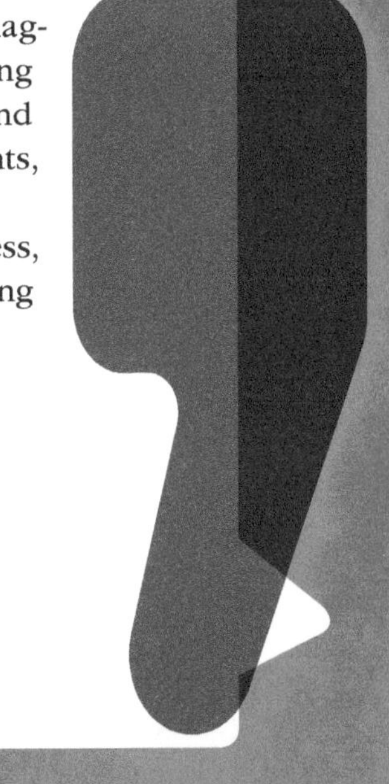

PRACTITIONER VIEWPOINT

Caroline Coyle, Caroline Coyle Consultancy, Sustainability for Tourism & Events

I came into the field of sustainable events at a key moment in its emergence as a professional discipline. London had just been appointed host of the 2012 Olympics, committing to the 'greenest Games ever,' and ISO 20121 in Sustainable Event Management was under development. There was a rush to understand the key issues for events and to identify measures to improve performance and accountability. My first notable project was to review a major international event for sustainability. I supplied intelligence, engaged with contractors on obstacles to change, and compiled a benchmark Sustainability Report. As the London Games approached, the organising committee established a set of requirements for sustainability for suppliers and contractors. I supported organisers of test events and contractors to the Games in achieving compliance, engaging with their suppliers and drawing up core documents, such as the Risk Register & Sustainable Event Management Plan.

Systems have been refined in the years since, and the professional standing of the corporate sustainability practitioner has increased under the auspices of bodies such as the Institute of Environmental Management & Assessment. Motivation for improving the sustainability of events varies, driven by regulation, client requirements or corporate ethics. The role of the sustainability practitioner is to engage with the parties concerned to turn aspiration into measurable achievement. Acknowledged in the profession as a lonely position, it requires a forensic attention to detail, and resilience to challenge assumptions.

Embarking upon the 2020s, we appear to be at another key turning point, with exponential growth in popular understanding of major global issues, such as climate change and plastic pollution, led in no small part by the world's youth. If event organisers fail to scrutinise the sustainability of their events, surely future clients and delegates will.

ACADEMIC VIEWPOINT

Dr Jane Ali-Knight, Professor in Festival and Event Management, Edinburgh Napier University

Sustainability is one of the key challenges facing the Festival and Event industry globally and the future of the industry lies with festival and event organisers having the expertise, knowledge and resources to be able to deliver sustainable events. Sustainability is not just about Greening but also about examining the social and economic viability to deliver events that are embedded in the local community, financially viable and bring true economic value to the destination. Policy makers and public funders are making sustainability a key component of any tourism-or events-related strategy or funding. Large, outdoor events using Greenfield sites can also have a huge impact on both the physical environment and the resident community, and the work that organisations like A Greener Festival (AGF) are involved in is vital to raise awareness of this challenge. As an AGF assessor I have been involved in conducting extensive environmental audits on festivals, leading them to achieve the well-respected AGF accreditation. The AGF Award Scheme has assessed and certified hundreds of festivals, events and venues worldwide, helping them to improve resource efficiency, environmental impact and ultimately become more sustainable. This is critical in rewarding and showcasing good practice as well as offering recommendations on how to reduce their carbon footprint. Sustainability underpins everything that we teach in our modules at Edinburgh Napier University, but we have also developed specific modules looking at the Impacts and Sustainability of Events and a module which addresses this specifically within the highly lucrative Business Event sector. The events student of the future needs to be educated and aware of the need to accelerate change and spread good practice to help develop a more sustainable festival and events industry.

REAL EVENT OUTCOME

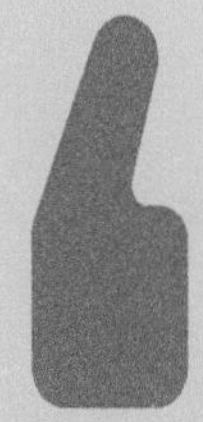

In practice there is really no other way than to 'roll up our sleeves and get our hands dirty'; to integrate with our client, to spend time observing and consulting from within the organisation, for a deeper understanding of the processes and the opportunities that exist. A bespoke rather than a generic approach adds value to the service we offer. Part of our professional remit is to engage the client; to lead the way and try to innovate the brief! This entails coming up with clear, meaningful objectives that can be measured (as part of ROO and ROI) and finding ways to support what the client is trying to achieve in terms of their own corporate sustainability goals. It is about mobilising change through the event experience, identifying sustainable 'hot spots' through an analysis of the issues that interested parties are most concerned about and where we can make the biggest difference, then building this into the design and experience of the event.

Sustainability is increasingly becoming the differentiator, with people and companies being more selective about which agencies they work for and with, the events they go to and even the products they buy. Tenders worth millions are now including sustainability as a key requirement. Over the past years, EcoEvents has supported clients, both to win these contracts and to achieve tangible improvements, such as a 30% reduction in energy consumption and to eliminate over 95% of single-use-plastic, which we are understandably proud of.

EVOLVING TECHNOLOGICAL INNOVATION

OBJECTIVE 1
Evolving technological innovation

INTRODUCTION TO EVENT-RELATED ISSUES

The industry continually faces new challenges from ever-increasing stakeholder expectations and the demands of consumers, competitors and clients, meaning organisers must keep abreast of the challenges and current issues facing the industry in order to lead in both quality and innovation. The issues that will be discussed in this chapter are by no means exhaustive, but can be identified as relevant and evolving in the industry at this current time and in the future.

TECHNOLOGICAL INNOVATION

Undoubtedly one of the fastest growing changes in the industry is the technological transformation, which has dramatically changed the way events have been executed and organised in recent years. This growth in technology has impacted the way we plan, execute and market events, as applications have changed the way people socialise and interact with each other. This in turn has brought about a new level of diversity, determining how all stakeholders experience events today.

Event professionals have to ensure that their workforce keep up to date with this fast-paced new marketplace and understand and possess the necessary skills to manage this new technology. This can be viewed as both an opportunity and a challenge for the industry. Some fear that this sudden surge of technological innovation may pose a threat to jobs within the industry. The fact that on-site experiences can now be recorded and posted within seconds online, makes events more prone to scrutiny than ever before. However, opinion still falls into two camps on this issue: David Rotman (2015) from the *Technology Review* argues that the impressive advance in computer technology is one of the main reasons for 'sluggish employment growth', but conversely a recent article written in *The Guardian* (Allen 2015) claims that the rise in technology has only benefitted employment within the industry, suggesting that rather than making humans obsolete, advanced technology can serve as a creator of jobs.

INTERNET CONNECTIVITY

Having sufficient internet connectivity has now become a major factor in the consumer buying decision process. Venues cannot run the risk of getting adverse negative publicity or bad reviews or ratings on social media sites, such as Trip Advisor, on account of unsatisfactory internet access or connectivity, so, in recent years, conference venues and hotels have had to finance the upgrade of their internet services to Broadband, with capacity for fibre optic speeds. Conference and event venues have also undergone a radical change in the way their customers can now book space and accommodation. This increased use of the internet has resulted in the emergence of specifically designed computer software, often tailor-made, using digital media to deliver a service or product to the customer online. It can be used for data collection, storage and the retrieval of documents. Online technology of this sort has reshaped how events currently run and has streamlined a lot of crucial processes, making them far easier to deliver. Booking engines such as the product iVvy, and other similar event management software products, are now being used by delegates, not only to search for, compare and book venues, but also to pay for function space, food and beverage provision, and group accommodation on the same portal. The emergence of the internet has also provided event companies with a much wider choice of suppliers, venues, real-time price setting, online registration and ticketing. Both client and venue information is easier to access and store through online portals, and this has eliminated much of the time-consuming paperwork that events can generate, thus reducing time and manpower.

THE USE OF SMARTPHONES AND MOBILE APPLICATIONS (APPS)

SOURCE: Image courtesy of Mike MacKenzie via flickr.com. Shared under the Creative Commons BY 2.0 license.

The increase in the use of smartphones and the amount of available mobile applications (apps) has also revolutionised the organisation of events today. Smartphone manufacturers have introduced a second screen system that involves transmitting relevant data directly on to the attendees' smartphone via an app. These applications are an efficient, sustainable and cost-effective way to convey information, by eliminating the need for paper and print. Applications, such as Eventboard and Wemmobi, are increasingly being utilised to allow attendees to book or purchase electronic tickets straight from their mobile phone, as has been discussed in Chapter 7. CrowdComms and EventMobi are suppliers who create bespoke event apps. CrowdComms director Felix-Stroud-Allen says:

> We have seen exponential growth in this sector, with event planners now seeing event apps as an integral part of their event, rather than nice to have ... Apps are eliminating the need for paper guides and providing an interactive medium for sponsors to position themselves dynamically in front of their audience.

Today applications are being used in many ways, such as enabling attendees to navigate the venue, for example using Google maps to pre-book parking slots at the venue, using applications such as RingGo or Pay by Phone parking, or an equivalent. This illustrates how technology can work to make the overall guest experience more satisfactory.

Recent research confirms that 63% of meeting planners are using apps and finding them beneficial to both organisers and attendees. Being able to communicate with other delegates using smartphones and tablets to access applications has become an essential event-planning tool. This allows delegates to join up with people with similar interests, or to chat about key topics. Further research by Guidebook (2014) shows that 88% of event professionals agreed that incorporating apps into events improves attendee engagement and helps them compete with non-event apps such as Candy Crush and Snapchat. Despite the existence of over 300-plus different event-related mobile applications, the meetings industry still does not appear to be making optimum use of time-saving devices, which now include some of the mobile applications shown in Table 9.1.

InitLive (www.initlive.com)	Designed for the management of volunteer and staff, this software system and app has proved effective for staff planning.
BlueStone Nexus (www. bluestonebd.com)	This smartphone-based app has been designed for business contacts exchange at events and exhibitions. It can capture business card information, distribute marketing information and integrate with CRM systems and robust analytics.
Event Pilot (ativsoftware.com)	Tailormade specifically for scientific/medical meetings, this app is an excellent planning tool, including features such as venue search capabilities, use of beacon technology, audience polling, slide distribution, online Q & A sessions and tracking.
Eventbase (www. eventbase.com)	This app uses beacon technology to assist in event networking. It allows delegates to enter interest areas into the app and link up with similar profiles.
Conferences.io (www. conferences.io)	An audience polling app which has a range of survey capabilities and analytics and integrates with PowerPoint.
Event Farm (www. eventfarm.com)	This app works to provide seamless delegate registration that can sync in a paperless format to multiple devices, with arrival alert notification for VIPS, with real-time analytics.

TABLE 9.1 Sample useful mobile applications

USE OF SOCIAL MEDIA SITES

Social media figures from the Office of National Statistics (2017) show that in the UK over 99% of adults aged 16–34 had used social media sites such as Instagram, Facebook, Snapchat, Twitter, Linked In, YouTube, and so on over a three-month period. These sites allow organisers to create pages based on the **target demographic** that enable the interested attendee to subscribe both pre- and post-event and to access information, such as video, slides and other shared content in advance. This information can be shared with attendees through all three phases: the planning stage, on-site, and the post-event stage, using tools such as Twitter, WhatsApp and Instagram, which enable organisers to be able to market to their target audience with far greater ease than in previous times and at a more reliable, affordable and realistic rate.

Target demographic a specific group of customers selected as having appropriate characteristics

DID YOU KNOW?

Today we have 16 billion connected internet devices, and in just four years' time there will be 40 billion connected devices.

65% of children entering primary school will end up working in job roles that don't even exist today. (According to Alec Ross, Senior adviser of innovation to Hillary Clinton 2016)

USE OF SOCIAL MEDIA AT FESTIVALS

Festivals such as Burning Man with its virtual festival BURN2 use a feature called 'Second Life', an online virtual world, developed and owned by the San Francisco-based firm Linden Lab to boost their marketing strategy. The Savonlinna Opera Festival in Finland has used **crowd sourcing** to create an online opera community for opera fans, to help develop new markets and promote specialist events.

Crowd sourcing
obtaining information or input into a task or project by enlisting the services of a large number of people, either paid or unpaid, typically via the internet

Radio Frequency Identification (RFID)
a type of wireless tag that connects and transmits information through electromagnetic waves using a longlife battery that can last up to two years

The Bonnaroo Music and Arts Festival is a four-day-long festival, which takes place every year in Tennessee, USA and attracts between 75,000 and 85,000 attendees. For the past few years, the festival has generated publicity by increasing its social media presence when announcing the line-up for the festival. Rather than announce it on their website, they created a playlist on the app Spotify, inviting attendees to listen to the artists, which gained 25,000 subscribers. The festival also utilised **Radio Frequency Identification (RFID)** technology.

This technology is able to store encrypted ticket details on a microchip, which has proven successful in preventing forgery and ticket touts. Each attendee was given a wristband which had the technology built into it. This wristband allowed attendees to check in at various portals around the festival and then post back to their Facebook accounts their precise location at the festival and what bands were performing there. This in turn allowed them to produce a unique Spotify playlist tracking all the music they had listened to at the festival. Over half the attendees participated in the scheme, scanning their wristbands and linking back to their social media accounts, which created unprecedented free publicity, generating an impressive 200,000 online posts to approximately 1.5 million Facebook users. Not surprisingly, this idea has subsequently been replicated worldwide. Festivals are also using blogging accounts such as Tumblr to post updates and create playlists and interviews with festival artists, and fans are encouraged to create their own online forums, where they can chat about the festival and also gain more information.

VIRTUAL REALITY (VR)

Although considered to still be in the early stages of development, virtual reality is another technological innovation that is transforming the delivery of today's event programmes. Products such as Sony's PlayStation give an idea of the potential that this technology could have on the industry in terms of virtual events and animated displays. The use of 5G wireless technology was recently showcased at the Pyeongchang 2018 Winter Olympic Games in South Korea, using data that transmits 20 times faster than 4G and allowing audiences to connect in 'real time', by transporting them 'virtually' into any meeting room, space or function.

At the 2018 Pyeongchang Games, global positioning system (GPS) enabled sensors to transmit locations and views through an app, which allowed spectators to experience the sporting event themselves from an athlete's perspective. Recorded footage from 60 cameras was placed on the helmets of one of the bobsleigh teams and transmitted on to virtual reality headsets. This enabled the spectators to experience the sensation of every spin and jump, from every angle of the ride.

REAL INSIGHT 9.1

THE USE OF VIRTUAL REALITY AT THE COACHELLA MUSIC FESTIVAL, USA IN 2012

In 2012, at the Coachella Valley Music and Arts Festival, a hologram of Tupac Shakur stunned 90,000 festivalgoers. Tupac, who died in 1996 after being shot four times in Las Vegas, was reunited on stage with Dr Dre and Snoop Dogg via holographic imagery.

The virtual performance was part of a show by Dr Dre and Snoop Dogg that saw rap artists such as Eminem and 50 Cent ignite the festival as they took to the stage one after another. But it was Tupac's holographic performance that blew the audience away. Tupac's short career and death meant fans and media alike never had a chance to see him perform live, save for some pre-recorded releases and posthumous guest appearances. These recordings continually drew media interest and gave him a huge following, making him one of the most popular artists in the world, even after his death.

SOURCE: Image courtesy of evsmitty, via Flickr.com. Shared under the Creative Commons BY 2.0 license.

At Coachella, this virtual performance resulted in 15 million YouTube views in just 48 hours. The hashtag #tupachologram was among the top ten tweeted topics for three weeks and there were more than 17 million Google search results for 'Tupac hologram' over the subsequent two weeks. Thousands of news stories appeared in print, online and on TV and radio. Sales of Tupac's music rocketed with more than 33,000 downloads of the rapper's top two singles and subsequent album sales increased by more than 500%.

Nick Smith, the company's president, told MTV it took several months of planning and four months of studio time to create the hologram. Smith declined to comment on the price of the project, but said a comparable project would cost from $100,000 to $400,000. By piecing together physical characteristics and movements from performances recorded before the rapper's death, the Tupac image was recreated on a computer. Using the latest in graphical and audio trickery, the company Digital Domain was able to add fresh movements and new dialogue to the act.

(Continued)

AV Concepts was charged with projecting the image of Tupac using IceMagic holographic technology to project the hologram on to the Coachella stage. This technology creates a life-like, life-size illusion of a 3D image and the other performers were able to interact with the dead rapper, walking around him and synching movements. Previously, AV Concepts had used similar holograms for Madonna, the Gorillaz, Celine Dion, and the Black Eyed Peas – helping to bring virtual performers to the world stage.

SOURCE: Adapted from www.cbsnews.com/news/tupac-coachella-hologram-behind-the-technology

OTHER TECHNOLOGICAL ADVANCEMENTS IN EVENTS

Cloud projectors models capable of projecting from the cloud directly from a server, without the need for a computer

Hybrid technology uses a combination of traditional face-to-face and virtual delivery of content

Live streaming watching video in real-time

In terms of on-site technological advancements, meetings and conferences now have the benefit of being able to use high-tech projectors, such as **cloud projectors**. This allows users to directly connect to their servers or online sites if they are not able to present at the conference in person. Whilst use of such technology could be seen as advantageous, it is predicted that delegates will always continue to look for a real experience, the real-life stimulation that face-to-face communication affords. It seems that rather than replacing face-to-face meetings, **hybrid technology** is now being used within the sector. Events are incorporating **live streaming** or pre-recorded material and enhancing conference content by showing live video material to increase audience engagement as part of the overall conference experience. This can prove a better solution than a purely virtual conference, where the technology can be complex. Poor audio quality can be detrimental to the overall conference programme, especially if delegates cannot hear or be heard. Sometimes insufficient bandwidth, noisy static, internet failure or a bad connection can ruin a virtual meeting. However, technology is improving all the time and virtual meeting technology (VMT) is increasingly being used to engage an audience, thus reducing costs and travel budgets and allowing delegates to interact with the programme content from their mobile devices. VMT also allows session speakers to communicate with delegates in real time and to share information across multiple markets and global business operations.

Skype and cloud-based videoconferencing is also used to communicate with delegates and speakers at conferences and corporate events. It can be used to support video group forums, particularly when delegates originate from different countries, and as a free resource, with free access to internet calls, Skype, Zoom, Houseparty and Facetime are becoming extremely cost-effective tools. There are other branded products on the market that have similar or improved features to these products and this type of technology is improving all the time.

THE USE OF ROBOTS IN EVENTS

The emergence of robot technology is on the rise and it is only a matter of time before this technology becomes a global phenomenon. At the Marriott hotel in Brussels, Belgium, robots are already being used to hand out room keys, animate meetings by reading out presentation notes, greet guests and for live-streamed monitors in the hotel's restaurants. In the Henn Na Hotel in Japan, robots run 90% of the hotel activity with only 10% being delivered by human employees. This could put traditional job roles, such as event planners and co-ordinators, at risk in future. Recent studies on this subject, including the 2018 Oxford Study, predict that within 20 years, 47% of existing jobs will be replaced in the United States by robots. This may have some positive outcomes, but could impact significantly on career opportunities for humans in the future and the professionalism of the industry in general.

- Human capital needs will be replaced by technological capital advances, so that event staff will become highly specialised as more and more functions are performed electronically.
- E-commerce will achieve full penetration of the market, resulting in a complete shift to online registration, ticket sales and tracking.
- The internet will be able to provide wideband real-time opportunities, resulting in hybridisation between live face-to-face and online virtual events, providing better yield management and guest interaction.
- Virtual reality will be used more widely at corporate events and festivals, amongst other event types, using sophisticated virtual reality goggles and an increased focus on gaming.
- Facial-recognition systems will be used more often at events, such as trade shows, concerts, festivals and sporting events to reduce queuing time and speed up delegate entry times.
- Event managers will also use facial-recognition technology to aid audience feedback, by placing cameras around the venue and recording audience reaction and emotion by their facial expressions.
- Digital business cards will be exchanged by the tapping together of two smartphones, which will enable contact details to be stored instantly.
- Blogging will change the face of the industry, particularly in sporting events, where independent bloggers and vloggers will contribute to the buzz surrounding the event and generate interest and ultimately increased participation.
- The duration will be shorter, partly as a result of the *TED* phenomenon, where attendees expect more digestible information in the form of short videos, thus allowing delegates to access information in their own time and preventing information overload and lack of retention.
- There will be complete systems integration, resulting in round-the-clock opportunities for guests who wish to forecast, attend and review their participation in an event.
- Conferences and business meetings will increasingly use webinars and webcasts, through applications like Skype and Zoom, to link up with presenters on a global scale.
- Overcrowding at indoor and outdoor events will be monitored using scalable technology at venue entrances and exits to control numbers.
- The use of wearable technology will increase to include watches, fitness trackers and tech jewellery, and planners will use this technology to transmit key detail, to communicate information about on-site inspections, menu options, travel directions, appointment updates, contact details and facial recognition.
- Sponsorship and brand opportunities will be improved by the use of 3D viewing systems. Venues will create a digital platform to deliver a fully three-dimensional customised view of luxury venues, such as Wembley Stadium in London, Stade de France in Paris or Maracana in Rio de Janeiro.

(Continued)

TABLE 9.2 (Continued)

- Drones will be used more at events, and as drone traffic increases, so will safety concerns and the amount of accidents caused by them on-site.
- Events will have full robotic capability and will be totally automated, enabling organisers to significantly expand the number of simultaneous events being produced, using fewer human staff.
- There will be interplanetary broadcasting, allowing guests of planet earth and guests of other planets to conduct interplanetary events using advanced communications technology!

TABLE 9.2 The future of the events industry

SUSTAINABILITY ISSUES IMPACTING THE INDUSTRY

Sustainable events are not just those that can endure indefinitely, they ... also fulfill important social, cultural, economic and environmental roles that people value. (Getz 2016: 70)

Responsible events are sensitive to the economic, socio-cultural and environmental needs within the local host community, and organized in such a way as to maximize the net holistic (positive) output. (Smith-Christensen 2009: 25)

Sustainability is an enduring, balanced approach to economic activity, environmental responsibility and social progress. (The British Standards Institute's definition of sustainability 2006)

TABLE 9.3 Definitions of sustainability

WHAT IS SUSTAINABILITY?

In its infancy, sustainability was seen as being all about environmental stewardship, principally protecting and conserving the natural environment and managing environmental resources responsibly and wisely. Sustainability encourages us to think about mankind's impact on the world in which we live and had its origins in the subject of ecology. As the concept grew and developed, these simple environmental principles were supplemented with concern for the social and cultural environment we live in.

One of the first major studies on sustainability was written by Gro Harlem Brundtland in 1987. The Brundtland commission and the UN World Commission on Environment and Development recognised that the current path of development not only had a negative impact on the natural environment, but also failed to successfully address social inequalities, both among nations and between nations, and could therefore not be sustained indefinitely. Brundtland's goals and vision for sustainability were developed much further at the first Rio Earth Summit in 1992, with commitment to Agenda 21, where the values of sustainability were specified as:

- Protecting human heritage
- Combating poverty
- Supporting health initiatives

- Improving education
- Changing political systems away from the denial of public interests
- Self-determination.

GO ONLINE

The milestone of events in Table 9.1 in the online Appendix shows how the issue of sustainability and awareness of it have developed over the last 40 years.

EVENT ETHICS

> In just a few years you will see that the work you do now will be industry changing. The communities, venues and contractors you interact with will all be influenced and changed by your involvement. **It's up to you** – motivated event managers and those training to enter the industry – to see sustainability as a must-take & to make changes happen. (Meegan Jones 2018: 10)

Do you agree or disagree with this statement?

SUSTAINABLE GUIDELINES

The recent focus on sustainable issues is partly the result of the increased awareness of the type of environmental disasters evidenced above and also the result of more recent discoveries, some of which were discussed at the United Nations Climate Change Conference, COP25, held in Madrid in 2019. This includes renewed evidence on the depletion of the ozone layer and resulting climate change, for example the impact of the ice caps melting in the Arctic and Antarctica. These discoveries have made us all more aware of the damage we are doing to our planet, resulting in a shift towards delivering more sustainable events. ISO 20121 guidelines were put in place:

- To set a recognisable sustainability policy
- To identify issues relevant to the business or event
- To set objectives for those issues
- To identify possible solutions for meeting those objectives
- To agree how to implement the solution
- To monitor and measure sustainability.

The guidelines were not prescriptive or mandatory, but recommended rather that organisations and companies implement the procedures shown in Figure 9.1 for each event organised.

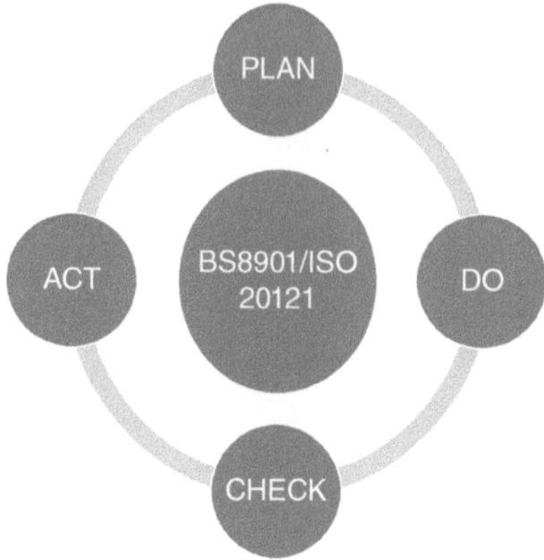

FIGURE 9.1 The sustainability process

The benefits of these guidelines are that the documentation provides a useful template and starting point, albeit with some necessary tweaking, monitoring and measurement, by the various event companies who have adopted it. The standard supports organisational learning, assists communication and strives for market differentiation and improved relations with suppliers. The reality is that in an ever increasingly procurement-driven industry, many agencies and suppliers cannot afford to ignore this template and need to implement it in order to guarantee market opportunities and selection as part of the bid process. This guidance document for managing sustainable development was a precursor for ISO 20121, the international standard, which specifies the requirements for Event Sustainability and was implemented for the first time during London 2012. The use of the standard is generally considered to be a positive outcome during and after the 2012 Games. At Rio 2016 it became a core part of the delivery and is one that is now internationally recognised and used within the industry.

The process of developing this policy began shortly after the bid for the London 2012 Olympic Games in 2005. In the bid to host the Olympics in the UK, London positioned itself to offer the first 'green Olympic Games.' This meant that London 2012 had a limited time to develop a plan for a new sustainable Event Management standard and tested BS8901 in the years leading up to the London 2012 Olympics, by setting out and implementing working objectives and practices at key events leading up to the London 2012 Games, such as Manchester International Festival (MIF), where the following initiatives were introduced:

- Renewable energy sources
- Energy-saving bulbs and sensors in kitchens and toilets
- Removing personal bins to increase recycling
- Printing double-sided
- Using eco-friendly cleaning products
- Using Fair-Trade products, such as coffees and teas, which adopt fair terms of trade for farmers and workers

- Using save-a-flush and Aqua-aid water filters
- Installing bike racks for staff and interest-free loans
- Collecting data on MIF travel and trying to estimate CO_2 emissions
- Offering ethical pension schemes for staff.

REAL INSIGHT 9.2

SUSTAINABILITY AND THE 2012 LONDON AND 2016 RIO OLYMPICS

SOURCE: www.flickr.com/photos/brianharringtonspier/7691420202

At the London 2012 Olympic Games, the International Olympic Committee (IOC) kept to its promise of delivering 'a greener games to encourage and support a responsible concern for environmental issues, to promote sustainable development' (IOC 2012), by regenerating the East End of London. Some of the environmental goals leading up to the London 2012 Games included setting a new standard for sustainable design and construction in the sports venues, ensuring that they could be reused in future events.

The Olympic Park was built on an old industrial site that was redeveloped to host the Games and has since become the largest new urban parkland in Europe for 150 years, offering recreation and green space to its residents and visitors. Further evidence of this includes the fact that the 'top ring' of the stadium was constructed using surplus gas supplies and the inclusion of sustainable

(Continued)

and recyclable materials. This allowed them to save over 400,000 tonnes of carbon dioxide.

BMW, one of the official partners of the London 2012 Olympics, supplied 240 low-emission electric and hybrid cars to transport camera equipment and athletes throughout the Games. The Queen Elizabeth Olympic Park is now open to the public and aims to continue the promises made in the Olympic bid, by promoting a healthy and sustainable lifestyle for the local community. This is still being reinforced through the Learning Legacy Project, which aims to share knowledge and the lessons learned through the construction of the Olympic Park. Residential properties in the park were designed to be zero carbon and water efficient, using responsible sourcing of materials to create a low environmental impact and nurture natural habitats and biodiversity, with good public transportation links to further reduce carbon emissions.

Although London's 2012 sustainable promise was centred around carbon footprint, waste management and delivering a green message, the Rio 2016 Olympic Games sustainability goals focused on people, planet and prosperity. In collaboration with the Dow Chemical Company, the Rio 2016 Olympic Games developed an environmentally friendly transportation solution by implementing B20 Biodiesel for event-sponsored cars, offsetting more than 2 million tons of CO_2, and pledged to plant 24 million seedlings in order to improve green space and reduce carbon footprint.

Three and a half thousand tons of recyclable waste were handled during the Rio 2016 Games and jobs were created due to this higher requirement for recycling activities. These were the first ever Games to introduce medals made from 100% recycled material. Silver medals, for example, were made from recycled mirrors, and gold medals were 100% mercury free.

However, concerns about water pollution health and safety in Rio led to the installation of barriers around the rivers where boats were employed to collect waste during the water-based competitions. Although these activities succeeded in cleaning up 50% of wastewater used in the aquatic activities, the pollution after water testing was still reported to be 30% below the recommended health and safety requirement for athlete safety, which caused controversy and negative publicity.

In order to canvas a more positive perception towards the Games, a waste-management initiative was introduced, which aimed to provide meals for the many homeless people living in the local community, supplied from the surplus food left over from the Games. Forty-five chef volunteers held cooking and nutrition classes. These were implemented to send a sustainable message to local communities, as a symbolic gesture to counter the negative reports circulating regarding the deforestation of the Brazilian rainforests, the Zika virus epidemic, high levels of crime and corruption, and the high levels of water pollution in Brazil.

Sustainability has become an area of increasing significance for event companies today, with many of them now embedding sustainability into the core of their business operations. This in turn will potentially help slow down global warming and reduce the impact on the environment. Huggins (2003), cited in Tassiopoulos (2010: 217), discusses how environmental considerations are likely to become a determining factor in the future and success of sporting events. Mega events need to consider their impact on the local society. Since London 2012 and Rio 2016, the legislation and the framework in which these environmental practices and initiatives are conducted, have ensured that host countries must clearly set out their vision and plans for environmental issues early in the bidding phase of these mega events.

SUSTAINABILITY IN EVENTS

There are a number of reasons why sustainability has been an increasing area of importance in the industry, or what we might term a 'hot topic.' Some of these reasons are as follows:

- Increase in awareness and knowledge in scientific terminology
- Growth of education
- More focus on values
- Revised law, policy and regulations concerning sustainability
- Competition differentiation in procurement terms
- Supply chain/related sectors
- Customer expectation.

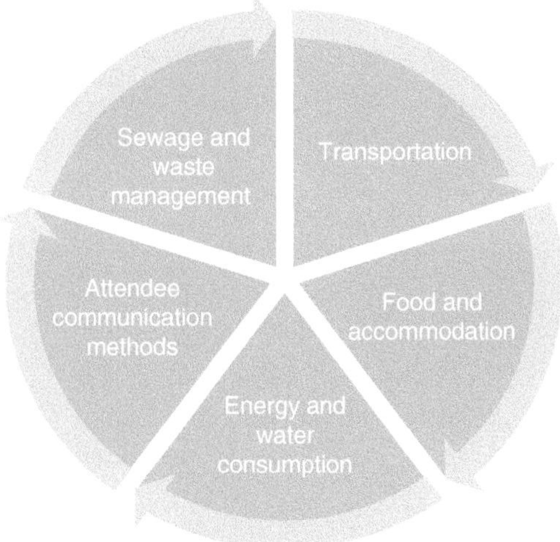

FIGURE 9.2 Areas of event sustainability

Jones (2018) also adds to this list, discussing the following ways that event organisations are trying to preserve the environment:

- Waste management and **resource recovery**
- Energy management

Resource recovery recycling, composting or energy generation in order to extract the maximum benefits from products

- Preservation and maintainable management of natural resources
- Green marketing to consumers
- Eco-efficiency.

Many smaller companies are also trying to incorporate sustainability into their company structure in order to position themselves as being environmentally conscious. One example of this is Brisbane-based Australian company Aaabiz Events and Venues, who state in their credential documentation that their policy is to deliver sustainable events, primarily concentrating on waste management, energy efficiency, procurement and resources, and to reinvest in local, social and economic communities.

Abu Dhabi in the United Arab Emirates recently launched a groundbreaking global forum to address the challenges of renewable energy and to promote international dialogue towards achieving a more sustainable future, by welcoming more than 32,000 participants from 170 countries to tackle the world's pressing issues in energy and sustainable development.

As previously mentioned, there is no global mandate which dictates a sustainable approach to business has to be adopted. However, these measures are to some extent governed by the law. The Companies Act 2006 (Strategic Report and Directors Report 2013) now requires that all UK-based companies record and report their greenhouse gas emission levels on their director reports. The following Real Insight illustrates a global events company that is trying to deliver a more sustainable service.

REAL INSIGHT 9.3

SUSTAINABILITY AT FIRST PROTOCOL

First Protocol is an international events agency with offices in Los Angeles, New York, Singapore and London. They were first established in 1996 and are owned and managed by their shareholders. They specialise in the design and delivery of high-quality live communications and their events range from large projects to small intimate VIP events, and they specialise in worldwide internal investor meetings and business-to-business events. They are also ISO 20121-certified for sustainability. Having the International Standard of Operations helps guarantee that their clients receive the same high standards globally across the whole of their offering and get the same service and treatment wherever they operate. Their sustainability aims are to raise customer and supplier awareness of green issues and to minimise the environmental impact on their operations. They strive to reduce their carbon emissions in line with the International Standard to ensure that there is a reduction of waste both in and out of their offices.

As with any new industry standards and policies, there are bound to be obstacles to change. According to the Meeting Professional International report (MPI.org 2018), only one in ten businesses indicated a likelihood of adopting the ISO 20121 accreditation. However, the International Standards Organisation advocates that all event companies and associated agencies need to adopt this policy in order to add value and credibility to their business profile. They believe that joining the scheme will allow event companies to be more financially successful, more socially responsible, as well as reducing their carbon footprint, thus supporting the planet whilst increasing their competitive advantage and profitability. Within the industry, resistance to implementing sustainable policies comes mostly from a general inertia to implement the policy. This could be due to time constraints, or a lack of knowledge about the Standards' aims, and sometimes even a lack of understanding of what sustainability actually is. Some believe that event companies are still not being sustainable enough in terms of environmental outcomes. Getz (2016) cites areas still falling short as the minimisation of waste, energy consumption, pollution, and the use of private transportation. He advocates protecting valuable resources for the future and adopting a more positive environmental attitude by reusing facilities and space, rather than building new ones, and, wherever possible, avoiding damage to wild habitat and ecological systems.

Possible resistance from the events industry to making changes in this area are the cost implications for implementing some of the measures and recommendations previously discussed. However, even making small changes to become more sustainable could reduce overall profit margins and therefore proves untenable for smaller agencies. A further obstacle is that there tends to be a degree of scepticism about the real impact that small changes, like those listed above, will actually make in terms of the overall impact on global sustainability.

REAL INSIGHT 9.4

SUSTAINABILITY AT THE 'BURNING MAN' FESTIVAL IN NEVADA AND GLASTONBURY FESTIVAL IN SOMERSET, UK

The 'Burning Man' festival takes places every year in the Nevada desert in a huge temporary city in the middle of the desert, in one of the harshest climates on the planet. Temperatures soar to over 100 degrees during the day, with dust storms and sub-zero temperatures at night-time. The annual Burning Man Festival attracts around 65,000 people for one week. The massive semi-circular campsite stretches for miles across the Black Rock desert in Nevada. The festival tries to use only environmentally friendly producers and stresses

(Continued)

that as an organisation, they have a low carbon footprint and base the concept on 'going back to basics'. Festival organisers only provide the entertainment, but attendees have to bring their own food, drinks and shelter, as no monetary transactions are allowed – only sharing, gifting and exchange. There are no shops or outlets and nothing to buy, except for the two essentials of ice and coffee. This forces all attendees to think creatively about reusing and recycling. The materials used during the festival are recyclable and biodegradable and the organisers make an effort to ensure that no rubbish is left behind and can be recycled wherever possible. At Burning Man water is valued as a precious commodity. Grey water is never thrown away but sent to shallow evaporation pools to be reused for other purposes. The organisers promote ride-sharing programmes to cut down on traffic and emissions and bus transportation ferries passengers to the festival from various popular points in California to also relieve traffic congestion.

These 'leave no trace' objectives are echoed at Glastonbury Festival which can attract up to 200,000 attendees over a weekend of live music. The festival recognises that having such a substantial number of attendees can create a significant amount of waste, which could negatively impact the farmland and local community. This may be one of the reasons Michael and Emily Eavis, the festival organisers, allegedly propose to change the location of the event from Worthy Farm in Pilton to the larger nearby site in the future. The concept of 'reduce, reuse and recycle' was introduced at this festival to encourage a decrease in waste that goes to landfill, by trying to get attendees to take items they can take back home with them. Glastonbury Festival states that 49% of waste is currently being recycled, including all cans, glass, paper, organic waste, and electric and electronic equipment.

The statement 'a tent is for life, not just for a festival' was also introduced to encourage attendees to invest more money in a better quality recyclable tent that could be used for many camping experiences and not just left at the site after the festival has taken place. After the 2017 festival, a litter picking crew of around 800 people were needed to clear the huge site of rubbish, and picked up an assortment of stray wellies, abandoned tents and discarded nitrous oxide canisters and balloons which had been used to inhale 'hippy crack', also known as laughing gas. An estimated 11 tonnes of clothes and camping gear are believed to have been abandoned, including 6500 sleeping bags, 5500 tents, 3500 airbeds, 2200 chairs, 950 rolled mats and 400 gazebos. It is thought that the festival organisers spent around £780,000 collecting the rubbish from across the site, while volunteers sifted through around 9 tonnes of glass, 54 tonnes of cans and plastic bottles, 41 tonnes of cardboard and 66 tonnes of scrap metal.

Nearly 200 tonnes of composted organic waste was removed from the site throughout the five-day festival. The fields of Worthy Farm were then returned to grazing land for dairy cows. Tractors carrying magnetic strips travelled across the site to pick up tent pegs while workers carried out a fingertip search to make sure no inch of the land remained unchecked. Workers have to be extra cautious of stray tent pegs as cows grazing the site have died in previous years after eating them. Generally, the clear-up operation can last up to six weeks, before the land can be restored to a working dairy farm.

At the 'Burning Man' Festival, it has been reported that even despite its utopian values, many attendees are incapable of letting go of the luxuries of modern life and their five-star standards, so it is not uncommon to see elaborate camps with fully stocked fridges and air conditioning. Glastonbury Festival organisers work closely with WaterAid and Greenpeace to deliver a more ecological and responsible festival and their presence can be seen all across the festival site. However, the Royal Geographical Society (2014) discusses the negative impacts of this festival, citing evidence of numerous traffic queues in the lead-up to and after the event, which significantly contribute to the pollution, as well as the clean-up operation afterwards. They also mention sewage disposal and water usage as other key areas of concern.

Both festivals showcased here have some way to go to be truly sustainable, but at least have started the important process of communicating to the delegates the significance of sustainability for the long-term future of the planet we inhabit.

THE FUTURE OF SUSTAINABILITY IN EVENTS

Despite resistance and scepticism from some events companies and agencies, it cannot be denied that overall the industry has started to become more environmentally aware over the last 20 years. According to Wrap (2015), the sector had a vision for zero waste to landfill by the year 2020. This basically means that all materials used at events will need to be recyclable. This is an ambitious target as currently the industry only recycles about 15% of waste. However, as it was possible to achieve this at the London 2012 Olympics and Rio 2016, it may not prove an unrealistic vision. It is evident that the industry has now become aware of the negative environmental impacts that are being created for future generations, and as a result today's events are experiencing increased pressure from consumers, who now expect them to be structured to reduce the negative impacts created. Companies and consumers alike concur that pollution, emissions, waste and exploitation of natural resources must be reduced and preserved, and strive to eliminate the use of plastic packaging, products and waste wherever possible in the sector.

Case (2012) advocates that events have always been designed to produce and impact cultural, social and economic legacy, but nowadays it is more about minimising negative impacts on the environment. This can be seen in the way that some events are being cancelled today, in order to placate the public's outrage over the potential damage they may cause to the environment. This reinforces the belief that events should not only strive to achieve sustainable development, but also be planned and managed in a sustainable way. With increased global concern about the irreparable damage being caused to the planet by climate change, it is likely that the call for increased sustainability and reduction will be a pressing and important issue for future generations in the industry.

GLOBALISATION WITHIN VARIOUS SECTORS OF THE EVENTS AND HOSPITALITY INDUSTRY

WHAT IS GLOBALISATION?

This word has become a 'buzzword' to describe the global integration that has taken place in the world in the last few decades. Globalisation could be described as the movement towards the expansion of economic and social ties between countries. This has led in recent times to the shrinking of the world in economic terms and has increased the need to balance local and global concerns, such as volatile political situations, trade deals, fluctuating markets and exchange rates, international relations and cultural diversity.

GLOBALISATION IN THE INDUSTRY

The growth of globalisation means that time and space are no longer barriers to trade; the increased speed of transactions resulting from internet, social media and mobile application usage, has dramatically shifted the industry over the last decade from a localised to a more global platform. Today many event companies have an international customer base and global suppliers and brands. Online research can help determine whether there is a wider international requirement for any event product or service on a global basis. It can also pinpoint whether any other event suppliers are currently working on a similar idea, and potentially provide the event owner with the opportunity to partner with another company or supplier to increase their global presence. This might potentially open up sponsorship opportunities, increase the target audience, or allow the client to recreate the event in multiple international destinations.

In economic terms, events are considered to be net generators of tourism, producing both additional visitors and revenue to a destination. There is an increased requirement to adopt certain types of events to attract the 'right' sort of tourism, such as a gastronomy

... globalisation is the process through which an increasingly free flow of ideas, people, goods, services and capital leads to the integration of economies and societies. (The International Monetary Fund (IMF))
... the defining feature of the global economy is not the flow of products and services, but the flow of international capital, information, people and resources. (Burbank et al. 2002)
As international travel, trade and communications increase, national boundaries and local differences are increasingly subsumed into the global marketplace. (Bowdin et al. 2011: 233)

TABLE 9.4 Definitions of globalisation

festival in Torino, Italy, a film festival in Cannes, a fringe comedy festival in Edinburgh, or a gay pride in San Francisco, all of which are financially viable for the destination. Many local and regional events are now attracting global attention, for example Notting Hill Carnival in London and Mardi Gras in Sydney, which both started as small local festivals but are now attracting a global audience and guests from all over the world.

These types of events reflect the aspirational lifestyle of this new urban middle class, with seemingly more **disposable income**, and can be linked to strategic changes in global bidding for events and increased marketing in these regions. Destinations are often marketed for the city's attributes and aspirations, like style, uniqueness, authenticity (Williams 2004). Essentially **cityscapes** are now in global competition with each other and it is the responsibility of cultural intermediaries, such as advertising and public relations agencies, to create positive impressions of destinations and market them accordingly.

Disposable income income remaining after the deduction of taxes

Cityscapes the urban equivalent of a landscape

Figure 9.3 shows areas of globalisation that are currently impacting the industry:

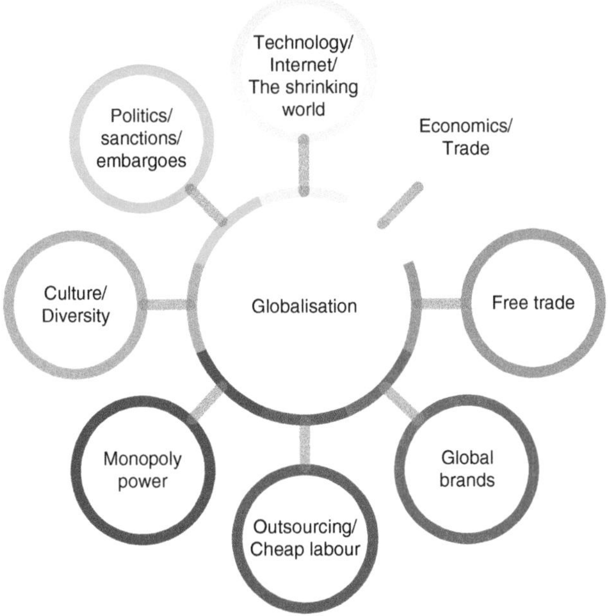

FIGURE 9.3 Areas of globalisation

THE RISKS AND BENEFITS OF BECOMING A GLOBAL INDUSTRY

The perceived benefit to an organisation of entering a global market is that they are able to reach a wider audience of potential customers and reduce any fluctuation in the business caused by seasonal adjustments or suppressed demand. Global saturation is not without potential risk however, so the decision to enter a global marketplace needs careful consideration, as the model in Figure 9.4 illustrates. Although the benefits of globalisation are clearly evident, **host communities** are now under more pressure to compete with other similar destinations, to develop more original and unique concepts for their events and festivals. This could ultimately prove a risk for some sectors of the industry who are not as cost-effective, creative or entrepreneurial as others. Large multinationals, whether they be event agencies, production companies or other suppliers, will be faced with the decision on whether to expand or to keep selling to a domestic market. This may depend on whether there are attractive and lucrative market opportunities available overseas.

Host communities a community of people in a certain destination hosting an event

In reaching this decision, the various suppliers and companies need to assess and evaluate a number of factors that may impact their potential success abroad. Firstly, the company or supplier will need to consider foreign market conditions and target their offering to countries that have an evident requirement for their products and services. Not all markets around the world are the same, or offer the same competitive advantage, business rates or growth opportunities. For example, it may cost significantly less and be equally viable to hold a meeting in Asia or Eastern Europe than in other parts of Europe or the world, and this may become a threat to those more expensive regions in a global marketplace with higher labour costs and a stronger currency.

Cultural and language barriers also need to be considered, as well as product viability in a country which may have different values, religious beliefs, traditions, customs and negotiation styles and practices. Lastly, the company would need to research any regulations or constraints, licensing restriction or political or governmental risks that could potentially limit the success of their expansion. International Standards are now required within the events industry to ensure seamless distribution of products and services around the world. Therefore, thorough research on setting up a business in a global marketplace should be conducted, including competitive advantage, as well as the cost of goods and labour, global accounting, legislation procedures and any licensing or contractual requirements. Economic factors and political stability within these foreign markets and shifting borders in times of growing political change can pose a threat to business expansion overseas and this would also need to be evaluated in the feasibility stage, by means of an intricate marketing strategy and detailed plan, as discussed in Chapter 4 of this book.

The factors of this decision process are illustrated in Figure 9.4.

THE FUTURE OF EVENT GLOBALISATION

It is easy to see how political events, the global economic turmoil, trade alliances, free trade movement and border controls, can shape and alter the stability of the

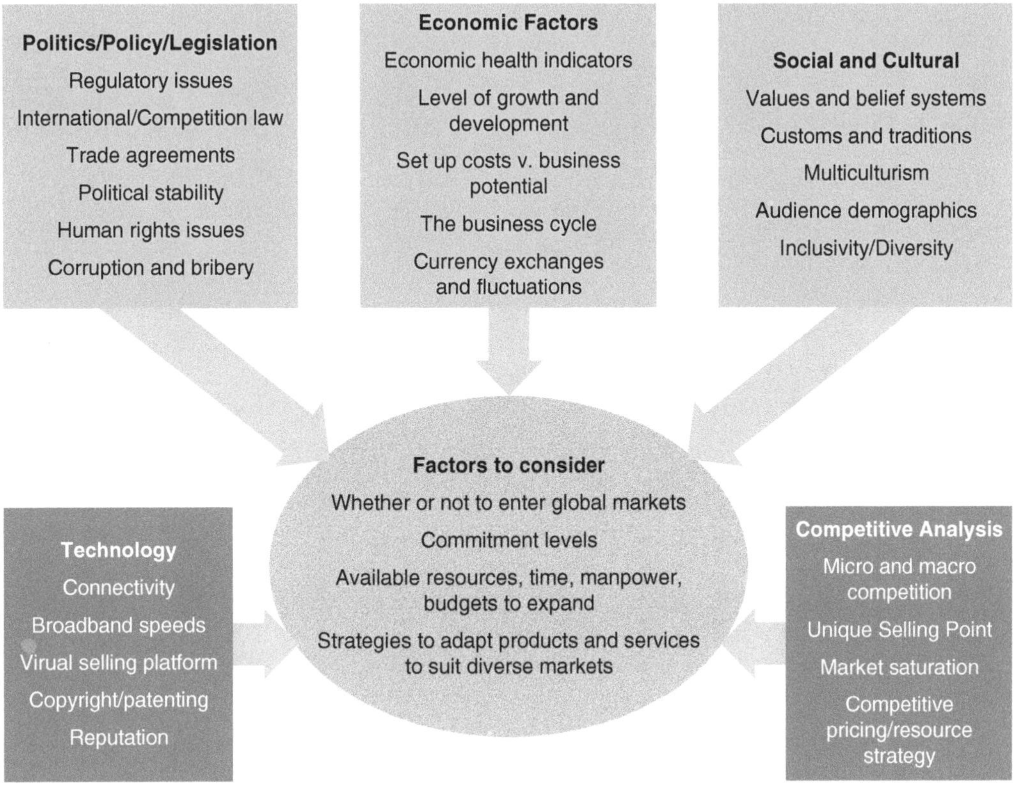

Politics/Policy/Legislation
Regulatory issues
International/Competition law
Trade agreements
Political stability
Human rights issues
Corruption and bribery

Economic Factors
Economic health indicators
Level of growth and development
Set up costs v. business potential
The business cycle
Currency exchanges and fluctuations

Social and Cultural
Values and belief systems
Customs and traditions
Multiculturism
Audience demographics
Inclusivity/Diversity

Factors to consider
Whether or not to enter global markets
Commitment levels
Available resources, time, manpower, budgets to expand
Strategies to adapt products and services to suit diverse markets

Technology
Connectivity
Broadband speeds
Virual selling platform
Copyright/patenting
Reputation

Competitive Analysis
Micro and macro competition
Unique Selling Point
Market saturation
Competitive pricing/resource strategy

FIGURE 9.4 Decision model for entering foreign markets

events industry. With many political changes now taking place in the world and an increase in global terror attacks, political disputes and health epidemics, events have been subject to many risks, as well as a new era of personal responsibility.

Although the world may be getting larger in terms of being able to trade in an open market, it is also shrinking because of increased visibility and the awareness that technological advancements in internet access and communication networks have afforded. Recent terror attacks have impacted European and other worldwide event destinations. Large corporations have begun reviewing their security measures for overseas travel, which has included increased contingency plans and duty of care measures. However, in an increasingly globalised and competitive event environment, being too risk averse could be very detrimental to future growth and expansion.

It is also worth remembering that although increased economic co-operation might increase globalisation in the events industry, existing trading such as the European Commission (EC), NATO and the World Trade Organisation (WTO) can also be areas that nations may want to dissociate themselves with for political, economic or other reasons, as has been seen in the way that alliances and border restrictions are constantly changing in the modern world.

OBJECTIVE 4

Current international legislation and regulatory requirements

CURRENT INTERNATIONAL LEGISLATION AND REGULATORY REQUIREMENTS

WHAT DOES REGULATION AND POLICY MEAN IN EVENTS?

Regulations dominate all aspects of our private and organisational lives and regulatory environments and policies shape future rules, laws and institutions. As previously discussed, the world is constantly changing, and organisations need to understand regulatory frameworks in order to formulate and implement strategies. Just like any other activity in society, events are subject to regulations and guidelines that influence their operation. Incidents such as Hillsborough Football Stadium UK in 1989 and The Love Parade disaster in 2010 in Germany brought about compulsory legislative changes in the industry, such as the introduction of all-seater stadiums and the development of compulsory training of football stewards, and led to the formation and implementation of appropriate regulation.

The reasons regulations generally exist in the events industry are:

- To aid effective planning
- To administer distributive and social justice
- To ensure the welfare and safety of all event stakeholders
- To avoid market failure.

... regulation in the UK refers to the various instruments (both formal legal instruments and such informal tools as 'guidance') used by government to control some aspects of the behaviour of a private economic actor. Regulation can also include rules issued by non-governmental bodies (e.g. self-regulatory bodies) to which governments may have delegated regulatory powers. All regulations are supported by the explicit threat of punishment for non-compliance. (OECD 2001)
... public policy is goal-directed processes by governments and their agencies, manifested in laws, regulations, decisions ... and intentions of governments regarding specific problems or general areas of public concern. (Getz 2016: 38)

TABLE 9.5 Definitions of regulation and policy

Types of regulation that relate to competition and protecting consumers cover areas such as maintaining government standards, protecting clients and customer interests, protecting the environment and fair marketing transactions, and can be illustrated in the three types of regulation detailed in Table 9.6.

Economic (Structural) Regulation	To regulate and provide parameters on who can enter a business environment and the prices they are able to charge for their products and services.
Social (Conduct) Regulation	To govern how any business or individual carries out activities and practices.
Administrative Regulation	To provide specific details and guidelines on implementing and enforcing policies.

TABLE 9.6 The various types of regulation

Office of Fair Trading
Sector regulators
OFWAT, OFGEM, OFCOM
Competition Act 1998
Fair Trading Act 1973
European Commission

TABLE 9.7 Regulatory institutions

Within the events industry, there are also the following areas to consider in terms of legislation and policy: finance, venues and other suppliers, programme and content, technical production, catering, outdoor events, security, cancellation, postponement, and insurance.

WHAT ARE EVENT POLICIES?

The most obvious public policy that relates to planned events is government funding. Policies are generally formed by governments, who put together regulations in order to guide the actions of all persons involved or connected with the organisation. Policies are guidelines for directors, committee members, employers and members and in the events arena might include:

- Policies on athlete doping in sport
- Policies in the service to members of an organisation or external customers
- Policies on crowd control in events
- Policies on financial management
- Policies on marketing and promotion
- A code of conduct for event participants
- Policies on risk, and health and safety.

In some cases, the policies set are mandatory and must be observed, to avoid contravening them. In most cases, however, policies are only put in place to act as guidelines and are therefore advisory rather than mandatory. For instance, an athlete found guilty of using a banned substance to enhance performance in **contravention** to a sporting body's policy on 'Drugs in Sport', will suffer an automatic ban from the sport. However, in the case of a person who has failed to observe the organisation's safety policy they will 'suffer the consequences'. Such consequences may range from nothing at all to the possibility of being sued.

Contravention
an action which offends against a law, treaty or other ruling

HASAW (Health and Safety at Work) was compiled by the Health and Safety Executive (HSE) in 1974 and is a public body that is responsible for the regulation and promotion of health and safety in the workplace, as well as employee welfare. HASAW itself has a whole series of legislation and regulations that it relates to such as:

- The Noise at Work Regulations
- The Reporting of Injuries, Diseases and Dangerous Occurrence Regulations (RIDDOR)

- The Control of Substances Hazardous to Health Regulations (COSHH)
- The Health and Safety (Signs and Signals) Regulations
- The Firework (Safety) Regulations.

The guidelines laid out in regard to general working practices help create a better understanding of the whole area of Health and Safety, as discussed in Chapter 6.

Another important event policy put in place to prevent overcrowding at events is the Occupational Health and Safety (OHS) Act. This ensures that organisers and venues alike create crowd control safety systems to comply with regulations under this area, such as installing safety measures for emergency evacuations, surveillance at venue entrances and exits, and conducting regular updated risk assessment reviews. This is also a legal venue requirement under The Management of Health and Safety at Work Regulations 1999 (MHSQ). The Control of Noise at Work Regulation 2005 is an example of a regulation that is often overlooked. It came into effect in the entertainment and music sector in 2008 and was set up to prevent long-term damage to the hearing of those working in close proximity to loud noises. The 2008 revision to the existing legislation made the correct procedures clearer for those working in the entertainment industry who were closely linked to music, such as festivals and concerts.

POLICY CONSTRAINTS

Any organisations and associations charged with the responsibility of formulating and developing a policy need to be aware that this policy may be constrained by the laws and regulations of parent organisations, umbrella organisations, regulatory bodies, community expectations, government policy and other legislation. Widespread consultation is paramount to successful policy formulation. Furthermore, an organisation that does not formulate policies may contravene government regulations and fail to conduct its affairs within expected community standards, thereby gaining an undesirable reputation with government funding agencies.

Policy making in events can be driven by governments and external agencies, or from consultation with the community or other stakeholders. From an event manager's perspective, policies provide a useful and necessary tool to ensure that staff carry out their tasks correctly and responsibly (Hall and Page 2006). Setting policies can therefore help decrease the amount of direct supervision by the manager, and at the same time increase the efficiency of work processes. However, as planned events can cross multiple areas, sometimes involving several levels of government, it is necessary to involve all stakeholders in the process of developing these event policies from the outset, as Figure 9.5 demonstrates.

REGULATIONS, LEGISLATION AND CODES OF PRACTICE

Common law tort
a civil wrong that unfairly causes someone else to suffer loss or harm, resulting in legal liability for the person who commits the act

Events are also covered by guidelines and codes of practice. One of the core legal principles of event management is understanding that, as an organiser, there is a 'duty of care' to adhere to. However, a mutual understanding alone is not contractually binding and therefore this understanding needs to be supported in some way by a **common law tort**. In event terms, this means the client will take

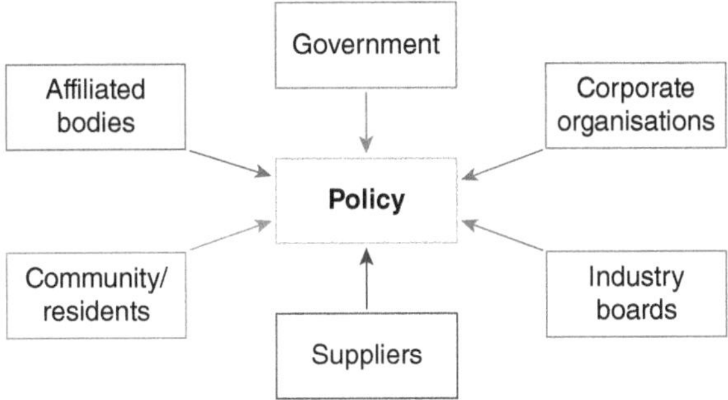

FIGURE 9.5 Policy stakeholders

action to prevent any foreseeable risks to all stakeholders involved. This extends beyond attendees to include crew, volunteers and suppliers, such as performers and entertainers, venue and catering staff, and so on, all of whom could be represented in a court of law.

Legislation is law that is made in parliament by elected representatives, i.e. members of parliament. Generally, the presiding government proposes new legislation, but any individual member of parliament can propose a law to be made or an amendment to existing law, providing they get a majority vote from other members of the parliament to agree and pass the legislation. Regarding the health and safety of event staff and volunteers, recent changes to legislation include the Corporate Manslaughter and Corporate Homicide Act 2007. This important act may result in the prosecution of management and companies who fail to comply with the health and safety standards set out by the HSE. This act removes the onus on the individual and makes the company and/or management culpable and liable for any staff errors and misconduct that may lead to causing harm to another.

The word 'harm' can take many forms such as injury, financial loss, or spoiling of a person's enjoyment of life. In many cases, such issues can be decided outside of the courtroom, but in cases where the harmed individual or individuals seek compensation or litigation for the damage, loss or suffering caused, they may decide to take the matter to a court to obtain an official judgment. This could be costly for the company being sued.

As the events arena is so varied, and much depends upon the type and size of event planned, it is not possible to follow one specific code or guideline. However, it is always the duty of the organiser to determine which licences, laws and legislation must be adhered to for each specific event and which governing bodies need to be notified and contacted. The emergency services certainly need advance information on what is being planned, especially if they are required to provide resources on-site. This means contacting the police, ambulance and fire services, especially if a firework display is planned or a large crowd expected. For the organisation of any large-scale festivals, an environmental health report needs to be filed, which will require input from district councils and the local police force, fire and emergency medical services, as well as hospital primary care facilities, and the highways and traffic agency, as detailed in Chapter 6.

RECENT CHANGES IN UK REGULATIONS

Regulations need to be amended from time to time. There are two revised health and safety regulations that came into effect from 1 October 2013. Recommendations were made by Ragnar Lofstedt, Professor of Risk Management at King's College London and the Director of King's Centre for Risk Management to the British government, who appointed the HSE to implement the changes. This did not alter the duties and responsibilities already placed on all stakeholders. The revisions were:

- The Health and Safety First Aid Regulations 1981 were amended to remove the requirements for the HSE to approve training and qualifications
- Low-risk workplaces like small offices only need a first aid box and one trained first aider
- High-risk workplaces need a fully trained and assessed first aider
- Reporting of Injuries, Diseases and Dangerous Occurrences Regulations (RIDDOR) 1995 made changes to clarify and simplify the reporting requirements, whilst ensuring all data collection is accurate
- RIDDOR classification of 'major injuries' to workers has been replaced with a shorter list of 'specified industries'
- The National Association for Environmental Management (NAEM) recognises that people and children may become lost during an event and has revised appropriate procedures for their care and repatriation
- The existing schedule detailing 47 types of industrial diseases has been replaced with eight categories or reportable work-related illnesses
- Fewer types of dangerous occurrences require reporting.

Codes of practice are available for almost everything and they lay down basic guidelines. For instance, there is a code of practice in relation to event stewarding and crowd safety services which is called BS 8406:2003, available at the website for the Royal Society for the Prevention of Accidents (ROSPA). This is a very useful place to get information on codes of practice for different activities at events and to find safety codes for the use of fireworks, for water-based leisure activities and other event activity.

Risk assessment and health and safety have been discussed in Chapters 2 and 6 of this book.

THE FUTURE OF REGULATION IN EVENTS

Compliance issues conforming to rules or policies

Although the industry is still reasonably robust, terrorist attacks have forced event companies to think more about **compliance issues**. For this reason, the corporate sector has also started to question the amount of non-essential conferences that they attend, particularly in high-risk countries. Some corporations have chosen to steer away from high-alert destinations, preferring smaller, more secluded cities to hold their events in and accommodating delegates in locally owned hotel groups rather than major international chains, which may be more likely to be targeted by extremists.

Event companies increasingly have to seek approval from their clients' security advisory committees before embarking on events in areas perceived to be of moderate to high risk. As the industry is becoming more professionalised, it is likely that in the future event companies will need to become more mindful of risk, outsourcing to specialists to undertake detailed risk assessment before delivery and ensuring that all staff are trained in all health and safety aspects. It is also probable that as the industry becomes liable to more litigation and criminal prosecution, some of the softer policies and guidelines that the industry is encouraged to follow will become more mandatory practices. In future, this may take the form of more prescriptive industry regulations, government acts and legislation, that industry stakeholders will need to comply with in order to ensure they are able to trade.

THE LINK TO SOCIAL RESPONSIBILITY

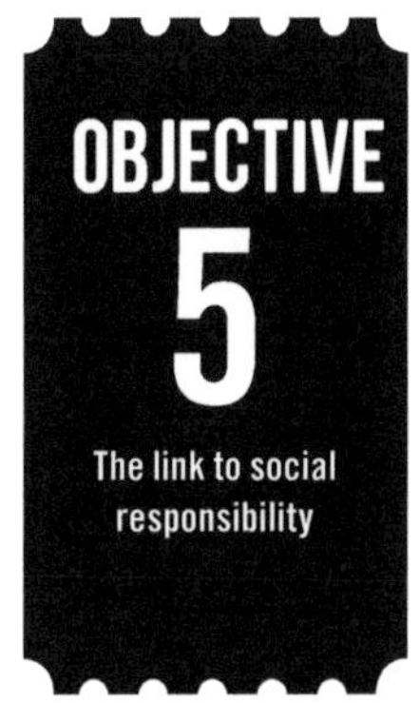

WHAT DOES CORPORATE SOCIAL RESPONSIBILITY (CSR) MEAN?

Also known as Corporate Responsibility, Accountability, Ethics, Corporate Citizenship or Stewardship and Responsible Entrepreneurship, CSR means that organisations are having to take further steps to improve quality of life for employees and their families, as well as for the local community and society at large.

In the 1980s and 1990s, the business world began to transform, and companies began to consider all stakeholders, rather than financial investors or customers alone. This transformation of business ethics impacted the way the events industry started to conduct itself professionally and changed stakeholders' expectations. Therefore, it can be said that CSR is predominantly a 20th century concept and has played a significant role in building the reputation of some of the world's leading event organisations.

... a concept whereby organisations consider the interests of society by taking responsibility for the impact of their activities on customers, suppliers, employees, shareholders, communities and other stakeholders, as well as the environment. (Carroll, 2008, cited in Crane et al. 2008: 107)

... there is only one social responsibility of business, to use its resources and engage in activities designed to increase its profits, so long as it stays within the rules of the game, which is to say it engages in open and free competition without deception or fraud. (Friedman 1970: 32)

... the responsibility of an organisation for the impacts of its decisions and activities on society and the environment through transparent and ethical behaviour ... consistent with sustainable development and the welfare of society; ... the expectations of stakeholders; is in compliance with applicable law and consistent with international norms of behaviour; and is integrated throughout the organisation. (The ISO 20060 Working Group on Social Responsibility, Sydney, February 2007)

TABLE 9.8 Definitions of CSR

As previously mentioned, consumers are becoming more demanding than ever before and event organisations are expected to communicate openly and honestly with customers, as well as building strong internal and external partnerships, in order to ensure long-term financial stability.

Putting workers' representatives on the boards of directors	Being transparent in financial reporting, i.e. publishing accounts
Putting quality before profit	Being honest and credible in advertising and not misleading customers
Being open and forthright in dealing with the public	Adhering to laws and regulations
Undertaking regular risk assessments in the workplace	Not doing something that needlessly endangers the consumer
Paying beyond the minimum wage, or adopting the living wage	Not discriminating against any person on the basis of age, sex, ethnicity or sexual orientation
Making sure people are properly equipped and trained to do their jobs	Adherence to working time directives
Provision of occupational health schemes	Being respectful, fair and open in employment practices
Recognising a union and an individual's right to join a union	Accepting the recommendations of an independent arbitration service
Paying a fair price for raw materials and manufactured products, e.g. not using suppliers who condone predatory practices in offshore manufacturing, such as child labour	Investing a percentage of profits in developing countries, e.g. health and education programmes

TABLE 9.9 Examples of CSR in business practice

WHO ARE THE 'DRIVERS' OF CSR?

Essentially there are two forces at work here: governments, who are naturally interested in the way businesses operate and their impacts on their employees and society at large; and businesses themselves who perceive there can be some specific advantages to adopting a programme of CSR. There is increasing awareness of the limits of government legislation and regulations to effectively solve all problems and issues, which is not always realistic, but CSR can offer an incentive for corporations to act in advance of regulations.

Governments and intergovernmental bodies, such as the United Nations, the Organisation for Economic Co-operation and Development (OECD) and the International Labour Organisation (ILO), have developed various compacts, declarations, guidelines, principles and other instruments that outline standards for what they consider to be acceptable business conduct. Today's CSR practices often reflect these internationally agreed goals and laws regarding human rights, the environment and anti-corruption policy.

The way companies behave is becoming a matter of increasing interest and importance in society. With private sector corporations, sometimes it is their sheer numbers that raise questions about their influence and accountability. However, even small and medium sized enterprises (SMEs) can have a significant impact on political, social and environmental systems.

WHY HAS THE CONCEPT OF CSR DEVELOPED WITHIN THE EVENTS INDUSTRY?

In past times, a number of serious and high-profile breaches of corporate ethics have resulted in damage to employees, shareholders, communities and the environment within the events industry. Examples include **embezzlement** of funds, employing cheap overseas labour and supplying goods and services to questionable regimes. In events, there are many examples of bad practice, as Real Insight 9.5 illustrates.

Embezzlement theft or misappropriation of funds placed in one's trust or belonging to one's employer

REAL INSIGHT 9.5

UNETHICAL PRACTICE IN EVENTS AT HEWLETT PACKARD IN THE USA

SOURCE: Image courtesy of WhisperToMe, via wikicommons.

Hewlett-Packard has been fined US$108 million (£66.8m) for bribing government officials with cash, gifts and luxury trips to secure massive contracts, including a contract worth an estimated €35m (£28m) with the Russian Prosecutor General's office.

HP pleaded guilty to breaching anti-bribery legislation and the Foreign Corrupt Practices Act after a long-running investigation conducted by the Department of Justice. International law enforcement partners and the FBI in the States found the technical giant had attempted to unethically buy business from government budget holders in Russia, Poland and Mexico. The company had run worldwide incentives, including trips to Las Vegas and private tours to the Grand Canyon, and also made non-travel-related gifts of cars, jewellery, clothing, furniture and electronics.

The Justice Department deputy assistant attorney General Bruce Swartz said in a statement:

(Continued)

> Hewlett-Packard subsidiaries, co-conspirators and intermediaries created a slush fund for bribe payments; set up an intricate web of shell companies and bank accounts to launder money; employed two sets of books to track bribed recipients, and used anonymous email accounts and prepaid mobile telephones to arrange covert meetings in order to hand over bags of cash.

Principal deputy assistant attorney general Marshall Miller said: 'Even more troubling was that the government contract up for sale was with Russia's top prosecutor's office.' He added: 'Today's conviction and sentencing are important steps in our on-going efforts to hold accountable those who corrupt the international marketplace.'

SOURCE: www.meetpie.com/Modules/NewsModule/NewsDetails.aspx?newsid=19495

In recent years and particularly the last decade, there has been a shift in the events sector that has prompted many companies to adopt different codes of conduct, principles and standards, as CSR has become increasingly integrated into contemporary events practices. Today corporate companies seek to integrate social, environmental and economic concerns into their values, culture, decision making and operations in a transparent and accountable way to establish better practices within the firm, create enhanced wealth and make improvements to society. In events these commitments and activities typically extend to:

- How the company runs its events programme
- Taking a moral or ethical position on operating practices
- Health and safety
- Environmental stewardship
- Human rights for all staff and volunteers
- Working conditions, including safety and health, working hours and staff wages
- Corporate philanthropy, volunteerism and community investment.

WHAT ARE THE BENEFITS OF ADOPTING A PROGRAMME OF CSR?

The business case for CSR differs depending on a number of factors. These include the company's size, nature of business, products, activities, location, suppliers, leadership and reputation. This means that the approach any individual company takes towards CSR can vary from strategic and incremental on certain issues, for example adopting an individual initiative on an equal opportunities policy, to becoming a mission-oriented CSR leader, where everything that the company does is influenced by CSR. The benefits that companies that adopt the principles of CSR stand to gain are shown in Table 9.10.

Benefits of adopting CSR in business
Effective governance and management of legal, social, environmental and economic risks in an increasingly complex market
The enhancement of reputation founded on values such as trust, credibility, reliability, quality and consistency
Enhanced ability to recruit, develop and retain staff, which can be the direct result of pride in the company's products and practices, or of introducing improved human resources practices, such as 'family-friendly' policies
Improvement in employee morale and loyalty, innovation, competitive advantage and market positioning, potentially leading to becoming a supplier to particular businesses
Improved ability to attract and build effective and efficient supply chain relationships and better stakeholder understanding of the organisation's objectives and activities translates into improved stakeholder relations
Enhanced ability to address change through regular stakeholder dialogue – better position to anticipate and respond to regulatory, economic, social and environmental changes
Better operational efficiencies and cost savings and more access to increased capital borrowing, as financial institutions are increasingly incorporating social and environmental criteria into their assessment of projects
More robust 'social licence' to operate in the community through enduring public, private and civil society alliances and overall business efficiency
Improved relations with regulators, as CSR procedures can help firms win approval for development with governments, and assist in the procurement of export assistance contracts

TABLE 9.10 Benefits of adopting CSR in business

In the events world, CSR can be demonstrated in practice through the adoption of regulated work hours, paid holidays, a safe working environment, the living wage, abolishment of **zero hours contracts**, diversity and inclusion policies, and fair labour practice. The events industry is proving to be far more transparent than in previous times, with agencies now explaining expenditure and profit margins to their clients and showing annual reports and financial documentation. Event companies and agencies are now more likely to engage and do business with suppliers who share the same ethical **codes of conduct**, contributing to a fair **supply chain**. London and Morfopulos (2010) and Davidson and Hyde (2014) advocate that it is now easier to sell a venue to a client if it is slightly more expensive, but transparent in the budget breakdown.

Zero hours contracts a type of contract between an employer and a worker where the employer is not obliged to provide any minimum working hours, while the worker is not obliged to accept any work offered

Codes of conduct a set of rules outlining the social norms and rules and responsibilities of, or proper practices for, an individual, party or organisation

Supply chain a system of organisations, people, activities, information and resources involved in moving a product or service from supplier to customer

WHAT ARE THE RISKS OF NOT ADOPTING A PROGRAMME OF CSR?

Communication and transparency are also major aspects of CSR and vital to the success of the industry as the planner looks to communicate its reputation and overall purpose to all stakeholders involved. Nowadays, in an increasingly procurement-driven environment, corporations cannot take the risk of not appearing to be socially responsible, as failure to engage in CSR could potentially:

- Jeopardise event companies' and agencies' ability to create wealth for themselves, so that they miss out on a market opportunity
- Increase the risk of legal or other responses, e.g. in some cases and countries fines and imprisonment or boycott of certain events, for example Russia's boycott of the 2016 Rio Olympic Games

- Result in failure to achieve a Unique Selling Point (USP) in a competitive arena
- Reduce the chance to adopt sound governance and ethical business practices in event delivery
- Alienate the events workforce and the local community in the host destination.

It is evident that both consumers and investors are showing increasing interest in supporting responsible business practices, with more companies publishing annual reports. In 2016 97.3% of people declared that they would be willing to make a monetary sacrifice to work for a socially responsible company. They are demanding more information on how companies are addressing risks and opportunities related to event issues. For this reason, adopting CSR within the events industry can help build share value, and ensure better stakeholder responsiveness to the market.

THE LINK BETWEEN CSR AND SUSTAINABILITY IN EVENTS

Over the years, there has been a general consensus that CSR is deeply rooted in the actions that businesses have to trade sustainably with an obligation and duty that go beyond their economic survival (Jones 2018). The link from sustainability to CSR in events involves instances where a company helps society by developing ethical products and practices that will benefit society and the environment, rather than just focusing on profitability, for example through the use of biodegradable products, reduction of waste, recycling and committing to cut down on plastic packaging and products, aiming to become a plastic-free environment. It also links to increased transparency, in terms of communicating sustainable strategies and progress, with more emphasis on the use of locally grown produce, organic and fair-trade food. CSR is an entry point for understanding sustainable development issues and responding to them as part of the overall event strategy.

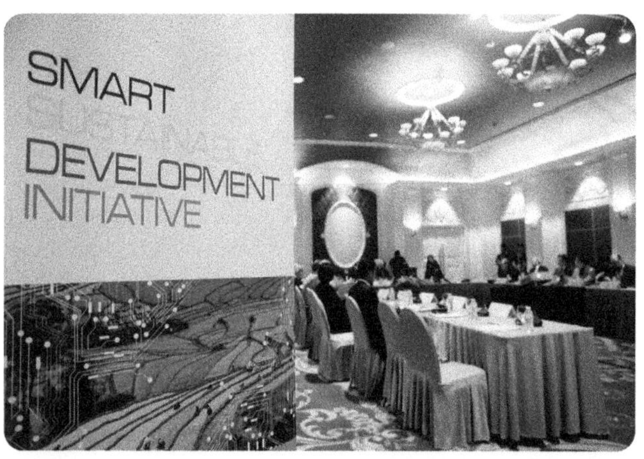

SOURCE: Image courtesy of ITU Pictures, via flickr.com. Shared under the Creative Commons BY 2.0 license.

Event agencies such as George P. Johnson are currently looking at ways to re-use event furniture, props and decorations, and use wireless applications to make fiscal savings, as well as reducing carbon footprint, linking technology to CSR as a more responsible way of managing the planet's resources.

THE LINK BETWEEN CSR AND GLOBALISATION IN EVENTS

As previously discussed, recent advances in communications technology, such as the internet and smartphones, are making it easier to manage business activities, report on business practice and initiate change globally. This means that nowadays there is greater cross-border and multinational trade, with a renewed focus on overseas enterprises and global supply chains. However, economic globalisation is increasingly raising CSR concerns in relation to human resource management practices, environmental protection, and health and safety in events, as these practices are not always exemplary. In New Zealand, for example, tobacco and alcohol companies have faced increasing criticism about the unhealthy nature of their products, such as fizzy drinks, confectionary, tobacco and fast food, which are linked to community sports events (CSEs) through sponsorship deals. Thus, setting uniform standards for ethical responsibility around sponsors and partnership affiliations and the promotion of healthy products becomes a global concern.

The international event agency Jack Morton states that as members of a global community, we can only be effective if we act sustainably. Indeed, many global event corporations feel the events industry should meet the same high standards in social and environmental care, regardless of culture differentiation and event origin. Although it is difficult for governments to monitor the activities of corporations across international borders, one positive aspect of globalisation, in terms of CSR, is that organisers can make informed decisions through a shared approach to common problems that may have already been experienced by other nations. This is particularly the case in terms of major and mega sporting and cultural events.

THE LINK BETWEEN CSR AND TECHNOLOGY IN EVENTS

The growth of technology, as reviewed earlier in this chapter, links to CSR through a reduction in paper usage. Documents can now be saved and filed online, and events have become increasingly ticketless. The International Association of Exhibitions and Events (IAEE) has recommended the elimination of paper-based materials at events, and the advent of devices such as smartphones, high-tech touch screens, virtual reality headsets and portable tablets are making this ever more achievable, so that paperless events may be a reality in the near future.

THE LINK BETWEEN CSR AND PHILANTHROPY IN EVENTS

Over the past decade, the corporate sector has changed its focus from being purely profit driven to one that promotes values such as philanthropy and altruism and aims to contribute to social or charitable causes. This can be seen through the increase in the amount of not-for-profit events which are now being organised in order to give something back to the community, or to raise funds for a specific charitable cause. It can also be seen in the increase of volunteerism that is now taking place throughout the event sector, much of which is for intrinsic, rather than for extrinsic, reasons.

THE LINK BETWEEN CSR AND LAW AND GOVERNANCE IN EVENTS

Despite the recent changes and many challenges that face the events industry, such as the global financial turmoil and ever-increasing security threats, CSR is not governed by law or regulations. CSR is still very much an optional choice for the industry at this time. The introduction of The Bribery Act 2010 established governmental assertion that organisations should act in a responsible way. Under this law, events have been forced to adjust their business negotiations or risk being accountable for corrupt practices, like accepting 'backhanders' or financial bribes to secure business contracts.

Many agencies now require all suppliers to sign a code of conduct, before entering into a contractual arrangement with them, as illustrated in the case study on Hewlett Packard in Real Insight 9.5 featured above. Since the introduction of this act in 2010, there has been a big decrease in corporate spending on entertaining clients in an attempt to win and retain future business. This act has especially impacted the public sector, defence, financial and pharmaceutical industries, which have become a lot more stringent about accepting corporate hospitality, gifts or anything that could be perceived as a bribe.

Another act that has changed how event managers and venues operate responsibly is the Disability Discrimination (DDA) Act 1995. The act looks to ensure that those who are physically or otherwise impaired are not disadvantaged or treated less favourably than others. It states that any service provider with any industry sector is required to make all the changes and adjustments needed to ensure and improve access for customers with a disability, or even potential customers. Also, the venue must make reasonable changes and practical building alterations to improve actual access to the venue as well as providing information to customers or guests that have impaired vision or hearing, and additional staff for those that need support. The Disability Rights Commission (DRC) states: 'the act makes it unlawful for a service provider to discriminate against a disabled person by refusing to provide a service which it provides to members of the public.' The act also aims to ensure that there is fair treatment for all employees and volunteers with disabilities.

In 2007 the Equality and Human Rights Commission (EHRC), in association with industry professionals, produced *Engaging with Disabled People: An Event Planning Guide*. This guide looks to offer advice and creative solutions for all aspects, including transportation, the design and layout of events. The original 1995 Disability and Discrimination Act was updated and revised in a piece of legislation that has become the Equality Act of 2010.

THE FUTURE OF CSR IN THE EVENTS INDUSTRY

Despite all the recent changes in regard to technology, globalisation, sustainability and philanthropy that have been discussed in this chapter, there are still no universally agreed standards or ethical guidelines on how event agencies or organisations should act. However, the recommended guidelines currently set are almost becoming unofficial or 'soft laws' as demands increase for the events industry to be more transparent, and to give something back to society and the community it operates in, rather than just to make a profit.

As previously discussed, one of the main areas of resistance to CSR is the short-term cost of introducing responsible events and the associated costs of training staff and applying new procedures. However, in the long term, not adopting CSR could cost a company even more, through possible loss of business and increased staff turnover. Advocates of CSR have argued that more responsible business performance and increased transparency can lead to cost savings and the ability to attract the right clientele. It is clear that all the factors of CSR discussed in this chapter will continue to develop and shape the way events are ethically and responsibly managed in future years.

HOW THE EVENTS INDUSTRY MAY CONTINUE TO CHANGE IN FUTURE

The issues discussed throughout this chapter, such as the spread of more accessible technological advancements, and the increasing pressure to reduce carbon footprints have brought about a 'curve ball', which is proving to be a difficult and complex issue to tackle within this industry. In this new events environment, the only constant is change, and organisers and delegates alike need to start to be more adept at dealing with volatile situations and more flexible and risk aware in their approach to planning.

According to a survey carried out by *Associations Meeting International* magazine in 2016, almost a third of international associations considered or actually cancelled a meeting because of the threat of terrorism and the perceived risk to delegates (AMI magazine 2016). Of the survey respondents 70% said that they felt the world was a more dangerous place than it was 10 years ago, and 74% said that as a result of these terror attacks, they had taken steps to secure additional security at their meetings. The event organiser now has a responsibility to be vigilant concerning public safety and the safety of delegates and guests.

Increased terrorism may make an even stronger argument for the need for event organisers to work closely with destination management companies (DMCs) in the countries they are operating in to ensure good access to local up-to-date knowledge and security data. If safety issues have risen in prominence, so has the whole area of data security, as high-profile data breaches at hotel chains, such as the 2015 Linux conference in Australia, have brought awareness of data security to the fore.

Data protection entails taking responsibility for clients' and delegates' physical and digital information and updating procedures to make sure the infrastructure is secure on an ongoing basis. Where appropriate, organisers are advised to work in conjunction with specialist IT departments and ensure that their supplier chain fully adheres to a commitment to data security and equipment and information they have access to during the event. The accreditation standard ISO 27001 enables corporations to follow **best practice** in the area of personal and company protection, protection of client data and sensitive information through **encryption** and safe data storage and the physical security of clients and event attendees. Event organisers and the venue have a duty of care to protect the attendee's data and **cyber security** in the location, by using tested and secure devices.

All the issues and areas discussed in this chapter that have had an impact on current event trends and practices in an ever-changing environment and uncertain political climate, will leave a lasting legacy that will ultimately completely change the face of the current industry.

Best practice
commercial or professional procedures that are accepted or prescribed as being correct or most effective

Encryption
the process of encoding messages or information in such a way that only authorised parties can read it

Cyber security
the protection of information systems from theft or damage to the hardware, the software, and to the information on them, as well as from disruption or misdirection of the services they provide

CHAPTER SUMMARY

CHAPTER SUMMARY QUESTIONS

1 How is virtual reality used in events?
2 In what way did the Brundtland Report become a guideline for global sustainability?
3 What do BS 8901, ISO 20121 stand for and why were they set up?
4 What event impacts are caused by globalisation?
5 When was the Disability Discrimination Act set up and why?
6 What are the main security risks affecting the events industry today?

DISCUSSION POINTS

- What resources/support do you feel are needed to make events more sustainable?
- Why has CSR become an issue for event companies today?
- How have recent changes in legislation impacted the events industry?

ACTIVITIES

- In groups, research the Erika Oil Spill ecological disaster.
- For an event you are planning, you have been told you should moderate the event to facilitate a disabled audience. What measures would you take?
- Which online mobile applications might you download and use at a conference to make the event planning process easier?

REFERENCES

Allen, K. 'Technology has created more jobs than it has destroyed, says 140 years of data', *The Guardian*, 18 August. Available at: www.theguardian.com/business/2015/aug/17/technology-created-more-jobs-than-destroyed-140-years-data-census (accessed 22 April 2020).

AMI Magazine (2016) Convene's 27th Annual Meetings Market Survey [online]. Available at: www.pcma.org/convene-27th-annual-meetings-market-survey (accessed 24 July 2018).

Bowdin, G., McDonnell, G., Allen, J. and O'Toole, W. (2011) *Events Management*, 4th edn. Oxford: Butterworth-Heinemann.

Brundtland Commission (1987) Our Common Future (ed. Volker Hauff). Oxon: OUP.

BSI group.com (2012) Available at: www.bsigroup.com/LocalFiles/en-AE/Sustainability/ISO%2020121/BSI-ISO20121-Product-Guide-MEA.pdf (accessed February 2020).

Burbank, M.J., Andranovich, G. and Heying, C.H. (2002) 'Mega events, urban development and public policy', *Review of Policy Research*, 19(3): 179–202.

Carroll, A.B (2008) 'A history of corporate social responsibility: Concepts and practices', in A. Crane, D. Matten, A. McWilliams, J. Moon and D.S. Siegel (eds), *Oxford Handbook of Corporate Social Responsibility*. Oxford: Oxford University Press, pp. 19–46.

Case, R. (2012) 'Event impacts and environmental sustainability', in S.J. Page and J. Connell (eds), *The Routledge Handbook of Events*. Oxford: Routledge.

Crane, A., McWilliams, D., Matten, J., Moon, J. and Siegel, D. (2008) 'A history of corporate social responsibility: Concepts and practices', in A. Crane, D. Matten, A. McWilliams, J. Moon and D.S. Siegel (eds), *Oxford Handbook of Corporate Social Responsibility*. Oxford: Oxford University Press, pp. 19–46.

Davidson, R. and Hyde, A. (2014) *Winning Meetings and Events for Your Venue*. Oxford: Goodfellow.

Equality and Human Rights Commission (2019) Engaging with disabled people: An event planning guide. Available at: www.equalityhumanrights.com/sites/default/files/housing-and-disabled-people-engaging-with-disabled-people-event-planning-guide.pdf (accessed 18 May 2020).

Friedman, M. (1970) 'The social responsibility of business is to increase its profits', *The New York Times Magazine*, 13 September.

Getz, D. (2016) *Event Studies: Theory, Research and Policy for Planned Events*. Oxford: Butterworth-Heinemann.

Guidebook (2014) State of mobile event technology [online]. Available at: https://guidebook.com/mobile-guides/mobile-event-tech-report-2014 (accessed 17 February 2017).

Hall, C.M. and Page, S. (2006) *The Geography of Tourism and Recreation: Environment, Place and Space*, 3rd edn. London and New York: Routledge.

Huggins, A. (2003) 'The greening of sporting events: Production of environmental management guidelines for eventing' in D. Tassiopoulos (2010) *Events Management*, 3rd edn. Claremont: Juta.

International Monetary Fund (IMF) Available at: www.imf.org/en/Research (accessed 15 August 2016).

International Olympic Committee (IOC) (2012) Available at: www.olympic.org/london-2012 (accessed 15 August 2016).

Jones, M. (2018) *Sustainable Event Management: A Practical Guide*, 3rd edn. London: Taylor Francis.

London, M. and Morfopulos, R.G. (2010) *Social Entrepreneurship*. New York and London: Routledge.

Meetings Professional International MPI (2016) Annual Review [online]. Available at: www.mpi.org (accessed 10 September 2017).

OECD (2001) What we do and how. Available at: www.oedc.org/about/whatwedoandhow (accessed 14 August 2016).

Office of National Statistics (ONS) (2017) Home internet and social media usage [online]. Available at: www.ons.gov.uk/peoplepopulationandcommunity/householdcharacteristics/homeinternetandsocialmediausage (accessed 5 December 2017).

The Royal Society for the Protection of Accidents (ROSPA) Homepage. Available at: www.rospa.com (accessed 2 October 2016]).

Ross, A. (2016) Hilary Clinton [online]. Available at: www.youtube.com/watch?v=LMh6UzHqeQk (accessed 2 December 2016).

Rotman, D. (2015) 'Who will own the robots?', *Technology Review*, June.

Smith-Christensen, C. (2009) 'Sustainability as a concept within events', in R. Raj and P.W. Sutton, *The Environment: A Sociological Introduction*. Cambridge: Policy Press.

Solomon, M., Marshall, G., Stuart, E., Mitchell, V. and Barnes, B. (2009) *Marketing People and Choices*. London: Pearson.

The Royal Geographical Society (2014) Annual review. Available at: www.rgs.org/about/the-society/annual-review (accessed 6 December 2017).

Williams, S. (2004) *New Directions and Alternative Tourism: Critical Concepts in the Social Sciences*, Volume IV. London and New York: Routledge.

Wrap (2015) Zero waste events: Achieving success [online]. Available at: www.wrap.org.uk/content/zero-waste-events (accessed 11 July 2016).

10

EVENT CAREERS, HUMAN RESOURCES AND CONSULTANCY

CHAPTER OVERVIEW

This chapter explores the emergence of increased professionalism within the industry. It discusses various career paths that exist within the event industry and evaluates what skills and qualifications are recommended to gain employment and start a successful career in events management. It will also look at different career routes into the events industry, including university-undergraduate and postgraduate studies, apprenticeships and internships. The chapter examines the transferable skills and more subject-specific skills that employers look for in new employees and graduates. In addition, this chapter will discuss the role of human resources in the sector, progression routes and corresponding pay scales.

CHAPTER OBJECTIVES

After reading this chapter, you will be able to identify and understand:

OBJECTIVE 1 The need for a professionalised industry

OBJECTIVE 2 Graduate entry, apprenticeships and other recognised qualifications

OBJECTIVE 3 Skills and attributes for a career in events

OBJECTIVE 4 Sourcing and applying for event-related work

OBJECTIVE 5 The role of human resources in events and hospitality

OBJECTIVE 6 Career paths and progression routes

Meet AHMAD AMIRAHMADI

Company owner

Specialising in the recruitment and managing of major sporting events within the UK and overseas

Ahmad graduated from Thames Valley University in 1992, with an Honours Degree in Event and Hospitality Management. He then joined Town and County Catering, as a catering manager at the Business Design Centre in Islington, London. After that he continued to expand his career working in the events division of Gardner and Merchant, which then became Sodexho. In 1999 he left Sodexho to start his own event agency, supplying staff and managing events all over the world. His career highlights to date have been working on the Rugby World Cup in Paris 2007, then London 2015 and Tokyo 2019. His favourite event is the Wimbledon Tennis Championship which takes place every July in London, which he has now worked at for more than 20 years. Another of Ahmad's career highlights was helping organise and manage the Queen's garden parties at Buckingham Palace, where on two separate occasions he was presented to HRH Queen Elizabeth II.

REAL EVENT CHALLENGE

The main challenge I experience year on year is dealing with the peaks and troughs of the event season and being able to predict head count for the events I recruit for in the summer months. For that reason, I employ mostly freelance or casual staff, with only a few permanent paid staff members. The biggest challenge I have is recruiting for Ascot races and Wimbledon, where I need to recruit in the region of 50 to 70 staff for each event. I also have to make sure I do this in time, so that there is time to interview, recruit and train staff within our company and also on site at each of the events, so they have time to cover all the necessary

Q&A

WHAT WAS YOUR FIRST JOB OUT OF UNIVERSITY?

I was a catering manager in London, providing food and beverage for in-house exhibitions, country living fairs and many other events.

WHAT HAS BEEN YOUR BEST CAREER ACHIEVEMENT TO DATE?

Having worked on the last three Rugby World Cups, France 2007, London 2015 and Japan 2019, I would say I have certainly enjoyed these the most, especially the last two. They are fun events to work on, with a great international perspective and really nice fans and customers. For all three of the Rugby World Cup events, my company recruited staff for the catering, security, ticketing and cleaning services.

WHAT DOES YOUR IDEAL DAY LOOK LIKE?

I like to be up early and get as much done in the morning as possible. If there is an event, I am usually on-site and well into my day by 8 am.

When there isn't an event on, I drive to my office at the Twickenham Rugby Stadium and start to conduct interviews, plan the week ahead, and so on.

YOUR HERO?

Slightly outside my own area of expertise, but I admire Jason Atherton and Michel Roux Junior. They started as chefs and have done so well; going on to run very successful restaurants and businesses. As a business owner myself, I find them both very inspirational.

BEST TRAVEL TIP?

Plan ahead and research the place you are going to even if you have been before. I have been to Tokyo at least 10 times, but before going there in the autumn I spent a lot of time researching what was new, in terms of things to do, places to eat, and so on.

risk assessment and security clearance, plus undergoing induction and training before commencing work at the events.

PRACTITIONER VIEWPOINT

Gilly Tajasque, Events Recruitment Specialist, Regan & Dean Recruitment

The event industry is a great sector to work in. You will start to build relationships there that you would be hard pressed to find in a normal office environment. It's dynamic, exciting and different, but it can also be hard work and labour intensive, so don't try to run before you can walk. Events take all sorts, so spend some time researching and finding out what sort you are and what area will suit you best.

Expose yourself to new challenges and keep a commentary or diary of your work experiences. Events are often intense, and memories can fade quickly after the moment has passed, so try to log it all if you can. Whether it has been a good or bad experience, always think how you might be able to use it in an interview when you're asked to talk about how you dealt with a challenge, or something that went wrong, and so on. Write down five key skills that you think an employer would benefit from if they employed you and try to find real examples to back these skills up.

Get as much experience as you can during your time at university or college. If possible, try to get an internship or a placement in a company, or develop your office skills, as most events roles need good IT skills and experience of being in an office.

ACADEMIC VIEWPOINT

Dr Rob Davidson, Visiting Fellow at the University of Greenwich and Managing Director of MICE Knowledge

For me, a clear priority in my teaching has always been to prepare students for employment in MICE or business events by letting them see the 'big picture' of this industry – how the various professionals such as meeting planners, destination management companies, venues and convention bureaus all work together to produce successful business events that meet the objectives of all the stakeholders. In my lectures focusing on the roles of these different professionals, I am constantly inviting the students to consider which roles they themselves are most attracted to as a career. But, regardless of which career they choose to follow in this industry, I believe that the 'big picture' overview they get will always help them to understand how everything fits together in the MICE world and how their chosen role contributes to the overall success of business events.

REAL EVENT OUTCOME

Throughout the winter months, I visit local universities and colleges that offer Hospitality and Events courses in London and the home counties, to recruit new students. I present the various work opportunities and try to sign up as many students as possible to work on these events in the summer. I usually manage to recruit enough students to cover all the summer sporting events, as they are pleased to have the opportunity to earn money and to get valuable work experience at the same time. They can also make some pretty good tips on top of their wages, providing they are prepared to work hard over those events.

I also advertise the positions through social media and word of mouth. The most important factor is to make sure the students can attend the half-day training session with our company and the two-day training session, which is held on-site, at both Ascot racecourse and the All England Club, better known as Wimbledon. The students are paid to attend the training sessions and the induction covers important aspects of the job, including risk assessment and a detailed health and safety briefing. Once on-site we offer students a 'buddying up' system, where they are able to shadow a more experienced member of the team initially until they get to grips with the role. The students really enjoy the experience, make new friends and sometimes even get to see a bit of the sporting action in their free time. We must be doing something right in this area because I've been working at Ascot for 20 years now and at Wimbledon for 27!

THE NEED FOR A PROFESSIONALISED EVENTS INDUSTRY

WHAT IS PROFESSIONALISM IN EVENTS?

Unlike the fields of Law, Engineering, Marketing, and so on, which have their own recognised professional organisations representing them, the events industry currently has no professional body or **accreditation** governing it. This means that theoretically anyone could set up as an in-event operator and practise, with no qualifications, training or expertise.

Accreditation the process in which certification of competency, authority or credibility is presented

The last century saw an events industry start to emerge, encompassing various sectors. The corporate sector in particular made calls to formally acknowledge this fast-growing industry. Consumers now demand professionally run events and there has been an increasing use of the term 'events professional'. The vision for a professionalised events industry is one supported by government to provide increased training, relevant industry-related qualifications, an increasing body of knowledge and a clear progression route. This echoes Wilensky's (1964) five-stage natural history of professionalism, which he defined as:

- The emergence of a full-time occupation
- The establishment of a training school
- The founding of a professional organisation
- The protection of the association by law
- The adoption of a formal code.

Middlehurst and Kennie (1997) discuss professionalism in terms of commercial vision, and customer and client satisfaction, with the emphasis being on sustained client relationships, excellence in leadership and management, entrepreneurial skills and demonstrable success through professional and profitable management of events. In more traditional employment areas, being a 'professional' is seen to be highly desirable, as it confers status and legitimises the industry.

Goldblatt (2002) lists the necessary skills to classify as an event professional as being able to research, design, plan, coordinate and evaluate. In 2003 Silvers first developed an Event Management Body of Knowledge (EMBOK) as a starting point for a multi-national and multi-disciplinary discussion. Her definition of an event manager is one who can 'oversee and arrange every aspect of an event, including researching, planning, organising, implementing, controlling and evaluating an event's design, activities and production.'

THREE KEY AREAS OF PROFESSIONALISM IN EVENTS

As with any profession, the industry needs to keep abreast of the many changes and advancements taking place in the industry and to make sure the events workforce continuously improves existing skills and knowledge. Enhanced competence and a commitment to service lead to credibility both within the industry and externally.

Research and studies that have looked at training and professionalism in the industry have identified the following three key areas:

- Information, advice and guidance
- Continuing professional development
- Qualification development.

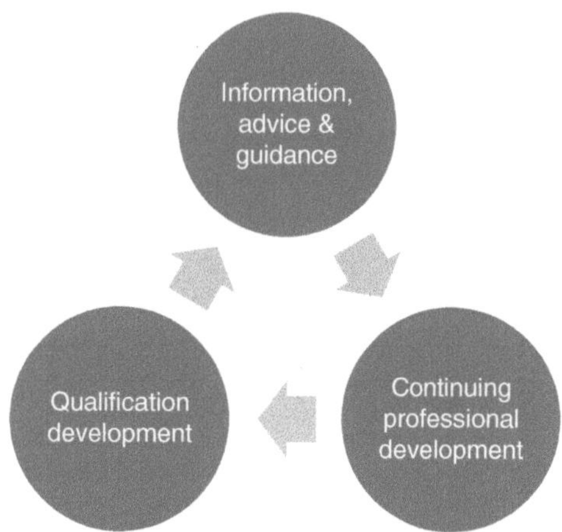

FIGURE 10.1 Key areas of training and professionalism needs in events

Competence goes beyond formal qualifications to the continuous development of the professional's knowledge, both theoretical and in practice. So that the continuous improvement of skills are current and can effectively represent the interests of the client and institution. (ACCED-I, 2002)
Professionalisation may be defined as a process by which occupations gain their standing as a profession by identifying attributes which separate professional work from that of other kinds. (Formadi and Raffai 2009)
Professionalism is being subjected to reforming pressures that contribute to shifts toward entrepreneurial professionalism in which the possession of managerial and entrepreneurial skills is increasingly valued by the professionals themselves, the professional practices are repositioned around a more business-like focus. (Boyce 2008: 87, cited in Formadi and Raffai 2009: 248)

TABLE 10.1 Definitions of professionalism

A NEW PROFESSIONALISM IN THE EVENTS INDUSTRY

Most stakeholders agree that, as a global industry, some sort of international standard or quality assurance needs to be introduced to the events industry, in order to monitor consistency and best practice. Many employers recognise the lack of professional qualifications for their employees, but are also unaware of what training courses are available and how they can gather the appropriate information. Consequently, most event training has been informal to date and does not necessarily result in a specific industry qualification or practical accreditation.

Whilst event employers are pleased to see that college and university courses are increasingly available and believe this is helping to professionalise the industry and equip learners for entry level into it, they also expressed concerns over a perceived lack of practical and industry experience and the extent to which some lecturers lack practical experience. They would like to see some formalisation around continuing professional development (CPD). This could take the form of accreditation in meetings (AIM) or alternative professional accreditation, for example a CPD qualification that would professionalise the industry, as well as facilitate progression routes and up-skill the workforce and suppliers.

In the UK, the Chartered Management Institute (CMI) has provided consultation and advice on how the Institute of Event Management (IEM) could operate within an educational and administrative framework. One short-term and relatively quick solution would be to develop a central CPD portal offering online and offline courses, designed to meet professional development needs. The course content could support the **core competencies** required by employers, professional bodies and sector skills councils. This would enable learners that enrol on bespoke courses to have access to a range of tools that help them identify skills needs, log learning hours and build a portfolio for assessment purposes. Rather than studying specific modules, existing event workers could claim for **Accreditation for Prior Experiential Learning (APEL)**. This portal could contain useful resources such as case studies, and study and e-learning material. There is also a need for this professional development to include regulatory content in order to protect the quality of services and the interests of both the employees and the client.

Core competencies a combination of multiple resources and skills that distinguish a business in the marketplace

Accreditation for Prior Experiential Learning (APEL) a mechanism of recognising an individual's expertise and prior experience

According to Brown (2014: 15) 'it's just that multiplicity and lack of common agreement that prevent the industry from being described as a profession'. However, some employers and event practitioners would argue that at this stage event management is still not a real profession. In order to determine whether there is a need or an impetus for the industry to progress to a professionalised industry, it would appear that further debate and discussion are needed.

QUALIFICATION DEVELOPMENT

Currently, there is a wide array of qualifications available to support work-based training, but no consistent **benchmarking** across the sector. The aim of higher education institutions is to accredit degrees in events management that can support skills development. The existing qualifications can be generic, for example health and safety, or sector-specific, for example food hygiene in catering. In some cases, the accreditation is industry-specific, such as certification in events management, or knowledge of temporary structures, such as pop-up stalls and marquees.

Benchmarking comparing one's business processes and performance metrics to industry bests and best practices from other companies

Although some **competence-based** qualifications are currently available to support continuing professional development, as previously mentioned, there are calls to

Competence-based an approach to teaching and learning more often used in learning concrete skills than abstract learning

develop these further. This could include more bespoke training packages developed to address specific skill needs. These courses could be standalone training programmes, accredited by a higher education institution or an awarding organisation. Considering the nature and history of the events market, it would appear there needs to be a consultation with industry to enable a better understanding of requirements at this level and whether the development of competence-based qualifications is the right solution.

One such bespoke training course is the MCI/CMP (Certified Meeting Professional) examinations. The Certified Meeting Professional (CMP) credential was developed by the Convention Industry Council (CIC) and recognises those who have achieved the industry's highest level of professionalism. The training is mostly delivered by internal staff with some external trainers. MCI also offers senior event staff the opportunity to achieve certification based on professional experience and a rigorous examination. The elite CMP community apparently now numbers more than 12,000 in 34 countries around the globe; however, the majority are currently North American based. To qualify as a candidate to take the CMP examination, staff members must fulfil the following three criteria:

- A minimum of three years' employment experience in meeting management
- Current, full-time employment in a meeting management capacity
- Responsibility and accountability for the successful completion of meetings.

As previously discussed, the need for professional well-educated staff within the event management industry has been driven by the need to develop the industry in a more strategic direction.

THE GROWTH OF INDUSTRY ASSOCIATIONS

Further indication of the existence of a professional event industry, is the growth and continuous development of industry associations. In the UK, the industry was previously served by the Travel, Tourism Services and Events National Training Organisation and more recently by People1st and the new Sector Skills Council (AEME 2016).

According to Crosetto and Salah (1997) and Kloss (1999: 71, cited in Arcodia and Reid's (2003) paper on the educational role of Arcodia and Reids (2003) paper on the role of Event Management Associations.

> the professional association exists to advance the standing of the members of the occupation or profession by setting educational and other standards governing the profession, advocating for public and private policies, aiding members in their professional development, and advancing professional practice through research and information dissemination.

There are now over 50 global associations representing different sectors of the events industry. This is because there are so many different skills and roles within the field. Some are specialist, others are general, but today event management associations are clearly providing a variety of educational opportunities to their members and have many networking opportunities and complimentary seminars to support and empower both new entrants and the existing events fraternity.

GRADUATE ENTRY, APPRENTICESHIPS AND OTHER RECOGNISED QUALIFICATIONS

BREAKDOWN ON UK/INTERNATIONAL EVENT DEGREE COURSES

Universities have put renewed emphasis on higher level skills and workforce development since the publishing of the Leitch report in 2006, so that higher education institutions have increased the focus on the employability of graduates after their studies. This has resulted in the design and implementation of more vocational programmes, the latest being foundation degrees and apprenticeships, where close liaison with employers, often with a period of industrial placement, is now part of the course design and required learning outcomes.

LEARNING THROUGH WORK

Work-based learning (WBL) has been an integral feature of higher education since the 1950s. Since that time, undergraduate courses have introduced a variety of programmes, ranging in duration, across a wide range of subject areas. Gray (2001) notes that placement courses have a relatively long history, where students attain skills and experience in the workplace linked to their subject domain. It is also recognised that with the increase in tuition fees, students today often need to work on a part-time basis whilst studying in order to finance their studies. Other schemes include building an element of assessed work experience into the course curriculum. Students are then usually required to submit some evidence of the work hours gained, together with some reflections and learning outcomes from their work-related role. Many events and hospitality courses are vocational in design and put the work-based, more practical aspects at the core of the programme.

REAL INSIGHT 10.1

VOCATIONAL COURSES IN CATERING

'I want to be a chef in a Michelin star restaurant and to work my way up in the industry. Always aim high!' Ashesh came to the UK three years ago after studying catering at college in his home country of Nepal. He always enjoyed watching cookery shows and competitions on TV, and knew he wanted to get into the industry. Since joining Eastleigh College, Ashesh has taken part in a variety of work experience placements and industry visits which have complemented his studies. His favourite experiences so far include taking part in the Holiday Inn takeover. Ashesh also gained a two-week work experience placement at the

(Continued)

Holiday Inn, where he got involved in front of house service, cooking in kitchens and managing the function facilities. Ashesh also enjoyed working with Michelin star chefs at Cambridge College, who taught him how to cook a 12-course menu focusing on fish as the main ingredient.

Working with employers and talented chefs has taught Ashesh a range of skills in the hospitality and catering industry, but his favourite part is the cooking! Over this year, Ashesh has competed in the WorldSkills regional and national competitions, where he has been required to create dishes of his own and display his culinary skills across a range of cuisines. Ashesh was chosen from the regional competitions in the summer of 2015 to progress onto the national competitions, where he was awarded a medal and invited to the next stage at the Skills Show in November.

Unfortunately, Ashesh was unable to compete in the global finals, but he is thrilled with the opportunities he has been given and what he has learned over the past few months. He said:

> This has been the toughest, hardest, but best experience I've ever had. It's so different to working at college – there's added time pressure which makes it mentally challenging. ... Competing in WorldSkills has helped me in so many ways, especially with formulating ideas for new recipes. You get to meet so many new people and talk about your industry, so it opens your mind to all the possibilities out there and different ways of doing things and encourages you to experiment and try something new.

PLACEMENT/'SANDWICH' COURSES

Traditionally, the student placement is a year long and is sandwiched between the course learning, usually at the end of the second or third year of study. In some programmes, the placement may be of a shorter duration or take the form of a vacation-based role or a series of shorter term work-based projects or part-time course-related work experience whilst studying. Recently there has been an increase in undergraduate programmes that allow students to opt for shorter work-based placements of about 6–10 weeks, or part-time work as part of the overall programme of study. A nominal wage is normally offered to the placement student by the employer, which helps off-set any course fees and to remunerate and incentivise the student for the hours worked whilst on placement.

Universities generally link a module related to course work which deals with the subject of learning through work. This provides the student with the opportunity to reflect on the skills and experience gained in the work placement. Students are normally visited by tutors during this time and assessed in their role together with the employer. This allows the placement tutor to deal with any potential problems the students may encounter. In many cases, the employer is happy to extend the placement or make a more permanent job offer to the student after graduating. It can be advantageous to the employer to assess the student's suitability for a long-term role from a safe stance and, having invested the time to train the student in the role, it can make sense to retain those students who have demonstrated the most promise.

STUDENT APPRENTICESHIPS

Previously, apprenticeships were only considered for traditional trades, such as plumbing, mechanics or hairdressing. However, they are now available in a range of subject disciplines, such as: business administration, development, consultancy, management, banking, leadership, finance, information technology (IT) and human resources (HR).

In the UK, more than 2.1 million apprenticeships have been created since 2010, which combine academic and practical training to provide new and attractive routes into the work environment. Backed by industry and top education institutions, they will help ensure the skills gap is being met in the future. Degree apprenticeships are similar to higher apprenticeships but differ in that they provide an opportunity to gain a full undergraduate (Level 6) or master's degree (Level 7). The courses are designed in partnership with employers, with part-time study taking place at a university or college. Apprentices split their time between university study and the workplace. The courses could take between three and six years to complete, depending on the level, though most take between two and four years, and involve part-time study at a college, university or an alternative training provider.

As with other apprenticeships, the cost of the course fees is shared between government and employers. This means the apprentice can earn a bachelors or even master's degree without paying any fees but earning a wage and getting real on-the-job experience in their chosen profession. As well as being suitable for school leavers as an alternative route to gaining a degree, the new qualifications are expected to strengthen the vocational pathway and be suitable for existing apprentices looking to progress in their career.

For the employer, especially small and medium-sized enterprises (SMEs), this provides a valuable opportunity to employ enthusiastic workers who will grow with the business, thus saving on recruitment fees. It also provides an ideal opportunity to train apprentices to the required industry standard. At the moment, the scheme only operates across England and Wales, although applications may be made from all parts of the UK. It is anticipated that the number of vacancies within the hospitality and tourism sectors will increase. In the future, this scheme is expected to extend to the area of event management and will be replicated on a global basis in other parts of the world.

Apprenticeship courses provide an excellent opportunity for those students who prefer to take a practical rather than an academic route into the events industry and earn money whilst studying for relevant qualifications. As with placement schemes, the advantages of being able to secure a job on completion of the degree apprenticeship cannot be underestimated for both the employee and the employer. Some of the advantages of this are that it:

- Delivers vocational training leading to a qualification
- Brings new skills, fresh ideas and creativity to the workplace
- Helps companies, especially SMEs, develop full-time staff
- Boosts productivity
- Benefits people at all stages of their career
- Helps companies attract, retain and motivate high-calibre staff
- Fills higher level skill gaps
- Trains existing and new employees to degree level or beyond
- Helps increase diversity in the workplace
- Increases new industry knowledge
- Allows the company to keep up with new technologies.

REMOTE STUDY OR DISTANCE LEARNING

Online learning is another viable option within further or higher education, allowing the student to learn the necessary event fundamentals without having to take whole days out of their busy schedule. This route could be ideal for mature or disabled students, or parents with childcare needs. It is also an alternative option for those already working but wishing to acquire the necessary skills and accreditation to change careers or improve career and promotion options.

In order to be successful within the events industry, an applicant needs resilience, tenacity and self-belief. They will also need to be able to multi-task, update social media feeds and organise marketing and promotional activities, as well as understand the legislation and health and safety and risk assessment elements that surround the industry today. Online learning can furnish anyone preferring not to study on a regular part-time or full-time programme the chance to obtain these valuable hard skills. The Open University and a new offshoot called FutureLearn work together with the world's top universities today, to create high quality online and **blended learning courses** across a range of disciplines. Studying remotely in this way is an alternative option to gain professional qualifications and pathways to other online degree courses.

Blended learning courses blended learning is an education course that combines online digital media with traditional classroom methods

PAID WORK EXPERIENCE

Many students who are studying for a degree in hospitality, events or tourism related courses today are increasingly looking for part-time paid employment to help fund them through their studies. According to the 2018 Department for Education and Skills Survey on student income and expenditure in the UK, 52% of full-time students were working at some point during study years one to three.

Among part-time students, this figure increased to 73%. This is a 'win–win' situation, as employers in the events and hospitality sector benefit from a flexible, cheap and trained pool of labour, whilst students are able to work to help finance their studies. Employing students on a part-time basis provides an attractive proposition to employers, allowing them to pay lower wages and reduce employee benefits as well as being able to increase or decrease hours in line with seasonal business demands.

The events and hospitality sector is ideal for part-time work, as seasonal adjustments provide employment opportunities for students at peak times, for example the period leading up to Christmas and the summer months.

Additional research indicates that, in addition to providing the student with financial rewards, regular part-time work also gives them the opportunity for personal development and networking with industry contacts. This might result in better employment prospects in the future. The college or university careers or placement services should be able to help students find paid work in relevant disciplines. It is also worth contacting local and national recruitment agencies, as well as regularly checking social media sites, such as LinkedIn, for any appropriate paid work available.

VOLUNTEERING

Volunteers tend to be used particularly at charitable, music, sporting and special events. Although the student or graduate gives their time usually out of generosity, volunteering can have many benefits. It is a great way to meet like-minded people, have a day out and enjoy an event for free, with only a low level of commitment. On a practical level, it is an excellent way to gain valuable event experience, self-esteem and confidence, which looks positive on any CV. Volunteering is a good way to network with relevant industry peers and contacts and is especially good for students and graduates who are looking to build up experience and knowledge of the events industry, as discussed in Chapter 1.

Volunteers are a great asset to the charitable sector, because of their expertise, availability and flexibility. Numerous charities now work closely with universities to ensure a consistent and skill-based stream of volunteers. However, for the event organiser, managing volunteers can be complicated, since by the very nature of volunteering, people give their time freely. The selection of volunteers is not always systematic and sometimes it is more a case of who feels like doing it, rather than who is best able to do it. Therefore, from a human resource perspective, recruiting and training can add to the complexity of managing a temporary events team.

For mega events, which require large numbers of volunteers, positions are usually advertised through schools, colleges, youth groups and online advertising. All age groups and demographics are considered, as volunteering can bring people back into the mainstream of work, allowing them to obtain the necessary skills for future paid employment.

Implementing a good human resource structure with a clear induction strategy is needed to monitor the volunteers and ensure overall customer satisfaction. When recruiting a volunteer base, it is important for the event manager to set out their expectations, including the purpose of the event, responsibilities and any remuneration. This will help create an atmosphere of trust, teamwork and respect. Event owners have started to set up bespoke online forums for the volunteers to help with any issues and information exchange about the event they are supporting, together with FAQs (frequently asked questions) and key training dates and schedules.

REAL INSIGHT 10.2

VOLUNTEERING AT THE NEW YORK MARATHON

Marta Fernandez, a 23-year-old graduate from Bilbao in Spain, wanted to experience the TCS New York City Marathon. She was spending some time in New York as part of her gap year. In 2016 she applied to volunteer through the J-1 Exchange Visitors Programme.

This is an initiative led by the US Department of State, which allows people from around the world to visit the United States on a special work or study visa, to stay for a period of time to learn skills for their future careers back home. Volunteerism has become a key part of the programme, as was evident when more than 1400 exchange visitors put on waterproof ponchos to man the water stations at miles 5 and 6 in Brooklyn and mile 18 in Harlem. This scheme now makes up 14% of the race's total volunteers.

SOURCE: Image courtesy of Exchanges Photos, via flickr.com.

Marta remarked on the experience: 'I made some great friends during the day. We cheered the runners and handed them out water as they passed by.' Some of the team were also holding out buckets to raise funds. She went on to say: 'I've watched the marathon on TV and online, but I've never seen it in real life. This race is one of the biggest events in NYC and I feel so lucky to experience it in such a multicultural environment.' Marta cheered and handed water out to the athletes in wheelchairs at the start of the race. She also got the opportunity to see the amazing costumes that some of the runners were wearing and saw at close hand some top athletes, including Olympic medallist and NYRR Team for Kids Ambassador Shalane Flanagan.

Marta added: 'We were still there when the final runner completed the marathon and saw the sweeper vans at the end. The runners really responded to our cheers. I will definitely volunteer again when I get back to Bilbao, as it's far more fun being a volunteer than a spectator and more rewarding too'.

INTERNSHIPS

An internship is a period of work experience that offers students and graduates valuable exposure to the working environment, often within a specific industry relating to their field of study. Internships can be as short as a week or as long as 12 months. They can be paid or voluntary; however, before starting an internship it is important to fully understand the remuneration available.

Internships can be found in a range of industry sectors. In events and hospitality, this might include a number of functional roles, such as sales, marketing, operations, design, production, management, IT, inbound and outbound groups, and many more. The internship is designed to furnish the graduate or employee with a variety of 'soft skills', including communication, personal effectiveness, presentation, creative problem solving and influencing skills.

'On-the-job' experience can often be as valuable as studying. It helps provide an understanding of the role and the work environment. Internships are great opportunities to speak directly to people who already have experience in the role. Internships test out skills in real-life situations and can provide an insight into a designated organisation or career path, allowing students to build on the theory learned at university, and helping to gain practical skills that will help strengthen their CV and increase their employability chances in future.

It is not unusual for career aspirations to change when faced with the true realities of a role. Internships can therefore be used to try a role out from a safe distance, before finally committing to a long-term career. This is also true for the employer, who can evaluate the graduate over time to decide whether they have the potential to offer a longer-term job role within the company or organisation. Following a successful internship, it is not unusual for employers to make a full-time job offer to their intern. Many employers use internships as a trial period and will already have plans to recruit on a permanent basis. For that reason, the intern should strive to make a good impression – turn up on time, be enthusiastic and show flexibility, adaptability and commitment.

Results from a recent survey conducted by Graduate Advantage (see allaboutcareers.com) indicate that internships do create jobs for graduates. The survey results showed that 81% of interns are now employed and 74% of those are either in permanent employment or on a long-term contract. Of these, 68% believe their internship helped them to gain their current position and an impressive 33% are still working with their internship organisation.

FREELANCE AND CONSULTANCY ROLES

Most event agencies use freelance staff on a regular basis. The nature of the events industry dictates that, as a seasonal industry, there are some periods that are busier than others in events. For this reason, it is sometimes more cost-effective for companies to recruit freelancers and contractors to work on a specific project, rather than employing a full-time member of staff and covering the cost of this overhead. Even though the freelancers' daily rates might be much higher than normal everyday staff rates at that level, it is still less expensive to hire them on a short-term contract and use their specific skills as and when required. Working in this way also has benefits for the freelancer or contractor too. It offers them a flexible way of working, particularly if they have family or other commitments. It can also provide variety, independence and freedom, plus new challenges, without the burden of office politics.

As a new entrant or graduate, it is quite unusual to start out as an event freelancer. This is because event employers tend to recruit freelance staff for their expertise, acumen and specific skills. However, there are still some freelance roles available for less experienced or junior event planners. When starting a career as a freelance events manager, it is important to be prepared to work on all types of projects. The longer the freelancer has been working in this way, the more they will be known and contacted. In time, the contractor or freelancer may be in a position to choose the projects they most want to work on. However, sometimes it is a case of working on a project just because it fits in with their timescale and availability.

Professionals who have either worked for an event agency or an in-house event division of a company, generally have the experience and knowledge to be able to adapt and deal with any situation. They tend to act as **trouble-shooters** and problem solvers. Sometimes they are expressly recruited to lead a fairly inexperienced team. However, most event agencies need freelancers to bolster their workforce when managing larger projects, for many roles including delegate and project management, or for additional on-site support.

Trouble-shooters skilled workers employed to locate trouble and make adjustments as necessary

There are also specialist event recruitment agencies that place freelancers, as well as permanent staff, on medium- or short-term contracts. Another way to actively network is by joining networks on social media. There are several groups available to join to share information, post CVs, contacts and inside information. One example is a LinkedIn group called Freelance Event Managers UK, which is a discussion forum with nearly 3000 members. Other similar freelance groups and forums, such as Freelance Event Professionals and Freelance Nation, also exist globally.

One of the advantages of freelancing is that it may be possible to accrue more free time or longer holidays than fixed-term employees, providing the freelancer has planned their time well and is in constant demand. However, it is worth noting in some cases that the opposite can also be true. Freelancers or contractors do not like to refuse any work or project in case they do not get approached again by that company, so sometimes tend to take on every project offered and end up working all year, without taking any leave.

For those deciding to pursue event projects as a freelancer or contractor, it may be advisable to set up as a limited company. The contract worker will need to understand their personal legal liability, such as tax requirements, and whether they need to register for VAT. As the contractor will be working for a variety of companies, rather than receiving salary through PAYE, they invoice the client for their time worked. They are therefore responsible for paying their own tax through self-assessment.

The annual tax return has now been abolished in favour of real-time online accounting. This can be a complicated and time-consuming process. At times therefore, it is advisable for freelancers or contractors to outsource to a tax specialist or accountant to help file tax returns and deal with other tax-related matters. The accountant will advise and instruct on how to claim for any costs and overheads incurred and ensure the right amount of tax is paid at the end of each tax year, and so on. It is important for the contractor to ensure that they have sufficient funds available to pay the amount of tax due, so being organised and having the skill to plan ahead are important attributes for any freelancer or contract worker.

OTHER ROUTES INTO THE EVENTS INDUSTRY

This chapter has talked about the routes into the events industry through undergraduate and postgraduate degree courses, apprenticeships and the accredited courses. However, there may be other routes into the events industry that do not require these qualifications. It may be possible to progress to a career in events through a secretarial or PA role within a corporate organisation. It may also be possible to enter into the industry in a junior role such as administrator and progress to managerial level. As the events industry is versatile and flexible, it is also possible to transfer from one sector of the hospitality industry, such as hotels, catering or tourism, into a more specifically event-related role.

There are also opportunities for the entrepreneur who sets up their own events company. They should spend some time initially evaluating the competition and trying to establish a Unique Selling Proposition (USP). This route is not without risk but can lead to financial reward and greater personal satisfaction. All these routes to enter a career in the events industry are possible; however, it is becoming an increasingly competitive and sought-after career choice and one that people aspire to, rather than just drifting in to. Therefore, a combination of relevant qualifications and proven industry experience seem to be the best formula to ensure an employer will want to take the application to the next level and beyond.

GO ONLINE

Tips for starting up an event business as an entrepreneur can be viewed in the online Appendix as Table 10.1.

SKILLS AND ATTRIBUTES FOR A CAREER IN EVENTS

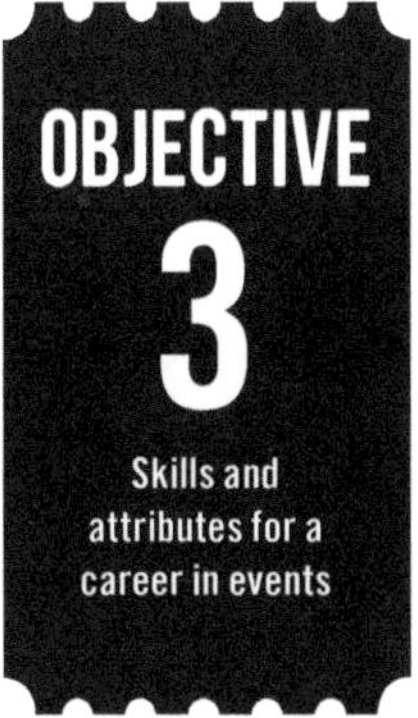

WHAT ARE 'SOFT SKILLS'?

In an increasingly competitive job market, the focus is shifting to the skills employers expect from today's university graduates. Various studies have continued to highlight the need for universities and colleges to improve graduate skills in readiness for the workplace. This has been in direct response to employer demand. University degree programmes have continued to examine the impact that skills acquisition has on a student, and their subsequent transfer to the workplace.

This has led practitioners from a variety of subject disciplines to adopt a more 'skills-based' approach to learning. These skills are not only subject or occupationally specific, but more generic or what we might term 'transferable' or 'soft' skills. These can be used either in the context of academic study or in the world of work. These generic or transferable skills can be gained through education, but also from previous jobs, voluntary work, sport, hobbies and interests. Some of the 'soft skills' that can be developed, either in an academic setting or in the workplace, include, according to Little (2000):

- Communication and interpersonal skills
- Social skills
- Problem-solving skills
- Team-working skills
- Organisational skills
- Project management skills
- Customer skills
- Financial awareness skills.

Additionally, there are behavioural skills or character traits that can be integrated into the learning experience, to prepare students for working life by familiarising them with the workplace culture. Personal attributes include areas such as trustworthiness, adaptability, commitment, integrity and the ability to deal with stress.

Harvey et al. (1997) suggest that employers found that graduates who had undertaken a period of work as part of their degree programme, possessed more of the skills needed for a successful career, such as team working, maturity, communication and interpersonal skills, as well as an enhanced awareness of the workplace culture.

In order to demonstrate to potential employers that they possess these skills and attributes, the applicant should provide examples of how their skill set matches the qualities and expertise stipulated within the job advertisement. They should also provide the employer with examples of how they have demonstrated the required skills in a previous work setting. It is a good idea too for the applicant to highlight the skills they have and those to work on in future. The applicant's curriculum vitae (CV) should be adjusted accordingly to reflect these skills, once the necessary experience has been acquired.

WHAT ARE 'HARD SKILLS'?

'Hard skills' are subject-specific skills and knowledge that will be required for a predetermined career path. Unlike 'soft skills', these are more tangible and generally learned through some form of education or training. Since many industries and professions have a specific list of required abilities to properly perform the job, they can also be termed job-specific skills. In order to secure an interview, it is essential for job seekers to list any 'hard skills' acquired on their resume or CV, and where possible to include evidence of these in practice.

Within event management, these skills might encompass areas such as destination knowledge, event policy, legislation, venue health and safety awareness, food and catering hygiene proficiency, and so on. University degrees and other event training courses normally seek to include a mixture of 'soft transferable skills' and more 'subject specific hard skills' within the programme. Gray (2001) notes that degree courses with placements enable students to attain hard skills and experience in the workplace linked to their subject domain. This is also the case for vocational courses, placements, work experience and internships. According to Tallantyre (2008), ongoing industry engagement between employers and university lecturers is also important when furnishing students with hard skills. This provides a valuable opportunity to update staff on the latest workplace methods and technology, thus keeping their own industry skills current and relevant.

HOW TO RECORD AND DEVELOP SKILLS

There are a number of self-assessment activities that can help aspiring event employees to reflect on, evaluate and develop these attributes and skills. Keeping a log of experiences is a valuable method for documenting skill acquisition. The log can then be added to and can be a useful tool to review previous work experience, to identify any gaps, to draw meaningful conclusions and to plan the next steps in learning through work.

- Working to deadlines and under pressure
- Negotiation skills
- Numeracy skills
- Decision making
- Research skills
- Flexibility and adaptability
- Ethical awareness and judgement
- Leadership and initiative
- Working with others
- Improving own learning and performance
- Problem solving and creativity
- Organisational skills
- Communication
- IT proficiency
- Languages

TABLE 10.2 Skills that employers require from event graduates and new employees

SOURCING AND APPLYING FOR EVENT-RELATED WORK

SOURCING EVENT-RELATED WORK AFTER GRADUATING

In an increasingly competitive job market, graduate employability is often difficult to find, particularly in the first year of leaving university, so having a clear strategy to help find that first full-time job is recommended. Event- or hospitality-related work may be available through the university careers service; today most universities offer post-graduation support for students. It is also advisable to start building contacts and networking within the industry. This may involve attending industry or association events, or career and placement fairs, with the aim of getting noticed.

Portals such as 'Job Match' and 'Indeed' help give an indication of career paths available in the industry. 'LinkedIn' has now developed into a recruitment as well as a networking platform. It is therefore important to register on the site, as well as on other social media channels. It is also worth remembering that the first job does not necessarily tie the jobseeker into a particular career path on a long-term basis. This may be a good time to explore all options and avenues and widen the search for graduate jobs.

There are also a number of specialised event management agencies that job seekers can register with in order to search for jobs and event roles. These agencies will require a current CV and may advise changes to it, based on their expertise and the position applied for. In some cases, the CV may need to be tailored each time to a specific role. It is possible that the agency may want to meet with the applicant before putting them forward for any available positions. The agency often acts as a 'go between', for the applicant and the employer, setting up the interview and negotiating the remuneration package, and so on. It is always advisable for the jobseeker to spend time with the recruitment agency, to try to build up a relationship with them. The agency fee for securing the placement is paid by the employer and may be charged out as a percentage of the new employee's overall salary. This is normally subject to them receiving a full-time permanent contract, after the initial probation period, which can be between three and six months, or in some cases as long as a year.

INTERVIEW SKILLS AND WORK EXPERIENCE

Being prepared and well organised are likely attributes of event management applicants, so compiling the correct documentation for the interview should be relatively straightforward. Making sure that the CV is constantly updated to reflect all work experience gained is also advised. The applicant should thoroughly research the company in advance of the interview and determine whether they have a mission statement or any core values. It is crucial to meticulously check the job description, or specification, to try to gauge exactly what the role is and what the employer is looking for, to plan out a strategy to demonstrate their skills and experience to best match the job advertised.

If possible, the jobseeker should prepare and rehearse a typical interview scenario with a trusted friend, colleague or tutor. Careers services or course tutors may be able to provide support in this area, possibly by arranging a 'mock' interview with the candidate in advance to prepare them for the type of questions they might be asked. It is good practice to anticipate likely questions and responses to the questions and provide examples and anecdotal evidence from previous work or volunteering experience. The interview process can inevitably be stressful, so for peace of mind and competitive advantage, the applicant needs to be as prepared as possible. It is recommended to look up directions on how to reach the interview, take plenty of drinking water, dress professionally for the interview and allow plenty of time to get there. It is also a good idea to bring an extra copy of the most recent CV to the interview, and a logbook detailing any event projects worked on, either whilst at college or university, or in the workplace, including any volunteering experience. If testimonials or references are available, they can be brought to the interview, although references will usually be sought by the recruitment agency or employer after the interview stage. Preparation is the key to success and the guidelines shown in Figure 10.2 should be followed.

Review skills, experiences and qualities

Check CV for content, consistency and accuracy

Anticipate questions and identify relevant examples

Prepare key selling points on the brand that is YOU

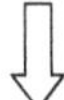

Research the organisation, by looking at websites, reports, articles, company literature and relevant press articles

Research the job and occupational area and potential progress paths

Source contacts that have knowledge of the organisation or sector

Make a personal visit or telephone call in advance

Prepare appropriate questions and demonstrate knowledge of current issues

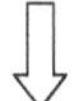

Practise a 'mock interview' with a friend, colleague, tutor or placement, or careers officer

FIGURE 10.2 Interview preparation

It is essential for the job seeker to prepare a CV, a work portfolio and other documentation in advance before registering with a recruitment agency, as a suitable position may be available immediately.

WHAT IS THE PURPOSE OF A CURRICULUM VITAE (CV)?

A curriculum vitae (CV) comes from Latin and when translated literally means 'the course of one's life'. This gives a big clue as to what a CV should be about – a person's life to date, but with most of the focus on the working life and outline of their educational and professional history. The purpose of a CV is to inform the employer about previous education, work experience, skills and interests and to promote these qualities in an attempt to persuade the employer to invite the applicant to interview. Most of all, a CV is a marketing tool to help sell the applicant to an employer. A curriculum vitae should be tailored to each position applied for and enclosed, together with a covering letter, whenever:

- An employer asks for a CV
- An employer states 'apply to …' without specifying the format
- Making speculative applications.

RECOMMENDATIONS FOR WRITING A GOOD CV

It is always advisable to keep a CV as brief as possible, preferably on two sides of paper, although the more work experience gained, the longer the CV is likely to be. Opinion is divided on whether it is good practice to enclose a photograph, but this may depend on the nature of the job and is by no means a pre-requisite. Professional language should be used throughout the CV, which should be proofed for any spelling errors before sending.

GO ONLINE

See the online Appendix (Table 10.2) for a handy checklist of items that should be included in any CV. Then, head over to the handouts section to access a sample CV.

DID YOU KNOW?

The average recruiter spends just 20 seconds looking at a CV.

PREPARING A WORK PORTFOLIO DETAILING PREVIOUS EXPERIENCE

It can be useful to take a work portfolio to the interview as this may make the jobseeker stand out from the competition. For example, it would be relevant to bring details on a practical university project, or experience gained on a specific event or events, in a previous work role. This might include any live event experience, where the portfolio could provide information on the following aspects that the applicant could discuss:

- Team information, including roles and responsibilities
- Operational considerations such as:
    - logistical and financial details
    - staff briefing sheets
    - venue information
    - accreditation
    - audience profiles, etc.

It is also beneficial to include as many visual examples of previous events worked on as possible, together with any testimonials from employers or clients, to provide additional evidence and lend credibility to the application.

WHAT SHOULD BE INCLUDED IN THE COVER LETTER?

When applying to jobs independently, a covering email or letter, together with a copy of a recent CV, should be sent. The covering letter or email should be brief and to the point. It should be written as a courtesy and should be focused on the specific job advertised. The letter should contain any additional information not included in a generic CV and should convey enthusiasm and passion for the role advertised. In some cases, it may be worth speculatively submitting a CV to larger organisations that tend to recruit new entrants on an ongoing basis.

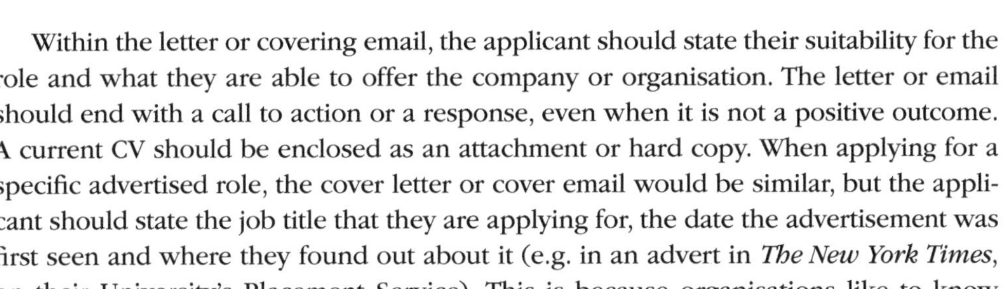

GO ONLINE

See a sample speculative covering letter or email along with the same CV in the handouts section of the online resources available at **study.sagepub.com/quick.**

Within the letter or covering email, the applicant should state their suitability for the role and what they are able to offer the company or organisation. The letter or email should end with a call to action or a response, even when it is not a positive outcome. A current CV should be enclosed as an attachment or hard copy. When applying for a specific advertised role, the cover letter or cover email would be similar, but the applicant should state the job title that they are applying for, the date the advertisement was first seen and where they found out about it (e.g. in an advert in *The New York Times*, on their University's Placement Service). This is because organisations like to know which of their advertising sources are attracting the most applicants. A covering letter or email for a specified role should clearly state the reasons why:

- The applicant is interested in this type of work or this particular job
- The company attracts them
- They would value the opportunity to work for this particular organisation
- They are the right candidate for the job.

The applicant should focus on the relevant skills, knowledge and expertise that best match the role advertised, and provide examples using their most recent qualifications and work experience as evidence.

HOW TO CONDUCT A GOOD INTERVIEW

All interviews are structured conversations; a meeting with an objective, aimed at gathering data about the applicant. Interviews are a very popular method of recruiting new staff, but do not always accurately predict whether or not a person will be able to carry out the advertised role sufficiently. There are many reasons why this is the case, including lack of training and experience, and fundamental errors in perception on behalf of the interviewer/s. The employer's objective is to find the best person for the job and to review the candidate's experience and abilities to find out:

- Can they do the job? (Skills, abilities, qualifications)
- Will they do the job? (Interest, attitude and motivation)
- How will they fit into the organisation? (Personality)

The employee's objective is to impress the employer and prove that they are the most suitable candidate for this position, to assess the position on offer and how it fits in with their career plans. Generally, there are three types of questions that are asked at interviews, which fall into the categories shown in Table 10.3.

Biographical	These questions are aimed at understanding how a person has got to this point, to assess if they are ready or experienced enough for the role, e.g. 'How many years' experience do you have in the events industry?'
Competency based	These questions are designed to be far more specific, to illustrate the attributes and skills of the applicant, e.g. 'Describe an occasion where you had to plan or organise something'.
Situational	These are questions which require the interviewee to respond to scenario or pre-set criteria, e.g. 'Describe a situation where you had a difficult decision to make and explain how you resolved this'.

TABLE 10.3 Interview question types

The competencies that the company are looking for and will want to see demonstrated through an open exchange in the interview are:

- Adaptability
- Innovation
- Teamwork
- Initiative
- Knowledge of the business
- Results driven
- Ability to solve problems and make difficult decisions.

1. What do you know about the organisation/company?
2. Why do you want to join our organisation/company?
3. What skills do you think you could bring to the role?
4. Describe yourself (in one word).
5. Why did you choose your university/course and what factors influenced your choice?
6. What work experience have you gained that might help you with this role?
7. Describe a situation where you worked well as part of a team.
8. Describe a situation where you have led a team or taken responsibility.
9. What are your strengths and weaknesses?
10. Describe a situation in which you used initiative to solve a problem.
11. What has been your greatest achievement?
12. What would you do in the following scenario ...?
13. Describe a situation in which you dealt with confrontation (for example with a difficult customer).
14. Describe a situation in which you influenced or motivated people.
15. What do you expect to be doing in five years' time?
16. What other careers have you considered/applied for?
17. Who else have you applied to/got interviews with?
18. What do you like doing in your spare time?
19. Would you be prepared to relocate if necessary?
20. Have you got any questions about the role?

TABLE 10.4 Typical interview questions

GO ONLINE

Further tips for interviews can be found in Table 10.3 in the online Appendix.

PROVIDING REFERENCES AND REFEREES

It is good practice to include two referees when applying for a job. One should be a business or work manager and the other could be a personal contact. It is fine to just provide their contact details, but it is good practice to seek the referee's permission in advance, as the employer may contact them direct before notifying the applicant. It may be worth asking a previous employer or college tutor to write a general testimonial, in letter or email form, for when a reference is required at short notice. Generally, the employer will approach the referee by email and may ask specific questions about the potential candidate.

GO ONLINE

These are generally a combination of open and closed questions regarding their honesty, punctuality, integrity, skills and attitude that can be accessed, as detailed in the sample reference form in the handouts section of the online resources.

THE ROLE OF HUMAN RESOURCES IN EVENTS AND HOSPITALITY

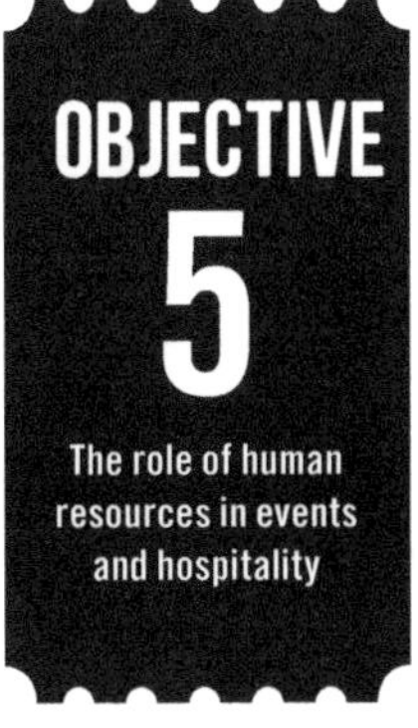

WHAT IS THE FUNCTION OF HUMAN RESOURCES?

> The design, implementation and maintenance of strategies to manage people for optimum business performance including the development of policies and processes to support these strategies and the evaluation of the contribution of people to the business. (Mullins 2010)

The role of human resources (HR) within a company is varied but may also depend largely on its size and structure. In a smaller event company, there may be no need for a specific HR manager or division. There are often elements of human resource management in every manager's or supervisor's job, and this function may be handled by the line manager or another administrative role within the organisation.

Generally, a line manager will be concerned with the actual implementation of policies and procedures, in so far as they affect their team and event operations, whereas an HR specialist will also be involved in the bigger picture for the organisation, setting and implementing these policies in the first place, as part of an ongoing organisational strategy. The role of a HR division or department generally involves:

- Recruitment and selection
- Learning and talent development/training
- Planning and succession

- Supporting the production of the job description
- Procuring the best recruitment method
- Provision of employee contracts
- Ensuring the quality of the induction process
- Provision of fair treatment for employees
- Provision of equal opportunities
- Managing diversity
- Motivating workers to achieve improved performance
- Employee counselling
- Talent management
- Employee well-being
- Payment and reward of employees.

WHAT TASKS AND ISSUES WILL AN HR MANAGER DEAL WITH?

An HR specialist can be involved in a wide range of issues, regardless of whether they operate in the events and hospitality sectors or other industries, and may operate at a higher level in the organisation. They will generally be responsible for supporting the organisation to achieve its strategic objectives and will also be required to offer specialist advice, administration and support to all staff, as well as advising personnel on company policy. The route to this role would normally involve obtaining relevant accreditation through CPD training and a relevant professional qualification, i.e. various levels of CIPD accreditation, in order to be able to fulfil all aspects of the role. Typical activities that might be undertaken by a HR department are:

- Training and staff induction
- Conducting job appraisals and performance monitoring
- Negotiation of salaries/pay increments
- Disciplining individuals
- Dealing with grievances
- Dismissal/redundancy.

TRAINING AND STAFF INDUCTION

The function of a company's HR or training division is to formulate a training policy and approved budget for the approval of the general manager and the company board. The Board should be kept informed of the implementation of the training policy, as well as receiving regular reports from the HR division on income and expenditure. Responsibilities of the HR role may involve the identification and review of all employee training requirements and procedures. The training or HR department of an organisation should keep abreast of the changing needs of all their employees, at all grades and categories. Their role is generally to support and encourage a culture of learning, identify the training or learning needs of the individual or department, and analyse how best to deliver the training or development course. Providing adequate staff training should help to build a sustainable business fit for the organisation, to meet their present and future needs. Staff training might be required at the induction stage, for a staff refresher course or following any new assignments or work responsibilities.

Continuous training in the workplace

Changes in event industry laws or regulations may demand ongoing employee training. This is particularly the case in the events industry, where legislation, such as The Bribery Act 2010, The Disability Discrimination Act 2010 and The Data Protection Act 2018 (see Chapter 9) may have significant impact on the accepted professional conduct of employees. Health and safety awareness should also be built into induction training. If the HR division is not able to provide any of the training requirements internally, they should work in partnership with educational institutions and training centres to provide this.

Part of the training function of any HR division is the preparation of operating and training manuals, other publications, teaching aids and the necessary material required for employee training. The training division of any large event company, agency or supplier should draw up a programme that aims to develop the internal staff members by:

- Supporting and encouraging a culture of learning
- Identifying the training or learning needs of the employee
- Analysing how best to deliver these needs
- Developing a training or development programme and evaluating its success
- Improving employees' knowledge, skills and attitudes to work
- Increasing output and sales, and employee loyalty
- Streamlining the recruitment process
- Reducing breakages, waste of materials and possible misuse of equipment
- Reducing accidents, absenteeism and staff turnover
- Providing less stress on management issues
- Planning future succession
- Building the brand and the image of the company to transmit to the outside world.

A key element of any organisation's training and learning strategy is targeting the long-term development of those identified as exceptionally high-performing or high-potential individuals, also known as 'talent', who are critical to long-term business success. To ensure a sustainable, successful organisation, HR would typically adopt an organisational strategy which includes the use of techniques, such as mentoring programmes with senior leaders, in-house development courses and project-based learning. This type of learning differs from training, as it seeks to balance the organisational needs with the individual's career management aspirations. This focuses on workforce capabilities, skills or competencies, and aligning roles to the people in the company, rather than just allocating them to existing roles, and allows the staff an ongoing learning platform within the workplace. Ongoing training is necessary in order to consistently innovate and make all staff within the organisation adaptable to change and self-development.

Staff induction programmes

A well-planned induction programme helps to integrate new employees into the organisation and to foster good staff relations and a sense of belonging. Induction training is important, as it helps to build up a two-way channel of communication between management and workers. It is usually undertaken by the HR department of any company or organisation and is designed to take place preferably on the first day, or even a week before the new entrant starts their job role. This formal orientation programme may take a day to deliver, or in some cases up to a week or longer. It should be designed to introduce new employees to the organisation and its policies, particularly regarding health and safety. Induction training normally covers the following:

- A brief history of the company, the nature of the business and its operation
- The company's organisational and reporting structure
- Policies and procedure
- Products and services
- Location of employee facilities
- Safety measures
- Grievances procedures
- Benefits and services for the employee
- Disciplinary procedures
- Opportunities for training, promotions and transfers.

During the induction training, the human resources or personnel officer should impart the information detailed above, together with some background detail on the company or organisation's current position in the industry, the company's mission statement, values and culture. More practical aspects, such as explaining any benefits the employee may be eligible for, such as annual leave, time in lieu, work breaks and rest periods, should also be included.

It is also an opportune time to go through the company first aid and health and safety regulations. Every induction session should include detailed fire, accident and emergency procedures training. Additionally, the session should cover a breakdown on company reporting structures, the probation and appraisal process and any disciplinary details. Most companies will provide staff with a manual during induction, itemising the above areas in more detail. This manual can be kept for future reference and built upon with any changes, additions or amendments.

CONDUCTING JOB APPRAISALS AND PERFORMANCE MONITORING

Further key functions that should be regularly undertaken by the human resources manager are job evaluation and appraisal, as 'a method of determining on a systematic basis the relative importance of a number of jobs' (ACAS 2012). Work appraisal provides a basis for a 'fair and orderly grading structure' but does not necessarily determine actual pay. Job appraisals tend to be held with staff once or twice annually and allow the line manager to discuss the staff member's performance, identify their strengths and weaknesses, find out what their aspirations and ambitions are and work out the quickest route to get there. Appraisals should be a positive experience, allowing both sides to have a positive, open and honest discussion, aimed at building the employee's career and potentially even leading to promotion or a pay increase.

NEGOTIATION OF SALARIES/PAY INCREMENTS

It is also the function of a personnel or HR manager to negotiate salaries and pay increments with employees. This could be in the recruitment stage, where the applicant may have a specific salary in mind. It might be necessary for the HR manager to negotiate back and forth with the candidate, until a mutually agreeable pay deal can be reached. Employers need to offer pay and conditions that will attract and retain good people. Employees also need to feel that their pay is 'fair'. Salary and other benefits can be used to reward individuals on merit and their worth to the organisation, in order to achieve organisational goals (Kearns 2000). The final package offered may include flexible benefits, allowing employees more choice on how they would like to be remunerated. For example, these benefits might include the opportunity to trade some pay for more holidays, a company car, flexible working hours, or a work from home policy.

Pay increases and promotions within an organisation may be awarded to an employee due to an increased grade, length of tenure in a company or seniority. Although remuneration tends to be linked to historical practices, pay and reward can also be used to apply 'pressure' on employee performance. It is often the case that employees leave one company and join a competitor because they are enticed by a better salary package. As the cost of recruiting and training a new staff member cannot be underestimated, HR specialists should aim to implement pay and reward strategies that will encourage and reward employees, attract new talent and aid the retention of existing staff.

DISCIPLINARY PROCEDURES

Discipline procedures can make a positive contribution to organisational performance and need not be viewed solely as negative, if used correctly, as they can help good employee relations and staff retention. Different countries will have their own governing bodies; however, within the UK, the disciplinary and grievances policy guidelines used within companies need to comply with the Advisory, Conciliation and Arbitration Service (ACAS) code of practice.

Within event and hospitality organisations, disciplinary and grievance procedures can be used as a preventative measure to avoid losing time, disruption and possible bad publicity caused by tribunal cases. The procedure should clearly state the disciplinary actions which may be taken and specify levels of authority for different layers of management. They should also provide information and evidence to persons subject to proceedings, prior to a disciplinary hearing. Within the workplace, disciplinary offences tend to occur in areas such as:

- Absenteeism
- Timekeeping
- Poor performance
- Contravening health and safety policies
- Internet misuse and abuse
- Theft
- Sexism
- Racism
- Fighting
- Threatening behaviour
- Alcohol/drug abuse.

HR can carry out either formal or informal actions, as part of the disciplinary procedure, and should inform the employee which course of action will be taken and make them aware of the appeals procedure. ACAS recommends mediation at each stage and some organisations include this as a formal part of the procedure. An informal action is normally the most appropriate way of dealing with alleged minor misconduct or unsatisfactory performance. This may just involve the supervisor or manager having a quiet word with the individual and can be a quick and easy way of sorting out a problem.

A formal route takes longer to implement. This requires a more in-depth investigation of the issue, followed by a letter to the employee, with any supporting documents. A meeting would then be scheduled between the employee and the HR manager, which may lead to further disciplinary or non-disciplinary action. After this meeting, the employee would receive a first written warning, or improvement note from HR. If the situation did not improve, a final written warning would be issued. In cases where no improvement is recorded, it could lead to dismissal or some other penalty. The employee would have an opportunity for representation at the meeting and a formal appeal procedure from a work colleague, companion or union representative, who is permitted to state or summarise the worker's case, to discuss points with the worker, to ask any questions of witnesses and to respond to any views expressed on the worker's behalf. Gross misconduct is a far more serious allegation. Any of the following allegations could lead to dismissal, even for a first offence:

- Theft
- Deliberate damage
- Fraud
- Incapacity to work because of drugs or alcohol
- Physical assault
- Sexual harassment
- Racial harassment
- Serious infringement of health and safety rules.

DEALING WITH GRIEVANCES

Grievances are complaints made by one employee against another. This may be for claims of unfair or discriminatory treatment, failure to act within the designated procedures, or a belief that the employer has failed to meet a common law duty of care (Banfield and Kay 2012). An employee may still raise a grievance against individuals, or the organisation itself, within 12 months of leaving the company, or indefinitely in severe cases, such as sexual harassment. All companies need to have a grievances procedure in place.

The employee should raise their grievance in writing with the immediate supervisor. An initial meeting should be set up between the line manager, a HR representative and the employee raising the grievance. If it is not possible to resolve the grievance following the meeting, the employee can request a meeting with a higher-level manager. Employers should ensure that the worker is aware of their right to be accompanied at the meeting and that mediation is possible at any stage. A Grievances

Procedure Rights of Appeal should be included at each stage and any records made should be kept confidential.

The employer must take reasonable action to protect employees from any harmful or damaging experiences. Most grievances are never formally raised with management, but the employee tends to leave the company as a result of the grievance. Even a line manager or HR specialist may not know the true reasons for someone leaving but staying in touch and encouraging the employee to speak about the issues first may prevent them leaving.

Exit interviews conducted by HR can identify any unacceptable situations. The risk of losing an employee in this way can be damaging to any event business, as they may join a competitor and could take valuable business with them. Industry contacts take time and hard work to build and maintain. Moreover, these grievances are now more visible to the wider world since the increase of social media.

DEMOTIONS/DISMISSALS/REDUNDANCIES

Another function of HR or personnel is to take action for demotions, dismissals and redundancies (as shown in Table 10.5):

Suspension	• When an employee is not permitted to work for a defined period of time, and pay is suspended. • This tends to be in situations of alleged employee misconduct, which need further investigation. • Employees are not permitted to apply their leave toward a suspension without pay.
Dismissal	• This is when an employee receives an involuntary termination of employment.
Demotion	• Often due to misconduct or poor performance. • The employee normally receives a decrease in the salary within their current pay grade, or is placed in a position at a lower pay grade.
Redundancies	• At some stage of their careers, most HR professionals will be involved in managing job losses. • The role of HR is to plan and scope the numbers likely to be involved and then agree some financial terms and payments for the employees, including their statutory rights. • Employees will normally be invited to volunteer for redundancy in the first instance. • Other involuntary redundancies are often necessary. • Formal notification in writing needs to be sent out to those selected for redundancy. • Sufficient time should be allowed for any appeal and to allow the employees to seek alternative employment. • It is often the function of HR to offer those made redundant, outplacement support, counselling and career coaching, dependent on their job level. • Guidance and advice should be available from the HR team to help redundant staff to source future work in the industry.

TABLE 10.5 Demotions/dismissals/redundancies

THE ROLE OF HUMAN RESOURCES IN THE RECRUITMENT PROCESS

In larger organisations, it is usually the role of the HR manager to research the role and gather the necessary information for any new position. They would also tend to write the job description and decide what skills, attributes and previous expertise to include in the job specification. Regardless of who puts the wording together, that person needs to be skilled enough to write a job description and to understand the role thoroughly. They will need to provide information on how the job links to other existing functions in the company. The job specification or description will vary, according to the nature and complexity of the role being advertised.

GO ONLINE

In the events industry, a sample job description might look as demonstrated in Table 10.4 in the online Appendix.

The following are characteristics that will help be successful in the recruitment process.

1. Attributes of candidate
2. Previous relevant experience
3. Relevant accreditation and qualifications
4. Skills, competencies and knowledge
5. Career development potential

TABLE 10.6 Five characteristics for successful recruitment

RECRUITMENT AND SELECTION

The catalyst for recruiting for a role within an event organisation is often when someone leaves. It may also be that, due to winning a new contract or event tender, more staff are required. Sometimes it is necessary to recruit due to a company reorganisation, or restructure, such as cutting management layers or hiring more graduates. With larger event and hospitality companies, recruitment could be linked to a longer term strategy of workforce planning. For example, the organisation may decide to recruit an annual intake of new graduates to guarantee a diverse range of skills within the company, rather than just focusing on their short-term needs.

Whilst recruitment is about attracting people from an appropriate talent pool, selection is concerned with the rational process of deciding which person to hire. For both procedures, there are basic guidelines which need to be followed. Employing staff for events is just like any other business that employs staff. Most recruitment systems will be simple, with stages that can be followed as a process, whenever there is a vacancy to be filled. These processes can be monitored and adapted with experience.

The process should be cost-efficient, as it is estimated, according to ACAS (Advisory, Conciliation and Arbitration Service), the average cost of recruiting and losing an employee in the UK is circa. £4500. For this reason, it is important to think of it as an opportunity to potentially review and redesign the position and to develop a strategy to recruit a suitable candidate, with the right skills base. It is also an opportunity to analyse the range of skills needed for the role and to determine the possibility of merging two jobs, or make the role part-time or job share. It is also an opportune time to consider whether the staff member might be able to work on a freelance or contract basis, work from home, or whether the role could actually become automated or dispensed with, in order to reduce overhead and salary costs.

It is worth spending time analysing the role and to treat recruitment as an investment, possibly by outsourcing to a professional event recruitment agency who will be able to use their expertise to employ the optimum candidate at the outset. This is particularly important, as recruiting staff that are wrong for the organisation can lead to:

- Increased labour turnover
- Increased costs for the organisation
- Lowering of morale in the existing workforce
- Discontentment and unrest
- Poor quality delivery/work ethic
- Severing the work contract voluntarily or involuntarily.

The recruitment process should be cost-effective in method and resources, in order to produce enough suitable candidates, but not too many. It should ensure identification of the most suitable candidate for the job and the organisation. The recruitment process should be deemed to be fair, so that the candidate is appointed on merit alone without prejudice. However, when appointing new staff, regrettably internal politics can and does often affect the ultimate decision.

RECRUITMENT METHODS

There is a varied selection of recruitment methods used today to attract potential job applicants. These include:

- Internal application
- Personal recommendation of a friend or colleague
- Internal website/bespoke websites
- Employment agencies – job centres, career fairs and events
- Institutions, universities/further education/graduate fairs.

THE SELECTION PROCESS

Selection is about making choices at various stages of the recruitment process. The initial selection phase might involve reviewing an application form or a CV, a face-to-face interview, a psychological assessment, an aptitude test or a Skype or FaceTime interview.

PSYCHOLOGICAL ASSESSMENT

Aptitude tests look at general mental skills, such as intelligence and awareness, or more specific things such as an ability to work with tools, or with customers, and so on, whereas personality profiles tend to assess work style, for example if the applicant is diligent or more relaxed as a character trait. Personality measurement often asks the job seeker to express opinions or make statements about their attitudes. These may be presented in the form of multiple-choice statements, one of which should be selected even if they do not completely apply. The results from this type of test usually produce multiple scores, each for a different personality aspect. Both forms of these tests are more evidence-based, and therefore adapted to be able to spot more suitable candidates for a specific role than a general interview.

While personality metrics can provide exceptional detail and accuracy, they require considerable skill and judgement, both to produce the metrics themselves and to understand what those metrics are telling us. These tests need to be used appropriately and require special and expensive training in order to analyse the data gathered. In some cases, it may be advisable to outsource to professionals or even hire a qualified psychologist.

ASSESSMENT CENTRES

These are widely used in graduate recruitment. An assessment centre uses any combination of objective selection techniques to measure the applicant's suitability for a job. It usually involves attending a venue along with other candidates for a day or a half day. Assessment centres provide an environment where several applicants compete with each other on a range of tasks, which are purposefully designed to demonstrate and test candidate capability. A variety of exercises undertaken are observed by a team of trained assessors, who will make hiring decisions based against a set of pre-determined criteria.

MANAGING CHANGE IN THE WORKPLACE

Change management is a systematic approach to dealing with change, both from the perspective of an organisation and the individual. Changes within the workplace may be provoked by some major outside driving force, for example substantial cuts in funding or the arrival of a new chief executive officer (CEO). It could be that an organisation wishes to evolve to a different level in their life cycle, which results in the management adopting a new strategy to accomplish its overall goals.

It can be very difficult to introduce change to an organisation. Failure to recognise and deal with this fact has been the cause of many project failures. Organisational change can include the management of changes to:

- The culture
- Business processes
- The physical environment
- Job design
- Staff roles and responsibilities
- Existing knowledge base
- Policies and procedures.

Resistance to change can be a defence mechanism for the employee, brought about by frustration and anxiety. In many cases, there is not so much a disagreement about the necessity of the new process, as much as fear of the unknown future and how to adapt to it. Employees sometimes worry that they will not be able to develop the new skills and behaviours that are required in a new work setting.

HR specialists should be trained in handling these types of interpersonal issues and be able to devise appropriate procedures. They should have the skills to be able to provide employees with specialist advice. It is their responsibility to ensure that line managers are suitably trained and know the company procedures and how to act on them. They should also constantly monitor these procedures.

ORGANISATIONAL STRUCTURES

Organisational structures are often a response to the growth of a business, where a defined reporting structure is needed to balance stability and change. HR functions need to respond quickly to changing resource requirements and internal structures. In larger hospitality organisations, the structure may be divided by a linear or functional structure, or by groups of activities. This helps combine the work functions of employees in a logical and efficient manner.

In the events and hospitality industries, job titles and associated duties vary according to the company and the current market conditions. It is usually the work function rather than the job title which identifies the various departments. So, within a conference hotel, two of the major operating divisions might be the Rooms division and the Food & Beverage division.

Within larger event and hospitality companies and organisations, more hierarchical structures still exist. The culture may dictate that individuals within this type

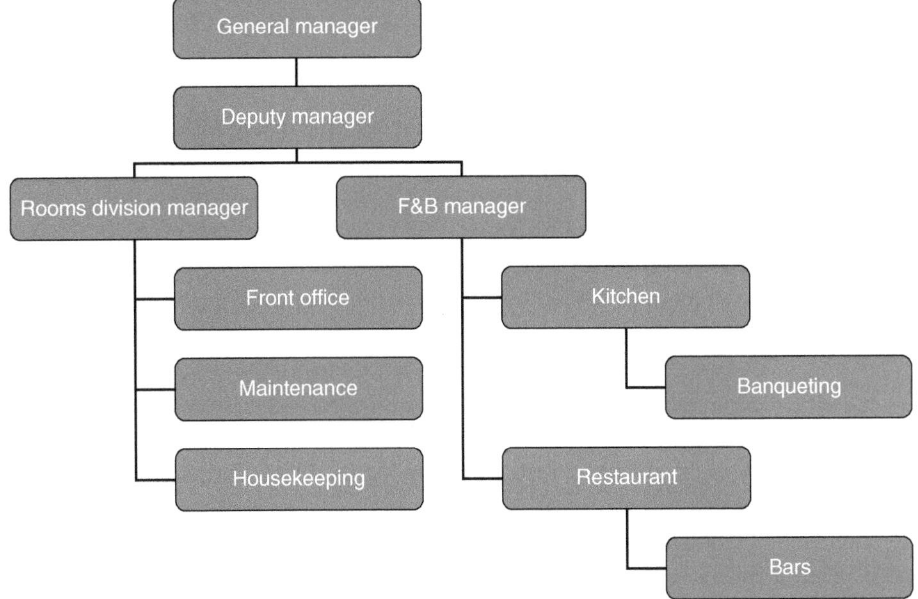

FIGURE 10.3 A sample conference hotel organisational structure

of organisational structure, have clear job roles and functions to perform. These roles and reporting structures are clearly specified within their job description and employees tend to follow the rules rather than work in a creative way. However, the industry is evolving and today organisational structures are changing to become 'flatter', with greater emphasis placed upon employee empowerment. Nowadays selecting the right people, investing in training, creating empowered employees and recognising and rewarding excellence are more important than traditional organisational hierarchies.

HOW DO HUMAN RESOURCES FUNCTION INTERNATIONALLY?

The emergence of a globalised events industry is one of the issues facing international human resource management today. There are many multinational event companies that employ a workforce originating from different countries throughout the world. Global organisations rely on complex supply chains to source, manufacture, design and deliver products and services. In a global marketplace, decisions are driven by the market rather than geography. For these types of international concerns, the following HR issues need to be considered:

- Increasing levels of international trade
- Greater financial flows around the world
- Growth of foreign investment
- The growing activities of multinational companies
- Local legislation
- Participation of women employees in overseas projects
- Equality issues in other countries
- Lack of equality on a global basis
- Managing cross-cultural issues or international HR management.

Evidence shows that most employment practices and corresponding policies remain nationally based. However, within the events and hospitality industries the influence of multinational firms and the pressure for convergence have created a need for greater transparency and transferability of human resources practices. Additional factors such as safety concerns, the costs of family, accommodation, schooling, health care and repatriation costs are other areas that the international HR manager will need to deal with.

There are also cultural and ethical issues to take into account when producing goods for overseas markets and the way fair trade is managed on an international level. This includes aspects such as payment of staff in low-paid countries, exploitation of migrant workers, human trafficking and the exploitation of overseas workers.

In some countries and societies, women still do not have equality in the workplace and there may be cultural and legal requirements regarding work roles that women are allowed to do. There is also disparity in the way organisational and hierarchical structures operate with some cultures. In the events and hospitality industries, the observance of protocol and etiquette can be very important. At times, an understanding of diversity and cultural awareness are needed in order not to cause offence when operating overseas. Managing cultural differences in a sensitive way can be a prerequisite for an international HR division or team.

EVENT ETHICS

Many companies' human resources departments have policies in place that force them to list online for public access any current openings – including when that employer has already earmarked the position for an internal candidate.

Do you think it is ethical to post out these phantom job roles externally?

In the UK, compliance with the Equality Act 2010 includes making it unlawful to discriminate against disabled individuals without justifiable reason. Also, employers must make reasonable adjustments to workplace or working arrangements.

Agree or disagree?

Do you think this is fair and have you seen any evidence of this within the events arena in your current work experience?

SOURCE: www.acas.org.uk

CAREER PATHS AND PROGRESSION ROUTES IN EVENTS

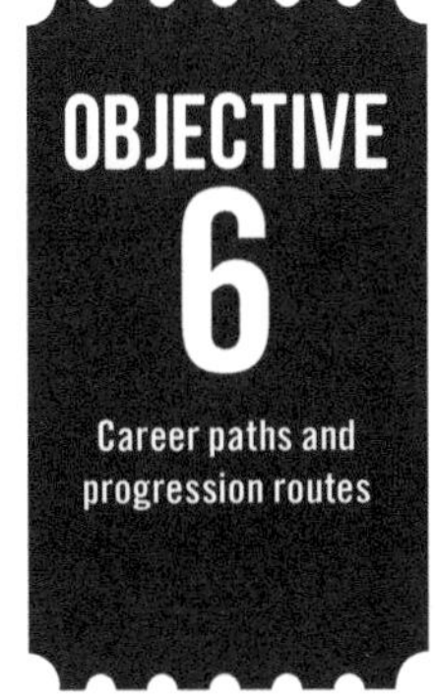

EVENT JOB SPECIFICATIONS

As already discussed in this chapter, the events industry offers a rich diversity of employment opportunities. As Rogers (2013: 225) states:

> Few people will become millionaires, but the rewards in terms of job satisfaction, fun, creativity and building friendships around the world are rich indeed.

As is the case with many event posts, the position may be temporary and only run for the duration of the event, so this also needs to be clearly stated. However, having produced a job description the recruiter will now need to produce a person specification, which is a list of qualifications and skills required. When applying for any job in the industry, it is essential for the applicant to look carefully at the job specification and try to match these with the skills and attributes they possess and their existing experience in the industry, or similar work sector. This is the time for the job seeker to think about building a unique brand and consider:

- What makes them different and marketable?
- What qualities set them apart from their peers?
- How might they add value to a company?

- What message are they giving out about their brand?
- How might they volunteer their services to acquire relevant experience?
- The value of 'word-of-mouth' marketing.

ADVERTISING FOR JOB ROLES

The main thing to remember with any job, paid or voluntary, is that the applicant needs to know exactly what the job role involves. Therefore, the employer or the organising committee should write out the job description, fully outlining the various tasks that need to be undertaken within it, before they advertise the role or outsource to an agency. The job description needs to be detailed but concise, and will of course include information on salary and any additional benefits or rewards.

In order to recruit event staff, job adverts in local papers, online or national papers, agencies will all be useful. The downside is that it will cost money to advertise the role in this way. Outsourcing to an agency probably gives the employer a better chance of accessing and evaluating the right people. Although there is also a cost involved, recruiting staff in this way can be far less time-consuming. As the agency should do most of the work, it may save the company or organisation money in the end, by allowing employers to concentrate on their own job roles and other responsibilities and leave the recruiting to the experts.

BREAKDOWN OF TYPICAL CAREER STRUCTURE AND TITLES OF ROLES

As already mentioned, there are no clearly defined progression routes or job titles within the events industry. Each organisation will have its own job titles and internal structure. For example, it may be possible to be called an operations assistant, operations executive or conference assistant at the same level of responsibility within an event management agency. However, assistant or executive are generally the lower points of entry, then progressing to manager and finally director level.

Each increase to the next level of responsibility is usually reflected in a salary increment. The progression route within the events industry tends to be quite fast, should the employee display the right skills, acumen and aptitude. The progression table (Table 10.5) in the online Appendix shows the various roles and levels which exist within the events industry.

CAREER PROGRESSION

Within the events industry, just as in any other professional field, career mapping and plotting the next career move are essential. It is not the starting but the finishing point that counts, and finding the quickest route to reach the dream job and salary package. It is good practice to consider a career route for the next 3, 5 or 10 years, to research that career path and how to achieve each phase of it, based on current and future skills and experience. An example of a possible career route and progression within the events industry is shown in Figure 10.4.

The career route outlined in Figure 10.4 is only one option. As already discussed, there are many roles and types of events within the sector, which may lead to a completely different career direction. It is also worth remembering that it is always possible to switch roles from one sector of the events industry to another. For example, with the right skills and expertise, it could be completely acceptable to transfer from a wedding planner to become a festival organiser. If the generic, 'soft skills' obtained are relevant, it may also be feasible to transfer from a completely different industry sector, such as retail or marketing, to an event role.

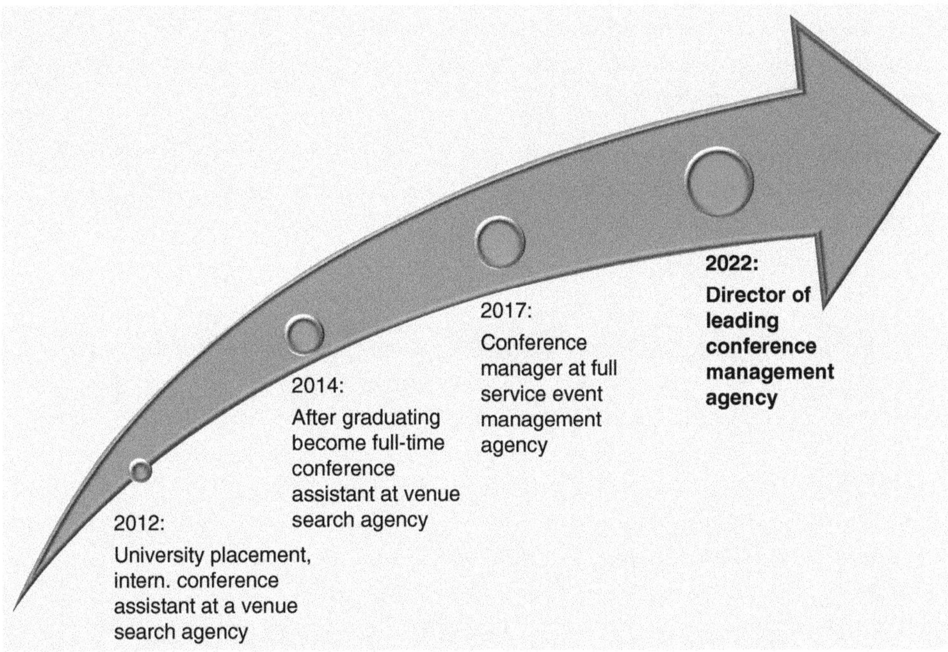
2012:
University placement, intern. conference assistant at a venue search agency
2014:
After graduating become full-time conference assistant at venue search agency
2017:
Conference manager at full service event management agency
2022:
Director of leading conference management agency

FIGURE 10.4 Possible career professions in event management

PAY SCALES, SALARY EXPECTATIONS AND OTHER REWARDS

Remuneration and reward systems are needed in every organisation to attract new talent and retain existing staff. Pay and reward systems are also used to recognise employees for their performance and individual merit, and can include non-monetary payment, sick pay, maternity or paternity pay, pensions and leave of absence. Reward systems are generally designed to motivate employees and are often awarded in cases where performance exceeds expectations. Pay scales are regularly benchmarked and tend to be commensurate with other organisations in the same sector – this is sometimes termed as market-related pay, which reflects industry norms.

Graded pay within organisations is usually based on incremental progression, which tends to be defined by the role in the company, or the length of time the employee has served there, and is more prevalent in the public sector. In the events industry, however, it is more common for individuals to be rewarded on their own merit. The remuneration package might comprise of a mix of basic salary, commissions or bonuses, or performance-related pay (PRP), based on the employee's overall worth to the organisation.

In reality, there are no set pay structures for the events industry and pay strategies are hybridised to achieve the best fit for the company and organisation concerned. However, salaries and extra rewards are often more transparent and accessible in the public sector, such as within governmental, health or educational event roles. Although the Equality Act 2010 states that it is unlawful for an employer to prevent or restrict discussion about pay that could be related to protected characteristics, the employer can still insist on confidentiality outside the organisation. Within the private sector of the events industry, remuneration packages are often still highly confidential and not to be disclosed or discussed with other staff members.

The following considerations may be taken into account when deciding on a strategy for staff remuneration:

- What the organisation can afford to pay
- What other organisations are paying for similar jobs and roles in the sector
- Local skills or expertise shortages which may increase demand
- National/international rates of pay
- The impact of casual labour or cheap migrant labour.

In the hospitality, tourism and events sector, the nature of the business often means that work is seasonal and increases during holiday periods, such as the summer, or over special cultural and religious festivals, for instance Christmas, Spring Break or Diwali. For this reason, short-term contracts tend to be issued to students or migrant workers, who are prepared to work on a short-term or temporary basis for wages.

The term wages tends to describe payments made weekly, often based on an hourly rate and/or paid in cash, for shorter term projects, or daily based work at a basic level with far less emphasis on job security. When paid in this way, it is less likely that any fringe benefits will be offered. Indeed, workers may be on a zero-hours contract, with no sick pay, leave or notice period required and only paid a minimum wage or lower. These types of 'casual workers' are often still paid 'cash in hand', and are often not required to pay income tax, dependent on the amount earned per annum. For this reason, some employees who may be illegal workers, or want to be exempt from paying emergency tax, are prepared to accept poor rates of pay and few additional benefits. With this sort of payment, the earning potential tends to peak early and this 'casual labour' lacks any defined career progression.

INTRODUCTION OF THE LIVING WAGE IN THE UK

The minimum wage varies from country to country. In June 2015 the UK government acted upon demand and enforced a national living wage for workers over 18. The minimum hourly pay rate in 2016 was £6.95, but the UK Living Wage was set at £8.45. Since then there has been much talk of introducing a Living Wage for all employees.

The Living Wage Foundation is a charity campaigning within the UK to persuade employers voluntarily to pay their employees a fair rate; it also provides services and support, including legal guidance, procurement frameworks and human resources assistance if required. The Living Wage Foundation website (2016) reported that 2747 employers had registered to the programme across the UK and 80% of employers believed that it had enhanced the quality of work and staff attitudes, reducing staff leaving rates by 25% since the introduction of the scheme (living.wage.org.uk).

According to Wills and Linneker (2012), in London over 10,000 families have been lifted out of poverty as a result of the Living Wage. In 2016 the Incentive Travel & Meetings Association (ITMA) and the Association of British Professional Conference Organisers (ABPCO) joined to launch a campaign to support a Living Wage in live events. However, the downside of this scheme is that the hospitality industry, which is traditionally one of the poorest paid, may be forced to cut positions if they have to adhere to these new pay rates. The Office for Budget Responsibility (2015) reported that as many as 60,000 jobs may be lost if employers are forced to increase salaries in line with the Living Wage.

SALARY EXPECTATIONS

The word salary is generally used to describe payments which are paid out monthly, normally directly into the employee's bank account, based on an annual gross (before tax) salary figure. With a salary payment, other fringe benefits, such as maternity and paternity leave, sick pay, the opportunity to take a sabbatical, and so on, are often part of the package offered. The long-term prospects are often seen as being more important than the immediate incentives, as the earning capacity tends to increase over time. A salary implies more job security, a long-term fixed contract and a career path that may lead to a future managerial role within the company or organisation.

As already discussed, in the private sector there are no fixed salary bands and salaries are very much at the discretion of the company involved and the specific skills set they are looking for. Generally, in any global capital, salaries will be higher in order to cover the high cost of living in the city.

OTHER REWARDS AND INCREMENTS

In addition to competitive salaries, employers need to offer conditions and benefits that will attract and retain a good workforce. Some flexible benefits that might be highly valued by potential employees are the opportunity to trade some pay for more holidays, healthcare, pensions, time off in lieu given for weekends worked, subsidised parking and a subsidised staff canteen. Employees also need to feel that their pay is 'fair'. But, typically, the reward package is less critical to employers' ability to achieve high performance than other, 'softer' aspects of the employment relationship. Woodruffe (1992) identifies three elements of the relationship critical to employability as: the potential for career advancement, the opportunity for personal development, and being part of a respect-worthy organisation.

According to the CIPD recruitment survey (2015), employees want to work for an organisation that they can feel proud of. In recent years, employers have begun to realise this and integrated this factor into their recruitment strategies and practices. New challenges, the opportunity to grow and develop, personal achievement, a sense of direction, respect and recognition, autonomy, balance and a sense of fun have all been identified as key components of job satisfaction. They are also cited as important elements of career design. In particular, there is an important link to satisfaction for employees who feel they have a satisfactory balance between their work and personal lives. With this in mind, employers need to think through how to guide and support their workforce to help achieve this balance.

CHAPTER SUMMARY

CHAPTER SUMMARY QUESTIONS

1 What are the main event associations within your country?
2 What do you understand by the term event professional?
3 What are the core duties and responsibilities of an event planner/coordinator?
4 What do you understand by the term HRM?
5 What is the difference between a human resources manager and a personnel manager?
6 What are the positives and negatives of freelancing in the events industry?

DISCUSSION POINTS

- How do you think the events industry should set about becoming a more professionalised industry?
- Since line managers seem to have a large part to play in people management, to what extent do you think human resource managers are necessary?
- Do you think event volunteering decreases opportunities for paid event roles?

ACTIVITIES

- Write up a brief combined job description/specification for an event marketing manager.
- Put together a job advert for an event manager, using the following headings:
  - Position title
  - Reporting to: (yourself or someone else)
  - Responsible for: (any other staff)
  - Job activities
  - Knowledge and skills
  - Previous work experience.
- Decide where to post the advertisement and which recruitment selection methods you would use and why.

REFERENCES

Advisory, Conciliation and Arbitration Service (ACAS) (2012) Available at: https://archive.acas.org.uk/media/3455/Annual-Report-2011---2012 (accessed 10 August 2019).

All about Careers. Available at: www.allaboutcareers.com (accessed 12 December 2019).

Arcodia, C. and Reid, S. (2003) 'Goals and objectives of event management associations', *Journal of Convention & Exhibition Management*, 5(1): 57–75.

Association of Collegiate Conference and Event Directors-International (ACCED-I) (2002) Available at: www.acced-i.org/page/Past_AC (accessed 5 June 2018).

Banfield, P. and Kay, R. (2012) *Introduction to Human Resources*, 2nd edn. Oxford: Oxford University Press.

Boyce, A. (2008) Professionalism meets entrepreneurialism and managerialism. In: E. Kuhlmann and M. Saks (eds) Rethinking Professional Governance: International Directions in Health Care. Bristol: Policy Press, pp. 77–95.

Brown, S. (2014) 'Emerging professionalism in the event industry: A practitioner's perspective', *Event Management*, 18(1): 15–24.

CIPD recruitment survey (2015) Available at: www.cipd.co.uk/Images/resourcing-talent-planning_2015_tcm18-11303.pdf (accessed 2 December 2019).

Crosetto, G. and Salah, T. (1997) 'National purchasing and supply management associations: A means to reinforce professional skills', *International Trade Forum*, 3: 28–34.

Foot, M. and Hook, C. (2012) *Introducing Human Resource Management*, 4th edn. London: Pearson Education.

Formadi, K. and Raffai, C. (2009) 'New professionalism in the events sector and its impact in Hungary', in T. Baum, M. Deery, C. Hanlon, L. Lockstone and K. Smith (eds), *People and Work in Events and Conventions: A Research Perspective*. Wallingford: CABI International, pp. 75–89.

Goldblatt, J. (2002) *Special Events: Global Event Management in the 21st Century.* Hoboken, NJ: Wiley & Sons.

Gray, D. (2001) *A Briefing on Work-Based Learning.* Bristol: HEFCE.

Harvey, L., Moon, S., Geall, V. and Bower, R. (1997) *Graduates' Work: Organisational Change and Students' Attributes.* Birmingham: Centre for Research into Quality, University of Central England, Birmingham and the Association of Graduate Recruiter.

Kearns, P. (2000) *Measuring and Managing Employee Performance.* London: FT/Prentice Hall.

Kloss, L. (1999) The 'Suitability and Application of Scenario Planning for National Professional Associations', *Nonprofit Management & Leadership,* 10(1): 71-83.

Leitch, S. (2006) *Leitch Review of Skills: Prosperity for all in the Global Economy – World Class Skills.* Norwich: HMSO.

Little, B. (2000) 'Undergraduates' work based learning and skills development', *Tertiary Education and Management,* 6: 119–35.

Livingwage.org.uk. Available at: www.livingwage.org.uk (accessed 30 September 2019).

Middlehurst, R. and Kennie, T. (1997) 'Leading professionals: Towards new concepts of professionalism', in J. Broadbent, M. Dietrich and J. Roberts (eds), *The End of the Professions? The Restructuring of Professional Work.* London: Routledge, pp. 50–68.

Mullins, L. (2010) *Management and Organisational Behaviour,* 9th edn. London: Prentice Hall.

Office for Budget Responsibility (2015) Available at: https://obr.uk/annual-report-and-accounts-2015-16 (accessed 10 June 2019).

Pilbeam, S. and Corbridge, M. (2010) *People Resourcing and Talent Planning: HRM in Practice.* Harlow: Pearson.

Rogers, T. (2013) *Conferences and Conventions: A Global Industry,* 3rd edn. London: Routledge.

Silvers, J.R. (2003) 'EMBOK: A theoretical and practical model for the event world', in U. Wünsch and H. Wachowiak (eds), *Facets of Contemporary Event Management – Theory and Practice for Event Success.* Bonn: International University Bad Honnef.

Silvers, J.R. (2008) `EMBOK: A theoretical and practical model for the event world', in U. Wunsch (ed.), Facets of Contemporary Event Management - Theory and Practice for Event Success. Bad Honnef, Germany: Verlag K.H. Bock.

Tallantyre, F. (2008) 'Foreword' in The Higher Education Academy, *Work-based Learning in Workforce Development: Connections, Frameworks and Processes.* York: The Higher Education Academy.

Wilensky, H.L. (1964) 'The professionalization of everyone?', *American Journal of Sociology,* 70(2): 137–58.

Wills, J. and Linneker, B. (2012) *The Costs and Benefits of the London Living Wage.* London: Queen Mary University of London.

Woodruffe, C. (1992) 'What is meant by a competency?', in R. Boam and P. Sparrow (eds), *Designing and Achieving Competency: A Competency-Based Approach to Developing People and Organizations.* Berkshire, UK: McGraw-Hill, pp. 16–30.

INDEX

Page numbers in *italics* refer to figures; page numbers in **bold** refer to tables.

CPSIA information can be obtained
at www.ICGtesting.com
Printed in the USA
BVHW012001190223
658820BV00008B/22

9 781473 948099